The Epic of Gilgamesh

Selected Readings from its Original Early Arabic Language

Including a New Translation of the Flood Story

Arabic Transliteration, Arabic and English Translations, Introduction, and Critique by

Saad D. Abulhab

Blautopf Publishing

B l a u t o p f Publishing
blautopfpublishing.com
New York

Colophon
English text set in *Arabetics Latte*, *Arial*, *Cambria*, and *Calibri*
Arabic text set in *Arabetics Latte* and *Arial*

Publisher's Cataloging-in-Publication Data

The Epic of Gilgamesh: Selected Readings from its Original Early Arabic Language.
Including a New Translation of the Flood Story / [Editor] Saad D. Abulhab
p. cm.
1. Gilgamesh. 2. Epic poetry, Assyro-Babylonian -- History and criticism.
3. Arabic Language – History. 4. Deluge. 5. Cuneiform inscriptions, Akkadian.
6. Epic poetry, Assyro-Babylonian -- Translations into English.
7. Epic poetry, Assyro-Babylonian -- Translations into Arabic.
I. Title. II. Gilgamesh. Selections. Akkadian. III. Gilgamesh. Selections. English.
IV. Gilgamesh. Selections. Arabic. V. Abulhab, Saad D.

PJ3771.G6 A235 2016
892.119–dc22
Library of Congress Control Number: 2016957056
CIP

ISBN: 978-0998172729 (hardcover)
ISBN: 978-1539315902 (paperback)

First Edition

Printed by Lightning Source©, an INGRAM© company

20 18 16 14 13 8 7 6 5 4 3 2 1

DEDICATION

To the two women of my life:

Fathiyyah Karim Abulhab, my late aunt and my true Mesopotamian heroine whose motherly care, devotion, and sacrifice, I shall never forget.

Sabine Gruber, my loving wife and the mother of our two wonderful girls; I could not have done the breakthrough work in this book without her understanding, support, and sincere friendship.

TABLE OF CONTENTS

An Introduction to the Language and Reading of the Epic of Gilgamesh

In the breakthrough research outlined in this book, the first of its kind, I examined more than 900 lines from the Standard Babylonian edition of the Epic of Gilgamesh, and all corresponding lines in the Old Babylonian edition and the Ugaritic fragments.* Specifically, I examined the first tablet, and the last two tablets, the tenth and eleventh, where the flood story was told. My goal was to study a sizable sample from the epic, utilizing the historical etymological Arabic references as primary tools and the modern linguistic references of Assyriology as secondary tools, in order to "dig out", as much as possible, the original language in which the epic was *actually* told. For my translation, I used the Cuneiform Latin transliterations prepared by a distinguished scholar of the epic, Andrew R. George, and consulted the most prevailing translations available today, for comparison.

Following three years of intensive work, my findings and conclusions are astounding. The epic, I found out, was a literary work written in a beautiful, powerful, and undisputable early Classical Arabic language! This early language, like the Classical Arabic language later recorded in the Quran, was clearly not the daily spoken language of any population center. The so-called Sumerian and Akkadian languages that the epic was recorded with, which we are told are unrelated languages, were in fact one evolving language, written with one evolving writing system, passing through two major time periods. Evidently, the Sumerian language had heavily used an earlier two-letter Arabic root system, while the Akkadian language had extensively used both, the two-letter and three-letter root systems, just like Classical Arabic.

The Sumerian Cuneiform script started as a pictorial script. It then evolved into a sound-based symbolic script, mainly representing consonants. This new script, like the Musnad script, could not adequately represent the complex and evolving Arabic language of its time, prompting the future Akkadian change. Evidently, the Akkadian Cuneiform writing system was a syllable-based system, incorporating both vowels and early forms of ligatures, creating a complex alphabetical writing system consisting of more than 700 syllables. This Akkadian approach was a genius approach to accurately record Early Arabic. It parallels, in significance, the standardization and codification of the

* The Standard Babylonian edition was written by a Mesopotamian priest named *Sîn-lēqi-unninni*. Scholars believe his name means 'Sîn (Moon God) is one who accepts a prayer', or possibly, if transliterated *Sîn-liqe-unninni*, means 'O Sîn! Accept my prayer'. However, as I will explain in Part 2.2.26, I believe this name is only a title, and it should be read *"man of* the god Sîn (Moon God) who accepts prayers".

current vocalized Arabic writing system, which was introduced by the Muslim Arabs more than two thousand years later.

Through my research, I learned that the language of the Sumerians is not a language of unknown origin. It is not of Hungarian, Turkic, Persian, or alien origin. It is, indeed, the earliest recorded Arabic language! The scribes of various copies of the Akkadian Standard Babylonian edition of the epic did not use Sumerian words to "showoff", as scholars of Assyriology teach today. These words were used to express older, precise Classical Arabic word usages. The Sumerian script was not a script of a foreign language borrowed by the Akkadians. It was the script of their common language, which was improved by them after taking over, just as the Abbasids improved the early Kufic script. The Akkadians and Sumerians are one people: early Arabs who had migrated north during different time periods. Neither the Akkadian nor the Sumerian language should be considered dead languages, as long as their words are still alive in the many impartial, historical Classical Arabic etymological references, which are readily available to the scholars of Assyriology!

As a high school student in Iraq, I attempted to read the Arabic translation from English of the Epic of Gilgamesh, several times. Each time, I gave up reading it, because I found its Western literary style language and allegories were difficult to absorb by my Mesopotamian Arabic mindset, and its content and stories were sometimes borderline nonsense gibberish. However, this time around, reading its events in its own words, as a translator, and reading the events surrounding its discovery, script decipherment, and translation by Western scholars of the 19th century, I was extremely thrilled. In fact, I felt like I was watching a most fascinating dramatic irony, worthy of a Shakespearean-like play!

For most "characters" of the epic, not only Noah, I found, were remarkably preserved, almost identically, in the stories and teachings told by the holy books and the preachers of the succeeding monotheistic religions, particularly and most accurately the Quran and Islam! And most of the 19th century characters working tirelessly to resurrect the epic, I found, were loyal diplomats, spies and army generals turned into archeologists and scholars. Like daring front-line soldiers, they skillfully penetrated the Islamic Arab Near East, establishing their NeoCrusader ideological order, in preparation for the upcoming conquests by the Christian white colonialist powers of Western Europe. They did not only succeed in marginalizing the Arabs and the Arabic language in the scholarly textbooks, but also in the minds of the Arab people!

It is quite an irony that the earliest known major Arabic literary work is classified today as "non-Arabic"; and the earliest, greatest, and *most relevant* literary work of mythology is downplayed today in the classrooms, in favor of the European mythology works that were introduced thousands of years later. The word irony is defined by Merriam-Webster, as the "incongruity between the actual result of a sequence of events and the normal or expected result." Denying the Classical Arabic language its roots and its pioneering literature work are not the only paradoxical ironies surrounding the Epic of Gilgamesh, though. After all, the epic itself was concluded with a more paradoxical irony. Following long laborious adventures, Gilgamesh, the hero of the epic, was finally able to secure a way to gain eternal life: the plant of longevity. However, on his way back, a snake ate the plant instead and gained his sought-after eternal life. In a sarcastic tone, a weeping Gilgamesh then pointed out his funny but sad irony: he had done an excellent job, not for himself, but for the ferocious creature of the den!

However, the irony of all ironies is the one indirectly outlined by Thomas Edward Lawrence, an Oxford trained British soldier, spy, and archeologist, a passionate expert of the history of the Crusaders, and a good student of another Oxford-trained scholar, Reginald Campbell Thompson, an Assyriologist, archeologist, Cuneiformist, and a student of Hebrew and Aramaic, who is credited with the introduction of the earliest baseline translation of the Epic of Gilgamesh. Lawrence wrote in his autobiography that tribesmen and townsmen of Arabic-speaking Asia are of a different race, not "just men in different social and economic stages," because there is no "family resemblance" in the "working of their minds." He further explained that the Arabs "were a limited, narrow-minded people, whose inert intellects lay fallow in incurious resignation." "Their imaginations were vivid, but not creative." "They have no organizations of mind or body. They invented no systems of philosophy, no complex mythologies".[*]

And yet, we have the following eye-opening facts for the Oxford-trained Lawrence and his esteemed Oxfordian colleagues. Based on the inscriptional evidence of the Epic of Gilgamesh, it was clearly written with early Classical Arabic language. Hence, it seems that the writers of this language (i.e. early Arab tribesmen settling north) have not only invented the earliest known mythology work on earth, the epic, but according to the stories of this epic, it seems like they have also invented the most important and lasting myth ever invented: the God of Heaven.

More ironies from the early years of Assyriology and the events leading to the discovery and translation of the Epic of Gilgamesh. The first man to decipher the Cuneiform symbols was the German schoolmaster Grotefend. That was in 1802. Yet, British major Rawlinson, who was born in 1810, is considered "the father of Assyriology". The man, who first discovered the tablets of the Epic of Gilgamesh near Mosul, was Rassam, an Iraqi Chaldean Christian man working for the British. Yet, we all point to Layard, the British man of French origins, as the founder of the epic. The first man to translate the Epic of Gilgamesh was George Smith, a British banknote engraver. That was in 1872. Yet, scholars would routinely point to Haupt, Jensen, or Thompson, as the earliest pioneering translators. In fact, A.R. George did not even mention George Smith in the introduction of his comprehensive translation of the epic!

No one did a better job describing those 9th century eventful years of Near East archeology than Kurt Wilhelm Marek (pen name C. W. Ceram), a German journalist and author who is known for his popular works about archaeology[†]:

"The decipherment of the cuneiform script was a true work of genius. It was one of human mind's most mastery accomplishment, and ranks with the greatest scientific inventions." "The first man to take a decisive step in the direction of deciphering cuneiform writing, however, was motivated neither by scholarly curiosity, nor by the scientific impulse. He was a German, in 1802 a young man of twenty-seven

[*] T. E. Lawrence. *The Seven Pillars of Wisdom: a Triumph*. New York: Doubleday, Doran & Company. Privately printed, 1926.

[†] C. W. Ceram. *Gods, Graves, and Scholars: the Story of Archaeology.* Translated from the German by E.B. Garside and Sophie Wilkins. Second Revised and Substantially Enlarged Edition. New York: Alfred A. Knopf. 1968.

employed as assistant master in the schools of Göttingen. This schoolmaster deciphered the first ten letters of a Cuneiform script simply in order to win a bet. The idea came to him while he was drinking with some comrades, who took him up when he offered to bet on his hunch."

"George Friedrich Grotefend was born on June 9, 1775, at Munden in Germany. He was trained at the Paedagogium, first in his home town, later at Ilefeld, after which he studied philology at Göttingen." "In 1849 he was pensioned off, according to law, and on December 15, 1853 he died."

"Improvements followed, yet, remarkable enough, more than thirty years had passed before anyone was able to make another significant advance. The next contributors to the science of Cuneiform decipherment were the Frenchman Emile Burnouf, and the German Christian Lassen, the investigations of both of whom were written up in 1836."

"In complete unawareness of Grotefend's, Burnouf's and Lassen's contributions," "British Major Henry Creswicke Rawlinson (1810-1895) deciphered, by a method very similar to Grotefend's, the names of three Persian kings", "using the same tablets that Burnouf had worked with." "When, in 1836, he discovered Grotefend's writings, comparison revealed that in many significant respects he had improved on the school master of Göttingen."

"The name of Champollion, decipher of the hieroglyphs, is widely known, yet, paradoxically enough, hardly anyone seems to have heard of Grotefend. His theory is never taught in the classroom, and many modern encyclopedias either ignore him entirely or dismiss him with a brief reference in the bibliography. Nevertheless, he and he alone, must be accorded priority in making possible the historical interpretation of Mesopotamian excavation."

"Priority, I say, for an Englishman, working independently, also succeeded in solving the riddle of the Cuneiform writing. These independent discoveries, incidentally, are typical of science. The Englishman's contribution to Assyriology did not appear, however, until 1846, sometime after Grotefend's interpretation had been revised and improved by Burnouf and Lassen."

"None the less, the Englishman must get credit for going far beyond his predecessors. He succeeded in bringing cuneiform writing out of the specialist's study into the university classroom, in developing methods of decipherment to a point where the original language could be taught like any other. It was he who forged the tool that made it possible to handle the mass of inscriptional material that steadily accumulated throughout the nineteenth century."

"It was in the fall of 1849 when Layard began to work on the mound of Kuyunjik, on the banks of the Tigris across from Mosul. There he found one of the greatest palaces of Nineveh. After four weeks' work he had opened up nine chambers of the palace of Sennacherib (704-681 B.C), one of the mightiest and bloodiest rulers of the Assyrian kingdom." "In Sennacherib's palace, he discovered two rooms apparently added by way of afterthought, which had functioned as library." "The use of the term *library* to describe theses rooms is not at all farfetched. The treasury of information discovered there by Layard comprised nearly thirty thousand "volumes". A library of clay tablets!" [This was the library built by Assurbanipal (688-626 B.C), who ascended the throne few years after Sennacherib's death.]

"Among the purely "literary" tablets were those recording the first great epic of world history, the saga of the terrible and splendid Gilgamesh, part god, part human. This Gilgamesh Epic is the most significant work produced by the Mesopotamian civilizations." "These particular tablets were not discovered by Layard. They were found by a man who, shortly before, had been freed from an unpleasant two-year imprisonment in Abyssinia by a rescue expedition." "Hormuzd Rassam, who actually made the find, was one of Layard's assistants. When Layard gave up archeology for a diplomatic career, Rassam was appointed by the British Museum to carry on the master's work." "Rassam was a Chaldean Christian, born in 1826 in Mosul, on the Tigris. In 1847, he began his studies at Oxford and in 1854 was employed as interpreter at the British residency in Aden. A short time thereafter, though hardly thirty years old, he was made deputy resident. In 1864 he went as a diplomat messenger to the court of King Theodore of Abyssinia."

"Modern history historians however, characteristically put little stress on the Epic of Gilgamesh. They cite ten or dozen lines, call it the 'wellspring of epic poetry,' and let it go at that. Actually it is the whole work that leads us back to the very cradle of the human race, and pads out the bones of our remotest ancestors with living flesh."

"The tracking down of the Gilgamesh Epic to the ancient sources was accomplished by a man who died only four years after completing the task." "This man was George Smith, another archaeological amateur, and a banknote engraver by profession, who was born on March 26, 1840 at Chelsea, in London. Smith was a self-taught man who at night in his little room gave himself over with unparalleled zeal to the study of the first publications of Assyriology. When he died prematurely, in 1876, at the age of thirty-six, he had already published a dozen books and linked his name with significant discoveries."

"In 1872, this erstwhile banknote engraver was sitting over the tablets that Hormuzd Rassam had sent to the museum, trying to decipher them." "As it happened, however, Smith was not interested particularly in the literary quality of the tablets per se. He was thrilled by the bare content of the tale, by the "what" rather than "how" of the legend."

"Bit by bit he unraveled the great deeds of Gilgamesh the strong." "Smith read the Ut-napishtim legend with eager eyes. As his initial excitement began to evolve in the certainty of a remarkable discovery, bigger and bigger gaps appeared in the narrative flow of the Rassam tablets. Smith had to reconcile himself to the fact that he had only fragments of the total inscription to work with. Indeed the most essential section of the story was entirely missing—that is, the conclusion."

"Later a powerful newspaper came to Georg's Smith aid. The London Daily Telegraph announced that it is offering the sum of a thousand Guineas to anyone who would go to Kuyunjik, find the missing Gilgamesh inscriptions, and bring them back to England."

"George Smith himself accepted the offer. He travelled the thousands of miles separating London from Mesopotamia," "Smith actually found the missing parts of the Gilgamesh Epic." "He brought home, altogether, 384 fragmentary clay tablets, among them the missing parts of the controversial story of Ut-napishtim. This tale was a variation of the Biblical legend of the Flood. Ut-napishtim, indeed, was none other than Noah!" "Impossible to question the fact that the primal version of the Biblical legend of the Deluge had been found." "This text in Cuneiform from the Gilgamesh Epic raised for Smith's generation the disturbing question: Was the Bible no longer the oldest historical source we had?"

The following paragraphs from *Discovering Gilgamesh* by Vybarr Cregan-Reid give more details about George Smith's excavations and his tragic death*:

"It was not until January 1873 that the Telegraph stepped in to offer the British Museum £1,000 for Smith to conduct further excavations. Taking travel advice from Arnold, Smith departed for Ottoman Iraq later that month."

"Digging began on May 7, and within three days he believed he had discovered more broken fragments of the "Deluge". In fact, he had discovered another long-lost poem: The Epic of Atrahasis. In Smith's own

* Vybarr Cregan-Reid. *Discovering Gilgamesh*. Manchester University Press. 2013.

words, "The proprietors of *The Daily Telegraph*, however, considered that the discovery of the missing fragment of the deluge text accomplished the object they had in view, and they declined to prosecute the excavations further... desiring to see it carried on by the nation." The brief excavation was over. The question of future funding would depend on Gladstone."

"Permission was granted and on a second dig (in 1874) Smith discovered Babylonian accounts of the creation, the fall of man, the pestilence, the Tower of Babel, and fragments of many other legends. But it was on the third excavation in 1876 that Smith ran into difficulties." "He left England in 1875, and was so delayed by Ottoman officials that he did not arrive at Nineveh until July 1876. By then, with temperatures already in the mid-40s, it was too late to dig. He fell ill."

"Smith's notebooks in the British Library recount his descent into delirium, and the final pages make for heartbreaking reading. He set off for England, but died before he got as far as Aleppo. He was 36, only four years into his career as an Assyriologist."

Following my brief and first encounter with the Chicago Assyrian Dictionary in early 2013, I became fairly convinced that the Akkadian words, I was investigating, were indeed Arabic words. Out of curiosity, I decided to translate a sample text from the Epic of Gilgamesh, corresponding to both the Old Babylonian Edition and the Standard Babylonian Edition, primarily using the old Arabic dictionaries. My sample comprised of the 50 lines where Gilgamesh revealed his two dreams about Enkidu to his mother. In my translation, I skipped reading the so-called Sumerian words, marked with capital letters, for a future investigation. After three months, I was so pleased with the result of my work; I decided to publish my first Arabic-based prototype translation. At the same time, I emailed A. R. George, on December 24th, 2013, attaching my Arabic-based draft translation of the first 19 lines of the Standard Babylonian edition, and asking for his feedback regarding my translation approach. George promptly replied, on December 27th, 2013, with the following:

"Thank you for your messages and draft translation of part of Gilgamesh. I am very sympathetic to your desire to study the text but I am not convinced that your methodology is capable of producing a more accurate rendering than the Assyriological method. The Assyriological method works when applied to ancient Babylonian and Assyrian documents of all kinds, from narrative poetry to private letters to scientific enquiry. It is this universal success as a decipherment tool, in producing coherent meaning in all kinds of contexts, that gives it scholarly legitimacy. May I recommend that you apply your method to another genre of Babylonian text, to test its ability to produce coherence?"

George's reply was accurate, honest, and a scholarly one. His usage of the term "Assyriological method" did not only explain the essence of the Assyriological approach, but it also justified, to me, the need for an Arabic-based approach. After reading George's response, I was more convinced and determined to continue my research. I thought the Assyriological method, no matter how effective and accurate, can only provide *speculated* word meanings. The historical Arabic etymological references, on the other hand, provide *actually-used* word meanings. Potentially, the Arabic "method" can bring to life the *actual* soundings of the original text, its linguistic style, and its rhymes and rhythms. Using the Assyriological method vs. actual language references is like using Google Translate vs. a qualified translator! It is like using a robot vs. human. A robot, of course *can* do a better job. The Assyriological method "robot", however, will never be able to do that, because it was "born" deformed. It was coded with a *speculated* language, not the *actual* language used in ancient Mesopotamia..

Speculation, of course, can be a very powerful and legitimate tool in scientific investigation, *if* it is based on actual and substantial evidence. Compiling a dictionary with speculated words meanings, based on real but very limited "hash-bosh" linguistic evidence, and a large but finite sample of discovered inscriptions written with multiple versions of an extremely complex script, is a risky scientific project; particularly, when such a project is conducted by hundreds, if not thousands, of editors, over a century-long time period. It would take only a few wrongly-speculated word meanings in a few inscriptions to cause a major ripple effect of inaccuracies. I have experienced such ripple effects myself using my Arabic approach. Choosing one wrong word meaning from the Arabic references, in one line, acted like a time bomb in other lines! In most cases, I have to admit, I chose word meanings not attested by the Assyriological method, mainly because I was not able to conclude the Arabic root of these words, at the first try. Each time after fixing my mistake, I was thinking out loud: "George was right again!"

Encouraged by my valuable, informational exchange with a prominent expert of the epic, I decided to completely translate Tablet I. Soon after, I discovered first-hand both, the indispensable value and the unquestionable limitation of the deciphering tools of Assyriology method. George's advice about "producing coherent meaning in all kinds of contexts" was an excellent advice. More and more, I realized that most of the words' meanings offered through these tools are not only accurate, but crucial to determine the correct corresponding Arabic root words. Only after studying these meanings, I was able to arrive to more accurate meanings through the historical Arabic references. In a way, the Assyriology method became my prototyping tool, and George's reading became my indicator to the accuracy of my reading.

The following is a step-by-step summary of my Arabic-based approach to translate an Akkadian-Sumerian text. First, I re-transliterated the Latin-transliterated words (of the Cuneiform words) of the text into all of their possible Arabic transliterations, following the guides of Part 2.1. Second, I eliminated the Arabic-transliterated words that have no corresponding Arabic root words in the old etymological references. Third, I validated the remaining Arabic-transliterated words by checking whether they have any common meanings in the references of *both* Classical Arabic and the Assyriology method. Finally, I determined which validated Arabic-transliterated words should be considered for the translation, by carefully examining their Arabic meaning usages, old and new.

Clearly, my Arabic-based approach, as summarized above, makes good use of the excellent deciphering tools of the Assyriology method. It would not work optimally without using them. The grammar rules outlined in these tools are indispensable, particularly when determining verb tenses. Even though words' meanings in the Assyriology dictionaries are basically speculated, they can be excellent indicators of the specific usages by the Akkadian and Sumerian Arabic languages. In fact, most of these meanings are either identical or close to the meanings provided in the old Arabic references. Occasionally, they are different. In such cases, one should determine the likely correct meanings by examining multiple usages from the old tablets.

Determining the underlining Arabic roots of a Latin transliteration of the epic is a very challenging and complex process, controlled by three important factors. First, Classical Arabic, according to its historical etymological references, had routinely exchanged letters of similar sounds. These replacements were sometimes based on geography, but most of the times they were based on sounds similarities. As a result, words pronounced differently can have the same meaning. Second, the languages of the Sumerians and Akkadians, according to references of the Assyriological method, had not only exchanged several letters and sounds over a long period of time, but also several scripts. Third, the 19th century scholars of Assyriology, rushing to translate a pile of Cuneiform tablets at hand, chose a limited and foreign Western script to transliterate the complex scripts of the sound-rich Mesopotamian languages. Of course, we will never know 100% how the texts of these buried ancient tablets, we laboriously dug out, actually sounded. However, because of the above factors, the actual sounds and letters of their texts became even more laborious to "dig out".

Incidentally, one of my earliest tasks, after translating more than 50 lines of the epic, was to determine whether either the Standard Babylonian edition or the Old Babylonian edition was indeed Babylonian poetry. I concluded they were not. Even though most of the lines in my Arabic based translation of three tablets of the Standard Babylonian edition were rhythmic, these lines were completely independent of each other. The epic sounds more like a musical story than a collection of poems. Current translations' attempts to pair lines in two, and sometimes three, are not only unconvincing, but have negatively affected the accuracy of these translations. However, evidently, the epic had included quotations and even poetry verses. Lines 262^{T10} and 263^{T10} of the Standard Babylonian edition sound like a beautiful Classical Arabic traditional vertical poetry verse:

ذا سَغبَ لَغَبْ ليعدِلُ كاءَ ذا   إنَ عِسْرِ خيا وعِسْرِ ليِفْحُ كاءَ ذا

The most rewarding outcome of my project was my conclusion that the language of the Sumerians was not a different, "non-Semitic", language. I have concluded, through my investigation, that the Sumerians were early Arab migrants, mostly from Eastern and Southern Arabia, sharing the same linguistic roots with the Akkadians (i.e. Arabic roots). Their language was *fortunately* written with an evolving primitive script which started pictorial but changed eventually into a mainly *consonant-based* Cuneiform script, before it was finally replaced with a *syllable-based* script by the Akkadians. I said "fortunately" because their writings seem to record the early beginnings of the language of their ancestors, in addition to their independently evolving language.

The syllable-based Akkadian Cuneiform script cleverly incorporated both vowels and ligatures. With a simple example Marek explained the way it works. "The sound *r* was expressed by six different signs, according to whether the intent was to indicate the syllables *ra*, *ri*, *ru*, *ar*, *ir*, or *ur*. But suppose one wished to reproduce the sound *ram*, or *mar*—that is, to add a consonant to ra, or ar—than an entirely new ideogram resulted from the new phonetic situation. Moreover, the pronunciation of the new ideogram could not be deduced from its component parts."

The description outlined above is *exactly* how the Arabic Naskh script works, with a minor difference: vowels are optional accents. For example, in the traditional Arabic Naskh script, the word Muhammad is written in at least three ways:

محمد محمد محمد

The first (from right) has four syllables, the second has three syllables, and the third has two syllables. In each word, each syllable has its own shape and phonetic value. Although all these words are actually pronounced Muhammad, but if one would pronounce them according to their discreet phonetic values, they will sound differently: mu-ha-ma-id, muh-ma-id, and muham-id, respectively.

As I mentioned before, in my first reading of the epic, I chose to postpone tackling the Sumerian words because I needed a larger text sample to deal with. Now that I have dealt with a reasonable number of them, I firmly believe, at least in the case of the epic, that these words have Arabic roots. In many instances, I was only able to arrive to intelligible and coherent line translations after transliterating these Sumerian words into Arabic and studying their various meanings. The explanation, given by the scholars of Assyriology, that these scattered Sumerian words were used by scribes in the Standard Babylonian edition for "showoff" is quite misleading. Why haven't the scribes of the much earlier Old Babylonian edition used them extensively, too?

For each so-called Sumerian word I studied in my epic sample, I was able to find its Arabic counterpart in the historical Arabic references, with identical meaning. At times, these words were combined with Akkadian components. Scholars of Assyriology explained that these Akkadian components serve as "hints" for the particular meaning intended via the Akkadian language. This may be so, but it was not always the case in my experience. In many cases, I found out that the combined Sumerian-Akkadian word and the individual Sumerian word have one identical meaning in the Arabic references. And yet, in other cases, the Akkadian components were used to grammatically qualify the Sumerian word in the sentence.

I do realize that my argument that Sumerian was as Arabic as Akkadian is a double-fold scholarly bombshell. I know of many Assyriology students and scholars who either firmly believe or willing to accept that Akkadian was, indeed, early Arabic. Not so with Sumerian! The main reason, scholars of Assyriology have argued, is that the tablet dictionaries discovered by Layard and Botta were bilingual dictionaries. Every time I hear this argument, I wonder: hasn't anyone heard of the Merriam Webster, the English-English dictionary, or Lisan al-Arab, the Arabic-Arabic dictionary! I believe the clay tablet "dictionaries" and "instruction manuals" discovered by Layard and Botta and used by Rawlinson, were both linguistic and scholarly script tools of a single evolving language and a single evolving script. Similar usage of such tools in later centuries can be seen in the field of Quranic studies. Scholars of *Arabic* differed constantly on how to pronounce and explain many *Arabic* words in the Quran because the early Kufic script lacked vowels.

Scholars of Assyriology have also argued that the grammar and sentence structures of the language of the Akkadians were different than that of Arabic. They pointed out that Arabic and Akkadian "have different morphology, especially of the verb, and that makes a big difference to parsing the verb forms". However, these written verb forms were governed by the Cuneiform *script* grammar rules. They do not indicate a unique *language* grammar feature. Some enthusiastically argued that in standard Akkadian, unlike in standard Arabic, verbs *typically* followed subjects. However, this language grammar feature of the Akkadian seems to be a feature of an evolving early standard Arabic rather than a unique language. The old language of Yemen, the earliest language of the Arabs, was similar! In fact, the Classical Arabic language of the Quran and pre-Islamic poetry has plenty of examples of atypical mixed-ordered verbs.

According to the scholars of Assyriology, the Akkadian was an East "Semitic" language and Classical Arabic was a West "Semitic" language. However, there is no inscriptional evidence supporting the existence of this so-called "Semitic" language. The term "Semitic", which was invented in the 19th century, is rooted in theology and has no scientific value. Furthermore, Classical Arabic, or *al-'Arabiyyah al-Fuṣḥa*, was (and still is) the formal language of the educated elite; the language of literature and formal communication. It was not, at any time period we know about, the spoken language of a specific geographical location. Ordinary people did not communicate with Classical Arabic in the cities of Hijaz. Similarly, the language of the Epic of Gilgamesh, which resembles that of pre-Islamic poetry, was not the spoken language of the Akkadian people, but a literary language.

The accomplished scholars of the Islamic Arab civilization classified the people of the Fertile Crescent as Nabataean Arabs. Some scholars called them Northern Arabs. They classified the ancient Mesopotamians as the earliest Nabataeans to differentiate them from the later Nabataeans of the Levant. The language of old Babylonia was the Nabataean language, they said. Islamic scholars' classification of the Mesopotamians and their language was far more accurate than the classification of modern Assyriology, according to the evidence of the Epic of Gilgamesh.

Another most rewarding outcome of my Arabic-based reading project was my ability to decipher the actual meanings and pronunciations of several important names of gods, persons, cities, mountains, and other entities. Understanding these names can help us accomplish a more accurate and coherent overall reading of the epic, and determine its linguistic classification and style. It can help us discover the identity of its characters, and their geographical and cultural settings. Realizing the actual names of ancient Mesopotamian gods can help us understand the evolution process of the concept of god and the background themes behind the monotheistic religions. While many of the currently told meanings, through the deciphering tools of the Assyriology method, are generally correct, many are not. On the other hand, using the old Arabic etymological references seems to consistently produce more meaningful names. In Part 2.2, I briefly outlined my examination of 33 major names, mostly from the selected sample of the epic in this book. For my examination, I did not only utilize major Arabic and Assyriology linguistic references, but also religious books and other relevant sources.

A key fact to realize about the names of Ancient Mesopotamia is that they were neither arbitrary nor unique. Multiple names can refer to a single entity, just as multiple words can share one meaning in any language. Most names of important gods and personalities seem to be titles or nicknames rather than first names. They were descriptive names, indicating the natures and roles of their holders. Aside from the pure linguistic nature of these multiple names, one must take into account that they were used over a long period of time in a large geographical area, going through a continuous process of script and language evolution. In my opinion, a key indication for the accuracy and validity of a given meaning of a name is that such meaning should be harmonious with the meanings of all other alternative names.

The following few examples can better illustrate my above observations. The Arabic meaning given by the historical references for the word "Ruqu", which was regularly used after the word Ut-napishtim, is identical to the meaning of the word "Noah". This, in turn, points out the meaning and etymology of the word Noah, and sheds light on the evolution of his character. All names referring to

Gilgamesh have one overall meaning according to the Arabic references: a stubborn (sometimes foolish) fighter. This, of course, fully matches his role and character, as told by the epic. The Assyriology method, on the other hand, did not only fail to explain his name, but had also led scholars to bizarre meanings like "The Ancestor is Young-man" (J.L. Hayes. *Manual of Sumerian Grammar and Texts*)!

Analyzing the *literal* Arabic name meanings of the three highest gods of Mesopotamia, Anu, Enlil, and Ea, I confirmed the following. Anu, from the Arabic word for sky *'an*, was the god of heavens, the *one* father god of all gods. Enlil was the trouble making god, *Iblīs* (Satan), the father of the underground *Jins* (ghosts). Having had a status of god, of course, matches the Islamic believes that *Iblīs* was initially a good character! God Ea (or IDIM), the soil and water related earthly god, is indeed Adam, the father of men! In the flood story of the epic, Ea (Adam) wanted to save men, while Enlil (*Iblīs*) wanted to annihilate them! Sounds familiar? The gods of ancient Mesopotamia, it seems, had only undergone a few slight role and rank changes over the past thousands of years. The rise of the monotheistic order was more like a house re-order event than a new revolutionary change.

Another good example to illustrate my above points is the following. The meanings of the names of the mountain that supposedly held or hid Noah's vessel, according to the Epic of Gilgamesh, *Mt. Namus* or *Mt. Niṣirt*, are identical to the meanings of the names of a mountain overlooking Mecca, *Mt. al-Amīn* (the keeper), or *Mt. Abu Qubays*. This mountain is part of a mountain chain named until today, *Ajyād*, the plural word for *Jawdiyy*. It was given several names, and was considered a holy mountain long before Islam because it supposedly hid the "black stone' of *Ka'bah* during the Flood! The Quran explicitly called the mountain holding Noah's ark, *Mt. al-Jawdiyy*, to indicate it was one of the *Ajyād* peaks. Most importantly, the meaning of the name *al-Jawdiyy* is identical to the meanings of all above-mentioned mountain names. After all, based on geographical facts alone, waters from a flooded Mesopotamia can *only* flow southward, not northward to mountainous Turkey!

Incidentally, Noah's ark was a round/elliptic raft, not a conventional ship, as clearly pointed out in its epic description, in the Hebrew references which named it *taybah* (*tay-baw')*, a sealed basket-like chest, in the Quran which named it *al-Fulka* (a round floating raft), and even in the Greek and Latin translations of *taybah*, where it was called Arca noae, clearly indicating it looked like a round sealed bi-valve shell.

This book was primarily written as a reference textbook for scholars and students of Assyriology, Arabic, linguistics, theology, and literature. However, those who are only interested in reading its selected epic translations can also use it. I am sure most trained scholars of Assyriology will *promptly* dismiss the work presented in this book. This would not be surprising, knowing that the field of Assyriology was molded from its inception with all sorts of questionable theses regarding the history of the Arabs and the Arabic language. I am also sure that my pioneering work in this book is not without inaccuracies or mistakes. Both, the literary language of the epic and the Classical Arabic language are too complex for anyone to claim absolute accuracy. Particularly when one takes into account, the inevitable inaccuracies associated with reading and deciphering a complex Cuneiform script, pieced together from thousands of clay inscriptions. I am not a trained scholar of Linguistics, Arabic, or Assyriology, but I am hopeful that the intellectually-curious, trained scholars and students of these fields will find my work a solid base to launch their own investigations.

Finally, I would like to share with my readers the following. Shortly before publishing this book, I contacted A. R. George, once again, regarding the upcoming publication of my selected translation of the epic. As a good teacher, he did not only respond promptly with a valid observation, but also gave me a challenging assignment to translate "a Babylonian text that is not in the public domain at all", to test the validity of my translation method. See George's respond below. I accepted Prof. George's challenging assignment and promptly replied with my translation of that text. Unfortunately, I did not hear back from him.

"With Gilgamesh you have had the benefit of 150 years of Assyriological research as an aid to understanding, even if you reject the premise of Assyriologists that the poem is composed in a language that is not Arabic but only distantly related to it. For me your translation work would gain legitimacy if it yielded similar results on less well-known material. I am wondering what you would make of a Babylonian text that is not in the public domain at all. Would you like to try your hand at translating the attached?"

Of course, the central thesis of my work, that is the language of the Epic of Gilgamesh was early Classical Arabic, has already gained legitimacy, because my work had clearly yielded similar results! Having "the benefit of 150 years of Assyriological research" is very helpful, but it is not a significant factor. The fact that one can use the old Classical Arabic etymological references to read the epic and to produce a similar, but even more accurate and coherent translation is, by itself, strong evidence that the language of the epic was early Arabic. Particularly, since theses references were written more than a thousand years before the discovery of the epic, which makes them both, effective and neutral tools. George's excellent test indicator for the legitimacy of my translation work and his assignment reminded me with one of the many interesting stories told by the talented Kurt Wilhelm Marek. I cannot find an easier argument to support my hypothesis, to demonstrate the overall scientific accuracy of my Arabic-based new translation, and to conclude this introduction, than to quote him, once again:

"When Rawlinson issued a public claim that he could read the most difficult of the Cuneiform scripts – like all great intellectual pioneers he was constantly beset and reviled – the Royal Asiatic Society in London did something seldom or never heard of in the history of scholarship."

"To the four greatest Cuneiform experts of the day – unknown to each of the others – the society sent a sealed envelope containing a newly discovered, lengthy Assyrian inscription with a note urgently requesting its decipherment."

"The four experts were Rawlinson, Talbot, Hincks, and Oppert. All went to work on the project about the same time, none knowing about the others, and each working according to his private methods. Finally all four returned their results in sealed envelopes, whereupon a commission examined the texts. The claims that had been so vociferously scoffed at by the public were brilliantly vindicated; it was definitely possible to read this supremely complicated syllabic writing. For all four texts agreed on essential points."

"In 1857 in London appeared *An Inscription by Tighlath-Pileser, King of Assyria*, translated by Rawlinson, Talbot, Dr. Hincks, and Oppert. There could not have been a more convincing proof of the scientific accuracy of the results, even though a diversity of approaches over paths heavily strewn with obstacles had been used."

Part 1

Translations and Arabic Transliterations

Reading Guide

Arabic and English translations are kept as close as possible to the linguistic style of the original texts

Arabic transliterations are centered and bold

Light-shaded words are Sumerian words

Superscript numbers refer to the “Words References Index” in Part 2.4

[ ] Alternative transliterations or translations

{ } Words or lines from another tablet copy

( ) Alternative words meanings or clarification nots

<> Words or lines from Ugaritic tablet fragments

... Missing words or lines

| | Assumed words or lines for lost text

Tablet 1
The Standard Babylonian Edition

(1) [235, 259, 349, 399]

ذا نَجْبَ <نَقْبَ> إِإِمُرُ عِضدِ [إِشدِ] [إِسدِ] <عِلدِ [إِلدِ]> مأتِ [مأثِ]

هو ذا الذي رأى المجهول [الكُلُّ (كامل الامور)] [الخالص (المطلق)]، تخوم [دعائم] الارض [الخصبة]

[هو ذا النقيبُ (العالمُ بكامل الامور) [النجيبُ (الفاضلُ في نوعه)] الذي رأى تخوم [دعائم] الارض [الخصبة]]

He who saw the unknown [the whole] [the absolute], the frontiers [pillars] of the [fertile] land

[He is the know-it-all [one of a kind] who saw the frontiers [pillars] of the [fertile] land]

(2) [184, 209, 284]

<أَلْكَكَتِ> إِإِدُوَ [إِهدُوَ] كَلَمُ [كَلأمُ] حَسٌّ

عرَف (تلقائيا) <دواخلها [شِعابها] المُتضامّة>، كان حاسا كل شيء [رؤيا الغيب]

He knew (instinctively) its <inner order [ways]>, he was aware of everything [the vision (of the unseen)]

(3) [91, 349]

جِشْجِمَش[دنجر] <بِلْجَمَس> ذا نَجْبَ <نَقْبَ> إِإِمُرُ عِضدِ [إِشدِ] [إِسدِ] <عِلدِ [إِلدِ]> مأتِ [مأثِ]

جِشجِمَش هذا الذي رأى المجهول [الكُلُّ (كامل الامور)] [الخالص (المطلق)]، تخوم [دعائم] الارض [الخصبة]

[هو ذا النقيبُ (العالمُ بكامل الامور) [النجيبُ (الفاضلُ في نوعه)] الذي رأى تخوم [دعائم] الارض [الخصبة]

Gilgamesh is he who saw the unknown [the whole] [the absolute], the frontiers [pillars] of the [fertile] land

[Gilgamesh is he, the know-it-all [one of a kind], who saw the frontiers [pillars] of the [fertile] land]

(4) [37]

<أَلْكَكَتِ> إِإِدُوَ [إِهدُوَ] كَلَمُ [كَلأمُ] حَسٌّ

عرَفَ (تلقائيا) <دواخلها [شِعابها] المُتضامّة>، كان حاسا كل شيء [رؤيا الغيب]

He knew (instinctively) its <inner order [ways]>, he was aware of everything [the vision (of the unseen)]

(5) [371]

<يحِطْمَ> مِتْحَرِتْ <فَرَقِ [بَرَكِ]>

<مفتشا > كل مكان <عن الانتصارات [الرفعة والعظمة]>

<He was searching> everywhere <for triumphs [glory]>

(6) [216, 402, 405]

نَبْحَرْ نَيمَقيَ ذا كَلَمُ {كَلَمَ} {كَلَمِ} <إإدي [إهدِي]>

حقق شمولية المعرفة (الخبرة) لكل شيء

He achieved the totality (the full extent) of knowledge (experience) of everything

(7) [244, 294, 424]

نِصِرْتَ [نِظِرْتَ] إإمُرْمَ كِتمتي [كتمتوَ] إفتوَ [إفتحوَ] { إفتيَ [إفتحَ]}

رأى المكتوم، بيّنَ (كشفَ) خفاياهُ

He saw the secret (matter), revealed its hidden details

(8) [11, 318, 587, 603]

أبْلَ [أُعْبُلَ] طِعِمَ [طيمَ] {طعِمُ [طيمُ]} <طعِمَ [طيمَ]> ذا لَمْ عَبُبُ {عَبُبِ}

حَمِلَ (جلب) عقلُ (معرفة) ما قبل الطوفان

He carried (brought back) the mind (knowledge) of (the time) before the Deluge

(9) [39, 226, 485, 554, 638]

أُرهَ <حَرانَ> رُقْتَ [رُقْتُم] إلِكِمَ [إلِكَمَ] <إلِكْ> آنِحْ و ذُفُسُحْ <ذُفْشُقْ [ذُبْشُقْ]>

ترسّلَ (ذهب) طريق بعيد [صعب]، مُعاني (مُتعب) و(لكن) ذو سعة صدر <ذو سعة نفس لحرص [منهمك]>

He travelled a difficult [far] road, (he was) enduring (tired) but tolerant <eagerly tolerant [occupied]>

(10) [39, 394, 498]

سَكِنْ [ثَكِنْ] إنَ نانَرو كَلُ مَنَحْتِ

<قَرْنُ ذومَ نَروَ كَل مَنَحْتِ>

وضع (ثبّت) [جَمَعَ] في نَروة (صخرة رقيقة) كلّ كفاحه

<ضمّن نَروة (صخرة رقيقة) كلّ كفاحه>

He set [collected] in a thin stone tablet, all his struggle (toil)

<He incorporated within a thin stone tablet, all his struggle (toil)>

(11) [61, 556, 629, 631]

أُعْفِسْ {أُعْفِسوَ} بَيض [بَيد] ذا عَنُوجكيع سُفُرِ {سُفُرُ} [ذُفُورِ {ذُفُورُ}]

أنجزَ (بني) سور عُروك مقام المناسم والانعام [مذبح القرابين]

He built the wall of Uruk-of-the-cattles-site [alter]

(12) [125, 135, 462, 563]

ذا حِيَنَّ [إيَنَّ] قُدُسِ ذوتُمُ {ذوتُمِ} عِلِيمْ

حيث (الذي فيه) المعبد المقدس، مقام [مستودع] الاعْلون [الانقياء] (الآلهة)

That of the holy temple, the site [the repository] of the high [the pure] (the gods)

(13) [61, 123, 299, 412, 460]

أمُرْ بَيض [بَيد] {دُورُ} ذو ذا كيما قِيي [جِيي] نِفْشُ

أُنظُر الى محيطه (سوره) الذي (نُسج) مثل خصال حبل الصوف

Look at its surrounding (wall) that is (woven) like wool robe strands

(14) [268, 353, 501, 623]

إتَبْلَسْ سَمِتا ذو [شَمِتا ذو] ذا لا يُماثَلْ مَمَّ

تأملْ بدقة (بدهشة وحيرة) سماته التي لا يُماثلوَ أيّا كان

Observe carefully (be astonished by) its features (details) that none [nobody] could match

(15) [168, 492, 621]

ضَبَطْمَ [جشْ] كُنْ **[قُنْ] ذا أُلْتُ أُلانُ**

إلتزِمْ مدرجات ستائر الحائط الخشبية لأوّلُ الأوّلين (اول الزمان)

Take on to the wall-protruding (wooden) steps of the ancient time

(16) [125, 543]

قِتْرُبْ أنَ حِينَّ [إينَّ] سُبَتْ [ثُبتُ] [دنجر] 15

إقتَرِبْ [تقرّب] الى المعبد، مسكن [مقامُ] الالهة إسْتار

Come near the temple, the seat of goddess Ishtar

(17) [46, 335, 338, 353]

ذا لْجَل **أركُوَ لا يُماثَلْ** لُعْ **مَمَّ**

هو ذا الذي لم يماثَلوَ ملكٌ بعده، (أو) ايّ رجل كان

[هو ذا الملك الذي لم يماثَلوَ بعده ايّ رجل كان]

He who no later king could match, (nor) any man

[He is the king who no man after him could match]

(18) [135, 231, 609, 629]

إعلِما إنَ عُجْ [عُقْ] بَيض [بَيد] **ذا** عُنوج[كيع] إيم**تَأَلَكْ**

<إعلِي بِلْجَمَس إنَ دُورِ ذا عُروك إإتَأَلَكْ>

إصعدْ (يا جِشْجِمَش)، في اعالي [حوالي] سور عُروك، ترسّلْ (إذهبْ) في كل الاتجاهات

<إصْعَدْ يا ابا الجَمَس، في اعالي [حوالي] سور عُروك، تجوّلْ>

Go up, (O, Gilgamesh,) in (to) the top of [around] the wall of Uruk, go in all directions

<Go up, O Gilgamesh, in (to) the top of [around] the wall of Uruk, wander around>

(19) [214, 521, 556, 588]

ضَمَنُ [طَأمَنُ] [تَأمَنُ] حِئِطَمْ سِج **صُبّو [ضُبّو]**

<ضَمَنَ [طَأمَنَ] [تَأمَنَ] حِئِطْ سِج **صُفّي>**

إستطلعْ نظام الحماية، طابوق المصبّات <المصافي> (المرازيب)

[إستطلِعْ نظام الحماية، تَفَحّصَ [تفحّصْ] الطابوق]

Explore the protecting apparatus, the brickwork of its waterways (gutters)

[Explore the protecting apparatus, examine the brickwork]

(20) [18, 521, 550]

ثُمّ سج ذو لا آجُرَت

<أمَا سج ذا لا آجُرَت>

بَعدَ إذْ (حقا ان) [(انظر) اذا ما كان حقا] طابوقه ليس آجرة (طابوق مطبوخ في فرن)

<أما (ألا) [أمَا (حقاً)] (ان) طابوقه ليس آجرة (طابوق مطبوخ في فرن)؟>

After all (indeed) [(see) If in fact] its brickwork is not kiln-fired

<Is it not [indeed] its brickwork is not kiln-fired?>

(21) [209, 379, 653]

و أسُّ <أُسّ> ذو لا إِدوَ [إهدوَ] 7 مُنْتَلْكُ

و اسُسُه ما وضعَ المرسلون السبعة

And its foundation, the seven messengers had not laid out

(22) [124, 146, 302, 365, 446, 507, 643]

سأر أورْ سأر [جش] كير [ميس] سأر حِسّو بتِرْ [فتِرْ] حي [إي] [دنجر] إسْتار

سأر (جزء كبير) مدينة، سأر حقول [بساتين]، سأر حفرة طين، شطر (نصف سأر) معبد إسْتار

A Sar (large part) is a city, a Sar is orchards, a Sar is a clay pit, half (Sar) is the Temple of Ishtar

(23) [446, 575]

3 <ثلاث> سأر و بتِرْ [فتِرْ] عنوج تَمْسحُ

3 سأر وشطر (نصفِ سأر) (تساوي) مساحة عُروك

Three Sar and a half is (equals) Uruk area

(24) [157, 597]

<فتيمَ [فتحمَ]> [جش] تُبْذِنَّ [طُبْذِنَّ] <تُبنِن [طُبنِن]> ذا [جش] عرن

إفتحْ [إكشفْ] خزانة اللوائح المصنوعة من خشب شجر العرن

Open [reveal] the (tablets) chest that is made of cedar wood

(25) [452, 666]

<فُطَرْ [بُطَرْ]> خَرقَلِ ذو ذا زَبَرْ

إفصل قضيب حديد قفلها (المصنوع من) الحديد

Separate the metal bar of its iron (made) lock

(26) [244, 279, 424]

فِتيمَ؟ [فتحمَ] كاء ذا نِصرْتِ [نِظرْتِ] ذو

إكشِفْ مفاجأة سرها المكتوم

Reveal the surprise (wonder) of its hidden secret

(27) [260, 395, 538]

إِلذيمَ [إِلتيمَ] طوبِ [نا] زاجن [زاقن] سِئتَسي <تِسَسي>

خُذ (استخرج) لوح حجر اللازَوَرد، إقرأ (إعْلِنْ) <لتقرأ (التعلَنْ)> (منه) بصوت عالي

Get (take out) the lapis lazuli stone tablet, read (declare) <to read (to declare)> (from it) loud

(28) [113, 353, 358]

مُوَ دنجرجِشْجِمَش دودوكُ [طوطُكُ] [دُعْدُعُكُ] {دودُكُم [طوطُكَم] [دُعْدُعُكَم]} كَلُ {كَلَ} مَرْضَاتِ {مَرْضَاتُم}

كُلُّمَا لجِشجِمَش من المغامرات (رواح ومجيء) [الشدائد] [العثرات]، كلّ المعانات

All of Gilgamesh's adventures [difficulties] [misfortunes], all the sufferings

(29) [139, 156, 502, 564]

سُطُرْ عُجْ [عُقْ] لُجَلمِيس ذا نُوْدُ عن [أن] جَثّ

<سُطُرْ أنَ لُجَل ذا نُوْد عن [أن] جَثّ>

تجاوز (شأناً) فوق [بين] (جميع) الملوك، داهية (معجزة) بهيئة (ببُنية جسد) انسان عظيم

<تجاوز (شأناً) على (مجرد) ملك (أكثر من ملك)، داهية (معجزة) بهيئة (ببُنية جسد) انسان عظيم>

Surpassed (in status) over [among] (all) kings, a miracle (in) a form (body build) of a master being

<Surpassed (in status) (more than) a (mere) king, a miracle (in) a form (body build) of a master being>

(30) [331, 391, 457, 481]

قَردُ [كَرْدُ] <قَرَدُ [كَرَدُ]> ليلِدْ {ليلِدُ} عُنوجكيع ريمُ {أمْ} مُتأكْفُ [مُتَكْفُ]

محاربٌ (بطلٌ) وليد عُروك، ريمٌ مجابه (مقدام) [مظفّر]

A warrior (a brave one) is the son of Uruk, a daring (confrontational) [conquering] wild bull (Arabian Oryx)

(31) [50, 212, 226, 437]

إلَكْ إنَ فَني {إجي [حَجي]} أذا ريدْ

تَرسّلَ (ذهب) في المقدمة (الواجهة)، صاحب ريادة (مقدام)

He went to the front, a daring leader

(32) [46, 518, 593]

أرْكُ {أرْكَ} إلَكْ {إلَكَم} تُكُلْتي سيسمِيس ذو

تَرسّلَ (حمل رسالة (تَفقّد)) المؤخرة، مُعْتَمَدُ مؤتمريه (جنوده)

He went (attended the needs of) the rear, the trusted one of his soldiers

(33) [82, 296, 549, 624]

كِبرُ (كِبرِ) ذأنُ [ضَنُّ] [دَنُّ] ظَلُلْ أمانِ ذو

جبروت كبير (عظيم)، ظلالُ (خيمةُ) رعيته (قومه)

A mighty might, the shade (the protector) of his subjects (people)

(34) [19, 149, 373, 393]

أجُوَ عزُّ [إزُّ] مُعبِطْ [مُئبِتْ] بَيض [بَيد] نا

هيجان منيعٌ (لا يقهر) [ملتهب] يشق (يُحطم) [يُذيب] سورٌ من صخر

An undefeatable [A blazing] eruption (outburst) smashing [melting down] a wall of stone

(35) [28, 102, 172]

ريمُ {أمْ} ذا دنجرلُجل باندا دنجرجِشْجِمَش جِتْمَلُ [جِتْمَلْ] حِمُقي

ريم (ابن) الإله لُجل باندا، جِشجِمَش، مكتملُ العزم (التفاني)

The wild bull (the son) of the god Lugalbanda, Gilgamesh, is perfect in vigor (strength)

(36) [6, 141, 151, 536, 638]

إنِقْ [عِنِقْ] أرحي {عَيب [عائب]} صِرتِ {صِرتُم} {ذا} ^ف^ريمة ^دنجر^نِنْسُن {^ف^ريمة ^دنجر^نِنْسُنَنَ}

ناقي (ماصِصُ) (راضعُ) صدر (ثدي) الحليب المتخثر [حليب الثدي المتخثر] لريمة ننسون (آلهة الحُسْنُ) [لغزالةُ الحُسنْ]

Suckling of the coagulated breast milk of the gazelle of (daughter of) Ninsun (the goddess of beauty) [of the Gazelle of Beauty]

(37) [172, 476, 523]

ذيحُ ^دنجر^جِشْجِمَش جِتْمَلْ [جِتْمَلْ] رَسُبُ

عملاقٌ (جبارٌ) جِشجِمَش، كاملٌ، قاصمٌ (بضربته)

Giant (is) Gilgamesh, perfect, devastating (crushing) (with strike)

(38) [197, 244, 406]

فَتحوَ [فَتَوَ] نيْرِبَتِ (نَيْرَبَتَم) ذا حُرساني (حُرسانو)

فتح [فتت (شق صخور)] اخاديد (ممرات) الجبال

He opened [crushed the stones of] mountains' passages

(39) [73, 173, 191, 313]

حِرُوَ [خِرُوَ] بُوْرِ ذا جُو كوري

حَفر [ثَقب] آبار باطن الصُقُعِ (صِعابِ الارض)

He excavated [dug] wells of hard lands' underground

(40) [11, 78, 121, 129, 574]

عِبِرْ عَبَّ طَمَتِ {طَمَتِم} دَجَلْةِ {دَجَلْتِم} عن [أنْ] ^دنجر^أُضُحِ {^دنجر^أُضُحَا} [^دنجر^وضُحِ {^دنجر^وضْحَا}]

عَبَرَ أمواج البحر الواسع (المحيط) حتى [الى] (موضع) مطلع الشمس

He crossed (swam through) the waves of the vast sea (the ocean) until [to] the (site of) sunrise

(41) [62, 214, 296, 389]

حَئَطْ كِبْراتِ {كِبْراتِم} مُسْتِعو بَلاطِ {بَلاطُ}

أحاط (تفقد) أطرافه، ساعيا الحياة الابدية

He explored (combed) its boundaries, pursuing (striving for) the eternal life

(42) [82, 289, 376, 485]

قَصِدْ [كَسِدْ] ذأنُ ذو [ضَنُّ ذو] [دَنُّ ذو] أنَ ^م^عُد ذي [^م^عُطْ ذي] {^م^عُد ذيتم [^م^عُطْ ذيتم]} رُوقِ {رُوقَ}

<ألِكْ قسقل أُتُرْ نَفُسْتِ رُقْتِ>

اعتمد (أمّ) جبروته (قوته) (للوصول) الى عُدْ ذي (معاد (دائم) الحياة) [عُطْ ذي (معطى الحياة)] (أُتانَفسْتم) البعيد المُتنحي (نوح)

<تَرسّل (ذهب) رحلة [طريق] أُتُرْ نَفسْتِ (مدام (دائم) الحياة) (أُتانَفسْتم) البعيد المُتنحي (نوح)>

He used his might to (reach) UD ZI (one with recurrent (permanent) life [life-given one]) (Uta-Napištim) the withdrawn and distant (Noah)

<He went (took on) the journey [road] of Utur-Napušti (one with permanent life: Uta-Napištim) the withdrawn and distant (Noah)>

(43) [53, 351, 390, 611, 647]

مُتِرْ [مُتئِرْ] مَحَزُ {مَحَزِ} أنَ أسرِ [أثْرِ] ذُونُ ذا أُحَلقُ {أُسَلفِتُ [أُسَلبِتُ]} عَبُبُ

أعاد الاحواز (الاراضي او الاملاك) الى اصحابها الذين ازالهم {دمرهم [سلبهم]} الفيضان (الطوفان)

He gave back the lands (properties) to their owners whom the flood had wiped out {destroyed [stole]}

(44) [41, 168, 439, 607]

مُكِنْ فَرْض [فَرْصِ] أنَ ميس عُجْ [ميس عُقْ] عفاتِ

طبق الفرائض (القوانين) على الناس العاقين (الملتوين)

He enforced the laws on the disobedient (crooked) people

(45) [276, 354, 539]

مَنّوُ ذا إتيَ ذو إثأنَنُ {إثتأنّنْ} أنَ لُجَلتي

من ذا الذي تنافس معه على الملوكية [ملوكيته]؟

Who is there who could have competed with him on the kingly status [his kingly status]?

(46) [245]

و كي دنجر جِشْجِمَش يقَبّوَ أنَكُما لُجَل

و (من ذا الذي) كجِشجِمَش، يزأر (يصرخ) "انا اكن [لكم] الملك؟"

And (who), like Gilgamesh, can shout "I am the king [your king]?"

(47) [331, 397, 551, 602]

دنجر جِشْجِمَش أُلْتُ أُومْ إأَلْدو [أَلْدو] نَبو سُمْ ذو [ثُمْ ذو]

جِشجِمَش، أوّلُ يوم وُلِدَ [حالا يوم وُلدَ]، نَبو كان إسمُهُ [نَبو كان بعده]

Gilgamesh, the first day he was born [right after the day he was born], Nabu was his name [Nabu was after]

(48) [31, 98, 539, 548]

ثِنِ {ثِتَ} ذو دنجِرمَ {دِنجِرأُمَ} ثُلُتَ ذو عَميلُتُ

ثُنْتينه {ثُنْتاه} (اثنين منه، ثُلثاه) إله، ثالثتهم بشر

Two (parts) of him (two-thirds) is god, his third (one) is human

(49) [97, 436, 500, 621, 652]

صَلَمْ فَقرِ ذو دنجِر مَه أُصِرْ

رقيقة وجميلة الإله رسمت شكل قوامه

The delicate and beautiful lady of god drew the shape of his figure

(50) [108, 156, 620]

أُلتَصْبِي جَثَّ ذو دنجر نؤديمُدْ

أحكم (أكمل) [نَصَبَ] هيئته (جسده) الإله نوديمُدْ [نؤديمُدْ] (الإله حيا: حافظُ الديمومة [الخِصْب]، المُديمُ، الدَّيُّومُ)

God Nudímmud (EA: keeper of land fertility [survival (existence)]) fitted (perfected) [erected] his form (body)

(51) [510]

... سَرُح [صَرُح] ...

... عظيم (فخم) ...

... majestic (gigantic) ...

(52) [319]

<II إنَ أمَتِ لَعَنْ ذو>

<II بالاذرع (طول) جذعه (جسمه) [ضخامته]>

<II in Cubit is (the height of) his body [immensity])>

(53) [65]

<4 إنَ أمَتِم بيرِتْ تَلَ [تُلَعْ] ذو>

<4 بالاذرع مابين كتفيه>

<4 in Cubit between his shoulders>

(54)

(55)

(56) [166, 365, 408, 410, 420, 448, 455]

نِجْكَ [نِجْخَ] جير ذو [غير ذو] 2\1 نندان فُرِسُ [فُرِتٌّ]

<نِكّاس جيرَ منْ ذو [غير منْ ذو] و قنا فُرِدُ ذو>

(كطول) سهم [نصلُ محراث] [ثلاث اضعاف الذراع] ساقه (الكعبُ للرُكبة) ، و (كطول) نصف نندان [عمود] رجله

<(كطول) سهم [ثلاث اضعاف الذراع] ساقيه (الكعبُ للرُكبة) و (كطول) رمح [قصبة بردي] رجليه>

An arrow [A plow blade] [A triple Cubit] (length) is his lower leg, half Nindan [half rod] his full leg

<An arrow [A triple Cubit] (length) are his two lower legs, and a spear [reed] (length) his full legs>

(57) [65, 315, 447]

6 كوس بيرِتْ فُرِدِ ذو

6 اذرع مابين افراد رجله (سعة خطوته)

Six Cubits between his legs (his step extent)

(58) [51, 408]

|3| كوس عَذارِتِ ذا | لَيتِ| ذو

<نِكّاس إجي دَو ميس ذا لَيتِ ذو>

|3| اذرع (طول) عذارتي لجام [خصلتي] صفحتي عنقه [خديه]

<(كطول) سهم [ثلاث اضعاف الذراع] غطاءي وجه صفحتي عنقه [خديه]>

|3| Cubits (is the length of) the bridle sides [quiffs (curls)] of his neck sides [cheeks]

<An arrow (length) [A triple Cubit] the face covers [quiffs (curls)] of his neck sides [cheeks]>

<أنَ ذا رأ [رَيْ] آ صُفْ [ضُفْ] فَني ذو>

على (منطقة) إرتكاز ذلك (الغطائين)، مصطفٌ [مزدحمٌ] وجهه

On that (area) of the base of that (the two covers), his face is assembled [crowded]

(59) 324, 581

طارَّ [طَرَّ] لَيتا ذو جيم ...

ملتحيا خديه كيما ...

Bearded are his cheeks, like ...

(60) 107, 272, 442, 612

عِتْقي <عَفَتْ [عَبَتْ]> فرتِ ذو أُخْتَنَبا كيما دنجر نِسَّابَ

ضفائر <عِقص (لفّات)> شعر رأسه طالت كما الإلهة نِسّابَة (إلهة الحبوب)

The tresses <curls> of his hair extended (down) as if (he is) the goddess Nissaba (goddess of grains)

<سَكِنْ [ثَكِنْ] فَرتَ كي عُقْنَتِ>

<مثبت [مجمع] [منضّد] شعر رأسه كأنما أنثى [أنثى مزينة]>

<His hair is set [arranged] as if (he is) a woman [a stylish woman]>

<ينَمْبُطَ [ينَبُطَ] سِنَ ذو كيمَ نِفخْ [نِفحْ] دنجر شَمسِ>

<تظهر [تلمع] أسنانه مثل شمس بازغة [مشرقة] >

<His teeth emerging [gleaming] like a rising [shining] sun>

(61) 172, 335, 523

إنَ ذَيحِ ذو جِثْمَلُ [جِئْتْمَلُ] لَعْلِ ذو

في ضخامته مثاليٌ [مكتملٌ] كِبْره (كِبر حجمه)

In (As for) his largeness, his huge size was perfect (complete)

(62) 119, 305, 501

إنَ سِمَتْ [شِمَتْ] كيعتِمْ [قيعتِمْ] دُمُقْ [دُمُجْ]

في وصف التحتيين (العامّة) (باللغة الدارجة)، مفتول ومصقول (مجدول)

In the description of lower (common) ones (in colloquial language), he was entwined and polished (well-built)

(63) 226

إنَ سُفُرُ [ذُفَورُ] ذا عَنُوجِ كيع ذوو يتألَكْ {يتَأنَلَكْ}

في [عند] مقام المناسم والانعام [مذبح القرابين] لعُروك، هو يتجول {بكبرياء}

In (when in) Uruk-of-the-cattles-site [alter], he wanders around {with pride}

(64) [479, 482, 608]

يُجْدَسَرْ ريمَ نِسْ شهقوَ رِيسُ [ريّ ذو]

يتجاسر (يتأمّر)، ريمَ السّوق (جِشجِمَش)، شاهقٌ رأسه

He lords (bullies) around, the commanding wild bull (Gilgamesh), (with) his head held high

(65) [260, 539, 585, 593]

أُل إإذي [إإتي] {إإذو [إإتو]} ثانينَمَ تَبُو جش تُكُل مِيس ذو

ما أوتي (ما له) ثانياً (موازيا)، (دوماً) منتصبة (مهلِكةً) عصاياه

He has no second (equal), his sticks are (always) erected

(66) [450, 484, 585]

إنَ فُكُ {فُكِ ذو} [بُكُ {بُكِ ذو}] تَبُو رُعْو ذو

في (عند) الثورة (الهيجان) [ثورته (هيجانه)]، على الاقدام منتصبين رعاياه

In (during) eruption [his eruption], his subjects are up on (their) feet

<إكْتَفلْ [إكْتَبِلْ] دنجر بِلْجَمَس 50 رُعِي>

<{أُوميذَمْ [أُوميتَمْ] إجَمّرْ غُرُسْ}>

<ضَمّ [حَبَسَ (حَجَزَ)] جلجامش 50 رعّية (بدفعة واحدة)>

<{ كل يوم ضَمّ [حَبَسَ (حَجَزَ)] شابا}>

<Gilgamesh took in [held (seized)] 50 subjects (at once)>

<{Every day he took in [held (seized)] a young man}>

(67) [178, 310, 660]

أُتَذَعْري [أُتَدَأري] <أُلتَذعِرْ [أُلتَدئِرْ]> غُرُس مِيس ذا عَنوج كيع إنَ كَوكتِ [خوختِ] [قوقتِ]

أرهب (أفزع) شباب عُروك بتسرّع (بدون تميز او عدل) [بحمق]

He pushed around (shoved) [terrorized] the young men of Uruk in haste (indiscriminately) [foolishly]

(68) [16, 53, 120]

أُل أُأمَشّرْ [أُأمَذّرْ] [أُأمَسَرْ] دنجر جِشْجِمَش دُمو [ذُمو] أنَ أدْ [عَدْ] ذو

ما فرّق (ميّز) [ترك] [حرر] جِشجِمَش إبن من (عن) [الى] أبيه

Gilgamesh did not differentiate [leave] [let go] a son from [to] his father

(69) [217, 287, 516, 639]

عُرا و مُسي يكَأدِرْ شَرِسْ [سَرِسْ] [شَرِذْ {شَرَذْ}]

نهارا وليلا يشتد (يزداد) شراسة [سوء] [شرا]

Day and night he was intensifying (pouring) cruelty [wickedness]

(70)

دنجر جِشْجِمَش ...

جِشجِمَش ...

Gilgamesh ...

(71) [533]

ذوو سيبمَ ذا عُنوج[كيع] ظُفُرِ [ذُفَورِ]

هو الراعي المطلق لعُروك مقام المناسم والانعام [مذبح القرابين]

He is the shepherd of Uruk-of-the-cattles-site [alter]

(72) [29]

أُل أُأمَشَّرْ [أأُمَذّرْ] [أأُمَسَرْ] [دنجر]جِشْجِمَش ... أنَ أمَ ذا

مافرق (ميّز) [ترك] [حرّر] جِشجِمَش |بنت| من (عن) [الى] أمها

Gilgamesh did not differentiate [leave] [let go] a daughter from [to] her mother

(73) [638]

<ذوو ريم ذنا ذنا أرحاتم>

<هو ريمهنّ، هنّ بقراته (الحلوب)>

He is their wild bull; they are his (milking) cows

(74) [583]

تَعَظِمْتَذِنَ؟ ..... إنَ فَني ذِنْ

استغاثتهُن .... امامهن

Their appeal? .... in front of them

(75) [557, 608]

جَسْرُ سُفُو [سُبُو] مُدُو ....

شقي، اهانته [تهجمه] ممتدة الى ...

A bully, his insult [his attack] was extended to ...

(76) [178, 276]

أُل أُأمَشّرْ [أأُمَذّرْ] [أأُمَسَرْ] [دنجر]جِشْجِمَش <بِلجَمَس> غُرْس تور [طور] <كَلّتْ صِهْرِتْ> أنَ مؤتي [معطي] ذا

ما فرّق (ميّز) [حرّر] جِشجِمَش <ابا الجَمَس> البنت العذراء [البنت الجارية] <العشيقة المُعدمة (الجارية)> من (عن) [الى] امرأتها (المتزوجة) [معيلتها (مالكتها)]

Gilgamesh did not differentiate [let go] a young virgin [young slave girl] <destitute young lover (slave girl)> from [to] her (married) woman [provider (owner)]

(77) [147, 193, 356, 457]

مَرأتْ قُرَدِ خِيرَت عِطلِ [عِتِلِ] {لَعُ غُرْس}

بنت المحارب، زوجة الرجل القوي الشاب

The daughter of the warrior, the wife of the young strong man

(78) [101, 265, 583]

تَعَظِمْتَذِنَ إسْتَنَما <إلْتَنَمي> [إسْتَنَمعا <إلْتَنَمعي>] [دنجر]15 <إستار>

استغاثتهُن (لعظمة الآلهة) رُفعت الى [سمَعتْ] الإلهة إستار

Their appeal (to the great gods) was raised to [heard by] the goddess [Ishtar]

(79) [139, 551, 669]

دنجر ميس سامَمِ عن ميس {عن} ذِكْرِ

(و) آلهة السماوات، أرباب {ربّ} القول (أصحابُ { صاحبُ} القرار)

(and) The gods of heavens, the lords {the lord} of saying (the decision makers)

<رِجْمُ مَرْضُ إكتَنَسَدا [إقتَنَصَدا] أنَ عني أن نيم>

<صوت المعاناة وصل الى سماء (الإله) أنيم>

<The voice of the suffering reached (up) to the heaven of (god) Anim>

(80)

.... سِيس ....

.... قال [قالت] [قالو] ...:

.... said ....:

(81) [595]

تَلْتَبْذِما {تَلْتَبْذِمَ} ريمَ كَأدرَ إنَ عَنوج كيع سُفُرُ [ذُفورُ]

"نَما في عُروك مقام المناسم والانعام [مذبح القرابين] ريمُ كَدر (مشاكل)

"A trouble-making wild bull had grown up (emerged) in Uruk-of-the-cattles-site [alter]

(82) [260, 585]

أل إإذي [إإتي] {إإذو [إإتو]} ثانينَمَ تَبُو جش تُكُل ميس ذو

ما أوتي (ما له) ثانياً (موازيا)، (دوماً) منتصبة (مهلِكةً) عصاياه

He has no second (equal), his sticks are (always) erected

(83) [450, 467]

إنَ فُكي [بُكي] سُتْبو رُعْو ذو

في (عند) ثورته (هيجانه)، ماشين دون البطئ [سائرين فوق العَنَقِ (مسرعين)] رَعاياه

In (during) (his) eruption, his subjects are tiptoe-walking [are rush-walking]

<إكْتَفَلْ [إكْتَبَلْ] بِلْجَمَس 50 رُعي>

<{أوميذَمْ [أوميتَمْ] إجَمّرْ غُرُسْ}>

<ضَمّ [حَبَسَ (حَجَزَ)] جلجامش 50 رعيّة (بدفعة واحدة)>

<{في كل يوم (يومياً) ضَمّ [حَبَسَ (حَجَزَ)] شابا}>

<Gilgamesh took in [held (seized)] 50 subjects (at once)>

<{Everyday he took in [held (seized)] a young man}>

(84) [660]

أُسْتَذعِرْ [أُسْتَدئِرْ] <أُتَذعِرِ [أُتَدئِرْ]> عِطلوتي ذا عُنوج كيع إنَ كَوكِتِ [خوخِتِ] [قوقِتِ]

أرهب (أفزع) شباب عُروك بتسرّع (بدون تميز او عدل) [بحمق]

He pushed around (shoved) [terrorized] the young men of Uruk in haste (indiscriminately) [foolishly]

(85) [1]

أُلْ أُأَمَشَرّ [أُأَمَذَرْ] [أُأَمَسَرْ] دنجرجِشْجِمَش دُمو [ذُمو] أَنَ أَدْ ذو

ما فرق (ميّز) [ترك] [حرّر] جِشجِمَش إبن من (عن) [الى] أبيه

Gilgamesh did not differentiate [leave] [let go] a son from [to] his father

(86) [163, 516, 639]

عُرا و مُسو {في} يكَأدِرْ شَرِسْ {شَرَسْ} [سَرِسْ {سَرَسْ}] [شَرِذْ {شَرَذْ}]

نهارا وليلا يشتد (يزداد) شراسة [سوء] [شرا]

Day and night he was intensifying (pouring) cruelty [wickedness] [in wickedness]

(87)

ذوو سيبِمَ ذا عُنوجكيع ظُفُرِ [ذُفورِ]

هو الراعي المطلق لعُروك مقام المناسم والانعام [مذبح القرابين]

He is the shepherd of Uruk-of-the-cattles-site [alter]

(88)

دنجرجِشْجِمَش ...

جِشجِمَش ...

Gilgamesh ...

(89)

ذوو رَعوذِنَمَ ...

هو راعيهم المطلق ...

He is their herding shepherd ...

(90)

جَسْرُ سُفُو [سُبُو] مُدُو ...

شقي، اهانته [تهجمه] ممتدة الى ...

A bully, his insult [his attack] was extended to ...

(91)

أُلْ أَمَشَرّ[أُمَذَرْ] [أُمَسَرْ] دنجرجِشْجِمَش فغُرُس تور [طور] أَنَ مؤتي [معطي] ذا

ما فرق (ميّز) [ترك] [حرّر] جِشجِمَش البنت العذراء [البنت الجارية] من (عن) [الى] امرأتها (المتزوجة) [معيلتها (مالكتها)]"

Gilgamesh did not differentiate [leave] [let go] a young virgin [young slave girl] from [to] her (married) woman [provider (owner)]"

(92) [457]

مَرأتْ قُرَدِ خيرَت عِطلِ [عتلِ]

بنت المحارب، زوجة الرجل القوي الشاب

The daughter of the warrior, the wife of the young strong man

(93) 83, 265

تَعَظِمْتَذِنَ إسْتَنَمي [إسْتَنَمَعِي] دنجرأنوم

استغاثتهم (لعظمة الآلهة) رُفعت الى [سَمَعَ] الأله أنيم

Their appeal (to the great gods) was raised to [heard by] the god Anim

(94) 85, 338

دنجرأُرُورُ إسُّوَ جَلْتوَ:

جلالته (الإله أنيم) أمر الإلهة أُرُورُ:

His highness (Anim) ordered the goddess Aruru (goddess of fertility):

(95) 59, 335, 572

"أتِ دنجر أُرُورُ تَبنيِ لَغْ

"انتِ (يا) أُرُورُ خلقت الرجُل

"You, Aruru, built (created) man

(96) 140, 572, 669

حِينِنَ بِنِيِ ذِكِرْ ذو

الآن إبني ذِكْره (رجله (مكافئه) القوي الشجاع)

Now, build his (his equivalent) strong daring man

(97) 325, 343, 352, 602

أنَ أومْ لِبِّ ذو لُوو [لُهو] ماخِر

الى يوم (قادم)، ليكن صُلبه معادلا له

For a (future) day, let his core (strength) be equal to him

(98) 334, 538, 554

لِيستَنَنُما عُنوج كيع ليستَفسِحْ

ليتحاربا، ليرتاح عُروك"

Let them fight teeth to teeth, to let Uruk rest"

(99) 40, 514

دنجر أُرُورُ آنِتَ {آنِتِ} إنَ سِمعِ ذا

الآلهة أُرُورُ، حالا، حين (عند) سَمع ذلك (أمر الاله أنيم)

The goddess Aruru, immediately, in hearing that (when she heard that) (Anim's order)

(100) 325, 572, 669

ذِكْرُ {ذِكِرْ} {ذِكْرِ} ذا دنجرأنيم {دنجر50} إبْتَني إنَ {أنَ} لِبِّ ذا

بَنَت (ضَمّت) ذَكَرُ (رَجلُ) الاله أنيم (المكافئ) في (الى) قلبها (داخلها)

She built (created) {appended} the (requested) man of the god Anim in {to} her heart (inside)

(101) [233, 540]

[دنجر]أُرورُ إمتَسِحي [إمتسي] شوو مِنْ ذا [شوو[مِنْ] ذا] { شوو مِنْ[مِيس] ذا}

الآلهة أُرورُ مسحت [فركت (الطين من)] طرف يديها [طرفيها] {أطراف يديها}

The goddess Aruru cleaned [rubbed (the mud) off] her hands' extremity [two extremities] {hands extremities}

(102) [132, 209, 222, 590]

طِيطَ {طِيطِ} إكتَرِصْ [إقتَرِصْ] إتأدي {إتأدو} إنَ عدن {ظِهرِ}

إقترصت (اخذت حفنة) طين، أوْصَلَتْه (وضعته) في البرية

[إقتَرصَ (إلتفّ) [تَجَمّعَ] الطين، وَصَلَ (وضع نفسه تلقائيا) في البرية]

She took a pinch of mud, she made it arrive (she put it) in the wild

[The clay spiraled [gathered], it arrived (instinctively) in the wild]

(103) [87, 457]

إنَ عدن [دنجر]أنكِدو إبْتَني قُرَدُ

في البرية، بنَت (خلقت) (أُرورُ) الإله أنكيدو، محاربٌ (بطلٌ)

In the wild, she built (created) god Enkido, a warrior (hero)

(104) [106, 225, 304, 349, 465]

عِيلِتِ {عِيلِتُ} قُلْتِ {موتُم} كِصِرْ [قِصِرْ] [خِصِرْ] [دنجر]نِنْورةَ

(من) سلالة (ابن) الهلاك {الموت}، فارسُ [مُعتمد)] الاله نِنْورةَ (اله النار والحرب)

(from) The ancestry of (son of) obliteration {death}, trooper [confidante] of god Ninurta (god of fire and war)

(105) [509, 541, 674]

ذُؤرْ [ذُعُرْ] {ذُؤرُ [ذُعْرُ]} شَعَرْتَ كَلُ زُمْرِ ذو [ضُمْرِ ذو]

إفتَرَشَ شعره كل جسمه

[مُذعرً (مُفزعً)، شعره (على) كل جسمه]

His hair was matted all (over) his body

[Frightening, his hair (over) all his body]

(106) [165, 412, 531, 631]

عُفُسْ [أُبُشْ] {نُفُشْ [نُبُسْ]} فَرَتُ جيم ذِنِثْتِ <عُقْنَتِ>

إنجازْ (هيئة) [تزيين] {نَفْشُ [خُصَلْ]}] شعر رأسه كأنما أنثى <أنثى مزينة>

His hair style [decoration] {fluff [tufts]} as if (he is) a female <a stylish woman>

(107) [1]

عِتِقْ فَرْتِ ذو أُخْتَنَبَ كيما [دنجر]نِسَّبَ [نِشَّبَ]

ضفائر شعر رأسه طالت كما الاله نِسَّبَ (اله الشعير ؟)

The tresses of his (head) hair extended as if (he is) the god Nissaba (of wheat?)

(108) [209]

لا إدَ [إهدَ] عُجُ ميس [عُقُ ميس] {دنجر ميس} و مأثَمَ [ميثَمَ]

لا يعرف الاعْلَون {الالهة} او الارض الخصبة (البلاد)

He does not know the high ones {the gods} or the fertile land (the country)

(109) [109, 337]

لُبُسِ {لُبُسْتِ} لابِسْ [لابِثْ] جيم دنجر ذاكَنْ

مرتديا ملابس مثل (ملابس) الإله ذاقَنْ (إله الماشية)

He is dressed in cloths like (that of) the god Dhakkin (of cattles)

(110) [276, 358, 551]

إتي مثَدَ ميس مَ يأكَلَ ثَمِّ

جاء مع الغزلان، يأكل العُشُب

(he came) With the gazelles, eating weed

(111) [68, 269, 362]

إتي بؤلِمْ [بُعْلِمْ] مَسقى يتِعفِرْ

(جاء) مع القطيع ، (في) المسقى [وقت السقي]، يتزاحمَ (يتهالكَ)

(he came) With the herd (at) the water hole [(at) drinking time], cramming

(112) [2, 270, 325, 401]

إتي نَمَسِيَ آ ميس يطِبْ لِبَّ ذو [لِهْبَ ذو]

(جاء) مع الحيوانات، (في) المياه، يطيب [يطفئ] قلبه [لَهيبه]

(he came) With the beasts (at) the waters, soothing his heart [flame]

(113) [185, 488]

صائدُ حَبِيكُ لُعُ

صياد، رجلُ حبال (فخّاخ)

A hunter, a rope trapper man

(114) [352, 451, 490]

إنَ فوتْ مَسْقِيِي ذا أذو أُسْتَمْخِرْ ذو

في (حينما) قرب المسقى الذي له (لأنكيدو)، إختاره (المسقى)

While near the water hole that is for him (Enkido), he (the hunter) chose it (the water hole)

(115) [451, 602]

1 نٍ أُومَ 2 آ و ثَلْثا إنَ فوتْ مَسْقِي |إذا أذو أُسْتَمْخِرْ ذو| كمن

يوم واحدٍ، ثانيا، وثالثا في (حينما) قرب المسقى الذي له (لأنكيدو)، إختاره

One day, second, and third while near the water hole that is for him, he chose it

(116) [437, 488, 654]

إِمُرْ ذومَ صائدُ أُسْتَحْرِرُ فَنو ذو

(فجأة) رآه الصياد (رأى أنكيدو) (فـ)بهت (إصْفرّ) وجهه [(فـ)سَخُنَ وجهه (تصبّبَ عرقا)]

(suddenly) The hunter saw him (Enkido), (and) his face became pale [his face heated (sweated)]

(117) [67, 254]

ذووَ و بؤلِ [بُعْلِ] ذو بِتُسْ [بِطُسْ] ذو إِرُما

هو (أنكيدو) وقطيعه بطبيعته الخضراء (مرعاهم) أكلا [اقاما]

He (Enkido) and his herd, grazed on [stayed put] in their green nature (prairie)

(118) [465, 654, 660]

إِنَّدِرْ أُسْحَرْ [أُشْحَرْ] إقْلَمَ [إقْمُلَمَ]

(الصياد) خاف [سقط من الخوف]، بَهُت (خمد) [فتح فمه] [فقد عقله (وعيه)]، عَجز عن الكلام [ضَعُف]

He was frightened [He collapsed from fear], he was shocked (frozen) [he opened his mouth] [he lost his mind], he was speechless [he was weak]

(119) [48]

|...| لِبَّ ذو فَنو ذو أَرْفُ

قلبه (داخله) كان |....|، وجهه (مظهره) كان ساكنا من الرعب

His heart (inside) was |....|, his face (look) was calm from horror (fear)

(120) [203, 288, 496]

يبَثي [يبَذي] سغبا لغب [لجب] إنَ كَرشِ ذو

يظهر [يتواجد] جوع إعياء وتعب في كرشه

An exhaustion hunger appears [exists] in his gut

(121) [623]

أنَ أَلِكْ أَرِهِ رُقُتِ فَنو ذو مَثْلُ

كَمن ترسل (جاء) طريق بعيد [صعب] مَثَلُ وجهه (مظهره)

His face (appearance) looks like as if for someone who had travelled a difficult (long) road

(122) [245, 435, 631]

صائدُ فا ذو إفْشَمَ [إعِفْسَمَ] [إعِفْشَمَ] يقبي مُوَرَ أنَ أبِ ذو

الصياد أطلق [جمع وأطلق] فمه (لسانه)، صارخا، قال الى ابيه:

The hunter let go [held and let go] his mouth (tongue), shouting, (he) said to his father:

(123) [264, 451]

"أبي إستَنْ [إستَأنْ] عِطلُ ذا إلِكَ أنَ فُوتِ مَسقِيي

"أبي، (هناك) رجلٌ واحد (معين) (و) الذي ترسّلَ (جاءَ) الى قرب المسقى

[أبي، تربّص (مكث وأنتظر) [تَوحّدَ] رجلٌ (ما) (و) الذي ترسّلَ (جاءَ) الى قرب المسقى]

"Father, (there is) one (certain) man who came by the water hole

[Father, a man who came by the water hole had stayed and awaited [had secluded himself]]

(124) [82, 138]

إنَ كور ذأنْ [ضَنْ] [دَنْ] حِمُقِ إإذو [إإتو]

في الصَّقعِ (أرضِ الصِعاب) قويا، أوتي (له) عزم (تفاني)

In the difficult land, he is mighty, he has vigor (strength)

(125) [304]

كيما كِصْرُ [قِصْرُ] ذا دنجرأنيم ذُأْنُنَ [ضُنُنَ] [دُنُنَ] حِمُقَ ذو

مثل فرسُ الاله أنيم جبروت (قوة) عزمه (تفانيه)

Like a horse of the god Anim is the might of his vigor (strength)

(126) [1]

يتَأنَلَكْ إنَ عُجُ [عُقُ] كوري كَ...

يتجول بكبرياء في اعالي [حوالي] الصُقُعِ (صِعابِ الارض) كَ...

He wanders around with pride in top of [around] the difficult lands ...

(127) [280]

كأنما إتي بؤلِم [بُعْلِم] إكَلَ |عو|

كأنما رافق القطيع، أكلَ |عُشُب|

As if he joined the herd, ate weed

(128) [166, 451, 498]

كأنما جير ميس [غير ميس] ذو إنَ فُوتْ مَسْقِيِيَ سَكْنَ

كأنما اقدامه [سيقانه] بقرب المسقى ساكنة (دائمة)

As if his feet [legs] are set (permanent) near the water hole

(129) [42, 57, 490]

فَلْهَكُمَا أُل أطِحا أنَ ذا أذو

كنت منهزما (خائفا) منه، لم أتقرب اليه

I was afraid of him, I did not come close to him

(130) [37, 73, 191, 626]

أُمْتَلِ بُؤرِ ذا أُحَرُو [أُخَرُو] أنَكو

أُمْتَلِيَ (مَلئَ) الحُفَرَ (فخاخ الارض المستورة) التي سوّيت [حفرت] انا نفسي

He filled the pits (hidden land traps) that I leveled up [dug out], myself

(131) [427, 488, 651, 661]

أُتَسِحْ نُبَلِيَ ذا أُثْني لو

اكتسحَ (اقتلع) احجاري التي أُحرِفُ بها (مسير القطيع) لها (للحُفر)

He swept away (pulled out) the stones that I divert with (the path of the herd), to them (to the pits)

(132) [458, 655]

أُسْتِلِيَ إِنَ قاتِيَ بِؤلَمْ [بُعْلَمْ] نَمَسا ذا عدن

إنتزع فيما (بين) طرفي يديّ القطيع، حيوانات البرية

He snatched from my hands the herd, the animals of the wild

(133) [398, 631]

أَل ينَمْدِئتَني أَنَ عِفِش [عِفِس] [إفِش] عدن

لم يدعني أكبّ (اواظب) على عمل المقام"

He did not let me go on (doing) the work of the site"

(134) [398, 631]

أبو ذو فاء ذو إفُشَمَ [إعِفُسْمَ] [إعِفُشْمَ] إقَبي إذكَرَ أَنَ صائدُ

أبوه اطلق [جمع وأطلق] فمه (لسانه)، صارخا [صرخ]، قال الى الصياد:

His father let go [held and let go] his mouth (tongue), shouting [shouted] , (he) said to the hunter:

(135) [356]

"مَرِ .... كور عَنُوج[كيع دنجر] **جِشْجِمَش**

بُنَي .... صَقعِ (ارض، ناحية) عُروكِ جِشْجِمَش

Son, ... the land of Uruk-of-Gilgamesh

(136)

.... حلُ عدن **ذو**

.... حوالي مقامه

.... around his seat (residence)

(137)

كيما كِصِرُ [قِصْرُ] ذا [دنجر] أنيم ذُأُنَنَ [ضُنُنَ] [دُنُنَ] حِمُقَ ذو

مثل فرسُ الاله أنيم جبروت (قوة) عزمه (تفانيه)

Like a horse of the god Anim is the might of his vigor (strength)

(138) [437, 492, 498]

ضَبطْ أُرْهَ إِنَ لِبّ عَنُوج[كيع] **سُكُنْ فنِيكَ**

إلتَزِمْ الطريق، ثبّت وجْهَتُكَ في (نحو) مركز عُروك

Take to the road, set your destination in (toward) the center of Uruk

(139)

.... حمُقْ لَعْ

.... عزم (تفاني) رجل

.... vigor (strength) of a man

(140) [153, 254]

ألكْ مَري [مَرأي] إتكَ حَرِمتُو سَمْحَت [شَمْخت] أُرِمَ

تَرسّل (اذهب) (يا) بني، خذ معك حُرمته سَمْحات [شَمْخات] الفاتنة

Go, son, take with you his harem Samhat [Shamkhat], the beautiful

(141) [82]

.... جيم ذأنُ [ضَنٌّ] [دَنٌّ]

.... مثل جبروت (قوة)

.... like the might of

(142) [255]

حينُمَ بُعْلُ يشَنِقُ [يسَنِقُ] أنَ مَسْقِي

بينما القطيع يتطلّع (يتوجه) الى [يُتخم عند] المسقى

While the herd is looking forward to (approach) [is overstuffing at] the water hole

(143) [244, 317]

ذيي ليسْحُطْ [ليشْحُطْ] لُبُسِ ذامَ ليفْتا [ليفْتحا] كُذُبْ ذا [كُزُبْ] ذا

هي، ليَسقُط (ليملص) ملبسُها، ليتَبيّن إغراءها

She should let her cloths drop (slip) to reveal her attractions

(144) [57, 490]

يأمَرْدِمَ يطِحا أنَ ذا أذي

سيراها، سيقترب إليها

He will see her, (he) will come near to her

(145) [237, 250]

ينَكِرْ ذو بؤلْ [بُعلْ] ذو ذا إربو عُجُ [عُقُ] عدن ذو

سيتجاهله قطيعه الذي ربّاه فوق [حول] (في كنف) مقامه"

The herd, which has raised him up within its site, will ignore (abandon) him"

(146) [368]

أنَ ملِكَ ذا أبي ذو ....

الى توجيه أبيه، ....

To the guidance of his father, ...

(147) [226]

صائدُ إتألَكْ ....

الصائد ترسّلَ (ذهب) ....

The hunter went ....

(148) [487, 498]

إضّبطْ أُرْهَ إنَ شأي عُنوج[كيع] إسْتَكَنْ [إثتَكَنْ] فَني ذو

إلتَزَمَ الطريق، في (نحو) مركز عُروك ثبّتَ وجْهَتَهُ

He took to the road, he set his face (his destination) in (toward) the center of Uruk,

(149)

أنَ لُجَل [دنجر]جِشْجِمَش ...... |إذَكَر|

الى الملك جِشجِمَش .... |قال|:

To the king Gilgamesh .... |said|:

(150) [451]

"إستَنَّنْ عِطلُ ذا إلكَ أنَ فُوتِ مَسقِيِي

"تربّصَ (مكثَ وانتظرَ) [اختبئَ] رجلٌ ترسّلَ (جاءَ) الى قرب المسقى

“A man who came by the water hole, stayed and awaited (sneaked) [hid out]

(151)

إنَ كور ذأنْ [ضَنْ] [دَنْ] حِمُقي إإذو [إإتو]

في الصَّقع (أرضُ الصِعاب) قويا، أوتي (له) عزم (تفاني)

In the difficult land, he is mighty, he has vigor (strength)

(152)

كيما كِصْرُ [قِصْرُ] ذا [دنجر]أنيم ذُأُنَنَ [ضُنُنَ] [دُنُنَ] حِمُقَ ذو

مثل فرسُ الاله أنيم جبروت (قوة) عزمه (تفانيه)

Like a horse of the god Anim is the might of his vigor (strength)

(153)

يتَأنَلَكْ إنَ عُجُ [عُقُ] كوري ......

يتجول بكبرياء في اعالي الصُقُعِ (صِعابِ الارض) .....

He wanders around with pride in top of [around] the difficult lands ...

(154)

كأنما إتي بُعْلِم |يأكَلَ عو|

كأنما مع القطيع |يأكلَ العشب|

As if |he eats weed| with the herd

(155) [451]

كأنما جير[ميس] [غير[ميس]] ذو إنَ فُوتْ مَسْقِيِيَ سَكَنْ [ثَكَنْ]

كأنما اقدامه [سيقانه] بقرب المسقى ساكنة (دائمة)

As if his feet are set (permanent) [legs] near the water hole

(156) [57]

فَلْهَكُمَ أُل أطِحا أنَ ذا أذو

كنت مهزوم (خائف) منه، لم أتقرب اليه

I was afraid of him, I did not come close to him

(157) [37]

أُمْتَلِي بُؤرِ ذا أُحَرُو أنَكو

مَلئَ الحُفَر (فخاخ الارض المستورة) التي سويتها انا نفسي

He filled the pits (hidden land traps) that I leveled up, myself

(158)

أُتَسِحْ نُبَلِيَ ذا أُثْني لو

اكتسحَ (اقتلع) احجاري التي أُحرِفُ بها (مسير القطيع) لها (للحُفر)

He swept away (pulled out) the stones that I divert with (the path of the herd), to them (the pits)

(159) [490]

أُسْتَلِيَ إنَ شوا مِنيَ بؤلَمْ [بُعْلَمْ] نَمَسا ذا عدِن

إنتزع فيما (بين) طرفي يديّ القطيع، حيوانات البرية

He snatched from my hands the herd, the animals of the wild

(160)

أُل إنَمْدِئنَني أنَ عِبِثْ {عِبِثِ} عدِن"

لم يجعلني أنال من عمل المقام"

He did not let me gain from the work of the site"

(161) [669]

جِشْجِمَش[دنجر] أنَ ذا ذوم إذَكَر أنَ صائدُ

جِشجِمَش اليه قال، الى الصياد:

Gilgamesh said to him, to the hunter:

(162) [488]

"ألِكْ صائدي إتِكَ حَرِمتُو سَمَحَت [شَمْخت] أُرُمَ

تَرسّل (اذهب) صائدي، خذ معك حُرمته سَمْحات [شَمْخات] الفاتنة

Go, my hunter, take with you his harem Samhat [Shamkhat], the alluring (seductive)

(163)

حِينُمَ بؤلَمْ [بُعْلَمْ] يشَنِقُ [يسَنِقُ] أنَ مَسْقِي

بينما القطيع يتطلّع (يتوجه) الى [يُتخم عند] المسقى

While the herd is looking forward to (approach) [is overstuffing at] the water hole

(164)

ذيي ليسْحُطْ [ليشْحُطْ] لُبُسِ ذامَ ليفتا [ليفْتحا] كُذُبْ [كُرُبْ] ذا

هي، ليَسقُط (لينملص) ملبسُها، ليتَبيّن إغراءها

She should let her clothes drop (slip) to reveal her attractions

(165) [57, 490]

يأمَرْذِمَ يطِحا أنَ ذا أذي

سيراها، سيقترب إليها

He will see her, he will come near to her

(166) [250]

ينَكِرْ ذو بُوْلْ [بُعلْ] ذو ذا إربُو عَجُ [عَقْ] عدِن ذو

سيتجاهله قطيعه الذي رباه فوق [حول] (في كنف) مقامه"

The herd, which has raised him up within its site, will ignore (abandon) him"

(167)

إلِكْ صائدي إتي ذو حَرِمتي ﻓ سَمْحَت [ﻓ شَمْخت] أُرمَ

تَرَسّلَ صائدَه، رافق (أخذ معه) حُرمته سَمْحات [شَمْخات] الفاتنة

Off went his hunter, (he) took with him his harem [Enkido's], the alluring (seductive)

(168) [290, 656]

إضبَطو أرَهَ أُسْتَذَرو [أُسْتَدَرو] حَرانُ {قسقل}

إلتزمو (الصائد والحُرمة) الطريق، إبتدءو الرحلة [اسرعو سوق قافلتهم]

They took to the road, (they) started the journey [harried their caravan]

(169) [3, 14, 220]

إنَ ثَلْث أومَ إنَ أشا [عَشا] مَدَنِ [عَطَنِ] [أدَنِ] إكْتَلْدُنِ

في اليوم الثالث، في حقل المأوى [المقام] أمسكو (توقفو) [ألقو انفسهم]

In the third day, in the refuge [site] field, they stopped [threw themselves down]

(170) [270, 649]

صائدُ و ﻓ حَرِمْتُ أنَ عُشْبِ ذونَ إتَّبْنِي

الصائد والحُرمة على عُشبه (الحقل) جلسو (ترقبّو)

The hunter and the harem, on its grass, sat (awaited)

(171) [274, 451]

1 نِ أومَ 2 آ أومَ إنَ فوتْ مَسْقِيي إتَّبْنِي <إتَّبْو>

يوم، يومان، بقرب المسقى جلسو (ترقبّو)

First day, second day, near the water hole, (they) sat (awaited)

(172) [257, 313]

كوردَ [قوردَ] بُعلُ مَسْقى يذأتِ [يذعَتِ] [يستئ] [يستَع]

(ثم) تكوّم (تكدّس) القطيع (في) المسقى [وقت السقي]، يتدافع بعنف

(then) The herd piled up (crammed) (at) the water hole [(at) drinking time], jostling

(173) [270, 325]

كوردَ [قوردَ] نَمَسِيَ آ^ميس^ يِطِبْ {يطِبُ} لبّ ذو [لِهْبَ ذو]

تكوّمت (تكدّسَت) الحيوانات (في) المياه، تُطيب [تُطفئ] قلبها [لَهَبها]

The beasts piled up (crammed) (at) the waters, soothing their hearts [flame]

(174) [225, 494]

و ذوو ^دنجر^أنكيدو عِيلِتَ ذو سَادُمَ

وهو ذا أنكيدو سلالته (اصله) الجبل

And there he was, Enkido, his ancestry (origin) is the mountain

(175)

إتي مثدَ^ميس^ مَ يأكَلَ عو

(جاء) مع الغزلان، يأكل العُشب

(he came) With the gazelles, eating weed

(176) [257, 269]

إتي بؤلِم [بُعْلِم] مَسقى يتِعفرْ {يذأتِ [يذعَتِ] [يستئ] [يستَع]}

(جاء) مع القطيع (في) المسقى [وقت السقي]، يتزاحم {يتدافع بعنف}

(he came) With the herd (at) the water hole [(at) drinking time], cramming {jostling}

(177) [271, 325]

إتي نَمَسِيَ آ^ميس^ يطِبْ {يطِفِي} لِهْبَ ذو

(جاء) مع الحيوانات (في) المياه، يطيب {يطفئ} لَهيبه [لهيب قلبه]

(he came) With the beasts (at) the waters, soothing {extinguishing} his flame [his heart flame]

(178) [31]

إإمُرْ ذُومَ سَمْحَتَ [شَمْخت] لعُلا [لُئلا] لُعُ {لعُلا [لُئلا] عمِيلُ}

نَظرت اليه سَمْحات [شَمْخات]، (الى) الرجل التيس [رضيع الكائن الوحشي]

Samhat [Shamkhat] looked at him, the he-goat (savage) man [the infant of the savage creature]

(179) [454, 497]

غُرس سَجَتا {سَجَتو} [سَجَسا {سَجَسو}] [شَجَتا {شَجَتو}] ذا قَبَلْتِي {قَبَلْتو} عدِن

ابن الطبيعة [الهمجية] ذا (القادم من) واجهة (عزُّ) البرية

The son of nature [savagery] of (from) the heart of the wilderness

(180) [254, 303]

أنُو ذووَ سَمْحَت [شَمْخت] رُميي كِرميك

"أنه هو (يا) سَمْحات [شَمْخات]، أرخي (أطلقي) فردتي عجزك

"This is he, Samhat [Shamkhat], loosen up (let go) your buttocks

(181) [244, 332, 639]

عُرْكَ {أُرك} فتيمَ [فتحمَ] كُذُبْك ليلقي

إكشفي (بيِّني) عُريكِ {جنسك} ليَجد (ليرى) إغراءاتك

Reveal your nudity {sexuality} so he can find (see) your attractions

(182) [124, 332, 412, 582]

إي تَثْمُت لِقيي نَفسُ

إيّاكِ ان [لا] تفزعي، خُذي جسده

Do not show fear, take on his body

(183) [57, 283]

يأمَرْكِمَ يطِحا أنَ كَا أذي

سيراك (عندما يراك)، سيقترب إليكِ (من اجلك)

He will see you; (he) will come near to you (because of you)

(184) [135, 392, 549, 609]

لُبُسكِ مُصِّمَ [مُضِّمَ] عُجُكِ [عُقُكِ] {عليكِ [حلكِ]} ليظِّلَكْ [ليصِّلَكْ]

اغسلي [أُنشري] ثيابك لتُظلّ (لتغطي) [لتنشف] عليك [حولك]

Wash [Spread (hang)] your clothes, let them shade (cover) [let them dry] over [around] you

(185) [335, 531, 556, 631,]

عِفْسِ [عِفْشِ] [حِفْشِ] [إفْشِ] [إبْسِ] ذومَ لُعلا [لُلا] سِبرْ ذِنِثْت

أنجزي (هيئي) [أطلقي] [إجمعي] له، (الى) التيس [الرضيع]، خبرةُ الانثى

Perform (prepare) [Collect] [Let go] [Spread] for him, (to) the he-goat [infant], the expertise of a woman

(186) [77]

دَدُ ذو {دَدُكَ} يحبَبُ {ليحَبَبُ} عُجُ [عُقُ] {عِلِ [حلِ]} عَدنكِ {عدن ذو}

ولَعَهُ {ولَعك} سيحوم {دعيه يحوم} فوق [حول] مقامكِ {مقامه}

His passion {your passion} will {let his passion} hover over [around] your {his} site

(187) [213, 250]

ينكِرْ ذو بُوْل [بُعلْ] ذو ذا إربُو إنَ عدن ذو

سيتجاهله قطيعه الذي رباه في (كنف) مقامه"

The herd, which has raised him up in its site, will ignore (abandon) him"

(188) [94, 254]

أرتَمِ {أرتَمُ} سَمْحَت [شَمْخت] دِهدَ [دِيدَ] ذا {دِهدا [دِيدا] ذو}

إرتمت (اسقطت ارضا) سَمْحات [شَمْخات] لباس وركها

Samhat [Shamkhat] threw (dropped) her skirt

(189)

عُر [أُر] ذا {ذو} إفْتيمَ [إفْتحِمَ] كُذُبْ ذا {ذو} إلقي

كشفت (بيَّنت) عُريها [جنسها]، وَجد (رأى) (أنكيدو) اغراءها

She showed her nudity [sexual appeal], he found (saw) her attraction

(190) [582]

أَل إثْمُتْ إلتقِي نَفِسُ

ما فزعت، التقت (استقبلت) جسده

She did not show fear, she received his body

(191) [549]

لُبُس ذا {ذو} {ذي} أُمَصِّمَ [أُمَضِّمَ] عُجُ [عُقُ] ذا {ذو} إصْلَكْ [إظْلَكْ]

غسلت [نشرت] لباسها، غطى [نَشَفَ] فوقها [حولها]

She washed [spread] her cloth, it shaded (covered) [dried out] over [around] her

(192) [531]

إعِفُسمَ [إعِفُشُمَ] [إحِفُشُمَ] [إفُشُمَ] [إإبُسُمَ] لُعُلا [لُلا] سبِرْ ذِنِثْتِ

أنجزت (هيئت) [أطلقت] [جمعت] له، (الى) التيس [الرضيع]، خبرةُ الانثى

She prepared (performed) [collected] [Let go] [spread] for him, (to) the he-goat [infant], the expertise of a woman

(193)

دَدُ ذو إحْبُبُ عُجُ [عُقُ] عدنِ ذا {ذو}

ولعه [ولعها] حام فوق [حول] مقامها {مقامه}

His passion [her passion] hovered over [around] her site {his site}

(194) [162, 585, 638, 639]

6 عُري و 7 مُساتِي {غِي ميس} دنجرأنكيدو تَبِيمَ سَمْحت [شَمْخت] {سَمْحتَ [شَمْختَ]} إرحيَ {يرحيَ}

لستة ايام وسبعة ليالي (كان) أنكيدو منتصبا، طحن {يطحن} سَمْحات [شَمْخات]

For six days and seven nights Enkido was erected, he pounded {was pounding} Samhat [Shamkhat]

(195) [258, 353, 621]

أَلتَ إشْبُعُو لَعَلَ ذا {لَعَلا ذا}

أولُّ ما (حالما) أشبعَ عطشه (الجنسي)

Right after he quenched his (sexual) thirst

(196) [498]

فَنِي ذو إسْتَكَنْ أَنَ {إنَ} عدن بُعْلِ ذو

وجهه (نظره) تركز على مقام قطيعه

His face (eye) was set at the site of his herd

(197) [249]

إإمُرَ ذومَ [دنجر]أنكيدو إرَفُضَ {إرَفُضُ} [إرَبُذَ {إرَبُذُ}] مثدا[مُيش]

(بعدما) رأت أنكيدو، رامت (تركت) [خففت قوائمها (جرت مسرعتا)] الغزلان

(after) They saw Enkido, the gazelles roamed (left) [lightened their legs (sped away)]

(198) [275, 561]

بُؤلْ [بُعُلْ] عدن إتَسِي إنَ زو ذو {سو ذو} {زُمُرِ ذو [ضُمُرِ ذو]}

أسيَ [إستخفّ] قطيع المقام {لهيئته} {(المنظر) جسمه}

The herd of the site was upset (hurt) at [belittled] his appearance {his body (look)}

(199) [235, 436, 619]

أُلْتَخِي [أُلْطَخِي] [دنجر]أنكيدو عُلُكَ (عُلُكُ) فَقَرْ ذو

دنّسَ أنكيدو طُهر (نقاء) قوامه (صُلبَه)

Enkido had defiled the purity of his figure

(200) [66, 149]

إتَرزَ [إتَعزِزَ] بِرْكا {بِرْكِيا} ذو ذا إلِكَ {إلَكَ} بُعُلْ ذو

تصلبتا رجلاه [ركبتاه] اللتان (طالما) ترسلتا (تقدمتا) قطيعه

His legs [knees], which (often) led his herd, stiffened

(201) [323, 625]

أُمْتَطو [دنجر]أنكيدو أُل كِيي ذا فَنِي لَسَنْ ذو

ابتعد (تنحى) أنكيدو، ليس مثل ما مضى لَسَنَه (قفزه)

Enkido was far behind, his jumping was not as before

(202) [184, 475]

و ذوو إإذي [إإتي] |طِعم [طِيم]| رَباضْ [رَباسْ] [رَباذْ] حَسِسَ

و (ليس مثل ما مضى) ما له هو من |معرفة| الحس الواسع [العميق] (بالمحيط)

And (not as before) the knowledge he has of broad [deep] sense (of surrounding)

(203) [274, 390, 503]

إتُوَرَرَم إتَثَبْ إنَ سَفَلْ [ثَفَلْ] حَرِمَتِي

عاد [تفرّدَ]، جلس (استقر) في سَفْلِ (تحت أمر) جاريته

He returned [became alone], sat under the order of his harem

(204) [236]

[ف]حَرِمتُم ينَّطَلا فَني ذا {فَني ذو}

جاريته (كانت) ترى من بعيد [تتمعنُ] وجهه

[(ل)جاريته، (كان) يتمعّنُ وجهها]

The harem (was) watching from far [(was) staring at] his face

[(of) His harem, he (was) watching from far [(was) staring at] her face]

(205) [161, 245, 514]

و ذا [ف]حَرِمتِي يقَبّوَ يسَمَعْ جَيسْتَ[مُنْ] ذو [جَسْتَ[مُنْ] ذو]

وصاحب الحُرمة (الصائد) (كان) يصرخ (انه) يسْمَعُ (صوت) وِطْئيه (وطئ خطواته)

[و(الكلام) الذي تصرخ حرمته تسْمَعُ أذنيه]

And that of the harem (the hunter) (was) shouting he is hearing the (sound of the) impact of his two steps

[And what his harem (was) shouting, his two ears (were) hearing]

(206) [381]

[ف]حَرِمتُ أنَ ذا ذومَ مُوَرَ أنَ [دنجر]أنكيدو

الحُرمة قالت اليه بنبرة عالية، الى أنكيدو:

The harem said to him with a loud voice, to Enkido:

(207) [119, 203, 299]

دَمْقَتا [دنجر]أنكيدو كيمَ {كيي} دنجر تَبَذي [تَبَثي]

"مفتول ومصقول (مجدول) انت، (يا) أنكيدو، مثل إلهٍ تظهر (تبدو)

"You are entwined and polished (well-built), Enkido, like a god you appear

(208) [249, 354]

أمَنِ إتّي نَمَسيَ تَرَفُضْ [تَرَبُذْ] عدنِ؟

من اجل ماذا (لماذا) مع الحيوانات تروم [تجري مسرعا] في البرية؟

For what (Why) do you roam [speed away] in wild with the animals?

(209) [325, 390]

ألْكَ لأُتَرُكَ {لأُتَرِكَ} أنَ لِبِّ {شأي} عُنوج[كيع] سُفُرُ {سُفُرْ} [ذُفَورُ {ذُفورْ}]

تَرسّل (تعال) لأعود بك في قلب (مركز) عُروك مقام المناسم والانعام [مذبح القرابين]

Come, I will return with you in the center of Uruk-of-the-cattles-site [alter]

(210) [101, 124]

أنَ حِي [إِي] عِلّمْ {حِنّ قُدُسُ} مُسَبْ {مُسَبُ} [دنجر]أنيم و [دنجر]إسْتار {[دنجر]15}

الى معبد الاعْلون (الالهة) [النقاء] {المعبد المقدس}، مسكن الاله أنيم والإلهة إستارْ

To the temple of the high ones (the gods) [purity] {the holy temple}, home of god Anim and goddess Ishtar

(211) [53, 172]

أشَر [أثَرْ] [أسَرْ] دنجرجِشْجِمَش جِتْمَلْ [جِتْمَلْ] حِمُقي {حِمُقَمْ}

حيث (فيها) جِشجِمَش مكتملُ العزم (التفاني)

Where Gilgamesh is perfect in vigor (strength)

(212) [608]

وكي [جيم] أم يُجْدَسَرُ {يُجْدَسَرِ} عُجْ [عُقْ] غُرس ميس

ومثل (كيما) ظبيُ وحشٍ يتجاسر (يتأمّر) فوق [حوالي] ابناء البلاد"

And like a wild bull lords (bullies) over [around] the people"

(213) [267, 350, 578]

يتَمَا ذُمَ {تأقَ ذومَ} مَجرْ قَبا ذا {قَباءَ}

عقل (منطق) كلامها المنفعل (صراخها) كان يتّمُه (يقنعه) {نبهَه (شوّقَهُ)}

The logic of her passionate cry [talk] was convincing him {made him alert (eager)}

(214) [325, 375, 389]

مُدُوَ [مُهْدُوَ] لِهْبَ [لِبّ] ذو يسعَا إبْرَ

قلبه كان يهديه (تلقائيا) ليسعى (الى) رفيق

His heart was guiding him (instinctively) to seek a comrade

(215)

دنجرأنكيدو أنَ ذا ذومَ مُوْرَ {مُوْرْ} أنَ حَرمْتِ

أنكيدو اليها قال بنبرة عالية، الى جاريته:

Enkido said to her with a loud voice, to his harem:

(216) [155, 200]

ألكي سَمْحَت [شَمْخت] قيرِني {قيرَني} إيّاذي

"ترسّلي (تعالي)، يا سَمْحات [شَمْخات]، ضُمّيني (خُذيني) [صاحبيني]

"Come, Samhat [Shamkhat], join (take) me [accompany me]

(217) [124]

أنَ حي [إي] علّمْ قُدُسِ مُسَبْ دنجرأنيم دنجرإسْتار

الى معبد الاعلْون (الالهة) [النقاء] المقدس، مسكن الاله أنيم (و) الالهة إستارْ

To the holy temple of the high ones (the gods) [of purity], home of god Anim (and) goddess Ishtar

(218) [172]

أشَر [أثَرْ] [أسَرْ] دنجرجِشْجِمَش جِتْمَلْ [جِتْمَلْ] حِمُقي (حِمُقَمْ)

حيث (فيها) جِشجِمَش مكتملُ العزم (التفاني)

Where Gilgamesh is perfect in vigor (strength)

(219)

وكي أم يُجْدَسَرُ {يُجْدَسَرِ} عُجُ [عُقُ] عُرَس ميس

ومثل (كيما) ظبيُ وحشٍ يتجاسر (يتأمّر) فوق [حوالي] ابناء البلاد

And like a wild bull lords (bullies) over [around] the people

(220) 166

أنَكو لأُجْرِ ذومَ ذأنْ [ضَنْ] [دَنْ] |حِمُقيا|

انا نفسي سأتحداه، قويا |عَزمي (تفانيي)|

I, myself, will challenge him, mighty is |my vigor (strength)|

(221) 638

|لألتَرِهْ| إنَ شأي عَنوج كيع **أنَكومي ذأنُ [ضَنُّ] [دَنُّ]**

|سأستقر| في مركز عُروك، انا نفسي (سأكون) له الجبروت (القوة)]

|I shall settle| in the center of Uruk; I, myself, will be the might for it

(222) 237, 501

|......| شِماتوَ [سِمَاتوَ] أُنَكَرْ

|......| سأغيّر الوضع (الوجهة؛ المصير)

|..........| I will change the situation (direction; destiny)

(223)

ذا إنَ عدن إألَدُ ذأنْ [ضَنْ] [دَنْ] حِمُقي إإذو [إإتو]

هذا الذي في البرية وُلد (يكون) قويا، أوتي (له) عزم (تفاني)"

He who was born in the wild is mighty, he has vigor (strength)"

(224)

|ذوو| ليأمُرَ فَنيكَ

"|هو| سيرى وجهك

|He| shall see your face

(225) 37, 203

.... يبَتُو [يبَذو] أنَكو لو إإدي [إهدي]

.... يظهرُ ، انا نفسي هديتُ (دلّلتُ) له (بدون علمه) [انا نفسي عَرفت له]

.... appears, I myself guided to (steered) him (without his knowledge) [I, myself, knew of him]

(226)

ألِكْ دنجر **أنكيدو أنَ عَنوج** كيع **ظُفُرِ [ذُفورِ]**

تَرَسّلْ (تعال)، يا أنكيدو، الى عُروك مقام المناسم والانعام [مذبح القرابين]

Go [come], Enkido, to Uruk-of-the-cattles-site [alter]

(227) 591, 665

أشَر [أثَرْ] [أسَرْ] غُرُس مَبس أزُهو طوق حبلا مَبس

حيث (فيها) زَهَو (تحلّى) [تفاخر] الشباب باطواق الحبال

Where the young men prided themselves with waistbands

(228) 261, 498, 602, 604

أوميذَمَ [أوميتَمَ] عود ... سَكِنْ [تَكِنْ] إزِنُ [إسِنُ]

كل يوم عيد ... أقيم إحتفال [تجمُّعْ إحتفالي]

Every day of holiday ... a festival [a festival gathering] is held

(229) 135, 641

أشَر [أثَرْ] [أسَرْ] أرتَصَنو عَلُوو

حيث (فيه) إحتفو بطبولهم

Where they celebrated with their drums

(230) 562, 572

و ف حَرْماتي شُوسُمَ بِنُتُو

والحريم بهيّات الاجساد

And the harems, gorgeous are their [in their] figures

(231) 192, 483, 626, 675

حيلي [حلي] زُؤنا مَلّا رِشاتِ {رشاتُم} [ريساتِ {ريساتُم}]

طيبات (متطيبات) بيضاوات (نقيات) [حُلوات (جذّابات)]، متبرجات (متزينات)، مَليئات رقة وتودد [تبختر]

Sweet (smelling) and white (pure) [Sweet (attractive)], primped, full with charm [vanity]

(232) 347, 387, 472, 650

إنَ مآلْ [مأئَلْ [مَعَلْ]] مُسي [مُشي] أَشَصُوَ رَبُوتُمْ {رَبُوتِ}

في الأسرّةِ، مساءا، نهض [تَهيّجَ] المسنين

In beds, at night, the elderly got up [aroused]

(233)

دنجر أنكيدو ذا لا إِدُو [إهِدُو] بَلاطَ {بَلاطِ}

(يا) أنكيدو الذي ما عرف (اهتدى الى) حياة التحضر (الرخاء والاستقرار) (بعد)

O Enkido, who had not known (yet) the civilized (settled) life

(234) 186, 284

لأكَليمْكَ [لأكَلئمْكَ] دنجر جِشْجِمَش هَدأَ {هَدؤوَ} [حَدأَ {حَدؤوَ}] لَعْ {عميلُ}

لأجعلك ترى جِشجِمَش، الرجل المُنعم (نِعْمَ الرجل)

I shall make you see Gilgamesh, a man at ease (the best-of-man)

(235) [235, 236]

أمُرْ ذا أذو أُطُلْ فَني ذو

أنظر له، تمعّن وجهه

Look at him, stare at (examine) his face

(236) [63]

عِطْلُتَ بَنِي بَلْتَ إإذي [إإتي]

مليء بالرجولة، له وقار (كبرياء)

He is built with manhood, he has dignity

(237) [317, 675]

زُؤنَ كُذْبَ كَلُ زُمْرِ ذو [ضُمْرِ ذو]

زينة إغراءه (في) كل (تفاصيل) جسمه

The adornment of his attraction is all over his body

(238) [82]

ذأنَ [ضَنَّ] [دَنَّ] حِمُقَ عُجُكَ عِلِكَ [حِلِكَ] {عُقكَ} إإذو [إإتو] { إإذي [إإتي]}

أوتي (له) قوة العزم (التفاني) فوقك (حولك)

He has the might of vigor (strength) over [around] you

(239) [163, 549]

لا ظَلِكُ [ضَلِكُ] ذا عُرا و غِي {مُسا و عُرا}

لا يمكن بلوغ هذا [لا غائبٌ هذا] ، نهارا وليلا {ليلا ونهارا}

He is unapproachable [He is not absent], day and night {night and day}

(240) [237, 515]

[دنجر]أنكيدو نُكِرَ شِرِتْسو [شِرِتْذو] {شِرِتْكَ}

(يا) أنكيدو اترك (أبعد عنك) شَرّهِ {شرّكَ}

Enkido, leave (stay away from) his harm {your harm (to you)}

(241)

[دنجر]جِشْجِمَش [دنجر]أُضو إرأمْ ذومَ

جِشجِمَش (هذا)، إله الشمس (إله الضوء) داعبه (رعاه)

(this) Gilgamesh, the god Shamash (god of light) caressed (embraced) him

(242) [86, 88, 475, 664]

[دنجر]أنوم [دنجر]إنليك و [دنجر]حيا [إيا] أُرَبِضو [أُرَبِسو] [أُرَبِذو] وزنُ ذو [أُزنُ ذو]

الاله أنيم، الاله إنليك (الشيطان: إله الجن والعواصف) والاله حيا (أدِم: إله المطر والخصب) وسّعو [عمّقو] [شحِذو] عِلمه [حدسه] [حصافته]

The god Anim, the god Enlil (Satan: god of ghosts and storms), and the god Ea (Adam: god of rain and fertility) expanded [deepened] [sharpened] his knowledge [sense] [wisdom]

(243) [226, 318, 494, 621]

لَمْ تألكا أُلْتَ سادِمَ

(حتى) قبل (ما) تترسّل (تترك) أولَ جبلٍ [جبل المنشأ]

(Even) before you come (down) from (left) the first mountain [the mountain of origin]

(244) [552]

دنجر جِشْجِمَش إنَ شأي عَنوج كيع ينَّطَلا شونَاتَكَ

جِشجِمَش في مركز عُروك كان يبصُر (من بعيد) حلمكَ

Gilgamesh, in the center of Uruk, was seeing (from far) your dream

(245) [69, 381, 552]

إتْبيمَ [إتْبغمَ] دنجر جِشْجِمَش شونَتَ {شونَتُو} بُرَرْ مُوَرَ (مُوْرْ) أنَ أمَ ذو

نهض جِشجِمَش يفسّر (يسرد) الحلم [حلمه]، قال بنبرة عالية الى امه:

[إبتغي جِشجِمَش (ان) يفسّر (يفهم) الحلم [حلمه]، قال بنبرة عالية الى امه:]

Gilgamesh rose up to reveal the dream [his dream], he said with a loud voice to his mother:

[Gilgamesh seeked to explain the dream [his dream], he said with a loud voice to his mother:]

(246) [236, 360]

أُمي مشجِ [مأشجِ] أطَلَ {أطَلُ} مُسيتيَ

’أمي، رأيت (من بعيد) ضوء ليلي ساطع عالي (بعيد)، عند مسائيَ

‘Mother, I saw (from far) a high (distant) bright night light, at my evening

(247) [38, 203, 378]

إبْثونمَ [إبّذونمَ] ملَ ميس {ملُ} عَنيِ

ظهرت {ظهر} [تواجدت {تواجد}] لي كواكب {كوكب} السموات

The stars {a star} of heavens appeared [I had] before me

(248) [132, 232, 304]

جيم كِصْرُ [قِصْرُ] ذا دنجر أنيم إمتَقوْتا [إمتَقُمتا] {إمتَنَقوْتوَ [إمتَنَقُمتوَ]} علِ [حلِ] {عُجْ [عُقْ]} عدنيَ

مثل فرسُ الإله أنيم وقع (هبط) فوق [حول] مقامي

Like a horse of god Anim fell (landed) over [around] my site

(249) [55, 82]

أعَسي ذومَ [أهَشّي ذومَ] ذأنْ [ضَنْ] [دَنْ] عليَ [حلِيَ]

طفتُ به [إنطَلَقت به] [طُرتُ به؟]، (كان) قويا (مهيمنا) عليّ [حولي]

I roamed him [unleashed him] [flew him?], (he was) mighty (overwhelming) over [around] me

(250) [335, 432, 618]

أُلْتَبْلَكَ ذومَ أَل إلَعيا [إلَئيا] نُسُّ [نُوس]

تلبَكْته (تعجّلته وخلطت عليه السوق والطريق)، ما خفت [ما أبطأتُ] سرعته

I rushed him around, I did not fear [I did not slow down] his speed

(251) [149, 349]

عُنوج كيع مأتُمْ [مأثُمْ] يأزَزْ [يعزَزْ] عُجُ ذو [عُقُ ذو]

عُروك الأرض [الخصبة] كان يتصلب [يقف ساكنة] حوله

Uruk-of-the-[fertile] land was hardening [was standing still] around him

(252) [349, 377, 449]

مأتُ [مأثُ] فُهرَتْ [فُخرَتْ] إنَ مُحِّ [مُخِّ] ذو

الارض [الارض الخصبة] كانت مجتمعةً [متشرفةً] في محيطه [بنقائه]

The [fertile] land was gathered [was honored] around him [in his purity]

(253) [269]

يتِعفرْ أمانُ عُجُ [عُقُ] عدِن ذو

كان القوم يتزاحم [يتهالكَ] فوق [حول] مقامه

The people were cramming over [around] his site

(254) [276, 352, 613]

غُرْس ميس يُكْتَمَرو [يُغْتَمَرو] عُجُ ذو [عُقُ ذو]

الشباب تحشدو [تجمعو] فوقه [حوله]

The young people were crowding over [around] his site

(255) [166, 335, 517, 628]

كي سهِر لَعي ينَشَقو جير ميس ذو [غير ميس ذو]

مثل أطفال رُضّعْ خائفين كانو يستنشقون (يشمّون) اقدامه [سيقانه]

Like scared babies, they were sniffing his feet [lower legs]

(256) [21, 54]

أرأمْ ذومَ جيم أساتَ عُجُ ذو [عُقُ ذو] أحُبُبْ

أرأمتمَ (داعبته) مثل إمراة، أحَبب (أُقبّل) فوقه [حوله]

I caressed (embraced) him like a woman, kissing (all) over [around] him

(257) [55, 209]

أعَسَسْ ذومَ [أهَشَشْ ذومَ] أتأدي ذو إنَ سَفْلِك [ثَفْلِكِ]

أطفتُه [أطْلَقْتُه]، أوْصَلْتُه (وضعتهُ) (تلقائيا) في سَفْلِك (تحت أمرتكَ)

I roamed him [unleashed him], I made him arrive (put him) under your command

(258) [59, 352]

و أتِ تُلتَمَخرِ ذو إتيَ

و انت إخترتيه إليّ'

And you chose him for me'

(259) [120, 137, 139, 209, 284, 375, 381]

أمي دنجر جِشْجِمَش عِمْقَتْ {إِنْقَمَتْ} مُدَتْ {مُداتو} [مُمدَتْ {مُمداتوَ} كلَم {كَلا} [كَلاَمَ {كَلأ}] إِدَ [إِمدَ] مُوَرْ أَنَ عَنْ ذا {دَمو ذو}

أميَ جِشجِمَش فكّرت عميقا {فهمت}، عالمة [مفسرة] كل شيء [رؤيا الغيب] عَرِفتْ، قالت بنبرة عالية الى سيدها {ابنها}

The mother of Gilgamesh thought deeply [understood], the interpreter of everything [the vision (of the unseen)] knew, she said with a loud voice to her master {her son}

(260)

ف ريمة دنجر نِنْسُن عِمْقَتْ {إِنْقَمَتْ} مُدَتْ {مُداتوَ} [مُمدَتْ {مُمداتوَ} كلَم {كَلا} [كَلاَمَ {كَلأ}] إِدَ [إِمدَ] مُوَرْ أَنَ دنجر جِشْجِمَش

ريمة ننسون فكّرت عميقا {فهمت}، عالمة [مفسرة] كل شيء [رؤيا الغيب] عَرِفتْ، قالت بنبرة عالية الى جِشجِمَش:

Rimat Ninsun thought deeply [understood], the interpreter of everything [the vision (of the unseen)] knew, she said with a loud voice to Gilgamesh:

(261) [38, 203]

إِبْثونِكَ [إِبّذونكَ] مُلْ مُس {مُلْ} أني [عَني]

'ظهرت {ظهر} [تواجدت {تواجد}] لك كواكب {كوكب} السموات

'The stars {a star} of heavens appeared [you had] before you

(262) [232, 262]

كيم كِصْرُ [قِصْرُ] ذا دنجر أنيم إِمتَنَقوّتو [إِمتَنَقُعتوَ] {شَبْمَش [شَبْ مُس]} عِلُ [حِلُ] (عَجُ [عَقُ]) عدنكَ

مثل فرسُ الاله أنيم إرتمى [وقع] {نَزو (وقع بجميع اطرافه) [نَزو (رفع جميع اطرافه)]} فوق [حول] مقامك

Like a horse of god Anim fell (landed) {was raising all hands (as if to copulate)} over [around] your site

(263)

تَعَسِيْ ذومَ [تَمَشِي ذومَ] ذأنْ [ضَنْ] [دَنْ] حِلِكَ (عَجِكَ [عَقَكَ])

طُفتَ به [طِرْتَ به؟] [إِنْطَلَقْتَ به]، (كان) قويا (مهيمنا) فوقكَ [حولكَ]

You roamed him [unleashed him] [flew him?], he was mighty (overwhelming) around [over] you

(264)

تُلْتَبِلْكِت ذومَ أَلْ تَلِعيا [تَلِئيا] {تَلَعيعن [تلعيأن] [تَلَئيعن تلئيأن]} نُسُّ [نُوسُ]

تَلبّكْته (تَعجّلته وخلطت عليه السوق والطريق)، ما خِفتَ [ما أبطأتَ] سرعته

You rushed him around, you did not fear [you did not slow down] his speed

(265) [209]

تَعَسَسْ ذومَ [تَمَشَشْ ذومَ] تأدِي ذو إِنَ سَفْلِيَ [ثَفْلِيَ]

أَطِفْتُه (ايلا) [أَطْلَقْتُه] [طِرْتَ به؟]، أَوْصلْته (وضعتُه) في سَفْلِي (تحت أمرتي)

You roamed him [unleashed him] around, you made him arrive (you put him) under my command

(266)

و أنَكو أُلتَمْخِرَ ذو {أُلتَمْخَر ذو} إتيكَ

و انا نفسي إخترتُه {سأختاره} لكَ

And I, myself, chose {shall choose} him for you

(267) [80]

تَرأمْ ذومَ جيم دَم تَحَبُبُ عُجْ ذو [عُقْ ذو]

ستداعبه مثل إمرأة، ستُحَبب (تُقبّل) فوقه (حوله)

You will caress (embrace) him like a woman, you will kiss (all) over [around] him

(268) [82, 205, 226, 386, 576]

يألكَكومَ ذأنُ [ضَنُّ] [دَنُّ] تَفُو مُشَرَبْ [مُشَذَبْ] إبْرِ

سيترسلُك (سيأتي لك)، قوة تفي [تجيب (عند الصعاب)]، منقذٌ للرفيق [لرفيقه]

He will come to you, a might to be loyal [to answer (when needed)], a savor of a [his] comrade

(269)

إنَ كور ذأنْ [ضَنْ] [دَنْ] حِمُقي إإذو [إإتو] { إإذي [إإتي]}

في الصَّقعِ (أرضُ الصِعاب) قويا، أوتي (له) عزم (تفاني)

In the difficult land, he is mighty, he has vigor (strength)

(270)

كيما كِصْرُ [قِصْرُ] ذا دنجر **أنيم ذأُنُنُ [ضُنُنُ] [دُنُنُ] {ذأُنَنَ [ضُنَنَ] [دُنَنَ]} حِمُقَ ذو {حِمُقا ذو}**

مثل فرسُ الاله أنيم جبروت (قوة) عزمه (تفانيه)

Like a horse of the god Anim is the might of his vigor (strength)

(271) [80]

تَرأمْ ذومَ جيم دَم تَحَبُبُ عُجْ ذو [عُقْ ذو]

ستداعبه مثل إمرأة، ستُحَبب (تُقبّل) فوقه (حوله)

You will caress (embrace) him like a woman, you will kiss (all) over [around] him

(272) [82, 283, 386]

ذوو ذأنُ [ضَنُّ] [دَنُّ] يُشْتَنَزَبْكَ [يُشْتَنَذَبْكَ] كا أذا {يُشَرَبْ [يُشَذَبْ] كا أذو}

هو (هذا) الجبروت [القوة]، سيدافع عنك مرارا لذاك {سيدافع لكَ}'

He, the might, will protect you often for that (for loving him) {will protect for you}'

(273) [558]

ثانتُمْ إتَأمرْ شونَتوَ

{|ثانِتُمْ إتَأمرْ| شُقُرُتْ شُونَتْكَ}

ثانياً رأى حلمه (حلم الفرس)

{|ثانياً رأى| نفيسُ (فرس نفيس شديد الحُمرة) حلمك}

For a second time he saw his dream (the horse dream)

{|For a second time he saw| the precious one (an ultra-red precious horse) of your dream}

(274) [101, 212]

إتْبيمَ [إتْبغمَ] يتأَربْ أنَ إج [حج] دنجر إستار أمَ ذو

نهض يطلب (المساعدة) الى مقدمة (أمام) الإلهة، أمه

[ابتغى يطلب (المساعدة) الى مقدمة (أمام) الإلهة، أمه]

He rose up, seeking (help) to the front of (before) the goddess, his mother

[He proceeded to seek (help) to the front of (before) the goddess, his mother]

(275)

دنجر جِشْجِمَش أنَ ذاذِمَ مؤَرْ أنَ أمَ ذو

جِشجِمَش قال اليها بنبرة عالية، الى امه:

Gilgamesh said to her with a loud voice, to his mother:

(276) [242, 568]

إفُنَ أمّاه أتأمَرْ ثانيتَ {ثانِتُمْ} شُتَّ [شُعُتَ] {مشجِ [مأشجِ]}

'مرة اخرى يا أمّاه رأيت شعاع ضوء بعيد {ضوء ليلي ساطع عالي (بعيد)} ثانيا

'Again, O mother, I saw a second far light ray {high (distant) bright night light}

(277) [526]

إنَ سيكَ ذا عُنوجِ كيع رَبيتُمْ

في سوق رابية عُروك

In the market of Uruk-of-the-hill

(278) [398, 449, 539]

حَصينُ نَديمَ عُجُ ذو [عُقُ ذو] فَهرِ {فَهرُ} [فَخْرِ {فَخْرُ}]

فرسٌ (كان) مُلقىً (مُرتمياً)، فوقه [حوله] تجمع [تفاخر]

A horse was lying down, there was a gathering [boasting] over [around] him

(279) [175]

عُنوجِ كيع مأتمْ [مأثُمْ] يأزَزْ [يعززْ] {جُبَزْ} عُجُ ذو [عُقُ ذو]

عُروك الأرض [الخصبة] كان يتصلب [كان يقف ساكنا] {كان جامدا} حوله

Uruk-of-the-[fertile] land was hardening [was standing still] {was frozen} around him

(280)

مأتُ [مأثُ] فُهُرَتْ [فُخُرَتْ] إنَ مُحِّ ذو [مُخِّ ذو] {إنَ عُجُ ذو [عُقُ ذو]}

الارض [الارض الخصبة] كانت مجتمعةً [متشرفةً] في محيطه [بنقائه] {في محيطه [بعلوّه]}

The [fertile] land was gathered [honored] around him [in his purity] {in his surrounding [in his highness]}

(281)

يتِعفِرْ أمانُ عُجُ [عُقُ] عدِنِ ذو

القوم كان يتزاحم [يتهالكَ] فوق [حول] مقامه [مقامه]

The people were cramming over [around] his site [over [around] him]

(282)

فُرُس ^ميس^ يكْتَمَرو [يِغْتَمَرو] عُجُ ذو [عُقُ ذو]

الشباب كانو يتحشدون [يتجمعون] فوقه [حوله]

The young people were crowding over [around] him

(283) [55, 209]

أعسَسْ ذومَ [أهشَشْ ذومَ] أتَدي ذُوَ {أتَدِذ} إنَ سَفْلِك [ثَفْلِك] {سَفْلِكُ [ثَفْلِكُ]}

طفتُ [انطلقتُ] به، أوْصَلتُه (وضعته) {موصلا (واضعا) اياه} في سَفلِكَ (تحت امرتك)

I roamed with him, I made him arrive (put him) {making him arrive (putting him)} under your command

(284)

أرأمْ ذوم كي أساتَ {دَمْ} عُجُ ذو [عُقُ ذو] أحُبُبْ

داعبته مثل إمرأة، أُحَبب (أُقبّل) فوقه [حوله]

I caressed (embraced) him like a woman, kissing (all) over [around] him

(285) [59, 352]

و أت تُلتَمْخِرِ ذو [تُلتَمَخَرِ ذو] إتيَ

و انت إخترتيه [ستختاريه] إليّ'

And you chose [will choose] him for me'

(286)

أمَ ^دنجر^ جِشْجِمَش عِمْقَتْ {إنْقَهَتْ} مُدَتْ {مُداتو} [مُهدَتْ {مُهداتوَ}] كَلَم {كَلا} [كَلأمَ {كَلأ}] إدَ [إهدَ] مُوْر {مُؤَرْ} أنَ دُمو ذا {دُمو ذو}

أميَ جِشجِمَش فكرت عميقا {فهمت}، عالمة [مفسرة] كل شيء [رؤيا الغيب] عَرِفتْ، قالت بنبرة عالية الى ابنها

The mother of Gilgamesh thought deeply [understood], the interpreter of everything [the vision (of the unseen)] knew, she said with a loud voice to her son

(287)

^ف^ريمة ^دنجر^ نِنْسُن عِمْقَتْ {إنْقَهَتْ} مُدَتْ {مُداتو} [مُهدَتْ {مُهداتوَ}] كَلَم {كَلا} [كَلأمَ {كَلأ}] إدَ [إهدَ] مُوْرَ {مُؤَرْ} أنَ ^نجر^ جِشْجِمَش

ريمة ننسون فكرت عميقا {فهمت}، عالمة [مفسرة] كل شيء [رؤيا الغيب] عَرِفتْ، قالت بنبرة عالية الى جِشجِمَش:

Rimat Ninsun thought deeply [understood], the interpreter of everything [the vision (of the unseen)] knew, she said with a loud voice to Gilgamesh:

(288) [235]

دُمو حَصينُ ذا تَأمُرُ إبْرِ {إبْرُ} {لَعْ}

'يا بُني، الفرس الذي رأيت رفيق {رجل}

'Son, the horse (that) you saw is a comrade {a man}

(289)

تَرْأَمْ ذوم جيم دَم تَحَبُبُ {تَحَبُبْ} عُجْ ذو [عُقْ ذو]

ستداعبه مثل أمه، ستُحَبب (تُقبّل) فوقه (حوله)

You will caress (embrace) him like a woman, you will kiss (all) over [around] it

(290) [37, 352]

و أنكو أُلتَمْخِرَ ذو {أُلتَمَخَرْ ذو} إتيكَ {كيْكَ}

و انا نفسي إخترته (ليكن) معك {من اجلك}

And I, myself, chose him (to be) with you {for you}

(291) [82]

يألَكَكُومَ ذأنُ [ضَنٌّ] [دَنٌّ] تَفُو مُشَرَبْ [مُشَذِبْ] إبْرِ

سيترسلكمَ (سيأتي لك)، قوة تَفي [تُجيب (عند الصعاب)]، منقذٌ للرفيق [لرفيقه]

He will come to you, a might to be loyal [to answer (when needed)], a savor of a [his] comrade

(292)

إنَ كور ذأنْ [ضَنْ] [دَنْ] حِمُقي إإذو [إإتو]

في الصَّقع (أرضُ الصِعاب) قويا، أوتي (له) عزم (تفاني)

In the difficult land, he is mighty, he has vigor (strength)

(293)

كيما كِصْرُ [قِصْرُ] ذا [دنجر] أنيم ذأُنَنَ [ضُنُنَ] [دُنُنَ] {ذأْنُنُ [ضُنُنُ] [دُنُنُ]} حِمُقَ ذو {حِمُقا ذو}

مثل فرسُ الاله أنيم جبروت (قوة) عزمه (تفانيه)'

Like the horse of the god Anim is the might of his vigor (strength)'

(294)

[دنجر]جِشْجِمَش أنَ ذاذمَ مُوْرْ أنَ أمَ ذو

جِشجِمَش اليها قال بنبرة عالية، الى امه:

Gilgamesh said to her with a loud voice, to his mother:

(295) [232,279, 338, 368, 435]

أماه إنَ كا{فيّ} [دنجر]إنليل مَلكْ {مَلكِ جَلي} ليمقُتَما {لينقُتَما} [ليمقُعتَما {لينقُعتَما}]

'أماه، بأمر [بمرجعية] الإله إنليل، المَلكُ (القوي القادر) { ملكُ الجلالات)}، ليَقَعُ (دعيه يقع) عليّ

'O Mother, by the order of god Enlil, the mighty one {the almighty}, let him fall upon me

(296) [37, 344, 368]

إبرِ مَلِكُ {مَلَكْ} {مَلَكَ} أنكو لأُرسيَ

رفيقٌ ملكٌ (قوي قادر)، لأُرسيَ (لأعتمدَ عليه) انا نفسي

A comrade, a mighty one, I, myself, can lean on

(297) [344, 368]

لأُرسيمَ {لأُرسِيَ} إبرِ مَلِكُ {مَلِكْ} أنَكو

لأُرسيَ (لأعتمدَ على) [دعيني أرسيَ (أعتمدَ على)] رفيقٍ مَلِكٍ (قوي وفي)، انا نفسي'"

Let me lean on a comrade, a mighty one, I, myself'"

(298)

إتأمَرْ {إتَأمْرَ} شونَاتي {مشجِ ميس ذو [مأشْجِ ميس ذو]}

(وهكذا) رأى (فهم) (جِشجِمَش) حُلميه {طيفَيه}

(Thus) he saw (understood) his two dreams {bright lights (night visions)}

(299) [235, 267]

|إنَا| فسَمْحَت [فشَمْخت] شونَتِي دنجرجِشْجِمَش يتَما أنَ دنجرأنكيدو

|فيما (بينما)| تَتِمُّ (تَنهي) سَمْحات [شَمْخات] (سرد) حُلمي جِشجِمَش الى أنكيدو

|Right when| Samhat [Shamkhat] was finishing (the recounting of) Gilgamesh's two dreams to Enkido

(300) [284]

إرتأمو كِلَّن

تعانقو (تداعبو) سويتا (كلاهما)

They hugged (caressed) each other

Tablet 2 (lines 1-46)
The Old Babylonian Edition (Penn Tablet)

(Correspond to lines 245-300 of Tablet 1 of the Standard Babylonian Edition)

(1) [91, 239]

إتبِيّمَ [إتبِغّمَ] [دنجر] جِش شونَتَم يِفَسرْ

نهض جِش يفسّر (يسرد) حلمه

[ابتغي جِش (ان) يفسّر (يفهم) الحلم [حلمه]]

Gish rose up to reveal the dream [his dream]

[Gish seeked to explain the dream [his dream]]

(2) [669]

إذَكَرَمْ أنَ أُمي ذو

قال الى امه:

He said to his mother:

(3) [387, 491]

أُمي إنَ ساعة مُسِيتيَا

"أمي، في ساعة (وقت) مسائي

"Mother, in [during] my evening hour (time)

(4) [226, 489, 568]

شَامْخاكُمَا أتَأنَلكْ

ترسّلْتُ (أطِلْتُ (رأيت عن بعيد)) شامِخُكِ (ضوءك العالي (نجمك))

I came across (I saw from far) your high one (your high bright light (star))

(5) [65]

إنَ بيرتْ عِطلوتِمْ [عِتلوتِمْ]

فيما (انا) بَين [حينما (انا) بينَ] الرجال الشباب الاقوياء

While (I am) in between (among) the young strong men

(6) 203, 453

إبّثونما {إفزرونَمْ} كأكَبو سَماءِي

ظهرت [تواجدت] {تفَرقت (إنتشرت)} لي كواكب السماوات

The stars of heavens appeared {dispersed (spread)} before me

(7) 232, 304, 485, 535

قِصْرُ [كِصرُ] {قِصْرُم [كِصرُم]} ذا دنجرأنيم إمقوُتْ [إمقُعُتْ] أنَ ظِهْرِيَ

فرسُ الإله أنيم وقع (هبط) الى خلفي [على مقامي] (تحت أمرَتي)

A horse of god Anim fell (landed) to my back (behind me) [on my site] (came under my command)

(8) 219

أعسِي ذومَ [أهشِي ذومَ] إكْتَبِتْ حلِيَ [علِيَ]

طُفتُ به [طِرتُ به؟] (اليلا) [إنطَلَقت به]، كَبَتَ (هَيمَنَ) عليّ

I roamed him [unleashed him] [flew him?], he overpowered (overwhelmed) me

(9) 335, 432, 618

أنِسْ ذومَ {أنِسُمَ} نُسَّ ذو ألْ إلْتِئِي [إلْتَعِي]

أسرعته (أسرعت سوقه)، ما خِفتُ [ما أبطأتَ] سرعته [علوّه؟]

I rushed him, I did not fear his speed [altitude?]

(10) 644

عُروك مأثُمْ [مأثُمْ] فَهِرْ [فَخِرْ] عِلِ [حلِ] ذو

أرض عُروك [الخصبة] تجمعت [تشرفت] عليه [حوله]

The [Fertile] Land of Uruk was gathered [honored] over [around] him

(11) 534, 628

عِتلوتُمْ {عِطلوتُمْ} يُنَسكو {يُنَشَقو [يُنَسَقو]} ظِيفِي ذو

الرجال الشباب الاقوياء يُشمّون [يُقبّلون] اقدامه [سيقانه]

The young strong men sniffed [kissed] his feet [lower legs]

(12) 451, 662

أُمدِمَ فُوتِي

تمددو [سجدو] أمامي

They extended (laid down) [knelt] in front of me (before me)

(13) 201, 662

يِمدِو إياتِي

يَمِدون (العون) لي [يمدونني (يعينوني)]

Extending out (their help) to me [helping me]

(14) [8, 55]

أعَسيا ذومَ [أمَشيا ذومَ] أبَلا ذو [أعبَلا ذو] [أبعَلا ذو] أنَ ظهرِكِ"

طافو به [أطلقوه]، حملوه (جلبوه) [وجهوه] الى خلفكِ [الى مقامكِ] (تحت أمرَتكِ)"

They roamed with him, they brought him [led him] to your back (behind you) [to your site] (brought him under your command)

(15) [375]

أمي دنجرجِش مُديتْ [مُهديتْ] كلَمَ [كلأمَ]

أم جِش، عالمة [مفسرة] كل شيء [رؤيا الغيب]

The mother of Jish, the interpreter of everything [of the vision (of the unseen)]

(16) [669]

إذكَرَمْ أنَ دنجرجِش

قالت الى جِش:

She said to Jish:

(17) [293, 299, 367]

مند [منذ] دنجرجِش ذا كيمَ كاتِ

"من الواضح [مُذ ان كان هذا]، يا جِش، هذا كأنما انت

"Clearly [Since this was], O Jish, this one like yourself

(18)

إنَ ظهرِ إإولِدمْ [يولِدمَ]

في البرية وُلِدَ

In the wild, he was born

(19) [494]

أربي ذو سادُوَ

إحتضنَه الجبل

The mountain reared (raised) him

(20) [59, 226, 573, 655]

تأمَرْذومَ |كِيمَ سَلْ| تَحَدو أتَّ

ستراه، |مثل طفل [رضيع]| ستلتزمه (ستتبناه) [ستفرحُ] أنت

You will see him, |like a child [an infant]| you will take him (adopt him) [you will rejoice]

(21) [147]

عتِلوتُمْ {عِطلوتُمْ} يُنَسكو {يُنَشَقو [يُنَسَقو]} ظيفي ذو

الرجال الشباب الاقوياء سيشمّون [سيقبلون] اقدامه [سيقانه]

The young strong men will sniff [kiss] his feet [lower legs]

(22) [589, 660]

تِطَرّاَ ذو {تِدِراَ ذوم} تُتُؤْمَ

ستقابله فجأة [ستخرج عليه فجأة]، ستتوأمه

You will face him suddenly; you will take him like a twin

(23)

تَتَرَسو أنَ ظِهْرِيَ

سترسيه [ستضعه] الى خلفي [في مقامي] (تحت أمرتي)"

You will anchor (put) him in my back (behind me) (you will bring him under my command)"

(24) [658]

أستِنْئِمَ {إتِلْئمَ} إتأمَرْ ثانيتَمْ

تأفف [نامَ]، رأى (حلما) ثانياً

He slept [wailed], he saw (a dream) for the second time

(25)

إتْبِي [إتْبِغ] يتَوأمْ أنَ أمِيَ ذو

نَهَض [بغي] يفضي الى امه:

He rose up [seeked] to disclose [to explain] to his mother:

(26)

أُمي أتأمَرْ ثانتَمْ

"امي، رأيت (حَلمت) ثانياً

"Mother, I saw a second one

(27) [136, 546, 617]

|أتأمَرْ عِ|مِيَ [حِمِي] عَلا إنَ سُوقِمْ

|رأيت| ضوءً ساطعاً بعيدا (عاليا) في السوقِ

|I saw| a distant (high) bright light in the market

(28) [644]

ذا عُروك رِبِيتِمْ

الذي في عُروك الرابية

Of Uruk-of-the-Hill

(29) [189]

حَصِينُ نَدِيمَ

فرسٌ (كان) مُلقىً (مُرتمياً)

A horse was lying (down)

(30)

عِلِي [حِلِي] ذو فَهْرُ [فَخْرُ]

فوقه [حوله] تجمع

A gathering was over [around] him

(31) [189, 539, 572]

حَصِينُمَ ثانِ [سَعْنِ] [شَعْنِ] بُنُ ذو

الفرس (هذا) (كان) غريبٌ [معيبٌ] [قبيحٌ] [رثٌ] [صغير] بنيانه (شكله)

The horse was strange [ugly] [shabby] [miniature] in his build (shape)

(32) [37, 573]

أمُرْ ذومَ أحْتَدو أنَكو

رأيته، التزمته (تبنيته) [فرحتُ] انا نفسي

I saw him, I, myself, took him (adopted him) [I, myself, rejoiced]

(33) [247]

أرأمْ ذومَ كِيما أساتِمْ

داعبته مثل إمرأة

I caressed (embraced) him like a woman

(34)

أُحَبُبْ عِلْ [حِلْ] ذو

أُحَبب (أُقبّل) فوقه [حواليه]

Kissing (all) over [around] him

(35) [332]

إلْكِ ذوم {إلْقِي ذوم} أستَكَنْ ذو

ترسلتُه (قُدْتُهُ) {أخَذْتُه}، أستَكِنُهُ (أضَعَهُ)

I went with him (led him) {took him}, placing (putting) him

(36) [22]

أنَ أهِيَ [أخِيَ]

الى [على] جانبي (كرفيق) [كأن أخي]

On my side (as a comrade) [Like my brother]

(37) [375]

أُمي [دنجر] جِش مُديَتْ [مُهديَتْ] كَلَمَ [كَلأمَ]

أم جِش، عالمة [مفسرة] كل شيء [رؤيا الغيب]

Mother of Jish, the interpreter of everything [the vision (of the unseen)]

(38) [262, 269]

إذَكَرَمْ {إسأقَرَمْ} أنَ دنجرجِش

قالت {أقرّت} الى جِش:

Said {Declared} to Jish:

(39)

(40)

(41)

(42)

(43)

آذُمْ [هذُمْ] أُسْتَمَخَرو إتيكَ

هذا لانه (الرجل) ساختاره (ليكن) معك

That is because he (this man) I shall choose (to be) with you

(44)

دنجرجِش شُوناتَمْ يفسَرْ

(بينما) جِش كان يفَسّر (يسرد) [يفَسّر (يفهم)] حلماه

(As) Jish was revealing [explaining (understanding)] his (two) dreams

(45) [352]

دنجرإنكيدو وَثِب مَخَرْ حَرِمتِم

إنكيدو كان جالس قبالة الحُرمة

Enkidu was seated before the harem

(46)

أرْتَأمو كِلالَنْ

(ثم) تعانقو (تداعبو) سويتا (كلاهما)

(then) They hugged (caressed) each other

Tablet 10 (lines 207-322) The Standard Babylonian Edition

(207) [91]

ᵐᵈجِشْتُكْ أنَ ذا ذُوم مؤرْ أنَ ᵐعُد ذيتم

جِشْتُكْ (جِشْ الحُمقْ) (جِشجِمَش) قال اليه، الى أُتانَفسْتم:

Gilgamesh said to him, to Uta-Napištim:

(208) [374]

لِيبلُطْ ᵐعُد ذي دُمْ [دُمْ] ᵐعُبَر تُوتُ

"ليحيا أُتانَفسْتم بن قومِ تُوتُ

"Long live Uta-Napištim, son of the people (tribe) of Tutu

(209) [11, 133]

|إذا| لو عِجِرِ [إجِر] عَبُبَ ذا أنَ دَ...

هذا الذي له، بعد الطوفان الذي الى [على]............

He who, for him, after the Deluge that .... to [on] ....

(210)

عَبُبَ مِنا أنَ ....

الطوفان الذي منه الى [على]........................

The Deluge, from which .... to [on] ....

(211)

(212)

ᵐعُد ذي أنَ ذا ذُوم مؤرَ أنَ ᵐᵈجِشْتُكْ

أُتانَفسْتم قال اليه، الى جِشْتُكْ (جِشجِمَش):

Uta-Napištim said to him, to Gilgamesh:

(213) [354, 463]

أمن أكْلا لِيتَاكَ قودُدُ فَنُكَ

"لمَ آكِلا (متآكلان، غائران) خَديكَ، قُودُدٌ (مقدّدٌ، متَشققٌ) وجهكَ؟

"Why are your cheeks sunken, your face slashed?

(214) [341, 458, 670]

لؤمُنْ شأيكَ قَتُوْ [قَثُوْ] زِمُكَ

(لِمَ) حزينٌ [غَضِبٌ] قلبكَ، مُجتثٌ كبرياءك [مظهرك]؟

(why) Your heart is sad [angry], your pride [appearance] is wiped out?

(215) [203, 288, 413]

يبَثِي [إبَذِي] نِسَتُ إنَ كَرشِكَ

(لِمَ) جوع شديد [ضعف] يظهرُ (ينتشرُ) [يتواجدُ] في بطنك؟

(why) A severe hunger [weakness] appears (spreads) [exists] in your gut?

(216)

أنَ ألِكْ أُرهِ رُقَتِ فَنُكَ مَثُلُ

(لِمَ) مَثَلُ وجهكَ كَمن ترسّل (جاء) طريق بعيد [صعبٌ] ؟

(why) Your face looks like as if for one who had travelled a difficult (distant) road?

(217) [2, 466, 508, 519]

إنَ آ سَرْبِ و ضِيتِ قُمُؤ فَنُكَ

(لِمَ) قَمُؤٌ [متسقّعٌ (محُرقٌ)] وجهُكَ بذلك السَيل المائي وضوء الشمس؟

(why) Your face was burnt in that water torrent and sunshine?

(218) [249, 320, 498]

و فَنْ لَبِ سَكْنَتَمَ [ثَكْنَتَمَ] تَرَفُضْ [تَرَبُذْ] عدن

و (لِمَ) وجهَ لبوةٍ واضعٌ (انت)، ترومُ البرية؟"

[و (لِمَ) حالَ لبوةٍ ساكنٌ (انت)، ترومُ البرية؟]"

And (why) are you dressed up (in) a lioness face, roaming the wild?"

[And (why) are you living the (living) condition of a lioness, roaming the wild?]"

(219)

[م د]جِشتُلْ **أنَ ذا ذُوم مُرَ أنَ** عُد ذي**تم**

جِشتُلْ (جش الشديد الحمق) (جِشجِمَش) قال اليه، الى أُتانَفسْتم:

Gilgamesh said to him, to Uta-Napištim:

(220) [584]

أمِنِ لا آكْلا طي[ميس] **آ لا قودُدُ فَنُوا**

"لِمَ لا آكِلا (غائران) خدّيَ، لا قُوددٌ (متَشققٌ) وجهيَ؟

"Why should my cheeks not be sunken, my face not be slashed?

(221)

لا لؤمُنْ لبي لا قَتُوْ [قَثُوْ] زِمُوا

(لِمَ) لا حزينٌ [غَضِبٌ] قلبيَ، لا مُجتثٌ كبرياءي [مظهري]؟

(why) My heart should not be sad [angry], my pride [appearance] should not be wiped out?

(222)

لا إبِثي [إبِذي] نِستَ إنَ كَرشيا

(لِمَ) لا (ما) ظهر (انتشر) [تواجد] جوع شديد [ضعف] في بطنيا ؟

(why) A severe hunger [weakness] should not have appeared (spread) [existed] in my gut?

(223)

أنَ ألكْ أُره رُقِت فَنوا لا مَثْلُ

(لِمَ) لا مَثَلَ وجهيَ كَمن ترسّل (جاء) طريق طريق بعيد [صعبٌ] ؟

(why) My face should not look like as if for someone who had travelled a difficult (distant) road?

(224)

إنَ آ {أذ} سرْبِ و ضيتِ لا قُمُؤ فَنوا

(لِمَ) لا قَمُؤَ [مسقّعٌ (مُحرقٌ)] وجهيَ بذلك السَيل المائي وضوء الشمس؟

(why) My face should not be burnt in that water torrent and sunshine?

(225)

و فَنْ لَبِ لا سَكْنَكُما [ثَكْنَكَما] لا أرَفَضْ [أربُذْ] عدن

و (لِمَ) وجهَ لبوةٍ ما واضعٌ أنا، (و) لا أرومُ البرية؟"

[و (لِمَ) حالَ لبوةٍ ما ساكنٌ أنا، (و) لا أرومُ البرية؟]"

And (why) I should not be dressed up (in) a lioness face, (and) not roam the wild?"

[And (why) should I not be living the (living) condition of a lioness, (and) not be roaming the wild?]

(226) [25, 309, 417, 579]

إبرِ كَوْدَنِ طَرِدُ عَكَنُ ذا كور [قور] **نمْرُ {نِمْرِ} ذا عدن**

رفيقي، البَغل الطليقُ، غَليظُ الصَّقعِ (أرضِ الصعاب)، نمْرُ { نمْرِ} البرية

My comrade, the free mule, the boor of the difficult land, the tiger of the wild

(227)

إنكيدو إبرِ كَوْدَنِ طَرِدُ |عَكَنُ ذا كور نمْرُ {نِمْرِ} ذا عدن| كمن

إنكيدو رفيقي، البَغل الطليقُ، غَليظُ الصَّقعِ (أرضِ الصعاب)، نِمْرُ { نمْرِ} البرية

Enkido my comrade, the free mule, the boor of the difficult land, the tiger of the wild

(228) [114, 415]

ذا دُعو**دُعُما نيلُوَ سادا**

نحن اللذين، مجتمعين [قاصدين] سوياً، نُالو (أدركو) (قمم) الجبال

It was we who, joining [going] together, reached the mountains (tops)

(229) [135, 419, 620]

عَلاءَ نِصْبَتُمَ ... عَلاءَ نِحْنَرُ [نِنَّحَرُ]

نَصبو (مصيدة) لعلاء، | ثم| نَحرو [إنَّحرو] علاءَ

Trapped 'Ala' |then| slaughtered 'Ala'

(230) [92, 157, 160, 274, 647]

نُسَلْفِتُ دنجرحُمبَبَ [هُمْبَبَ] ذا إنَ جشطحر [جشطير] جشعرن أتْبو [عَشْبُوَ]

سَوّيا بالارض (دَمّرا) حُمبَبَ [هُمْبَبَ] الذي كان يقيم في [يقتات على] غابة شجر العرن [قِشّ (بقايا) خشب شجر العرن]

Leveled (wiped out) [d]Humbaba who was living [feeding] on the Cedar Forest [cedar wood remains]

(231) [409, 636]

إنَ نَيْرَبَيتِ ذا كورِي نِدُكُ هُرمَخ ميس [عُرمَخ ميس]

في ممرات الجبال دَكّو (قتلو) الاسود (الكائنات المفترسة)

Killed lions [ferocious creatures] in the mountain passages

(232) [82, 113, 276, 358]

إبرِ ذا أرأمُ ذو ذأنِتْ [ضَنِّتْ] [دَنِّتْ] إتيا دودُكُ [طوطُكُ] [دُعْدُعُكُ] كَلَ مَرْضَاتِ

رفيقي الذي أحِبُّهُ بقوة (جداً)، (الذي) رافقني المغامرات (الرواح والمجيء) [الشدائد] [العثرات]، كلّ المعانات

My comrade whom I love so much, who joined me (in) the adventures [the difficulties] [the misfortunes], all the sufferings

(233) [113]

إنكيدو إبرِ ذا أرأمُ ذو ذأنِتْ [ضَنِّتْ] [دَنِّتْ] إتيا دودُكُ [طوطُكُ] [دُعْدُعُكُ] إكَلُ مَرْضَاتِ| كمن

إنكيدو رفيقي الذي أحِبّهُ بقوة (جداً)، (الذي) رافقني المغامرات (الرواح والمجيء) [الشدائد] [العثرات]، كلّ المعانات

Enkido my comrade whom I love so much, who joined me (in) the adventures [the difficulties] [the misfortunes], all the sufferings

(234) [289, 527]

إقْصُدَنَ [إكْسُدانِ] ذو صِمات عَمِيلُتِ

قَصُدَنّهُ قَدرُ الانسان (الجنس البشري)

The destiny of mankind reached [pursued] him

(235) [10, 639]

6 عُرِي و 7 مُساتِي عُجْ ذو [عُقْ ذو] أبكِ

لستة مغرُبيات وسبعة ليالي فوقه [حوله] أبكي

(For) six sunsets and seven nights, I was crying over [around] him

(236) [14, 459]

أُل أُمَدِنْ [أَعطِنْ] [أدِنْ] [أطِنْ] ذو أنَ قِبيرِ

لم أأويه [ادعه] [أعطيه] الى الدفن

And I did not let him rest [I did not give him up] to burial

(237) [15, 43, 596]

عَدي [عَتي] ثُوْلتُ إمقوْتَم [إمقُعُتَم] إنَ أفّ ذو

حتى سقطت ثُلّةً (ثلة يرقات الدود) في (من) أنفهِ

Until after [Until] a (maggot) pack fell in (from) his nose

(238) [660]

أذعُر [أذأُر] ....

أخافُ ......

Fearing ....

(239) [42, 349]

مُوتَ [مُوتا] أفْلَهْمَا أرَفُض [أرَفُض] عدن

الموت [موته] جعلني أهرب، (جعلني) أروم البرية

Death [His death] made me run away, (made me) roam the wild

(240) [30, 219]

أمَتْ [همَتْ] إبرِيا كَبْتَتْ عُجْيا [عَقْيا]

قَدَرُ [همّ (حزنُ) [أمر]] رفيقي كان كابتً (مهيمنً) [هيمَنَ] عليّ

The fate [grief [matter]] of my comrade was overwhelming (too much) on me [overwhelmed me]

(241)

أره رُقتَ أرَفُض [أرَفُض] عدن

(جعلني) في طريق صعب (بعيد) أرومُ البرية

(it made me) Roam the wild on a difficult (distant) road

(242)

همَتْ إنكيدو إبريا |كَبْتَتْ عُجْيا[عَقْيا]| كمنَ

همّ (حُزنُ) [أمر] إنكيدو رفيقي كان كابتً (مهيمنً) [هيمَنَ] عليّ

The sorrow [matter] of (for) my comrade Enkido was overwhelming (too much) on me [overwhelmed me]

(243)

حَرَنُ رُقتَ |أرَفُض [أرَفُض] عدن| كمنَ

(جعلني) في رحلة صعبة [بعيدة] أروم البرية

(it made me) Roam the wild on a difficult (distant) journey

(244) [299, 345, 465]

كيْكي لأسْكُتْ كيْكي لأقُلْ [لأقْهلْ] أنَكو

(إذ) كيف، كيف لي أن أسكت (أعْرِضْ)، كيف، كيف لي أن أقلَّ [أقهلَ] (أضعفَ)، انا نفسي؟

How, how could I stay silent (abandon), how, how could I do less (weaken), I myself?

(245) [136, 590]

إبرِ ذا أرأمُ يتَعمِي طِيطتْ

رفيقي الذي أُحبّ كان يتوارى طيناً (بطينٍ)

My comrade, whom I love, was being buried in mud

(246)

إنكيدو إبرِ |ذا أرأمُ يتَعمي طيطِتْ| كمن

رفيقي إنكيدو الذي أُحبّ كان يتوارى طيناً (بطينٍ)

My comrade Enkido, whom I love, was being buried in mud

(247) 415

أنَكو أُل كي ذا ذومَ أنحلَمَ [أنيلَمَ]

انا، نفسي، سوف لا أنْحَل [أُنالُ]، كما هو

I, myself, will not lie down [will not be taken], like him

(248) 76, 123, 585

أُلْ أتبا دُرْ [دورْ] دَرْ [دَهر]

لا أنهض [(سوف) لن أهلَكُ] دوار الدهرِ (الى ابد الدهر)"

Not to rise [I will not vanish] round the age (through eternity)"

(249)

جِشْجِمَش أنَ ذا ذُوم || مُرَ أنَ مُعْد ذي دنجر

جِشجِمَش قال اليه، الى أُتانَفسْتم:

Gilgamesh said to him, to Uta-Napištim:

(250) 29, 207

أنَكو أُمَا لأُلكِمْ مُعُد ذي روقَ [روقِ] ذا يدَبُبُذْ لأُمُرْ

"أنا نفسي كنت لابد[علمت انني يجب] ان أترَسّل (أذهبُ) لأرى أُتانَفسْتم البعيد المُتنحي (نوح) الذي يُملي عدلاً

"I, myself had to [knew I should] go to see Uta-Napištim the withdrawn and distant (Noah) who promotes justice

(251) 52, 284, 313

أسْخُرْ ألِكَ {ألَكْ} || كَل ذِنَ كور مُبس **{كور كور** مُبس**}**

تَرسلتُ (ذهبت) أُذلّلُ (أقهرُ) [أدورُ ذاهبا وآيبا] كلّوَ صُقُعِ (صِعابِ الارض) {صِعاب صِعابِ الارض}

I went overcoming [circling back and forth] all those difficult lands {difficult, difficult lands}

(252) 358, 578

إعتِتْقَا [إعتِتّقا] || كور مُبس **مَرضُتِ**

تجاوزت مرارا أراض [جبال] مظلمة وَعِرة

I passed (crossed), repeatedly, through dark and rugged lands [mountains]

(253) 129, 574

وإتِتعْبِرَا كَل ذِنَ طَماتُم

وعَبرتُ مرارا كلّ تلك البحار

I crossed, repeatedly, all those seas

(254) [258, 270, 437, 568]

شتَّ طَبْتَ || أَل إشبُعو قَنُوا

{|أ|كو أَما شتِّ طَبْتُ أَل إشبُعو قَنُوا}

نوماً طيباً (رغيداً، هنيئا)، أَل (ما) شَبَعَ وجهي

{عرفت، نفسي، (ان) وجهي ما شَبُعَ نوماً طيباً (رغيداً، هنيئا)}

My face did not sate soothing (peaceful) sleep

{I knew, myself, (that) my face did not sate soothing (peaceful) sleep}

(255) [79, 474, 657]

أُسْتعزقْ [أُسْتئزقْ] [أُلْتعزقْ [أُلْتئزقْ]] رَأمَني إنَ دَلَفُ [دلَفِ]

(و)شَقَّقَ وقَشَّرَ [سَلَخَ] ذاته (الوجه) ببطئ (تدريجياً)

It (the face) slashed and peeled [skinned] its own, bit by bit (gradually)

(256) [524]

سِرعانيا سغبا لغب **أمتَلِ**

مصاريني إمْتَلت جوع إعياء وتعب

My intestines filled up with exhaustion hunger

(257) [26, 39, 354]

مِنا أكْتِسِر إنَ مَنَحْتِيا

أيّما (نزرٌ قليل) أُحْرَزْت (انا) في كفاحي؟

What (little) have I achieved in my struggle (toil)?

(258) [152, 289, 324, 337, 458]

أنَ ليتْ ^ف^سَبِئتْ أل أقصُدَمَ [أكسُدَمَ] لُبُسْتِ إقْتي

أَل (لَمْ) أبْلغ ولو السَّبِئَةِ (الخمّارة)، (و) أُجتُث (تَهرأ) مَلبَسي

I did not even reach the alewife (and) my clothes got wiped (worn) out

(259) [49, 70, 369, 407, 409, 417]

آدُكْ أسَ بوصَ نيسَ نمرِ مِنْدِنَ

دَكيتُ (قتلت) عَسَ (دب)، بَوصَ (ضبع)، ميسَ (ذئب)، نِمرِ، مدّين (أسد)

I killed bear, hyena, wolf, panther, lion,

(260) [5, 68, 401, 600]

آلَ تُرَحَ بوْلَ [بُعْلَ] و نَمَسيا ذا عدن

أيلَ (وعل)، تُرح (ماعز الجبل)، قطيع وحيوانات البرية

caribou (ibex), mountain goat, herd and beasts of the wild

(261) [315, 659, 663]

عُضو ^ميس^ **ذونَ أأكلْ [أكألْ]** كؤس ^ميش^ **ذونَ [**كُمس ^ميش^ **ذونَ] أُطَبَخْ**

(كي) أأكلُ أعضاءهم، أشوي (اجفف) جلودهم [أشوي كراعينهم]

(in order to) To eat their organs, to barbecue (burn-dry) their skins [to barbecue their limbs]

(262) [279, 327]

ذا سغبا لغب ليعدِلُ كاءَ ذا

"ذا جوعُ إعياءٍ وتعبٍ (الجائعُ المُتعب) ليُنصف (ليسوّي) ثغرهُ (جوفه)

“He who is hungry and exhausted shall do justice to (shall level) his cavity (abdomen)

(263) [144, 145, 279, 443]

إنَ عسرِ خيا وعسرِ ليفْحُ كاءَ ذا

بعِسرِ خواء (نبت يابسٍ شائك يؤكل في المجاعة) وعِسر (قِير مائع) ليَسُد (ليملئ) ثغرهُ (جوفه)"

With a thorny famine plant and asphalt, he shall seal (fill) his cavity (abdomen)”

(264) [56, 200, 347]

أذوَ [هذوَ] إياذي مِئلُكَ || لا |أُمعلكُ ....|

هذا لأنهم (الحيوانات) كانو مستعجلين (قافزين) لي (لأجلي)، ما |أُخِذو ....|

That is because they (the animals) were rushing (jumping) for me; they were not |taken ....|

(265) [56, 186, 347, 433]

أذوَ [هذوَ] إياذي فأ أدِء [فَدِء] [هَدإ] |أُمعلكُ ....|

{إياذي فأ أدِء [فَدِء] [هَدإ] |أُمعلكُ ....|}

هذا لأنهم (الحيوانات) |أُخِذو ...| غنيمةُ إنقاذ [فِدية، قُربان)] [هَديّة] لي (لأجلي)"

{هم |أُخِذو ...| غنيمةُ إنقاذ [فِدية، قُربان)] [هَديّة] لي (لأجلي)"}

That is because they (the animals) were |taken ...| (as) a saving booty [a sacrifice] [a gift] for me”

{They (the animals) were |taken ...| (as) a saving booty [a sacrifice] [a gift] for me”}

(266)

مُدُ ذيتم أنَ ذا ذُوم موَرَ أنَ دنجرجِشْجِمَش

أُتانَفسْتم قال اليه، الى دنجرجِشْجِمَش:

Uta-Napištim said to him, to Gilgamesh:

(267) [413, 601]

أمنِ دنجرجِشْجِمش نِستَ تُرتنئِدِ أتَّ؟

"لم يا جشجمَش تبتغي الشقاء (الاعياء) أنت؟

“Why, Gilgamesh, do you repeatedly go after drudgery (exhaustion)?

(268)

ذا إنَ عضو دِنجر مِلِيس وعَميلُتِ بَنأتَ

(أنت) الذي من عضو (صنف، عنصر) الآلهة والبشر بنائه

(You) who in (from) the kind [in (from) the components] of gods and human is his build

(269) [631]

ذا كيمَ {جيم} أدكَ و أمك |إعِفُسُنِكَ [إعِفُشُنِكَ]|

(أنت) الذي مثل أباك وأمك |أنجزوك (خلقوك) (الالهة)|

(You) who like your father and mother |they (the gods) made you|

(270) [330, 363]

مَتِما [دنجر] **جِشْجمش أنَ ليكِ |تُرتنئدِ أتَّ|؟**

منذ متى [حتى متى] يا جشجِمش الى احمق مجنون |تَنحدرُ أنتَ|؟

Since when [Until when], Gilgamesh, to a crazy fool |you decline|?

(271) [158, 168, 209, 245, 274]

[جش]**جوزع [جوزا] إنَ وكَن إإدوَمَ تِثِبْ [تِشِبْ] إقْبوكَ**

هَيَّوْ جَوزَعُ (مصطبة عالية، عرش) في الوكن (المجلس، الوكر)؛ إتّثِبْ [إتّشِبْ (إرتقي، إعتلي)]، قالو لكَ

They prepared a throne in the assembly; sit [ascend], they told you

(272) [14, 199, 516, 525]

نَدْنَ أذو أنَ ليكِ تُرْشُمِ {سِكَرِ} جيمَ إنْنَ [حِنْنَ] .....

(بينما) أعطو له، الى الاحمق المجنون، حثالةً جعة {جعةً} كأنها نفاية شحم محمص (دهن) ....

(while) They gave to him, to the crazy fool, beer sediment {beer} like the remains of a roasted fat (ghee) ....

(273) [316, 592]

طَحُ [طَح] وكُكُشا جيم ....

(أعطو له) طحين نخالة (قشور) وشعير كأنه ....

(they gave him) A grinded husk and malt (barley) like ....

(274) [337, 361]

لابِسْ مَشخَندَ جيم ....

مُرتديا (الاحمق المجنون) رداء فضفاض كأنه ....

He (the crazy fool) is dressed in a baggy gown like ....

(275) [128]

و ذا أذو جيم نِيبيخِ يِبخْ [عِبخْ] ....

وله (الرداء) (نسيج) مثل نسيج صوف خشن لحبل ثخين ......

And it (the gown) has (a fabric) like a rough wool fabric of a thick rope .....

(276) [56, 260, 368]

أذوَ [هذوَ] لا إإذُوَ [إإتُوَ] مَلِكِ ....

هذا لأنه (الاحمق المجنون) ما أوتي مَلِكً (آمرً) ....

That is because he (the crazy fool) has no leader ....

(277) [30, 368]

أمَتْ مِلْكِ [همَتْ مِلْكِ] لا إإذُوَ [إإتُوَ] ....

ما أوتي (عرف) (ما له) قَدْرُ مِلْكِ (قيمة التوجيه) [مِلاكُ الامر (صلاحُ الامر)] ....

He does not have (know) the value of guidance [the righteousness] ....

(278) [344]

إإذي [إإتي] رِسي ذو دنجر جِشْجِمَش ....

خُذ (استخلص) عِبرته، يا جشجِمش ....

Get (extract) his lesson, Gilgamesh ....

(279) [40, 139, 626]

أأنو عَن [أنْ] ذونُ مَلا ذا ....

هؤلاء (أمثاله) سيدهم |يقرر ......| مَلا ذا (مدى عمرهم)

Those (like him), their master |decides ....| their life span

(280)

(281) [74, 111]

.... دنجر30 و دِنجر مبس مُسيتي ....

.... القمر وآلهة الليل ....

.... the moon and the gods [of the night] ....

(282) [74, 111]

إنَ في دنجر30 إلَكْ ....

في الليل يترسّلَ (يذهَبَ) القمر.............................

In the night the moon goes (disappear) ....

(283) [79]

دَلْفُمَ دِنجر مبس ....

الالهة تتقدم تدريجيا................................

The gods move forward (appear) one by one ....

(284) [499, 639]

عِرا لا سَكِفُ ....

جماعة، لا (افرادا) مُتخبطين ....

As a group (side by side), not trampled ....

(285)

ألتُ فَنْ سَكَنْ [ثَكِنْ] ....

أوّلُ ما (حالما) قام الحال (بدأ الوجود) ....

Right when the state of being (existence) was established ....

(286) [312]

أتَّ كُفُدْمَ [كُفُتْمَ] ....

أنت .... خُطّةَ (غاية) ....

You .... the plan (goal) of ....

(287) [113, 577]

تَفْتُكَ [تَفْتُقَ] آ فيء دو ....

(أنت) تتجرأ (تتحدى) [تغير] بذلك قرار الجميع (القرار الجماعي) ....

(you are) challenging [changing], in that (that way), the decree of all (the unanimous decree) ....

(288) [675]

ثُمَّ دنجر **جِشْجِمَش حي [إي]** دنجر ميس **زَنئن ....**

بَعْدَ إذ (حقا) يا جِشجِمَش معبد الآلهة هو ملجأ ....

After all (indeed), Gilgamesh, the temple of gods is the refuge ....

(289) [219]

حِي [إي] دنجر15 ميس ....

معبد الآلهات ....

The temple of goddesses ....

(290)

ذِنا .... دنجر ميس ....

هم .... الآلهة ....

They .... the gods ....

(291)

أنَ .... إعِفُس [إعِفُشْ] ....

الى [على]...................... هيؤ [أنجزو] ....

To [on]................................... they prepare [made] ....

(292) [219, 261]

.... أنَ قِيثتم ....

.... الى [على] القِسمة والنصيب (الحظ) ....

.... to [on] fate and destiny (lot) ....

(293) [288, 398]

.... ينَمدؤ .... كرشي ذو

.... يعطو .... بدنه

.... give (provide) .... his body

(294) [675]

زَنئن ....

.... المُجهِّز (الرزاق)

.... the provisioner (provider)

(295)

(296) [332, 354, 501]

|ذوو| إلقُو أنَ سِمْتِ ذو [شِمْتِ] ذو ....

|هو| ألقَوْهُ (وجهوهُ) الى طريقه (مصيره) ....

|He,| they made him find (they directed him) to his road [to his destiny] ....

(297) [79, 332]

أتَّ تَدَلِفْ مِنا تَلقو

أنت تهْرمُ [تهْزلُ]؛ ماذا تلقي (تُحْرز) (انت)؟

You are aging [attenuating]; what are you finding (gaining)?

(298) [39, 79]

إنَ دَلَفِ تُنَحا رمأنكَ

ببطئ (أنت) تؤذي [تُتْعب] ذاتك

Slowly, you are hurting [tiring] your own

(299) [487]

سأي ميس كَ نِسَتَ {سغبا لغب} تُمالا

(أنت) تملئ مصارينك جوع شديد {جوع إعياء وتعب}

You are filling your intestines with severe hunger {exhaustion hunger}

(300) [485, 598, 604]

رُقُتُ تُقَرَبْ عُد ميس كَ

(أنت) تُقَرّب البعيد، (تقرب) مواعيدك [أيامُك] (الاخيرة)

You are bringing the faraway closer, your (final) dates [days]

(301) [43, 162, 190, 551]

عَميلُتُم ذا جيم جحي عَفي [أفي] هَصِفِ [حَصِفِ] |آ| سُومْ ذو [ثُمْ ذو]

الرجل ذا مَثَلُ قَصبَةِ أجمة (قصبة هور) مكسورة [مَقصية]، |ذلك| حُكمه (مَصيره) [ما بعده (مستقبله)]

A man is like a snapped off [an eliminated] reed in a canebrake, |that| is his fate [his afterward (his future)]

(302) [119, 295]

عِطلَ دَمْقا [دَمْجا] قصقلت دَمِقْتُم [دَمِجْتُم]

الشاب المفتول المصقول (المجدول)، الشابة المفتولة والمصقولة (المجدولة)

The entwined and polished (well-built) young man, the entwined and polished (well-built) young woman

(303) [349, 638, 655]

أُرُهِت |عَدي [حَدي] حَيا|ذونُمَ يسَلَكْ موتِ

بعجلة (قبل الاوان)، |حتى حياتهمُ| يَسلبُ الموت

Hurriedly (prematurely), death abducts |even their lives|

(304) 235, 349, 353

أُل مَمَّ موتُ {موتُم} يأمَرْ

لا أحدا يرى الموت

No one sees death

(305) 335

أُل مَمَّ ذا موتِ يأمَرْ فَني ذو

لا أحدا، لهذا الموت، يرى وجههُ

No one, of this death, sees its face

(306) 480, 514

أُل مَمَّ ذا موتِ || رِجْمَ ذو يسّمَعْ

لا أحدا، لهذا الموت، يسمع صرخته (صوته)

No one, of this death, hears its scream (voice)

(307) 19, 190, 335, 349

أجُّ موتُم || هَاصِفِ {هَاصِفْ} [حَاصِفِ {حَاصِفْ}] لُعَتِم {عَميلُتِ}

أجيجُ الموت [بطش الموت الذي لا يقهر] هو قاهر [قاصي] الرجل

The burst [This undefeatable force] of death is the destroyer [eliminator] of man (mankind)

(308) 124, 363, 631

إمّتِمَ نِعفُسا [نِعفُشا] {يعفُسْ [يعفُشْ]} حَيِ [إِيِ]

طالما (كلما) نحن نبتني {هو يبتني} صرحا

As long as we build {he builds} a palace

(309) 363, 455

إمّتِمَ نِقَنَّنُ قِنُّ

طالما (كلما) نحن نقتني [نحتكر] مُلكا (اضافيا)

As long as we acquire [monopolize] (more) property

(310) 149, 180, 363, 518

إمّتِمَ سيس ميس || يئزُزُ [يعزُزُ]

{إمّتِمَ سيس ميس يئزُزُ [يعزُزُ] خالا}

طالما (كلما) ينتزع [يستحوذ] الاخوان

{طالما (كلما) يتنازع [يستحوذ] الاخوان ميراثا}

As long as brothers snatch [confiscate]

{As long as brothers snatch [confiscate] inheritance share}

(311) [203, 667]

إمّتمَ زعرتُم {زعرتُ} [زيرتُم {زيرتُ}] || يبتّي [إبَذي] إنَ كور

طالما (كلما) تظهر (تنتشر) [تتواجد] الزَعارَةُ (الشراسة وسوء الخلق) [العداوة والبغضاء] في الصُقع (الارض)

As long as viciousness and immorality [animosity and hatred] spreads [exists] in the land

(312) [55, 206, 227, 603, 626]

إمّتمَ حيد إهِشا || علّو أعُبْلَ

{إمّتِمَ حيد إهِشَمَ مِلا {مِلْ} أعُبْلَ}

طالما (كلما) نشط (انطلق) (إرتفع) النهر ، (و)حَمل (جلب) العلو (الفيض)

As long as the river got energized (rose) (and) carried (brought) the flood

(313) [246, 285, 403]

كُلِك || إقِلفا {إقِلِف} إنَ حيد

(و)طاف المُعيل الراحل [الحبيب] في النهر

(and) The departing provider [The loved one] floated in the river

(314) [121, 236, 437]

فَنو ذا { فَنو ذو} ينّطَلو {ينّطَلَ} فَنْ {فَنو} دنجر أضو سي [دنجر وضو سي]

وجهه يحدّق بوجه الشمس

(with) His face staring (at) the face of the sun

(315) [203, 253, 621]

ألتُ ألانُما || ألّ يبتّي [إبَذي] مِما

أول بأول (حالا ، بلحظة)، لا يظهر [لا يوجد] له (لا يملك) اي شيء

At once (instantly), he does not have anything

(316) [20, 279, 349, 655]

سَلو {سَلُ} و ميتُ || كي أخامِذْمَ {سَلُّ و ميتُم كي كا أخا مِذْمَ}

المخطوف و الميت، كأنهم أخا مِذْمَة (نُطْفة) {كأنهم بهيئة أخا مِذْمَة (توْم)}

The abducted and the dead, they are like {they are like the form of} brothers of one semen-drop (like twin)

(317) [500, 652]

ذا موتِ {موتُم} || ألْ يأصِرُ صَلَم ذو

للموتِ، هم (الآلهة) لم يرسَمو شكل قوامه

Of death, they (the gods) did not draw (determine) the shape of its figure

(318) [61, 287, 327, 335]

لُعلُوَ [لُثُلوَ] لُعْ بَيض [بَيد] أَلْ إكْرُبَ كَرَبِ إنَ كور

لُعُلا [لُثُلا] لُعْ عدِلْ أُلتَ إكْرُبُ إذو

أبدية الرجل المتوحش [البدائي]، ما وهبتها (الآلهة) هبتاً في الصُقعِ (الارض)

{(لكن) مساواة الرجل المتوحش [البدائي]، وهبتها (الآلهة) أولا (من البداية)}

They had not granted the eternity of savage [early] man, as a grant, in the land

{(but) They had granted the equality of savage [early] man, from the beginning}

(319) [84]

دنجرأنونَ كي دنجر ميس || جَل ميس فَهْرو

جلالات أنونَّ كي (ملائكة الإله أنو في الارض)، جلالات الآلهة، كانو مجتمعين

Their majesties the Anunnaki (god Anim's angles on earth), their majesties the gods, were in assembly

(320) [103, 260, 289, 305, 501, 572]

دنجرمَميتُمْ [دنجرمَمي] بَنَتْ سِمْتِ كي ذونو {سِمْتِ ذونو} سِمَتو {سِمْتِ ذو} إِذيمَ [إِاتيمَ]

الآلهة مَميتم {مَمي} (آلهة الموت)، مُستخبرتا [متناولتنا (بالتفصيل)] القرار معهم {قرارهم}، أعطت قرارها

Goddess Mamitum {Mami} (goddess of death), (after) repeatedly inquiring [discussing in detail] the decree with them {their decree}, gave her decree

(321)

إِسْتَكْنو موتُ || و بَلاطَ {إِلْتَكَنْ موتِ و بَلاطُ}

هم أقامو (وضعو) الموت والحياة

They (the gods) established (set) death and life

(322) [209, 539, 604]

ذا موتِ || أَلْ أُدّو عُدْ ميس ذو

{ذا موتُو أَلْ أُدّو عُدْ ميس ذو ثانِذْ أُلتَدُو}

للموت، (هم) ما عرّفو (كشفو) مواعيده [أيامه]"

{للموت، (هم) ما عرّفو (كشفو) مواعيده [أيامه]؛ (هم) عَرّفوها (كَشفوها) بطريقة ثانية (اخرى)}"

Of death, they had not made known (revealed) its dates [days]"

{Of death, they had not made known (revealed) its dates [days]; they made them known (revealed them), differently}"

The Story of the Flood

As Told by Ut-napishtim (Noah) to Gilgamesh

(See lines 8 to 206 of the following Tablet 11)

Tablet 11
The Standard Babylonian Edition

(1)

دنجر جِشْجِمَش أنَ ذا ذُوم مؤرَ أنَ م عْد ذي رُوقِ

جِشْجِمَش قال اليه، الى أُتانَفسْتم البعيد المُتنحي (نوح):

Gilgamesh said to him, to Uta-Napištim the withdrawn and distant (Noah):

(2)

أنّطَلاكُمَ عُد ذي {عُد ذيتم}

"(عندما) أتمَعن النظر فيك، (يا) أُتانَفسْتم

"(as) I stare at you, Uta-Napištim

(3) 201, 354, 539

مِناتُكَ أُلْ ثَانا كيي إياتِما أتَّ

قُدرتُك (حجمك) ليس مختلف (استثنائي)، مثليَ أنت

Your capacity (size) is not different (exceptional), you are like me

(4) 201, 539

و أتَّ أُلْ ثانَتا كيي إياتِما [إياذِما] أتَّ

و أنت لست مختلفاً (استثنائياً)، مثليَ أنت

And you are not different (exceptional), you are like me

(5) 210, 599, 631

جُمُرْكا {جُمُرْكو} لبِّ [لهبِ] أنَ عِفِسْ [عِفِشْ] تُقُنْتِ {تُقُنْتو}

مُجْمِرً (مفحمً) قلبي [لهبي] على [الى] إنجاز معركة

Burning (eager) is my heart [inner flame] to conduct a battle

(6) 22, 398, 535

|و| أهِي نَدَتْ عِلي [حِلي] ظِهْرَكَ

|ولكن| يدي سقطت (شُلّت) فوق [حول] مقامك

|But| my hand had dropped (paralyzed) over [around] your site

(7) 149, 168, 389

أتَّ كيْكي تَعَزِزِمَ [تَأزِزِمَ] إنَ وكّن دنجر ميس بَلاطَ تَسْعوَ {تَسْعَأُم}

كيف، كيف أنت وقفت في مجلسُ الآلهة، (و) سَعيتَ {سعيت الوصول الى} الحياة الابدية؟"

How, how had you stood in the assembly of gods, (and) seeked {seeked to reach} the eternal life?"

(8)

م عُد ذيتم أنَ ذا ذُوم مُرَ أنَ دنجر جِشْجِمَش

أُتانَفسْتم قال اليه، الى جِشْجِمَش:

Uta-Napištim said to him, to Gilgamesh:

(9) 30, 244, 424

لأُفْتيكَ دنجر جِشْجِمَش أمَتْ [همَتْ] نِصِرْتِ [نِظِرْتِ]

"لأُكاشفُكَ، يا جِشْجِمَش، أمرُ سرٍ

"I shall reveal to you, Gilgamesh, a matter of secret

(10) 245, 283, 448

و فِرِسْتِ ذا دنجر ميس كا أذا لأُقْبِكَ

و لأُخبركَ (عن) غامضُ شأن (فعل) [حكم] الآلهة، لذاك (الامر) [لكَ]

And I shall tell you (about) an inner (hidden) deal [judgement] of the gods, for (regarding) that (matter) [for you (only)]

(11) 559

أُورُ شُرِبَّكْ [شُرِبَّعكْ] أُورُ ذا تَدُو ذو أتَّ

مدينة شُرِبَّأك [شُرِبَّعَك] (قاطع [بعج، وادي] ضفاف النهر [الارض اللينة])، المدينة التي تعرفها انت

The city of Shuruppak (riverside [soft land] valley [groove]), a town that you know yourself

(12) 172, 208

|أُورُ ذا إنَ| جوّ حيد فُراتِ سَكْنُ

|المدينة التي في| مُنْخَفض (غور) نهر الفرات ساكنة (واقعة)

The city that is located in the Euphrates depression (valley)

(13) 320, 598

|آ ذووا| {أُورُ ذوو} لَبِرْمَ [لَبِنْمَ] دنجر ميس قَرْبُ ذو {قَرْبُتْ}

| هي تلك (التي)| {هي المدينة (التي)} كانت الآلهة ماكثةً [انتهو] قُربُها {قريباً (منها)}

It is that (one) (that) {It is the city (that)} the gods were lodged [had ended] near it {near}

(14) 267, 498

|أنَ| سَكَنْ عَبُبِ {عَبُبُ} عُبْلَ لِبَّ [لِهبَ] ذونُ دنجر ميس جَلَ ميس

حتى حمل (أراد) قلبهم قيام الطوفان، جلالاتُ الآلِهَة

|Till| their hearts carried (decided) on setting the Deluge, their majesties the gods

(15) 16, 267, 368

إتْمَمَ [إتْمَما] أد ذونُ دنجرأنوم

الإله أنيم، ابيهم، أتَمّ (وافق)

The god Anim, their father, finalized (approved)

(16) 457

مَلِك ذونُ قُرَدُ دنجرإنليل

ملِكُهم كان الإله المحارب (البطل) إنليل

Their king (leader) was the fighter (hero) god Enlil,

(17) 89, 176, 179

جُزَلا ذونُ [جُذَلا ذونُ] دنجرنِنْورة

مستخدمهم (حاجبهم) كان الإله ننورة

Their officer (chamberlain) was the god Ninurta

(18) 89, 176

جوجَلا ذونُ دنجرعَنُّج

أُمَّعَتهم (خادمهم) كان الإله عَنُّج (التابع؛ الخادم)

Their puppet (servant) was the god Ennugi (the follower; the servant)

(19) 86, 104, 267

دنجرنِنْسِكُ دنجرحيا إتي ذونُ تَمِمَا [تَميمَا]

الإله حَيا، الإله الناسكُ (الذي يُسقي ويُخصب)، كان مغلوبا معهم

God Ea, the god Ninsiku (one who waters and fertilizes), was finalized (overpowered) with (by) them (the three gods)

(20) 30, 297, 539

أمَتْ [همَتْ] ذونُ أُثنا أنَ كِكِش [كِكِشُ]

(لذا) كرَّرَ (سرَّب لفعل الخير) أمرُهم [همَّتُهم (خطتهم)] الى (عبر) جدار القصب:

(thus) He repeated (leaked for good deed) their matter [their determination (plan)] to (via) the reed fence:

(21) 211, 297

كِكِشْ كِكِشْ {كِكِشُ كِكِشُ} إجَرْ [حجَرْ] إجَرْ [حجَرْ]

"ياسياج القصب، ياسياج القصب! يا جدار الحجر، يا جدار الحجر!

"Reed fence, reed fence! Brick wall, brick wall!

(22) 184, 211

كِكِشُ سِمَعمَ إجَرُ [حجَرُ] حِسَسْ

إسمع ياسياج القصب! إنتبه يا جدار الحجر

Listen, O reed fence! Beware, O brick wall!

(23) [374, 559]

لَعُ شُرِبّأكوَ [لَعُ شُرِبّعكوَ] دُمُ [ذُمْ] مُعُبَر دنجرتُوتُ

يا رجل شُرِبّكا [شُرِبّعكا] بن قوم تُوتُ

O man of Shuruppak, son of the people (tribe) of Tutu

(24) [169, 633]

أُقُرْ [عُقُرْ] حيِ [إِيِ] بِني [بِنو] جشماعَ

إلتزم (لاتبرح) الصرح (البيت)، إبني عوّامة (جارية)

(عوّامة (فُلْكَ [فُلْكَة]) نوح: سفينة خشبية مدورة اسطوانية مغلقة تشبه الكُفّة، الطَبْقَة، القُصعة، العُلبة، او الصحيفة، لها ارضية وسقف مقوسين، وقطر وعمق متساويين)

Stay [Do not leave] home, build a wooden raft

(Noah's raft: a closed round floater, with arched floor and roof, and equal diameter and depth)

(25) [53, 389, 411, 668]

مُذِرْ [مُسِرْ] نِيج توقُما سِعِي ذي ميس

أُتْرُكْ [تحرّر من] السَعيُ لحفظ المال والاملاك [الغنى]، إسعى (لحفظ) الأنفُس (الارواح)

Abandon [Free yourself from] seeking (to save) wealth, seek (to save) lives

(26) [62, 348, 412, 667]

مَكُرَ [مَكُرُ] زعِرْما نَفِستُ [نَفِستِ] بُلِطْ

إنْبُذُمَ العِقار، إحْيِ [إحفظ] النفس [الحياة]

Spurn land property, revive [keep on] the soul [life]

(27) [284, 412, 429, 547]

سُلِمَ نُعُمُنْ نَفْساتِ كَلَمَ إنَ لِبِّ [شأيِ] جشماع

أسْلِم (إحْفِظ) نُعُمُ الأنفاس (أنفاس (كائنات) الأنْعام (المواشي والدواجن)) كلها في داخل العوّامة

Safeguard the livestock (cattle) beings (the farm animals), all of them, inside the raft

(28) [572]

جشماعَ ذا تَبني أتَّ

العوّامة هذه التي ستبنيَ أنتَ

The raft that you will build

(29) [343, 354, 370, 572]

لوو [لُهو] مِنْدُدَ [مِدُّدَ] مِناتُ ذا {مِناتُ ذو}

لتكن لها ممتدة (كبيرة) قدرتها (حجم استيعابها)

For her, let her capacity (size) be extended (large)

(30) [46, 343, 371, 475]

لوو [لُهو] مِتْحُرْ رُبُضَ [رُبُسَ] و مؤرَكْ ذا

ليكن لها متماثل (متساوٍ)، وسعها [عمقها] وحوضها [امتدادها]

For her, let her breadth [depth] and basin [stretch] be corresponding (equal)

(31) [12, 549]

كيم أبزُ [عبْزُ] [أفزُ] [عفْزُ] ذا أذي ظُلكْ ذي

مثل عَبزُ ([أكمة (تلّة) [طاسة] [حُدبة] [قوس]) لها، غطائها"

Like an Abzu (a hill [a hunch] [a bowl] [an arc]) to it, its roof (should look)"

(32) [68]

أنكو إديمَ [إهديمَ] مُوْرَ أنَ دنجرحيا بَعليا

انا نفسي عَرفتُم [إهتديتُمَ] (تلقائيا)، قلت الى الإله حَيا، ربّيَ:

I, myself, understood [was guided] (instinctly), I said to god Ea, my lord:

(33) [68, 245, 299, 350]

أمجرْ بِعلِ ذا تَقُبا أتّ كيأمْ

"سأقبل (سأطيع) يا رب ما تَقولَ، حرفيا

"I shall accept (I shall obey), O lord, what you say, exactly:

(34) [209, 631]

أتَئِذْ أنكو عَفُسْ

سأؤدي انا نفسي الانجاز

I, myself, shall do the job

(35) [42, 299, 520, 624, 643]

كيم لأفُكْ أورْ أمانُ و شيبُتُمْ

كيف سأفكُّ (سأترك) المدينة، الرعية والشيبة؟"

How should I leave the city, the subjects and the elderly?"

(36) [115]

دنجرحيا فاء ذو إعفُسْمَ [إعفُشْمَ] ضَجًا {يقَبِ}

الإله حَيا أطلق [جمع وأطلق] فمه (لسانه)، ضاجّاً {صارخا (مُلقنا)}

God Ea let go [held and let go] his mouth (tongue), shouted {shouted (loudly)}

(37) [201, 639]

مُوْرَ {يذكَرَ} أنَ عرْ ذو إياتو

قال {قائلا} الى خادمه، اليّ:

He said {Saying} to his servant, to me:

(38) [245]

و أتّ كيأمْ تَقَبا ذونُتُ:

"وأنت ستقول (بصوت عالي) حرفيا لهم:

"And you shall say (loudly), verbatim, to them:

(39) [200, 367, 667]

مِندمَ [مِندمَ] إياذي دنجرإنليك يزِعرانِم [يزيرانِم]

من الواضح [مُذ ان أصبح] الإله إنليك ينبُذني [يضمر العداوة والبغضاء لي]

Clearly, the god Enlil [Since the god Enlil] is rejecting me [harboring animosity and hatred toward me]

(40) [274, 643]

أُلْ أُثَبْ إنَ أورُكُنُمَ

سوف لن أقيم (انا) في مدينتكم

I shall not stay (live) in your city

(41) [498, 534, 633]

إنَ قَقَرْ دنجرإنليك أُلْ أسكنَ {أسَكنْ} ظيفِياما {ظيفِيا}

في جُحرِ (مُستَقر) الإله إنليك سوف لن أسكن (أثبت) قدميّ [ساقي]

In god Enlil's den (dwelling-place), I shall not set my feet [my lower legs]

(42) [12, 274, 640]

أُرَدْمَ أنَ أبزُ [عَبْزُ] [أفزُ] [عَفْزُ] إتي دنجرحيا بَعليا أثْبَكُ

سوف أعود (انا) الى العَبزُ، سوف أُقيم مع الإله حَيا، ربّيَ

I shall go back to the Abzu, I shall live with god Ea, my master

(43) [283, 431, 645]

أنَ كا أذونُ أُسَزْنَنَكُنُذي نُخسَمَ [نُهسَمَ [نُهشَمَ]]

اليكمُ (من اجلكم)، سأتوسله ان يَنعمكم [يُمطركم] التزاحم [التناهش] (الكثرة (الخير))

To you (for your sake), I shall ask him to bestow upon you [to shower you] the rush (the abundance)

(44) [194, 308, 385, 453]

خِصِبْ [خِضِبْ] مَعشيِ ميس [مُشعِن ميس] فُزُرْ كود ميس مَ [كُوء ميس مَ]

خصبٌ (كثرةٌ) من الطيور، أسرابٌ من الاسماك

Plenty of birds, flocks of fishes

(45) [129, 366]

.... ميسرا حِبُرَمَ

.... فرحة اليُسر والغنى

.... the joy of ease and wealth

(46) [316, 513]

إنَ سَحَرْ |أُسَزْنَنَكُنُذيَ| كُكِي

في السَحْرِ (قبيك الصبح)، |سأتوسله ان يَنعمكم [يُمطركم]| الخبز اليابس [البيض]

Before dawn, I shall ask him to bestow upon you [shower you] eggs [dried bread]

(47) [219, 330, 501, 645]

إنَ ليلاتِ أُسَزْنَنَكُنُذيَ سَمُتْ كِباتِ [كِبادِ]

في الليل، سأتوسله ان يَنعمكم [يُمطركم] سيل من القمح [الخُثرة (اللبن)]"

At night, I shall ask him to bestow upon you [shower you] a flow of yogurt [wheat]"

(48) [353, 417, 513]

مِمُو سَحْرِ إنَ نَمَرِ

كُلُّمَ (طوال) السَحر (قبيل الصبح)، عند (منذ) أوّل بياض الصُبح الداكن

All time long, before dawn, (starting) at the earliest morning dark white

(49) [349, 376, 449]

أنَ كاء أتْرَ حَسِسْ يفَخُرْ [يفَهُرْ] مأتُمْ

على باب أتْرَ حَسِسْ (حاد الحس (المعرفة بالمحيط): كنية لعطا نفستم)، يتجمع تجمعاً

At the door of Atra-Hasis (the one with sharp sense: Uta-Napištim), a crowd was gathering

(50) [342, 432, 434]

لغ نَجار نَسيَ فأسُ

النجار ماضيا بفأسه

The carpenter proceeding with his ax

(51) [7, 336, 432]

لغ عَدْكِد نَسي أبَنْ [عَبَنْ] ذو

قاطع القصب ماضيا بهراوته

The reed cutter proceeding with his cudgel (club)

(52) [17]

عَجا سِلِجَ ذو؟ نَسي؟ ....

.... ماضيا بهراوته المصنعوة من خشب الاسفندان

.... proceeding with his maple wood club

(53)

لغ غُرُس ميس يـ.............................

الشباب الاشداء |يحملون| ....

The young strong men |carrying| ....

(54) [277, 445, 520]

شيبُتي يزَبِلو فتِلتَ

المسنين (الشيبة) يحملون (بالزبل) الحبال

The elders carrying (in baskets) ropes

(55) [311, 366, 432]

ثَرُو [سَرُو] نَسي كُفْرَ

الثري [السيد] ماضيا بالقير

The rich [the master] proceeding with the tar (bitumen, asphalt)

(56) [195, 322]

لَفْنُ {لَفْنِ} [لَبْنُ {لَبْنِ}] |....| حِثِحْتُ أُأبْلَ [أُعُبْلَ]

المعدم [الكادح الفقير] جلب |....| العمل المُضني المتطلب

The working poor brought in |....| the needed (necessary) hard labor

(57) [182, 209]

إنَ خَنْسِ أومِ أتَأدي بُنى ذو

في اليوم الخامس إتأديت (وضعت) بنيانها (هيكلها الخارجي):

In the fifth day, I did (I put) its external structure:

(58) [127, 177, 224, 421, 505]

1 إكو جور ذا 10 نندان تأم شَهقا إجر[ميس] [حجر[ميس]] ذا

فدان (مساحة) دائرتها، حوالي 10 نندان إرتفاع [10 نندان إرتفاع كل من] حياطينُها

An acre (the area of) its circle, as much as 10 Nindans [10 Nindans each,] the height of its walls

(59) [296, 352, 377, 421]

10 نندان تَأم {10 نندان أم} إمْتَحِرْ كِبِرْ مُحّ ذا

حوالي 10 نندان ساوى (امتدّ) طوق عاليها (فوهتها) [قطر محيطها]

[حوالي 10 نندان ساوت (امتدّت) {10 نندان ساوت (امتدّت)} اطراف عاليها [محيطها]]

As much as 10 Nindans equaled (extended) the rim of its top [the diameter of its surrounding]

[As much as 10 Nindans [10 Nindans each] equaled (extended) the edges of its top [surrounding]]

(60) [15, 319, 490, 652]

أدي لَأَنْ ذا ذا أذي إإصِرْ ذي

أديت (وضعت) فواصلها (الداخلية)، لها (لهذه الفواصل) انا رسمتها (صممتها):

I did (I put) its (internal) dividers, to them (the dividers), I drew (designed) them:

(61) [540, 642]

أُرْتَجِبْ ذي أنَ 6-تو [6-شُعُ] [6-شوُ]

دعمتُها الى (عبر اضافة) ستةً [6 أجزاء] [6 اطراف] (سقوف)

I supported it (the raft) by (adding) 6 parts (decks)

(62) [448, 540]

أفْتَرَسِ ذي {ذو} أنَ 7-تو [7-شُعُ] [7-شوُ]

قسمتها (عرضيا) الى سبعةً [7 اجزاء] [7 اطراف] (اقسام)

I divided it (horizontally) to 7 parts (sections)

(63) [448, 540, 598]

قَرْبِتو [قَربِ ذو] أفْتَرَسْ أنَ 9-تو [9-شُعُ] [9-شوُ]

قسمت قربتها (بطنها) الى تسعةً [9 اجزاء] [9 اطراف]

I divided its interior belly (vertically) to 9 parts (compartments)

(64) [2, 32, 167, 383]

جاج جش ميس اميس إنَ مورُب ذا لو أمْحَصْ {لو أمْحَص} {لوو [لهو] |أمْحَصْ|}

سدّادت مياه عند خواصرها (جوانبها الخارجية)، كبَسْتُ (ضَغَطْتُ ودقّيْتُ) لها {كبسْتُ، لتكن لها}

Water (sealing) plugs on its waists (sides), I squeezed (I pushed and pounded) for it {to let it have}

(65) [15, 195, 448]

أمُرْ فَرِسُ [فَرِصُ] وحِثِحْتُمْ أدي

رأيت (تفحصت) حجم كورها (تقعرها) و أديت (وضعت) العمل المُضني المطلوب:

I observed (examined) its half sphere (concave) size and did (put) the needed hard labor:

(66) [58, 166, 277, 298, 311]

3 سأر كُفْرِ أتَبَكْ أنَ كيرِ {جير}

3 سأر (3×3600 وحدة وزن) قير (خام) رميت على شكل دفعات (تدريجيا) الى الفرن

I Sar (3x3600 mass units) of raw bitumen, I threw in portions (gradually) to the oven

(67)

3 سأر {6 سأر} عِسر |.....| أنَ لِبِّ

3 سأر (3×3600 وحدة حجم) {6 سأر (3×3600 وحدة حجم)} زفت (قير مائع) |أطليت| على داخلها

3 Sar (3x3600) {6 Sar (6x3600} volume units of melted bitumen (asphalt), I |coated| on the inside

(68) [157, 171, 198]

3 سأر عرن ميس نَسْ جش سُسُكْ {جش شُسُكْ} ذا يزَبِكُ إجِس [إجِز]

3 سأر (3×3600 وحدة وزن) (من) الحبوب ما كان يحمل (بالزبائل) حمالي النقل بالشوكة (النقالة)

3 Sar (3x3600 mass units) of grain that the fork (dolly) transportation porters were carrying (in baskets)

(69) [24, 141, 148]

عِزُبْ سأر إجِس [إجِز] ذا إأكُلُ نِقُ

ضع جانبا (فيما عدا) سأر (3600 وحدة وزن) من الحبوب التي استهلكها عمل الخبز الحواري [أكلوها خبزا حواري]

Set aside (aside from) one Sar (3600 mass units) of grain that the bread making consumed [that they consumed as bread]

(70) [340, 453]

2 سأر إجِس [إجِز] ذا أُفَزِرُ لَغْ مألح

2 سأر (2×3600 وحدة وزن) من الحبوب ما أفرزَ (خزّنَ) الملّاح

2 Sar (2x360 mass units) of grain that the shipwright set aside (stored)

(71) 174, 602, 624, 659

أنَ أُمانَتِ أُطَبِخْ جُدُ ميس

الى الرعية (العمال) شويت النوق المسمّنة (المعلوفة)

For the subjects (workers), I barbecued fattened camels

(72) 497, 606

أشْجِتْ [أسْجِتْ] [أسْجِسْ] عُدو نيتَ ميس أوميتَمَ

ذبحتُ [أسجيت (مدّدتُ)] (لهم) العَدوِيّة (صغار الغنم)، كل يوم

I slaughtered young sheep (for them), every day

(73) 159, 314, 516

تِرِشْ كُرُعُنُ [كُرُؤنُ] [كُؤرُنُ] إجِس [إجِز] و جِعَتِ [جِسْتِ]

جعة (بيرة)، شرابُ حبوب، ونبيذ شعير!

Beer, grain drink, and barley wine!

(74) 206, 362

أماني أسْقِي كيمَ أ ميس حيدمَ

سقيت (رويت) رعيتي (عمالي)، مثلما (تفعل) مياهُ نهرٍ

I irrigated (hydrated) my subjects (workers), like the waters of a river (do)

(75) 23, 261, 631

إزِنُ [إسِنُ] يعفِسو [يعفِشو] كيي {كيما} أوم أكِتِمَ [أقِتِمَ]

هم كانو يهيؤ (الى) إحتفال [تجمُّعْ إحتفالي] مثل (احتفال) يوم العام الجديد

They were preparing (for) a festival [a festival gathering] like (the festival of) the New Year's Day

(76) 444

دنجرأُضو |إنَ أضِح أنَ| فِسّاتي [فِتّاتي] [بِسّاتي] قاتي أدي

عند شروق الشمس، وضعت يدي على اجزاء متفرقة (لها)

At sun's rise (sunrise), I put my hand on miscellaneous parts (of it)

(77) 210, 470

لَمْ دنجرأُضو رَبي [رَبِع] جِش ماع جَمْرَت

قبل إرتفاع الشمس (منتصف النهار)، كانت العوّامة مهيئة

Before sun's high (noon), the raft was ready

(78) 555

.... سُفْسُقَمَ

|نَقل العوّامة الى المياه| كان صعبا جدا

|Moving the raft to the waters| was very difficult

(79) [135, 166, 346,426, 503]

جرْ [جعرْ] ماع مُعج ميس [موج ميس] نتّعبْلو [نتّأبلو] علِتْ و سَفْلِتْ

بقينا نسحب حبال لجام السفينة، من الاعلى و الاسفل

[بقينا نحمل [ننقل (نجلب)] دحاريج (نقل) السفينة المنزلقة، من الخلف والمقدمة]

We kept pulling the ship harness ropes, from top and bottom

[We kept carrying [moving (bringing)] the ship slip-away (rolling) logs, from back and front]

(80) [15, 530]

عَدي [عَتي] إنَ آميس | إلِكُ سِنفَتْ ذو [ثِنِبتْ ذو]

حتى ترسّلَ (ذهب) سَنفُها (حزام (حبل اللجام) [ثلثاها] |في المياه|

Until its harness (rope) belt [Until two thirds of it] went in the waters

(81) [143, 260, 353]

مِمَّ إِذوَ [إِإتوَ] أأصَنْ ذي

كُلما أوْتِيتُ (مَلكتُ) حَمّلْتُها (العوّامة)

All what I had, I loaded aboard it (onboard)

(82) [143, 306]

مِمَّ إِذوَ [إِإتوَ] أأصَنْ ذي كهو بَهبّار [قهو بَهبّار]

كُلما أوْتِيتُ (مَلكتُ) من معدن الفضة حَمّلْتُها

All what I had of silver metal, I loaded aboard it (onboard)

(83) [143, 307]

مِمَّ إِذوَ [إِإتوَ] أأصَنْ ذي كهو سئِج [قهو سئِج]

كُلما أوْتِيتُ (مَلكتُ) من معدن الذهب حَمّلْتُها

All what I had of gold metal, I loaded aboard it (onboard)

(84) [143, 668]

مِمَّ إِذوَ [إِإتوَ] أأصَنْ ذي {كِمنْ} نُعْمَنْ ذي ميس كَلَمَ

كُلما أوْتِيتُ (مَلكتُ) من نُعُمُ الأنفاس (أنفاس (كائنات) الأنْعام (المواشي والدواجن)) حَمّلْتُها {اخفيتها}، كلها

All what I had of livestock (cattle) beings (farm animals), all of them, I loaded aboard it (onboard)

(85) [300, 655]

أُسْتَلي الى شأي جش ماع كَلَ كِيمْتيا و سلاتيا

إنتزعت (أرسلت) الى داخل العوامة كل مُقربيّ وسلالتي (ابنائي)

I grabbed (rushed) to the inside of the raft all my kith and kin

(86) [120, 284, 622, 624, 655]

بُعلْ عدن أُمَمْ عدن دُمْ ميس أُماني كَل ذُنُ أُسلَي

قطعان البرية، كائنات (دواب) البرية، أبناء رعيتي (عمالي)، إنتزعت (أرسلتُ) كلهم (فيها)

Herds of the wild, creatures of the wild, my subjects (workers), I grabbed (rushed) all (in)

(87) [14]

هَدَنَ دنجرأضو إسْكُنُم

إله الشمس حَدّدَ المهلة الزمنية:

The god Shamash had set the grace period (deadline):

(88) [501]

إنَ سَحَرْ كُكي إنَ ليلاتِ يُسَزْنَنْ سَمُتْ {سَمُتُ} كِباتِ [كِبادِ]

'في السَحَرِ (قبيلَ الصبحِ) خبزً يابس [بَيضً]؛ في الليل سيزُخُّ [سيَنْعَمُ] بسيلٍ من الطحين [الخُثرة (اللبن)]

'Before dawn, dried bread [eggs]; at night, he will shower [bless] with a flow of wheat [yogurt]

(89) [169, 279, 406, 443]

إرِبْ أنَ لبِّ جشماعمَ فيحَ كاءكَ {جشماع}

أُدْخُل الى قلب العوّامة، صُبْ (أقفل باحكام) بابُكَ {العوّامة}'

Enter to the inside of the raft, cast (seal) your door {the raft}'

(90) [220]

هَدَنَ ذوو |ثانيتم| إكتَلْدَ

أكدّ (كرر) هو |للمرة الثانية| المهلة الزمنية:

He stressed (repeated) |again| the grace period:

(91) [501]

إنَ سَحَرْ كُكي إنَ ليلاتِ يُسَزْنَنَ {يسَزْنَن} سَمُتْ {سَمُتُ} كِباتِ [كِبادِ]

'في السَحَرِ (قبيلَ الصبحِ) خبز يابس [بَيضً]؛ في الليل سينْعَمُ [سيزُخّ] سيل من القمح [الخُثرة (اللبن)]'

'Before dawn, dried bread [eggs]; at night, he will bestow upon [shower] a flow of wheat [yogurt'

(92) [236]

ذا أُوم أتَطَلْ بُنَى ذو

لذاك اليوم، نظرت عن بعيد حاله (مناخه)

Of that day, I look from far (observed) its condition (weather)

(93) [42, 268]

أُوم أنَ يتَبَلْسي فُلُهْتَ إإذي [إإتي]

(ذلكَ) اليوم، الى من يتمعن بدقة، أوتي (له) رعب (كان مرعب)

That day, to the one observing carefully, had fright (was frightening)

(94) [169]

إإرُبْ أنَ لبِّ جشماع أفْتَيَحَ بابي

دخَلتُ الى قلب العوّامة، صَبيّت (أغلقت باحكام) بابي

I entered to inside of the raft; I casted (sealed) my door

(95) [340, 372, 443]

أنَ فَيحِيِ ذا جِش ماع مُفُزُرْ دنجر كُرجَل لَعْ مألح

الى مُغلقُ العوّامة، فُزُرْ كُرجَلْ (سيد الجن، إنليل) (المنشق عن إنليل)، الملاّحُ

To the caster (sealer) of the raft, Puzur-Kurgal (Enlil's defector), the shipwright

(96) [14, 71, 126]

حي جَلْ [إي جَلْ] [إيجَلْ] أتهدِنْ [أتعطِنْ] [أتأطِنْ] [أتدِنْ] عَدي [عَتي] بُثيِي [بُذيِي] ذو

آويت (أعطيت) قصر الجلالة، (و)حتى محتوياته

I let to rest (I gave up) the palace of majesty, (and) even its contents

(97)

ممُو سَحْرِ إنَ نَمَرِ

كُلُّمَ (طوال) السَحر (قبيل الصبح)، عند (منذ) أوّل بياض الصُبح الداكن

All time long, before dawn, (starting) at the earliest morning dark white

(98) [48, 135, 259, 264, 500]

إعلَمَ إستُ {ألتُ} عِضِدْ[إشِدْ] عني عُرفَتُم ظَلِمْتُم

عَلَتْ (ظهرت فوق) أول تخوم السماء (الأفق) غيمة سوداء

A black cloud rose (showed) over the far horizon

(99) [100, 254, 480]

دنجرعِسْكُرْ [دنجرعِسْقُرْ] إنَ لبٌ ذا إرتَأمَمَ {إرتَجُمْ}

الإله عِسْكُر [عِسْقُر] (إله الظلام والرعد) في قلبها رَعد (توعّدَ صارخا)

The god Askar (Haddad: god of darkness and thunder) thundered (threatened loud) inside it

(100) [92, 112, 226, 352]

دنجرسُلاّتْ و دنجرحانِشْ إلَكو إنَ مَخرِ

الإله سُلاّتْ (إله السلب والنهب) و الأله حانِشْ (إله السبي) ترسّلا (ذهبا) في المقدمة

The god Sullat (god of looting) and the god Hanish (god of captivity) went in the front

(101) [179, 226]

إلَكو جُزَلا مبس {جُزَلُو} [جُذَلا مبس {جُذَلُو}] كورو و مأتُمْ

ترسّلو (قادو) المستخدمين (الجنود) جبالا وارض

They went with (led) the officers (soldiers) over mountains and land

(102) [90, 580, 627]

تَركُل دنجرأراكَل [دنجرهراكَل] يُنَسح {يِنَسَحْ}

الإله هراكَل (فوق الجبّار) كان يُذري (يكتسح) الدحاريج (دحاريج نقل ورسو السفن)

The god Errakal (the over mighty) was pulverizing (sweeping) the logs (ship rolling and mooring logs)

(103) [84, 99, 226, 352, 648]

إلَكْ دنجرنِنُورة مِخرِ {مِخرَ} يُسَعَرْ ذي

استرسل (جاء) الإله نِنْورةَ (اله النار والحرب)، يحرق المواخر (السفن والسدود)

The god Ninurta (of fire and war) passed by, burning the ships and weirs

(104) [55, 99]

دنجرأَنُنَّكي إعِسُو [إمِشو] دِفَراتِ

أَنُنَّ كي (ملائكة الإله أنو في الارض) طافو بالمشاعل [أطلقو المشاعل]

The Anunnaki (god Anim's angles on earth) roamed with [unleashed] the torches

(105) [610]

إنَ نَمْرِرِ ذونُ أُحَمَطُ مأتُمُ

بسوادهم وبياضهم وحمرتهم (الوان النمر: الوان الموت عند العرب)، رقّطو الارض

With their black, white, and orange/red (tiger colors: Arabs death colors), they spotted the land

(106) [202, 654]

ذا دنجرعِسكُرْ [دنجرعِسقُرْ] سُحَرَتُ [سُحَرَسُ] يبُوْو [يبغوَ] عَنِي

(بينما) سِحرُ (فسادُ) الإله عِسْكُر [عِسْقُر] كان يبوء (يحوز على) [يبغي (يطغي على)] السماء

(as) The spoiling (ruining) act (force) of the god Askar was taking over [encroaching] the sky

(107) [75, 390]

مِمَّ نمرُ أنَ دُهُمَتْ {دُهُمَتِ} أَتَرُ

كلّما كان أبيضا داكنا، الى سواد معتم عادَ

All that was dark white, to a pitch-dark (color) returned

(108) [174, 215, 251]

إرْهِصْ كور جيم جُد ...... إحْفِيَ ذي

عَصُرَ (سحق) أصقاع الارض مثل جملُ |معصرة الزيت| دار حولها (مرارا)

He pressed (crushed) the land, like |an oil compressor| camel he (repeatedly) circled it

(109) [377]

ا نْ أُومِ مَحُو ....

في يوم واحد، .... الريحُ [العاصفة] ....

In one day, the wind [storm] ....

(110) [183, 278]

خَنطِتْ [حَنْطِتْ] يزَقُمَ ...... كورا عَبُبُ

حالا [بعدوانية]، كان الطوفان يبتلع .... أصقاع الارض

Immediately [with a grudge], the Deluge was swallowing (submerging) .... of the lands

(111) [202, 291, 454, 607]

كيمَ قَبْلِ عُجُ [عُقُ] عُجْ ميس [عُقْ ميس] أُبَؤَوَ [أُبَغوَ] كَذُذُ [كَثُثُ]

كما (في) معركةٍ، باءَ (حاز) [بغي (طغي)] الترابُ (الرمل) فوق الناسَ

Like (in) a battle, the sand took over [encroached] the people

(112) [22]

أَلْ يأمَر أخو أخا ذو

لم يستطع الاخ ان يرى أخيه

A brother could not see his (own) brother

(113) [209, 288, 607]

أَلْ أُتَدى عُجْ ميس [عُقْ ميس] إنَ كَرَسِ [كَرَثِ] {عَنِ}

لم يستطع الناس ان يتواصلو ببعضهم في دمار التكدس [الدمار] {الحَبسةِ}

People could not connect with each other in the pileup ruin [the ruin] {the entrapment}

(114) [11, 42]

دنجر.دنجر {دنجر ميس} إفتَلْمو عَبُبَمَ

أخاف الطوفان (حتى) الآلهة

The Deluge frightened (even) the gods

(115) [135, 184]

إتَحَسُ [إتَحتُ] إتَعْلو أنَ عنِ ذا دنجر أنيم

أقلعو [أسرعو]، ارتفعو الى سماء الإله أنيم

They left [rushed], they went up to the haven of god Anim

(116) [168, 285, 471, 635]

دنجر ميس كيمَ عُرجِ كُنُنُ إنَ كَمات رَبْصُ

الآلهة كانت مختبئة كالضباع، متربّصة [مستلقية] في المخابئ

The gods were like hiding hyenas, waiting [lying down] in the hideouts

(117) [347, 538]

يسَسي دنجر إستار مألتِ {كيمَ ألتِ}

(بينما) الإلهة إستار كانت تقرأ بصوت عالي بيان (شهادة) {كأنما بيان (شهادة)}

(as) The goddess Istar was reading aloud {as if} a testimony (witness statement)

(118) [270, 397]

أُنَمْبيَ {أُنَمْبا} دنجر مَه {دنجر بَعَلْتَ دنجر ميس} طَبَتْ رِجْمَ

رقيقة وجميلة الإله {حبيبة الآلهة} صرخت باكيتا [رفعت] صرخةً صادقة (صريحة):

The lady of god {the sweetheart of gods} screamed (while weeping) [raised up] an honest (candid) outcry:

(119) [390, 590, 621]

أُومُ أُلوَ أنَ طيطي لُوو [لُهو] إِإتُرْمَ

’(حقا) كأولُ يومه، الى الطين، ليكن له (قد) عادَ!

‘(indeed) Like his first day, to the mud, let him (the human) be returned to it!

(120) [56,150, 245, 352, 449]

أذو [هذو] [آسو] أنكو إنَ مَخَرْ {فُهُرْ} دنجر دنجر **أقْبُو** ^ف^ هولْ

ذلك لانني انا نفسي، في مقدمة (أمام) {في مجمع} الآلهة، كنت قد زئرتُ (صرخت): يا هولة [حولة] (الى الحرب)

That is because I, myself, in front of {in the assembly of} the gods, had shouted: O, the one of horror (war)

(121) [150]

كيي أقْبِي إنَ مَخَرْ {فُهُرْ} دنجر دنجر ^ف^ هولْ

كيف لي أن زئرتُ (صرخت) في مقدمة (أمام) {في مجمع} الآلهة: يا هولة [حولة] (الى الحرب)

How could I had shouted in front of {in the assembly of} the gods: O, the one of horror (war)

(122) [611]

أنَ حُلُقْ عُجْ ^ميس^ **يا [**عُقْ ^ميس^ **يا] قَبْلَ أقْبِمَ**

(و)دَعوتُ الى معركة لإبادة بشريا

(and) declared a battle for the annihilation of my people

(123) [331, 425]

أنكومَ أُلَدا نِأسوآمَ

إني انا نفسي من يولد ذُرية البشر

It is I, myself, who give birth to the breed of people

(124) [308, 574, 626]

كيي دُمْ ^ميس^ كود ^حا^ [كوء ^حا^] **أُمَلى تَمْتَمَ**

(الان) هم مثل ذريات الاسماك يملؤون البحر!‘

(now) Like the breeds of fish, they fill the sea!’

(125) [10, 566]

دنجر.دنجر {دنجر ^ميس^} **ذُتْ** ^دنجر^ **أنُنَّكي بكو إتي ذا**

الآلهة، بالذات أنّنَكي، كانو يبكون معها

The gods, particularly the Anunnaki, were crying with her

(126) [10, 53, 274, 413, 430]

دنجر ^ميس^ **أسْرُ أُثْبي إنَ بِكِتِ**

{إنَ نُؤرُبْ نِستَ بَكوَ إتي ذا}

الآلهة كانو مغلوبين (غاصّين)، وهم جالسين، بالبكاء

{بإعياء صاخب كانو يبكون معها}

The gods were taken over (were overwhelmed), while sitting, by crying

{With noisy exhaustion, they were crying with her}

(127) [72, 294, 332, 493, 504]

ذَبَ {كَتْمَ} شَفْتَ ذونُ لِقاء بُخْريتِ

ذَبُلت (يبست) {دَكُنت} شفاههم نتيجة الاجتفاف

Their lips were dry {became dark} as a result of dehydration

(128) [639]

6 عُرا و مُساتي {و7 مُساتي}

لستة ايام وليالي {وسبعة ليالي}

For six days and nights {and seven nights}

(129) [256, 377, 468, 648]

إلَكْ سَعَرُ عَبُبُ مِحْوَ يسَفَنْ كور

{إلَكْ سَعَرُ رَعْدُ {رَأدُ} مِحْوَ عَبُبُ |يسَفَنُ كور|}

تَرسّل (جاء) سعير (أجيج) الطوفان، لمحوةٍ (ارض مغطاة بالماء) يَقشطُ (وجه) الارض

تَرسّل (جاء) سعير (أجيج) الرعد، لمحوةٍ (ارض مغطاة بالماء) كانت عاصفة الطوفان |تَقشطُ| (وجه) الارض

The hell of the Deluge came by, peeling the (face of) earth (turning it) to a flat water-covered land

{The hell of thunder came by, the Deluge |was peeling| the earth (turning it) to a flat water-covered land}

(130) [289]

7-وَ أُوم إنَ قَصَدِ [كَسَدِ]

عند مجيء سابعُ يوم

At the arrival of the seventh day

(131) [273, 377, 454]

طَرَقْ [تَرقْ] ذوو عَبُبُ قَبْلَ

{إطَرَقْ [إتَرَقْ] مِحْوَ |عَبُبُ|}

(اخيرا) هادئة كانت هي، معركة الطوفان

{هدأت عاصفة |الطوفان|}

It was (finally) quiet, the battle of the Deluge

{The battle of the Deluge quieted}

(132) [32, 181]

ذا إمتَخْضُ [إمتَحْصُ] كيمَ {جيم} حالْتِ

هذه التي مَخضت [ضغطت وضربت] مثل انثى في اول حمل (مخاض)

It, which had labored [had pushed and pounded] like a female in the first pregnancy (labor)

(133) [11, 24, 39, 230, 234, 654,]

إإنَحْ [إإنَخْ] عَبَ أُسْحَرِرْ إمْحَلُ {إمْعَكْ} عَبُبُ إكلاً {إكلوْ}

تنحى (انحسر) البحر، بهت (خمد)، شدّة (محنة) {إعصار} الطوفان انتهت {انتهى}

The sea pulled back (down) (subsided), fell still, the worst {the tempest} of the Deluge ended

(134) 268, 465, 574

أبَلْسَمَ {أبَلْسَ} أومَ {طَمَتِ} سَكِنْ قُلْ

تأملت يومها {البحر}، هدوء (صمت) مطبق

I observed that day {the sea}, complete quiet (silence) had set in

(135) 284, 390, 425

و كُلَتْ تَأنسيتِ إِإتُرَ أنَ طيطي

وكل البشر عادو الى الطين

And all people had returned back (turned) to clay

(136) 371, 639, 655

كِيمَ عُري مِتْحُرَتْ أُسَلُ

مثل عراء (فضاء الارض) اصبحت الوديان مستوية

Like an open (empty) land, the valleys were leveled

(137) 43, 61, 232, 244, 412, 605

أفْتِ [أفْتِح] نَفَسَمَ أُضا [عُضا] إِمْتَقعُتْ عُجُ [عُقُ] بيض [بَيد] أفيا

فتحت متنفسا (ثقب)، حزمة ضوء وقعت فوق محيط أنفي (خدي)

I opened a breathing hole, a beam of light fell (landed) over [around] the surrounding of my nose

(138) 10, 274, 614

أُقْتَمِسْمَ [أُكْتَمِسْمَ] أتَشِبْ أبَكي

غِصت (قرفصت)، جلست ابكي

I sank (squatted), I sat down crying

(139) 43, 96

عُجُ [عُقُ] بَيض [بَيد] أفيا إِلَكَ دِمَعا

فوق محيط أنفي (خدي) ترسّل (سال) الدمع

Over [around] the surroundings of my nose (my cheeks), the tears came (down)

(140) 244, 268, 296

أبَلِسْ كِبراتِ [كِبراتُ] فَضوُ [فَتوُ] {عنُ} عَبَ

تأملت اطراف فضاء {سماء} البحر

I scanned the edges of the sea space (expanse) {the sea sky (horizon)}

(141) 135, 400, 569

أنَ 12 تأم {14 تأم} إعْتَلى نَجو

على حوالي 12 {حوالي 14} (طرف) [على كل من 12 {14} (طرفا)]، إعْتلى (ظَهَرَ) مرتفع ارضي

On as many as 12 {14} (edges) [On each of the 12 {14} (edges)], a high land mass rose (appeared)

(142) [418, 662]

أنَ كور **نيموس {نَيْظير} {أنَ نَيْموس {نَيْظير}} إِتَمدْ [إعتَمدْ]** جش ماع

على {جبلْ} نَيْموس {نَيْظير} (حافظُ (سرِّ) الخير: الجبل الامين (الجودي)، احد قمم سلسلة جبال أجياد في مكة) إتمَدَت (إستوت: إعتدلت؛ إستقرت؛ إنتهت) [(إرتكَزت (رست؛ استقرت)] العوّامة

On {Mount} Naymūs [{Mount} Naydhīr] (keeper of the good (secret): *Mt. al-Amīn* (*al-Jawdiyy*), one of the peaks of the *Ajyād* mountains chain in Mecca), the raft leveled (rested; ended) [anchored]

(143) [14, 313, 418, 432, 492]

كورو كور**نَيْموس [**كور**نَيْظير]** جش ماع **إضْبَطْمَ أنَ ناس ألْ يهدِنْ [يعطِنْ] [يأطِنْ] [يأدِنْ]**

جبلُ نَيْموس {نَيْظير} إلتزَمَ (حَفظَ) العوّامة، الى الماء السريع لم يعطي (يستسلم)

Mount Naymūs [Naydhīr] held (kept) the raft; to the fast water, it did not give up

(144) [313, 418]

1-ن أومُ {أومَ} 2-اَ أومُ {أومَ} كورو **نَيْموس {نَيْظير} |**جش ماع **إضْبَطْمَ أنَ ناس ألْ يهدِنْ [يعطِنْ] [يأطِنْ] [يأدِنْ]|**كمن

يوما واحدا، يوما ثانيا، جبلُ نَيْموس {نَيْظير} إلتزَمَ (حَفظَ) العوّامة، الى الماء السريع لم يعطي (يستسلم)

First day, second day, Mount Naymūs [Naydhīr] held (kept) the raft; to the fast water, it did not give up

(145) [313, 418, 478]

3-تا {تَلْتا} أومُ {أومَ} 4-اَ أومُ {أومَ} كورو **نَيْموس {نَيْظير} |**جش ماع **إضْبَطْمَ أنَ ناس ألْ يهدِنْ [يعطِنْ] [يأطِنْ] [يأدِنْ]|**كمن

ثالثا يوم، رابعا يوم، جبلُ نَيْموس {نَيْظير} إلتزَمَ (حَفظَ) العوّامة، الى الماء السريع لم يعطي (يستسلم)

Third day, fourth day, Mount Naymūs [Naydhīr] held (kept) the raft; to the fast water, it did not give up

(146) [313, 418]

5-سو {5-تا} 6-سا {5-تا أومَ 6-تا أومَ} كورو **نَيْموس {نَيْظير} |**جش ماع **إضْبَطْمَ أنَ ناس ألْ يهدِنْ [يعطِنْ] [يأطِنْ] [يأدِنْ]|**كمن

خامسُ يوم، سادسا يوم، جبلُ نَيْموس {نَيْظير} إلتزَمَ (حَفظَ) العوّامة، الى الماء السريع لم يعطي (يستسلم)

Fifth day, Sixth day, Mount Naymūs [Naydhīr] held (kept) the raft; to the fast water, it did not give up

(147) [289]

7-و أومَ {أومُ} إنَ قَصَدِ [كَسَدِ]

عند مجيء سابعُ يوم

At the arrival of the seventh day

(148) [53, 584, 650]

أأشَصِمَ طع مَعشي [مُشعِن] **[**طَنُو مَعشي [مُشعِن]**] أمَسَرْ**

رفعت طير حمام، حررته

I lifted a dove, I set it free

(149) [241, 390, 584]

إلكْ طع مَعشي [مُشعِن] **[**طَنُو مَعشي [مُشعِن]**] إإتَرَمَ {يفرَمَ}**

تَرَسّل (ذهب) طير الحمام، (ثم) عادَ [(بقي) يحومَ (يدور)]

The dove went, it returned [(kept) circling around]

(150) [52, 240, 355, 631]

مَنْزَزُ أُلْ إعقَسْ ذومَ [إعقَشْ ذومَ] [إبّثْ ذومَ [إبّذْ ذومَ]] {إأقَدا ذوم} إسَخْرَ

أرض نزيزة ما ظهرت له [تواجدت له] {اشرفت (ظهرت) له}، قُهر (أُحبط) [بقي ذاهبا وآيبا]

A wet land had not appeared to it [became available to him], it was frustrated [it went back and forth]

(151) [53, 528, 650]

أُأشَصِمَ سئم مَعشي [مُشعِن] أُأمَسَرْ {أُأمَسِرْ}

رفعت طير سنونو، حررته

I lifted a swallow, I set it free

(152) [390]

إلِكْ سئم مَعشي [مُشعِن] إإتُرَمَ {يفِرَمَ}

تَرَسّل (ذهب) طير السنونو، (ثم) عادَ [(بقي) يحومَ (يدور)]

The swallow went, it returned [(kept) circling around]

(153) [52]

مَنْزَزُ أُلْ إعقَسْ ذومَ [إعقَشْ ذومَ] [إبّثْ ذومَ [إبّذْ ذومَ]] {إأقَدا ذوم} إسَخْرَ

أرض نزيزة ما ظهرت له [تواجدت له] {اشرفت (ظهرت) له}، قُهر (أُحبط) [بقي ذاهبا وآيبا]

A wet land had not appeared to it [became available to him], it was frustrated [it went back and forth]

(154) [45, 53, 650]

أُأشَصِمَ غَريبَ أُمَسَرْ {أُمَسِرْ}

رفعت غُراب، حررته

I lifted a raven, I set it free

(155) [45, 633]

إلِكْ غَريبَ قَرُرَ ذا آ ميس إإمُرَ

تَرَسّل (ذهب) الغراب، رآى رُسُب المياه

The raven went, it saw waters sediments

(156) [24, 62, 390, 661]

يأكَلْ يسَحِ يتَأرِ أُلْ إسَخْرَ

كان يأكلُ، يسيحُ، يتواتر (يحدّ البصر)، ما قُهر (أُحبط) [ما بقي ذاهبا وآيبا]

It was eating, cruising (roving), tracking (aiming), it was not frustrated [it did not go back and forth]

(157) [141, 231, 578]

أُأشَصِمَ أنَ 4 يم ميس أتَقي نِيقا

رفعت ذبيحة الى جهات الارض الاربعة [الى البحار الاربعة] واتقيت (ضحيت)

I lifted up an offering (sheep) to the four cardinal directions [to the four seas] and sacrificed (it)

(158) [560, 671]

أسكُنْ سُرْقينُ [سُرْجينُ] إنَ عُجُ [عُقُ] زيقورة كورِ

اقمت بخور في اعالي [حوالي] زيقورة (قمة) الجبل

I held incense (session) in the top of [around] the mountain peak

(159) [116, 615]

7 و 7 دوك أداجور [دوك أداقور] أُكْتِنْ

دخّنْتُ (بخّرْتُ) سبعة و (ثم) سبعة قوارير (اخرى)

I fumed (smoked) seven and (then) seven (more) flasks

(160) [58, 503, 528]

إنَ سَفْلِ ذونُ أتَبَكْ جحي جش عرن و شم جعر

في اسفلهم (في قعر القوارير او في النار تحت القوارير)، رميت بدفعات (تدريجيا)، قصب، خشب عرن، و عطر ورق الآس

In their underneath (in the flasks or in the fire beneath them), I threw, in portions (gradually), reed, cedar wood, and myrtle leaves scent

(161) [143, 252]

دنجر ميس **إإصِنو عِريسَ [إريسَ]**

الآلهة شمّت العطر

The gods smelled the savor

(162) [115, 143, 252, 270]

دنجر ميس **إإصِنو عِريسَ [إريسَ]** ضُجَ **{طابَ}**

الآلهة شمّت عطر طيب (حلوٌ)

The gods smelled the sweet {soothing} savor

(163) [449, 537, 672]

دنجر ميس **كيم زُنْبيي [سُنْبيي]** عُجُ [عُقُ] عَنْ تِشْكُرْ **إفْتَهْرو**

الآلهة، كالعقارب (المنافقين)، تجمعت فوق [حول] سيد (معطي) الشكُر (العرفان)

The gods gathered, like scorpions (hypocrites) [flies], over [around] the giver of the gratitude (the sacrifice)

(164)

ألتُ ألانُما دنجر مَه **إنَ كَسَدِ ذو [قَصَدِ ذو]**

رقيقة وجميلة الإله (أرورُ) ، أول بأول (فورا)، عند وصولها

The lady of god (Aruru), immediately, at her arrival

(165) [55, 416, 545, 631]

إعِسِي [إهِشِي] [إإشِي] [إإسي] نيم ميس جَلَ ميس **ذا** دنجر**أنوم إعِفُشوَ [إعِفُسوَ] كيي ضُحي ذو**

استخَفّت بجلالات منافقين الإله أنيم، جعلتهم مثل اضحوكتها:

She belittled their majesties the hypocrites of god Anim; she made them like her laughingstock:

(166) [35, 40, 173]

دنجر ميس هنوتمْ {هنُوتي} لوو [لُهو] نا زاجن [نا زاغن] جوّيا [جُعْيا] آ [أيا] أمْسِي

'الآلهةُ هنا [هذه]، ليكن لهم (ليلبسو) أحجار لازورْد باطنيا [إستيا] (جماميصيَ)، يجب ان لا (كي لا) أنساها

'The gods, herein, let them have (wear) the lapis lazuli stones of my interior [bottom] (i.e. my feces), (so) I should not forget them

(167) [34, 40, 76, 184]

أُد ميس {أومي} هنوتمْ {هنُوتي} لأُحْسُسَمَ {أحسُسَمَ} أنَ دهرِت آ [أيا] أمْسِي

الأيام هنا [هذه]، لأندب (لأرثي) {سأندب (سأرثي)} على مدى الدهر، يجب ان لا (كي لا) أنساها

These days, herein, I shall mourn forever, (so) I should not forget them

(168) [560]

دنجر ميس ليألِكُني أنَ سرْقين [سرْجين]

لتترسل (لتأتي) الآلهة الى البخور

The gods should come to the incense (session)

(169) [560]

دنجر إنليل آ [أيا] يألِكَ أنَ سرْقين [سرْجين]

الإله إنليل يجب ان لا يترسل (يأتي) الى البخور

(but) the god Enlil should not come to the incense (session)

(170) [226, 560]

أذو [هذو] لا إمْتَلْكُمَ {إمْتَلِكُم} إسْكُنَ عَبُبُ

هذا أنه (ذلك لأنه) ما تَماسكَ (تّصرّف بتهوّر)، أقام الطوفان

That is (because) he had not restrained himself (he acted carelessly), he established the Deluge

(171) [288, 354]

و عُجْ ميس يا إمْنو أنَ كَرَسِ [كَرَثِ]

و منّى (جعل قَدَرُ) ناسيَ الى دمار التكدس [الدمار]'

And he fated (destined) my people to the pileup ruin [to the ruin]'

(172) [289, 621]

ألتُ ألانُما دنجر إنليل إنَ كَسَدِ ذو [قَصَدِ ذو]

الإله إنليل، أول بأول (فورا)، عند وصوله

The god Enlil, immediately, at his arrival

(173) [149]

إإمُرْ جش ماعَمَ إعتَزِزْ {إتَزِزْ} دنجر إنليل

رأى العوّامة، تعزز (تصلب) الإله إنليل

He saw the raft; Enlil toughened (became angry)

(174) [95, 326, 626]

لِباتِ {لِباتَ} إمتَلي {إمتَلى} ذا دنجر.دنجر{دنجر ميس} دنجر يجِيجي

إمتلئ غضبا من الآلهة، آلهة يجيجِ (ياجوج وماجوج: جن باطن الارض):

He was filled with rage of (at) the gods, the Igigi gods (the underground *jinns* or ghosts):

(175) [392]

آأما {آنما} أُصي {أُصو} [هُصي {هُصو}] نَفِسْتِ

'هامنا (إجلبو) الكائن الحي الخارج (الهارب) [هامنا أخرجو [إجلبو] الكائن الحي]

'Over here (bring over here), the escaped living being [Over here (bring out here), the living being]

(176) [40, 62]

آ [أيا] يِبْلُط لَعْ إنَ كَرَسِ [كَرَثِ]

يجب ان لا يحيى رجل في دمار التكدس [الدمار]'

No man should survive in the pileup ruin [the ruin]'

(177) [115, 118]

دنجر نِنْورةَ فاء ذو ضُوُمَ ضُجَا

الإله ننورة أطلق [ضَمّ وأطلق] فمه، ضاجّاً {صارخا}

The god Ninurta let go [held and let go] his mouth (tongue), shouting

(178)

مُوَرَ {مُوَرْ} أنَ قُرَدِ دنجر إنليك

قال الى المحارب (البطل) الإله إنليل:

He said to Enlil the warrior (hero):

(179) [354]

مَنُمَ ذا لا دنجر حيا أمَتُ [هِمَتْ] {أمَتْ [هِمَتْ]} يبنّي

'من ذا الذي غير الإله حيا (يستطع ان) يحقق (مثل) هذا الامر [المخطط]؟

'Who other than the god Ea can accomplish (such) matter (plan)?

(180) [209, 556]

و دنجر حيا إإديمَ [إهديمَ] كَلَ سِفْرِ [سِبْرِ]

فالإله حيا قد اكتسب كل المهارات [الخبرات]'

For the god Ea had acquired all the skills [the experiences]'

(181) [115, 119, 245]

دنجر حيا فاء ذو ضُوُمَ ضُجَا

الإله حيا أطلق [ضَمّ وأطلق] فمه (لسانه)، ضاجّاً {صارخا}

The god Ea let go [held and let go] his mouth (tongue), shouting

(182)

مؤرَ { مؤرْ} أنَ قُرَدِ {قُرَدُ} دنجرإنليكْ

قال الى المحارب (البطل) الإله إنليك:

He said to Enlil the warrior (hero):

(183) [9]

أتّ أبجَلْ دنجر ميس قُرَدُ

'أنت أبجَل (عظيم) الآلهة، محاربٌ (بطل)

'You are the most revered of the gods, a warrior (hero)

(184) [226]

كيي كيي {كيْكي} لا تَمْتَلكَمَ عَبُبُ تَسْكُنْ

كيف، كيف لا تتماسك (كيف تتصرف بتهّور)، (و) تقيم الطوفان؟

How, how could you not restrain yourself (how could you act carelessly), (and) instate the Deluge?

(185) [47, 196, 662]

بعِلْ خطئ {أرْن} إعمِدْ [إإمِدْ] خِطأَ ذو

(على) صاحبُ (فاعلُ) الخطيئة، إعتمد (افرض مُعادل) [ساوي] خطيئته

(on) The one of a sin (on the perpetrator of a sin), impose the equal of [equalize (match)] his sin

(186) [164, 662]

بعِلْ جئِلتِ [غيلَتِ] إعمِدْ [إإمِدْ] جئِلتْ [غيلَتْ] ذو

(على) صاحبُ (فاعلُ) فعل الشر [الاعتداء] إعتمد (افرض مُعادل) [ساوي] فعل شرّه [اعتداءه]

(on) The one of evil-doing [of offence] (on the perpetrator of evil-doing [of offence]), impose the equal of [equalize (match)] his evil-doing [his offence]

(187) [204, 254, 544]

رُميي آ [أيا] إبتِقْ [إبتِكْ] [إفتقْ] شُدُدْ آ [أيا] إرْمُ

أرخي، يجب ان لا (كي لا) يصبح مقطوعا؛ شدّ، يجب ان لا (كي لا) يصبح راخيا

Loosen up, so it would not be broken; tighten up, so it would not be loose

(188) [33, 498]

أمَكِ {أمَكُ} تَسكُنَ {تَسكُنُ} عَبُبُ {عَبُبَ}

بدلاً من ان تُقيم الطوفان

Rather than you instate the Deluge

(189) [512, 585]

عُرمَخْ [هُرمَخ] ليتْبَمَ عُج ميس [عُقْ ميس] ليَصْهِرْ [ليصحِرْ]

لينتصب (ليظهر) كائنٌ مفترسٌ [اسدٌ] ليُبيدْ الناس المُسيئين

A ferocious creature [A lion] could rise (appear) to eliminate the offenders (the disobedient)

(190) [498]

أمَكِ {أمَكُ} تَسْكُنَ {تَسْكُنُ} عَبُبُ {عَبُبَ}

بدلاً من ان تُقيم الطوفان

Rather than you instate the Deluge

(191) [512, 585, 634]

هُرْبَرَ ليتْبَمَ عُجُ ميس [عُقَ ميس] ليَصَهرْ [ليصَحرْ]

لينتصب (ليظهر) ذئب [داهيةً] ليُبيدْ الناس المُسيئين

A sly creature [A wolf] could rise (appear) to eliminate the offenders (the disobedient)

(192) [498]

أمَكِ {أمَكُ} تَسْكُنَ {تَسْكُنُ} عَبُبُ {عَبُبَ}

بدلاً من ان تُقيم الطوفان

Rather than you instate the Deluge

(193) [195, 497, 498]

حُثَحُ ليسَكِنْمَ كور ليشْجِتْ

ليُقيمُ (ليعِمُّ) الجفاف، ليذبح (ليكتسح) الارض (الصُقع)

A famine could settle (pervade) to slaughter (to sweep) the land

(194) [90, 498]

أمَكِ {أمَكُ} تَسْكُنَ {تَسْكُنُ} عَبُبُ {عَبُبَ}

بدلاً من ان تُقيم الطوفان

Rather than you instate the Deluge

(195) [497]

إراء دنجر [هراء دنجر] ليتْبَمَ كور {عُجُ ميس [عُقَ ميس]} ليشْجِتْ

لينهض (ليظهر) الإله هرا (هراكَل) ليذبح (ليكتسح) الارض {الناس المُسيئين}

The god Erra (Errakal) could rise (appear) to slaughter (sweep) the land {the offenders (the disobedient)}

(196) [448]

أنكو أُل أفتا فرِسْتِ دنجر ميس جَلَ ميس

انا ، نفسي، لم أكشف غامضُ شأن (فعل) [حكم] جلالاتُ الآلهَة

I, myself, did not disclose the internal (hidden) deal [judgement] of their majesties the gods

(197) [376, 514, 552, 556, 646]

أتْرَ حَسِسْ شونَتَ أُسَبِرِ ذومَ فرِسْتِ دنجر ميس إسْمَعَ

انا جعلت أتْرَ حَسِسْ يختبر (يرى) حلماً، هو سمعَ غامضْ شأن (فعل) [حكم] الآلهَة

I made Atra-Hasis experience (see) a dream, he heard the internal (hidden) deal [judgement] of the gods

(198) [140, 368]

حينِنَمَ مِلِكْ ذو مِلْكُ

اما الآن (ف)لآمره (الإله إديم) الامرُ ‘

And now, the guidance (the decision) is (up) to his guider (his owner) (i.e. Ea)’

(199)

إعْلَمَ دنجر إديم أنَ لِبٍّ جش ماع

(بعد ذلك) صعد الإله إديم (ساقي الارض: الإله حيا) الى قلب العوّامة

(then) The god IDIM (the one who waters the soil: god EA) went up to the heart of the raft

(200) [135, 200, 458, 492, 655]

إضْبَطْ قاتيامَ أُلْتَلَنِيَ {أُسْتَلَنِيَ} إياذي

مَسكَ يداي، إنتزعني لي

He held my hands, he took me out

(201) [209, 531, 614, 655]

أُسْتَلِي أُسْتَقْمِسْ [أُسْتَكْمِسْ] ذِنِثْتِ إنَ يديا [حديا]

انتزع الإمرأة (زوجتي) (و) أجْلَسَها القرفصاء، بجنبي

He pulled out the female (my wife) (and) made her squat at my side

(202) [65, 149, 228, 287, 451]

إلفُتْ [إلفُسْ] فوتْنيما يأزَزْ [يعزَزْ] إنَ بيرِنِ يكَرَبَنَذي

لَفُتَ (أدارَ) [لَمسَ] واجهتينا [جبينينا]، يقف ساكنً بيننا، يهبُنا:

He turned [touched] our fronts [our foreheads], standing still between us, granting us:

(203)

إنَ فَنا مُعُد ذي عَميلوتُمَ

’في السابق، أُتانَفسْتم (كان) بشر

‘In the past, Uta-Napištim (was) human being

(204) [136, 380, 432]

حينِنَمَ مُعُد ذي و مؤنُثْ [مؤنُسْ] ذو لوو [لُهو] حمُو كيمَ دنجر ميس نَسيمَ

اما الآن، أُتانَفسْتم و إمرأته (زوجته)، ليكن لهم مصير مثل (مصير) آلهة ماضين (راحلين)

From now on, Uta-Napištim and his woman (his wife), let them have a destiny like preceding (bygone) gods

(205) [206, 274, 435, 485]

لوو [لُهو] أثِبْمَ مُعُد ذي إنَ رُوقِ إنَ فيي حِيدْ ميس

ليكن لهم أن يقيمُ أُتانَفسْتم بعيدا، في (عند) فم (منبع) الانهار‘

Let it be for them that Uta-Napištim shall dwell far away, in (at) the mouth (source) of the rivers’

(206) [274, 332]

إلْقونِمَا إنَ رُوقِ إنَ فيي {كاء} حِيدْ ميس أُسْتَثِبونِنِ

(وهكذا) ألقوني (أخذوني) بعيدا، في فم (منبع) الانهار، أأوَوْني

(and so) They took (put) me far away at the mouth (source) of the rivers, they made me settle

(207) [283, 449]

حينِنَمَ أنَ كا أذا مَنو دنجر ميس يُفَهَرَكُمَ

اما الآن، الى ذلك (من اجل ذلك) [إليك (من اجلك)]، من (ذا الذي) سيجمع الآلهة؟

And now, who will assemble the gods for (achieving) that [for you]?

(208) [202, 276, 602]

بَلاطَ ذا تُبَؤوَ [تُبَغوَ] تُؤتا أتّ

الحياةَ التي تصبو [تبغي] أن تُعطى (لك) أنت،

The (eternal) life that you aim [want] to be given,

(209) [124, 154, 226, 571]

جَنَأ إي تَتِلْ 6 عُري و 7 مُساتي

(هيا) أكِبْ لها، إياك أن [لا] تستلقي (تَنَم) لستة ايام وسبعة ليالي"

(come) Work hard for (it), do not lay down (sleep) for six days and seven nights"

(210) [65, 274, 447]

كيمَ أثبُمَ إنَ بيريت فُردِي ذو

كأنما جلس في ما بين فردتيه (رجليه) (قَرفصَ)

He sat in between his legs (crouched)

(211) [228, 412, 568]

شِتٌّ كيمَ عِمْبَري ينُفُش عُجُ ذو [عُقُ ذو]

النوم، مثل غبار [طيب العنبر] ينتشر فوقه [حوله]

Sleep, like dust [Ambergris perfume], is spreading (blowing) over [around] him

(212) [357]

مْعُدْ ذي **أنَ ذا ذومَ** مُؤرْ **أنَ مَرْهِتِ ذو**

أُتانَفسْتم قال اليها، الى إمرأته (زوجته):

Uta-Napištim said to her, to his woman (wife):

(213)

أمْرِ لَعْفُرُس **ذا يرِسوَ بلاطُ**

’أنظري الى (هذا) الرجل الشاب الذي ينوي (يطلب) الحياة (الابدية)!

‘Look at this young man who intends (wants) (eternal) life!

(214) [229, 412]

شِتُّ كيمَ عِمْبَري ينُفُش مُجُ ذو [عُقْ ذو]

النوم، مثل غبار [طيب العنبر] ينتشر فوقه [حوله]'

Sleep, like dust [Ambergris perfume], is spreading (blowing) over [around] him'

(215) [357]

مَرْهتو أنَ ذا ذومَ مُوْرْ أنَ ᵐعُد ذي

إمرأته (زوجته) قالت اليه، الى أُتانَفسْتم:

His woman (wife) said to him, to Uta-Napištim:

(216) [228, 329]

لُفُسمَ ليجألْتا لُعُ

'إلفِتْه (أدِرْه) [إلمسْهُ] ليَفزْ (ليستيقظ) الرجل

'Divert him [Touch him], let the man be startled (awakened)

(217) [390, 547]

حَرانِ إلِكَ ليتوْرْ إنَ سُلْمَ

ليرجع (عبر) الطريق (الذي) ترسّلَ (جاء)، بالسلامة

Let him go back (through) the road he went (came), in safety

(218) [390, 392]

كاء جَل أُصا [مُصا] ليتوْرْ أنَ ماتِ ذو

ليرجع (عبر) الباب العظيم (الذي) خرج (منه)، الى أرضه'

Let him go back (through) the great gate he exited, to his land'

(219)

ᵐعُد ذي أنَ ذا ذومَ مُوْرْ أنَ مَرْهتِ ذو

أُتانَفسْتم قال اليها، الى إمرأته (زوجته):

Uta-Napištim said to her, to his woman (wife):

(220) [473]

رأجَتْ عَميلُتُ يرأجِجْكِ

'البشر منافق، (قد) يخدعك

'Human is deceitful, he can deceive you

(221) [142, 154, 303, 479, 498, 652]

جَنّأ عِفيِي كُرُماتي ذو [قُرُماتي ذو] سِئتَكِني إنَ ريسِ ذو

هيا (أكِبي)، اتركي له خُبْزاته، ضعيها عند رأسه

Go on, leave him his breads; set (put) them by his head

(222) [211, 571]

و أُومِ ذا إتِلُ إنَ إجَرِ [حِجَرِ] أصْري

واليوم الذي إستلقى به (نامَه)، وثّقيه في حجر'

And the day in which he laid down (he slept) (through), document it in a brick (in a stone)'

(223) [303, 498]

ذيي إعِفِي كُرُماتي ذو [قُرُماتي ذو] إسْتَكَني إنَ ريسِ ذو

هي، تركَت له خُبْزاته، وضعتها عند رأسه

She left him his breads; she set (put) them by his head

(224) [209]

و أُومِ ذا إتِلُ إنَ إجَرِ [حِجَرِ] أُدَّ ذو

واليوم الذي إستلقى به (نامَه)، عَرّفتْه [علّمته] في حجر

And the day in which he laid down (he slept) (through), she showed [marked] it in a brick (in a stone)

(225) [264, 303, 493]

إسْتَ ذَبُلَتْ كُرُمَتْ ذو [قُرُمَتُ ذو]

الخُبزة [خُبزَتُه] الاولى كانت ذابلة (يابسة)

The first [His first] bread was dry

(226) [388, 477]

2-تُمْ مُسُكَتْ 3-تُمْ رَطْبَتْ

الثانية كانت جلدية (ملساء)، الثالثة كانت رَطِبة (مبْتَلّة)

The second was leathery (rubbery), the third was damp (soggy)

(227) [243, 286]

4-تُمْ إفْتَصي [إفْتضي] [إبْتَضي] [إفْتَصعي] كأمَنْ ذو

الرابعة رَشّحَت (عَرِقَت) رغيفة يانسونها

His fourth, its Anise loaf oozed (sweated)

(228) [209, 520]

5-تُمْ شِئِبَ [شِئِفَ] إتأدي

الخامسة جلبت (أنْتَجتْ) [وصلها (أصابها)] العفن

The fifth brought in (produced) [was reached (stricken) by] mold

(229) [60]

6-تُمْ بَسْلَتْ

السادسة كانت مطبوخة ومجففة (جاهزة للأكل)

The sixth was baked and dried (fresh)

(230) [228, 329, 441, 511]

سَبُعتُمْ إنَ فَتيمَ إلْفُسمَ إجألتا {إجألتمَ} لَعْ

(بينما) السابعة في طراوتها، لَفَتَهُ (أداره) [لمَسَه] (أُتانَفسْتم)، فَزَّ (استيقظ) الرَجلْ

(while) The seventh was tender, he (Uta-Napištim) diverted [touched] him, the man got startled (awakened)

(231)

دنجرجِشْجمَش أنَ ذا ذُوم مُوَرَ أنَ مُعْد ذي رُوقِ

جِشْجمَش قال اليه، الى أُتانَفسْتم البعيد المُتنحي (نوح):

Gilgamesh said to him, to Uta-Napištim the withdrawn and distant (Noah):

(232) [40, 568, 638]

أنمِتْ شِتُّمْ إرْهوَ عِليا [حِليا]

'حالما سكن النومُ فوقي [حولي]،

'As soon as sleep settled over [around] me,

(233) [183, 228, 570]

خَنْطِتْ [حَنْطِتْ] تَلْتَفْتَنما تَدَنْكَني [تَدَعْكَني] أتَّ

حالا [بفضاضة]، انت لفَتّني (أدِرْتني) [لَمَسْتني]، أزعَجتني (أنهَضتني)'

Immediately [Rudely], you diverted me [touched me], disturbed (aroused) me'

(234)

مُعْد ذي أنَ ذا ذُوم مُوَرَ أنَ دنجرجِشْجمَش

أُتانَفسْتم قال اليه، الى جِشْجمَش:

Uta-Napištim said to him, to Gilgamesh:

(235) [303, 354]

ألكما دنجرجِشْجمَش مُؤنا كُرُماتكَ [قُرُماتكَ]

'تَرَسّلْ (تعالَ) (يا) جِشْجمَش، عَلّمْ [عدد] خُبزاتكَ

'Come, Gilgamesh, mark [count] your breads

(236) [209, 283, 571]

و أُوم ذا تَتلُ لُوو [لهو] أدَكَ [عِدكَ] كا أذا

واليوم الذي إسْتَلْقَيتَ به (نُمْته)، ليكن له (إعطيه) تعليمُكَ [عَدُّكَ] (للخبز) لذاك (اليوم) [لكَ]

And for each day that you laid down [slept], let it have (give it) your mark [count] (for the bread) for that (day) [for you]

(237)

إسْتَت ذابلُت كُرُمَتَكَ [قُرُمَتَكَ]

خُبزَتُكَ الاولى كانت ذابلة (يابسة)

Your first bread was dry

(238)

2-تُمْ مُسُكَتْ 3-تُمْ رَطْبَتْ

الثانية كانت جلدية (ملساء)، الثالثة كانت رَطِبة (مبْتَلّة)

The second was leathery (rubbery), the third was damp (soggy)

(239) [286]

4-تُمْ إفْتَصي [إفْتضي] [إبْتَضي] [إفْتَصعي] كأمَنْك

الرابعة، رَشّحَت (عَرقَت) رغيفة يانسونك

The fourth one, your Anise loaf oozed (sweated)

(240) [532]

5-تُمْ شئِفَ إتأدي 6-تُمْ بَسْلَتْ

الخامسة جلبت (أنْتَجتْ) [وصلها (أصابها)] العفن، السادسة كانت مطبوخة ومجففة (جاهزة للأكل)

The fifth one, brought in (formed) [was reached (was struck) by] mold, the sixth was baked and dried (fresh)

(241)

7-تُمْ إنَ فَتيمَ ألْفُتْكَ أنكو {تَتَجألتا أتَّ}

(بينما) السابعة في طراوتها، لَفَتُّكَ (أدرْتك) [لمَسْتَكَ] أنا نفسي {فَزَّيت (استيقظت) أنت}'

(while) the seventh was tender, I, myself diverted [touched] you {you got startled (awoke)}'

(242)

جِشْجِمَش أنَ ذا ذُوم مُرَ أنَ مُعْد ذي رُوقِ

جِشْجِمَش قال اليه، الى أُتانَفسْتم البعيد المُتنحي (نوح):

Gilgamesh said to him, to Uta-Napištim the withdrawn and distant (Noah):

(243) [4, 226, 631]

كيْكي لأُعفُس [لأُعفُش] مُأتْ ذي {مُأتْ ذيتم} أأكَنِ {أأيكا} لأُلِكْ

'كيف، كيف لي ان أواصلْ، أُتْ ذي (مؤتى الحياة) (أُتانَفسْتم)، اي مكانٍ لاذهَبْ؟

'How, how should I proceed, Ut ZI (the life-given one: Uta-Napištim), where should I go?

(244) [134, 492]

|عضو|^مبس^ يا أُضَبطُ {أُضَبطَ} عَكيمُ

حجز أعضائيا القابضُ (الموت)

The Gripper has seized my organs

(245) [347, 349, 498]

إنَ حِي [إي] مأليا [مَعليا] أَثِبْ موتُم

في غرفة سريريَ [أريكَتي] يقيمُ الموت

In my bed's room [my bed-chamber], death dwells

(246)

و أشَر [أثَرْ] [أسَرْ] |فانيا| لأُسكُنْ ذوو موتمَ

وحيث سأضع [سأثبّت] |قدمي [وَجهي]|، هو ذا الموت!'

And wherever I will set |my foot [my face]|, there he is: death!'

(247) [340, 382]

مُعْد ذي أنَ ذا ذُوم مُرَ {إذكَرَ} أنَ مُعُرْسَنَبِ مألَحِ

أُتانَفسْتِم قال اليه، الى عُرْسَنَبِ (حامي الابدية) الملاّح:

Uta-Napištim said to him, to Ur-šánabi (the protector of eternity), the shipwright:

(248) [209, 282, 404, 667]

مُعُرْسَنَبِ كأرُ [خأرُ] ليأديكَ نِعْبِرُ ليزعَرْكَ

'(يا) عُرْسَنَبِ، ليُخرجِكَ (ليتخلص منك) الخَورُ، لينبذُكَ المِعْبَرُ (سفينة العبور)

'O Ur-šánabi, may the gulf extract you (get rid of you), may the crossing boat reject you

(249) [22, 113, 673]

ذا إنَ أهي ذا دودو ميس كُ [طوطُ ميس كُ] [دُعْدُع ميس كُ] أهْ ذا زُمعِ

هذا (الخور) الذي (جرت) في سواحله العديد من المغامرات (رواح ومجيء) [الشدائد]، إرتَعِدْ (خوفا) (من) ساحله

That (gulf), where many adventures (took place) at its shores, tremble in fear (when) at its shore!

(250) [226, 437]

لُعْ ذا تألكا فَنَاتُ

الرجل الذي ترسّلتَ (مَضيتَ) أمامه (قُدْتَ)

The man who you came ahead of (you led; you brought here)

(251) [223, 436, 626]

إكتَسُوَ مَلْؤُ فقَرْ ذو

إكتَسي (تغطى بشعر متعقّد) ملؤ (كاملُ) قوامه (جسده)

His full body is covered with matted hair

(252) [119, 388, 458, 663]

مَسْكُوَ أُقتَتُوَ دُمُقْ [دُمُجْ] عضو ميس ذو

جلوده الحيوانية إستأصلت (قَلّلَت) مجدولية (بُرْم وصُقْل) أعضاءه (جسده)

His hides (animal leather clothes) took away (lessened) the entwined and polished look of his organs (of his body)

(253) [68, 332, 401]

لِقي ذومَ مُعُرْسَنَبِ أنَ نَمْسي بِعلْ ذومَ [بِئلْ ذومَ]

إلتَقيه (خُذْهُ)، (يا) عُرْسَنَبِ، الى ناموس (وعاء العِلْم: حوض العلِو [النقاء]) أربابه (آلهته)

[إلتَقيه (خُذْهُ)، (يا) عُرْسَنَبِ، إرْشِده الى الناموس (وعاء العِلْم: حوض العلو [النقاء])]

Take him, Ur-šánabi, to the washtub of highness [washtub of purity] of his lords

[Take him, Ur-šánabi, direct him [bring him] to the washtub of highness [washtub of purity]]

(254) [2, 135, 233, 364, 626]

مَلْئَ ذو إنَ مِئي {أ ميس} كيم {جيم} علِي ليمْسح [ليمْسي]

ليُنظّف [ليَفْرك] في الماء، مثل عالٍ [نقيٍ] (إله)، ملؤهُ (كامله)

Let him clean [rub off] his fullness (his whole body) in the waters, like a high one [a pure one] (like a god)

(255) [209, 388, 574]

ليأدي مَسْكِي ذومَ ليبئل [ليبعل] [ليأبل [ليعبل]] طَمْطَمْ

ليتخلص من جلوده الحيوانية، ليتَولّاها [ليحملها (ليجلبها)] البحر (بعيدا)

Let him get rid of his hides (animal leather clothes), let the sea take them over [carry (bring) them away]

(256) [270, 565, 674]

طَابُ {طَابُم} صُفُو {صَفُو} {لو صُفُو} زُمْرُ ذو [ضُمْرُ ذو]

(و) طِيبً (عِطرً) إدلك {إدلك له} جسمه

(with) Fine oil (perfume), anoint (massage) his body {for him}

(257) [209, 440, 456, 495]

لُوو [لُهو] حُدُثْ {حُدُثُ} فَرْسِجُ [بَرْزَجُ] ذا قَقادِ ذو {سَجدُ ذو}

ليكن له مُجددا {مُجددْ} نطاق رأسه (عمامته)

Let him have his head band (his turban) made anew (be renewed)

(258) [63, 337, 492, 586]

تِحْديقَ {تِحْديقِ} لُوو [لُهو] لابِسْ ضُبَطْ بَلْتِ ذو

عباءةً ليكن له، مرتديا، قَدْرَ (بما يناسب) وقاره

Let him have a robe dressed, befitting his dignity

(259)

عَدي [عَتي] يألَكُ أنَ أورَ ذو {كور ذو}

(و)حتّى يترَسّل (يذهب) الى مدينته،

(and) Until he goes (home) to his city,

(260) [226, 289, 638]

عَدي [عَتي] يقصَدُ [يكسَدُ] أنَ أُرِه ذو

حتى يصلُ الى (يجدُ) طريقه،

Until he arrives to his way (finds his way home),

(261) [131, 209, 328, 532]

تِحْديقُ شِئِفَ آ [أيا] يأدي {يأدما} حديثُ ليدئص [ليدئض]

العباءة، يجب ان لا يَصلُها (يُصيبها) شَعَثٌ (تجعد وسخ وتشقق)؛ يجب ان تبقى غير منقوصة (مَصونةً) جديدةً'

The robe should not be afflicted by untidiness (should not become untidy); it should stay intact, new'

(262)

إلِقي ذومَ [م]عُرْسَنَبِ أنَ نَمْسي أُبِئِلْ ذومَ [أُبعِلْ ذومَ]

لقاهُ (أَخَذَهُ)، عُرْسَنَبِ، الى ناموس (وعاء العِلْم: حوض العِلو [النقاء]) أربابه (آلهته)

[لقاهُ (أَخَذَهُ)، عُرْسَنَبِ، أرْشَدَهَ [جَلَبَهُ] الى الناموس (وعاء العِلْم: حوض العِلو [النقاء])]

Ur-šánabi took him to the washtub of highness [washtub of purity] of his lords

[Ur-šánabi took him, he directed him [he brought him] to the washtub of highness [washtub of purity]]

(263)

مَلْئُ ذو إنَ مِئي {آ[ميس]} جيم عِلِي إمْسِحِي [إمْسِي]

نَظّفَ [فَرَكَ] في الماء، مثل عالٍ [نقيٍ] (إلهٍ)، مِلؤهُ (كامله)

He cleaned [rubbed off] in the waters his fullness (his whole body), like a high one [a pure one] (like a god)

(264) [315]

إدِي كُؤس[ميس] ذومَ أُبِئِل [أُبعِل] [أُبِل] [أُعبِل]] طَمْطَمْ

تَخلّصَ من جلوده الحيوانية، تَولّاها [حملها (جلبها)] البحر (بعيدا)

He got rid of his hides (animal leather clothes), the sea took them over [carried (brought) them away]

(265) [565]

طَابُ {طَابُم} إصَفُو {إصَفِي} زُمُرْ ذو [ضُمُرْ ذو]

دَلَكَ جسمَهُ طِيبً (عِطرً)

(with) Fine oil (perfume), he anointed (massaged) his body

(266) [131]

أُتَحَدِثْ فَرْسِجُ [بَرْزِجُ] ذا سَجدُ ذو

جُدّدَ (أُستُحْدُثَ) نطاق رأسه (عمامته)

His head band (his turban) was made anew (was renewed)

(267)

تِحْديقَ {تِحْديقِ} لابِسْ ضُبَطْ بَلْتِ ذو

عباءةً، كان مرتديا، ضَبْطُ (بما يناسب) وقاره

He was dressed in a robe befitting his dignity

(268)

عَدي [عَتي] يألَكُ أنَ أورُ ذو {كور ذو}

(ف)حتّى يترَسّل (يذهب) الى مدينته،

(making sure,) Until he goes (home) to his city,

(269)

عَدي [عَتي] يقَصَدُ [يكَسَدُ] أنَ أُرهِ ذو

حتَى يصِلُ الى (يجِدُ) طريقه،

Until he arrives to his way (finds his way home),

(270)

تحْديقُ شئِفَ آ [أيا] يأدِما حدِيثُ ليدِئص [ليدِئض]

العباءة، يجب ان لا يَصِلُها (يُصيبها) شَعثٌ (تجعد وسخ وتشقق)؛ يجب ان تبقى غير منقوصة (مَصونةً) جديدةً

The robe should not be afflicted by untidiness (should not become untidy); it should stay intact, new

(271) [253]

[دنجر]جِشْجِمَش و [m]عُرْسَنَبِ إرْكَبُو [جش]ماعَ

جِشْجِمَش و عُرُسَنَبِ عَلَوْ (ركبو) العوّامة

Gilgamesh and Ur-šánabi boarded the raft

(272) [170, 209, 253, 553]

[جش]مأجلَ إإدوَ [إهدوَ] ذونُ إرتَكْبُو

هيؤ (أعدّو) [وضعو في الماء] العوّامة المدورة التي هم (كانو قد) إعتَلَوْ (ركبو) (من قبل)

They prepared (equipped) [put (launched)] the round raft, which they had (previously) boarded

(273)

مَرْهِتو أنَ ذا ذومَ مُوْرْ أنَ [m]عَدَ ذي

إمرأته (زوجته) قالت اليه، الى أُتانَفسْتم:

His woman (wife) said to him, to Uta-Napištim:

(274) [39, 117, 266]

[دنجر]جِشْجِمَش دوكَ [دعُكَ] إأنَحا إأثُطا

’جِشّجِمَشْ دَوّى (دَبَّ) [تزاحم]، ناح (عانى)، جَرّ الخُطى (تَجَشم)

‘Gilgamesh rushed [jostled], endured, (and) incurred (struggled)

(275) [276, 390]

مِنا تَأتنَا ذوما يتأَرْ أنَ كور ذو [قور ذو]

أيّما (نزرٌ قليك) آتيتَهُ (أعطيه) (وهو) يرجع الى أرضه؟‘

What (little) have you given him (as) he returns (back) to his land?’

(276) [55, 448]

و ذوو إعسِي [إهشِي] فَرِسَ [دنجر]جِشْجِمَش

وبينما هو، جِشّجِمَش، (قد) حرّكَ (أطْلقَ) المُرْدي (خشبة التّسْير)

As he, Gilgamesh, moved (unleashed) his punting-pole

(277) [57, 296]

[جش]ماعَ أُطِحا أنَ كِبْرِ

(و)العوامة اقتربت الى الساحل

(and as) The raft moved closer to the shore

(278)

مُعُد ذيتم [مُعُد ذي] أنَ ذا ذُوم مُؤرْ أنَ دنجر جِشْجِمَش

أُتانَفسْتم قال اليه، الى جِشْجِمَش:

Uta-Napištim said to him, to Gilgamesh:

(279) [266]

دنجر جِشْجِمَش تألكا تأنَحا تأثطا

'(يا) جِشّجِمَشْ، (أنت) تَرَسّلتَ (جئتَ)، نُحْتَ (عانيتَ)، جَرّيتَ الخُطى (تَجَشّمْتَ)

'Gilgamesh, you came, you endured, (and) you incurred (struggled)

(280) [276, 390]

مِنا أتّناكوما تتأرْ أنَ كورِكَ [قورِكَ]

أيّما (نزرٌ قليلٌ) آتيتُكَ (أعطيتك) (وانت) ترجع الى أرضك؟

What (little) have I given you (as) you return (back) to your land?

(281) [244]

لأُفْتيَ دنجر جِشْجِمَش أمَتْ [همَتْ] نصِرْتِ [نظِرْتِ]

لأُكْشِفُ، يا جِشْجِمَش، أمرُ سرٍ

I shall reveal, Gilgamesh, a matter of secret

(282) [13, 245]

و أدْخَل ذا دنجر ميس كا أذا لأُقْبكَ

و لأُخبْرْكَ (عن) غامضُ شأن (فعل) الآلهة، لذاك (الامر) [لكَ]

And I shall tell you (about) an inner (hidden) deal of the gods, for (regarding) that (matter) [for you (only)]

(283) [130, 283, 551]

ثَمُّ ذوو كيمَ حدتِ إنَ جوّ أبْزُ| سكَنْ [ثَكنْ]

عُشبٌ هو مثل مَحد (السكاكين)، | في اعماق الأبزُ| ساكنٌ

It is a weed like a knife sharpener, located |under the Abzu|

(284) [36, 522]

سحِلْ ذو جيم أمُرْدنِمَ [أمُرْدِمَّ] يُسَحَلْ |قاتي منك|

شوكه (الناعم) [مِبْرَدِه] سيكْشِطُ (سيجْعَلْ) يداك كثمرة عليق (ملطاء)

Its (fine) thorns [Its file (rasp)] will scrape (make) your hands like a skinless (huskless) berry

(285) [550, 551]

ثُمّ ثَمَّ ذا أذو يقصَدَ [يكَسَدَ] قتاكا

اذا ما العُشب هذا، له تَصِلُ يداكَ

If that weed [After that weed], your hands reach to it

(286)

|...................... بلاطُ ....|

|....... ستحصل على الحياة الابدية|'

|.......... you will gain the eternal life|'

(287) [40, 514]

جِشْجِمَش[دنجر] آنيتو إنَ سَمعَ ذو

جِشّجِمَشْ، حالا ، حين (عند) سَمع ذلك

Gilgamesh, immediately, in hearing that (when he heard that)

(288) [469]

إفتي [إفَتَحي] رأطا |............. أنَ عبْزُ|

كَشَفَ [فَتحَ] منفذا مائيا |............ الى العَبْزُ|

He uncovered [opened] a waterway |......... to the ABZU|

(289) [393, 534, 637]

أرَكَسْ [أُركَزْ] نا[ميس] كَبْتُتَ أنَ [إنَ] ظيفي ذو

قَلَبَ رأسا على عقب [نكّسَ الى الاسفل] (رمى الى العَبْزُ) صخور مربوطة الى [في] قدميه [سيقانه]

He flipped upside down (threw downward into the Abzu) stones [tied] tightened (fastened) to [in] his feet [lower legs]

(290) [12, 209]

إلْدُ ذومَ [إدُّ ذومَ] أنَ عَبْزُ ....

(الصخور) أوْصَلته (سَحبته عميقا) الى العَبْزُ ....

They (the stones) made him arrive (pulled him deep) to the Abzu ....

(291) [551, 661]

ذوو إلقيَ ثَمَمَ إسُحا {إسُحْ ذو} ....

هو وجدَ عُشْبَه [العشب]، إقتلعه ......

He found his plant [the plant]; he swept it away (pulled it out) .....

(292) [204, 534]

أبَتقْ نا[ميس] كَبتُتَ إنَ ظيفي ذو

قَطع الصخور المربوطة في قدميه [سيقانه]

He cut loose the stones fastened in his feet [lower legs]

(293) [263, 296, 574]

طَمطَمْ إسكَا ذو [إسكُتو] أنَ كِبْرِ ذو

القاهُ (قَذفه) البحر الى الساحل

The sea threw him away (ejected him) to the shore

(294)

دنجر جِشْجِمَش أنَ ذا ذُوم مُوَرَ أنَ مُعُرْسَنَبِ مألَحِ

جِشْجِمَش قال اليه، الى عُرْسَنَبِ الملّاح:

Gilgamesh said to him, to Ur-šánabi, the shipwright:

(295) [141, 414]

مُعُرْسَنَبِ ثَمُ هانُو ثَمُ نقيتِ [نكيتِ]

'يا عُرْسَنَبِ، هذا العُشْبُ عُشْبُ الخلاص (النجاة) [عُشبُ الشدّة (الضيق)]

'O, Ur-šánabi, this weed is the plant of deliverance (salvation) [the plant for (against) hardship]

(296) [64]

ذا لَعُ إنَ لبِّ ذو يقصَدو [يكسَدو] نفْسَتْ بِلُرُ [نَفْسَتْ بِئِصُ]

للرجل، (هذا العشب) يُوصِلُ (يَمنحُ) الى قلبه نَفَسُ العيش (الحياة) [ومض [دَلَف] الحياة (نبض القلب)]

For a man, it delivers the living breath [the wink (spark) [trickle (flow)] of life] (the heartbeat) in his heart

(297) [8]

لأبعِلْ ذو [لأعبلْ ذو [لأبلْ ذو]] أنَ عَنوجِ كيع سفُرِ { عَنوجِ كيع سفُرُ} [عَنوجِ كيع ذُفورِ {عَنوجِ كيع ذُفورُ}]

سأحمله [سأجلبه] الى عُروك مقام المناسم والانعام [عُروك مذبح القرابين]

I shall carry it [bring it] to Uruk-of-the-cattles-site [Uruk-of-the-alter]

(298) [24, 239, 520]

لأتأكلْ [لأذاكلْ] شيبَمَ ثَمَّ لألْتَحُكْ

سأأكل العُشبَ عجوزاً، لأُجرّبْ

I shall feed the weed to an old man, to test

(299) [512, 520]

ثُمْتَ [ثُمْ ذو] شيبُ {شيبِ} إصَفِرْ لَعُ

(فقط) بعدما [اذا ما] العجوزُ صَغُرَ (صارَ) شاباً

If [(only) After] the old man grew into a young man

(300) [24, 390, 512]

أنكو لأأكُلما لأتوُر أنَ صِغْرِياما {أنَ ذا صُغْرِياما}

أنا، نفسي، سأأكُله لأعود الى شبابيا {الى ما لشبابي (الى عهد شبابي)}'

I, myself, shall eat it to go back to my youth {to that of my youth (the age of my youth)}'

(301) [81, 218]

أنَ 20 طَعنَ [ظَعنَ] إكْسُفُو كُسافُ

على (بَعْدَ) 20 رحلة (فرسخ) كَسَرو كسرة (خبزٍ) (أخذو استراحة للأكل)

After 20 journeys (leagues), they broke a (bread) piece (they took a meal break)

(302) [428, 498]

أنَ 30 طَعنُ [طَعنُ] إسْكُنُو نوبَتَ [نُبَطَ]

على (بَعْدَ) 30 رحلة (فرسخ) نزلو نوبةً (مَوْرِد: منهل)

After 30 journeys (leagues), they stopped by a watering place

(303) [73, 292]

أُمُرْمَ بؤرُ [بؤرَ] دنجرجِشْجِمَش ذا كَصو [كَصُعُ] آميس ذا

جِشْجِمَش رأى بئرُ (منبعُ) مياهه العذبة (الباردة)

Gilgamesh saw the source of its fresh (cold) waters

(304) [248, 640]

أُوْرِدْ أنَ لِبِّمَ آميس يرمُكْ

ذهب الى وسط المياه لينتعش

He went to the middle of the waters to refresh

(305) [143, 384, 412]

مؤس إأتأصِن نفِس ثَمُ

ثعبانٌ شَمّ نفس (رائحةَ) العشب

A snake smelled the scent of the weed

(306) [55, 135, 506]

سَقُمَتْ إعلَمَ ثَمُ إعسِي [إهشي]

إرتفع بهدوء، خَبَطَ [نَهَشَ] العُشب

Quietly, it raised, it snatched [snapped] (ate) the weed

(307) [209, 390, 464]

إنَ تأرِ ذو إتأدي قُلِفْتِ {قَلِفْتم}

في (عند) عودته، تخلص من (سَلَخ) جلدً

On its return, it got rid of (sloughed) a skin

(308) [10, 274]

إنَ أوميذُمَ [أوميتُمَ] دنجرجِشْجِمَش إتَثِبْ يبكي

في كل يوم، جِشْجِمَش جلسَ يبكي

Every day, Gilgamesh sat down crying

(309) [43, 96, 117]

عُجْ [عُقَ] بَيض [بَيد] أفّ ذو دوكَ [دعْكَ] {إلَكَ} دِمَعا ذو

فوق [حول] محيط أنفه دبّ (انهمر) {ترسّل (سال)} دمعُهُ

Over [Around] the surrounding of his nose (his cheeks), his tears rushed {went} down

(310)

|دنجر جِشْجِمَش أنَ ذا ذُوم مُوْرَ| أنَ مُعُرْسَنَبِ مألَحِ

|جِشْجِمَش قال اليه،| الى عُرْسَنَبِ الملّاح:

|Gilgamesh said to him,| to Ur-šánabi, the shipwright:

(311) [22, 39, 209, 354]

أنَ مَنيا مُعُرْسَنَبِ إِأنَحا يدا {أما}

'الى مَنْ (ذا الذي) لِيَ، عُرْسَنَبِ، عانت (كافحت) يداي

'For whom of mine, Ur-šánabi, my arms struggled (endured)

(312) [80, 603]

أنَ مَنيا إِأبلِي [إِعبِلِي] دَمُ لبِّيا

الى مَن (ذا الذي) لِيَ، تَحامَلَ غيظا (غَلي) دَمُ قلبيا

For whom of mine, the blood of my heart roiled (boiled)

(313) [119, 122, 474, 498]

ألْ أسْكُنْ دُمْقَ [دُمْجَ] {دُنْقِ [دُنْجِ]} أنَ {إنَ} رَأْمَنيا

أنا ما ضَمنت (أنجزت) عملا متقنا الى {في} ذاتي

I have not secured (I have not achieved) a well done job to {in} (for) my own

(314) [119, 631, 633, 636]

أنَ عَرمَخْ [هُرمَخْ] ذا قَقارُ {قَقارِ} دُمْقِ [دُمْجِ] {دُمْقَ [دُمْجَ]} أعتَفُسْ [أعتَفُشْ]

(ولكن) الى كائنِ الجُحْرِ المفترس (الثعبان)، أنا أنجزت عملا متقنا

(but) To the ferocious creature of the ground (den) (the snake), I have achieved a well done job

(315) [140, 209, 432]

حينِنَ أنَ 20 طَعنُ [ظَعنُ] هدُوَ ينَسمَ {ينَسا}

(اما) الآن، على (بَعْدَ) 20 رحلة (فرسخ)، فموج (البحر) العالي يمضي بسرعة

Now, after 20 journeys (leagues), the high (sea) tide is proceeding too fast

(316) [58, 244, 469, 630]

رأطُ {رأطَ} كيي أفْتُوَ [أفْتَحُوَ] أتبَكْ عُنُتّو

المنفذ (الارضي)، لكَيْ أكْشِفُه، رميت به حبال خطوة بخطوة

The (underground) tunnel, to uncover it [as I was uncovering it], I threw (down) ropes into it, step by step

(317) [184, 276, 305, 498]

أُتا آتِتا {آتا} ذا أنَ كيا {إِتيا} إسكُنُ أنكو لو أحِسْ

أيّ شيئاً سآتيَ (سأجد)، مَوْضوعاً ليرافقني (ليوجهني)، كي أحسُّ انا نفسي (طريقي) له

What can I find that is placed to accompany (guide) me, so I, myself, can feel (my way down) to it?

(318) [148]

و جِشْ**ماع إتعْزبْ إنَ كبْرِ**

و (قد) تركت انا [ايضا] العوّامة في (عند) الساحل'

And I had [also] left the raft at the shore (now)'

(319) [218, 281]

أنَ 20 طَعنْ [ظعنْ] **إكْسُفو كُسافَ**

{.......................... كَانِنفَ [كأنِنفَ]}

على (بَعْدَ) 20 رحلة (فرسخ) كَسَرو كسرة (خبز) (أخذو استراحة للأكل)

{.......................... وجبة غذاء [إستراحة غذاء]}

After 20 journeys (leagues), they broke a (bread) piece (they took a meal break)

{..................... meal [meal break]}

(320)

أنَ 30 طَعنْ [ظعنْ] **إسْكُنُو نوبَتَ [نُبَط]**

على (بَعْدَ) 30 رحلة (فرسخ) نزلو نوبةً (موْرِد: منهل)

After 30 journeys (leagues), they stopped by a watering place

(321)

إقصَدونمَ [إكَصَدونمَ] أنَ لبِّ عَنوجكيع **ظُفُرِ [ذُفورِ]**

(أخيرا) وصلو الى مركز عُروك مقام المناسم والانعام [مذبح القرابين]

(finally) They arrived to the center of Uruk-of-the-cattles-site [alter]

(322)

دنجر**جِشْجِمَش {**م دنجر**جِشْتُكْ} أنَ ذا ذُوم** مُوْرَ **أنَ** م**عُرْسَنَبِ** مألح

جِشْجِمَش {جِش تُكْ} قال اليه، الى عُرْسَنَبِ الملّاح:

Gilgamesh said to him, to Ur-šánabi, the shipwright:

(323)

إعلِمَ م**عُرْسَنَبِ إنَ** عَجْ [عَقْ] بَيض [بَيد] **ذا** عَنوجكيع **إتَلَكْ**

'إصعدْ، يا عُرْسَنَبِ، في اعالي [حوالي] سور عُروك، ترسَّلْ (إذهبْ) في كل الاتجاهات

'Go up, O Ur-šánabi, in (to) the top of [around] the wall of Uruk, go in all directions

(324) [214, 565]

ضَمَنُ [طَأمَنُ] [تَأمَنُ] حِيْطِمَ سج صُبّو [ضُبّو]

<ضَمَنَ [طَأمَنَ] [تَأمَنَ] حِيْطْ سج صُفّي>

إستطلعْ نظام الحماية، طابوق المصبّات <المصافي> (المرازيب)

[إستطلعْ نظام الحماية، تفحّصْ الطابوق]

Explore the protecting apparatus, the brickwork of its waterways (gutters)

[Explore the protecting apparatus, examine the brickwork]

(325)

ثُمّ سِج ذو لا آجُرَت

بَعدَ إذْ (حقا ان) [إنظر اذا ما] طابوقه ليس آجرة (طابوق مطبوخ في فرن)

After all (indeed) [(see) If (in fact)] its brickwork is not kiln-fired

(326)

و أُسُّ ذو لا إإدوَ [إهدوَ] 7 مُنْتَلْكُ

و اسُسُه ما وضعَ المرسلون السبعة

And its foundation, the seven messengers have not laid out

(327) [643]

1 سأر أُورُ[كي] 1 سأر [جش] كِيرِ[ميس] 1 سأر حِسّو بِتِرْ [فِتِرْ] حِي [إِي] [دنجر]إسْتار

1 سأر (جزء كبير) مدينة، 1 سأر حقول [بساتين]، 1 سأر حفرة طين، شطر (نصفِ سأر) معبد إسْتار

One Sar (large part) is a city, one Sar is orchards, one Sar is a clay pit, half (Sar) is the Temple of Ishtar

(328)

3 <ثلاث> سأر و بِتِرْ [فِتِرْ] عُنوج[كيع] تَمْسِحُ

3 سأر وشطر (نصفِ سأر) (تساوي) مساحة عُروك‘"

Three Sar and a half is (equals) Uruk area’”

Part 2

Appendixes and Indexes

1

Letters Substitutions Guides

al-Jibūrī Letters Substitutions Rules

From: *Qamūs al-Lughah al-Akkadiyyah al-'Arabiyyah*

Akkadian Arabic throat letters (أ، ح، هـ، ع، غ، ض، ظ، ث، ذ) **=> Hamzah** (') **=> ē, ī, ū, û , ā, â**

<u>e.g.</u> ba'lum = bēlum بعل | ḫaqlum = ēqlum حقل | ĝrub = ērub غرب

Nūn (n) **with sukūn** (stop) **+ Arabic lip letter** (b, p, m) **=> Arabic lip letter repeated** (bb, pp, mm)

<u>e.g.</u> kanpum => kappum | anpum => appum

Letter with sukūn (stop) **+ Arabic teeth letter** (t, d, ṭ, s, š) **=> Lām + Arabic teeth letter** (t, d, ṭ, s, š)

<u>e.g.</u> išdu => ildu | išṭur => ilṭur | iššī => ilšī | ištakan => iltakan | ušubtu => ušultu

Mīm (m) **+ Arabic teeth letter** (t, d, ṭ, s, š) **=> Nūn** (n) **+ Arabic teeth letter** (t, d, ṭ, s, š)

<u>e.g.</u> imdud => indud | imtu => intu | amiš => aniš | imtanum => intanum

Rā'(r) **+ Nūn** (n) **=> Nūn** (n) **+ Nūn** (n) **=> NūnNūn** (nn)

<u>e.g.</u> arnu => annu | ibqurnisu => ibqunnisu

Two assimilated letters => Nūn (n) **with sukūn** (stop) **+ One assimilated letter**

<u>e.g.</u> inazziq => inanziq | inaddi => inandi | immagar => imangar | nammuri => nanmuri

Two words joind by two assimilated letters L1-L2 => One word, repeated assimilated letter L2

<u>e.g.</u> şit-šamaši => şissamiši | sinm-yattum => sinyyatum | umam-kal => umakkal

Strong Sumerian letter sounds => Akkadian letter sounds

ث => ش   ذ => ط   ذ => ئ   ذ => ز   ظ => ص   ض => ص   ق <=> ك

Arabic Letters Substitutions

From: *Lisān al-ʿArab*

ت <=> ظ	س (+ ق،ط،غ،خ،غ) => ص	ز <=> س	أ <=> ع
ت <=> ض	س <=> ش	ز <=> ص	أ <=> هـ
ذ <=> ث	س <=> ت	ك <=> ق	ب <=> م
ذ <=> ض	ف <=> ب	م <=> ن	د <=> ط
	ت <=> ط	ن => ر	د <=> ذ

Latin Arabic Letters Substitutions

Compiled by the Author through his Research

Latin Letter	Possible Arabic Letter(s)	Latin Letter	Possible Arabic Letter(s)
A (àáāâ)	ا أ آ ع هـ	S	س ش ص ظ
B	ب	Š	ش س ذ ض ث ظ
D	د ذ ض ط	Ṣ	ص ض ظ
E (èē)	أ إ ي ح ع غ هـ	T	ت ط ث ذ
G	ج ق غ	Ṭ	ط ت
H (ẖ)	خ ح هـ	U (úū)	ؤ و ع
I (ìī)	إ ي ع ح هـ	W	و
K	ك ق خ	Y	ي
L	ل	Z	ز ذ ص ظ
M	م	ʾ Hamzah	أ ع غ ح هـ ض ظ ث ذ
N	ن	a	◌َ
P	ف ب	e	◌َ ◌ِ
Q (ḵ)	ق ك	i	◌ِ
R	ر	u	◌ُ

2

Names Pronunciations and Meanings

1. ABZU (*also* ENGUR, apsû, engurru, imgura) [Noah's arc (*Epic:* ^{giš}MÁ; *Bible*: taybah, tawbah; *Quran*: fulkah, fulk)]

<u>*Epic of Gilgamesh*, Tablet II (A. George translation):</u>

Lines 29-31: *"Her* (the ship) *dimensions should all correspond. Her breadth and length should be the same. Cover* her with a roof, like the ABZU."

Lines 59: *"Ten rods each, the edges of her* (the ship) *top were equal."*

Lines 42: *"I shall go down to the ABZU to live with Ea, my master."*

Lines 289-290: *"Heavy stones he tied on his feet. They dragged him down to the ABZU."*

Lines 292-293: *"He cut loose the stones (from his feet). The sea cast him up on its shore."*

<u>*Wikipedia:*</u>

ʿAbd Allah ibn ʿAbbas, a contemporary of Muhammad, wrote that Noah was in doubt as to what shape to make the ark, and that Allah revealed to him that it was to be shaped like a bird's belly and fashioned of teak wood.

<u>*worldwideflood.com*:</u>

"Ark" comes from the Latin word *arca* which means box or chest. In the trail from Greek to Latin to English we find *Noah's Ark* and the *Ark of the Covenant* sharing the same term. In Genesis, the Hebrew term is *tebah,* which is used in only one other place - the basket of baby Moses. The Masoretic Hebrew text describes Noah's ark using the term *tebah* {taw-bah} or *tbh*. It is not easy to establish the meaning of *tebah* because it appears in only two places - Noah's Ark and the reed basket of baby Moses. Such disparate objects (a colossal ship and a tiny baby basket) have kept many scholars guessing. Obviously it can't mean either "ship" or "basket" specifically. On the basis of this association there might be a number of meanings - anything from 'boat' to 'life saver'. It does not refer to the Ark of the Covenant.

<u>*Merriam-Webster:*</u>

Noah's ark shell: ark shell; *especially*: a common ark shell (*Arca noae*)
Origin and Etymology of noah's ark: so called from the supposed similarity to Noah's ark (Genesis 6:14–20)

<u>*Strong's Concordance:*</u>

tebah (Phonetic Spelling: tay-baw') noun feminine ark: properly *chest, box* (compare Late Hebrew תֵּבָה); probably Egyptian loan-word from *T-b-t*, *chest, coffin*; vessel in which infant Moses was laid among reeds

Exodus 2:3 (made of papyrus, גֹּמֶא), Exodus 2:5; vessel which saved Noah and his family, with animals, during flood (m5 κιβωτός): Genesis 7:1,7,9,17,23; Genesis 8:6,9 (twice in verse).

<u>Quran:</u>
فَأَوْحَيْنَا إِلَيْهِ أَنِ اصْنَعِ الْفُلْكَ بِأَعْيُنِنَا وَوَحْيِنَا فَإِذَا جَاءَ أَمْرُنَا وَفَارَ التَّنُّورُ ۙ فَاسْلُكْ فِيهَا مِنْ كُلٍّ زَوْجَيْنِ اثْنَيْنِ وَأَهْلَكَ إِلَّا مَنْ سَبَقَ عَلَيْهِ الْقَوْلُ مِنْهُمْ ۖ وَلَا تُخَاطِبْنِي فِي الَّذِينَ ظَلَمُوا ۖ إِنَّهُمْ مُغْرَقُونَ (سورة المؤمنون: 27)
وَقِيلَ يَاأَرْضُ ابْلَعِي مَاءَكِ وَيَا سَمَاءُ أَقْلِعِي وَغِيضَ الْمَاءُ وَقُضِيَ الْأَمْرُ وَاسْتَوَتْ عَلَى الْجُودِيِّ ۖ وَقِيلَ بُعْدًا لِلْقَوْمِ الظَّالِمِينَ (سورة هود: 44)
إِنَّا لَمَّا طَغَا ٱلْمَآءُ حَمَلْنَـٰكُمْ فِى ٱلْجَارِيَةِ لِنَجْعَلَهَا لَكُمْ تَذْكِرَةً وَتَعِيَهَآ أُذُنٌ وَٰعِيَة (سورة الحاقة:)
فَأَنْجَيْنَاهُ وَمَنْ مَعَهُ فِي الْفُلْكِ الْمَشْحُونِ (سورة الشعراء: 119)
وَآيَةٌ لَهُمْ أَنَّا حَمَلْنَا ذُرِّيَّتَهُمْ فِي الْفُلْكِ الْمَشْحُونِ (سورة يس: 41)
وَإِنَّ يُونُسَ لَمِنَ الْمُرْسَلِينَ (139) إِذْ أَبَقَ إِلَى الْفُلْكِ الْمَشْحُونِ (140) فَسَاهَمَ فَكَانَ مِنَ الْمُدْحَضِينَ (141) فَالْتَقَمَهُ الْحُوتُ وَهُوَ مُلِيمٌ (142) فَلَوْلَا أَنَّهُ كَانَ
مِنَ الْمُسَبِّحِينَ (143) لَلَبِثَ فِي بَطْنِهِ إِلَىٰ يَوْمِ يُبْعَثُونَ (144) (سورة الصافات: 139-144)
اللَّهُ الَّذِي سَخَّرَ لَكُمُ الْبَحْرَ لِتَجْرِيَ الْفُلْكُ فِيهِ بِأَمْرِهِ (سورة الجاثية: 12)

<u>From references of the Assyriology method, and using al-Jibouri rules</u>:
ABZU = apsû = cosmic underground water; a ritual water container in a temple
ENGUR = engurru = imgura = cosmic underground water; subterranean waters
pilku = filku =boundary, zone, sector = what encircles an area
MÁ = MA = ship; house; land; country = Ūta-napištim ship = Noah's ship
eleppu = MÁ = ship; boat = Ūta-napištim ship = Noah's ship

<u>From Hebrew:</u>
tebah = tay-baw' = taw-bah = closed box/chest; closed coffin (has shell-like oval shape) = Noah's arc; Moses's basket

<u>From Greek and Latin:</u>
arca noae = Noah's arc = sea shell = a marine, closed round/oval shaped, bivalve shell
Noah's ark = Noah's arc = ship that resembles the closed round/oval shaped bivalve shell

<u>From Arabic references</u>
abzu = ʿabzu = afzu = ʿafzu = ʿafsu = ʿanjurra = ʿImjura = hill, bulge, haunch, arc
ʿabzanu = a washbowl to wash ones hands and face; coffin
maʿa = to melt; self flow with ease
MÁ <=> māʿu = melting object; an object flowing by itself with ease (i.e. floating ball) => closed round raft
kiffah = qiffah = qiṣʿah = any round object like cup or pan; scale pan; round boat used in Iraq to cross river
eleppu <=>ʿilibbu = ʿilbah = qiṣʿah = round object like cup or pan (closed or open) => closed round raft
fallaka = falka = circulated
falk = any circular object; a young woman's breast; a sea wave
fulku (plural of falaku) = sea waves
fulkah = jariyah = Noah's arc = a ship that circulats in water =
tabaha => tā-buwah = tābut = closed coffin; the closed chest/box of the thoracic cage
araka = arraka = covered => arku = something roofed by a dome-like cover
arīka = a bed like a ship roofed by a dome-like cover
al-mashḫūn = filled up; rapid; hostile

أبزُ = عَبْزُ = أفزُ = عَفْزُ = عفس = عِنْجُر = عِنْجرّة = عِمْجرة = أكمَة (تلّة)؛ حُدبة؛ تقويس؛ عنجرة؛ طاسة؛ القفزُ (على شكل قوس)

أبزنُ = طاسة؛ حوض للغسل؛ تابوت

أرَكَ = أرّكَ = غطى وستر => أرْكُ = ما هو مغطى (مستور) بغطاء شبيه بالقبّة

أريكة = كسفينة، سرير مغطى (مستور) بغطاء شبية بالقبّة

فَلْكُ = مستدير؛ مدار؛ ثدي البنت الصغيرة؛ موج

فُلكُ = جمع فَلْكُ = امواج

فُلْكَ = فُلْكة = عوامة (جارية) تدور بالماء

تبه = التابُوه (لغة اهل يثرب) = التابوت؛ القفص الصدري وما يحويه تشبيها بالصندوق

كِفّة = قُفّة = قصعة = كل شيء مستدير مثل قدح او اناء؛ كفة ميزان؛ قارب مدور يستخدم في العراق حتى اليوم لعبور النهر

عِلِبُ = عِلبة = قِصعة = قدح او اناء مستدير مغلق او مفتوح => قارب مدوّر مغلق

ماعُ = ميعُ = الجاري = ما يجري مُنْبَسِطاً في هِيئَةٍ (مثل كرة في ماء) ؛ ما يسيل او ينساب

المشحون = المملوء؛ السريع؛ العدائي

"أفز: أَبو عمرو: الأَفْزُ، بالزاي، الوثْبةُ بالعَجَلَة."

"أبز: أَبَزَ الظَّبْيُ يأْبِزُ أَبْزاً وأُبوزاً: وثَبَ وقَفَزَ في عَدْوِه. قال ابن السكيت: الأَبَّازُ القَفَّازُ."

"بَزِيَ وبَزا يَبْزُو، وهو أَبْزَى، والأُنثى بَزْواء: للذي خرج صدره ودخل ظهره؛ وربما قيل: هو أَبْزَى أَبْزَخ كالعجوز البَزْواءِ والبَزْخاء التي إذا مشت كأَنها راكعة وقد بَزِيَتْ بَزىً؛ والبَزاءُ: إنحناء الظَّهْرِ عند العَجُزِ في أَصل القَطَنِ، وقيل: هو إِشرافُ وَسَطِ الظهر على الاسْتِ، وقيل: هو خروج الصدر ودخول الظهر، وقيل: هو أَن يتأَخر العَجُز ويخرُج."

"الأَبْزَنُ: شيءٌ يُتَّخَذ من الصُّفْر للماء وله جَوْف، وقد أَهمله الليث؛ ابن بري: الأَبْزَنُ شيء يَعْمَله النّجار مثل التابوت؛"

"تبه: التابُوه: لغة في التابوت، أَنصاريّة."

"تبت: التَّابُوتُ: الأَضْلاعُ وما تَحْويه كالقَلْب والكَبِد وغيرهما، تشبيهاً بالصُّنْدُوق الذي يُحْرَزُ فيه المَتاع أَي أَنه مكتوب موضوع في الصُّنْدُوق. وقال: التابُوه لغة في التَّابُوتِ، أَنصارية؛"

"توب: وذكر الجوهريّ في هذه الترجمة التابوت: أَصله تابُوَةٌ مثل تَرْقُوَة، وهو فَعْلُوَةٌ، فلما سكنت الواو انْقلبت هاءُ التأْنيث تاءً. وقال القاسم بن معن: لم تَختلف لغةُ قُريشٍ والأَنصارِ في شيءٍ من القرآن إِلاَّ في التَّابُوتِ، فلغةُ قريش بالتاءِ، ولغةُ الأَنصار بالهاءِ. قال ابن بري: التصريفُ الذي ذكره الجوهري في هذه اللفظة حتى ردَّها إِلى تابوت تَصْرِيفٌ فاسِدٌ؛ قال: والصواب أَن يُذكر في فصل تبت لأَنَّ تاءَه أَصلية، ووزنه فاعُولٌ مثل عاقُولٍ وحاطُوم، والوقْفُ عليها بالتاءِ في أَكثر اللغات، ومن وقف عليها بالهاءِ فإِنه أَبدلها من التاءِ، كما أَبدلها في الفُرات حين وقف عليها بالهاءِ، وليست تاءُ الفرات بتاءِ تأْنيث، وإِنما هي أَصلية من نفس الكلمة. قال أَبو بكر بن مجاهد: التَّابُوتُ بالتاءِ قِراءة الناس جميعاً، ولغة الأَنصار التابُوهُ بالهاءِ."

"العَفْزُ: الملاعبة. يقال: بات يُعافِزُ امرأَته أَي يُغازِلُها؛ قال الأَزهري: هو من باب قولهم بات يُعافِسُها فأَبدل من السين زاياً. والعفازةُ: الأَكَمَةُ. يقال: لَقِيته فوق عَفازَة أَي فوق أَكَمَة. الأكَمَةُ: معروفة. غيره: الأَكَمَةُ تَلٌّ من القُفِّ وهو حَجر واحد. ابن سيده الأَكَمَة القُفُّ من حجارة واحدة، وقيل: هو دون الجبال."

"العَفْسَ: الضرب على العَجُز. وعَفَسَ الرجلُ المرأَة برجله يَعْفِسها: ضربَها على عجيزتها يُعافِسُها وتُعافِسُه، وعافَسَ أَهله مُعافَسَة وعِفاساً، وهو شبيه بالمُعالجة.والمُعافَسَة: المُداعَبة والمُمارَسَة؛ يقال: فلان يُعافِس الأُمور أَي يُمارِسُها ويُعالجها."

"عَنْجَرَ الرجل، إذا مدَّ شفتيه وقلبهما. والعُنْجورةُ: غلاف القارورة. قال: والعُنْجُهُ والعُنْجُهَةُ القُنْفُذَة الضَّخْمة."

"أرك: والأَرِيكَةُ، كسفينةٍ: سَرِيرٌ في حَجَلَةٍ، أو كلُّ ما يُتَّكَأُ عليه من سَريرٍ ومِنَصَّةٍ وفِراشٍ، أو سَرِيرٌ مُنَجَّدٌ مُزَيَّنٌ في قُبَّةٍ أو بيتٍ، فإذا لم يكن فيه سَرِيرٌ، فهو حَجَلَةٌ. والحَجَلَةُ، محرَّكَةً: كالقُبَّةِ، ومَوْضِعٌ يُزَيَّنُ بالثيابِ والسُّتورِ للعَروسِ. وأرَّكَها تَأْرِيكاً: سَتَرَها بها."

"فلك: الفاء واللام والكاف أصلٌ صحيح يدلُّ على استدارةٍ في شيء. وأَفْلَكَ وفَلَّكَ وتَفَلَّكَ: اسْتَدارَ. من ذلك فَلْكة المِغزل بفتح الفاء ، سمِّيت لاستدارتها؛ ولذلك قيل: فَلَّكَ ثَدْيُ المرأة، إذا استدار. ومن هذا القياس فَلَك السماء. وأمَّا السفينة فتسمَّى فُلْكا. ويقال إنَّ الواحد والجمعَ في هذا الاسم سواء، ولعلَّها تسمَّى فُلْكاً لأنَّها تدار في الماء. والفُلْكُ، بالضم: السفينةُ، ويُذَكَّرُ، وهو للواحِدِ والجميعِ، أو الفُلْكُ التي هي جمعٌ: تَكْسِيرٌ للفُلْكِ التي هي واحدٌ. الفَلَكُ: مَدارُ النجوم، والجمع أَفْلاك. والفَلَكُ موج البحر."

"ماع: ماع الشيءُ يَميعُ: جَرَى على وجْهِ الأَرْضِ مُنْبَسِطاً في هِيئَةٍ"

"ميع: ماعَ والدمُ والسَّرابُ ونحوه يَمِيعُ مَيْعاً: جرى على وجه الأَرض جرْياً منبسطاً في هِينةٍ، وأَماعَه إِماعَةً وإِماعاً؛"

"علب: والعُلْبةُ: قَدَحٌ ضخْم من جلود الإبل. وقيل: العُلْبة من خشب، كالقَدَحِ الضَّخْم يُحْلَبُ فيها. وقيل: إنها كهيئةِ القَصْعَةِ مِن جِلد، ولها طَوْق من خشب. ومنه حديث خالد: أَعطاهم عُلْبَةَ الحالبِ أَي القَدَحَ الذي يُحْلَبُ فيه؛ والعِلْبةُ: غُصنٌ عظيم تُتَّخذ منه مِقْطَرةٌ؛"

"قصع: والمِصْحَنَة: إناء نحو القَصْعة. القَصْعةُ: الضَّخْمةُ تشْبع العشرة، والجمع قِصاعٌ وقِصَعٌ. وقَصَّعَ الضبُّ: سدّ باب جحره، وقيل: كل سادٍّ مُقَصِّع. ابن الأَعرابي: قُصَعةُ اليَرْبُوعِ وقاصِعاؤه أَن يَحْفِرَ حَفِيرةً ثم يسد بابها؛"

"كفف: كفَّ الشيءَ يكُفُّه كَفّاً: جمعه. وكل مستدير كِفة نحو كِفة الميزان."

"قفف: القُفَّةُ: الزَّبيل، الأَزهري: القفة شجرة مستديرة ترتفع عن الأَرض قدر شبر وتيبس فيشبه بها الشيخ إذا عسا فيقال: كأَنه قُفَّة."

"شحن: قال الله تعالى: في الفُلك المَشْحُونِ؛ أي المملوء. الشَّحْنُ: مَلْؤُكَ السفينة وإِتْمامُك جِهازَها كله. شَحَنَ السفينة يَشْحَنُها شَحْناً: مَلأَها، وشَحَنَها ما فيها كذلك. والشِّحْنَةُ: ما شَحَنها. والشَّحْنُ: العَدْوُ الشديد. وشَحَنَتِ الكلابُ تَشْحَنُ وتَشْحُنُ شُحُوناً: أَبْعَدتِ الطَّرَد ولم تَصِد شيئاً؛ المُشاحِنُ: المُعادي. والتَّشاحُنُ: تفاعل من الشَّحْناء العداوة؛"

Therefore:

ABZU = a underground bowl-shape sea filled with cosmic water; a washbowl filled with ritual water in a temple

MÁ (Ūta-napištim raft) = Noah's raft = a closed raft/floater with a round/oval belly and a dome-like roof

Noah's ark = Noah's arc = tebah (tay-bawah) = fulkah = Noah's closed (coffin-like) round/oval raft/floater

al-fulki al-mashḫūn = the rapid hostile waves

أبزُ = بحر من المياه الكونية بشكل طاسة تحت الارض؛ حوض بشكل طاسة مليء بمياه المراسيم (الشعائر) الدينية في المعابد

سفينة اتا نفستم = سفينة نوح = ماغُ = فُلكَ = تَيبوة = عوامة (جارية) مغلقة (كالتابوت) ذات جوف مدور\بيضوي وسقف يشبة القبة

الْفُلْكِ الْمَشْحُونِ = الامواج السريعة الغاضبة

Author's Notes: From the above evidence, it seems that ancient Mesopotamians believed the earth had a half sphere/oval shape, or a bowl shape. They have apparently believed that the bottom bowl-like part of this half sphere was filled with cosmic/divine waters, which was the source of waters for all seas, lakes, and rivers, and therefore life on earth. This sea of underground water was called ABZU. Believing in this half sphere shape clearly explains why the pre-Galileo monotheistic religions insisted the sun rotated around the earth. Gilgamesh needed to tie heavy stones to his legs to be dragged down to the bottom of the ABZU, and was eventually cast up on the sea shore after cutting loose these stones (Lines 289-293 of the Epic). This indicates that the ABZU according to their beliefs was under the sea and the entire earth, but was connected to it via openings.

The clear description of Noah's ark in the Epic, in addition to the linguistic evidence of the words used to name it in Hebrew, Latin, and Arabic; all indicate that it was a closed round/oval capsule/raft, not a conventional long ship. The emphasis of all given names was that it was "closed", just like a coffin, a sea shell, or oval chest/basket. This central point was confirmed by the usage in the epic of the word "sealed". According to George, Line 31 of the epic said "*Cover* her with a roof, like the ABZU", which could mean "cover her just as the ABZU is covered". However, examining the line carefully, it actually said *"Like an Abzu, to it, its roof"*, meaning "like ABZU shape, its roof should look like". The ABZU looked like a bowl or hill.

The Hebrew word *tebah* (*tay-bawah*), for coffin, which was used in the Bible to name Noah's ark, was primarily emphasizing it was a closed body. The word *tay-bawah* or *tā-buwah* is indeed the Arabic word *tābut*, for coffin, not a loan/foreign word in any form or shape! It is a very well-known variant Arabic word used by the people of Northern Hijaz, primarily *Yathrib* (modern day *al-Madinah al-Munawwarah*), which was one of the major Jewish centers in the Arabian Peninsula before Islam.

Was the Deluge triggered by an earthquake, tsunami, or a meteor in Mesopotamia?

Because the flood story in the Quran provided a credible name for Noah's arc's resting mountain that was identical in meaning to the name provided by the epic, researches should examine its flood story more closely (see Part 2.2.31). According to the Quran, the flood started after a water eruption from *al-tannūr* by a command from god حَتَّى إِذَا جَاءَ أَمْرُنَا وَفَارَ التَّنُّورُ. The Quran further said that this eruption was accompanied by heavy flooding and rain storms. Despite the clear meaning offered by the Arabic references for *al-tannūr*, "any erupted water from the ground", some Islamic scholars said *al-tannūr* was an actual mud oven, the common literal meaning of the word *tannūr*, explaining further that a water-spitting oven was god's signal to Noah about the start of the flood. Other Islamic scholars explained that *al-tannūr* was the historical *'Ayn Wardah* spring in Syria. The first explanation seems to be a desperate, meaningless, attempt to explain the word. The second one is a very serious one and should be examined.

The scenario of a water eruption from the ground, as a result of a volcano, earthquake/tsunami, or a meteor accompanied by severe rain storms and flooding around Mesopotamia is a very feasible one. However, assuming that the eruption started at *'Ayn Wardah* spring somewhere in Syria, is not a strong assumption because of one important reason: no one seems to know where that *'Ayn Wardah* spring is located exactly! A better hypothesis strongly points to Sawa Lake, located about 36 miles west of ancient Uruk, in southern Mesopotamia, where the flood supposedly occurred, according to many historical accounts. Scientists believe this lake is relatively young and was formed around 5000-10000 years ago, which is a very good match for a reasonably-assumed Deluge date.

Scientists theorized that Sawa Lake feeds "from the Euphrates through a system of joint cracks and fissures which transport water to aquifers beneath it". They theorized further that its "water does not dry up because of the equilibrium state between water feed and evaporation". However, despite the severely falling water level of the Euphrates River in the past decades, the lake continued to maintain its relatively-constant water level. This is why it was historically given the Arabic name *sawa*, meaning "the same". Unlike other water springs in the Iraqi desert, Sawa Lake water is excessively salty. The water level of Sawa Lake is 1-4m higher than its adjacent land, 5-7m higher than the water level of the Euphrates, and 17-20m higher than the water level of Shatt al-Arab and the Persian Gulf. Logically, a much larger and stable water body than the Euphrates is needed to maintain the water level of such highly elevated lake that is exposed to extreme high temperatures most of the year. One cannot rule out that Sawa Lake is feeding from deeper underground aquifers connected to the nearby Gulf, which was covering all southern Iraq long time ago!

In fact, the Arabs, before Islam, believed Sawa Lake was the cause of a major flood covering the vast Samawah desert around the sixth century CE. Even today, the local people of southern Iraq believe Sawa Lake's water was the source of the flood. Historically, the people of the area avoided this lake because they believed it was inhabited by ghosts. Recall, the god Enlil is the father of ghosts! From a distance, Sawa Lake looks like a round/oval bowl, filled with a constant level of peculiar thick water, sitting on high hill. In another word it looks like the ABZU! It is very possible, therefore, that the people of ancient Mesopotamia had believed this lake was a divine lake inhabited by their gods and was filled with cosmic waters feeding from (connected to) the underground ABZU. In fact the Iraqis had historically called Sawa Lake the "Lake of Secrets". Considering the geological and geographical facts of Sawa Lake and its surroundings, and taking into account the collective memory of the local people in the area, before and after Islam, it is very reasonable to assume the Quran was actually referring to an erupted Lake Sawa as *al-tannūr*. Lake Sawa eruption could have been caused by a meteor forming the lake, an earthquake, or a tsunami in the nearby Gulf.

Wikipedia:
Sawa lake (Arabic: بحيرة ساوة) is an Endorheic basin located in the Iraqi governorate of Muthanna near to the Euphrates River, some 23 kilometres (14 mi) to the west of Al-Samawa city. This lake has no inlet or outlet but, its feeds water from Euphrates through a system of joint cracks and fissures which transport water to aquifers beneath it. water's level fluctuates during dry and wet seasons. Water does not dry up because of the equilibrium state between water feed and evaporation. Lake Sawa is a unique body of water in Iraq since characterized by highest salinity value among Iraqi inland bodies water.The water level in the lake is one of the manifestations of the lake, which gives something of aesthetic and strangeness. Strangeness reflected the fact that the water level in the lake is higher than the adjacent land around the lake by 1-4 meters. Add to that, the water level of the lake is also higher than the water level of the Euphrates River by 5-7 meters which flow near the lake to the east side and the Shat Al-Arab and Persian Gulf by 17-20 m. A formations of gypsum are surrounding the lake, in some cases these a gypsum formations reach 6 m tall. They are formed due to evaporation of salty water and sedimentation of salt in shallow banks of lake. A formations of gypsum works as a dam prevent water flow from the lake on surrounding areas.

عن بحيرة ساوة في مصادر متعددة:
بحيرة ساوة هي بحيرة مغلقة مالحة تقع في محافظة المثنى العراقية قرب نهر الفرات، 23 كلم غرب مدينة السماوة. لاتملك بحيرة ساوة انهار تصب فيها أو تخرج منها إنما تتزود بالمّياه الجوفية من تحت البحيرة والتي ترشح اليها من نهر الفرات عبر الصدوع والشقوق. تشكلت البحيرة خلال عصر الهولوسين قبل عشرة الالف سنة. البحيرة التي يطلق عليها العديد من الأسماء مثل أم الأسرار والبخيلة والبطة تبلغ مساحتها 12/5 كلم^2 تحيط بها الصحراء من كل جانب، ويبلغ عرضها نصف كيلو متر في أضيق منطقة، أما طولها فيبلغ قرابة الـ5 كيلومتر، وعرضها في أوسع منطقة فيها يبلغ 2 كيلو متر، والغريب أن الذاهب إلى البحيرة لا يشعر بوجودها ولا يصدق بان هذه المعجزة تعيش وسط تلك الصحراء، منابع مياه البحيرة مدفونة في أعماقها، ومستوى مياهها ثابت منذ تكوينها، وحينما تُسحب منها المياه عبر قنوات، تتكثف مياهها على هيئة أحجار كلسيّة، والبحيرة مسوّرة طبيعياً بسياج كلسي يتضمن كهوفاً تنتشر على ضفافها وارتفاع السور يبلغ خمسة أمتار. تعددت الأسماء والسر غائب يقول المسرحي ماجد الوروار إن الكثير من الحكايات والأساطير والأسرار تعيش في عقول الناس وتتحدث عن هذه الجزيرة، وكانت وصايا أجدادنا وآبائنا كلها تصب في وجوب الحذر من البحيرة وعدم التواجد قربها ليلا من غير تعاويذ، لوجود أشباح وعفاريت تعيش فيها، مؤكدا أنها مجرد إشاعات لا أكثر، فالكثير من اهل السماوة يزورونها ليلا ويقضون ساعات جميلة يتمتعون بالهواء الطلق ومشاهدة أمواجها والطيور التي تزور ضفافها ليلا. وبشأن التسميات، قال سميت بالبطة لان شكلها لناظرها من الأعلى يشبه البطة تماما، ولكون تاريخ تكوينها غير معروف وكذلك مصدر مياهها وتركيبته الكيمياوية سميت بـ(أم الأسرار)، اما تسميتها (البخيلة) لكون الكثير من الفلاحين الذي كانت لديهم مزارع قريبة منها حاولوا أن يشقوا منها قنوات لسقي أراضيهم، لكنها شاهدوا بأم أعينهم كيف يتكلس الماء ويتحول إلى أحجار كلسية تسد تلك القنوات. مولد النبي وإيوان كسرى واختلفت آراء العديد من الباحثين بشأن تاريخ وجودها، فهناك العديد من الروايات يتناقلها أبناء السماوة منهم من يقول: إن البحيرة فاضت يوم مولد النبي (ص)، وإنها ستعلن جفافها مع ظهور الإمام المهدي (ع) كما يقول احد أبناء المدينة، والبعض يقول إن البحيرة كانت الرافد المائي لطوفان النبي النوح وهي بقايا ذلك الطوفان، ورأي آخر يربط ما بينها وما بين اهتزاز إيوان كسرى ولذا أن البحيرة تشكل ما يشبه اللعنة عند الفرس.

الحافظ أبو بكر محمد بن جعفر بن سهل الخرائطي. هواتف الجان
وروى ذلك الحافظ ابن عساكر. ثم أورد ذلك المعافي بن زكريا الجريري فقال: وأخبار سطيح كثيرة، وقد جمعها غير واحد من أهل العلم. والمشهور أنه كان كاهناً، وقد أخبر عن النبي صلى الله عليه وسلم، وعن نعته، ومبعثه. وروي لنا بإسناد الله به أعلم، أن النبي صلى الله عليه وسلم سئل عن سطيح فقال: نبي ضيعه قومه. قلت: أما هذا الحديث فلا أصل له في شيء من كتب الإسلام المعهودة، ولم أره بإسناد أصلاً. ويروي مثله في خبر خالد بن سنان العبسي، ولا يصح أيضاً، وظاهر هذه العبارات تدل على علم جيد لسطيح، وفيها روائح التصديق، لكنه لم يدرك الإسلام كما قال الجريري، فإنه قد ذكرنا في هذا الأثر أنه قال لابن أخته: يا عبد المسيح إذا كثرت التلاوة، وظهر صاحب الهراوة، وفاض وادي السماوة، وغاضت بحيرة ساوة، وخمدت نار فارس، فليس الشام لسطيح شاما، يملك منهم ملوك وملكات على عدد الشرفات، وكل ما هو آت آت. ثم قضى سطيح مكانه، وكان ذلك بعد مولد رسول الله صلى الله عليه وسلم بشهر- أو شية - أي أقل منه، وكانت وفاته بأطراف الشام مما يلي أرض العراق، فالله أعلم بأمره وما صار إليه.

قرآن:
حَتَّى إِذَا جَاءَ أَمْرُنَا وَفَارَ التَّنُّورُ قُلْنَا احْمِلْ فِيهَا مِنْ كُلٍّ زَوْجَيْنِ اثْنَيْنِ وَأَهْلَكَ إِلَّا مَنْ سَبَقَ عَلَيْهِ الْقَوْلُ وَمَنْ آمَنَ ۚ وَمَا آمَنَ مَعَهُ إِلَّا قَلِيلٌ (40) وَقَالَ ارْكَبُوا
فِيهَا بِسْمِ اللَّهِ مَجْرَاهَا وَمُرْسَاهَا ۚ إِنَّ رَبِّي لَغَفُورٌ رَحِيمٌ (41) وَهِيَ تَجْرِي بِهِمْ فِي مَوْجٍ كَالْجِبَالِ وَنَادَى نُوحٌ ابْنَهُ وَكَانَ فِي مَعْزِلٍ يَابُنَيَّ ارْكَبْ مَعَنَا وَلَا تَكُنْ

مَعَ الْكَافِرِينَ (42) قَالَ سَآوِي إِلَى جَبَلٍ يَعْصِمُنِي مِنَ الْمَاءِ ۚ قَالَ لَا عَاصِمَ الْيَوْمَ مِنْ أَمْرِ اللَّهِ إِلَّا مَنْ رَحِمَ ۚ وَحَالَ بَيْنَهُمَا الْمَوْجُ فَكَانَ مِنَ الْمُغْرَقِينَ (43)
وَقِيلَ يَا أَرْضُ ابْلَعِي مَاءَكِ وَيَا سَمَاءُ أَقْلِعِي وَغِيضَ الْمَاءُ وَقُضِيَ الْأَمْرُ وَاسْتَوَتْ عَلَى الْجُودِيِّ ۖ وَقِيلَ بُعْدًا لِّلْقَوْمِ الظَّالِمِينَ (44) (سورة هود: 40-44)

تفسير الميسر: ونبع الماء بقوة من التنور-وهو المكان الذي يخبز فيه- علامة على مجيء العذاب
تفسير الجلالين: وفار التنور للخباز بالماء وكان ذلك علامة لنوح

"غاضَ الماءُ يَغِيضُ غَيْضاً ومَغِيضاً ومَغاضاً وانْغاضَ: نقَص أو غارَ فذهبَ، وفي الصحاح: قَلَّ فنضَب. وفي حديث سَطيح: وغاضَت بُحَيْرةُ ساوَةَ أي غارَ ماؤها وذهَب. وغاضَه هو وغَيَّضَه وأَغاضَه، يتعدّى ولا يتعدّى، وقال بعضهم: غاضَه نقَصه وفَجَّرَه إلى مَغيض."
"سَواءُ الشيءِ مِثْلُه، والجمعُ أَسْواءٌ؛ ويقال: ساوى الشيءُ الشيءَ إذا عادَلَه."
"التَّنُّورُ: الذي يُخبَزُ فيه. وقوله تعالى: "وفارَ التَّنُّورُ". قال رضي الله عنه: هو وجهُ الأرض. والتَّنُّور وَجْهُ الأَرض، فارسي معرَّب، وقيل: هو بكل لغة. وفي التنزيل العزيز: حتى إذا جاء أَمْرُنا وفار التَّنُّورُ؛ قال علي، كرم الله وجهه: هو وجه الأَرض، وكل مَفْجَرِ ماءٍ تَنُّورٌ. قال أبو إسحق: أعلم الله عزّ وجل أن وقت هلاكهم فَوْرُ التَّنُّور، وقيل في التنور أقوال: قيل التنور وجه الأرض، ويقال: أراد أن الماء إذا فار من ناحية مسجد الكوفة، وقيل: إن الماء فار من تنور الخابزة، وقيل أيضاً: إن التَّنُّور تَنْوِيرُ الصُّبْح. وروي عن ابن عباس: التَّنُّورُ الذي بالجزيرة وهي عَيْنُ الوَرْدِ، والله أعلم بما أراد. قال الليث: التنور عمت بكل لسان. قال أبو منصور: وقول من قال إن التنور عمت بكل لسان يدل على أن الاسم في الأصل أعجمي فعرّبتها العرب فصار عربيّاً على بناء فَعُّول، والدليل على ذلك أن أَصل بنائه تنر، قال: ولا نعرفه في كرم العرب لأنه مهمل، وهو نظير ما دخل في كلام العرب من كلام العجم مثل الديباج والدينار والسندس والاستبرق وما أشبهها ولما تكلمت بها العرب صارت عربية."

2. ^{d}AN (*also* ^{d}Anu)

Ancient Mesopotamian Gods and Goddesses:
Sumerian *an* means "heaven, sky". In Akkadian he is *Anu. An/Anu* belongs to the oldest generation of Mesopotamian gods and was originally the supreme deity of the Babylonian pantheon. Consequently, his major roles are as an authority figure, decision-maker and progenitor. In heaven he allots functions to other gods, and can increase their status at will; On earth he confers kingship, and his decisions are regarded as unalterable. An/Anu is sometimes credited with the creation of the universe itself, either alone or with *Enlil* and *Ea. An/Anu* frequently receives the epithet "father of the gods," and many deities are described as his children in one context or another.

Written forms:
Sumerian: an; Akkadian: ^{d}a-nu, ^{d}a-num, an-nu, d60

Normalised forms:
An, Anu(m)

From Arabic references:
an/anu (used in connection with the sky) = what resides or appears in sky and heavens
"ويقال: لا أفعله ما أنّ في السماء نجمٌ، أي ما كان في السماء نجمٌ، لغةٌ في عَنَّ. قال ابن الأعرابيّ: العَنان: ما عَنَّ لك من شيء. قال الخليل: عَنان السَّماء: ما عَنَّ لك منها إذا نظرتَ إليها."

Therefore:
AN = anu = anum = God of heavens

عن = أن = عنو = أنو = إله السماوات

Author's Notes: The Akkadian names *anu* and *anum* are identical linguistically to the so-called Sumerian name *AN*. The additions of the "u" vowel and the letter "m", are for emphasis. The name and roles *of Anu*, the god of heavens, indicates he was indeed a *one* supreme god/lord, residing above, who was later re-introduced by the monotheistic Mesopotamians as their one god following some minor alterations to his nature and functions. In other words, the pre-monotheistic Arabs were already believing in one god but they had ascribed him partners (in the words of the Quran they were *Mushrikim*)

3. Anunnaki (a group of gods)

Ancient Mesopotamian Gods and Goddesses:
The term Anunna indicates a group of gods in the Mesopotamian pantheon. Later on, it is sometimes used to describe the underworld gods (as opposed to the gods of heaven, the Igigi). A recent and comprehensive study of the term Anunna is still lacking; such a study is made more difficult by the term having slightly different meanings in different time periods. The most likely suggestions translate the term as something like "Those of princely seed,"

Written forms:
Sumerian: ^{d}a-nun, ^{d}a-nun-na, ^{d}a-nun-na-ke$_4$-ne, ^{d}a-nun-ke$_4$-ne
Akkadian: ^{d}a-nun-na-ki, e-nun-na-ki, e-nu-uk-ki, ^{d}e-nu-uk-ki;

From references of Arabic and the Assyriology method:
KI = earth
an/anu = god of heavens

Using Arabic grammar:
a-nun = a-nun-na = e-nun-na = group of mini an/anu-related beings

Therefore:
anunna-ki = group of mini an/anu-related beings on earth = angles of god anu on earth
عَنُنّا كِع = عَنُنّا قِع = عَنُنّا كي = كائنات إله السماوات الصغيرة في الارض = ملائكة إله السماوات في الارض

Author's Notes: From Arabic, the word *anunnu* عَنُنّا is plural of the word *anu* عَنُ meaning mini *anu*-related beings. Doubling the letter "n" which stands for Arabic *shaddah*, adding an additional "n", and adding the letter "a" at the end, were used for diminution, plural, and possession. The final *ki* clearly stands for earth. After realizing how close is the ancient god *Anu* to the monotheistic god, one cannot resist but to describe these *Annunaki* as nothing more than the angles (the mini gods) of god *a-nu* on earth!

The relation of *a-nun-na-ki* to *a-nu* is the same as that of *en-kik-ka* عَنكِكا to *en-ki* عَنكي. Except that in the plural word *en-kik-ka* عَنكِكا the letter "k", instead of the letter "n", was doubled and added. Accordingly, the name *en-kik-ka-ki* means the angles (mini gods) of god *en-ki* on earth.

enkikka-ki = group of mini anki (Ea)-related beings on earth = angles of god anu on earth
عَنكِكا كِع = عَنكِكا قِع = عَنكِكا كي = كائنات الاله هيا (أديم) الصغيرة في الارض = ملائكة إله السماوات في الارض

4. ᵈAruru

<u>*Wikipedia:*</u>
Aruru, Belet-Ili (lady of the gods, Akkadian). Aruru, the goddess of creation.

<u>From Arabic references:</u>
aruru = fertility; delicate
MAḪ = delicate
DINGIR = god
bēlet = lady

"ومعنى أرَارَ أرَقَّ. ورِيْرِ القومُ: أخْصَبوا، و~ البلادُ: أخْصَبَتْ. وأرارَ اللّهُ مُخَّه: رَقَّقَه."
"مَهِهْتُ: لِنْتُ. ومَهَّ الإبِلَ: رَفَقَ بها. وسيرٌ مَهَهٌ ومَهاهٌ: رفيق. والمَهاهُ: الطراوةُ والحُسْنُ؛ وليس بعَيْشِنا مَهَهٌ ومَهاهٌ أي حُسْنٌ؛"
"البَعْلُ: الزوجُ، والجمع البُعولَةُ. ويقال للمرأة أيضاً بَعْلٌ وبَعْلَةٌ."

<u>Therefore:</u>
Aruru = the fertile one; the delicate one = goddess of fertility
DINGIR.MAḪ = the delicate (one) of god = حسناوة (رقيقة) الإله
bēlet-ilī = the lady of the gods = سيدة الالهة

5. ᵈEa *(also* ᵈEnki, ᵈNudimmud, ᵈIDIM, ᵈNiššiku, ᵈgašam)

<u>*Ancient Mesopotamian Gods and Goddesses:*</u>
Enki is spelled in Sumerian as ᵈen-ki or ᵈam-an-ki. In Akkadian, Ea's name is commonly spelled ᵈE2.A but it is unclear to which language this name belonged originally. In literary texts, Enki/Ea was sometimes known by the alternative names Nudimmud or Niššiku, the latter originally being a Semitic epithet TT (nas(s)iku "prince") that was then reinterpreted as a pseudo-logogram TT ᵈnin-ši-kù. He had a number of epithets TT, including 'stag of the abzu' and 'little Enlil'.

<u>Written forms:</u>
ᵈé-a; ᵈEN.KI; EN.KI-GA.KAM2; ᵈ40; ᵈ60; ᵈIDIM, ᵈnu-dím-mud, ᵈnin-ši-kù

<u>Normalized forms:</u>
Enki, Enkig, Nudimmud, Niššiku, Ea

<u>*Wikipedia:*</u>
Enki is a god in Sumerian mythology, later known as Ea in Akkadian and Babylonian mythology. He was the deity of crafts (gašam); mischief; water, seawater, lakewater (a, aba, ab), intelligence (gestú, literally "ear") and creation (Nudimmud: nu, likeness, dim mud, make beer). In Sumerian E-A means "the house of water". Enki (Ea) (Samael) (NUDIMMUD) of the Immortals (Lord of the Earth and Waters).

<u>Author's Notes:</u> God Ea was the good-doing god. He is the master of the earth and the creator of fertile soil. He is not only connected with humans, but his earliest name was *IDIM* which is clearly derived from the Arabic root word أدم, like the name *Adam*. Furthermore, he was in a continuous conflict with a stubborn, evil-doing, man-hating god named Enlil, whose name's exact Arabic linguistic meaning and derivation is identical to that of *Iblīs* (Satan). The gods *Idim* and *Iblīs* were the highest ranking Mesopotamian gods after *Anu*, the one and *only* one god of heavens. God Ea is no doubt the earlier version of the Monotheist Adam!

God Ea was referred to by many names/titles. Some of the meanings of these names, as provided by scholars of the Assyriology method, do not make sense. Below, I will explain their meanings utilizing the Arabic etymological references:

^{d}é-a

From Arabic references:
é-a = ẖaya = of rain and land fertility
é-a = haya = of creation

حَيا = المطرُ والخِصْبُ
هيا = الخَلق

"أَحْيا القومُ، أي صاروا في الحَيا، وهو الخِصْبُ. وقد أتيت الأرض فأَحْيَيْتُها، أي وجدتها خِصبةً." "ما أدري أيُّ هَيِّ بن بَيٍّ هو، معناه أي أيُّ الخَلْقِ هو."

Therefore:
é-a = god of rain and land fertility; god of creation

^{d}nin-ši-kù

According to al-Jiburi rules:
ninšikù = niššiku

From Arabic references:
našaka (v.) = to pour water on
nāšiku (adj.) = green, fertile, watered

"نَسَكْتُ الشيء: غسلته بالماء وطهَّرته، فهو مَنْسوكٌ. ونَسَكَ الثَّوْبَ أو غيرَهُ: غَسَلَهُ بالماءِ فَطَهَّرَهُ. وأرضٌ ناسِكَةٌ: خَضْراءُ حَديثَةُ المَطَرِ."

Therefore:
niššiku = the one who waters the land; the one who makes green and watered (fertile) land
نِسّيك = نِنسِكُ = المُنَسَكُ، المُطهِّر، الغاسلُ، الذي يسقي الماء، الذي يُمطر، الذي يجعل الارض خضراء مُسقاة (خصبة)

^{d}nu-dím-mud

From Arabic references:
nu = for us, our; distant; keeper
dímu = steady quite rain, continuance, survival, land watering (fertility), mud
mud = to keep
dím-mud = survival (existence)

"والمُدامُ: المَطَرُ الدائمُ. دامَ يَدُومُ ويَدامُ دَوْماً ودَواماً ودَيْمومَةً، ودِمْتَ، بالكسرِ. تَدُومُ نادِرَةٌ. والدَّيُومُ والدَّوْمُ: الدائمُ. ودامَ: سَكَنَ، ومنه: الماءُ الدائمُ، والدِيمَةُ، بالكسر: مَطَرٌ يَدومُ في سُكونٍ بلا رَعْدٍ وبَرْقٍ. وأرض مَدِيمَةٌ ومُدَيَّمَةٌ: أصابتها الدِّيَمُ، وأصلها الواو؛"
"ونَوَّيْتُه تَنْوِيةً أي وَكَلْتُه إلى نِيَّتِه. ونَوِيُّك: صاحبُك الذي نيته نيّتك؛ ونَواهُ اللهُ: حفظه؛"

Therefore:
nu-dím-mud = keeper of (our) land fertility; keeper of (our) survival (existence)
نُوديمُدْ = حافظ الخِصْب؛ حافظ الديمومة = المُديم = الدَّيُومُ

^{d}EN.KI

From references Arabic and the Assyriology method:
En = lord
KI = earth

"العَنوة: الطاعة. ويقولون: العاني: العبد."
"والقاعُ والقاعةُ والقِيعُ: أرض واسعةٌ سَهْلة مطمئنة مستوية حُرّةٌ لا حُزُونةَ فيها ولا ارْتِفاع ولا انْهِباط، تَنْفَرِجُ عنها الجبالُ والآكامُ، ولا حَصَى فيها ولا حجارةَ ولا تُنْبِتُ الشجر، وما حَوالَيْها أَرْفَعُ منها وهو مَصَبُّ المِياهِ، وقيل: هو مَنْقَعُ الماء في حُرِّ الطين."

Therefore:
EN.KI = lord of the land (earth)

عَن كِع؛ عَن قِع = عَن كي = سيد الأرض

^{d}EN.KI-GA-KAM

From Arabic references:
GA = watered land
KAM = kham =

"الجَعْوُ: الطين. يقال: جَعَّ فلانٌ فلاناً إذا رماه بالجَعْوِ وهو الطين. والجَيْئَةُ -بالفتح أيضاً-: الموضعُ الذي يجتمع فيه الماء، وكذلك الجِئَةُ مثال جِعَةٍ، الجِيّة، بغير همز: الموضع الذي يجتمع فيه الماء كالجِيئَةِ، وقيل: هي الركيَّة المُنْتِنَة. وقال ثعلب: الجِيَّة الماءُ المُسْتَنْقِعُ في الموضع."
"الخامَةُ: الرّطْبة من النّبات والزّرْع. أرضٌ خامَةٌ: وخِمَةٌ. والخامةُ الغَضَّةُ الرَّطْبَةُ من النبات."

Therefore:
EN.KI-GA-KAM = lord of the wet (fertile) watered land (earth)
عَن كِع جَأ خَم ؛ عَن قِع جَأ خَم = عَن كي جَأ خَم = سيد الأرض المسقية الرطبة (الخصبة)

^{d}Enkig

EN.KI-G = EN.KI-GA = lord of the watered land

عَن كِعْجَ [قِعْجَ] = سيد الأرض المسقية

^{d}IDIM

From Arabic references:
Adam (v.): to make water flow; to water
Adīm (adj.) one who makes water flow; flat land; top soil

أدَمَ، أدِمَ، أدُمَ، فهو آدِم، آدَمْ (فَعَلَ، فَعِلَ، فَعُلَ فهو فاعِلْ، فاعَلْ)
أأْدَمَ، أيْدَمَ، أوْدَمَ، فهو أيْدِيم (آدِم)، أوْدُوم (آدَمْ) (فَعْلَلَ، فَيْعَلَ، فَوْعَلَ فهو فَيْعِيلْ (فاعِلْ)، فَوْعُولْ (فاعَلْ))

"وائْتَدَمَ العودُ: جَرَى فيه الماءُ. وأَدَمَةُ الأَرض: وجهُها؛ وأَدَمَةُ الأَرض: باطِنُها، وأَدِيمها، وَجْهُها، وأَدِيمُ الليل: ظلمته. وقيل: هو من أُدْمة الأَرض، وهو لَوْنُها، قال: وبه سمي آدم أَبو البَشَر. واختُلف في اشتِقاق اسم آدم فقال بعضهم: سُمِّيَ آدم لأَنه خُلِق من أَدَمةِ الأَرض. الأَصمعي: الإِيدامةُ أَرض مُسْتَوية صُلْبة ليست بالغَليظة، وجمعها الأَياديمُ، قال: أُخِذَتِ الإِيدامةُ من الأَديمِ؛ ويقال للسِّقاء: ابنُ الأَدِيم."

Therefore:
IDIM = aydim = ādim = one who makes water flow (waters); one of (who makes) the fertile land
أيْدِيم = آدِم = ساقي الارض = ذا (سيد، أبو) الارض (التراب)

^{d}gašam

<u>From Arabic references:</u>
jasama = to cover land with water
jašam = jassam = one who covers land with water

"والجَسِيمُ: ما ارتفع من الأرض وعلاه الماء؛"

<u>Therefore:</u>
gašam = God who covers land with water

<u>Author's Notes:</u> Compare the consistent rational meanings offered by the Arabic references with some of the bizarre meanings provided through the Assyriology method decipherment tools, like "the house of water", "likeness make beer", "god of crafts", or "the prince".

6. ^{d}Enkidu

<u>Wikipedia:</u>
Enkidu (EN.KI.DU_3 "Enki's creation") is a central figure in the Ancient Mesopotamian *Epic of Gilgamesh.* Enkidu was formed from clay and saliva by Aruru, the goddess of creation, to rid Gilgamesh of his arrogance. Older sources sometimes transliterate his name as Enkimdu, Eabani, or Enkita.

<u>Mythology Dictionary</u>:
At times, referred to as Enkidu, Ea-bani, Ea-bani, Eabani, Eabani, Engidu, Engidu, Enkita, Enkita, Enkimdu, Enkimdu or Enbilulu.

<u>Author's Notes:</u> The current meaning of Enkidu, "Enki's creation", contradicts directly with the fact that Enkido was actually created, according to the epic, by the goddess *Aruru* following the command of god *Anu*, not the god *Enk*i. Additionally, this meaning does not match with meanings of Enkido's alternative names.

^{d}en-kidu

<u>From Arabic references:</u>
en = lord
kidu = hardship
"والكَيْدُ: الحرب. الكَيْدُ: السَّوْق. وتَكَأَّدَتْه الأُمورُ إذا شقت عليه. أَبو زيد: تَكَأَّدْتُ الذهابَ إلى فلان تَكَؤُّداً إذا ما ذَهَبْتَ إليه على مَشَقَّةٍ. ويقال: تَكَأَّدَني الذهابُ تَكَؤُّداً إذا ما شق عليك. وتَكَأَّدَ الأَمْرَ: كابَدَه وصَلِيَ به؛ والكَأْداءُ: الشِّدَّةُ، والظُّلْمُ، والحُزْنُ، والحِذارُ، واللَّيْل المُظْلِمُ. والكَؤُداءُ: الصُّعَداءُ. وهو يَكُودُ بنفسِه: يَجودُ. الكَوْدُ: المَنْعُ. يقال: أَوْكَدْتُه وأَكَّدْتُه وآكَدْتُه إيكاداً، وبالواو أَفصح، أَي شَدَدْتُه. والكَدا المنع. الكَدُّ: الشدّة في العَمَلِ وطَلَبُ الرزقِ والإِلحاحُ في مُحَاوَلَةِ الشيءِ."

<u>Therefore:</u>
en-kidu = lord of hardship and strenght

عن كدأ [عن كيد] [عن كأد] = سيد الشدة والمشقة

^{d}eabani

<u>From Arabic references:</u>
abani = hardship, stone, strength
ea-abani = en-abani = lord of hardship/hardness

عَعبن = عن عبن = اله الشدة، اله الشدة

"العَبْنُ، (بالفتح): الغِلَظُ في الجِسْمِ، والخُشُونَةُ. ورجل عَبَنَّى: عظيم. والعُبْنُ من الدواب: القَوِيّاتُ على السير، الواحد عَبَنَّى. رجل عَبَنَّك: صُلْب شديد."

Therefore:
Eabani = lord of hardship

عَبَنِ = سيد الشدة

ᵈen-gidu

From Arabic references:
gidu = vigor; strenght

"والجَدَدُ الأرض الصلبة. والجَدِيدُ: المَوْتُ. الجدُّ في الأمرِ والمبالغةُ فيه من هذا؛ لأنه يَصْرِمه صَرِيمةً ويَعْزِمُه عزيمة. وعالِمٌ جِدُّ عالِمٍ، بالكسر: مُتَنَاهٍ بالِغُ الغايَةِ.
وحَيْسٌ جَعْدٌ ومُجَعَّدٌ: غَليظٌ. والجَعْد من الرجال: المجتمع بعضه إلى بعض."

Therefore:
en-gidu = lord of hardship

عن جعد [عن جِدّ] = سيد الشدة

ᵈen-kita

From Arabic references:
kita = vigor; strenght

"والكَتِيتُ: صوتٌ في صَدْر الرجل يُشْبِهُ صوتَ البَكارة، من شدَّةِ الغَيْظ؛ وكَتَّ الرجُلُ من الغَضَب. وفي حديث وَحْشِيٍّ ومَقْتَلِ حمزة، وهو مُكَبّسٌ: له كَتِيتٌ أي هديرٌ وغَطيط."
"وكاتَعَهُ الله تعالى: قاتَلَهُ. والتَّكاتُعُ: التَّتابُعُ. ورجل كُتَعٌ: مُشَمِّرٌ في أمره، وقد كَتِعَ كَتَعاً وكَتَعَ؛ وقيل كَتَعَ تَقَبَّض وانضمّ كَكَنَع. وكاتَعه الله كقاتَعه أي قاتَله، وزعم يعقوب أَنَّ كاف كاتعه بدل من قاف قاتَعَه."
"والكِنْتَأْوُ، كَسِنْدَأْوٍ: الجَمَلُ الشديدُ."

Therefore:
en-kita = lord of hardship

عن كِتّ [عن كعتَ] = اله الشدة

ᵈen-kimdu

From Arabic references:
kimdu = sorrow; hardship

"ابن سيده: والكَمَد أَشدُّ الحزن. ورجل كامدٌ وكَمِدٌ: عابِسٌ. والكَمعدُ: هَمٌّ وحُزن لا يستطاع إمضاؤه. الجوهري: الكَمَدُ الحزن المكتوم. والكَمْدُ، بالفتح وبالتحريكِ: تَغَيُّرُ اللَّوْنِ، وذَهابُ صَفائِهِ، والحُزْنُ الشديدُ."

Therefore:
en-kimdu = lord of sorrow = lord of hardship

عن كِمدُ = اله الحزن (الشدة)

ᵈen-bilulu

From Arabic references:
bilulu = bilu = tolerance; steadfastness

"وهو بَعْلٌ على أهله أي ثِقْلٌ عليهم. والبَعَل الدَّهَش عند الرَّوع. فقال: البَعْل ما رَسَخ عُروقه في الماء فاسْتَغْنَى عن أن يُسْقَى؛ واستبْعل النخلُ إذا صار بَعْلاً. وبَعَل على الرجل: أَبى عليه."

Therefore:
en-bilulu = lord of tolerance (hardship)

عن بِعْلُلْ = اله التحمل والرسوخ (الشدة)

7. ^{d}Enlil (*also* ^{d}Ellil, ^{d}KUR.GAL, ^{d}Amurri)

Wikipedia:
Enlil (nlin) EN (Lord) + LÍL (Wind), "Lord (of the) Storm" is the God of breath, wind, loft and breadth (height and distance). Sometimes rendered in translations as "Ellil" in later Akkadian. Enlil was one of the supreme deities of the Mesopotamian pantheon. He decreed the fates, his command could not be altered, and he was the god who granted kingship.

Ancient Mesopotamian Gods and Goddesses:
There has been much debate concerning the writing, etymology, and hence meaning of Enlil's name. These elements are important to discuss because they also relate to an analysis of this deity's functions. The writing and reading of this deity's name is not certain (see below), and even if we do read den-líl, the translation of "líl" is contentious. The Sumerian word "líl", whose Akkadian equivalent is zaqīqu, means "ghost, phantom, haunted" but a translation of Enlil's name as "Lord Ghost" makes little sense in the context of his mythological attestations. The interpretation of líl as "wind" is apparently a secondary development of the first millennium BCE, which has led to an interpretation of Enlil's name as "Lord Wind" or "Lord Air". This interpretation has led some scholars to reconstruct a vertically ordered cosmology that consisted of the gods An (heavens), Enlil (atmosphere), and Enki (earth), but this remains very problematic.

Written forms: ^{d}en-líl, ^{d}50, ^{d}nu-nam-nir
Normalized forms: Enlil, Ellil

From references of Arabic and the Assyriology method, and using al-Jibouri's rules:
lílu >> lillu = fool, ghost, storm, chaos, hate
zaqīqu = ghost, phantom, haunted

لَبْسُ؛ بَلْسُ؛ لَيلُ؛ جَنَنُ: إختلاط، حيرة، يأس، ظلام، تَخفّي
إلْبيسْ؛ لِبيسْ – احمق، ملتبس، حائر، يائس، مظلم، مُتخفي (جِنْ، مَلاك، شبح)
إبْلِيسْ؛ بِلِيسْ – احمق، ملتبس، حائر، يائس، مظلم، مُتخفي (جِنْ، مَلاك، شبح)، شيطان

إلْبِيلْ >> إلّيلْ >> إنليلْ – احمق، ملتبس، حائر، يائس، مظلم، مُتخفي (جِنْ، مَلاك)
لِبيلُ (لِبِيلْ)>> لِيلُّ (لِيلْ) >> لِلْلُ (لِلْ) – احمق، ملتبس، حائر، يائس، مظلم، مُتخفي (جِنْ، مَلاك، شبح)

أَلَّ (ألل): عَصُفَ (أبرق، سبب إضطرب واختلاط، أسرع خاطفا)؛ جَنَّنَ واربك (دَفع قفاه متخفيا) ؛ حَقَدَ (يأس، حار، شكك، حسد)
أَلُّ (غُلُّ، لُبْسُ): عاصفة (بَرق وإضطرابْ (إختلاطْ) وإسراعُ خاطفْ)؛ جَنٌّ وارباك (دفع القفا بتخفّي)، حِقْدْ (يأس وحيرة وشَكْ وحَسدْ)
لَئِلَ: أبرق

لِيلُ (لِلْ) – عاصفة (بَرق وإضطرابْ (إختلاطْ) وإسراعُ خاطفْ)؛ جِنْ، احمق، شبح؛ حِقْدْ (يأس وحيرة وشَكْ وحَسدْ)
إلّيلْ >> إنليلْ – العاصِف (مُولّد العواصف والفوضى والاضطرابات)، الجِنُّين (مُولّد الجُن والاشباح والارباك)، المُحقّد (مُولّد الحقد والحسد والشك)

"اللَّيْلُ: عقيب النهار ومَبْدَؤُه من غروب الشمس. الليث تقول العرب هذه لَيْلةٌ لَيْلاءُ إذا اشتدَّت ظُلمتها، ولَيْلٌ أَلْيَل. وليلٌ أَلْيَلُ: شديد الظلمة؛ وأَلالَ القومُ وأَلْيَلوا: دخلوا في الليل. وأَلْبَسَ لَيْلٌ لَيْلاً: ركِبَ بعضُه بعضاً."

"اللُّبْسُ، بالضم: مصدر قولك لَبِسْتُ الثوبَ أَلْبَس، واللَّبْس، بالفتح: مصدر قولك لَبَسْت عليه الأمر أَلْبِسُ خَلَطْت. واللَّبْسُ واللَّبَسُ: اختلاط الأمر. لبَسَ عليه الأَمرَ يَلْبِسُه لَبْساً فالْتَبَسَ إذا خَلَطَه عليه حتى لا يعرف جِهَتَه. وفي المَوْلَدِ والمَبْعَثِ: فجاء المَلَكُ فشقَّ عن قلبه، قال: فَخِفْتُ أَن يكون قد الْتُبِسَ بي أَي خُولِطْت في عَقْلي، من قولك في رَأْيِهِ لَبْسٌ أَي اختلاطٌ، ويقال للمجنون: مُخالَط. والْتَبَسَ عليه الأمر أَي اختلَطَ واشْتَبَه. والتَّلْبيسُ: كالتَّدْليس والتَّخليط، شُدِّد للمبالغة، ورجل لَبَّاسٌ ولا تقل مُلَبِّس. والمِلْبَسُ: الليل بعَيْنه كما تقول إِزارٌ ومِئْزَرٌ ولِحافٌ ومِلْحَفٌ؛ واللَّبْسُ: اختِلاطُ الظلام. ورجل البِيسٌ: أَحمق. وفي شرح القاموس: ورجل لبيس، بكسر اللام. أحمق."

"والإِبْلاسُ: الحَيْرة؛ ومنه الحديث: أَلم تر الجِنَّ وإِبلاسَها أَي تَحَيُّرَها ودَهَشَها. البَلَسُ، محركةً: من لا خير عندَهُ، أو عندَهُ إبْلاسٌ وشَرٌّ، وأبْلَسَ: يَئِسَ، وتَحَيَّرَ، ومنه: إبليسُ."

"والجِنَّة :الجنون؛ وذلك أنّه يغطّي العقل. وجَنَانُ الليل: سوادُه وسَتْرُه الأشياءَ. قال: ولولا جَنَان الليل أدْرَكَ رَكْضُنا بذِي الرِّمْث والأَرْطَى عِياضَ بنَ ناشِبِ. ويقال جُنُون الليل، والمعنى واحد. وجَنَان النّاس مُعْظَمُهم، ويسمَّى السَّوَادَ. وجُنُونُه وجَنانُهُ: ظُلْمَتُهُ، واخْتلاطُ ظَلامِهِ. والجَنانُ: الثَّوبُ، واللَّيْلُ أو ادْلِهْمامُهُ. والجُنَّةُ، بالضم: كلُّ ما وَقَى، وخِرْقَةٌ تَلْبَسُها المرأةُ تُغَطِّي من رأسِها ما قَبَلَ ودَبَرَ غَيْرَ وَسَطِهِ، وتُغَطِّي الوجْهَ وجَنْبَي الصَّدْرِ، وفيه عَيْنانِ مَجُوبتانِ كالبُرْقُعِ. والجِنَّةُ، بالكسر: طائفةٌ من الجِنِّ. والجِنُّ ولدُ الجانّ. ابن سيده: الجِنُّ نوعٌ من العالَم سمُّوا بذلك لاجْتِنانِهم عن الأَبصار ولأَنهم اسْتَجَنُّوا من الناس فلا يُرَوْن، والجمع جِنانٌ، وهم الجِنَّة. وفي التنزيل العزيز: ولقد عَلِمَت الجِنَّةُ إِنهم لَمُحْضَرُون؛ قالوا: الجِنَّةُ ههنا الملائكةُ عند قوم من العرب، وقال الفراء في قوله تعالى: وجعلوا بينه وبين الجِنَّةِ نَسَباً، قال: يقال الجِنَّةُ ههنا الملائكة، يقول: جعلوا بين الله وبين خَلْقِه نَسَباً فقالوا الملائكةُ بناتُ الله، ولقد عَلِمَت الجِنَّةُ أَن الذين قالوا هذا القولَ مُحْضَرون في النار. والجِنِّيُّ منسوبٌ إِلى الجِنِّ أَو الجِنَّةِ."

"وزِيقُ الشيطانِ: لُعابُ الشمس. ولُعَابُ الشَّمْس: شيء تَراه كأنه يَنْحَدِر من السماءِ إذا حَمِيَتْ وقامَ قائمُ الظَّهيرة؛ قال الأَزهري: لُعَابُ الشَّمْسِ هو الذي يقال له مُخَاطُ الشَّيْطانِ. وقد زَقا الصَدى يَزْقو ويَزْقى زُقاءً، أي صاح. وكلُّ صائحٍ زاقٍ. والزَقْيَةُ الصيحةُ."

"والغَليلُ: الحِقْدُ، وغل الغِلالَةَ: لَبِسها، وهي بالكسر شِعارٌ تحتَ الثوبِ. كالغُلَّةِ، بالضم، والغَلْغَلَةُ: السُّرْعَةُ، وتَغَلْغَلَ: أسْرَعَ. وغل الثوبَ: لبِسْتُه تحت الثيابِ."

"الأَلُّ: السرعة، والأَلُّ الإسراع. قال ابن بري: أَلَّ دُفع في قفاه. والإِلُّ الحِقد. ويقال: ما له أُلَّ وغُلَّ؛ قال ابن بري: أُلَّ دُفع في قفاه، وغُلَّ أَي جُنَّ. والأَلُّ الصِّيَاحُ.

والهمزة واللام في المضاعف ثلاثة أصول: اللّمعان في اهتزاز، والصّوت، والسّبَب يحافَظ عليه. قال الخليل وابن دريد: ألّ* الشيءُ، إذا لمع. وتلألأ البَرْقُ: لَمَعَ."

Therefore:
Elíl = Ellil = Enlil = ilīl = illil = inlil = ilbīs = iblīs = Satan = the fool devil; the creator of the jinn (genies, the ghosts) and crazy ones; the desperate; the creator of storms, turbulences, anxiety, and chaos; the instigator of hate, jealousy, and skepticism

إلْيِيلُ = إلّيل = إنليل = إلْبِيسُ = إبْلِيسُ = الشيطان الاحمق؛ اليائسُ، مُولد العواصف والاضطرابات والخوف والفوضى؛ مولد الجِنْ والمجانين؛ المحرض على الحقد والغيرة والشك

EN.LIL = Lord (creator) of the Jinn (genies, the ghosts); Lord (creator) of storms, turbulences, anxiety, chaos; Lord (creator) hate, jealousy, and skepticism = Satan

عَنْ ليلْ = سيد (مولد) الجِنْ؛ سيد (مولد) العواصف والفوضى والاضطرابات؛ سيد (مولد) الحِقدْ و الغيرة والشك = إبليس، الشيطان

^{d}nun-nam-nir

From Arabic references, and using al-Jibbouri's rules:
namara = to threaten, to be angry, to bluster

"ونَمَرَ وتَنَمَّرَ: غَضِبَ، وساءَ خُلُقُهُ. وتَنَمَّرَ: تَمَدَّدَ في الصَّوْتِ عندَ الوَعِيدِ، وتَشَبَّهَ بالنَّمِرِ، و~ له: تَنَكَّرَ، وتَغَيَّرَ، وأوعَدَهُ، لأَنَّ النَّمِرَ لا يُلْقَى إلاَّ مُتَنَكِّراً غَضْبانَ، وسَمَّوْا: نِمْرانَ، بالكسر. ونَمِرَ الرجلُ ونَمَّر وتَنَمَّر: غَضِب"

Therefore:
numma-nir >> nu-nam-nir = the angry one who threatens and blusters = Enlil = Satan

نَمَرَ، نَمْنَرَ فهو نُمْنِرْ >> نُنَمْنِر = المتوعّدْ، المهدّدْ، الغاضبْ = إنليل = الشيطان

dKUR.GAL

Wikipedia:

Although the word for earth was Ki, Kur came to also mean land, and Sumer itself, was called "Kur-gal" or "Great Land". "Kur-gal" also means "Great Mountain" and is a metonym for both Nippur and Enlil who rules from that city. Ekur, "mountain house" was the temple of Enlil at Nippur. A second, popular meaning of Kur was "underworld", or the world under the earth. Kur was sometimes the home of the dead, it is possible that the flames on escaping gas plumes in parts of the Zagros mountains would have given those mountains a meaning not entirely consistent with the primary meaning of mountains and an abode of a god. The eastern mountains as an abode of the god is popular in Ancient Near Eastern mythology. The underworld Kur is the void space between the primeval sea (Abzu) and the earth (Ma). Kur is almost identical with "Ki-gal", "Great Land" which is the Underworld (thus the ruler of the Underworld is Ereshkigal "Goddess of The Great Land".

From references of Arabic and the Assyriology method, and using al-Jiburi's rules:

KUR = underworld
GAL = great, almighty
KUR.GAL = great of the underworld; great of twisting

كور = قور = قعُر = باطن الارض
جل = عظيم
كُرجَل = عظيم باطن الارض؛ عظيم اللُف والبرم

"والكُرَّجِيُّ: المُخَنَّثُ. وكَرَّجَ وتَكَرَّجَ أي فَسَدَ وعَلاهُ خُضْرةٌ."
"كور: الكاف والواو والراء أصلٌ صحيحٌ يدلّ على دُوْرٍ وتجمُّع. من ذلك الكوْر: الدَّور. يقال كار يَكُورُ، إذا دار. وقال النضر: كل دارة من العمامة كَوْرٌ، وكل دَوْرٍ كَوْرٌ. وتكْوِيرُ العمامة: كَوْرُها. وكارَ العِمامَةَ على الرأس يَكُورُها كَوْراً: لاثَها عليه وأَدارها؛ الجوهري: الكُورَةُ المدينة والصُّقْعُ، والجمع كُوَرٌ. والصَّقْعُ: رَفْعُ الصَّوْتِ؛ وصَقَع في كل النَّواحِي يَصْقَعُ: ذَهَبَ؛ ابن سيده: والكُورَةُ من البلاد المِخْلافُ، وهي القرية من قُرَى اليمن؛ وقيل: التَّكْوِير الصَّرْع، ضرَبه أَو لم يضربْه. والاكتيارُ: صرعُ الشيءِ بعضُه على بعضٍ. واسْتَكار: أَسْرع. وكُور وكُوَيْرٌ والكَوْر: جبال معروفة؛ وكُرْت الأَرض كَوْراً: حفرتُها. وقيل: كَرَيْت النهر كَرْياً إِذا حفرته. وكَرا الأَرضَ كَرْواً: حفَرها وهو من ذوات الواو والياء. وفي حديث فاطمة، رضي الله عنها: أَنها خرجت تُعَزِّي قوماً، فلما انصرفت قال لها: لَعَلكِ بَلغْتِ معهم الكُرَى؟ قالت: معاذَ اللهِ هكذا جاء في رواية بالراء، وهي القُبور جمع كُرْيةٍ أَو كُرْوةٍ، من كَرَيْتُ الأَرض وكَرَوْتُها إِذا حفرتها كالحُفرة؛ ومنه الحديث: أَن الأَنصار سأَلوا رسول الله، صلى الله عليه وسلم، في نهر يَكْرُونه لهم سَيْحاً أَي يَحْفِرُونه ويُخْرِجون طينه."

Therefore:

KUR.GAL = Master of the underworld (the jinn); Master of twisters (storms) = Enlil = Satan
كَرجَلْ = عظيم باطن الارض (الجن)؛ عظيم اللُف والبرم (الاعاصير)

dAmurri

From Arabic references:

ʿamr = what rises of voice or wind; mixer
ʿamru = name of Satan
zbu ʿamrah = that who brings death and destruction

عمر = كل ما يرتفع من صوت او ريح
العومرة = الاختلاط والجُلبة
عمرو = اسم شيطان
ابو عَمْرة = اذا حل هو بقوم حل بهم البلاء

"عمر: العين والميم والراء أصلان صحيحان، أحدهما يدلُّ على بقاءٍ وامتداد زمان، والآخر على شيءٍ يعلو، من صوتٍ أو غيره. وأيُّ ذلك كان فهو من العلوّ والارتفاع على ما ذكرنا. قال أهلُ اللغة: والعَمَار: كلُّ شيء جعلتَه على رأسك، من عِمامةٍ، أو قَلَنْسُوة أو إكليل أو تاج، أو غير ذلك، كلُّه عَمار.
وقال قوم: العَمار يكون من رَيحَان أيضاً. قال ابنُ السِّكِّيت: العَمَار: التَّحيَّة. يقال عمَّرك الله، أي حيّاك. ويجوز أن يكون هذا لرفع الصوت. وممكن أن يكون الحيُّ العظيم يسمى عمارة لما يكون ذلك من جلبة وصياح. والعَوْمَرَةُ: الاختلاطُ، والجَلَبَةُ، وجَمْعُ الناسِ، وحَبْسُهُم في مكانٍ. وعَمْرٌو: اسْمٌ، جمعه أعْمُرٌ وعُمُورٌ، واسمُ شَيْطانِ الفَرَزْدَق، وعامِرٌ: اسمٌ، وقد يُسَمَّى به الحَيُّ، وعُمَرُ، مَعْدولٌ عنه في حالِ التَّسْمِيَةِ. وعُمَيْرٌ وعُوَيْمِرٌ وعَمَّارٌ ومَعْمَرٌ وعِمْرانُ وعُمارَةُ ويَعْمَرُ، كيَفْعَلُ: أسْماءٌ. وأبو عَمْرَةَ: كُنْيَةُ الإفلاسِ والجُوعِ، ورجُلٌ كان إذا حَلَّ بِقَومٍ، حَلَّ بِهِم البلاءُ من القَتْلِ والحَرْبِ. وأَبو عَمْرة: الإِقْلالُ؛ قال: إِن أَبا عَمْرة شرُّ جار وقال: حلّ أَبو عَمْرة وَسْطَ حُجْرَتي وأَبو عَمْرة: كنية الجوع."

<u>Therefore:</u>
Ammuri = one who cause rising wind; that who brings death and distruction = Enlil = Satan

عَمُرٌ = جالب الرياح والاصوات العالية، جالب البلاء = ابليس ابو الجن = الشيطان

<u>Author's Notes:</u> Without a doubt, the god *Enlíl/Elíl* was the predecessor of Satan (Arabic *Iblīs*) characteristically and linguistically. According to Islamic literature *Iblīs* was the "father of *jinn* (ghosts)" and Adam was the "the father of human kind". Muslims believe he was initially honored by god and was living in heaven with the angles (this explains his verified god status in ancient Mesopotamia), but later he was condemned for his evil-doing, and was sent to live on earth. Accordingly, stubborn *Iblīs* had disobeyed god, refusing to kneel to Adam. In Arabic *Iblīs* is commonly referred to as "the *foolish* devil" (al-*Shaytan al-Ahmaq*), clearly matching the Akkadian and Sumerian meanings "fool" and "ghost" for *LIL*.

8. ᵈEnnugi

<u>*Wikipedia:*</u>
Ennugi in Sumerian and Akkadian mythology is the attendant and throne bearer of Enlil (Ellil)

<u>From Arabic references:</u>
ʿanj = the yes-man, the follower, the servent
nug = working with adulation
adulation = act or instance of complying; obedience to a request,etc,unworthy submission,or the capacity to yield

العنج = التابع، الأمعة، الخادم
نوج = العمل بمراءاة

"والرجل يَعْنُج إليه رأسَ بعيره، أي يجذِبُه بخِطامه. قال أبو زيد: العَنْج: جذبُك رأسَها وأنت راكبُها. وتقول العرب: عِناج أمْرِ فلان، أي مَقاده ومِلاك أمره."
" ناجَ يَنُوجُ إذا راءى بِعَمَلِه."

<u>Therefore:</u>
En-nugi = one of adulation works = servant
Ennugi = the yes-man god, the follower god, the servent god

عن نوج = صاحب العمل بمراءاة = الخادم
عَنُوجِ = الاله التابع، الأمعة، الخادم

9. ^{d}Erra (*also* ^{d}Errakal)

<u>*Ancient Mesopotamian Gods and Goddesses:*</u>
Erra is God of war and plagues, who later became closely associated with the underworld god Nergal. Erra was an especially war-like and violent god, who is often understood to be a bringer of pestilence. There is some debate, however, regarding the exact nature of his destructive functions. One of Erra's common epithets TT is 'warrior' and another is 'lord of plague and carnage'. This second epithet has been alternatively translated as 'lord of affray and slaughter' by Roberts 1971, who argues that Erra's destructive power is associated with famine rather than pestilence. He claims that textual evidence indicates that Erra should be thought of as a god of famine rather than pestilence.
Erra's name is usually written in later sources as ^{d}ER$_{3}$.RA, although several variant spellings are attested in different periods including ^{d}ER$_{9}$(= GIR$_{3}$).RA. Older spellings of the name of Erra might include the spelling ^{d}KIŠ-ra, although this reading has been highly contested. Roberts 1971 gives a possible etymology TT for Erra's name as deriving from the Semitic root for "to scorch" or "char" giving Erra the meaning of "scorching" or "scorched". He therefore suggests that Erra was originally a personification of the "scorched earth" resulting from a grass or forest fire, who in time came to personify famine more generally - especially famine arising from the burning of land, such as during war. This interpretation however is not universally accepted.

<u>From Arabic references:</u>
èrra = harra = to kill
èrrakal = èrraqal = haraqal = over mighty

هرا = قتل
أراكل (هراكل) = أراقل (هراقل) = فوق الجبار

"وأَهْرَأَ الرَّجُلَ: قَتَله. والهُرَاءُ اسم شَيْطانٍ مُوَكَّل بِقَبِيح الأَحْلام."
"الرَّقْلة مثل الرَّعْلة: النخلةُ التي فاتت اليد وهي فوق الجَبَّارة؛ وأَرْقَل القومُ إِلى الحرب إِرْقالاً: أَسرعوا؛ وفي حديث جابر في غزوة خيبر: خرج رجل كأَنه الرَّقْل في يده حربة. عَرْكَلٌ: اسم. والحَرْكَلَة الرَّجَّالة كالحَوْكَلَة؛"

<u>Therefore:</u>
èrra = the killer
èrrakal = èrraqal = haraqal = the over mighty

هراء = القاتل
أراكل (هراكل) = أراقل (هراقل) = الفوق الجبار

10. ^{d}Gilgamesh (*also* ^{d}GIŠ; ^{d}GIŠ-gím-maš; ^{d}bìl.ga.mes; ^{md}GIŠ-TUK)

<u>*Wikipedia:*</u>
Gilgamesh (*Gilgameš,* originally Bilgamesh) is the main character in the *Epic of Gilgamesh*, an Akkadian poem that is considered the first great work of literature, and in earlier Sumerian poems. In the epic, Gilgamesh is a demigod of superhuman strength who builds the city walls of Uruk to defend his people and travels to meet the sage Utnapishtim, who survived the Great Flood. His name means something to the effect of "The Ancestor is a Young-man", from Bil.ga = Ancestor, Elder and Mes/Mesh3 = Young-Man.

<u>From Arabic references:</u>
GIŠ = jiḥsh = jiḥs = fighter, defender, loner
GIŠ = jish = rough, tough

GIŠ = jaysh = outburst, eruption
gím-maš = Jíḥmash = rigid, tough
gím-maš = Jímash = stubborn, tough
gím-maš = Jímas = rigid, tough
bìl = lord of, lord of, father of
ga.mes = Jímas = rigidness
TUK = tuk = tawk = tayk = the extremely crazy one, the foolish, crazy

جحش = متفرد، متوحد، مقاتل، مدافع
جش = مقاتل، مدافع
جيش = ثائر
جمش = جمس = متصلب، عنيد، جامد
نك = توك = تيك = شديد الحمق، مجنون

"جَحَشَ عن القوم: تَنَحّى. وقال أَبو حنيفة: الجحيش الفَرِيد الذي لا يَزْحَمُه في داره مُزاحِمٌ. يقال: نزل فُلانٌ جَحِيشاً إذا نزل حرِيداً فريداً. وجاحَشَ عن نفسه وغيرها جِحاشاً: دَافَعَ. الليث: الجِحاش مدافعةُ الإنسان الشيءَ عن نفسه وعن غيره، وقال غيرُه: هُوَ الجِحاش والجِحاس، وقد جاحَشَه وجاحَسَه مُجاحَشَة ومُجاحَسَة: دافعَه وقاتَلَه. وفي حديث شهادة الأَعضاء يوم القيامة: بُعْداً لكُنْ وسُحْقاً فعَنْكُنّ كُنْتُ أُجاحِشُ أَي أُحامِي وأُدافعُ. والجِحاش أَيضاً: القتال. ابن الأَعرابي: الجَحْشُ الجهاد، قال: وتُحَوّلُ الشينُ سِيناً؛ وأَنشد: يَوْماً تَرانا في عِرَاكِ الجَحْشِ، نَنْبُو بأَجْلال الأُمُورِ الرُّبْشِ أَي الدَّواهِي العِظام. وجاحَشَهُ: أي دافعه. والجَحيشُ: المتنحّي عن القوم. جَحَسَ في الشيء جَحْساً: دَخَل فيه. وجَحَسَ جِلْدَه: إذا كَدَحَه؛ مثل جَحَشَه والجَحْسُ: القتل، قال: يوماً تراني في عِراكِ الجَحْسِ، تَنبو بأجلال الأمور الرُّبسِ. والجِحاس في القتال: مثل الجِحاش، قال الأصمعي: جاحَسْتُه وجاحَشْتُهُ: إذا زاحَمْتَ، وأنشد لأبي جِمَاس: والصَّقع في يوم الوغى الجِحاسِ."
"رجُلٍ أَجَشِّ الصوتِ أَي في صَوته جُشّة، وهي شِدّة وغِلَظ. الجيم والياء والشين أصلٌ واحد، وهو الثَّوران والغَلَيان."
"والجَمِيش الذي لا نَبْتَ به. الجَمْش: الصَّوتُ. أَبو عبيدة: لا يُسْمِعُ فلانٌ أُذُناً جَمْشاً يعني أَدنى صوتٍ؛ يقال لِلَّذي لا يَقْبَل نُصْحاً ولا رُشْداً، ويقال للمُتَغابي المُتَصامِّ عنك وعمَّا يلزمه. قال: وقال الكلابي لا تَسْمَعُ أُذُنٌ جَمْشاً أَي هم في شيء يُصِمّهم يَشتغلون عن الاستماع إليك، هذا من الجَمْش وهو الصوت الخفيّ."
"الجيم والميم والسّين أصلٌ واحد، من جُمُوس الشَّيء. يقال: جَمَس الوَدَك إذا جَمَدَ. جُموسُ الوَدَكِ: جُموده. والماءُ جامِسٌ، أي جامدٌ. الجامُوسُ: م، مُعَرَّبُ كاوْمِيش ج: الجَواميسُ، وهي جامُوسَةٌ. وجُمُوسُ الوَدَكِ: جُمُودُهُ، أو أكثَرُ ما يُسْتَعْمَلُ في الماءِ: جَمَدَ، وفي السَّمْنِ وغيره: جَمَسَ. والجامِسُ من النَّباتِ: ما ذَهَبَتْ غُضُوضَتُهُ. و~ من التَّمْرِ: اليابِسُ، والبُسْرَةُ أرْطَبَ كلُّها، وهي صُلْبَةٌ لم تَنْهَضِمْ بعدُ، وبالفتح: النارُ. وليلةٌ جُماسِيَّةٌ، بالضم: بارِدَةٌ، يَجْمُسُ فيها الماءُ. وصَخْرَةٌ جامِسَةٌ: ثابِتَةٌ في مَوْضِعِها."
"الجَحْمَش: الصُّلب الشديد. وامرأة جَحْمَش وجُحْموش: عَجُوز كبيرة."
"توك، تيك: أَحمق تائِكٌ: شديد الحمق، ولا فعل له؛ وأَحْمَقُ تائِكٌ: شَديدُ الحُمْق، (وقد تاكَ) يَتيكُ. وأحْمَقُ باكٌ تاكٌ: لا يَدْري صَوابَه من خَطائِهِ. التِّكَّةُ: واحدة التِكَكِ. ويقال فلانٌ أحمقُ فاكٌ تاكٌ. وهو إتباعٌ له، وبعضهم يفرده ويقول: أحمقُ تاكٌ. وما كنتُ تاكّاً، ولقد تَكَكْتُ بالفتح تُكوكاً. قال الكسائي: يقال أَبَيْتَ إلاّ أن تَحْمُقَ وتَتُكَّ. والتاكُّ: الهالك مُوقاً. يقال: أَحمق تاكّ، وقيل: أَحمق فاكّ تاكّ إتباع له، بالغُ الحمقِ، والجمع تاكُّون وتَكَكَةٌ وتُكَّاك كضَرَبَةٍ وضُرَّابٍ وتُكُك كبُزُل، وما كنتَ تاكّاً ولقد تَكَكْتَ، بالفتح، تُكُوكاً. قال الكسائي: يقال أَبيتَ إلا أَن تَحمُق وتَتُكَّ، وقد تَكَّهُ النبيذُ مثل هَكَّهُ وهَرَّجه إذا بلغ منه. والتَّكِيكُ: الذي لا رأْي له، وهو بيّن التَّكاكة؛ عن الهجري؛ وأَنشد: أَلم تَأْت التَّكاكةُ قد تَراها، كقَرْنِ الشمسِ، باديةً ضُحَيّا؟ التهذيب: ابن الأَعرابي تُكَّ إذا قطع. وتَكَّ الإنسان إذا حَمُق، قال: والتِّكَّكُ والفُكَّكُ الحَمْقى القُيَّق."

<u>Using al-Jibouri rules to derive Gilgamesh (glgmš):</u>
Jish-jimash = Jishshijimash = Jiljimash
Jish-jimas = Jishshijimas = Jiljimas
Jiḥsh-jimash = Jishshijimash = Jiljimash
Jiḥsh-jimas = Jishshijimas = Jiljimas

جِشّجِمَش = جِلْجِمَش
جِشّجِمَس = جِلْجِمَس
جحشِجِّمَش = جيشِجِّمَش = جِلْجِمَش
جحشِجِّمَس = جيشِجِّمَس = جِلْجِمَس

Therefore:
GIŠ = the fighter, the defender, the loner
GIŠ-gím-maš = Gilgamesh = the stubborn loner, the stubborn fighter
GIŠ-gím-mas = Gilgamesh = the tough loner, the rigid loner, the tough fighter, the rigid fighter
bìl.ga.mes = the one of toughness, the one of rigidness, the tough fighter, the rigid fighter
GIŠ-TUK = the foolish (stubborn) loner, the foolish (stubborn) fighter, foolish GIŠ

جشْ = المقاتل، المدافع، المتنحي
جشْجِمَشْ = جلْجمش = المتنحي العنيد، المدافع العنيد، المقاتل العنيد
جشْجِمَشْ = جلْجمش = المتنحي المتصلب، المدافع المتصلب، المقاتل المتصلب
بِلْجَمِس = بِعلجَمِس = ابو الصلابة، صاحب الصلابة
جِشْتُكْ = المتنحي شديد الحمق (عنيد)، المدافع شديد الحمق (عنيد)، المقاتل شديد الحمق (عنيد)، جِش الشديد الحمق

Author's Notes: Since Gilgamesh was given several names. This clearly indicates these names were only titles or nicknames. My Arabic linguistic analysis concluded similar overall meanings for all his names. Prominent Iraqi scholar of Akkadian and Sumerian, Ṭāhā Bāqir, wrote decades ago that some Akkadian texts indicated that the name Gilgamesh meant 'the front fighter'*. He was very close, indeed! Utilizing the inadequate references of the Assyriology method to provide bizarre meanings like "The Ancestor is a Young-man" is disappointing.

The clear proof that the name Gilgamesh is only a title/nickname is actually given in line 47 of the Standard Babylonian edition of the Epic of Gilgamesh itself. The line explicitly said his actual name at birth was *Nabu* meaning "the high one". The exact Latin/Arabic transliteration of line #47 in the first tablet, according to A. R. George is:

GIŠ-gím-maš ul-tu u-um i'-al-du na-bu šum-šú
جِشْجِمَش أُلْتُ أُومْ إِالْدو نَبو سُمْ ذو

George translated that line "Gilgamesh was his name from the day he was born". In his translation, he *effectively* omitted translating the word *na-bu*, or assumed it was from the verb *nabû* (Arabic *nabu'a*) meaning "was called". However, the Arabic-based translation of the line is actually "Gilgamesh, the first day he was born [first, the day he was born], Nabu was his name"
"جِشجِمَش، أوّلُ يوم وُلِدَ [اولا، يوم وُلدَ]، نَبو كان إسمُهُ"

Notice, the name mdGIŠ-TUK was preceded by "md", not just "d". This may signify that the foolishness qualification was given to Gilgamesh the man, not the god, meaning "man of *the foolish god GIŠ*".

11. dHaniš

Gilgamesh: The New Translation:
Haniš (god of destruction)

From Arabic references:
ẖanasha = to drive out and take captives

---

* *Malḥamat Jiljamish: Ūdīsat al-'Irāq al-Khālidah*. Baghdad. 1956. pg. 19

"والمَحْنوشُ: المَسُوقُ جِئْتَ به تَحْنِشُه أي تَسُوقُه مُكْرَهاً. قال: حَنَشَه وعَنَشَه إذا ساقَه وطرَدَه."

Therefore:
ḫániš = one who drive take captives = اله السبي

12. Humbaba (*also* Huwawa)

Wikipedia:
In Ancient Mesopotamian religion, Humbaba (Assyrian spelling), also spelled Huwawa (Sumerian spelling) and surnamed the Terrible, was a monstrous giant of immemorial age raised by Utu, the Sun. Humbaba was the guardian of the Cedar Forest, where the gods lived, by the will of the god Enlil, who "assigned [Humbaba] as a terror to human beings".
His face is that of a lion. "When he looks at someone, it is the look of death". "Humbaba's roar is a flood, his mouth is death and his breath is fire! He can hear a hundred leagues away any [rustling?] in his forest! Who would go down into his forest!" In various examples, his face is scribed in a single coiling line like that of the coiled entrails of men and beasts, from which omens might be read. Another description from Georg Burckhardt translation of Gilgamesh says, "he had the paws of a lion and a body covered in thorny scales; his feet had the claws of a vulture, and on his head were the horns of a wild bull; his tail and phallus each ended in a snake's head."

From Arabic references and using Arabic grammar:
ḫuwāʾ (plural) = creatures sticking to ground like snakes
ḫuwāʾa (single) = ḫuwā = ḫuwā-wa = any creature sticking to ground like snakes
huwām (plural) = poisonous creatures wandering the ground like snakes
hāmma (single) = humma = humba = humba-ba = any poisonous creature wandering the ground like snakes

الحُوَّاء (جمع) = كائنات ضخمة لازقة بالارض كالحيات
الحُوَّاءَةُ (مفرد) = الحُوَّا = الحواوة = كائن ضخم لازق بالارض كالحية
الهُوامُ (جمع) = كائنات سامة تهيم بالارض كالحيات
الهامّة (مفرد) = الهُمّة = الهُمْبة = الهُمْبَبَة = الهُمْبابة = كائن سام يهيم بالارض كالحية

"والحُوَّاء: نَبْتٌ يشبه لون الذِّئبِ، واحدته حُوَّاءَةٌ. وقال أَبو حنيفة: الحُوَّاءَةُ بقلة لازقة بالأَرض، والحُوَّاءة: الرجل اللازم بيته، شبّه بهذه النبتة. والحَيَّة: من الهوامّ معروفة، تكون للذكر والأُنثى بلفظ واحد وحَوى الحَيَّةِ: انطواؤها؛ وجمع الحَويَّةِ حَوايا وهي الأَمعاء، وجمع الحاوِياءِ حَوَاوٍ على فَوَاعِلَ، وكذلك جمع الحاوية؛ وتَحَوَّى أَي تَجَمَّع واستدارَ. يقال: تَحَوَّت الحَيَّة."
"الهَوْمُ: بُطْنانُ الأرضِ. والهَوّامُ، كشَدَّادٍ: الأسَدُ. والأهْوَمُ: العظيمُ الهامَةِ. والهَمِيمُ: دوابُّ هوامِّ الأَرض. والهوامُّ: الحيَّاتُ وكلُّ ذي سَمٍّ يَقْتُلُ سَمُّه. والهوامُّ ما كان من خَشاش الأَرض نحو العقارب وما أَشبهها. وقال ابن بُزُرْج: الهامّة الحيّةُ والسامّة العقربُ. يقال للحية: قد همّت الرجلَ، وللعقرب: قد سمَّته"
"وقد مرّ.العَرَنْدَد: الصُّلْب من كلِّ شيء. قال:وهذا ممّا زيدت فيه النُّون، وضُوعفت الدّالُ لزيادة المعنى. والأصل العُرُدُّ، وهو القويُّ. . قال:وهذا ممّا زيدت فيه النُّون، وضُوعفت الدّالُ لزيادة المعنى. العَمَرَّط: الجَسُور الشَّديد. [و] يقال عَمَرَّد، وهذا من العُرُدّ، وهو الشَّديد، والميمُ زائدة، والطاء بدلٌ من الدال.العَقَنْباة: الدَّاهية من العِقْبان، والجمع عَقَنْبَيَات. وهذا ممّا زيدت فيه الزوائد تهويلاً وتفخيماً. وهو أيضاً مما يوضِّح ذلك الطَّريق الذي سَلكناه في هذه المُقايَسات، لأنَّ أحداً لا يشكُّ في أنَّ عَقَنْبَاة إنَّما أصلها عُقَاب، لكن زيد فيه لِما ذكرناه. فافهَمْ ذلك.عَنْقَفير: الدَّاهية. وهذا مما هُوِّل أيضاً بالزِّيادة. يقولون للدَّاهية عَنْقاء، ثمَّ يزيدون هذه الزِّياداتِ كما قد كرَّرنا القول فيه غيرَ مرّة.عَلْطَمِيسٌ: جاريةٌ تارَّة حسَنَة القَوام. وناقةٌ عَلطَميس: شديدةٌ ضَخْمة. والأصل في هذا عَيْطَمُوسٌ واللام بدل من الياء، والياء بدل من* الواو."

13. ^{d}Igigi/Igigu (a group of gods)

Wikipedia:

Igigi was a term used to refer to the gods of heaven in Sumerian mythology. Though sometimes synonymous with the term "Annunaki," in one myth the Igigi were the younger gods who were servants of the Annunaki, until they rebelled and were replaced by the creation of humans.

Ancient Mesopotamian Gods and Goddesses:

This Semitic term describes a group of possibly seven or eight gods. It is likely that the god Marduk was one of them, but the total membership in this group is unclear and likely changed over time. Like the term Anunna, the term Igigu is equally complicated and in need of a comprehensive new study. Igigu, which is likely of Semitic origin, indicates a group of gods in the Mesopotamian pantheon. It is, however, not entirely clear what distinguishes the Igigu from the Anunna. A Sumerian logographic equivalent of the term Igigu is nun-gal-e-ne, to be translated as "the great princes/sovereigns." This term is mentioned in a literary text that has been ascribed to the princess Enheduanna, daughter of king Sargon, the founder of the Old Akkadian dynasty (Inana C, ETCSL 4.7.3 l. 2). This particular composition is only attested in Old Babylonian manuscripts and it is unclear whether an older date can be proven. According to Edzard (1976-80: 39) it is possible that nun-gal-e-ne was originally an epithet of the Anunna gods that later became identified with the Igigu under influence from Akkadian. The Igigu and Anunnaki are frequently attested in literary, mythological, and religious (incantations and prayers) texts until the end of the cuneiform tradition. The Igigu are mentioned, among others, in the Anzu myth, in Enāma eliš TT, and the Erra poem, all of which are attested in manuscripts of the first millennium BCE.

Written forms:

logographic: dnun gal-e-ne, dnun-gal-meš;

syllabic and pseudo-logographic: i-gi-gu, i-gi-gi, ^{d}i-gi$_4$-gi$_4$, ^{d}i-gi$_4$-gi$_4$-ne, i-gi$_4$-gu, ^{d}í-gì-gì (the latter appears first in ninth century BCE)

Normalized forms:

Igigu, Igigi

From Arabic references and using al-Jibouri rules:

nagala = majala = to erupt, be thrown, come from uder

ajaja = to erupt, to cause fire

نجل = مجل = يرمي، يسيل، ينبثق، يخرج من تحت

اجج = انبثق، ثار، حرق

"وفي حديث يأْجوج ومأْجوج: وتَجْأَى الأَرضُ مِنْ نَتَنِهِمْ حينَ يموتون"

"الأَجِيجُ: تَلَهُّبُ النار. وأَجَّةُ القومِ: حفيفُ مشيِهم واختلاطُ كلامِهم، كلُّ ذلك عن ابن دريد. واليأْجوجُ: مَن يَئِجُّ هكذا وهكذا. والأَجُوجُ: المُضِيءُ النَّيِّرُ. وأَجَجَ، كمَنَعَ: حَمَلَ على العَدُوِ. ويَاجوجُ ومَاجوجُ، من لا يَهْمِزُهُما يَجْعَلُ الألفينِ زائدتينِ، من يَجَجَ ومَجَجَ، وقرأ رُؤْبَةُ: آجوجَ وماجوجَ، وأبو مُعاذٍ: يَمْجوجَ. والأَجُوجُ: المُضِيءُ النَّيِّرُ. ويأْجُوجُ ومأْجُوجُ: قبليتان من خلف الله، جاءَت القراءَة فيهما بهمز وغير همز. قال: وجاءَ في الحديث: أَن الخلق عشرة أَجزاء: تسعة منها يأْجوجُ ومأْجوجُ، وهما اسمان أَعجميان، واشتقاقُ مثلهما من كلام العرب يخرج من أَجَّتِ النارُ، ومن الماء الأُجاج، وهو الشديد الملوحة، المُحْرِقُ من ملوحته؛ قال: ويكون التقدير في يأْجُوجَ يَفْعول، وفي مأْجوج مفعول، كأَنه من أَجِيج النار.؛ قال: ويجوز أَن يكون يأْجوج فاعولاً، وكذلك مأْجوج؛ قال: وهذا لو كان الاسمان عربيين، لكان هذا اشتقاقهما، فأَمَّا الأَعْجَمِيَّةُ فلا تُشْتَقُّ من العربية؛ ومن لم يهمز، وجعل الأَلفين زائدتين يقول:

ياجوج من يَجَجْتُ، وماجوج من مَجَجْتُ، وهما غير مصروفين؛ قال رؤبة: لو أَنَّ يَاجُوجَ ومَاجوجَ معا، وعَادَ عادٌ، واسْتَجاشُوا تُبَّعا ويَأْجِجُ، بالكسر: موضع؛ حكاه السيرافي عن أَصحاب الحديث، وحكاه سيبويه يَأْجَجُ، بالفتح، وهو القياس، وهو مذكور في موضعه."

"نجج: نَجَّ الشيءَ من فيه نَجًّا: كمجَّه. ابن الأَعرابي: مَجَّ ونَجَّ، بمعنى واحد؛ نَجَّتِ القُرْحَةُ تَنِجُّ، بالكسر، نَجًّا ونَجِيجاً: رَشَحَت؛ وقيل: سالَتْ بما فيها. ونَجْنَجَ في رأْيه وتَنَجْنَجَ: اضطرَبَ. واليَنْجُوجُ والأَنجُوجُ: العود الذي يُتبَخَّرُ به؛"

"مجج: مَجَّ الشرابَ والشيءَ مِن فيه يَمُجُّه مَجّاً ومَجَّ به: رَماه؛ يقال: أَحمق ماجٌّ للذي يسيل لعابه؛ وقيل: هو الأَحمق مع هَرَمٍ، وجمع الماجِّ من الإِبلِ مَجَجةٌ، وجمع الماجِّ من الناس ماجُّونَ، ومَجْمَجَ الكِتابَ: خَلَّطَه وأَفسَدَه.

"نجل: النون والجيم واللام أصلان صحيحان: أحدهما يدلُّ على رَمْيِ الشيء، والآخَر على سعةٍ في الشَّيء. فالأوَّل النَّجْل: رمْيُك الشَّيء. يقال: نَجَل نَجْلا. ويقال: استنجل الموضعُ، أي كثُر به النَجْلُ، وهو الماء يَظْهَرُ من الأرض."

"مجل: وقيل: المَجْل أَن يكون بين الجلد واللحم ماء. والمَجْلةُ: قِشرة رقيقة يجتمع فيها ماء من أَثر العمل، والجمع مَجْلٌ ومِجالٌ. والمَجْل: أَن يُصيب الجلدَ نارٌ أَو مشقَّة فيَتَنَفَّط ويَمْتلئ ماء. والرَّهْص الماجِلُ: الذي فيه ماء فإِذا بُزِعَ خرج منه الماء، ومن هذا قيل لِمُسْتَنْقَع الماء ماجِل؛ هكذا رواه ثعلب عن ابن الأَعرابي، بكسر الجيم غير مهموز، وأَما أَبو عبيد فإِنه روى عن أَبي عمرو المَأْجَل، بفتح الجيم وهمزة قبلها، قال: وهو مثل الجَيْئةِ، وجمعه مآجِل؛ الماجِلُ: الماء الكثير المجتمع؛"

نجل: نُجّلين -> نُنْجَلين -> مُجّلين -> مجوج = ماجوج
نجل: نُنْجَلْ ميس -> مُنْجَلْ ميس -> مُجّلين -> مجوج = ماجوج
أجج: إجيج -> يجيج = ياجوج

nun galene = nungalene = nuggalene = muggalene => magug = magog
nun-gal^{meš} = nuggal^{meš} = muggal^{meš} => magug = magog
igigu = igigi = yigigi = yigigu => yagug

<u>Gog and Magog / Yagog and Magog from historical relegious references:</u>
<u>Christian Courier:</u>
Who are ‘Gog and Magog,’ that surround and threaten the ‘saints,’ as mentioned in Revelation 20:7-8? Here is the full text that elicits consideration.

“And when the thousand years are finished, Satan shall be loosed out of his prison, and shall come forth to deceive the nations which are in the four corners of the earth, Gog and Magog, to gather them together to the war: the number of whom is as the sand of the sea. And they went up over the breadth of the earth, and compassed the camp of the saints about, and the beloved city: and fire came down out of heaven, and devoured them” (Revelation 20:7-9)

“Revelation 20:1-6 describes a period of 1,000 years wherein Satan is “bound,” and the people of God “reign” (i.e., they have a peaceful regime compared to times of exceedingly fierce persecution). The 1,000 years symbolically represent an era of full victory for Christian people (not a literal millennium with Christ reigning upon the earth from Jerusalem, as millennialists allege.”

“Observe, then, that following this epoch of relative tranquility, Satan is loosed again for a “little season” (20:3b) — a signal that persecution is about to be unleashed again with a brief though intense fury. There will be an attempt to “deceive the nations,” likely either by destroying the Scriptures (as such was attempted in the “Dark Ages”), or, at the very least, by nullifying their influence in the hearts of people.”

“At the same time, Satan will make a last-ditch effort to crush the children of God. This he will attempt through a certain agent, divinely allowed to be at his disposal (as in the case of Job’s persecution — chapter 1). This instrument of evil is called “Gog” and “Magog” (the Greek article qualifies both nouns, suggesting a single unit). Some contend that “Magog” is merely the realm of “Gog” (see below). This force will "surround the camp of the saints" in what appears to be certain victory. But the Lord will have the final word; "fire" descends from heaven destroying the enemy."

"The background behind the names "Gog" and "Magog" is found in the book of Ezekiel, where certain hostile forces come against Israel. Ezekiel was instructed to denounce these enemies and prophesy their overthrow by the Lord himself. Here is the text:

"(1) Now the word of the Lord came to me, saying, (2) "Son of man, set your face against Gog, of the land of Magog, the prince of Rosh, Meshech, and Tubal, and prophesy against him, (3) "and say, 'Thus says the Lord God: "Behold, I am against you, O Gog, the prince of Rosh, Meshech, and Tubal. (4) "I will turn you around, put hooks into your jaws, and lead you out, with all your army, horses, and horsemen, all splendidly clothed, a great company with bucklers and shields, all of them handling swords. (5) "Persia, Ethiopia, and Libya are with them, all of them with shield and hel. (6) "Gomer and all its troops; the house of Togarmah from the far north and all its troops-many people are with you met" (Ezekiel 38:1-6).

"The identification of this evil entity has long been a point of controversy among Bible scholars. Clearly, though, Ezekiel's "Gog" represented a sinister power that came against ancient Israel, but was defeated."

<u>يأجوج ومأجوج في الاسلام:</u>

<u>في القرآن:</u> سورة الكهف (93-99): حَتَّى إِذَا بَلَغَ بَيْنَ السَّدَّيْنِ وَجَدَ مِنْ دُونِهِمَا قَوْمًا لَا يَكَادُونَ يَفْقَهُونَ قَوْلًا (93) قَالُوا يَا ذَا الْقَرْنَيْنِ إِنَّ يَأْجُوجَ وَمَأْجُوجَ مُفْسِدُونَ فِي الْأَرْضِ فَهَلْ نَجْعَلُ لَكَ خَرْجًا عَلَى أَنْ تَجْعَلَ بَيْنَنَا وَبَيْنَهُمْ سَدًّا (94) قَالَ مَا مَكَّنِّي فِيهِ رَبِّي خَيْرٌ فَأَعِينُونِي بِقُوَّةٍ أَجْعَلْ بَيْنَكُمْ وَبَيْنَهُمْ رَدْمًا (95) آتُونِي زُبَرَ الْحَدِيدِ حَتَّى إِذَا سَاوَى بَيْنَ الصَّدَفَيْنِ قَالَ انْفُخُوا حَتَّى إِذَا جَعَلَهُ نَارًا قَالَ آتُونِي أُفْرِغْ عَلَيْهِ قِطْرًا (96) فَمَا اسْطَاعُوا أَنْ يَظْهَرُوهُ وَمَا اسْتَطَاعُوا لَهُ نَقْبًا (97) قَالَ هَذَا رَحْمَةٌ مِنْ رَبِّي فَإِذَا جَاءَ وَعْدُ رَبِّي جَعَلَهُ دَكَّاءَ وَكَانَ وَعْدُ رَبِّي حَقًّا (98) وَتَرَكْنَا بَعْضَهُمْ يَوْمَئِذٍ يَمُوجُ فِي بَعْضٍ وَنُفِخَ فِي الصُّورِ فَجَمَعْنَاهُمْ جَمْعًا.(99)

سورة الانبياء (96): حَتَّى إِذَا فُتِحَتْ يَأْجُوجُ وَمَأْجُوجُ وَهُمْ مِنْ كُلِّ حَدَبٍ يَنْسِلُونَ

<u>في الحديث:</u> "إن يأجوج ومأجوج ليحفرون السد كل يوم حتى إذا كادوا يرون شعاع الشمس، قال الذي عليهم: ارجعوا فستحفرونه غدا، فيعيده الله أشد ما كان، حتى إذا بلغت مدتهم، وأراد الله أن يبعثهم على الناس حضروا، حتى إذا كادوا يرون شعاع الشمس قال الذي عليهم: ارجعوا فستحفرونه غدا إن شاء الله، واستثنوا، فيعودون إليه وهو كهيئته حين تركوه، فيحفرونه ويخرجون على الناس، فينشفون الماء، ويتحصن الناس منهم في حصونهم، فيرمون سهامهم إلى السماء، فترجع وعليها كهيئة الدم الذي أجفظ، فيقولون: قهرنا أهل الأرض، وعلونا أهل السماء. فيبعث الله عليهم نغفا في أقفائهم فيقتلهم بها، والذي نفسي بيده إن دواب الأرض لتسمن وتشكر شكرا من لحومهم ودمائهم"

Gog = Leader of the Magog
The land of Magog = the land where the Magog live
Gog and Magog = Gog (the leader) and all the Magog

<u>Therefore:</u>
Igigi and Nungelene = Igigi and Nuggelene = Igigi and Muggelene = Yajuj and Majuj = Yagog and Magog = Two groups of genies associated with the god Enlil (Satan), the father of the genies (ghosts). The Yagog group lives aboveground while the Magog group lives underground. They come out and work together to annihilate the human kind through fire and destruction.
إجيجي و ننْجلين = إجيجي و نجّلين = إجيجي و مجّلين = ياجوح وماجوج = مجموعتين من شياطين الجن من اتباع الإله إنليل (إبليس)، ابو الجن. الياجوج يعيشون فوق الارض والماجوج تحت الارض. يخرجان ويعملان سويتا للقضاء على البشر عبر الحريق والدمار.

<u>Author's Notes:</u> Both the nature and Arabic linguistic derivations of the *Igigi* gods indicate they are the earlier version of the mysterious Gog and Magog (Arabic Yagog and Magog) that are mentioned

in the holy books. According to these books they are associated with Satan (Enlil). In the flood story of the epic, the *Igigi* gods were Enlil's "ghost" troop. They were the counterparts of the *Annunaki* gods (angles of god Anu in earth) and the *Enkikkaki* gods (angles of Ea in earth)!

14. ᵈIškur (*also* ᵈAdad)

Ancient Mesopotamian Gods and Goddesses:

According to what became the dominant genealogy, Iškur/Adad's father is the sky-god An/Anu. However, in Sumerian literature Iškur is sometimes the son of Enlil; the disparity probably reflects two local traditions. A mother of Iškur/Adad is mentioned only once, in an Old Babylonian prayer where Iškur is called the son of Uraš. Iškur's wife is the goddess Medimša; Adad's wife is Šala. Although the use of the sign for Sumerian IM, 'wind' to write his name is transparent, the etymology of Sumerian Iškur is unknown; it may be an otherwise obsolete Sumerian word, or borrowed from a language that was neither Sumerian nor Semitic. Akkadian Adad (also Addu) is derived from the Semitic root hdd, 'to thunder' - in West Semitic the storm god is called Hadda, Haddu or Hadad, and the Akkadian word addu means 'thunderstorm'.

Written forms:

ᵈiškur (IM), ᵈ10, ᵈa-da-ad, ᵈad-da-a, ᵈ'à-da

Normalized forms:

Iškur, Adad, Addu, Haddu

From Arabic references:

adada = hadada = to thunder, to threaten, to make loud voice
ʿaskara = to make dark, to make the dark of a sand storm

"عَسِكَ به عَسَكاً، فهو عَسِكٌ: لَصِق به ولَزِمَه، وكذلك سَدِكَ، وزعم يعقوب أن كاف عَسِك بدل من قاف عَسِق."
"عَسِقَ به يَعْسَقُ عَسَقاً: لزق به ولزمه وأُولِعَ به، وكذلك تَعَسَّق؛ والعَسَقُ الظلمة كالغَسَقِ؛ عن ثعلب؛ وأَنشد: إِنَّا لَنَسْمو، للعَدُوِّ حَنَقا، بالخيل أَكْداساً تُثِيرُ عَسَقا. كنى بالعَسَقِ عن ظلمة الغبار."
"العَسْكَرةُ: الشدة والجدب؛ وعَسْكَرَ الليلُ: تَراكَمَتْ ظُلْمتُه."
"الهَدُّ: الهَدْمُ الشديد والكسر كحائِط يُهَدُّ بمرَّة فَيَنْهَدِم؛ والهَدّة: صوت شديد تسمعه من سقوط ركن أَو حائط أَو ناحية جبل، تقول منه: هَدَّ يَهِدُّ، بالكسر، هديداً؛ والهَدُّ والهَدَدُ: الصوت الغليظ، والتَّهَدُّدُ والتهْديدُ والتَّهْدادُ: من الوعيد والتخوف. والهَدْهَدُ قيل في تفسيره: أَصواتُ الجنّ ولا واحد له. الهَدادِ والهَدِيدُ والفَدِيدُ: الصوتُ."

adddu = haddu = hadad = one who makes thunder
iškur = one who makes dark storm

هدّو = هَداد = الرعّاد
عِسكُر = عِسقُر = مسبب العواصف المظلمة

15. ᵈIštar (*also* ᵈInanna)

Wikipedia:

Ishtar (English pronunciation) is the Mesopotamian East Semitic (Akkadian, Assyrian and Babylonian) goddess of fertility, love, war, and sex. She is the counterpart to the earlier attested Sumerian Inanna, and the cognate for the later attested Northwest Semitic Aramean goddess Astarte. Ishtar was an important deity in Mesopotamian religion which was extant from c.3500 BCE, until its gradual decline between the 1st and 5th centuries CE in the face of Christianity.

Wikipedia:
Inanna's name derives from *Lady of Heaven* (Sumerian: nin-an-ak). The cuneiform sign of Inanna however, is not a ligature of the signs *lady* (Sumerian: nin) and *sky* (Sumerian: an). These difficulties have led some early Assyriologists to suggest that originally Inanna may have been a Proto-Euphratean goddess, possibly related to the Hurrian mother goddess Hannahannah, accepted only latterly into the Sumerian pantheon, an idea supported by her youthfulness, and that, unlike the other Sumerian divinities, at first she had no sphere of responsibilities. The view that there was a Proto-Euphratean substrate language in Southern Iraq before Sumerian is not widely accepted by modern Assyriologists.

Ancient Mesopotamian Gods and Goddesses:
Inana/Ištar is by far the most complex of all Mesopotamian deities, displaying contradictory, even paradoxical traits. In Sumerian poetry, she is sometimes portrayed as a coy young girl under patriarchal authority. Inana/Ištar is equally fond of making war as she is of making love: "Battle is a feast to her". Inana/Inanna is the Sumerian name of this goddess. It is most often etymologically interpreted as nin.an.a(k), literally "Lady of the heavens". A different interpretation translates her name as "Lady of the date clusters." The Semitic name Ištar originally belonged to an independent goddess that was later merged and identified with the Sumerian Inana. The meaning of her name is also unclear.

Written forms:
Inana: ^{d}INNIN, ^{d}in-nin, ^{d}in-ni-na, i-ni-en-na, en-nin, ^{d}en-ni-na, ^{d}in-na-na, in-na-na, in-na-an-na, na-na, ni-in, nin, ni-in-ni, ^{d}nin$^{?}$-ni-na, ^{d}nin-an-na, ni-in-na-na, ^{d}ir-ni-na
Ištar: $eš_4$-tár, $^{d}eš_4$-tár, $^{(d)}$IŠTÁR, ^{d}iš-tar, ^{d}15 (= IŠTÀR)

Normalised forms:
Inana: Inana, Inanna
Ištar: Ištar, Eštar, 'Aštar, Ištar, Ashtar

Strong's Definitions:
astēr (as-tare) a star (as strown over the sky), literally or figuratively: star.

Religion Facts:
The four-pointed star symbol in Christianity is usually styled to resemble a cross. Also known as the Star of Bethlehem or natal star, this star represents both Jesus' birth and the purpose for which he was born. It is used especially for church decoration during the Advent and Christmas seasons.

From Arabic references and grammar:
istar = ishtar = four, fourth
Inana = feminine for anu

إستار = إشتار = اربعة، ربع
عِنانة = عِنِينْ = عِنان = عِنينة = تأنيث عنو

"سَتَرَ الشيءَ يَسْتُرُه ويَسْتِرُه سَتْراً وسَتَراً: أَخفاه؛ والإِسْتارُ، بكسر الهمزة، من العدد: الأَربعة؛ قال جرير: إِنَّ الفَرَزْدَقَ والبَعيثَ وأُمَّه وأَبا البَعِيثِ لَشَرُّ ما إِسْتار أَي شر أَربعة، وما صلة؛ ويروى: وأَبا الفرزْدَق شَرُّ ما إِسْتار وقال الأَخطل: لَعَمْرُكَ إِنَّني وابْنَيْ جُعَيْلٍ وأُمَّهُما لإِسْتارٌ لَئِيمُ وقال الكميت: أَبلِغْ يَزِيدَ وإِسماعيلَ مأْلُكَةً، ومُنْذِراً وأَباهُ شَرَّ إِسْتارِ وقال الأَعشى: تُوُفِّي لِيَوْمٍ وفي لَيْلَةٍ ثَمانِينَ يُحْسَبُ إِستارُها قال: الإِستار رابعُ أَربعة. ورابع القوم: إِسْتَارُهُم. قال أَبو سعيد: سمعت العرب تقول للأَربعة إِسْتار لأَنه بالفارسية جهار فأَعْربوه وقالوا إِستار؛ قال الأَزهري: وهذا الوزن الذي يقال له الإِستارُ معرّب أَيضاً أَصله جهار فأُعرب فقيل إِسْتار. ويقال لكل أَربعة إِستارٌ. يقال: أَكلت إِستاراً من خبز أَي أَربعة أَرغفة. الجوهري: والإِسْتَارُ أَيضاً وزن أَربعة مثاقيل ونصف، والجمع الأَساتير. وأَسْتارُ الكعبة، مفتوحة الهمزة."

"ابن الأَعرابي: شَتِرَ انقطع، وشُتِرَ انقطع. وشَتَرَ ثوبه: مَزَّقَهُ. وقد شَتِرَ يَشْتَرُ شَتَراً وشُتِرَ أَيضاً مثل أَفِنَ وأُفِنَ. وفي حديث قتادة: في الشَّتَرِ ربع الدية، وهو قطع الجفن الأَسفل والأَصل انقلابُه إِلى أَسفل."

" أفن: أَفَنَ الناقةَ والشاةَ يأْفِنُها أَفْناً: حلَبها في غير حينها، وقيل: هو استخراجُ جميع ما في ضرعها. قال أَبو منصور: ومِن هذا قيل للأحمق مأْفونٌ، كأَنه نُزِع عنه عقلُه كلُّه. وفي حديث عليّ: إِيّاكَ ومُشاوَرَةَ النساء فإِن رأْيَهنّ إِلى أَفْنٍ؛ الأَفْنُ: النقصُ."

Therefore:

Ištar = Eštar = 'Aštar = Istar = Ashtar = The goddess of four (fertility, love, war, and sex)

Inana = Goddess of heavens

إستار = إشتار = آلهة الاربعة (الاخصاب، الحب، الحرب، الجنس)

عِنانة = عِنِينٌ = عِنان = عِنينة = آلهة السماوات

Author's Notes: Having the meaning of "goddess of four" and being identified with the old Sumerian Goddess of Heavens *Inanna*, the Goddess *Ishtar* was very likely associated with a particular star in Heavens. Since the Ishtar continued her role as an important deity in the Near East until the rise of Christianity between the 1st and 4th centuries CE, and since much of the old Mesopotamian myths had survived in the monotheistic religions, it is very likely she was replaced under Christianity by the four-pointed star cross symbol to represent Jesus. According to Christianity, "The four-pointed star symbol in Christianity is usually styled to resemble a cross. Also known as the Star of Bethlehem or natal star, this star represents both Jesus' birth and the purpose for which he was born." The fact that the name *Istar* is linguistically identical to the Greek word *astēr*, for "star", is hard to ignore.

16. dLugalbanda

Wikipedia:

Lugalbanda is a character found in Sumerian mythology and literature. His name is composed of two Sumerian words meaning "young/fierce king" (lugal: king; banda: young, junior, small; but also fierce)

From references of Arabic and the Assyriology method, and using al-Jibouri rules:

LU = man

GAL = mighty

LUGAL = LU-GAL = mighty man = king, master

baddada = to get rid or didperse something so that it does not exist any longer

badda = banda = huge, strong, fierce

لُعُ = الذي يقاتل على ما يؤكل = رجل

جَل = جليل = عظيم

لُعُجَل = لُعُ جَل = لُجَلْ = الرجل العظيم = الملك، السيد

بدد = فرَق، انهى الشيء

بدّ = بند = قوي، عظيم

"وقال الهجيميّ: البَنْدُ عَلَمُ الفُرْسانِ؛ وأَنشد للمفضل: جاؤُوا يَجُرُّون البُنُودَ جَرَّا. قال النضر: سمي العلم الضخم واللواءُ الضخمُ البَنْدَ."
"بَدَّهُ يَبُدُّهُ بَدّاً: فرَّقه. والتبديد: التفريق. يقال: شملٌ مُبَدَّدٌ. وتَبَدَّدَ الشيء: تفرّق. والبِدَّةُ، بالكسر: القوّة. واسْتَبَدَّ فلان بكذا أَي انفرد به؛ والأَبَدُّ: الرجل العظيم الخَلق؛ ورجل أَبَدُّ وفي فخذيه بَدَدٌ أَي طول مفرط."
"وجَلَّ الشيءُ يَجِلُّ جَلالاً وجَلالةً وهو جَلٌّ وجَلِيلٌ وجُلال: عَظُم، والأُنثى جَلِيلة وجُلالة. والتَّجِلَّة: الجَلالة، اسم كالتَّدْوِرَة والتَّنِهيَة؛ والتَّجالُّ التعاظم. يقال: فلان يَتَجالُّ عن ذلك أَي يترفع عنه. وجَلَّ الرجل جَلالاً، فهو جَلِيل: أَسَنَّ واحْتُنِك؛ وجُلُّ كل شيء: عُظْمه. والجَلَل: الأَمر العظيم."
"واللَّعو: السيء الخُلُق، واللَّعْوُ الفَسْلُ، واللَّعْوُ واللَّعا الشَّرِه الحَريص، رجل لَعْوٌ ولَعاً، منقوص، وهو الشره الحريص، قال الليث: يقال كلبة لَعْوةٌ وذِئبة لَعْوةٌ وامرأَة لَعْوة يعني بكل ذلك الحريصة التي تقاتل على ما يؤكل"

Therefore:
Lugalbanda = Lugal-banda = lugal-bàn-da = the fierce king = the mighty king

لُجَلْ بَنْدَ = الملك العظيم

17. ^{d}Mamitu (*also* ^{d}Mamitum)

Wikipedia:
In Mesopotamian mythology Mamitu was the goat-headed goddess of destiny, who decreed the fate of the new-borns. She was also worshipped as goddess of the oath, later a goddess of fate and a judge in the underworld, where she lives with the Anunnaku. She is occasionally regarded as a consort of Nergal. In some passages, she is also known as a demon of irrevocable curses. Mamitu is supposedly related to the Babylonian god Anu. Other spellings: Mammitu, Mammetum, Mammetu.

From Arabic references:
mamitu = mamitum = she who has dead ones or has someone dead

مميت = صاحبة الاموات

"غيره: المَوْتُ والمَوَتانُ ضِدُّ الحياة. والمَوْتُ السُّكونُ. ومَرَةٌ مُمِيتٌ ومُمِيتةٌ: ماتَ ولدُها أَو بَعْلُها، وكذلك الناقةُ إِذا مات ولدُها، والجمع مَمَاويتُ."

Therefore:
Mamitu = Mamitum = Mami = goddess of death or fate

مَميتُ =مَميتُم = مَمي = آلهة الموت

18. ^{d}Ninsun (*also* ^{d}Ninsunana, ^{d}Ninsumun, ^{d}Ninsumuna, ^{d}Rimat-Ninsun)

Wikipedia:
Ninsun or Ninsuna ("lady wild cow") is a goddess. Ninsun is called "Rimat-Ninsun", the "August cow", the "Wild Cow of the Enclosure", and "The Great Queen". In the Tello relief (the ancient Lagash, 2150 BC) her name is written with the cuneiform glyphs as: DINGIR.NIN.GUL where the glyph for GUL is the same for SUN2. The meaning of SUN2 is attested as "cow".

Ancient Mesopotamian Gods and Goddesses:
Ninsumun is primarily known as the mother of legendary king Gilgameš. She appears in this function already in the Sumerian Gilgameš tales dating to the Old Babylonian period (or possibly earlier) and continues to be mentioned in the Standard Babylonian *Epic of Gilgameš*. In the Standard Babylonian version, in the first part of Tablet III, she pleads with the sun-god Šamaš on behalf of her son. Ninsumun's name was originally read Ninsun. More recently the reading Ninsumun has been proven to be more accurate. The name appears to be a genitive construction, meaning "Lady of the wild cows"

<u>Written forms:</u>
^{d}nin-sún, ^{d}nin-súmun, ^{d}nin-súmun-na (= ^{d}nin-súmun-ak), ^{d}nin-súmun-ka

<u>Normalised forms:</u>
Ninsun, Ninsuna (both obsolete), Ninsumun, Ninsumuna, Ninsumunak

<u>From references of Arabic and the Assyriology method, and using al-Jibouri rules:</u>
ninsun = plural of woman
nin = single lady
sun = sunun = usun = sumun = nusum = related to fatness, beauty, creation, goodness, good progeny
nin-sun = nin-sunun = nin-usun = nin-sumun = nin-nusum = lady beauty; lady good progeny
nissun = nin-sun = missun -> maysun = one with good looking face and body
NIGUL = wideness, fullness, progeny, good progeny
NIN.GUL = NIN.NIGUL = Lady wide-eyes (beauty), lady good progeny

النِّسون -> النِنْسون = جمع إمرأة
نِنْ = إمرأة
سُنْ = سُنُنْ = أُسُنْ = سُمُنْ = نُسُمْ = متعلق بالسمن، الحُسن، الطيبة، الخُلق، كرم النسل
نِنْسُنْ = نِنْسُنُنْ = نِنْسُمُنْ = امراة الحُسن، امرأة كرم النسل
نِسّون = نِنسون = مِسّون -> ميسون = حسنة القد والوجه
نجل = سعة، امتلاء، نسل، كرم النسل
نِنْ نُجل = نِنْجُل = نجلاء = الواسعة العينين الجميلة (مثل غزالة)، الكريمة النسل

"النِّسْوةُ والنُّسْوة، بالكسر والضم ، والنِّساء والنِّسْوانُ والنُّسْوان: جمع المرأَة من غير لفظه، كما يقال خِلفةٌ ومَخاضٌ وذلك وأُولئك والنِّسُونَ (* قوله «والنسون» كذا ضبط في الأصل والمحكم أَيضاً، وضبط في النسخة التي بأيدينا من القاموس بكسر فسكون ففتح.)"
" أبو عمرو: المَسْنُ المُجون. يقال: مَسَنَ فلان ومَجَنَ بمعنى واحد. ومَيْسونُ: اسم إمرأَة (قوله «وميسون اسم إمرأة» أصل الميسون الحسن القد والوجه، عن أبي عمرو قاله في التكملة)."
"وأَرضٌ سَمِينة: جَيِّدة التُّرْب قليلة الحجارة قوية على ترشيح النبت. وقيل: معنى يَتَسَمَّنُون يحبون التَّوَسُّعَ في المَآكل والمَشارِب، وهي أَسباب السِّمَنِ. وفي حديث آخر: ويَظْهَرُ فيهم السِّمَنُ. وأَسْمَنَ القومُ: سَمِنَتْ مواشيهم ونَعَمُهم، فهم مُسْمِنون. وفي التهذيب: السُّمْنة دواء تُسَمَّن به المرأَةُ. والسَّمّانُ: أَصْباغ يُزَخْرَفُ بها، اسم كالجَبّان. والسَّمْنُ: سِلاءُ اللَّبَنِ. والسَّمْنُ: سِلاءُ الزُّبْد، والسَّمْنُ للبقر، وقد يكون للمِعْزَى؛"
"وروي عن الفراء: السِّنُّ الأكل الشديد. وسَنَّنَ المَنْطِقَ: حَسَّنه فكأَنه صقَله وزينه؛ والسُّنَّة: الوجه لصَقالتِه ومَلاسته، وقيل: هو حُرُّ الوجه، وقيل: دائرته. وقيل: الصُّورة، وقيل: الجبهة والجبينان، وكله من الصَّقالة والأَسالة. ورجل مسنون الوجه: حَسَنُه سهْله؛ عن اللحياني. وسُنَّة الوجه: دوائره. وسُنَّةُ الوجه: صُورته؛ والسُّنَّة: السيرة، حسنة كانت أَو قبيحة؛ والسُّنَّة: الطبيعة؛ وسُنَّت الأَرض فهي مَسنونة وسَنِينٌ إذا أُكل نباتها؛"
"وأَسِنَ لا غير: استدارَ رأْسُه من ريح تُصيبه. والأُسُن: بقيَّة الشحم القديم. وسَمِنت على أُسُنٍ أَي على أَثارَةَ شحم قديم كان قبل ذلك. أَبو عمرو: تأَسَّنَ الرجلُ أَباه إذا أَخذ أَخْلاقَه؛ يقال: هو على آسانٍ من أَبيه أَي على شَمائلَ من أَبيه، وأَخْلاقٍ من أَبيه، واحدُها أُسُنٌ مثل خُلُقٍ وأَخلاق؛ وقال ابن الأَعرابي: الأُسُنُ الشبَهُ، وجمعُه آسانٌ؛"
"والنَّسِيمُ: الريح الطيبة. يقال: نَسَمت الريحُ نسيماً ونَسَماناً. والنَّيْسَمُ: كالنسيم، نَسَم يَنْسِمُ نَسْماً ونَسِيماً ونَسَماناً. والنَّسَمُ كالنفَس، ويقال: نَسَّمْتُ نَسَمة إِذا أَحْيَيْتَها أَو أَعْتَقْتَها. ونَسَمَ الشيءُ ونَسِمَ نَسَماً: تغيَّر، وخص بعضهم به الدُّهن. والنَّسَمُ: ريحُ اللبَن والدسَم. وقال بعضهم: النَّسَمة الخَلْقُ، يكون ذلك للصغير والكبير والدوابِّ وغيرها ولكل من كان في جوفِه رُوحٌ حتى قالوا للطير؛"
"النَّجْل: النَّسْل. والمِنْجَل الرجل الكثير الأَولاد، والناجِلُ: الكريم النَّجْل. وفي حديث الزبير: عينين نَجْلاوَيْن؛ عين نجلاء أَي واسعة."
"والجَوْل: الوَعِل المُسِنُّ؛ عن ابن الأَعرابي، والجمع أَجْوال."
"نَيْسان: الشَّهْرُ السّابِعُ من الشُّهُورِ بالرُّوْمِيَّة."

<u>Therefore:</u>
Ninsun = Ninsunun = Ninsumun = NIN.GUL = goddess of beauty; goddess of good progeny
Rimat-Ninsun = the gazelle of beauty

نِنْسُنْ = نِنْسُنُنْ = نِنْسُمُنْ= نِنْجُل = آلهة الحُسن، آلهة كرم النسل

ريمة ننسون = غزالة الحُسن

<u>Author's Notes:</u> According to the deciphering tools of Assyriology, the name *Ninsun* means "Lady of the wild cows" or "Lady Wild-cow". This meaning does not only make no sense, but it also confuses her alternative name/title *Rimat-Ninsun*. If one would accept the current meaning, then *Rimat-Ninsun* should be translated "Wild-cow Lady Wild-cow", a complete non-sense!

19. dNinurta (*also* dNimurta)

<u>Wikipedia:</u>
Ninurta was a Sumerian and the Akkadian god of hunting and war. He was worshipped in Babylonia and Assyria and in Lagash he was identified with the city god Ningirsu. In older transliteration the name is rendered Ninib and Ninip, and in early commentary he was sometimes portrayed as a solar deity. A number of scholars have suggested that either the god Ninurta or the Assyrian king bearing his name (Tukulti-Ninurta I) was the inspiration for the Biblical character Nimrod.

<u>Mythology Dictionary:</u>
The Sumerian war-god, god of farming, floods, and wind. Son of Enlil and Ninlil or Ninmah. Son of Inanna, some say. Consort of Gula. When Zu stole the Tablets of Destiny from Enlil, Belet-Ili gave birth to Ninurta and sent him to recapture the Tablets. After a long battle, he killed Zu and returned the Tablets to Enlil. He fought the demon Asag with huge stones which he later used to make mountains to hold back the flood-waters of Kur. He has a magic weapon known as Sarur and a doubleedged scimitar. Some say that these weapons, Sarur and Sargaz, were cyclones which he controlled. In some accounts, he is the same as Ninib. Occasionally identified as Ninurta, Nimurta, Nimurta, Ninurta, Nin Ur, Nin Ur, Ninurta, Ninurash, Ninurash, Ninurta, Sharuk, Sharuk or Sarur.

<u>From Arabic references and grammar, and using al-Jibouri rules:</u>
nur = fire, white light
nar = fire, war
nin-urta = nin-warata = niwwarata = niwwurah = one who make fire, war, and battle
nim-urtu = nim-waratu = nim-warah = one who makes war and battle; one who has hate and anger

النُّورُ = النار، النور، اللون الابيض
النار = الحرب
النُّورَةُ = النِنْورَةُ = الذي يضرم النارُ ويقيم الحرب
نَمَرَ = تَنَمّرَ = غضب، تنكر، اقام الحرب والقتل
النِمْوَرة = الذي يقيم الحرب ويرتكب القتل

"والنُّورُ الضياء. والنار: معروفة أُنثى، وهي من الواو لأَن تصغيرها نُوَيْرَةٌ. وانْتارَ من النُّورَةِ، قال: ولا يقال تَنَوَّرَ إِلا عند إِبصار النار. والنَّوْرُ والنَّوْرَةُ، جميعاً: الزَّهْر، وقيل: النَّوْرُ الأَبيض والزهر الأَصفر وذلك أَنه يبيضُّ ثم يصفر، وجمع النَّوْر أَنوارٌالتهذيب: والنُّورَةُ من الحجر الذي يحرق ويُسَوَّى منه الكِلْسُ ويحلق به شعر العانة. ونارُ الحرب ونائِرَتُها: شَرُّها وهَيْجها."
"نمر: النون والميم والراء أصلانِ: أحدهما لونٌ من الألوان، والآخر يدلُّ على نُجوعِ شراب.فالأوَّل النَّمِر، معروف، من اختلاط السَّواد والبياض في لونِه، غير أنَّ البياضَ أكثر. ونَمَّرَ وجهَه أي غَيَّره وعَبَّسَه. يقال: لبس فلان لفلان جلدَ النَّمِرِ إذا تنكر له، قال: وكانت ملوك العرب إذا جلست لقتل إنسان لبست جلود النمر ثم أَمرت بقتل من تريد قتله. وفي حديث الحُدَيْبِية: قد لبسوا لك جُلودَ النُّمورِ؛ هو كناية عن شدة الحقد والغضب تشبيهاً بأَخْلاقِ النَّمِر وشَراسَتِه."

Therefore:
Ninurta = god of war and fire

نِنُورَةُ = إله الحرب والنار

20. ᵈNissaba (*also* ᵈNidaba)

Mythology Dictionary:
A Sumerian goddess of wisdom and writing. Daughter of An. In some accounts she is equated with Ninlil. On occassion, known as Nissaba, Nisaba or Nisaba.

Ancient Mesopotamian Gods and Goddesses:
The goddess' name is first attested in the Ur archaic texts as ᵈNAGA (in later times ᵈŠE.NAGA). The Akkadian reading of this name is uncertain. The readings Nis(s)aba (traditional) and Nidaba are primarily based on Akkadian pronunciation columns in lexical texts where writings such as *ni-is-sà-ba/ni-da-ba* are encountered. The reading Nidaba is preferred here. Nanibgal and Nun-baršegunu ("Lady whose body is the flecked barley") are alternative names of the same goddess. The former appears mainly as a praising epithet, whilst the latter is used essentially in agricultural contexts.

Written forms:
Nis/daba: ᵈnis/daba(ŠE.NAGA), ᵈnís/daba(NAGA)
Nanibgal: ᵈnanibgal(AN.NAGA), ᵈnánibgal(AN.ŠE.NAGA)
Nubaršegunu: ᵈnun-bar-še-gu-nu, ᵈnun-bar-še-gùn-nu

Normalized forms:
Nisaba, Nissaba, Nidaba, Nanibgal, Nunbaršegunu.

From references of Arabic and the Assyriology method, and using al-Jibouri rules:
nassab = nashshab = naddab = widely knowledgeable one who knows origins; one who throw arrows and spears; one who deals with arrows and spears and their lookalikes: grain spikes

النسّاب = النشّاب = الندّاب = الحكيم واسع العلم الذي يقتفي الاثر والاصل؛ الذي يرشق ويرمي السهام او الرماح؛ الذي يتعامل مع السهام او الرماح واشباهها كسنابل الحبوب

"ونَسَبْتُ فُلاناً إِلى أَبيه أَنْسُبه وأَنْسِبُهُ نَسْباً إِذا رَفَعْتَ في نَسَبه إِلى جَدِّه الأَكبر. الجوهري: نَسَبْتُ الرجلَ أَنْسبُه، بالضم، نِسْبةً ونَسْباً إِذا ذَكَرْتَ نَسَبه، وانْتَسَبَ إِلى أَبيه أَي اعْتَزَى. ورجل نَسِيبٌ مَنْسُوب: ذو حَسَبٍ ونَسَبٍ."
"عن ابن الأَعرابي وحده. نشب: نَشِبَ الشيءُ في الشيءِ، بالكسر، نَشَباً ونُشوباً ونُشْبةً: لم يَنْفُذْ؛ والنُّشَّابُ: النَّبْلُ، واحدتُه نُشَّابة. والنُّشَّابُ: السِّهامُ. والنُّشَبةُ من الرجال: الذي إِذا نَشِبَ بشيءٍ، لم يَكَدْ يُفارِقُه. الجوهري: نَشِبَ الشيءُ في الشيءِ، بالكسر، نُشوباً أَي عَلِقَ فيه؛ وأَنْشَبْتُه أَنا فيه أَي أَعْلَقْتُه، فانْتَشَبَ؛"
"ندب: النون والدال والباء ثلاثُ كلماتٍ: أحداها الأثَر، والنَّدْب الفَرَس الماضي. وعندنا أنّ النَّدْبَ في الأمر قريبٌ من هذا؛ لأنَّ الفقهاء يقولون: إنَّ النَّدْب ما ليس بفرض. ونَدَبَ الميتَ أي بكى عليه، وعَدَّدَ مَحاسِنَه، يَنْدُبه نَدْباً؛ وتقول: رَمَيْنا نَدَباً أي رَشْقاً؛ ونَدَبْنا يومُ كذا أي يومُ انْتِدابِنا للرَّمْي."

Therefore:
Nissaba = Niddaba = Goddess grains of wisdom

21. dŠakkan (*also* dšumuqan)

Wikipedia:
Šumugan (Shumugan, Šumuqan, Šakkan, Šamkan, Amakandu) is, in Sumerian mythology a god of the river plains. In creation myth he is given charge by the god Enki over the flat alluvial lands of southern Mesopotamia. He is also known as a god of cattle who dwells in the court of the underworld goddess Ereshkigal. Šumugan's father is Shamash, the sun god, and he may derive from the similar god Lahar.

From Arabic references:
šá-kkan = šumu-qan = šumu-gan = šam-kan = of qan = of cattles, of underground waters
ذا كَنْ = ذُمُ قَنْ = ذَم قَنْ = ذا المواشي، ذا ماء باطن الارض

"والقِنْقِنُ والقُناقِنُ، بالضم: البصير بالماء تحت الأَرض، وهو الدليل الهادي والبَصيرُ بالماء في حَفْرِ القُنِيِّ، والجمع القَناقِنُ، بالفتح. قال ابن الأَعرابي: القُناقِنُ البصير بجرّ المياه واستخراجها، وجمعها قَناقِنُ؛ قَنَوْت الشيء قُنُوًّا وقُنْواناً واقْتَنَيْتُه: كسبته. وله غنم قِنْوة وقُنْوة أَي خالصة له ثابتة عليه، والكلمة واوية ويائية. وقَنَوْت العنزَ: اتخذتها للحلبَ. وفي الحديث: أَنه نَهى عن ذبْح قَنِيّ الغَنم. قال أَبو موسى: هي التي تُقْتَنَى للدرّ والولد، واحدتها قُنْوَة وقِنْوة، بالضم والكسر، وقِنْية بالياء أَيضاً. يقال: هي غنم قُنْوة وقِنْية. وقال الزمخشري: القَنِيُّ والقَنِيَّةُ ما اقْتُني من شاة أَو ناقة، فجعله واحداً كأَنه فعيلَ بمعنى مفعول، قال: وهو الصحيح، والشاة، قَنِيَّةٌ، فإِن كان جعل القَنيّ جنساً للقَنِيّةِ فيجوز، وأَما فُعْلة وفِعْلة فلم يجمعا على فَعِيل. وقَنيُّ الغَنم: ما يتخذ منها للولد أَو اللبن. الجوهري: قنوت الغنم وغيرها قِنْوة وقُنْوة وقَنيت أَيضاً قِنْية وقُنْية إذا اقتنيتها لنفسك لا للتجارة؛ وتقول العرب: من أُعْطِيَ مائة من المَعز فقد أُعطي القِنى، ومن أُعطي مائة من الضأْن فقد أُعطِيَ الغِنى، ومن أُعطي مائة من الإبل فقد أُعطِي المُنَى. والقِنى: الرِّضا."

Therefore:
Šákkan = Šumuqan = Šumugan = Šamkan = god of cattles and underground water
ذقّان = ذَكّان = ذَمْكان = ذُمُقان = ذُمُجان = إله المواشي ومياه باطن الارض

22. dSiduri (*also* fsa-bit)

Wikipedia:
Siduri is a character in the Epic of Gilgamesh. She is an "alewife", a wise female divinity associated with fermentation. In the earlier Old Babylonian version of the Epic, she attempts to dissuade Gilgamesh in his quest for immortality, urging him to be content with the simple pleasures of life. She dwells by the sea at the ends of the earth. Siduri's name means "young woman" in Hurrian, and may be an epithet of Ishtar. Hurrian: ancient people, originally from Armenia, who settled in Syria and northern Mesopotamia during the 3rd–2nd millennia BC and were later absorbed by the Hittites and Assyrian
Mythology Dictionary:
A Babylonian goddess of brewing. A manifestation of Ishtar. She tried to persuade Gilgamesh to give up his search for immortality in favour of earthly pleasures and, when he refused, told him how to find Utnapishtim. She is depicted as a serpent. At times, called Siduri, Sabatu, Sabatu, Sabitu, Sabitu, Shiduri, Shiduri, Shidduri, Shidduri, Siduru, Siduru, Sithapishtim, Sithapishtim, Shidurri, Shidurri, Egyptian Tenemet, Egyptian Tenemet, Sitnapishtim or Sitnapishtim.

From Arabic references:
sadara = to circle
siddūr = siduri = one who circulates (stir)
sadru = dizziness
dūr; dār = to circle
dārah = wine making container
ši-duri = The woman who circulates (stirs, mixes) to make wine/beer = alewife

saba'a = to sell wine
saba' = wine
sabbā' (sabbi'ah (f.)) = wine maker/seller
sa-bit = = wine/beer maker/seller woman

سَدر = دار، خلط
الدارة = وعاء صنع الخمر
سبيئة = السبأ = الخمر
سبُاء = خمار
السِدّور = الدوّارة، الخلّاطة = التي تخلط وتدوّر في اناء لتصنع الخمر = الخمّارة
السَـبّـيـئةُ = الخمّارة

"السِّدْرُ: شجر النبق، واحدتها سِدْرَة وجمعها سِدْراتٌ وسِدِراتٌ وسِدَرٌ وسُدورٌ. وفي الحديث: الذي يَسْدَرُ في البحر كالمتشحط في دمه؛ السَّدَرُ، بالتحريك:
كالدُّوارِ، وهو كثيراً ما يَعْرِض لراكب البحر. وأَنشد ثعلب: وكأَنَّ بِرقع، والملائك تحتها، سدر، تواكله قوائم أَربع قال: سدر يَدُورُ. وقوله تعالى: عند
سِدْرَةِ المُنْتَهى؛ قال الليث: زعم إِنها سدرة في السماء السابعة لا يجاوزها مَلَك ولا نبي وقد أَظلت الماءَ والجنةَ، قال: ويجمع على ما تقدم. وفي حديث
الإِسْراءِ: ثم رُفِعْتُ إِلى سِدرَةِ المُنْتَهَى؛ قال ابن الأَثير: سدرةُ المنتهى في أَقصى الجنة إِليها يَنْتَهِي عِلْمُ الأَوَّلين والآخرين ولا يتعدّاها."
"سَبَأَ الخَمْرَ يَسْبَؤُها سَبْأً وسِباءً ومَسْبَأً واستَبَأَها: شَراها. ومنه سميت الخمر سَبِيئةً. والسَّبَّاءُ بَيَّاعُها. وهي السِّباءُ والسَّبِيئةُ، ويسمى الخَمَّار سَبَّاءً. ابن
الأَنباري: حكى الكسائي: السَّبَأُ الخَمْرُ، التهذيب: السُّبْأَةُ: السَّفَر البعيد"
"والنجم إذا هوى[1] ما ضل صاحبكم وما غوى[2] وما ينطق عن الهوى[3] إن هو إلا وحي يوحى[4] علمه شديد القوى[5] ذو مرة فاستوى[6] وهو بالأفق
الأعلى[7] ثم دنا فتدلى[8] فكان قاب قوسين أو أدنى[9] فأوحى إلى عبده ما أوحى[10] ما كذب الفؤاد ما رأى[11] أفتمارونه على ما يرى[12] ولقد رآه نزلة
أخرى[13] عند سدرة المنتهى[14] عندها جنة المأوى[17] إذ يغشى السدرة ما يغشى[16] ما زاغ البصر وما طغى[17] لقد رأى من آيات ربه الكبرى[18]"
(قرآن: 53: 1- 18)

<u>Therefore:</u>
Siduri = The alewife goddess

سِدوري = الآلهة الخمّارة

<u>Author's Notes:</u> Curiously, the name, location, and role of the goddess *Siduri* is too identical to that of *Sidrat al-Muntaha* سِدْرَةِ المُنْتَهى (*Sidrah* of the extreme limit or end) that was mentioned in the Quran. Islamic scholars suggested it was a Lote tree (Arabic and Aramaic *nubk tree*) located by the waters at the far end of heaven in the seventh sky that no one, including kings or prophets, can ever pass. The goddess *Siduri*, according to the Epic of Gilgamesh is an alewife residing at the far end of earth by a sea that no one can pass. It can not be a coincidence that both *Sidrah* and *Siduri* have feminine Arabic names with identical meaning. It can not be a coincidence that both were residing by waters at the far edge of their universe and were assigned the task of guarding an access gate to gods' territories!

The goddess *Siduri* is another remarkable example of an old Mesopotamian character finding its way as a new character or symbol in the monotheistic religions. According to the Muslims, Prophet Muhammad was raised up to this *Sidrah* tree (Arabic "*nubk*") during his midnight journey from Mecca to Jerusalem (*al-Isrā'*). And according to the Christians, the roman soldiers "put together a garland of flexible boughs (Aramaic "*nubk*") which were bushes filled with long sharp thorns, created a crown of thorns and placed it upon Jesus's head" during his crucifixion. Hence the name Christ's thorn tree.

23. ᵈSin (*also* ᵈEN.ZU, ᵈ30)

<u>*Wikipedia:*</u>
The Semitic moon god Su'en/Sin is in origin a separate deity from Sumerian Nanna, but from the Akkadian Empire period the two undergo syncretization and are identified. The occasional Assyrian spelling of ᵈNANNA-ar ᵈSu'en-e is due to association with Akkadian na-an-na-ru "illuminator, lamp", an epitheton of the moon god. The name of the Assyrian moon god Su'en/Sîn is usually spelled as ᵈEN.ZU, or simply with the numeral 30,

<u>*Ancient Mesopotamian Gods and Goddesses:*</u>

<u>Name and Spellings</u>
Su'en/Sin**:** first attested at Ebla from ca. 2400 BCE; spelled ᵈEN.ZU, but read Su'en in Sumerian names, and Sin in Akkadian names. From the Old Babylonian period onward: ⁽ᵈ⁾30, clearly related to the close connection between the moon and the month.

<u>Written forms:</u>
Su'en/Sin: ᵈEN.ZU, ⁽ᵈ⁾30

<u>Normalized forms:</u>
Nanna, Su'en, Sin, Suen, Dilimbabbar, Ashimbabbar (obsolete)

<u>From Arabic references and the Assyriology method:</u>
Su'en/Sin = face, beauty, image, face circle
ZU = shape, appearance, image

سِنْ = سؤن = حُسن، وجه، صورة، دائرة الوجه
زيُّ = هيئة، منظر، زي، حُسن

"وسَنَّنَ المَنْطِقَ: حَسَّنه فكأَنه صقَله وزينه؛ والسُّنَّة: الوجه لصَقالتِه ومَلاسته، وقيل: هو حُرُّ الوجه، وقيل: دائرته. وسُنَّة الوجه: دوائره. وسُنَّةُ الوجه: صُورته؛ والمَسْنون: المُصَوَّرُ. ويقال: امْضِ على سَنَنِك وسُنَنِك أي على وجهك. وتَسَنَّنَ الرجلُ في عَدْوِه واسْتَنَّ: مضى على وجهه؛"
"ومن الباب الزِّيّ: حُسْن الهيئة. والزِّيُّ: اللِّباسُ والهَيْئَة، وأَصله زِوْيٌ، تقول منه: زَيَّيْته، والقياس زَوَّيْتُه. ويقال الزِّيُّ الشارَةُ والهَيْئَةُ؛ قال الراجز: ما أَنا بالبَصْرة بالبَصْرِيِّ، ولا شبيه زِيُّهم بزِيِّي وقرئ قوله تعالى: هُمْ أَحْسَنُ أَثاثاً وزِيّاً؛ بالزاي والراء. قال الفراء: من قَرأَ وزِيّاً فالزِّيُّ الهيئة والمَنْظر، والعرب تقول قد زَيَّيْتُ الجارِيةَ أَي زَيَّنتُها وهَيَّأْتها. وقال الليث: يقال تَزَيّاً فلان بزِيٍّ حسن، وقد زَيَّيْته تزِيَّةً."

<u>Therefore:</u>
Sin =
EN.ZU = of the beautiful face circle (moon)

سن = اله الوجه المدور الحسن (القمر)
عن زيو = الإله سيد (صاحب) الوجه المدور الحسن (القمر)

24. ᵈSullat

<u>*Gilgamesh: The New Translation*</u>:
Sullat (god of despoilment (looting))

<u>From Arabic references:</u>
salla = istalla = stole
istilāb = theft
šúllat = one who steals

سلّ = استل = سرق، سلب
استلاب = سرقة

"السَّلُّ: انتزاعُ الشيء. وانْسَلَّ فلان من بين القوم يَعْدو إِذا خرج في خُفْيَة يَعْدُو. والسَّلَّة والإسلال: السَّرقة."

<u>Therefore:</u>
Sullat = šúllat = god of looting and thievery

سلّات = اله السلب والنهب

25. ᵈUTU (*also* ᵈUTU.È, ᵈUTU.È.A, ᵈŠamaš)

<u>*Ancient Mesopotamian Gods and Goddesses:*</u>
Šamaš the all-seeing, Mesopotamian sun god, who was associated with life, justice, divination and the netherworld. Šamaš (Sumerian Utu) is the god of the sun. He brings light and warmth to the land, allowing plants and crops to grow. At sunrise Šamaš was known to emerge from his underground sleeping chamber and take a daily path across the skies. As the sun fills the entire sky with light, Šamaš oversaw everything that occurred during the daytime. He thus became the god of truth, judgements and justice. Šamaš also played a role in treaties, oaths and business transactions, as he could see through deceit and duplicity. As a defender of justice, the sun god also had a warrior aspect. Utu's name is spelled ᵈutu in Sumerian, and Šamaš's name retains this logogram in Akkadian. The name Šamaš is a variant form of the Akkadian word for sun, *šamšu* (compare Arabic *šams*, Hebrew *šemeš*).

<u>First-millennium written forms include</u>:
20; ᵈ20; ᵈUTU-KAM; ᵈUTU$^{-ši}$; ᵈUTU$^{-šu}{}_{2}$; ᵈša$_2$-maš; ᵈša$_3$-maš$_2$; ᵈša$_2$-maš; šu-ša$_2$-na-ku.

<u>Normalised forms include:</u>
Šamaš, Šamši, Šamšu

<u>From references of Arabic and the Assyriology method, and using al-Jibouri rules:</u>
tu = dhu; utu = udhu = wutu = wudhu = sun; light; cleaness and clarity
e = È = È.A = ḫıyi = ḫiya = to live; to rise
utu'e = UTU + È = UTU + È.A = sunrise

ت = ض؛ أُتؤ، وتؤ = أُضؤ، وضؤ = أُضو، وضو = الضوء، الشمس، الحسن والنضافة، الوضوح
حي = حيا = الحياة، البزوغ، البقاء
أُتُؤح، وتُؤحِ = أُضُؤح، وضؤحِ = أُضُح، وضحِ = ارتفاع النهار، بزوغ الشمس والضياء

"الضَّوءُ والضُّوءُ، بالضم، معروف: الضِّياءُ، وجمعه أَضْواءٌ. وهو الضِّواءُ والضِّياءُ. التهذيب، الليث: الضَّوْءُ والضِّياءُ: ما أضاءَ لك. وقد ضاءَتِ النارُ وضاءَ الشيءُ يَضُوءُ ضَوْءاً وضُوءاً وأَضاءَ يُضِيءُ. وأَضَاءَتْه، يَتعدَّى ولا يَتعدَّى. أَبو عبيد: أَضاءَتِ النارُ وأَضاءَها غيرُها، وهو الضَّوْءُ والضُّوءُ، وأَمَّا

الضِّياء، فلا همز في يائه. وأَضاءَه له واسْتَضَأْتُ به. الوَضَاءَةُ: الحُسنُ والنظافة، تقول: وَضُؤَ الرجُل: أي صار وَضِيئاً، والمرأة وَضِيْئة. ويقال: تَوَضَّأْتُ أَتَوَضَّأُ تَوَضُّؤاً ووُضُوءاً، وأَصل الكلمة من الوضاءة، وهي الحُسْنُ. والوَضاءة الحُسْنُ والنَّظافةُ. وقد وَضُؤَ يَوْضُؤُ وَضَاءة، بالفتح والمدّ: صار وَضِيئاً، فهو وَضِيءٌ من قَوْم أَوْضِياءَ، وَوِضَاءٍ ووُضَّاءٍ. وفي حديث عائشة: لَقَلَّما كانتِ امرأَةٌ وَضِيئةٌ عند رجل يُحِبُّها. الوَضَاءة: الحُسْنُ والبَهْجةُ. يقال وَضُؤَتْ، فهي وَضِيئةٌ."

"الوَضَحُ: بياضُ الصبح والقمرُ والبَرَصُ والغرةُ والتحجيلُ في القوائم وغير ذلك من الأَلوان. التهذيب: الوَضَحُ بياض الصُّبْح؛ الضَّحْوُ والضَّحْوَةُ والضَّحِيَّةُ على مثال العَشِيَّة: ارْتِفاعُ النهار. والضَّحاءُ، ممدودٌ، إِذا امْتَدَّ النهارُ وكرَبَ أَن يَنْتَصِفَ؛ قال الله تعالى: والشمسِ وضُحاها؛ قال الفراء: ضُحاها نَهارُها، وكذلك قوله: والضُّحى واللَّيْلِ إِذا سَجا؛ هو النهارُ كُلُّه؛ قال الزَّجاج: وضُحاها وضِيائها. والضُّحى: حينَ تَطْلُعُ الشَّمْسُ فَيَصْفو ضَوْءُها. والضَّحاء: ارْتِفاعُ الشَّمْس الأَعلى. والضُّحى، مقصورة مؤَنثة: وذلك حينَ تُشْرِقُ الشَّمْسُ."

"ضحي: الضاد والحاء والحرف المعتل أصلٌ صحيحٌ واحدٌ يدلُّ على بُروز الشيء. فالضَّحَاء: امتداد النَّهار، وذلك هو الوقت البارز المنكشف. قال: ويقال ضحِيَ الرَّجلُ يَضْحَى، إذا تعرَّضَ للشَّمْس، وضَحَى مثْلُهُ. ويقال اضْحَ يا زيد، أي ابرُزْ للشَّمْس."

"ويوم شامسٌ وقد شَمَس يَشْمِسُ شُموساً أَي ذُو ضِحٍّ نهارُه كله، وشَمَس يومُنا يَشْمِسُ إِذا كان ذا شمس. ويوم شامِسٌ: واضِحٌ، الليث: الشمس عَيْنُ الضِّحِّ؛ قال: أَراد أَن الشمس هو العين التي في السماء تجري في الفَلَكِ وأَن الضِّح ضَوْءُه الذي يَشْرِقُ على وجه الأَرض."

"قال: وسأَلت أَبا عليّ عن فسادِه، فقال: العلة أَن أَصل البدل في الحروف إِنما هو فيما تقارب منها، وذلك نحو الدال والطاء، والتاء والظاء، والذال والثاء، والهاء والهمزة، والميم والنون، وغير ذلك مما تدانت مخارجه."

"والحَيُّ من كل شيء: نقيضُ الميت، والجمع أَحْياء. وقوله تعالى: رَبَّنا أَمَتَّنا اثْنَتَيْن وأَحْيَيْتَنا اثنتين؛ أَراد خَلَقْتنا أَمواتاً ثم أَحْيَيْتَنا ثم أَمَتَّنا بعدُ ثم بَعَثْتَنا بعد الموت حقال الأَصمعي: أَنشد بعضُ العرب بيتَ ذي الرمة: فقُلْتُ له: ارْفَعْها إِليكَ وحايِهَا برُوحِكَ، واقْتَتْه لها قِيتَةً قَدْرا وقال أَبو حنيفة: حَيَّت النار تَحَيُّ حياة، فهي حَيَّة، كما تقول ماتَتْ، فهي ميتة؛ وقال أَبو حنيفة: أُحْيِيَت الأَرض إِذا اسْتُخْرِجَت. وأَحْيا الله الأَرضَ: أَخرج فيها النبات. وحَيَّا الخَمْسين: دنا منها؛ عن ابن الأَعرابي. والحَيَّةُ: الحَنَشُ المعروف، اشتقاقه من الحَياة في قول بعضهم؛ قال سيبويه: والدليل على ذلك قول العرب في الإِضافة إِلى حَيَّةَ بن بَهْدَلة حَيَوِيٌّ، فلو كان من الواو لكان حَوَوِيّ كقولك في الإِضافة إِلى لَيَّة لَوَوِيٌّ."

<u>Therefore:</u>
UTU = god of Sun; god of light and clarity

أُتو = أضو = إله الشمس، إله الضوء والوضوح

26. mdSîn-Lēqi-Unninni

dSin = God of the moon

<u>From references of Arabic and the Assyriology method:</u>
lēqi = to find, to receive, to accept
unninni= prayer, compassion

لقي = يلقي، يحصل
أنن = شكوى، أنين

"وكلُّ شيءٍ استقبل شيئاً أَو صادفه فقد لقِيَه من الأَشياء كلها. وتَلَقَّاه أَي استقبله. وفلان يَتَلَقَّى فلاناً أَي يَسْتَقْبِله. والرجل يُلَقَّى الكلام أَي يُلَقَّنه. وقوله تعالى: إِذ تَلَقَّوْنَه بأَلسنتكم؛ أَي يأْخذ بعض عن بعض."
"أَنَّ الرجلُ من الوجع يَئِنُّ أَنيناً ورجل أَنّانٌ وأُنانٌ وأُنَنةٌ: كثيرُ الأَنين، وقيل: الأُنَنةُ الكثيرُ الكلام والبَثِّ والشَّكْوَى"

<u>Therefore:</u>
mdSîn-lēqi-unninni's = *man of* the god Sîn (Moon God) who accepts prayers
م دنجر سِنْ لقي أنَنِ = رجل إله القمر الذي يستقبل الشكوى (الصلاة)

<u>Author's Notes:</u> Scholars believe *mdSîn-Lēqi-Unninni* was a name of a person based on the following entry from a Neo-Assyrian list:

IŠKAR dGIŠ-gím-maš ša pi-i md30-le-qi-un-nin-ni ....
Translated: Series of Gilgamesh from the mouth of mdSîn-le-qi-un-nin-ni ...

They believe the name ^{md}*Sîn-lēqi-unninni*'s means "Sîn (^{d}30: the Moon God) is one who accepts a prayer", or, less probably, if transliterated *Sîn-liqe-unninni*, it means "O Sîn! Accept my prayer". According to W.G. Lambert, in the above line, "the term *ša pi-i* signifies authorship".*

However, such name would be peculiar, and would not conform to the styles of other Mesopotamian names, as seen in this section. The letters "md" before the name could mean he was both human and god, like Gilgamesh, who was referred to ^{md}GIŠ-TUK at some point. According to my possible reading of the md before the title ^{md}GIŠ-TUK, the name ^{md}Sîn-lēqi-unninni would then be a title meaning "man of the god Sîn (Moon God) who accepts prayers".

27. ^{m}pu-zu-ur-^{d}KUR.GAL (*also* puzur-^{d}Amurri)

KUR.GAL = amurri = Enlil

Therefore:
puzur-KUR.GAL = puzur-amurri = the defector from Enlil = Enlil's defector

فُزُرْ كُرجَل = فُرُزْ كُرجَل = فزر عَمُرِّ = فرز عَمُرّ = المنشق عن إنليل = منشق إنليل

28. ^{m}Ubara-^{d}tutu (*also* Ubar-tutu)

Wikipedia:
Ubara-tutu (or Ubartutu) of Shuruppak was the last antediluvian king of Sumer. He was said to have reigned for 18,600 years. Ubaratutu lived until the deluge swept over the land, like Lamech, the father of Noah.

^{m}u-bar-^{d}tu-tu (^{m}ubara-^{d}tu-tu). The Epic of Gilgamesh labels Atrahasis (Atrahasis) as the son of Ubara-Tutu, king of Shuruppak, on tablet XI, 'Gilgamesh spoke to Utnapishtim, the Faraway... O man of Shuruppak, son of Ubara-Tutu'. The Instructions of Shuruppak instead label Atrahasis (under the name Ziusudra) as the son of the eponymous Shuruppak, who himself is labelled as the son of Ubara-Tutu. At this point we are left with two possible fathers: Ubara-Tutu or Shuruppak. Many available tablets comprising The Sumerian King Lists support The Epic of Gilgamesh by omitting Shuruppak as a ruler of Shuruppak. These lists imply an immediate flood after or during the rule of Ubara-Tutu. These lists also make no mention of Atrahasis under any name. However WB-62 lists a different and rather interesting chronology – here Atrahasis is listed as a ruler of Shuruppak and gudug priest, preceded by his father Shuruppak who is in turn preceded by his father Ubara-Tutu. WB-62 would therefore lend support to The Instructions of Shuruppak and is peculiar in that it mentions both Shuruppak and Atrahasis.

From references of Arabic and the Assyriology method:
ʿUbru = a group of people, tribe
Tutu = name of a person, name of a tribe

عُبْرُ = عُبار = قومُ
توت = اسم شخص، اسم قبيلة
"الليث: لَمَكُ أَبو نوح، ولامَكُ جدُّه، ويقال: نوح بن لَمَك، ويقال: ابن لامَك."

---

* George, A.R. *The Babylonian Gilgamesh Epic: Introduction, critical edition and cuneiform*, page 27.

"وفي حديث ابن عباس: أَن ابن الزبير آثَرَ عَليَّ التُّوَيتَاتِ، والحُمَيْدَاتِ، والأُسامات؛ قال شمر: هم أَحْياءٌ من بني أَسَدٍ: حُمَيْدُ بن أُسامةَ بنِ زُهَيرِ بن الحارث بنِ أَسَدِ ابن عبد العُزَّى بن قُصَيٍّ، وتُوَيتُ بنُ حَبيب بنِ أَسدِ بن عبد العُزَّى بن قُصَيٍّ، وأُسامةُ بنُ زُهير بن الحارث بن أَسَد بن عبد العُزَّى بن قُصَيٍّ."
"ويقال: فلان في ذلك العِبر أَي في ذلك الجانب. وعَبَرْت النهرَ والطريق أَعْبُره عَبْراً وعُبوراً إِذا قطعته من هذا العِبْر إِلى ذلك العِبر. وعبر السَّفَر يعبُره عَبراً: شَقَّة؛ والعُبْر، بالضم: الكثير من كل شيء، وقد غلب على الجماعة من الناس. والعُبْر جماعة القوم؛ هذلية عن كراع. ومجلس عِبْر وعَبْر: كثير الأَهل. وقوم عِبير: كثير. والعُبْرُ قبيلة."

<u>Therefore:</u>
Ubartutu = the tribe of Tutu

عُبَر تُوتُ = قوم او قبيلة توتُ

<u>Author's Notes:</u> According to Western scholars, it was believed that *Ubartutu* have reigned for 18,600 years. This ridiculous number further suggests that Ubar-tutu was not a name of a person, but a dynasty that had ruled for a long time, up to the Deluge period. The fact that various tablets had indicated different names for the father of Ut-napishtim also supports this assumption. In Arabic, it is common to call a descent of group x "son of group x". Islamic scholars identified Noah's father name as *Lamak*. The historical Arabic references identified Tutu as a possible name of a founder of a *Bani Asad* tribe called *al-Tuwaytat*. This would strongly suggest that Noah's father was originally from *Najd*, the heart of Arabia, and the home of the *Bani Asad* tribes.

29. ^{m}Ur-^{d}šánabi (*also* ^{m}Sursunabu, ^{m}Amēl-^{d}Éa, ^{m}Awīl-Ea)

<u>Role Playing in Sumer and Akkad:</u>
Enlil gave to Puzur-Amurri a new name, Uršanabi, to mark immortal life and a new cycle of servitude. Puzur-Amurri oversaw the construction of this vessel that he would have between his hands as the floodwaters rose to drown all he had ever known. Just as he was told, he lied to the other citizens of Šuruppak about the ark, telling them only that his Prince had incurred Enlil's wrath and, in consequence, was heading into exile in a far-away land. This terrible lie haunts Puzur-Amurri to this very day, but not as much of the memory of the days that followed.

<u>A. R. George:</u>
Ur-šanabi (Sursunabu). The ferryman of Ūta-napišti in the Standard Babylonian Epic of Gilgameš. His name is spelled ^{m}Ur-šánabi and ^{m}Ur-^{d}šánabi in first-millennium manuscripts of the epic from Nineveh and Babylonia, but ^{m}Ur-šu-na-be in an early Neo-Assyrian manuscript from Kalḫu. In the Hittite paraphrase of the epic his name occurs as ^{m}(U)-ur-ša-na-bi and ^{d}Ur-ša-na-bi. An Old Babylonian tablet, probably from Sippar, gives his name as Su-ur-su-na-bu, in which initial /s/ is inexplicable. Outside the epic the name appears in a bilingual list of personal names, ^{m}Ur-šánabi! = ^{m}Amēl(lú)-^{d}É-a. Names on the pattern Ur-DN/GN are typical of Sumerian anthroponymy, but the element šánabi "two-thirds" is not, and it is likely that the name U. represents a learned coinage of the late Old Babylonian period, deriving from the common Akkadian name Awīl-Ea "Man of Ea". Another suggestion links the fraction two-thirds with Gilgameš's constitution as "two-thirds god" and takes the name U. to mean "servant of Gilgameš"

<u>From references of Arabic and the Assyriology method:</u>
Ur-šánabi = band or entrance of eternity
Ur-^{d}šánabi = band or entrance of the eternal divine life
Sur-sunabu = wall of eternity = protector of eternal life
Amēl-Éa = Awīl-Ea = Man of Ea

عُرْ سَنَب = سوار او مدخل الابدية
عُرْ الاله سَنَبِ = سوار او مدخل الابدية الالهية (نوح)
سور سَنَبِ = سور الابدية = حامي الابدية
عميل حيا = عويل الاله حيا (آدم) = رجل الاله حيا (آدم)

Therefore:
Ur-^{d}šánabi = Sur-sunabu = the protector of eternity
Ur-šánabi = Ur-^{d}šánabi = protector of the eternal divine life
Amēl-^{d}Éa = Awīl-^{d}Ea = the man of god Éa

Author's Notes: Puzur-Amurri (or Puzur-KURGAL), Enlil's defector, was Ut-napishti's ferryman who oversaw the construction of his ark/ship. As per lines 35-47 of the Epic, the god Ea (Adam) told Ut-napishti (Noah) to tell the people of Šuruppak that he has incurred Enlil's wrath, and therefore he was heading into exile to live with his god Ea in the Abzu. Effectively, Ea had asked Ut-napishti (and Puzur-Amurri) not to inform the people about the upcoming flood. This means Puzur-Amurri was god Ea's collaborator, as it is clearly evidenced by his other names Awīl-Ea, and *^{m}Amēl(lú)-^{d}Éa*, meaning (Ea's man).

After the end of the flood, Ea—not Enlil—granted eternal life to Ut-napishti and his wife according to Line 199 of the epic. The ferryman Puzur-Amurri then took on another role/title after Ut-napishti was placed in the faraway mouth of the rivers and was granted the eternal life. In his new role, he was entrusted by god Ea to protect the secret water way leading to Ut-napishti dwelling. It is clear, therefore, that Puzur-KURGAL was given the title Ur-šanabi (or Sur-sunabu), meaning "the protector of eternity", by Ea—not Enlil— as a reward for both protecting Ut-napishti during the Deluge in the past, and keeping secret the location of his hiding, thereafter.

30. ^{m}Ūta-napišti (*also* ^{m}UD-ZI, ^{m}ut-ZI, Atra-Hasis, Ūtur-napišti, Ziusudra, Tuttu)

Wikipedia:
Atra-Hasis ("exceedingly wise") is the protagonist of an 18th-century BCE Akkadian epic recorded in various versions on clay tablets. The Atra-Hasis tablets include both a creation myth and a flood account, which is one of three surviving Babylonian deluge stories.The name "Atra-Hasis" also appears on one of the Sumerian king lists as king of Shuruppak in the times before a flood. A few general histories can be attributed to the Mesopotamian Atrahasis by ancient sources; these should generally be considered mythology but they do give an insight into the possible origins of the character.

Mythology Dictionary:
Atrahasis, a king of Shurupak. The Babylonian Noah. Son of Ubar-Tutu, some say. Warned by Enki, he survived the flood sent by Enlil in his ship Preserver of Life, saving also his wife, animals, plants and seeds. He was granted immortality by Ea or Enlil. Some accounts refer to two people of this name - one, the survivor of the Sumerian flood, the other said to be the father of Utnapishtim, the survivor of the Babylonian version. Also identified as Atrahasis, Amahasis, Amahasis, Atarhasis, Atarhasis, Atra-chasis, Atra-chasis, Atraharsis, Atraharsis, Atrahis, Atrahis, Atramhasis, Atramhasis, Hasis-Atra, Hasis-Atra, Superwise, Superwise, Utnapishtim, Utnapishtim, Pir-napishtim, Uta-napishtim, Utanapishtim, Utnapishti, Uta-naptishtim, Babylonian Atrahasis, Sumerian Ziusudra, Edjo, Wadjet, Atra-hasis, Atra-hasis, Atrah(ars)is,

Atrah(ars)is, Syrian Ut(a)napishtim, Syrian Ut(a)napishtim, Ziusudra, Ziusudra, Ziudsudda, Ziusuttu, Tut(t)u, Syrian Utnapishtim or Xithuthros.

<u>From references of Arabic and the Assyriology method:</u>

ZI = napišti = life, soul
'Ūta = 'ut = given
ʿUD = 'utur = recurrent, repeated = permanent (eternal)
sudra = cycled = permanent (eternal)
ʿatra = strong, excessive, exceeding
ḫasis = sense
Tuttu = a son of (descendant) Tutu

ذي = ذيت = ذات = نفسُ، حياة
أُتا = عُطا = مؤتى، مُعطى
عُودُ = مُعاد، دائم
أُتُرْ = مُعاد الكرّة، مُدام، دائم
عَتْرا = شديد
حَسِس = حس، احساس

"عادَ إليه يَعودُ عَوْدَةً وعَوْداً: رجع. العَوْدُ: الرُّجوعُ. و العَوْدُ: ثانِي البَدْءِ. والمَعادُ: المصيرُ والمرجعُ. والمُعاوِدَةُ: الرجوع إلى الأمر الأوَّل. وعاوَدَهُ بالمسألة، أي سأله مرة بعد أخرى. والمُعاوِدُ: المُواظِبُ، والبَطَلُ. واسْتَعادَه: سأَله أن يَفْعَلَه ثانياً، وأن يَعودَ. وأعادَه إلى مكانِه: رَجَعَه، وأعاد الكَلامَ: كَرَّرَه."
"وأَتَرْتُ الشيءَ: جئت به تارةً أُخرى أي مَرَّةً بعد مرة؛ قال: ومنه يقال أَتْأَرْتُ النَّظَرَ إِليه أي أَدمته تارةً بَعْدَ تارةٍ. وأَتْأَرتُه بصري: أَتْبَعْته إِياه. والتَّارَةُ: الحين والمَرَّة، أَلفها واو، جَمْعُها تاراتٌ وتِيَرٌ؛ والتَّوْرُ الرسول بين القوم، عربي صحيح؛ ابن الأعرابي: التَّورَةُ الجارية التي تُرسَلُ بين العُشَّاق. أبو عمرو: فلان يُتارُ على أَن يُؤْخَذَ أَي يُدار على أَن يؤْخذ؛
"قال ابن خالويه: النَّفْس الرُّوحُ، والنَّفْس ما يكون به التمييز، والنَّفْس الدم، والنَّفْس الأَخ، والنَّفْس بمعنى عِنْد، والنَّفْس قَدْرُ دَبْغة. ونَفْس الشيء: ذاته؛ والنَّفْس: الجَسَد؛ ويقال للعَيْن نَفَسٌ."
"والإِعْطاء والمُعاطاةُ جميعاً: المُناوَلة، وقد أَعْطاهُ الشيءَ."
"والإِيتاءُ: الإِعْطاء. آتى يُؤَاتي إِيتاءً وآتاهُ إِيتاءً أَي أَعطاه. ويقال: لفلان أَتْوٌ أَي عَطاء. وآتاه الشيءَ أَي أَعطاه إِيَّاه. وفي التنزيل العزيز: وأُوتِيَتْ من كلِّ شيء؛ ورجل مِيتاءٌ: مُجازٍ مِعْطاء."
"وناقةٌ مِعْطارٌ ومُعْطِرٌ: شَديدة؛ وناقةٌ عَطِرَةٌ ومِعطار، أي كريمة."
"عتَرَ الرُّمْحُ وغيره يَعْتِر عَتْراً وعتَراناً: اشتدّ واضطرب واهتز؛ وعَتَر الذكَرُ يَعْتِر عَتْراً وعُتُوراً: اشتدّ إنعاظُه واهتز؛ ورجل مُعَتَّر: غليظٌ كثير اللحم. والعَتَّار: الرجل الشجاع، والفرس القوي على السير، ومن المواضع الوَحْش الخشن؛"
"وأَنشد ثعلب: وكأَنَّ بِرقع، والملائك تحتها، سدر، تواكله قوائم أَربع قال: سدر يَدُورُ."
"وفي حديث ابن عباس: أَن ابن الزبير آثَرَ عَليَّ التُّوَيتَاتِ، والحُمَيْدَاتِ، والأُسامات؛ قال شمر: هم أَحْياءٌ من بني أَسَدٍ: حُمَيْدُ بن أُسامةَ بنِ زُهَيرِ بن الحارث بنِ أَسَدِ ابن عبد العُزَّى بن قُصَيٍّ، وتُوَيتُ بنُ حَبيب بنِ أَسدِ بن عبد العُزَّى بن قُصَيٍّ، وأُسامةُ بنُ زُهير بن الحارث بن أَسَد بن عبد العُزَّى بن قُصَيٍّ."

<u>Therefore:</u>

Ūta-napišti = the life-given one
Ut-ZI = UD-ZI = the life-given one
UD-ZI = one with recurrent (eternal) life; the life-given one
Ūtur-napišti = one with recurrent (eternal) life
Ziu-sudra = one with cycled (eternal) life
Atra-Hasis = one with exceeding (strong) sense
Tuttu = Son of the Tutu (Tuwaytat) tribe

أُتا نَفِستِ = مؤتى (معطى) التفس (الحياة)
أُتْ ذي = مؤتى (معطى) الحياة

عُطْ ذي = مُعطى الحياة
عُدْ ذي = مُعاد (دائم) الحياة
أُتْرْ نَفِستِ = مُدام (دائم) التفس (الحياة)
ذيُ سُدرا = مُدار (ابدي) الحياة
عَتَرا حَسِسْ = شديد (مرهف) الحس
تُتّو = ابن (من قوم) تُويتُ (االتويتات فخد من بني اسد)

<u>Author's Notes:</u> All of the names above are clearly nicknames or titles that were given to Ut-napishti at different periods and occasions, and by different population centers. For example, in the Epic of Gilgamesh, he was only referred to as *Atra-Hasis* (the one with exceeding (strong) sense) *after* god *Ea* (Adam) told the gathering of gods that he did not reveal the secret of the flood to Ut-napishti and that Ut-napishti had *sensed* it himself. As for the name *Tuttu*, this is an adjective of *Tutu* meaning "related to *Tutu*", just as *ʿAllāwī* is an adjective of *ʿAlī* meaning "related to *ʿAlī*", and *Ḫassūn* is an adjective of *Ḫasan* meaning "related to *Ḫasan*".

In fact, the Arabs commonly refer to important personality with several titles at once. This was apparent in the case of Ut-napishti as he was routinely referred to as *ᵐUD-ZI ru-ú-qu*. The second additional word ru-ú-qu (Arabic rūqu روق), which means "the distant" or "the withdrawn", is identical in meaning and grammar to the Arabic word *nūḫu* نوح, or Noah. The title Noah was the preferred title of Ut-napishti in his new monotheistic role, after is "eternal" life status was reduced to few centuries long only. The name Noah is clearly not the first name of the monotheistic prophet, as it's commonly believed, based on bible scholars' claim that Noah was a "masculine proper name, from Hebrew Noah, literally rest". Following are the Arabic derivations of the name Noah:

<u>CAD:</u> anāḫu = tired; troubled; wandering around; depressed
<u>Arabic:</u> aniḫu = tired; troubled; depressed; gone far away; became distant, became resigned
ru-ú-qu = rūqu = distant, withdrawn, pure, caring, concerned
nu-ú-ḫu = nūhu = Noah = the tired one, the troubled, the distant, the far away, the resigned
أناح = أبْعَدَ، نحّا، اخذ بعيدا
نَوح = المتنحي، المبتعد، البعيد، الحزين، المهموم، المتعب
روق = نوح = المتنحي، البعيد، الخالص، الحريص، المهموم

"ورَوْقُ الإِنسان: هَمُّه ونَفْسه، إِذا أَلقاه على الشيء حِرْصاً قيل: أَلقَى عليه أَرْواقَه؛ كقول رؤبة: والأَرْكُبُ الرامُون بالأَرواقِ ويقال: أَكل فلانٌ رَوْقَه وعلى رَوْقِهِ إِذا طال عُمُره حتى تَتَحاتَ أَسنانُه. والأَرْواقُ: الأَثْقالُ؛ وربما قالوا: رَوَّقَ الليلُ إِذا مَدَّ رِواقَ ظُلْمته وأَلقى أَرْوِقَته. ابن الأَعرابي: الرَّوْقُ السَّيِّد، والرَّوْقُ الصافي من الماء وغيره، والرَّوْقُ العُمُر. يقال: أَكل رَوْقَه."
" النَّحْوُ: القصد، والطريق. ونَحَّيْتُهُ عن موضعه تَنْحِيَةً، فتَنَحَّى. ونَحى الشيء يَنْحاه نَحْياً ونَحَّاه فتَنَحَّى: أَزاله. التهذيب: يقال نَحَّيْت فلاناً فتَنَحَّى؛ وإِبِل نَحِيٌّ: مُتَنَحِّيةٌ ؛ وانتحى الفرَس في جَرْيه أي جَدَّ. واسْتَنَاحَ: ناحَ، واسْتَنَاحَ الذِّئْبُ: عوى. والمَناحةُ والنَّوْحُ: النساء يجتمعن للحُزْن؛ واستناحَ الرجلُ: بَكَى حتى اسْتَبْكَى غيره؛ ونُوحٌ اسم نبي معروف ينصرف مع العُجْمَةِ والتعريف."

31. ᵏᵘʳNimuš (*also* ᵏᵘʳNiṣir)

<u>Wikipedia:</u>
Mount Nisir (also spelled Mount Niṣir, and also called Mount Nimush), mentioned in the ancient Mesopotamian Epic of Gilgamesh, is supposedly the mountain known as today as Pir Omar Gudrun (elevation 9000 ft. (approx. 2743 m)), near the city Sulaymaniyah in Iraqi Kurdistan. The name may mean

"Mount of Salvation". According to the Epic of Gilgamesh, Mt. Nisir is the resting place of the ship built by Utnapishtim. Despite the precise descriptions in the Epic of Gilgamesh, the curious have never attempted to search for the remains of the giant ship on Mt. Nisir. An alternative translation of "Mount Nisir" in the Epic of Gilgamesh XI,141a is based on the ambiguous words: "KUR-ú KUR ni-sir held tight the boat." The Sumerian word KUR can mean land or country or hill, but not mountain. In Akkadian, KUR with the phonetic complement -ú is read as shadû which can mean hill or mountain. The second KUR is a determinative indicating that nisir is the name of a hill or land or country (or in Akkadian a mountain). But Thompson read this determinative as matu, an Akkadian word for country. The country Nisir may have got its name from nisirtu which means a locality that is hidden, inaccessible, or secluded. Hence the boat may have grounded on an inaccessible hill.

<u>From references of Arabic and the Assyriology method:</u>
KUR = Mountain
niṣirtu = ni-ṣir-tu = secret
niṣir = ni-ṣir = nay-ṣir = keeper for good
nimuš = ni-muš = nay-muš = nā-muš = secret, keeper of good secret, name of Jibra'il (Gabriel)
Judi (s.) (pl. ajyad) = doer of good, keeper of good

<u>نمس:</u> نَيمس = ناموس = السر، حافظ سر الخير
<u>نظر:</u> نَيظر = ناظور= الحافظ للخير
<u>جود:</u> جوديّ (جودياء) (مفرد) (ج: أجياد) = الكساء (الغطاء)؛ الحافظ للجود (الجيد)؛ الحافظ للخير

"وقيل يا أرض ابلعي ماءك ويا سماء أقلعي وغيض الماء وقضي الأمر واستوت على الجودي وقيل بعدا للقوم الظالمين (سورة هود)"
"والجُودِيُّ: جبلٌ بالجزيرةِ اسْتَوَت عليه سفينةُ نوحٍ، عليه السلام"
"والجُوديُّ: موضع، وقيل جبل، وقال الزجاج: هوَ جبل بآمد، وقيل: جبل بالجزيرة استوت عليه سفينة نوح، على نبينا محمد وعليه الصلاة والسلام؛ وفي التنزيل العزيز: واستوت على الجوديّ؛ وقرأَ الأَعمش: واستوت على الجودي، بإِرسال الياء وذلك جائز للتخفيف أَو يكون سمي بفعل الأُنثى مثل حطي، ثم أُدخل عليه الأَلف واللام؛ عن الفراءِ؛ وقال أُمية ابن أَبي الصلت: سبحانه ثم سبحاناً يعود له، وقَبلنا سبَّح الجُوديُّ والجُمُدُ."
"وأَجياد: جبل بمكة، صانها الله تعالى وشرّفها، سمي بذلك لموضع خيل تبع، وسمي قُعَيْقِعان لموضع سلاحه."
"وحسب المصادر العربية الاسلامية فان جبل او سلسلة جبال أجياد سميت بذلك لانها كانت موضع خيل تبع، وسميت قُعَيْقِعان لموضع سلاحه."
" وقد جاد جَوْدة وأَجاد: أَتى بالجَيِّد من القول أَو الفعل. ويقال: أَجاد فلان في عمله وأَجْوَد وجاد عمله يَجود جَوْدة، وجُدْت له بالمال جُوداً."
"والجودِياء، بالنبطية أَو الفارسية: الكساء؛"
"والنامُوسُ: المَكْرُ والخِداع. والتَّنْمِيسُ: التَّلْبيس. ويقال للشَّرَكِ نامُوس لأَنه يُوارَى تحت الأَرض؛ والنَّاموس: جبريل، صلى الله على نبينا محمد وعليه وسلم، وأَهل الكتاب يسمون جبريل، عليه السلام: الناموس. وفي حديث المَبْعَث: أَن خديجة، رضوان الله عليها، وصفت أَمر النبي، صلى الله عليه وسلم، لِوَرَقَة بن نَوْفَل وهو ابن عمها، وكان نصرانياً قد قرأَ الكتب، فقال: إِن كان ما تقولين حقّاً فإِنه ليَأْتِيه الناموس الذي كان يأْتي موسى، عليه السلام، وفي رواية: إِنه ليأْتيه النَّاموس الأَكبر. أَبو عبيد: النامُوس صاحب سر المَلِك أَو الرجل الذي يطلعه على سِرِّه وباطن أَمره ويخصه بما يستره عن غيره. ابن سيجه: نامُوسُ الرجل صاحبُ سِرِّه، وقد نَمَسَ يَنْمِسُ نَمْساً ونامَسَ صاحبَه مُنامَسَةً ونِماساً: سارَّه. وقيل: النامُوسُ السِّرُّ، مثل به سيبويه وفسره السيرافي. ونَمَسْتُ الرجلَ ونامَسْتُه إِذا سارَرْته؛ ونَمَسْتُ السِّرَّ أَنْمِسُه نَمْساً: كَتَمْتُه. والمُنَامِسُ: الداخل في الناموس، وقيل: النامُوس صاحب سِرّ الخير، والجاسُوسُ صاحب سِرّ الشر، وأَراد به وَرَقَةُ جبريلَ، عليه السلام، لأَن الله تعالى خصه بالوحي والغيب اللذين لا يطَّلع عليهما غيره."

<u>About the mountains of Mecca and the location of Mt. al-Jawdi from historical Arabic references:</u>
بنيت الكعبة بين جبلين يطلق عليهما تسمية الاخشبين (الجبلين). والأخشبان جبلان في مكة هما جبل أبي قبيس، او الامين، وله قمة واحدة، وجبل أجياد (قعيقعان) وهو متعدد القمم مكونا بذلك سلسلة جبلية. وحسب المصادر الاسلامية، فقد سأل جبريل (الناموس) النبي محمد، بعد اضطهاد واهانة قريش له، ان اراده ان يطبق الاخشبين على مكة لمعاقبة قريش. وبذلك يشكل هذان الجبلان سلسلة جبلية متصلة واحدة عرفت باسم اجياد، تطل هذه السلسلة الجبلية على المسجد الحرام من المشرق. وكلمة أجياد هي كلمة جمع لكلمتي جيد وجودي. والاخيرة تعني حافظ الجود او حافظ سر الخير.
اما جبل أبي قبيس فقيل انه سمي بذلك لأن رجلاً يقال له: أبو قبيس، أول من قام بالبناء عليه او لأن الحجر الأسود أقتبس منه. ويعتقد ايضا ان جبل قبيس كان أول جبل وضع على الأرض. وكان جبل أبي قبيس يسمى في الجاهلية الأمين لأن الركن الأسود كان فيه مستودعاً عام الطوفان فلما بنى إبراهيم الخليل البيت نادى أبو قبيس أن الركن مني بموضع كذا وكذا وقيل أتى به جبريل من الجبل وسلمه إلى إبراهيم. وحسب المصادر الاسلامية سمي ابو

قبيس بالجبل الأمين بسبب احفاظه بأمر من الله بالحجر الأسود في بطن الجبل. وقد سمي جبل ابو قبيس ايضا بمغارة الخنس أو مغارة الكنس، بمعنى مغارة الاختباء.
وحسب المصادر العربية الاسلامية ايضا، فان الربوة التي بنيت عليها الكعبة تتصل بأصل جبل أبي قبيس .وأصل الصفا الذي يبدأ السعي منه عند الحج يقع في أسفل أبي قبيس في مقابلة ركن الحجر الأسود وان انشقاق القمر حصل عليه وذلك معجزة للرسول محمد.
وروي أيضاً أن النبي عليه الصلاة و السلام كان مرة في مكة المكرمة في مكان يقال له أجياد فنزل عليه جبريل الأمين عليه السلام متشكلاً في صورة بشرية.

<u>إسماعيل بن عمر بن كثير القرشي الدمشقي. البداية والنهاية.</u> 20 جزء. دار عام الكتاب. 2003
وروى علباء بن أحمر، عن عكرمة، عن ابن عباس قال: كان مع نوح في السفينة ثمانون رجلا معهم أهلوهم، وأنهم كانوا في السفينة مائة وخمسين يوما، وأن الله وجه السفينة إلى مكة فدارت بالبيت أربعين يوما، ثم وجهها إلى الجودي فاستقرت عليه فبعث نوح عليه السلام الغراب ليأتيه بخبر الأرض، فذهب فوقع على الجيف فأبطأ عليه، فبعث الحمامة فأتته بورق الزيتون، ولطخت رجليها بالطين، فعرف نوح أن الماء قد نضب، فهبط إلى أسفل الجودي فابتنى قرية، وسماها ثمانين، فأصبحوا ذات يوم، وقد تبلبلت ألسنتهم على ثمانين لغة؛ إحداها لغة العربي، فكان بعضهم لا يفقه كلام بعض، فكان نوح عليه السلام يعبر عنه". وقال قتادة وغيره: ركبوا في السفينة في اليوم العاشر من شهر رجب فساروا مائة وخمسين يوما (ص273)، واستقرت بهم على الجودي شهرا، وكان خروجهم من السفينة في يوم عاشوراء من المحرم، وقد روى ابن جرير خبرا مرفوعا يوافق هذا، وأنهم صاموا يومهم ذلك.

<u>Author's Notes:</u> According to the flood story in the Quran, Noah's ark (*al-Fulk*: the round floater) was held by a mountain named *al-Jawdiyy*. The above historical, geographical, and linguistic facts indicate that the Quran was referring to one of the mountains of the *Ajyād* mountain chain of Mecca. The city of Mecca was built on a high land connecting two mountains. One is to the east of the city and the other to its west. The eastern mountain, *Mt. Ajyād*, has multiple peaks. The western mountain, *Mt. Abu Qubays*, has one peak. The two mountains are physically connected to form a single mountain chain referred to as the *Ajyād* mountain Chain. Since the word a*jyād* is a plural of *jawdiyy* then any peak/mountain of the *Ajyād* chain, including *Mt. Abu Qubays,* can therefore be called *Mt. al-jawdiyy.* In fact, the Arabs before Islam called *Mt. Abu Qubays*, *Mt. al-Amīn* (the keeper or hider of good) because they believed it hid the sacred "black stone" of *Ka'bah* during the flood! Continuing in their steps, the Muslims further believed *Jibra'īl* (Gabriel) (also called *al-Nāmūs*) had brought this "black stone" from that mountain to Abraham who then built the *Ka'bah* house of Mecca around it. Also according to the Muslims, *Jibrā'īl* revealed the first words of the Quran to Prophet Muhammad in a cave located on another peak of the *Ajyād* chain. *Mt. Abu Qubays* (or *Mt. al-Amīn*) was also called *Magharat al-kans* or *Magharat al-khans*. Both names mean "the Hiding Cave". Evidently, the epic had not only hinted the location of the resting mountain by confirming the meaning of the name *al-Jawdiyy* through its identical meaning name *Nimūš*, but also in its description of that mountain surrounding area. According to the epic, when Ut-napishti got out of the ship he saw several nearby high land islands not covered by waters. In other words, his ship was held by a mountain peak closely surrounded by several other congregating peaks.

Most Assyriology scholars claim *Mt. Niṣir* (or *Mt. Nimuš*) is either *Mt. Pir Omar Gudrun,* near *al-Sulaymāniyah* city of northern Iraqi Kurdistan, or *Mt. Arārāt* of eastern Turkey. Some Bible-inspired scholars have even claimed that they have satellite pictures of Noah's Ark wreckage deep under *Mt. Arārāt*! However, assuming the flood waters of the Deluge had flown north to the high mountainous land goes against the facts of Mesopotamian geography and geology. Both the Old Testament and the Epic of Gilgamesh said Noah, himself, was exiled *far away* near the mouth of the two rivers (Turkey). However, this has nothing to do with where his floating ark was held at the first place. The Tigris and Euphrates flow southward. It is impossible for Noah's round floating vessel to land in northern

Mesopotamia. Logically, it must have landed in a mountainous area in the Arabian Peninsula, southwest of the Euphrates River, like Mecca.

Scholars of the Islamic Arab civilization said *Mt. al-Jawdiyy* was located in *al-Jazīrah*; a term usually refers to the whole Arabian Peninsula. However, most scholars claimed it was the *al-Jazīrah* area near Mosul city of northern Iraq, even though no such mountain had ever existed there! Some scholars like *al-Masʿudī* and *Ismāʿīl al-Dimashqī*, explicitly pointed to Mecca being a destination of the Noah arc, but they did not indicate it was the location of the *Mt. al-Jawdiyy*. Instead, they contradicted themselves and agreed with the rest of the scholars who claimed that mountain was in northern Iraq. In his 20 volumes book, *"al-Bidāya wa-al-Nihāya", al-Dimashqi* wrote that "God had directed the ship toward Mecca. It circulated around the house (al-Kaʿbah) for 40 days, then it was directed to Mt. al-Jawdi and it settled on it." As for *al-Masʿūdī* his opinion can summarized from most Arabic references in the following paragraph. "The ark began its voyage at Kūfa in central Iraq and sailed to Mecca, circling the Kaaba before finally traveling to Mount Judi, which surah 11:44 states was its final resting place. This mountain is identified by tradition with a hill near the town of *Jazīrat ibn Umar* on the east bank of the Tigris in the province of Mosul in northern Iraq, and Masudi says that the spot could be seen in his time." Notice that the mountain location given by *al-Masʿūdi* theory was only "identified by tradition"! However, the epic explicitly said Noah was exiled, after being pulled from his rested ship, far away to the mouth of the rivers [Turkey]. Turkey is not far away from Mosul, it is adjacent to it. Macca, on the other hand, is far away from Turkey.

According to Islamic tradition, Mecca was built long before 2000 BCE. The first known map of the world (front cover) that was produced by the Babylonians around 1000 BCE listed a city called *Bit Yaqinu*, which I think was Mecca.* The map placed this city close to the sea, *proportionally distant* to the far southwest of Babylon. Scholars of Assyriology say *Bit Yakinu* is "the territory of an Aramaean tribal group settling around the southern Euphrates".* However, the city in the map was *near a sea*, not the Euphrates River, and the word *Bit means* "house", not "territory". The name *Bit Yaqinu* (Arabic *Bayt al-Yaqīn)* means "house of knowledge, believe, and certainty", clearly refereeing to Abraham's house of Mecca, which was also called *al-Bayt al-ʿAtīq* (old house) and "*Bayt Allah*" (house of god). In fact, many quoted Ismael (Abraham's son) calling it *Bayt al-Yaqīn*, from *Sa*ḫ*i*ḫ *al-Bukharī.* †

"اليَقِينُ: العِلْم وإزاحة الشك وتحقيقُ الأَمر، وقد أَيْقَنَ يُوقِنُ إيقاناً، فهو مُوقِنٌ، ويَقِنَ يَيْقَن يَقَناً، فهو يَقِنٌ."
قرآن: "فلما بلغ معه السعي قال يا بني إني أرى في المنام أني أذبحك فانظر ماذا ترى قال يا أبت افعل ما تؤمر ستجدني إن شاء الله من الصابرين"
صحيح البخاري: "قال إبراهيم : يابنى إنى أرى فى المنام أني أذبحك فانظر ماذا ترى؟ قال إسماعيل : يا أبت افعل ما تؤمر ستجدنى إن شاء الله من الصابرين تربى فى بيت اليقين والتسليم لله رب العالمين"

32. Shuruppak (*also* Shuruppag)

Wikipedia:

Shuruppak or Shuruppag (Sumerian: "The Healing Place") was an ancient Sumerian city situated about 35 miles south of Nippur on the banks of the Euphrates at the site of modern Tell Fara in Iraq's al-Qādisiyyah Governorate.

---

* Clay tablet of the map is kept in The British Museum (http://www.britishmuseum.org). Collection Number: 92687

† I could not locate the exact page number of this commonly-used quotation from *Sa*ḫ*i*ḫ *al-Bukharī*

<u>From Arabic references:</u>
šurup = šurub= shurub = riverside; soft land
pak = ba'k = baʿk = ba'g = baʿg = fa'g = Groove; Valley
šurup-pak = šurup-pag = riverside groove; riverside vally; softland groove; softland vally

شُرُبْ = شُرُبَة = ارض لينة، ناحية مجاورة للنهر
بَعْج = بَأج = بَعْك = بَأك = فَأج = بعج، قاطع، وادي، متسع
شُرُبَّك = شُرُبَّج = قاطع ضفاف النهر؛ وادي ضفاف النهر؛ قاطع الارض اللينة؛ وادي الارض اللينة

"والشَّارِبةُ: القوم الذين مسكنهم على ضَفَّة النهر، وهم الذين لهم ماء ذلك النهر. والمَشْرَبَةُ، وتُضَمُّ الرَّاءُ: أرضٌ لَيِّنَةٌ دائِمَةُ النَّباتِ. والشَّرَبَّةُ أَرض لَـيِّـنَة تُنْبِتُ العُشْبَ، وليس بها شجر؛ وشَرِيبٌ، وشُرَيْبٌ، والشُّرَيْبُ، بالضم، والشُّرْبُوبُ، والشُّرْبُبُ: كلها مواضع. والشُّرْبُبُ في شعر لبيد، بالهاءِ؛ قال: هل تَعْرِفُ الدَّار بسَفْحِ الشُّرْبُبَه؟ والشُّرْبُبُ: اسم وادٍ بعَيْنِه. قال زهير: وإلاَّ فإنَّا بالشَّرَبَّةِ، فاللِّوى، * نُعَقِّر أُمّاتِ الرِّباع، ونَيْسِرُ وشَرَبَّةُ، بتشديد الباءِ بغير تعريف: موضع؛ قال ساعدة بن جؤية: بِشَرَبَّةٍ دَمِث الكَثِيبِ، بدُورِه * أَرْطًى، يَعُوذُ به، إذا ما يُرْطَبُ يُرْطَبُ: يُبَلُّ؛ وقال دَمِث الكَثِيب، لأَنَّ الشُّرَبَّةَ موضع أَو مكان؛"
"والبائِجُ: عِرْقٌ في الفَخِذِ. والبائج عرق محيط بالبدن كله، سمي بذلك لانتشاره وافتراقه. والبائجةُ: ما اتسع من الرمل."
"بعج: الباء والعين والجيم أصل واحدٌ، وهو الشَّقّ والفَتْح. قال الخليل: باعِجَةَ الوادي حيثُ ينبعِج ويتَّسع. قال:قال أبو زياد: [و] أبو فقعس: الباعجة الرُّحَيْبَة الصغيرة بَعَجَتِ الوادي من أَحَدِ جانبَيْه؛ وهي مِن مَنابت النّصيّ. قال النَّضر: الباعجة مكان مطمئنٌّ من الرِّمال كهيئة الغائط، أرض مَدْكوكة لا أسناد لها، تُنبت الرِّمْث والحَمْضَ* وأطايب العُشْب. وباعِجَةُ الوادي: حيث يَنْبَعِجُ فيَتَّسِع، والباعِجَة: أَرْضٌ سَهْلَةٌ تُنْبِتُ النَّصِيَّ؛ وقيل: الباعِجَةُ آخر الرَّمْلِ، والسُّهولَةُ إلى القُفِّ. والبَواعِجُ: أماكِنُ في الرَّمل تَسْتَرِقُّ، فإذا نبت فيها النَّصِيُّ كان أَرَقَّ له وأَطيبَ؛"
"الفَيْجُ والفِيجُ: الانْتِشارُ. والفائجَةُ: مُتَّسَعُ ما بَيْنَ كُلِّ مُرْتَفِعينِ، والفَيْجُ: مُعَرَّبُ: بَيْك، والجَماعَةُ مِنَ النَّاسِ. أَبو عمرو: الفائِجُ البِساطُ الواسِعُ من الأَرض؛"
"والمُباوِكُ: المُخالِطُ في الجِوارِ والصحابةِ. وتَبوكُ: أرضٌ بين الشامِ والمدينةِ."
"وبُعْكُوكة الوادي: وسطه."

<u>Therefore:</u>
Šuruppak = Šurubba'ak = Shuruppaʿag = Šuruffa'ak = the riverside valley city
شُرُبَّك = شُرُبّأك = شُرُبعَج = شُرُفعَج = مدينة وادي جوار النهر

<u>Author's Notes:</u> There is no linguistic evidence that the so-called Sumerian name *Shuruppak* meant literally "The Healing Place". The excavation site at *Tell Fara* where this city was presumably located is about 30 miles east of the modern day Iraqi city of *al-Dīwāniyah*. It was presumably located on the bank of an old branch of the Euphrates River. Unlike the Tigris River, the Euphrates River splits into many braches south of Baghdad, before uniting again north of Basra. Studying the historical maps of southern Iraqi rivers confirmed the existence of such river branch up until early last century. The Arabic meaning "riverside valley city" further support that assumption.

33. UNUG^{ki} (*also* Uruk^{ki})

<u>Wikipedia:</u>
Uruk (^{URU}UNUG; Arabic: وركاء, *Warkā'*; Sumerian: Unug; Akkadian: *Uruk*; Aramaic/Hebrew: אֶרֶךְ *Erech*; Ancient Greek: Ὀρχόη *Orchoē*, Ὠρύγεια *Ōrugeia*) was an ancient city of Sumer and later Babylonia, situated east of the present bed of the Euphrates river, on the dried-up, ancient channel of the Euphrates River, some 30 km east of modern As-Samawah, Al-Muthannā, Iraq. The Arabic name of Babylonia, *al-ʿIrāq*, is thought to be derived from the name *Uruk*, via Aramaic (*Erech*) and possibly Middle Persian (*Erāq*) transmission. In myth and literature, Uruk was famous as the capital city of Gilgamesh, hero of the Epic of Gilgamesh. It is also believed Uruk is the biblical Erech (Genesis 10:10), the second city founded by Nimrod in Shinar.

<u>From references of Arabic, Hebrew, and the Assyriology method:</u>

Ki = land

ארך (*'arak*) = to be long or to prolong.

ʿanaja = ʿanaqa = ʿaraqa = extended

ʿunuj = ʿunuq = ʿuruq = the extended one

ʿunuj^{ki} = ʿunuq^{ki} = ʿuruq^{ki} = the extended land

عنج = عنق = عرق = امتد

عنوج = عنوق = عروق = ما هو ممتد

عنوج^{كي} = عنوق^{كي} = عروق^{كي} = الارض الممتدة

"وأَرَك الرجل بالمكان يَأْرُك ويأْرِك أُرُوكاً وأَرِك أَرَكاً، كلاهما: أَقام به. الأَراكُ، كسَحابٍ: القِطْعَةُ من الأرْضِ"

"عنج: العين والنون والجيم أصلٌ صحيح واحدٌ يدلُّ على جَذْبِ شيء بشيء يمتدّ، كحبلٍ وما أشبهه. عَنَجَ الشيءَ يَعْنِجُه: جَذَبه. وكلُّ شيء تَجْذِبه إليك، فقد عَنَجْتَه. قال أبو عبيدة: العُنجوج من الخيل: الطويل العُنق، والأنثى عنجوجة."

"عنق: العين والنون والقاف أصلٌ واحد صحيح يدلُّ على امتدادٍ في شيء، إمَّا في ارتفاعٍ وإمَّا في انسياح. وجَمْعُ تُعْنوقٍ، بالضمِّ: للسَهْلِ مِنَ الأرضِ. والمُعْنِقُ، كمُحْسِنٍ: ما صَلُبَ وارْتَفَعَ من الأرْضِ وحَوالَيْهِ سَهْلٌ."

"عرق: العين والراء والقاف أربعة أصولٍ صحيحة. والأصل الرّابع: الامتداد والتَّتابع في أشياءَ يتبع بعضُها بعضاً. وقال آخر:ومن هذا الباب: العِرَاق، وهو عند الخليل شَاطئ البحر. وسمِّيت العِراقُ عِراقاً لأنَّه على شاطئ دِجلَة والفرات عِدَاءً حتَّى يتّصل بالبحر. والعِراق في كلام العرب: شاطئ البَحْر على طُوله. قال الدُّريدي: "سمِّيت العِراق لأنَّها استكفَّتْ أرضَ العرب "، أي صارت كالِكفاف لها. وذُكر عن أبي عمرو بن العلاء أنّ العِراق مأخوذ من عروق الشّجر، وهي مَنابِت الشَّجر."

<u>Therefore:</u>

UNUG = Uruk = ʿIrāq = the extended land along the river shore

عنوج = عروق = عراق = الارض الممتدة بمحاذاة شاطئ النهر؛

<u>Author's Notes:</u> The above derivations of the names UNUG and Uruk, for Iraq, illustrate beyond doubt that using the Arabic etymological references can not only produce more meaningful and coherent translations than using the deciphering tools of the Assyriology method, but sometimes it is our only way to read the Akkadian and Sumerian texts *correctly*. More than a thousand years ago, the famous Muslim scholar *al-Khalīl* explained that the name Iraq meant "the extended land along the two rivers' shores". He was 100% right! Keep in mind, he did not know then about our modern discoveries indicating the old name of Iraq was *'UNUG*, which according to the old Arabic references has the exact meaning of *'Uruq*. The above derivations should also put to rest the claim that the name UNUG is a non-Akkadian, non-Arabic, so-called Sumerian name. It should also be noted from the above that the meanings of UNUG or Uruk have nothing to do with the biblical-inspired meanings of Erech "length, or Moon-town". In fact the Hebrew meaning of Erech is identical to its Arabic meaning. Furthermore, the geographical location, classification, and the linguistic derivation of historical Uruk, whether it was a city, a territory, or both, do not indicate it was the ancient counterpart of the modern Iraqi city of *al-Warkā'*.

3

Lines with Significantly Different Translations, Compared*†

<table>
<tr><td rowspan="3">17^{T1}</td><td>SA</td><td>He who no later king could match, (nor) any man
[He is the king who no man after him could match]</td></tr>
<tr><td>AG</td><td>that no later king can replicate, nor any man</td></tr>
<tr><td>MK</td><td>such as no later king or man ever equaled!</td></tr>
<tr><td colspan="3"><u>Notes:</u> Current translations assumed line 17^{T1} was completing the previous line. However, this line seems like an independent line needed to reintroduce Gilgamesh just before the writer “invited” him metaphorically in line 18^{T1}, without naming him, to climb the wall and inspect its foundation. The evidence of the Ugaritic tablet, where the writer addressed Gilgamesh by name, is clear. In fact, line 1^{T1} introduced Gilgamesh using an exact opening phrase “He who” in the meaning of “Here is he who”.</td></tr>
<tr><td rowspan="2">18^{T1}
<20^{U}>
19^{T1}
20^{T1}
<25^{U}>
21^{T1}
<26^{U}></td><td>SA</td><td>Go up, (O, Gilgamesh,) in (to) the top of [around] the wall of Uruk, go in all directions
<Go up, O Gilgamesh, in (to) the top of [around] the wall of Uruk, wander around>
Explore the protecting apparatus, the brickwork of its waterways (gutters)
[Explore the protecting apparatus, examine the brickwork]
After all (indeed) [(see) If in fact] its brickwork is not kiln-fired
<Is it not [Indeed] its brickwork is not kiln-fired?>
And its foundation, the seven messengers had not laid out
<And its foundation, the seven messengers had not laid out></td></tr>
<tr><td>AG</td><td>“Go up on to the wall of Uruk, and walk around</td></tr>
</table>

* Several prominent translations were consulted for the comparisons in this section, but only four are shown. Andrew R. George (AG) translation is the most comprehensive and scholarly translation of the epic available today. This translation pays very close attention to the modern Akkadian and Sumerian language and grammar rules of the Assyriologist method, and to the actual text of the epic. Maureen G. Kovacs (AK) translation is another excellent translation with substantially similar outcome to George's. This translation takes a more open approach to text of the epic without scarifying its authenticity. Morris Jastrow and Albert T. Clay (MJ) translation of corresponding lines from the Old Babylonian Edition (Column I of the Penn Tablet), was the earliest translation but is still a good one. Reginald Campbell Thompson (RT) translation was fully referenced for the new translation, but only selectively included in this section. Published in 1928, this translation is considered “one of the baseline translations” of the Epic of Gilgamesh.

† AG translations from: Andrew R. George. *The Babylonian Gilgamesh Epic: Introduction, Critical Edition and Cuneiform Texts.* Oxford University Press, 2003. MK translations from: Maureen Gallery Kovacs. *The epic of Gilgamesh.* Stanford University Press. 1989. RT translations from: R. Campbell Thompson. *The Epic of Gilgamesh, Complete Academic Translation: Translated from cuneiform tablets in the British Museum literally into English hexameters.* Forgotten Books. 2007. First published 1928. MJ translations from: Morris Jastrow; Albert T. Clay. *An Old Babylonian Version of the Gilgamesh Epic.* Yale Oriental Series Vol. IV, 3. Yale University Press. 1920

<table>
<tr><td></td><td></td><td><Go up, O Gilgameš, on to the wall of Uruk, 21 walk around>
survey its foundation platform, inspect the brickwork!
(See) if its brickwork is not kiln-fired brick,
<thus: "Is not its brickwork kiln-fired brick,>
And if the Seven Sages did not lay its foundations!
<did the seven sages not lay its foundations?></td></tr>
<tr><td></td><td>MK</td><td>Go up on the wall of Uruk and walk around,
examine its foundation, inspect its brickwork thoroughly.
Is not (even the core of) the brick structure made of kiln-fired brick,
and did not the Seven Sages themselves lay out its plans?</td></tr>
<tr><td colspan="3"><u>Notes:</u> The writer of the epic was emphasizing in the lines above the miraculous fact that the wall was not made of the usual kiln-fired bricks and the foundation was not laid out by the seven experts, as usual. This was the reason for his call for inspection or close examination, either for protection or confirmation.</td></tr>
<tr><td>36[T1]</td><td>SA</td><td>Suckling of the coagulated breast milk of the gazelle (daughter) of Ninsun [Gazelle of Beauty]</td></tr>
<tr><td></td><td>AG</td><td>Suckling of the exalted cow, Wild-Cow Ninsun
{Suckling of the exalted cow of the Wild-Cow Nisunanna}</td></tr>
<tr><td></td><td>MK</td><td>son of the august cow, Rimat-Ninsun;</td></tr>
<tr><td colspan="3"><u>Notes:</u> After the previous line told us about Gilgamesh's vigor and determination, this line pointed out that even as a baby he was vigorous enough to suck the thick coagulated breast milk of his mother. The name Ninsun, as it was explained above, was not associated with cows. Baby Gilgamesh did not feed from a cow's breast!</td></tr>
<tr><td>43[T1]</td><td>SA</td><td>He gave back the lands (properties) to their owners whom the flood had wiped out {destroyed [stole]}</td></tr>
<tr><td></td><td>AG</td><td>Who restored the cult-centers that the Deluge destroyed</td></tr>
<tr><td></td><td>MK</td><td>who restored the sanctuaries (or: cities) that the Flood had destroyed!</td></tr>
<tr><td colspan="3"><u>Notes:</u> The line after this line explained further that Gilgamesh had enforced the law on (crooked) people. AG and MG ignored translating the part "ana aš-ri-šú-nu".</td></tr>
<tr><td>45[T1]</td><td>SA</td><td>Who is there who could have competed with him on the kingly status [on his kingly status]?</td></tr>
<tr><td></td><td>AG</td><td>Who is there that can be compared with him in kingly status,</td></tr>
<tr><td></td><td>MK</td><td>Who can compare with him in kingliness?</td></tr>
<tr><td colspan="3"><u>Notes:</u> The writer used a-na, meaning "to" or "on", but not "in", after the verb "to second" in its past tense.</td></tr>
<tr><td>47[T1]</td><td>SA</td><td>Gilgamesh, the first day he was born [right after the day he was born], Nabu was his name</td></tr>
<tr><td></td><td>AG</td><td>Gilgamesh was his name from the day he was born</td></tr>
<tr><td></td><td>MK</td><td>Whose name, from the day of his birth, was called "Gilgamesh"?</td></tr>
<tr><td colspan="3"><u>Notes:</u> AG effectively ignored translating the word na-bu. MG arbitrarily converted the line into a question, linking it to the line before, in order to translate the word na-bu in the meaning of "was called". Arguably, one can translate the line "Gilgamesh was called his name from the day he was born", but why would one need to add na-bu as a verb meaning "was called" if one can just say "Gilgamesh was his name from the day he was born"? To assume na-bu was a verb/adjective does not make sense grammatically or logically. The writer of an epic about the well-known Gilgamesh did not need to inform his readers that "Gilgamesh was his name from the day he was born" because such a line would not be of any informative value! On the other</td></tr>
</table>

<table>
<tr><td colspan="3">hand, treating the word as an adjective/name to inform the readers that Gilgamesh's actual name was Nabu, originally, is not only informative and necessary, but is the only grammatically correct reading. After all, the name Nabu was commonly used in ancient Mesopotamia.</td></tr>
<tr><td rowspan="3">56[T1]</td><td>SA</td><td>An arrow [A plow blade] [A triple Cubit] (length) is his lower leg, half Nindan [half rod] his full leg
<An arrow [A triple Cubit] (length) are his two lower legs, and a spear [reed] (length) his full legs></td></tr>
<tr><td>AG</td><td>A triple Cubit was his foot, half a rod his leg</td></tr>
<tr><td>MK</td><td>N/A</td></tr>
<tr><td colspan="3"><u>Notes:</u> Gilgamesh's dimensions, according to the epic, proportionally matched those of a man. See measurements below. Gilgamesh was a human, not a wild bull! However, accepting the current Assyriology Method translation of the word GÌR (Akkadian: šēpu) as foot, would mean Gilgamesh's foot length was half of his leg's length. This would defy the physics of walking! According to the historical Arabic references šēpu is the lower extremity of the leg below the knee.
<u>Below are Gilgamesh's approximate dimensions and ratios according to the epic:</u>
Height ~ 11 cubits ~ 15.4 ft ~ 4.6 m
Leg (like spear) ~ 0.5 Nindan (pol) = 6 Cubits = 8.4 ft ~ 2.5 m
Lower leg (like arrow) ~ 3 Cubits = 4.2 ft = 1.2 m
Step (stride) = 3 cubits = 4.2 ft = 1.3 m
Shoulder width = 4 Cubits = 5.6 ft = 1.7 m
Ratio of foot to leg (according to AG) ~ 1.2 /2.5 ~ 48% (Normal 35%)
Ratio of foot to height (according to AG) ~ 1.2 /4.6 ~ 26% (Normal 16%)
Ratio of shoulder width to height ~ 1.7/4.6 ~ 32% (Normal 28%)
Ratio of leg length to height ~ 2.5/4.6 ~ 54% (Normal 47%)</td></tr>
<tr><td rowspan="3">58[T1]</td><td>SA</td><td>3 Cubits (is the length of) the bridle sides [quiffs (curls)] of his neck sides [cheeks]
<An arrow (length) [A triple Cubit] the face covers [quiffs (curls)] of his neck sides [cheeks]>
<On that (area) of the base of that (the covers), his face is assembled [crowded]></td></tr>
<tr><td>AG</td><td><a triple cubit the whiskers(?) of his cheeks>
<To . . . of his face></td></tr>
<tr><td>MK</td><td>N/A</td></tr>
<tr><td colspan="3"><u>Notes:</u> Examining images of Gilgamesh, there seems to be a bridle-like curly face cover attached just under his cheek bones.</td></tr>
<tr><td rowspan="3">62[T1]</td><td>SA</td><td>In the description of lower (common) ones (in colloquial language), he was entwined and polished (well-built)</td></tr>
<tr><td>AG</td><td>by human standards [by the standards of the earth], he was very handsome</td></tr>
<tr><td>MK</td><td>N/A</td></tr>
<tr><td colspan="3"><u>Notes:</u> Being handsome is an earthly human standard, exclusively. Why would the writer need to mention it? This line is referring to a lower colloquial description, using the formal classical Arabic word dumuq.</td></tr>
<tr><td rowspan="2">65[T1]
66[T1]
83[T1]</td><td>SA</td><td>He has no second (equal), his sticks are (always) erected
In (during) eruption [his eruption], his subjects are up on feet
In (during) his eruption, his subjects are tiptoe walking [are rush walking]</td></tr>
<tr><td>AG</td><td>He has not any equal, his weapons being ready,
his companions are kept on their feet by the ball.
his companions are kept on their feet by the ball</td></tr>
</table>

<table>
<tr><td></td><td>MK</td><td>There is no rival who can raise his weapon against him.
His fellows stand (at the alert), attentive to his (orders ?),
His fellows stand (at the alert), attentive to his (orders ?),</td></tr>
<tr><td>94^{T1}
95^{T1}
96^{T1}
97^{T1}</td><td>SA</td><td>His highness (Anim) ordered the goddess Aruru:
"You, Aruru, built man
Now, build his (his equivalent) strong daring man
For a (future) day, let his core (strength) be equal to him</td></tr>
<tr><td></td><td>AG</td><td>They summoned Aruru, the great one
"You, O Aruru, created man:
Now create what he suggests!
Let him be equal to the storm of his heart,</td></tr>
<tr><td></td><td>MK</td><td>and (the gods) called out to Aruru:
"it was you, Aruru, who created mankind(?),
now create a zikru to it/him.
Let him be equal to his (Gilgamesh's) stormy heart,</td></tr>
<tr><td colspan="3"><u>Notes:</u> Line 93^{T1} informed the reader that the complaints about Gilgamesh had finally reached god Anu. Therefore, he was the one giving the orders of the following lines to Aruru, not all gods collectively.</td></tr>
<tr><td>113^{T1}
114^{T1}
115^{T1}
116^{T1}
117^{T1}</td><td>SA</td><td>A hunter, a rope-trapper-man
While near the water hole that belongs to him (to Enkido), he (the hunter) chose it (water hole)
One day, second, and third, while near the water hole that belongs to him, he chose it
(suddenly) The hunter saw him, (and) his face became pale [his face heated (sweated)]
He (Enkido) and his herd, grazed on [stayed put] in their green nature (prairie)</td></tr>
<tr><td></td><td>AG</td><td>A hunter, a trapper-man,
Came face to face with him by the water-hole
One day, a second and a third, he came face with him by the water-hole.
The hunter saw him and his expression froze,
He and his herds—he went back to his lair</td></tr>
<tr><td></td><td>MK</td><td>A notorious trapper
came face-to-face with him opposite the watering hole.
A first, a second, and a third day, he came face-to-face with him opposite the watering hole.
On seeing him the trapper's face went stark with fear,
and he (Enkidu?) and his animals drew back home.</td></tr>
<tr><td colspan="3"><u>Notes:</u> In lines 116^{T1} - 121^{T1} the writer first pointed out and then elaborated about the hunter's state of shock upon seeing Enkido. One would be shocked after a first face-to-face encounter, not after three days of face to face meetings, as current readings suggest! Besides, in line 129^{T1}, the hunter clearly told his father that he did not dare to meet Enkido face-to-face.</td></tr>
<tr><td>125^{T1}</td><td>SA</td><td>Like a horse of god Anim is the might of his vigor (strength)</td></tr>
<tr><td></td><td>AG</td><td>his strength is as mighty as a lump of rock from the sky [a lump of god Anu]</td></tr>
<tr><td></td><td>MK</td><td>his strength is as mighty as the meteorite(?) of Anu!</td></tr>
<tr><td></td><td>RT</td><td>Like to a double of Anu's own self [his strength] is enormous,</td></tr>
<tr><td colspan="3"><u>Notes:</u> Current translations claim the word kiṣru, which appeared in line 125^{T1} and many other lines of the epic, meant meteorite. However, in the historical Arabic etymological references this word means "horse". In Arabic, the root words qaṣra, kaṣara, and qasara, can mean "to conquer" "to defeat" "to imprison". Even modern Assyriology references gave the word kaṣara the same meanings as of Arabic. Furthermore, they</td></tr>
</table>

gave the word *kiṣru* the meaning "troop". Clearly, this word is not the same as the Arabic/Akkadian words *kisru*, or *kirṣu*, meaning "a piece of". When Gilgamesh revealed his first dream to his mother, in later lines, he indicated that his people had kissed/smelled the *legs* of this *kiṣru* and he was roaming/rushing it around and caressing it like a woman. A fast falling meteorite hitting earth and settling in a deep hole would not have any type or legs! Also, when Gilgamesh revealed his second dream, he complained that he was seeing *its* (the horse) dream *again* but this time he called it *ḫaṣinu*, which clearly means "small horse" in Arabic. The epic used other words identifying *kiṣru* as a horse, like *šuqrat* (*shuqrat*), meaning "precious reddish horse" according to Arabic. See below:
CAD: kirṣu "piece"
CAD: kaṣāru "to defeat; to conquer; to surround; to besiege"
CAD: kiṣru "troop"
قسر (لسان العرب) القَسْرُ: القَهْرُ على الكُرْه. قَسَرَه يَقْسِرُه قَسْراً واقْتَسَرَه: غَلَبه وقَهَره، وقَسَرَه على الأَمر قَسْراً: أَكرهه عليه، واقْتَسَرْته أَعَمُّ.
قصر (لسان العرب) وقَصَرَ الشيءَ يَقْصُره قَصْراً: حبسه؛ ومنه مَقْصُورة الجامع؛ ويقال للمَحْبُوسة من الخيل: قَصِير؛ وقَصَرَ الشيءَ يَقْصُره قَصْراً: حبسه؛ والقَصِيرُ خلاف الطويل.
كصر (لسان العرب) أبو زيد: الكَصِيرُ لغة في القَصِير لبعض العرب.

180^{T1} 181^{T1}	SA	"This is he, Samḫat [Shamkhat], loosen up (let go) your buttocks Reveal your nudity {sexuality} so he can find (see) your attractions
	AG	*"This is he, Samḫat! Uncraddle your bosom; Bare your sex so he may take in your charms!*
	MK	*"That is he, Shamhat! Release your clenched arms, expose your sex so he can take in your voluptuousness.*
	RT	*"Tis he, O girl! O, discover thy beauty, thy comeliness shew (him), So that thy loveliness he may possess—(O), in no wise be bashful,*

Notes: The word *kirimmu*, meaning "clasped arms for cradle" in the modern Assyriology references, was stretched in the current translations to mean "bosom" or "chest". However, there was no indication in the epic that Samḫat's hands were held in a cradle position (clenched) when she saw Enkido. Why assuming the hunter had asked her to release her arms in order to show her breast then? In Arabic, the word *kirmah* means "buttock. The word *kirimayki* means "buttocks", the most effective sexual symbol in Mesopotamia and elsewhere. In fact, according to line 188^{T1}, the first action taken by Samḫat to attract Enkido was dropping her skirt.

184^{T1}	SA	Wash [Spread (hang)] your clothes, let them shade (cover) [let them dry] over [around] you
	AG	*Spread your clothing so he may lie on you*
	MK	*Spread out your robe so he can lie upon you,*

Notes: Recall from line 108^{T1}, savage Enkido did not know "people or country". Surely, he did not sleep on beds or sheets. Samḫat did not need to spread her cloth on the floor so that Enkido would "lie over her", as we are told by current translations. The Arabic word *maṣaṣa* means "to wash". Approaching the water-hole to wash her cloths and hang them around for privacy makes more sense.

201^{T1} 202^{T1}	SA	Enkido was far behind, not as before was his jumping And (not as before) the knowledge he has of broad [deep] sense (of surrounding)
	AG	*Enkido was diminished, his running was not as before, but he had reason, he was wide of understanding*
	MK	*Enkidu was diminished, his running was not as before. But then he drew himself up, for his understanding had broadened.*

<table>
<tr><td colspan="3"><u>Notes:</u> Line 202^{T1} explained why Enkido was unable to jump as before. Pointing out that he "had reason" or "drew himself up" because he had "broad understanding" is incomprehensible. At least not to the author of this book!</td></tr>
<tr><td rowspan="3">214^{T1}</td><td>SA</td><td>His heart was guiding him (instinctively) to seek a comrade</td></tr>
<tr><td>AG</td><td>His heart (now) wise was seeking a friend</td></tr>
<tr><td>MK</td><td>Becoming aware of himself, he sought a friend.</td></tr>
<tr><td colspan="3"><u>Notes:</u> The writer emphasized in this line that Enkido was led instinctively by higher powers to meet his future comrade, Gilgamesh.</td></tr>
<tr><td rowspan="3">228^{T1}</td><td>SA</td><td>Every day of holiday … a festival [a festival gathering] is held</td></tr>
<tr><td>AG</td><td>Every day […] a festival is held,</td></tr>
<tr><td>MK</td><td>(where) every day is a day for some festival,</td></tr>
<tr><td colspan="3"><u>Notes:</u> The word UD means "the returning day", or holiday.</td></tr>
<tr><td rowspan="3">239^{T1}
240^{T1}</td><td>SA</td><td>He is unapproachable [He is not absent], day and night
Enkido, leave (stay away from) his harm (way) {your harm (way)}</td></tr>
<tr><td>AG</td><td>he is unsleeping by day and by night
O Enkidu, get rid of his [your] sinful intention</td></tr>
<tr><td>MG</td><td>without sleeping day or night!
Enkidu, it is your wrong thoughts you must change!</td></tr>
<tr><td colspan="3"><u>Notes:</u> Gilgamesh could not been "unsleeping" day and night because he had even had dreams according to the epic. In line 240^{T1} Samḫat advised Enkido to avoid confronting Gilgamesh because he, not Enkido, was a harmful one.</td></tr>
<tr><td rowspan="3">246^{T1}</td><td>SA</td><td>"Mother, I saw (from far) a high (distant) bright night light, at my evening</td></tr>
<tr><td>AG</td><td>"O mother, the dream that I saw in the course of this night</td></tr>
<tr><td>MK</td><td>"Mother, I had a dream last night.</td></tr>
<tr><td colspan="3"><u>Notes:</u> In Arabic, the word MÁŠ.GI means "a high (distant) bright night light". It also means "night vision" or "dream" according to references of the Assyriology Method. If Gilgamesh had really meant "dream" with MÁŠ.GI he would not added "in the course of this night" or "last night", since he had just woke up and headed to his mother.</td></tr>
<tr><td rowspan="4">248^{T1}
249^{T1}
250^{T1}</td><td>SA</td><td>Like a horse [a trooper] of god Anim fell (landed) over [around] my site
I roamed him [unleashed him] [flew him?], (he was) mighty (overwhelming) over [around] me
I rushed him around, I did not fear [I did not slow down] his speed</td></tr>
<tr><td>AG</td><td>like lump of god Anu (lumps of rock from the sky) they kept falling towards me.
I picked one up but it was too much for me,
I kept trying to roll it but I could not dislodge it.</td></tr>
<tr><td>MK</td><td>and some kind of meteorite(?) of Anu fell next to me.
I tried to lift it but it was too mighty for me,
I tried to turn it over but I could not budge it.</td></tr>
<tr><td>RT</td><td>When something like unto Anu's own self fell down on my shoulders,
(Ah, though) I heaved him, he was o'erstrong for me, (and though) his grapple
Loosed I, I was unable to shake him (from off me): (and now, all the meanwhile),</td></tr>
</table>

Notes: See line 125^{T1} above, regarding the word *kiṣru.* Clearly, *kiṣru* is singular. There are many possible Arabic transliterations and meanings for the word *áš-ši or áš-šá-áš.* The meaning of "roaming" fits well with *kiṣru* being a horse or trooper, though. Notice, the earlier translation by RT did mention any meteorite or rock.

257^{T1} **258^{T1}**	SA	I roamed him [unleashed him], I made him arrive (put him) under your command And you chose him for me"
	AG	*I picked it up and set it down at your feet,* *and you, you made it my equal"*
	MK	*I laid it down at your feet,* *and you made it compete with me."*

Notes: Current translations do not tell us why Gilgamesh was able to pick up the rock and lay it at his mother's feet, even though he was not able to dislodge it earlier. The old Babylonian edition (in the Penn Tablet) explicitly indicated that the crowd helped Gilgamesh *bringing* that *kiṣru* to his mother.

262^{T1} **263^{T1}** **264^{T1}** **265^{T1}** **266^{T1}**	SA	Like a horse of god Anim fell (landed) {was raising all hands (as if to copulate)} over [around] your site You roamed him [unleashed him] [flew him?], he was mighty (overwhelming) around [over] you You rushed him around, you did not fear [slow down] his speed You roamed him [unleashed him], you made him arrive (put him) under my command And I, myself, chose {shall choose} him for you
	AG	*like lump of god Anu (lumps of rock from the sky) they kept falling towards you.* *you picked one up but it was too much for me,* *you kept trying to roll it but you could not dislodge it.* *You picked it up and set it down at my feet,* *and I, I made it your equal*
	MK	*and the meteorite(?) of Anu which fell next to you,* *you tried to lift but it was too mighty for you,* *you tried to turn it over but were unable to budge it,* *you laid it down at my feet,* *and I made it compete with you,*

Notes: The writer of line 262^{T1} in another tablet copy of the epic replaced the verb *im-ta-qu-ut* (meaning "fell") by the word *ŠUB.MEŠ.* AG *assumed* a missing *šá* (meaning "of") before that word in order to translate it as a plural of *ŠUB* (meaning "rock"), leaving the sentence without a verb! In Arabic, the verb *shaba* (or *shabmash*) is used in conjunction with horses in the meaning of "to raise hands (as if to copulate)". Grammatically, either ŠUB.MEŠ or *ŠUB.^{MEŠ}* seems to be describing an action. I treated it as an adjective in the meaning of "was raising all hands".

شَبا (القاموس المحيط) شَبا: عَلا، و شَبا الفَرَسُ: قامَتْ على رِجْلَيْها،

شبا (لسان العرب) والشِّبابُ، بالكسر: نَشاطُ الفرَس، ورَفْعُ يَدَيْه جميعاً. وشَبَّ الفرسُ، يَشِبُّ ويَشُبُّ شِباباً، وشَبِيباً وشُبُوباً: رَفَعَ يَديه جميعاً، كأَنه يَنْزُو نَزَواناً

273a^{T1} **273b^{T1}**	SA	|For a second time he saw| the precious one of your dream (the ultra-red precious horse) For a second time he saw his (the horse) dream
	AG	*Favourable and precious was your dream"* *He saw a second dream*
	MK	*Your dream is good and propitious!"* N/A

<u>Notes:</u> Current translations failed to explain line 273^{T1}. According to AG this line has two variants from two separate editions. In the first variant, he treated the line as part of the previous section, reading the beginning part of the line [*dam-gat šu-qu-rat* ...] or [*Favourable and precious*]. Previously, though, he transliterated that same part [... *i-ta-mar / šu-qu-rat* ...] which is the correct way in my opinion. In other words, the two variants are: $273a^{T1}$ [*šá-ni-tum i-ta-mar šu-qu-rat šu-na-at-ka*] and $273b^{T1}$ [*šá-ni-tum i-ta-mar šu-na-at-tú*]. AG's Assumption that the missing first word was *dam-qat* seems like a desperate attempt to read the word *šu-qu-rat*. This word, which means "precious" according to the Assyriology method and to Arabic, was used in Arabic to describe a *rare and precious ultra-red horse*. If we accept AG's assumption that line $273a^{T1}$ was part of the previous section, then we must accept that the next section had started with the line "*Gilgamesh said to her to his mother*" without informing the reader first that he had seen a second dream. This was not the case with the first dream when it was introduced by the same writer.

276^{T1} 277^{T1} 278^{T1}	SA	Again, O mother, I saw a second far light ray {high (distant) bright night light} In the market of Uruk-of-the-hill A horse was lying down, there was a gathering [boasting] over [around] him
	AG	*And again, O mother, I have seen a second dream.* *In a street of Uruk-Main-Street,* *an ax was lying and people were gathered around it.*
	MK	*"Mother, I have had another dream:* *At the gate of my marital chamber* *there lay an axe, and people had collected about it.*
	RT	*'[Mother], a second dream [did I] see:* *[Into Erech, the high-wall'd],* *Hurtled an axe, and they gather'd about it: [the meanwhile, from Erech]*

<u>Notes:</u> Even though, *SILA* can mean "street" or "market", the equivalent word used by the old Babylonian tablet was *su-ḵi-im*, or *su-qi-im*, the Arabic word for "market". The word *ẖa-ṣi-nu*, when pronounced *kha-ṣi-nu* (*khaṣinu* خصين), means "axe" in Arabic. However, this Akkadian word can also be pronounced *ẖa-ṣi-nu* (or *ẖaṣinu* حصين) which means "horse" or "smaller horse" in Arabic. The Cuneiform *ẖa* syllable symbol was used for three different sounds.

خصن (لسان العرب) ابن الأَعرابي: من أَسماء الفأْس الخَصِينُ والحَدَثانُ والمِكْشاح.
حصن (لسان العرب) والحِصَانُ: الفحلُ من الخيل، والجمع حُصُنٌ. قال ابن جني: قولهم فرَسٌ حِصانٌ بَيِّنُ التحصُّن هو مُشْتَقٌّ من الحَصانةِ لأَنه مُحْرِز لفارسه، كما قالوا في الأُنثى حِجْر، وهو من حَجَر عليه أي منعه. وتَحَصَّنَ الفَرَسُ: صارَ حِصاناً.

283^{T1} 284^{T1} 285^{T1}	SA	I roamed with him, I made him arrive (put him) {making him arrive (putting him)} under your command I caressed (embraced) him like a woman, kissing (all) over [around] him And you chose [will choose] him for me"
	AG	*I picked it up and set it down at your feet,* *I loved it like a wife, and I caressed and embraced it,* *and you, you made [you will make] it my equal"*
	MK	*I laid it down at your feet,* *I loved it and embraced it as a wife,* *and you made it compete with me."*

<u>Notes:</u> The word *aẖ-bu-ub* (from *ẖub* حب) can also mean "to kiss" in southern Iraqi dialect.

288^{T1} 289^{T1} 290^{T1}	SA	"Son, the horse (that) you saw is a comrade {a man} You will caress (embrace) him like a woman, you will kiss (all) over [around] it And I, myself, chose him (to be) with you {for you}

	AG	"My son, the axe you saw is a man [a friend], *you will love him like a wife, and caress and embrace him,* *and I, I shall make him your equal.*
	MK	*"The axe that you saw (is) a man.* ... (that) you love him and embrace as a wife, but (that) I have compete with you."

Notes: Even in dreams, people associate a living being with another living being, not an axe.

295^{T1} **296^{T1}** **297^{T1}**	SA	"O Mother, by the order of god Enlil, the mighty one {the almighty}, let him fall upon me A comrade, a mighty one, I, myself, can lean on Let me lean on a comrade, a mighty one, I, myself"
	AG	*"O mother, by Counsellor Enlil's command may it befall me!* *I will acquire a friend, a counsellor,* *a friend, a counsellor, I will acquire"*
	MK	*"By the command of Enlil, the Great Counselor, so may it to pass!* *May I have a friend and adviser,* *a friend and adviser may I have!*

Notes: The Arabic word *malik*, is a complex and well-established one. Assuming a single Akkadian meaning (i.e. adviser or counselor) is misleading. The basic meaning of the root word *mlk* indicates "might and righteousness" according to the well-known Arabic etymological reference, *Maqāyīs al-Lughah*. The meaning of "counsellor" or "advisor" for *malik* is correct, but in this case the meaning "mighty" is the one most connected to the descriptions of both Enlil and Enkido. Besides, arrogant Gilgamesh was never in dire need for a counsellor!

3^{P} **4^{P}**	SA	"Mother, in (during) my evening hour (time) I came across (I saw from far) your high one (a high (distant) bright night light (star))
	AG	*oh mother during the course of my night* *I walked hale and hearty*
	MJ	*Mother, during my early night hours,* *I became strong and moved about*

Notes: Lines 3 and 4 in the in the Old Babylonian edition (Penn Tablet), combined, can be transliterated:
um-mi i-na šá-at mu-ši-ti-ia šá-am-ḫa-ku-ma at-ta-na-al-la-ak
The above combined line directly corresponds to line 246^{T1} of the Standard Babylonian edition, which was transliterated: *um-mi MÁŠ.GI aṭ-ṭu-la mu-ši-ti-ia*

6^{P} **7^{P}** **8^{P}** **9^{P}**	SA	The stars of heavens appeared {dispersed (spread)} before me A horse of god Anim fell (landed) to my back [on my site] (under my command) I roamed him [unleashed him] [flew him?], he overpowered (overwhelmed) me I rushed him, I did not fear his speed [altitude?]
	AG	*Then the stars of sky hid from me,* *a piece of the sky fell down to me.* *I picked it up, but it was too heavy for me,* *I pushed at it but I could not dislodge it.*
	MJ	*And from the starry heaven* *a meteor(?) of Anu fell upon me:* *I bore it and it grew heavy upon me,* *I became weak and its weight I could not endure.*

<table>
<tr><td colspan="3"><u>Notes:</u> AG's updated transliteration of the word ib-ba-šú-nim-ma to ip-zi-ru-nim, Arabic "spread", confirmed my alternative transliteration of ib-ba-šú-nim-ma, as Arabic ibbathunima, meaning of "spread"</td></tr>
<tr><td rowspan="3">12^{P}
13^{P}
14^{P}</td><td>SA</td><td>They extended (laid down) [knelt] in front of me (before me)
Extending out (help) to me [helping me]
They roamed with him, brought him [led him] to your back [your site] (under your command)</td></tr>
<tr><td>AG</td><td>I braced my forehead and
they helped me push,
I picked it up and carried if off to you.</td></tr>
<tr><td>MJ</td><td>It was raised up before me.
They stood me up.
I bore it and carried it to thee.</td></tr>
<tr><td colspan="3"><u>Notes:</u> The word ab-ba-la-áš-šú from abālu can mean "carried", but it can equally mean "brought". A carrier brings an object from point A to point B.</td></tr>
<tr><td rowspan="3">22^{P}
23^{P}</td><td>SA</td><td>You will face him suddenly; you will take him like a twin
You will anchor him behind me (under my command)"</td></tr>
<tr><td>AG</td><td>You will embrace him and
will bring him to me</td></tr>
<tr><td>MJ</td><td>Thou wilt spare him and
wilt endeavor to lead him to me</td></tr>
<tr><td colspan="3"><u>Notes:</u> I was not able to confirm the meanings, "spare" or "embrace" for either word in line 22^{P}. The Arabic meanings, on the other hand, matched well with the rest of the story.</td></tr>
<tr><td rowspan="3">26^{P}
27^{P}
28^{P}
29^{P}
30^{P}
31^{P}</td><td>SA</td><td>"Mother, I saw a second one
|I saw| a distant (high) bright light in the market
Of Uruk-of-the-Hill
A horse was lying
A gathering was over [around] him
The horse was strange [ugly] [shabby] [miniature] in his build (shape)</td></tr>
<tr><td>AG</td><td>"O mother, I have had another dream.
|..............| in the street
of Uruk-the-Town-Square,
an axe was lying
with a crowd gathered around.
The axe itself, it was strange of shape;</td></tr>
<tr><td>MJ</td><td>"My mother, I have seen another
|Dream.| My likeness I have seen in the streets
Of Uruk of the plazas.
An axe was brandished,
and they gathered about him;
And the axe made him angry.</td></tr>
<tr><td colspan="3"><u>Notes:</u> AG re-transliterated line 27^{P} as follows: "x x x me-e UL.A i-na su-ḳi-im". Previously, it was read "... at-mar e-mi-a i-na su-ḳi-im". Clearly, the word e-mi-a is the same as e-me-e. This word means "bright light" or "high", and with UL.A (high) would give the same meaning as MÁŠ.GI in Arabic. Therefore, lines 26, 27, and 28, combined, in the Old Babylonian edition (Penn tablet) should be transliterated:
"um-mi a-ta-mar šá-ni-tam xxx e-mi-a UL.A i-na su-ḳi-im šá Uruk^{ki} ri-bi-tim"
This would match lines 276 and 277, combined, in Tablet I of the Standard Babylonian edition:</td></tr>
</table>

"ip-pu-un-na-a AMA-a a-ta-mar šá-ni-tum MÁŠ.GI ina SILA šá UNUG[ki] re-bi-tum"		
213[T10] **214**[T10] **215**[T10]	SA	"Why your cheeks are sunken, your face slashed? (why) Your heart is sad [angry], your pride [appearance] wiped out? (why) A severe hunger [weakness] appears (spreads) [exists] in your gut?
	AG	*"Why are your cheeks hollow, your face sunken, your mood wretched, your feature wasted? (Why) is there sorrow in your heart,*
	MG	*"Why are your cheeks emaciated, your expression desolate! Why is your heart so wretched, your features so haggard! Why is there such sadness deep within you!*
Notes: Current translations used multiple words of identical meanings to compensate for the limitation of the Assyriology method: hollow ~ sunken; wretched ~ wasted ~ haggard. This limitation was very clear in the translation of the words *ni-is-sa-tu* or *SAG.PA.LAGAB*. The Assyriology references gave them the exact meaning "sorrow". This led translators to all kind of strange translations. Arabic references gave the two words the accurate meanings of "hunger" or "extreme exhausting hunger", respectively.		
217[T10]	SA	(why) Your face was burnt in that water torrent and sunshine?
	AG	*Why is it your face is burnt by frost and sunshine,*
	MK	*so that ice and heat have seared your face!*
Notes: Gilgamesh came to Ut-napishti via sea waters. Frost does not accumulate on see waters. The Arabic meaning of the word *šar-be*, "water torrent", is more fitting.		
250[T10]	SA	"I, myself had to [knew I should] go to see Uta-Napištim the withdrawn and distant (Noah) who promotes justice
	AG	*I thought, "I will go and find Uta-napišti the Far-Away, of whom people talk"*
	MK	*"That is why I must go on, to see Utanapishtim whom they call 'The Faraway'"*
Notes: The word *i-dab-bu-bu-uš* (Akkadian: to speak) is from Arabic root *dababa* meaning, "to fill the land justice". دبب (لسان العرب) وأَدَبَّ البِلادَ: مَلأَها عَدْلاً		
254[T10] **255**[T10] **256**[T10]	SA	My face did not sate soothing (peaceful) sleep {I knew, myself, (that) my face did not sate soothing (peaceful) sleep} It (the face) slashed and peeled [skinned] its own, bit by bit (gradually) My intestines filled up with exhaustion hunger
	AG	*My face did not have enough of sweet sleep I scourged myself by going sleepless. I kept filling my sinews with pain;*
	MK	*that is why (!) sweet sleep has not mellowed my face, through sleepless striving I am strained, my muscles are filled with pain.*
Notes: One does not scourge a face by going sleepless! The word *da-la-pu* indicates "gradualness" and "slowness" according to Arabic references.		
262[T10] **263**[T10] **264**[T10]	SA	'He who is hungry and exhausted shall do justice to (shall level (fill)) his cavity (abdomen) With a thorny famine plant and asphalt, he shall seal (fill) his cavity (abdomen)' That is because they (the animals) were rushing (jumping) for me; they were not taken ....

265^{T10}		That is because they (the animals) were taken … (as) a saving booty [a sacrifice] [a gift] for me”
	AG	*May they bar the gate of sorrow,* *May they seal its doorway with bitumen and asphalt!* *Because of me they shall not |…| the dancing,* *because of me, happy and carefree, they will … |…|”*
	MK	*The gate of grief must be bolted shut,* *sealed with pitch and bitumen!* *As for me, dancing ...* *For me unfortunate(!) it(?) will root out ..."*
	RT	*“let them bolt her gate . . .* *with pitch and bitumen . . . .* *……………………..* *……………………..”*

Notes: After Gilgamesh told Ut-napishtim that he had to kill all kinds of animals, eat their organs, and use their skins, he justified his actions by *throwing in* a beautiful two part rhymed classical Arabic poem/quotation verse (lines 262^{T10} and 263^{T10}), which are literally transliterated in Arabic, based on AG’s Latin transliteration: إنَ عِسْرِ خيا وعِسْرِ لِيفْحُ كاءَ ذا   ذا سغبا لغب ليعدِلُ كاءَ ذا
Gilgamesh, who is two-third god, then continued to explain that he did not take the lives of these animals by force, but these animals had sacrificed themselves by jumping *voluntarily* at him to save his life. The above remarkable Classic (vertical) Arabic poetry is not only an indisputable evidence that Classical Arabic poetry pre-dated Islam by thousands of years, but also clear evidence that the Akkadian/Sumerian language of the epic is indeed, early Classical Arabic. Current translations of lines 262^{T10}, 263^{T10}, 264^{T10}, and 265^{T10} are not only wrong, but illogical. For sure, arrogant Gilgamesh who was ready to do battle with Ut-napishtim to capture the eternal life was not an animal right advocate! He was a brutal king who declared himself half god, and gods enjoy sacrifices.

267^{T10}	SA	“Why, Gilgamesh, do you repeatedly go after drudgery (exhaustion)?
	AG	*Why, Gilgamesh, do you constantly chase sorrow?*
	MK	*"Why, Gilgamesh, do you ... sadness?*

Notes: Gilgamesh was chasing “eternal life”, not “sorrow”. He pursued a challenging and exhausting goal.

270^{T10}	SA	Since [until] when, Gilgamesh, |you decline| to a crazy fool?
	AG	*Did you ever, Gilgamesh, … to the fool?*
	MK	*Have you ever... Gilgamesh ... to the fool ...*

Notes: This line confirms Gilgamesh was considered a “fool” after he decided to roam the wild, following Enkido’s death. That is why he was given a new title GIŠ-TUK (the foolish (stubborn) loner).

297^{T10} **298^{T10}** **299^{T10}** **300^{T10}** **301^{T10}**	SA	You are aging [attenuating]; what are you finding (gaining)? Slowly, you are hurting [tiring] your own You are filling your intestines with severe hunger {exhaustion hunger} You are bringing the far ones closer, your (final) dates [days] A man is like a snapped off [eliminated] reed in a canebrake, |that| is his fate [his afterward (future)]
	AG	*You, you kept toiling sleepless (and) what did you get?* *You are exhausting yourself with ceaseless toil,* *You are filling your sinews with pain,*

		Bringing nearer the end of your life [your distant days] *Man is one whose progeny is snapped off like a reed in the canebrake:*
	MK	*You have toiled without cease, and what have you got!* *Through toil you wear yourself out,* *you fill your body with grief,* *your long lifetime you are bringing near (to a premature end)!* *Mankind, whose offshoot is snapped off like a reed in a canebreak,*
Notes: Line 303^{T10} was not an opening sentence to introduce the following two lines regarding the untimely deaths of young men and women, but an independent line to provide a beautiful quotation regarding the unescapable fate of man. The next two lines are very informative on their own and do not need an introduction. The word *šùm-šú* does not mean "whose progeny" or "offshoot", but "his fate" or "his afterward (future)". To assume it meant "whose progeny" would not work grammatically, either.		
308^{T10} **309^{T10}** **310^{T10}** **311^{T10}** **312^{T10}** **313^{T10}** **314^{T10}** **315^{T10}** **316^{T10}** **317^{T10}** **318^{T10}** **319^{T10}** **320^{T10}** **321^{T10}** **322^{T10}**	SA	As long as we build a palace As long as we acquire [monopolize] (more) property As long as brothers snatch [confiscate] {As long as brothers snatch [confiscate] inheritance share} As long as viciousness and immorality [animosity and hatred] spread [exists] in the land As long as the river got energized (rose) (and) carried (brought) the flood (and) The departing provider [The loved one] floated in the river (with) His face staring (at) the face of the sun At once (instantly), he does not have anything The abducted and the dead, they are like brothers of one semen-drop (twin) Of death, they (the gods) did not draw (determine) the shape of its figure. (and) They had not granted savage [early] man's eternity, as a grant, in the land: {(but) They had granted savage [early] man's equality from the beginning:} Their majesties the Anunnaki (god Anu's angles on earth), their majesties the gods, were in assembly The goddess Mamitum {Mami} (goddess of death), repeatedly inquiring [discussing in detail] the decree with them {their decree}, gave (the man) his destiny They established (set) death, and life Of death, they had not made known (revealed) its dates [days]" {Of his death, they had not made known (revealed) its dates [days]; they made them known (revealed them), differently}"
	AG	*At some time we build a household,* *At some time we start a family,* *At some time the brothers divide,* *{At some time the brothers divide shares,}* *At some feud feuds arise in the land.* *At some time the river rose (and) brought the flood,* *the mayfly floating on the river.* *Its countenance was gazing on the face of the sun,* *Then all of a sudden nothing was there!* *The abducted and the dead, how alike they are!* *They cannot draw the picture of death.* *The dead do not greet man in the land.* *{Mortal man is imprisoned. After they blessed me,}* *The Anunnaki, the great gods, were in assembly,* *Mammitum, who creates destiny, made a decree with them: {made a decree:}* *Death and life they did establish,* *The day of death they did not reveal'*

<table>
<tr><td rowspan="2"></td><td>MK</td><td>For how long do we build a household?
For how long do we seal a document!
For how long do brothers share the inheritance?
For how long is there to be jealousy in the land(!)!
For how long has the river risen and brought the overflowing waters,
so that dragonflies drift down the river!'
The face that could gaze upon the face of the Sun,
has never existed ever.
How alike are the sleeping(!) and the dead.
The image of Death cannot be depicted.
(Yes, you are a) human being, a man (?)!
After Enlil had pronounced the blessing,'"
the Anunnaki, the Great Gods, assembled.
Mammetum, she who forms destiny, determined destiny with them.
They established Death and Life,
but they did not make known 'the days of death'".</td></tr>
<tr><td>RT</td><td>"Shall we for ever build house(s),
for ever set signet (to contract),
Brothers continue to share,
or among [foes (?)] always be hatred?
(Or) will for ever the stream (that hath risen) in spate bring a torrent,
Kulilu-bird [to] Kirippu-bird . . . . ?
Face which doth look on the sunlight . . .
presently (?) shall not be 1 . . .
Sleeping and dead [are]r alike,
from Death they mark no distinction
Servant and master, when once thy have reach'd [their full span allotted],
Then do the Anunnaki, great gods, ...
Mammetum, Maker of Destiny with them, doth destiny settle,
Death, (aye), and Life they determine;
of Death is the day not revealéd."</td></tr>
<tr><td colspan="3">Notes: The above important lines give us a very interesting glimpse to Ut-napishtim's (Noah's) ideological believes. Apparently, he was not only the first monotheistic prophet on earth, but also the first socialist ideologue! The Deluge, he believed, was not only gods' punishment for people's moral sins, a key theme in all monotheistic religions, but also people's excessive desire to accumulate wealth. God Enlil's (Satan) exploitation of the Deluge to eliminate the humankind, and god Ea's (Adam) action to spare Noah life, do not contradict with that, since god Ea had accepted (obeyed) the collective decision of the gods to enact a flood to punish people.
In line 318[T10], Uta-napishtim tells Gilgamesh the gods did not give man an eternal life as a grant, clearly alluding to his exceptional case when he was granted eternal life for his good deed. This theme is identical to the monotheistic religions' theme that a human will be given an eternal life in heaven, after death, as a reward for his good behavior. Mistranslating a rather clear and easy Arabic word im-ma-ti-ma إمّتِما (إنَ متى ما), which literally means "at any time" but also means "as long as", the current translations had completely missed the powerful point and beautiful language of this section of the Epic, which can be summarized in the following:
As long as people behaved greedy and committed sins, as long as the river rose up to punish them with the flood, and the loved one is abducted by its waters, floating with his face gazing at the face of the sun. Instantly, he lost everything! The abducted and the dead look alike; they (the gods) did not draw an image of death, (and) they did not grant mankind eternal life, as a grant, on earth {in another edition: (but) they have granted mankind equality}: The Goddess Mamitum, after consulting with the rest of the gods in a</td></tr>
</table>

<table>
<tr><td colspan="3">meeting, announced the fate of man; they (the gods) had established death and life, (but) they had not revealed the days of death.</td></tr>
<tr><td rowspan="3">9^{T11}
10^{T11}</td><td>SA</td><td>"I shall reveal to you, Gilgamesh, a matter of secret
And I shall tell you (about) an inner (hidden) deal [judgement] of the gods, regarding that (matter) [for you (only)]</td></tr>
<tr><td>AG</td><td>"I will disclose to you, Gilgamesh, a secret matter,
and I will tell you a mystery of the gods</td></tr>
<tr><td>MK</td><td>"I will reveal to you, Gilgamesh, a thing that is hidden,
a secret of the gods I will tell you!</td></tr>
<tr><td colspan="3"><u>Notes:</u> The word ka-a-šá likely means "for that" or "for this". Less likely, it also means "for you", when addressing a masculine noun, like the word ka-a-šú does.</td></tr>
<tr><td rowspan="3">16^{T11}
17^{T11}
18^{T11}
19^{T11}</td><td>SA</td><td>Their king (leader) was the fighter (hero) god, Enlil,
Their officer (chamberlain) was the god Ninurta
Their puppet (servant) was the god Ennugi (the follower, the servant)
The god Ea, Ninsiku (one who waters and fertilizes), was finalized (overwhelmed) with (by) them (the three gods)</td></tr>
<tr><td>AG</td><td>their counsellor, the hero Enlil;
their chamberlain, Nintura,
their inspector of waterways, Ennugi,
With them the Prince Ea was under oath likewise,</td></tr>
<tr><td>MK</td><td>Valiant Enlil was their Adviser,
Ninurta was their Chamberlain,
Ennugi was their Minister of Canals.
Ea, the Clever Prince(?), was under oath with them</td></tr>
<tr><td colspan="3"><u>Notes:</u> It is rather clear from these lines that the god Ea had not really agreed to the Deluge, but only accepted the collective secret decision by the gods in the assembly to punish the humankind by a flood. The flood decision was pushed by the three gods Enlil, Nintura, and Ennugi, who secretly planned and executed the all-out Deluge, instead. Line 19^{T11} informs the reader how god Ea, who was apparently suspicious of their plan, had secretly whispered his warning words about the upcoming Deluge to the reeds, so that Ut-napishtim (Noah) can hear.</td></tr>
<tr><td rowspan="4">24^{T11}</td><td>SA</td><td>Stay [Do not leave] home, build a wooden raft</td></tr>
<tr><td>AG</td><td>demolish the house, build a boat!</td></tr>
<tr><td>MK</td><td>Tear down the house and build a boat!</td></tr>
<tr><td>RT</td><td>a dwelling Pull down, (and) fashion a vessel (therewith);</td></tr>
<tr><td colspan="3"><u>Notes:</u> According to the current translations of lines 95^{T11} and 96^{T11} Ut-napishtim (Noah) told Gilgamesh that he had given his palace and all its belongings to pu-zur-KUR.GAL (Enlil's defector), the sailor was secretly working with god Ea (Adam). However, according to the same translations, Ea had asked Ut-napishtim earlier in line 24^{T11} to "demolish the house". This is a clear contradiction. The correct meaning of the word ú-qur from Arabic is "stay (don't leave)", not "demolish". Logically, one must ask why would god Ea ask Ut-napishtim to waste valuable time and demolish his palace.</td></tr>
<tr><td rowspan="2">27^{T11}</td><td>SA</td><td>Safeguard the livestock (cattle) beings (farm animals), all of them, inside the raft</td></tr>
<tr><td>AG</td><td>Put on board the boat the seed of all living creatures!</td></tr>
</table>

<table>
<tr><td></td><td>MK</td><td>Make all living beings go up into the boat.</td></tr>
<tr><td></td><td>RT</td><td>every creature Make to embark in the vessel.</td></tr>
<tr><td colspan="3"><u>Notes:</u> Current translations claimed the word NUMUN نُغَم was a Sumerian word meaning “seed”. This is possible, since in Arabic it could mean “the tiny ones”, referring to “seed”. However, this Arabic word seems to be an equivalent of the word anʿām انعام, which has another appropriate meaning here: “livestock”. There were no Giraffes on Noah arc or in Mesopotamia. Noah was simply asked to save the important animals around him. This of course indicates that the Deluge was a local event, not a global one!</td></tr>
<tr><td>29^{T11}
30^{T11}</td><td>SA</td><td>For her, let her capacity (size) be extended (large)
For her, let her breadth [depth] and basin [stretch] be corresponding (equal)</td></tr>
<tr><td></td><td>AG</td><td>her dimensions should all correspond:
her breadth and length should be the same,</td></tr>
<tr><td></td><td>MK</td><td>its dimensions must measure equal to each other:
its length must correspond to its width.</td></tr>
<tr><td colspan="3"><u>Notes:</u> Both of the above lines started with the same word lu-ú. Current translations of the two lines are repetitive. Ea could not have asked in one line “to make her dimensions equal” then asked in the following line the same, “make her breadth and length (her dimensions) equal”. The Arabic word mun-du-da is same as mud-du-da مدد, which means “be extended”.</td></tr>
<tr><td>55^{T11}
56^{T11}</td><td>SA</td><td>The rich [the master] proceeding with the tar (bitumen, asphalt)
The working poor brought |….| needed hard work</td></tr>
<tr><td></td><td>AG</td><td>The rich man was carrying bitumen,
The pauper brought the …. tackle.</td></tr>
<tr><td></td><td>MK</td><td>The child carried the pitch,
the weak brought whatever else was needed.</td></tr>
<tr><td colspan="3"><u>Notes:</u> Older wealthy masters do not carry heavy bitumen! Poor workers do.</td></tr>
<tr><td>64^{T11}
65^{T11}</td><td>SA</td><td>Water (sealing) plugs on its waists (sides), I squeezed (pushed and pounded) for it {I squeezed, to let her have them}
I observed (examined) its half sphere (concave) size and did (put) needed hard work:</td></tr>
<tr><td></td><td>AG</td><td>I struck the water pegs into her belly.
I found a punting-pole and put the tackle in place.</td></tr>
<tr><td></td><td>MK</td><td>I drove plugs (to keep out) water in its middle part.
I saw to the punting poles and laid in what was necessary.</td></tr>
<tr><td colspan="3"><u>Notes:</u> One cannot use a punting-pole to move an acre-sized ship, loaded with people, animals, and grain! Besides, Noah’s ship was a floater, not a conventional ship. It was not driven by punting poles.</td></tr>
<tr><td>76^{T11}
77^{T11}</td><td>SA</td><td>At sun-rise, I put my hand on miscellaneous parts (of it)
Before sun-high (mid-day), the raft was ready</td></tr>
<tr><td></td><td>AG</td><td>At sun-rise to the oiling I set my hand;
before sundown the boat was finished.</td></tr>
<tr><td></td><td>MK</td><td>… and I set my hand to the oiling(!).
The boat was finished by sunset.</td></tr>
<tr><td colspan="3"><u>Notes:</u> According to references of the Assyriology method the term ereb šamši meant “sunset”. The word ereb غرب means “to set or go down”, but not the word ra-bé-e in the phrase of line 76^{T11}, la-am ^{d}UTU ra-bé-e.</td></tr>
</table>

<table>
<tr><td colspan="3">In Arabic, the word ra-bé-e ربي means "vertically risen", which is the position of the sun at noon.</td></tr>
<tr><td rowspan="4">84^{T11}
85^{T11}
86^{T11}</td><td>SA</td><td>All what I had of livestock (cattle) beings (farm animals), all of them, I loaded aboard it
I grabbed (rushed) to the inside of the raft all my kith and kin
Herds of the wild, creatures of the wild, my subjects (workers), I grabbed (rushed) all (in)</td></tr>
<tr><td>AG</td><td>I loaded aboard it whatever seed I had of living things, each and every one.
All my kith and kin, I sent aboard the ship,
I sent aboard animals of the wild, creatures of the wild, persons of every skill and craft</td></tr>
<tr><td>MK</td><td>All the living beings that I had I loaded on it,
I had all my kith and kin go up into the boat,
all the beasts and animals of the field and the craftsmen I had go up.</td></tr>
<tr><td>RT</td><td>All I possess'd of the seed of all living [I laded aboard] her.
Into the ship I embark'd all my kindred and family (with me),
Cattle (and) beasts of the field (and) all handicraftsmen embarking.</td></tr>
<tr><td colspan="3"><u>Notes:</u> After a flood recedes, plants flourish by themselves. Besides, one does not preserve animal lives by saving their "seeds". The vague phrase of the current translations, "seed of living things", is a failed attempt to decipher the word NUMUN.</td></tr>
<tr><td rowspan="3">90^{T11}
91^{T11}</td><td>SA</td><td>He stressed (repeated) |again| the grace period:
"Before dawn, dried bread [eggs], at night, he will bestow upon [shower] a flow of wheat [yogurt]"</td></tr>
<tr><td>AG</td><td>that time had arrived–
"In the morning he will rain down bead cake, in the evening, a torrent of wheat."</td></tr>
<tr><td>MK</td><td>That stated time had arrived
In the morning he let loaves of bread shower down, and in the evening a rain of wheat.</td></tr>
<tr><td colspan="3"><u>Notes:</u> According to the current translations of lines 87^{T11}, 88^{T11}, and 89^{T11}, Ut-napishtim said to Gilgamesh: "the god Shamas had set the deadline and told me 'He (Ea) will rain bread and wheat, go into the ship and seal the hatch'". Then immediately after, line 90^{T11} and 91^{T11} were translated "That time had arrived. 'He (Ea) will rain bread and wheat'", without explaining who said what this time. Was it Ut-napishtim or the writer? Then again, why would either one say "he will rain" if time had arrived? It should be "he rained". In the Arabic etymological references, the word ik-tal-da is the same as the word ik-tad-da, from the roots kadda and kalada. They both mean "to cease" or "to insist". Accordingly, in lines 90^{T11} Ut-napishtim was telling Gilgamesh that God Shamas had repeated/re-emphasized what he told him earlier in line 88^{T11}, and then he re-stated the exact message of line 88^{T11} in 91^{T11}.
الكَدُّ (القاموس المحيط) الكَدُّ: الشِّدَّةُ، والإِلْحاحُ، والطَّلَبُ، وأكَدَّ، واكْتَدَّ: أمْسَكَ،</td></tr>
<tr><td rowspan="3">101^{T11}</td><td>SA</td><td>They went with (led) the officers (soldiers) over mountains and land</td></tr>
<tr><td>AG</td><td>"throne-bearers" traveling over mountain and land.</td></tr>
<tr><td>MK</td><td>heralds going over mountain and land.</td></tr>
<tr><td colspan="3"><u>Notes:</u> Notice, the Akkadian word gu-za-lá in line 19^{T11} is the same as the so-called Sumerian word GU.ZA.LÁ in this line.</td></tr>
<tr><td>103^{T11}
104^{T11}
105^{T11}
106^{T11}
107^{T11}</td><td>SA</td><td>The god Ninurta (of fire, and war) passed by, burning the ships and weirs
The Anunnaki (god Anu angles on earth) roamed with [unleashed] the torches
With their black, white, and orange/red (tiger colors: Arabs death colors), they spotted the land
(as) The spoiling (ruining) act (force) of god Askar was taking over [encroaching] the sky
All that was dark white, to a pitch-dark (color) it returned</td></tr>
</table>

108^{T11} 109^{T11} 110^{T11} 111^{T11} 112^{T11} 113^{T11}		He pressed (crushed) the land, like |an oil compressor| camel he (repeatedly) circled it In one day, the wind [storm] .... Immediately [with a grudge], the Deluge was swallowing (submerging) .... of the lands Like (in) a battle, the sand took over [encroached] the people A brother could not see his (own) brother People could not connect with each other in the pileup ruin [the ruin] {in the entrapment}
	AG	*Nintura going (by), made the weirs overflow* *The Anunnaki bore torches aloft,* *Setting the land aglow with their brilliance.* *The still calm of the Storm God passed across the sky,* *All that was bright was turned into gloom.* *Like an ox he trampled the land, he smashed it like a pot,* *for one day the gale ....* *Quickly it blew and the Deluge ......the east wind,* *like a battle the cataclysm passed over the people* *One person could not see another,* *nor people recognize each other in the destruction.*
	MK	*forth went Ninurta and made the dikes overflow.* *The Anunnaki lifted up the torches,* *setting the land ablaze with their flare.* *Stunned shock over Adad's deeds overtook the heavens,* *and turned to blackness all that had been light.* *The... land shattered like a... pot.* *All day long the South Wind blew ...,* *blowing fast, submerging the mountain in water,* *overwhelming the people like an attack.* *No one could see his fellow,* *they could not recognize each other in the torrent.*
Notes: Current translations explained line 108^{T11} rather strangely. For example, AG likened the storm to an Ox tramping the land and smashing it like a pot, a weak metaphor. MG gave up. The actual meaning of the line in Arabic is a powerful and beautiful one, though. In this line Ut-napishtim likened the repeatedly circulating Deluge storm to a repeatedly circulating camel in an oil pressing apparatus. Using blind-folded circulating camels to cold press oil from seeds is still being done in Arabia, even today!		
114^{T11} 115^{T11} 116^{T11} 117^{T11} 118^{T11} 119^{T11} 120^{T11}	SA	The Deluge frightened (even) the gods They left [rushed], they went up to the haven of God Anu The gods were like hiding hyenas, waiting [lying down] in the hideouts (as) The goddess Istar was reading aloud a testimony (a witness statement) {as if a testimony (a witness statement) The lady of god {the sweetheart of gods} (Aruru) shouted, weeping, an honest (candid) outcry: (indeed) Like his first day (the human), to the mud, let him be returned to it! That is because I, myself, in front of {in the assembly of} the gods, had shouted: O, the one of horror (on to the war) How could I had shouted in front of {in the assembly of} the gods: O, the one of horror (on to the war)
	AG	*Even the gods took fright at the Deluge!* *They withdrew, they went up to the heaven of Anu.* *The gods were curled up like dogs, lying out in the open.* *The goddess, screaming like a woman in childbirth,* *Belet-ili, the sweet-voiced, wailed aloud:*

<table>
<tr><td></td><td></td><td>"Indeed the past has truly turned to clay,
Because I spoke evil in the assembly of gods.
How was it I spoke evil in the assembly of gods,</td></tr>
<tr><td></td><td>MK</td><td>The gods were frightened by the Flood,
and retreated, ascending to the heaven of Anu.
The gods were cowering like dogs, crouching by the outer wall.
Ishtar shrieked like a woman in childbirth,
the sweet-voiced Mistress of the Gods wailed:
'The olden days have alas turned to clay,
because I said evil things in the Assembly of the Gods!
How could I say evil things in the Assembly of the Gods,</td></tr>
<tr><td colspan="3"><u>Notes:</u> If the scared gods went to the comfort of god Anu's heaven, why would they be curling or cowering in the open, or by an outer wall! The word kun-nu-nu, means "hidden" in Arabic. Accordingly, the line was saying, the gods went up to hide and wait, like hyenas in hideouts.
Line 117^{T11} started a new paragraph telling the reader that while the Goddess Istar was announcing something to the gods (in Anu's heaven), the goddess Aruru started shouting, interrupting her. In line 132^{T11} the word ẖa-a-a-al-ti was translated correctly by all as "woman in childbirth". However, line 116^{T11} used the word ma-li-ti (and in another edition a-lit-ti), not ẖa-a-a-al-ti. This word means "a testimony" or "a witness statement". Notice, this word was followed a verb meaning "announcing loud" or "reading loud".</td></tr>
<tr><td>123^{T11}
124^{T11}
125^{T11}
126^{T11}
127^{T11}
128^{T11}
129^{T11}</td><td>SA</td><td>It is I, myself, who give birth to the breed of people
(now) Like the breeds of fish, they fill the sea!"
The gods, particularly the Anunnaki, were crying with her
The gods were overwhelmed, while sitting, with crying
{With a noisy exhaustion, they were crying with her}
Their lips were dry {became dark} as a result of dehydration
For six days and nights {and seven nights}
The hell of the Deluge came by, peeling the (face of) earth (turning it) to a flat water-covered land
{The hell of thunder came by, the Deluge |was peeling| the (face of) earth (turning it) to a flat water-covered land}</td></tr>
<tr><td></td><td>AG</td><td>It is I that give birth (to them)! They are my people!
(Now) like so many fish they fill the sea!"
The gods, the Anunnaki, were weeping with her,
the gods were humble, sitting in tear,
{wet-faced with sorrow, they were weeping with her,}
their lips were parched, being stricken with fever.
For six days and seven nights,
was blowing the wind, the downpour, the gale, the Deluge laying flat the land.
{was blowing the wind, the Deluge, the gale laying flat the land.}</td></tr>
<tr><td></td><td>MK</td><td>No sooner have I given birth to my dear people
than they fill the sea like so many fish!'
The gods--those of the Anunnaki--were weeping with her,
the gods humbly sat weeping, sobbing with grief(?),
their lips burning, parched with thirst.
Six days and seven nights
came the wind and flood, the storm flattening the land.</td></tr>
<tr><td colspan="3"><u>Notes:</u> Line 125^{T11} used the word šu-ut ذت which seems to be the equivalent of the modern Arabic word بالذات meaning "particularly".</td></tr>
</table>

<table>
<tr><td rowspan="3">133^{T11}</td><td>SA</td><td>The sea pulled back (down) (subsided), fell still, the worst {the tempest} of the Deluge ended</td></tr>
<tr><td>AG</td><td>the tempest grew still, the Deluge ended.</td></tr>
<tr><td>MK</td><td>The sea calmed, fell still, the whirlwind (and) flood stopped up.</td></tr>
<tr><td colspan="3"><u>Notes:</u> There were definitely three parts in this line.</td></tr>
<tr><td rowspan="3">136^{T11}</td><td>SA</td><td>Like an earth space (empty land) the valleys were leveled</td></tr>
<tr><td>AG</td><td>The flood plain was level like a roof.</td></tr>
<tr><td>MK</td><td>The terrain was as flat as a roof.</td></tr>
<tr><td colspan="3"><u>Notes:</u> Roofs are not necessarily leveled. They are not endless in size or space, either. Using “roof” as a metaphor is not only weak, but incorrect. The word ú-ri عري is clearly from Arabic root word ‘ara عرا.</td></tr>
<tr><td rowspan="3">156^{T11}
157^{T11}</td><td>SA</td><td>He was eating, cruising (roving), tracking (aiming), he was not frustrated [he did not go back and forth]
I lifted up an offering (sheep) to the four cardinal directions [to the four seas] and sacrificed (it)</td></tr>
<tr><td>AG</td><td>It was eating, bobbing up and down, it did not come back to me.
I brought out an offering and sacrificed to the four corners of the earth {to the four Winds}</td></tr>
<tr><td>MK</td><td>It eats, it scratches, it bobs, but does not circle back to me.
Then I sent out everything in all directions and sacrificed (a sheep).</td></tr>
<tr><td colspan="3"><u>Notes:</u> Hard to believe Ut-napishtim had such sharp eyes to see the raven “scratches” itself from a mile away!</td></tr>
<tr><td rowspan="4">163^{T11}
164^{T11}
165^{T11}
166^{T11}
167^{T11}</td><td>SA</td><td>The gods gathered, like scorpions (hypocrites) [flies], over [around] the giver of the gratitude
The lady of god (Aruru), immediately, at her arrival
She belittled their majesties the hypocrites of god Anu; she made them like her laughingstock:
These gods, herein, let them have (wear) the lapis lazuli stones of my interior [bottom] (i.e. feces), I should not forget them (so I don’t forget them)
These days, herein, I shall mourn for ever, I should not forget them (so I don’t forget them)</td></tr>
<tr><td>AG</td><td>the gods gathered like flies around the sacrificer.
As soon as Belet-ili arrived,
she lifted aloft the great flies that Anu had made when he wooed (her):
“O gods, let these be lapis lazuli (beads) around my neck,
so that I remember these days and never forget them!</td></tr>
<tr><td>MK</td><td>and collected like flies over a (sheep) sacrifice.
Just then Belet ili arrived.
She lifted up the large flies (beads) which Anu had made for his enjoyment(!):
'You gods, as surely as I shall not forget this lapis lazuli around my neck,
may I be mindful of these days, and never forget them!</td></tr>
<tr><td>RT</td><td>(aye,) the gods did assemble like flies o’er him making the off’ring.
Then, on arriving, the Queen (of the gods) the magnificent jewels
Lifted on high, which Anu had made in accord with her wishes;
‘O ye Gods! I will (rather) forget (this) my necklet of sapphires,
Than not maintain these days in remembrance, nor ever forget them.</td></tr>
<tr><td colspan="3"><u>Notes:</u> The word iš-ši اسي، اشي، هشي، عسي in line 165^{T11} means “belittled” or “felt sorry for”.
والأَشّاش: الهَشّاش. واسْتَهشّهُ: اسْتَخَفَّهُ. عس: العين والسين أصلانِ متقاربان: أحدهما الدنوُّ من الشّيء وطلبُه، والثاني خِفَّةٌ في الشيء. وأَسِيتُ عليه أسىً: حَزِنْت.
The word ṣu-ḫi-šú, even according to references of the Assyriology method, means “his/her joke or</td></tr>
</table>

<table>
<tr><td colspan="3">laughter". The word *ṣu-ḫi* is clearly not a verb.
Lines 163^{T11} used the word *zu-um-bé-e,* meaning "scorpions", or "insects", according to Arabic. Line 165^{T11} used the so-called Sumerian word NIM نيم meaning "hypocrite", according to Arabic. Daring to attend Ut-napishtim's thanking sacrifice to the gods after they had enacted the horror of the Deluge, clearly points out that these gods had acted like "hypocrites" or "scorpions", not "flies".</td></tr>
<tr><td rowspan="3">**170^{T11}**</td><td>SA</td><td>That is because he had not restrained himself (he acted carelessly), he established the Deluge</td></tr>
<tr><td>AG</td><td>*because he lacked counsel and caused the Deluge*</td></tr>
<tr><td>MK</td><td>*because without considering he brought about the Flood*</td></tr>
<tr><td colspan="3">Notes: Another clear indication that Enlil was the lead god behind the Deluge.</td></tr>
<tr><td rowspan="3">**184^{T11}**
185^{T11}
186^{T11}</td><td>SA</td><td>(on) The perpetrator of a sin, impose (the equal of) [equalize (match)] his sin
(on) The perpetrator of offence, impose (the equal of) [equalize (match)] his offence
Loosen up, so it would not be broken; tighten up, so it would not be loose</td></tr>
<tr><td>AG</td><td>*On him who commits a sin, inflict his crime!*
on him who does wrong, inflict his wrong-doing!
Slack off, lest it be snapped! Pull taut, lest it become slack!</td></tr>
<tr><td>MK</td><td>*Charge the violation to the violator,*
charge the offense to the offender,
but be compassionate lest (mankind) be cut off,</td></tr>
<tr><td colspan="3">Notes: The three lines above sound like rhymed classical Arabic poetry verses or just quotations. The moral theme of the first two lines are repeated in the Quran: "لا يجرمنكم شنآن قوم على ان لا تعدلو اعدلو هو اقرب للتقوى"</td></tr>
<tr><td rowspan="3">**198^{T11}**
199^{T11}</td><td>SA</td><td>And now, the guidance (the order) is to his guider (i.e. IDIM)"
The god IDIM (god Ea) went up to the heart of the raft</td></tr>
<tr><td>AG</td><td>*Enlil came up into the boat*
And now, consider what is to be done with him."</td></tr>
<tr><td>MK</td><td>*Now then! The deliberation should be about him!'*
Enlil went up inside the boat</td></tr>
<tr><td colspan="3">Notes: Current translations of line 198^{T11} assume that the writer of the Epic had mistakenly written IDIM instead of Enlil. For example, AG wrote in the footnote of his translation: *corruptly "king Ea".* This assumption is simply wrong. Line 198^{T11} followed a long verbal attack by IDIM against Enlil. Stating after that it should be up to him (IDIM) to decide the fate of Ut-napishtim (Noah) is the only logical conclusion/reading. Therefore, it was indeed the god IDIM (Adam), not Enlil, who gave Ut-napishtim (Noah) the eternal life. He was the one saving him, to start with. This is very clear, at least according to the Standard Babylonian edition of the Epic.</td></tr>
<tr><td rowspan="3">**204^{T11}**</td><td>SA</td><td>From now on, Uta-Napištim and his woman, let them have a destiny like (that of) preceding (bygone) gods</td></tr>
<tr><td>AG</td><td>*but now Uta-Napištim and his woman shall be like us gods!*</td></tr>
<tr><td>MK</td><td>*But now let Utanapishtim and his wife become like us, the gods!*</td></tr>
<tr><td colspan="3">Notes: The current translations of line 204^{T11} are definitely inaccurate. The god Ea did not make *Ut-napishtim a* god like himself or other gods. This is why *Ut-napishtim* was never referred to as god in the literature. God Ea gave *Ut-napishtim* the fate of a *passing (retired? dead?)* god. This fate was to have"eternal life" in gods' heavens.
Incidentally, if the story of a man building a floating raft (i.e. Noah) to avoid a major flood was a true story,</td></tr>
</table>

<table>
<tr><td colspan="3">then it seems that that man had actually died, but the Mesopotamian people wanted to *believe* otherwise, by claiming he was given an eternal life! This is typical of Mesopotamia and elsewhere. I still remember as a kid how people had refused to believe that their beloved leader, Gen. Abdul Karim Qasim, was actually killed after the CIA-sponsored coup of 1963. Some claimed they have seen him years later!</td></tr>
<tr><td rowspan="3">**207^{T11}**
208^{T11}
209^{T11}</td><td>SA</td><td>And now, who will assemble the gods for (all) that [for you]?
The (eternal) life that you aim [want] to be given,
(come) Work hard for (it), do not lay down (sleep) for six days and seven nights"</td></tr>
<tr><td>AG</td><td>*But now, who will bring the gods to assembly for you,
so you can find the life you search for?
Come, for six days and seven nights do not sleep!'*</td></tr>
<tr><td>MK</td><td>*"Now then, who will convene the gods on your behalf,
that you may find the life that you are seeking!
Wait! You must not lie down for six days and seven nights."*</td></tr>
<tr><td colspan="3"><u>Notes:</u> In the current translations, the combining of line 207^{T11} and line 208^{T11} by "so", "that", or else, in order to create one question/sentence, was assumptive, not grammar-based. The Arabic word *gana'*, in the beginning of line 209^{T11}, is rather clear, it means "work hard on":
جنأ (لسان العرب) وأَجْنَأَ الرَّجُلُ على الشيء: أَكَبَّ؛</td></tr>
<tr><td rowspan="3">**227^{T11}**</td><td>SA</td><td>His fourth, its Anise loaf oozed (sweated)</td></tr>
<tr><td>AG</td><td>*his forth flour-cake had turned white,*</td></tr>
<tr><td>MK</td><td>*the fourth turned white, its ...,*</td></tr>
<tr><td rowspan="3">**239^{T11}**</td><td>SA</td><td>The fourth one, your Anise loaf oozed (sweated)</td></tr>
<tr><td>AG</td><td>*your fourth flour-cake had turned white,*</td></tr>
<tr><td>MK</td><td>*your fourth turned white, its ...*</td></tr>
<tr><td colspan="3"><u>Notes:</u> According to the current translations, the fourth bread (AG claimed it was a *flour-cake*!) became white (i.e. produced mold). However, according to the same translations, the fifth bread produced mold (i.e. had whitish color).</td></tr>
<tr><td rowspan="3">**244^{T11}**
245^{T11}
246^{T11}</td><td>SA</td><td>The Gripper (death) has seized my organs
In my bed's room [bed-chamber] death dwells
And wherever to set |my foot [my face]|, there he is: death!"</td></tr>
<tr><td>AG</td><td>*The Thief has taken hold of my [flesh]
In my bed-chamber Death abides,
and wherever I might turn [my face], there too will be Death."*</td></tr>
<tr><td>MK</td><td>*The Snatcher has taken hold of my flesh,
in my bedroom Death dwells,
and wherever I set foot there too is Death!"*</td></tr>
<tr><td colspan="3"><u>Notes:</u> The word in line 244^{T11} was *ek-ke-mu* (عكيم), which means "the gripper". It seems that old Mesopotamians had nicknamed death "the gripper" القابض because it confiscates/grips the human body.
عكم (لسان العرب) العين والكاف والميم أصلٌ صحيح يدلُّ على ضمٍّ وجمع لشيء في وعاءٍ. ويقال: ما عَكَمَ عن شتمي، أي ما انقبض.</td></tr>
<tr><td rowspan="2">**248^{T11}**
249^{T11}</td><td>SA</td><td>"O Ur-šánabi, may the gulf extract you (get rid of you), may the crossing boat reject you
That (gulf), where many adventures (took place) at its shores, tremble in fear at its shore!</td></tr>
<tr><td>AG</td><td>*"Ur-šánabi, may the quay reject you, may the ferry scorn you!
You who used to walk on its shore, suffer absence from it!*</td></tr>
</table>

	MK	*"May the harbor reject you, may the ferry landing reject you! May you who used to walk its shores be denied its shores!*

<u>Notes:</u> The word DU.DU.^{MEŠ}-ku was used in several lines of the epic in the meaning of "adventures". Using the qualifier ^{MEŠ} for plural, it is could not been a Sumerian verb meaning "to walk".

253^{T11} **254^{T11}** **255^{T11}** **256^{T11}** **257^{T11}** **258^{T11}**	SA	Take him, Ur-šánabi, direct [bring] him to the washtub of highness [purity] [Take him, Ur-šánabi, to the washtub of highness [purity] of his lords] Let him clean [rub off] his fullness in the water, like a high [pure] one (like a god) Let him get rid of his hides, let the sea take them over [carry (bring) them away] (With) fine oil (perfume) anoint {anoint to him} his body Let him have his head band (his turban) made anew {be renewed} Let him have a robe dressed, befitting his dignity
	AG	*Take him, Urshanabi, get him to the washtub, let him wash his matted hair as clean as can be! Let him cast off his hides and the sea carry (them away)! Soak his body so fair! Let the kerchief of his head be renewed! Let him be clad in a royal robe, the attire befitting his dignity!*
	MK	*Take him away, Urshanabi, bring him to the washing place. Let him wash his matted hair in water like ellu. Let him cast away his animal skin and have the sea carry it off, let his body be moistened with fine oil, let the wrap around his head be made new, let him wear royal robes worthy of him!*

<u>Notes:</u> In addition to the meanings "sweet", "fair", and "good", the Arabic word *ṭābu* طيب also means "fine oil", or "perfume", even in the modern Arabic language.
In the footnotes of his translation, after pointing out the word *te-di-qa* تحديقة meant *kerchief*, AG explained that "*modern Iraqis call it chafiyah*". He is right. The reader should take note that according to the above important lines, translated almost identically by all scholars, Gilgamesh had to dress a *kafiyah* (كفية), a head-band (*ʿiqal* عقال), and a robe (*ʿaba'ah* عباءة) to look presentable. Sounds familiar? With this exact general outfit being worn by the Iraqi Arabs, even today, Gilgamesh and his people (i.e., the Sumerians) must have been Arabs, speaking the Arabic language!

271^{T11} **272^{T11}**	SA	Gilgamesh and Ur-šánabi boarded the raft They prepared (equipped) [put (launched)] the round raft, which they had (previously) boarded
	AG	*Gilgamesh and Ur-šánabi boarded the boat, they launched the craft, they crewed it themselves.*
	MK	*Gilgamesh and Urshanabi bearded the boat, they cast off the magillu-boat, and sailed away.*

<u>Notes:</u> Here is a simple question regarding AG's translation of line 272^{T11}: why would anyone need to point out that Gilgamesh and Ur-šánabi had crewed the boat "themselves"? Who else was there to join them back to Uruk? Incidentally, according to historical Arabic references, the word *magillu* (like *eleppu*) means "a round container":

مجل (لسان العرب) المجلة: الصَّحيفة؛ علب (لسان العرب) العُلْبة: قدحٌ من خشب

276^{T11} **277^{T11}** **278^{T11}**	SA	As he, Gilgamesh, moved (unleashed) his punting-pole, (and as) The raft moved closer to the shore, Uta-Napištim said to him, to Gilgamesh:

	AG	*And he, Gilgamesh, raised the punting-pole, he brought the boat close to shore. Utanapishtim spoke to him, to Gilgamesh:*
	MK	*Then Gilgamesh raised a punting pole and drew the boat to shore. Utanapishtim spoke to Gilgamesh, saying:*
Notes: Very clearly, the word "And", which line 276^{T11} started with, meant "As", consistent with Arabic grammar. This meaning is also consistent with the actual event sequence taking place, according to the three lines.		
281^{T11} **282^{T11}** **283^{T11}** **284^{T11}**	SA	"I shall reveal to you, Gilgamesh, a matter of secret And I shall tell you (about) an inner (hidden) deal of the gods, regarding that (matter) [for you (only)] It is a weed like fine-thorn plant [It is a weed like a knife sharpener], located |under the Abzu| Its (fine) thorns [Its file (rasp)] will scrape (make) your hands like a skinless (huskless) berry
	AG	*I will disclose, Gilgamesh, a secret matter, and [I will] tell you a mystery of [the gods]. It is a plant, its [appearance] is like box-thorn, its thorn is like the dog-rose's, it will prick your hands.]*
	MK	*I will disclose to you a thing that is hidden, Gilgamesh, a... I will tell you. There is a plant... like a boxthorn, whose thorns will prick your hand like a rose.*
	RT	*Gilgamish, I will reveal thee a hidden matter . . . I'll tell thee: There is a plant like a thorn with its root (?) [deep down in the ocean], Like unto those of the briar (in sooth) its prickles will scratch [thee],*
Notes: The word *eddittu* حديّة could have been used as name of a "fine-thorn plant". However, this word means "knife sharpener" in Arabic. It is important to realize here that our tough hero, Gilgamesh, was not a young naïve kid who needs someone to explain to him that *"thorns will prick your hand like a rose"*. It is obvious that a thorn would prick a hand. The life-giving plant of the Abzu had a sharpener-like stem, capable of pealing the skin of someone's hand while pulling it out.		
295^{T11} **296^{T11}** **298^{T11}** **299^{T11}** **300^{T11}**	SA	"O, Ur-šánabi, this plant is the plant of deliverance (salvation) [the plant for (against) hardship] For a man, it delivers the living breath [the wink (spark) [trickle (flow)] of life] (the heartbeat) in his heart I shall feed the weed to an old man, to test (only) After [If] the old man is grown (to) young man I, myself, shall eat it to go back to my youth {to that of my youth (the age of my youth)}"
	AG	*Ur-šánabi, this plant is the "plant of heartbeat", by which means a man can recapture his vitality. I will feed some to an old man and put the plant to the test. Its (or his) name will be "The Old Man Has Grown Young", [If the old an grows young (again)] I will eat some myself and go back to how I was in my youth.*
	MK	*"Urshanabi, this plant is a plant against decay(!) by which a man can attain his survival(!). I will bring it to Uruk-Haven,*

		and have an old man eat the plant to test it. *The plant's name is 'The Old Man Becomes a Young Man.'"* *Then I will eat it and return to the condition of my youth."*

Notes: Assuming the word *šum-šu* in line 299T11 means "its name" would lead us to a Native American sounding name in Mesopotamia: *'The Old Man Has Grown Young', or 'The Old Man Becomes a Young Man'*! AG's alternative reading of the word *šum-šu* as *šum-ma* ثَمّ is the correct reading. The word *šum-šu* was actually *šum-tu* ثُمتَ consistent with classical Arabic.

ثمم (لسان العرب) وثُمَّ: حرفُ عطفٍ يدلُّ على الترتيب والتراخي، وربَّما أدخلوا عليها التاء

306T11 **307T11**	SA	Quietly, it raised, it snatched [snapped] (ate) the weed On its return, it got rid of (sloughed) a skin
	AG	*Silently it came up and bore the plant off;* *as it turned away it sloughed a skin.*
	MK	*silently came up and carried off the plant.* *While going back it sloughed off its casing.'*
	RT	*Darted he up [from the water (?)], and snatch'd the plant,* *uttering malison As he drew back.*

Notes: Why (and how) would that snake carry the plant? It is very clear the snake ate that plant on the spot, because it supposedly sloughed a skin *before* leaving on its way back, which could not have happened if it had only carried the plant away! In line 306T11, the Assyriology method failed once again in reading the word *iš-ši*. The Arabic meaning "snatched" for *iš-ši* is more fitting. In fact, the earlier translation by RT used this meaning, possibly because it was the logical one, or because RT had consulted the Arabic references. After rising up quietly (i.e. sneakily), the snake must perform a fast act like snatching/biting something, not quietly carrying away something!

والأَشَّاش: الهَشَّاش. واسْتَهَشَّهُ: اسْتَخَفَّهُ. وهشَشْتُ الورَقَ أَهُشُّه هَشّاً: خبَطْتُه بِعصاً ليَتحاتَّ؛ والتَّعسْعُسُ: الشَّمُّ، وطَلَبُ الصَّيْدِ. عس: العين والسين أصلانِ متقاربان: أحدهما الدنوُّ من الشَّيء وطلبُه، والثاني خِفَّةٌ في الشيء.

310T11 **311T11** **312T11** **313T11** **314T11** **315T11** **316T11** **317T11** **318T11**	SA	*Gilgamesh said to him, to Ur-šánabi the shipwright:* "For whom of mine, Ur-šánabi, my arms struggled (endured) For whom of mine, the blood of my heart roiled (boiled) I have not secured (I have not achieved) a well done job to {in} (for) my own (but) To the ferocious creature of the ground (hole) (the snake), I have achieved a well done job Now, after 20 journeys (leagues), the high (sea) tide is proceeding too fast The (underground) tunnel, to uncover it [as I was uncovering it], I threw (down) ropes in it, step by step What can I find that is placed to accompany (guide) me, so I, myself, can feel (my way down) to it? And I had left the raft at the shore (now)"
	AG	*He spoke to Ur-šánabi the boatman:* *"[For whom] of my (kind), Ur-šánabi, did my arms grow exhausted,* *for whom of my (kind) ran dry the blood of my heart?* *Not for myself did I established a bounty,* *[for] the "Lion of the Earth" I have done a favour* *Now for twenty leagues the tide has been rising!* *When I opened the channel I abandoned the tools:* *what thing would I find that was placed (to serve) for my landmark?* *Had I only turned away,* *and left the boat on the shore!"*

	MK	*"Counsel me, O ferryman Urshanabi! For whom have my arms labored, Urshanabi! For whom has my heart's blood roiled! I have not secured any good deed for myself, but done a good deed for the 'lion of the ground'!" Now the high waters are coursing twenty leagues distant,' as I was opening the conduit(?) I turned my equipment over into it (!). What can I find (to serve) as a marker(?) for me! I will turn back (from the journey by sea) and leave the boat by the shore!"*
<u>Notes:</u> For several lines, the current translations of the epic claimed the word *UR.MAḪ* was a Sumerian word meaning "lion". However according to Arabic, this word means "ferocious creature", which would include a lion. And while the word *qaq-qa-ri* can mean earth, even according to references of the Assyriology method, it also means "ground; underworld; lower; down below". Therefore, the term "*UR.MAḪ šá qaq-qa-ri*" in line 314^{T11} means "the ferocious creature of the ground (hole)", clearly refers to the snake that ate the plant. Reading lines 316^{T11}, 317^{T11}, and 318^{T11} correctly requires some analysis and explanation. The Abzu, according to the evidence of the epic, was an underground sea of cosmic/divine water, in the shape of a bowl. Its water, it seems, was feeding oceans, seas, rivers, and lakes located on a flat surface of a half-sphere-like earth. In other words, the Abzu was the lower portion of this half sphere earth, but it was connected to all water bodies via channels. Therefore, one can reach the Abzu via deep tunnels located on high grounds or openings located in the bottom of the sea. Gilgamesh, after hearing about a plant for eternal life located in the bottom of the Abzu, he quickly found/opened a tunnel, *through the ground*, it seems. He used ropes to feel his way down in the deep darkness of that tunnel, until he reached the waters of the Abzu. He then tied heavy stones to his lower legs and jumped into the Abzu sea, in order to reach its bottom floor and pluck that fine-throne plant. Finally, he cut loose the heavy stones off his lower legs, and was brought up by the waters via the openings beneath the sea, to be thrown on the opposite shores of the cosmic, bitter river sea. The word *ú-nu-tú* does mean tools, as current translations indicated. However, according to the historical Arabic references, it also means fixed set of "ropes". Ropes can explain why Gilgamesh could not have reused them again. It seems that he used the same ropes to climb down and then to tie the heavy stones. Ropes are tools, of course, but they are not equipment. Possibly, he had more ropes in the boat, but he explained that he had abandoned that boat on the opposite shores, close by Uta-Napištim (Noah).		
323^{T11} 324^{T11} 325^{T11} 326^{T11}	SA	"Go up, O Ur-šánabi, in the top of [around] the wall of Uruk, go in all directions Explore the protecting apparatus, the brickwork of its waterways (gutters) [Explore the protecting apparatus, examine the brickwork] After all (indeed) [(see) If in fact] its brickwork is not kiln-fired And its foundation, the seven messengers had not laid out
	AG	*"Go up, Ur-šánabi, on the wall of Uruk, and walk around survey its foundation platform, inspect the brickwork! (See) if its brickwork is not kiln-fired brick, And if the Seven Sages did not lay its foundations!*
	MK	*"Go up, Urshanabi, onto the wall of Uruk and walk around. Examine its foundation, inspect its brickwork thoroughly— Is not (even the core of) the brick structure made of kiln-fired brick, and did not the Seven Sages themselves lay out its plans?*
<u>Notes:</u> In the beginning of the epic, the writer asked Gilgamesh, metaphorically, to clime the walls of Uruk to inspect them. In the above closing lines, we are told by the writer that Gilgamesh had asked *Ur-šánabi*, as they arrived in Uruk, to clime its walls to inspect them. This was possibly to indicate that *Ur-šánabi* was awarded a new role, by Gilgamesh this time, as the protector of Uruk.		

Words References Index*

#	Word in Epic	Line# Tablet#	Modern Assyriology References (ePSD, CAD, AALD)* / Notes	Arabic References
1	a a-a a-a a-a a-a	38^{U} 166^{T10} 167^{T10} 169^{T10} 176^{T10}	AALD: a (dem pron) (or ā, aya) (a, a-a) ذلك؛ هؤلاء؛ كلمة آرامية	أيَا (القاموس المحيط) إيا (الصّحّاح في اللغة) أيا (الصّحّاح في اللغة) أيا (لسان العرب) أ (القاموس المحيط)
2	A.^{MEŠ} A.^{MEŠ} A.^{MEŠ} A.^{MEŠ}	112^{T1} 217^{T10} 64^{T11} 254^{T11}	ePSD: a a [WATER] wr. a Akk. mû; rihûtu	أاءٌ (القاموس المحيط) أوأ (لسان العرب)
3	A.ŠÀ	169^{T1}	ePSD: ašag ašag [BUTTERFLY] wr. a-šag$_4^{mušen}$ Akk. kurmittu ašag [FIELD] wr. a-šag$_4$; ašag; $^{a-šag}$$_4$ašag Akk. eqlu AALD: *eqlu (s. m. f.)	حقل (مقاييس اللغة) وشج (مقاييس اللغة) وشج (لسان العرب) عشش (لسان العرب)
4	a-a-ka-ni a-a-i-ka-a	243^{T11} 243^{T11}	AALD: akkana (adv.) (akkanu, akkani) هنا؛ الآن AALD: ayikāni (interr.) أين؟ AALD: ayikī'am (interr.) (ayika, ayaka, ayak) أين؟	وكن (لسان العرب) أيك (لسان العرب) الأيْنُ (القاموس المحيط) أين (مقاييس اللغة) أين (لسان العرب)
5	a-a-la	260^{T10}	ePSD: ayyalu ayalum [STAG] wr. aya-lum Akk. ayyalu simul [STAG] wr. si-mul Akk. ayyalu	أيل (لسان العرب)
6	ÁB	36^{T1}	ePSD: ab ab [COW] wr. ab$_2$ "cow" Akk. arhu; littu	عيب (لسان العرب) عيب (مقاييس اللغة) العَيْبُ (القاموس المحيط)
7	a-ba-an-šu	51^{T11}	ePSD: abnu na [STONE] wr. na$_4$; na; ^{na}$_4$na Akk. abnu niĝkiluha [STONE] wr. ^{ĝeš}niĝ$_2$-ki-luh-ha Akk. abnu za [BEAD] wr. za; za$_2$ Akk. abnu	العَبْنُ (القاموس المحيط) عبنك (لسان العرب) عبن (لسان العرب) أبن (مقاييس اللغة) أبن (لسان العرب)

* Word groupings are based on their classifications in both Arabic and modern Assyriology linguist references, and on the relevancy of their meanings in the new translation of this book. ePSD is the electronic version of the Pennsylvania Sumerian Dictionary. CAD is the Chicago Assyrian Dictionary. AALD is the Akkadian Arabic Language Dictionary, a concise Arabic version of CAD. Arabic root words references from *al-Bahith al-Arabi* database (www.baheth.info), which includes the major five historical Classical Arabic etymological references.

8	*ab-ba-la-áš-šú* *li-bil* *lu-bil-šu*	14[P] 255[T11] 297[T11]	See *ub-la* See *bu-lim*	
9	*ABGAL*	183[T11]	ePSD: abgal abgal [PROFESSION] wr. ab_2-gal Akk. ? abgal [SAGE] wr. $abgal_2$; abgal Akk. apkallu	بجل (مقاييس اللغة) بَجَّلَهُ (القاموس المحيط) بجل (لسان العرب)
10	*ab-ki* *a-bak-ki* *i-bak-ki* *ba-ku-ú* *bi-ki-ti* *ba-ku-ú*	235[T10] 138[T11] 308[T11] 125[T11] 126[T11] 126[T11]	ePSD: bakû er pad [WEEP] wr. er_2 pad_3 Akk. bakû er šeš [WEEP] wr. er_2 $šeš_4$ Akk. bakû šeš [WEEP] wr. $šeš_4$; $še_8$-$še_8$; $še_8$; $šeš_2$; $šeš_x$(|A.IGI|); $šeš_3$; $še_x$(|IGI×A|) Akk. bakû	بكو/ء (مقاييس اللغة) بكا (لسان العرب)
11	*a-bu-bu* *a-bu-bi* *a-ab-ba* *a-bu-be* *A.AB.BA* *a-bu-ba-am-ma*	8[T1] 8[T1] 40[T1] 209[T10] 133[T11] 114[T11]	ePSD: abūbu uru [FLOOD] wr. uru_2; uru_{18}; uru_5 Akk. abūbu ePSD: ab ab [SEA] wr. ab; a-ab-ta "sea" Akk. tâmtu	هبب (لسان العرب) عبب (لسان العرب)
12	*ABZU*	31[T11] 32[T11] 290[T11]	See Part 2.2.1 See also *up-piš* See also *mu-ab-bit* ePSD: abzu abzu [WATER] wr. abzu; $abzu_x$(|UMUM×KASKAL|) Akk. apsû ePSD: apsû abzu [WATER] wr. abzu; $abzu_x$(|UMUM×KASKAL|) Akk. apsû engur [WATERS] wr. engur; im-gu-ra Akk. apsû; engurru	engur عنجه (الصّحّاح في اللغة) عجه (لسان العرب) عنجر (لسان العرب) العَنْجَرَةُ (القاموس المحيط) عنجر (الصّحّاح في اللغة) تنر (لسان العرب) غيض (لسان العرب) غوص (لسان العرب) سوا (لسان العرب) أبت (لسان العرب) أفت (لسان العرب) أبد (لسان العرب) أفد (لسان العرب) أبض (لسان العرب) عفس (لسان العرب) أبس (لسان العرب) بسا (لسان العرب) فسأ (العباب الزاخر) فسا (لسان العرب) بزخ (لسان العرب) بزا (لسان العرب) أبز (لسان العرب) أفز (لسان العرب) عفز (لسان العرب) أكم (لسان العرب)
13	*AD.ḪAL*	282[T11]	See also *pu-ri-su* ePSD: AD.HAL adhal [COPPER] wr. ad-hal Akk. erû adhal [SECRET] wr. ad-hal AD See *AD-šú*	دَخَلَ (القاموس المحيط) دخل (الصّحّاح في اللغة) دخل (لسان العرب)

			ḪAL See ḪA.LA	
14	*a-dan-ni* *ad-din-šu* *na-ad-na-áš-šú* *a-dan-na* *at-ta-din* *id-din*	169^{T1} 236^{T10} 272^{T10} 87^{T11} 96^{T11} 143^{T11}	See also *EDIN* See also *dan-nu* See also *i-du-ú* See also *dan-nu* ePSD: nadānu šum [GIVE] wr. šum$_2$; ze$_2$-eĝ$_3$ Akk. nadānu AALD: adannu (s.)	أذن (لسان العرب) أذِنَ (القاموس المحيط) ذنِن (لسان العرب) الذَّنينُ (القاموس المحيط) دنن (لسان العرب) دنا (لسان العرب) دنا (الصّحّاح في اللغة) دُونَ (القاموس المحيط) دون (لسان العرب) أدن (لسان العرب) وطن (لسان العرب) أطن (لسان العرب) عطن (لسان العرب) عطا (لسان العرب) هدن (مقاييس اللغة) هدن (لسان العرب)
15	*a-di* *a-di* *ad-di* *ad-di*	237^{T10} 80^{T11} 60^{T11} 65^{T11}	See *i-du-ú* See also *ḫa-di-'-a* ePSD: adi enna [UNTIL] wr. en-na; an-ma; en; en$_7$ Akk. adi AALD: *adi (prep.) (hadi, hadu, qadi, qadu)	حَدِيَ (القاموس المحيط) حتا (لسان العرب) عد (مقاييس اللغة) عدد (لسان العرب) عدو (مقاييس اللغة) عدا (الصّحّاح في اللغة) عَدا (القاموس المحيط) عدا (لسان العرب)
16	*AD-šú* *AD-šú-nu*	68^{T1} 15^{T11}	ePSD: AD ad [BEAD] wr. ad ad [LOG] wr. ad; ^{ĝeš}ad ad [VOICE] wr. ad Akk. rigmu adda [FATHER] wr. ad-da; ad Akk. abu	See *i-du-ú*
17	*a-ga-si-li-ga-šu*	52^{T11}	See *UGU* ePSD: agasalakku agasilig [AX] wr. aga-silig Akk. agasalakku silig [AX] wr. ^{ĝeš}silig; ^{ĝeš}silig$_5$ silig [BED] wr. ^{ĝeš}silig Akk. mayyaltu silig [CEASE] wr. silig "to cease" silig [HAND] wr. silig$_2$; silig$_4$ Akk. lupnu; qātu; rittu silig [MIGHTY] wr. šilig; šilig$_6$ Akk. šagapūru	عجا (لسان العرب) سلج (لسان العرب)
18	*a-gur-rat*	20^{T1}	dinig [KILN] wr. dinig; dinig$_3$; di-ni-ig Akk. kūru; nappašu; nappāhu AALD: agurru (s.) (akurru) الكورة، الفرن لحرق الطابوق؛ حجر لرصف الارضيات، الآجر، نوع من الحجر	الكُورُ (القاموس المحيط) أجر (لسان العرب)
19	*a-gu-ú* *ag-gu*	34^{T1} 307^{T10}	ePSD: agû aga [TIARA] wr. aga; aga$_3$ Akk. agû aĝi [WAVE] wr. a-ĝi$_6$ Akk. agû izid [WALL] wr. iz-zi; i-zi Akk. agû; igāru kurku [FLOOD] wr. ku-kur; kur-ku; kur-ku$_4$ Akk. agû men [TIARA] wr. men; men$_4$ Akk. agû	هجج (لسان العرب) أجّ (مقاييس اللغة) أجج (لسان العرب)
20	*a-ḫa-meš-ma*	316^{T10}	See *a-ḫi-ia*	مذذ (لسان العرب) مذي(لسان العرب)

			ePSD: māšu maš [TWIN] wr. Maš Akk. māšu mašmin [TWIN] wr. Mašmin Akk. māšu	
21	*ah̲-bu-ub*	256^{T1}	ePSD: habû dubul [DRAW] wr. du-bu-ul Akk. habû ePSD: habbu umun [PIT] wr. umun$_{10}$; umun$_{11}$; umun$_{12}$; umun$_{5}$; umun$_{6}$ Akk. habbu; hammu	حبب (لسان العرب)
22	*a-h̲i-ia* *a-h̲i* *a-h̲u* *a-h̲a-šú* *a-h̲i-šá* *ah̲-šá* *Á-a*	36^{P} 6^{T11} 112^{T11} 112^{T11} 249^{T11} 249^{T11} 311^{T11}	See also *i-da-a-a* ePSD: ahu a [ARM] wr. a$_2$ Akk. ahu; idu gu [NECK] wr. gu$_2$ Akk. ahu; kišādu; tikku pap [RELATION] wr. pap Akk. abu; ahu; ašarēdu; zikaru šeš [BROTHER] wr. šeš Akk. ahu zag [SIDE] wr. zag Akk. ahu; idu; imittu; ishu; mişru; pāţu	أحح (لسان العرب) عها (لسان العرب) أهه (لسان العرب) أخخ (لسان العرب) هيا (لسان العرب) هوا (لسان العرب)
23	*a-ki-tim-ma*	75^{T11}	ePSD: akītu akiti [FESTIVAL] wr. a$_2$-ki-ti; a$_2$-ki-te; a$_2$-ki-tum Akk. akītu	الأقْتُ (القاموس المحيط) وقت (الصّحاح في اللغة) وقت (لسان العرب)
24	*ak-kal* *ak-la* *i-ku-lu* *ik-lu* *ik-la* *ik-kal* *lu-šá-kil* *lu-kul-ma* *lu-šá-kil*	261^{T10} 213^{T10} 69^{T11} 133^{T11} 133^{T11} 156^{T11} 298^{T11} 300^{T11} 398^{T11}	ePSD: akalu aš [FLOUR] wr. aš Akk. akalu; upumtu ninda [BREAD] wr. ninda; inda Akk. akalu u [PLANTS] wr. u$_2$ Akk. akalu; rîtu; šammu ePSD: akālu gu [EAT] wr. gu$_7$ Akk. akālu rig [EAT] wr. rig$_7$ Akk. akālu; haţāpu; re'û; šatû; sarāpu ePSD: ikkillu akkil [NOISE] wr. akkil; akkil$_2$ Akk. ikkillu; rigmu; tanūqātu; šīsu ašša [LAMENTATION] wr. ašša$_2$ Akk. ikkillu; rigmu gukiri [CRY] wr. gu$_3$-^{ĝeš}kiri$_6$; gu$_3$-kiri$_6$ Akk. ikkillu makkaš [LAMENTATION] wr. makkaš$_2$; makkaš Akk. ikkillu tal [CLAMOR] wr. tal$_3$; ti-il; tal; tal$_4$; tal$_5$; ta-il; til Akk. ikkillu; tanūqātu; šīsu	أكل (مقاييس اللغة) كلأ (الصّحاح في اللغة) كالَ (القاموس المحيط) أكل (لسان العرب)
25	*ak-kan-nu*	226^{T10}	akkannu akkanum [DONKEY] wr. ak-ka-nu-um Akk. akkannu dubdubu [BIRD] wr. dub$_2$-dub$_2$-bu^{mušen} Akk. akkannu; suttinnu; šagaşu	عكن (لسان العرب)
26	*ak-te-šìr*	257^{T10}	See also *ki-şir* AALD: kašāru (v.) (see kašēru) يُصلح، يُعمّر؛ ينجح، ينجز	كسر (مقاييس اللغة) كسر (الصّحاح في اللغة) كسر (لسان العرب) كَسَرَهُ (القاموس المحيط)
27	*al-ka-ka-ti*	2^{U}	See *il-li-kam-ma*	
28	*AM*	35^{T1}	See also *ri-i-mu* ePSD: am am [BIRD] wr. am^{mušen}	أيِم (لسان العرب)

			am [BULL] wr. am Akk. rīmu	
29	*AMA* *um-ma* *um-ma*	72^{T1} 25^{U} 250^{T10}	See also *šum-ma* ePSD: ama ama [CHAMBER] wr. e$_2$-MI; ama$_5$; a$_2$-mi Akk. maštaku ama [MOTHER] wr. ama Akk. ummu ePSD: ama'atud ama'atud [SLAVE] wr. ama-a-tud; ama-tu "house-born slave" Akk. dušmû; wardu ePSD: UM samag [BIRTHMARK] wr. samag$_3$; samag$_2$; samag$_4$; samag$_6$; samag Akk. umşatu; šullu tehi [APPROACH] wr. tehi$_2$; tehi Akk. ţehû tehi [DISEASE] wr. dih$_2$ um [ROPE] wr. um Akk. ummu AALD: uma: الان AALD: ulla: حسنا، اداة نفي، لا، الان AALD: ūma (adv.) (ūmu) في هذا اليوم، اليوم AALD: umma (adv.) (Old Akk: enma, amma) اداة تسبق الكلام المباشر او غير المباشر "يقول"	أما (لسان العرب) أمَ (مقاييس اللغة) أمم (لسان العرب) أوم (لسان العرب) الأوامُ (القاموس المحيط) أمَّهُ (القاموس المحيط)
30	*a-mat* *a-mat* *a-mat* *a-mat-su-nu*	240^{T10} 277^{T10} 9^{T11} 20^{T11}	ePSD: amatu adus [PLANK] wr. ad-us$_2$ Akk. amatu; aduššu inim [WORD] wr. inim; e-ne-eg$_3$ Akk. amatu AALD: amatu (s.) (awatu, awutu, abutu): الامر، القرار، المسألة، الشأن، الشيء، أخبار، تقرير، اشاعة، سر، صيغة النص، المحتوى، الاتفاقية،	عمت (مقاييس اللغة) عمت (لسان العرب) أمت (مقاييس اللغة) أمت (الصّحاح في اللغة) أمت (لسان العرب) أوا (لسان العرب) هبت (مقاييس اللغة) هبت (لسان العرب) هَمَتَ (القاموس المحيط) الهَمُّ (القاموس المحيط) همي (لسان العرب) همم (لسان العرب)
31	*a-me-lu-tu* *a-me-la/lu* *a-me-lu-tùm-ma* *a-me-lut-tu*	48^{T1} 178^{T1} 203^{T11} 220^{T11}	See also *LÚ* ePSD: amēlu ili [MAN] wr. i$_3$-li$_2$ Akk. amēlu lu [PERSON] wr. lu$_2$; mu-lu; mu-lu$_2$; lu$_{10}$; lu$_6$ Akk. amēlu; ša lulu [MAN] wr. lu$_2$-lu$_7$; lu$_2$-lu$_7^{lu}$ Akk. amēlu; lullû na [MAN] wr. na Akk. amēlu ur [MAN] wr. ur Akk. amēlu za [MAN] wr. za Akk. amēlu ePSD: amēltu (s.) المرأة الحرة، مرأة من مركز ادنى او غير محدد ePSD: amēlûtu (s.) البشرية، الجنس البشري، الناس (كبار، صغار، ذكور، اناث)، اي شخص، اي واحد، الجندي، العامل، المستتخدم، العبد	أمل (لسان العرب) عمل (لسان العرب)
32	*am-ḫaş* *am-ḫas-si* *im-taḫ-şu*	64^{T11} 64^{T11} 132^{T11}	See also *im-ta-si* ePSD: mahāşu sag [BEAT] wr. sag$_3$; sag$_2$ Akk. mahāşu	محس (العباب الزاخر) محس (لسان العرب) مَحَسَ (القاموس المحيط) معس (لسان العرب)

			<u>šu rah</u> [BEAT] wr. šu rah$_2$ Akk. mahāşu <u>tu</u> [BEAT] wr. tu$_{14}$ Akk. mahāşu; ţurru <u>tuku</u> [BEAT] wr. tuku$_5$ Akk. mahāşu	محص (مقاييس اللغة) مَحَصَ (القاموس المحيط) محص (لسان العرب) حيض (لسان العرب) خوض (لسان العرب) خض (مقاييس اللغة) مخض (مقاييس اللغة) مَخَضَ (القاموس المحيط) مخض (لسان العرب)
33	*am-ma-ki* *am-ma-ku*	188^{T11} 188^{T11}	See also *a-na-ku-ma* AALD: ammaki (adv.) (ammaku) see makû بدلا من AALD: makû (v.) ماكو، لا يوجد AALD: -māku اداة تشير الى شيء موجود او خيالي: يستعمل بعد الافعال والمفعول به AALD: māku (s.) (makû) ماكو، الغائب AALD: makû (s.) الجاسوس، الغائب؛ الفقر ، العوز ، الحاجة	اما (لسان العرب)
34	*am-ma-ti* *am-ma-tim*	34^{U} 35^{U}	See also *KÙŠ* ePSD: ammatu <u>akuš</u> [FOREARM] wr. a$_2$-kuš$_3$; a$_2$-1(diš)-kuš$_3$ Akk. ammatu <u>anaš</u> [WHY?] wr. a-na-aš Akk. ammatu <u>igiĝal</u> [UNIT] wr. ^{ĝeš}igi-ĝal$_2$ Akk. ammatu <u>kuš</u> [UNIT] wr. kuš$_3$ Akk. ammatu	أمت (مقاييس اللغة) أمت (الصّحّاح في اللغة)
35	*am-ši* *am-ši*	166^{T11} 167^{T11}	ePSD: mašû <u>ĝeštug ulu</u> [FORGET] wr. ĝeštug$_2$ u$_{18}$-lu Akk. mašû <u>halam</u> [FORSAKE] wr. ha-lam; gel-le-eĝ$_3$ Akk. halāqu; lapātu; lemnu; mašû <u>uh</u> [FORGOTTEN] wr. uh$_6$ Akk. mašû <u>Note:</u> mašû = našû	مسح (لسان العرب) مسأ (العباب الزاخر) مَسَأَ (القاموس المحيط) نسي (مقاييس اللغة) نسأ (لسان العرب) نسا (لسان العرب)
36	*a-mur-din-nim-ma*	284^{T11}	ePSD: amurdinnu <u>ĝeštinkira</u> [BERRY] wr. ^{ĝeš}ĝeštin-kir$_4$-ra; ^{ĝeš}ĝeštin-gir$_2$-ra; ^{ĝeš}ĝeštin-kir$_4$; ^{ĝeš}ĝeštin-gir$_2$ "a berry" Akk. amurdinnu	ردن (لسان العرب) مرد (مقاييس اللغة)
37	*a-na-ku-ma* *ana-ku* *ana-ku* *ana-ku* *a-na-ku* *a-na-ku* *a-na-ku* *a-na-ku*	4^{T1} 130^{T1} 157^{T1} 225^{T1} 266^{T1} 290^{T1} 296^{T1} 32^{P}	ePSD: annû <u>ul</u> [PRONOUN] wr. ul-la; ul "a demonstrative pronoun" Akk. annû; ullû AALD: *anāku (pron.) (انا + أكو) انا AALD: kû (adj.) (kûm, kuāu, kuwāu) f. (kattu, kuātu, kuwātu) pl. (kuttun) يعود اليك، لك	أنن (لسان العرب) كو (مقاييس اللغة) كون (لسان العرب) كنن (لسان العرب)
38	*AN-e*	247^{T11} 261^{T11}	See *EN*	
39	*a-ni-ḫ* *ma-na-aḫ-ti* *tu-un-na-ḫa* *i-na-ḫa* *i-na-ḫa* *e-na-ḫa* *i-nu-uḫ* *ma-na-aḫ-ti-ia*	9^{T1} 10^{T1} 298^{T10} 274^{T11} 311^{T11} 311^{T11} 133^{T11} 257^{T10}	See also *ru-uq-ta* ePSD: anāhu <u>kušu</u> [TIRED] wr. kuš$_2$; kuš$_2$-u$_3$ Akk. anāhu ePSD: manahtu <u>akuš</u> [TOIL] wr. a$_2$-kuš$_2$ "toil, labor" Akk. manahtu	عيس (لسان العرب) نوخ (مقاييس اللغة) نوخ (لسان العرب) نخخ (لسان العرب) أنح (لسان العرب) أنح (مقاييس اللغة) نحا (الصّحّاح في اللغة) نحا (لسان العرب)

			AALD: anāẖu (v.) ينوح، يكدح؛ متعب، منهك؛ اكتفى؛ يتسكع، يتألم؛ في غم، مكتئب؛ يغني، يخرج صوت عويل	التَّناوُحُ (القاموس المحيط) نوح (مقاييس اللغة) نوح (لسان العرب) نحح (لسان العرب) منح (مقاييس اللغة) منح (لسان العرب)
40	*an-ni-ta* *an-nu-tum* *an-nu-ti* *a-a-um-ma* *a-a-nu-um-ma* *an-ni-miš* *a-nu* *an-ni-tú*	99[T1] 166[T11] 167[T11] 176[T11] 176[T11] 232[T11] 279[T10] 287[T11]	See also *e-nin-na* ePSD: anumma aše [NOW] wr. a_2-še Akk. anumma ePSD: annu anna [APPROVAL] wr. an-na Akk. annu nanam [CONSENT] wr. na-nam Akk. annu u'ul [CONSENT] wr. u_4-ul Akk. annu AALD: *annu (adv.) الان AALD: *anīna (adv.) الان AALD: annittān (adv.) آنئذٍ، بعدئذ، هذا اذن AALD: annu (pron.) (see anna) (anniu, hanniu, f. annitu) هذا، ذلك AALD: anna (adv.) (anni, annu) نعم AALD: anna (interj) (see annāma) الان، فعلا AALD: anāma (conj.) حالاً AALD: annimmiš̱ (adj.) حالاً AALD: annû (pron.) (anniu, hanniu, f. annītu) هذا، ذلك AALD: anmû (dem. pron.) (anamu) هذا AALD: anūtu (s.) مهنة، منزلة لاعلى الالهة (أنو) مع علامة الاله AALD: anūtu (s.) أداة، معدّات AALD: anna (interj.) (annāma) الان، فعلا AALD: anna (adv. Indecl.) (anni, annû) نعم AALD: anumma (adv.) (anummi, anummu) الآن، هنا AALD: anummānum (adv.) see anummu هناك AALD: anummē (interj.) (anummamē) هُنا، ها هُنا AALD: anummû (dem. pron.) (f. anummūtu) هذا المذكور آنفا	أنن (لسان العرب) هلم (لسان العرب) هنا (الصّحّاح في اللغة) هنا (لسان العرب) هنا (لسان العرب)
41	*a-pa-a-ti* *ap-pat*	44[T1] 31[U]	See also *ap-pi-šu* ePSD: appātu šītu kiritab [BRIDLE] wr. [kuš]$kiri_3$-tab Akk. appātu šītu; aššatu šītu ePSD: appat ša imēri zib [DONKEY-BRIDLE] wr. zib_2 Akk. appat ša imēri	عفت (مقاييس اللغة) عفت (لسان العرب) عبت (لسان العرب) عبأ (لسان العرب) عفا (لسان العرب)
42	*ap-laẖ-ma* *pal-ẖa-ku-ma* *lu-pu-ul* *pu-luẖ-ta* *ip-tal-ẖu* *ip-la-ẖu*	129[T1] 239[T10] 35[T11] 93[T11] 114[T11] 114[T11]	ePSD: palāhu ni teĝ [FEAR] wr. ni_2 $teĝ_3$ Akk. palāhu; šahātu šu e [BLESS] wr. šu e_3 Akk. waşû; palāhu; karābu ePSD: puluhtu ni [FEAR] wr. ni_2; e; ne_4 Akk. puluhtu AALD: pālilu (s.) الطليقة (للجيش)، الراكض، المتقدم AALD: pallākum (s.) ارض ممسوحة	فلح (لسان العرب) بله (لسان العرب) بلح (مقاييس اللغة) فَلَخَهُ (القاموس المحيط) فلل (الصّحّاح في اللغة) فلل (لسان العرب) فلو (مقاييس اللغة) فلا (لسان العرب) أفَلَ (القاموس المحيط) افل (لسان العرب) فَلَّهُ (القاموس المحيط)

43	*ap-pi-šu* *ap-pi-ia* *ap-pi-ia* *ap-pi-šú* *a-pi*	237^{T10} 137^{T11} 139^{T11} 309^{T11} 301^{T10}	ePSD: appu kiri [NOSE] wr. $kiri_3$ Akk. Appu ePSD: apu abum [FUNERARY MOUND] wr. a-bu-um Akk. apu ePSD: ipu arhuš [WOMB] wr. arhuš; $arhuš_2$; $arhuš_5$; $arhuš_6$ Akk. ipu; rîmu uš [MEMBRANE] wr. $uš_3$; $uš_5$; $uš_6$ Akk. ipu; silītu; silītu AALD: apu (s.) (abu) القصب الثخين، اجمة (غابة) قصب AALD: apu (s.) الحفرة؛ معنى غير اكيد Note: al-juburi rule: anpi -> appi	أفف (لسان العرب) أف (مقاييس اللغة) افف (العباب الزاخر) أنف (لسان العرب) عفا (لسان العرب)
44	*a-ra-le-e* *i-rat-su-nu*	41^{T9}	Hayds إنحرافات؛ جحيم؛ دارُ البَوَار : جَهَنَّم	
45	*a-ri-bi* *a-ri-bi-ma*	154^{T11} 155^{T11}	ePSD: arabû arabu [BIRD] wr. a_{12}-ra_2-$bu^{mušen}$; $adab^{mušen}$; a_2-$tab^{mušen}$; $^{udu\text{-}bu}adab^{mušen}$ Akk. arabû; usābu ePSD: Akk. āribu "rook, jackdaw; crow, raven" ePSD: ereb šamši utušuš [SUNSET] wr. utu-$šu_2$-uš; utu-$šuš_2$ Akk. ereb šamši ePSD: erēbu[rook] buru [BIRD] wr. $buru_4^{mušen}$; gu-$ur_2^{mušen}$; $buru_{15}^{mušen}$; $buru_{16}^{mušen}$; $buru_6^{mušen}$ Akk. erēbu[rook] AALD: *āribu (s.) (ēribu, hērebu or arību, erēbu, herēbu) الغراب، الغداف (غراب اسود)، نبات، سمكة	غرب (لسان العرب)
46	*ár-ku-ú* *ar-ka* *ár-ku* *mu-rak-šá*	17^{T1} 32^{T1} 32^{T1} 30^{T11}	See also EGIR ePSD: arkatu aga [REAR] wr. a-ga; a-ba Akk. arkatu eĝir [BACK] wr. eĝir; $eĝir_5$(LUM); $egir_4$; $eĝir_6$($MURGU_2$) Akk. arkatu ePSD: arāku gid [LONG] wr. gid_2 Akk. arāku AALD: marāku (s.) (see arākû) الطول، الامتداد AALD: arākû (v.) يطول، يمتد، يدوم طويلا، يتأخر	ورك (لسان العرب) عرك (لسان العرب) أرك (لسان العرب) رك (مقاييس اللغة) ركك (الصّحاح في اللغة) ركا (لسان العرب)
47	*ár-ni*	185^{T11}	See also ^{ĝeš}ERIN AALD: arnu (s.) (annu) ذنب، اثم، جريمة	أرن (مقاييس اللغة) أرَن (القاموس المحيط) ارن (الصّحاح في اللغة) أرن (لسان العرب)
48	*ar-pu* *ur-pa-tum*	119^{T1} 98^{T11}	ePSD: erpetu dungu [CLOUD] wr. dungu Akk. erpetu; upû zela [CLOUD] wr. ze_2-la Akk. erpetu ePSD: erēpu ša ūmi	عرف (مقاييس اللغة) عَرَفَةُ (القاموس المحيط) عرف (لسان العرب) رفا (لسان العرب) أرف (لسان العرب)

			<u>ud šuš</u> [DARKEN] wr. ud šu$_2$ Akk. erēpu ša ūmi	
49	*asa*	259[T10]	ePSD: asu <u>az</u> [BEAR] wr. az; ^{ĝeš}az "bear; ~ figurine" Akk. asu <u>az</u> [MYRTLE] wr. ^{ĝeš}az; ^{ĝeššim}az "myrtle" Akk. asu	See *áš-ši-šu-ma*
50	*a-šá-red*	31[T1]	ePSD: ašaredu <u>ušum</u> [SNAKE] wr. ušum "first and foremost; noble; snake" Akk. ašaredu; bašmu; gitmālu	رود (لسان العرب)
51	*a-šá-rit-ti*	58[T1] 37[U]	See also *IGI.DU.*[MEŠ]	عذر (لسان العرب) عذر (مقاييس اللغة) وجد (لسان العرب) دعع (لسان العرب) جبب (الصّحَاح في اللغة) الجَبَبُ (القاموس المحيط) جعب (لسان العرب) الجَوْبُ (القاموس المحيط) جوب (لسان العرب)
52	*as-ḫur* *is-saḫ-ra* *is-saḫ-ra* *is-saḫ-ra*	251[T10] 150[T11] 153[T11] 156[T11]	See also *šèr-ri* See also *uš-ta-aḫ-ri-ru* ePSD: sahāru <u>dub</u> [GO AROUND] wr. dab$_6$; dub Akk. lawû; sahāru <u>gur</u> [TURN] wr. gur Akk. sahāru; târu <u>niĝin</u> [ENCIRCLE] wr. niĝin$_2$; niĝin Akk. esēru; lawû; sahāru; târu; târu; sahāru; ṣâdu <u>šu niĝin</u> [MAKE A ROUND TRIP] wr. šu niĝin$_2$; šu niĝin Akk. sahāru ePSD: šaharru <u>sadua</u> [NET] wr. sa-du$_3$-a Akk. šaharru <u>sahar</u> [POROUS?] wr. sahar$_2$ Akk. šaharru <u>sahar</u> [VESSEL] wr. ^{dug}sahar; ^{dug}sahar$_2$ Akk. šaharru ePSD: sahirru <u>sahir</u> [NET] wr. sa-hir Akk. Sahirru AALD: sihru (s.) (sahru) الحافة، الحاشية، الحدّ؛ الانعطاف، الانحراف؛ حافة، احاطة؛ تماما؛ انواع من الحجر	شخر (لسان العرب) سخر (مقاييس اللغة) سَخِرَ (القاموس المحيط) سخر (لسان العرب) سهر (لسان العرب) سهر (مقاييس اللغة) See *šèr-ri*
53	*aš-ri-šú-nu* *áš-ri-šu-nu* *ú-maš-šar* *a-šar* *muš-šir* *aš-ru* *ú-maš-šar* *ú-maš-šar* *ú-maš-šar* *ú-maš-šir*	43[T1] 43[T1] 68[T1] 211[T1] 25[T11] 126[T11] 148[T11] 151[T11] 154[T11] 154[T11]	See also *šu-nu* ePSD: ašru <u>ki</u> [PLACE] wr. ki Akk. ašru; erṣetu; mātu; qaqqaru; šaplû ePSD: ašāru <u>na deg</u> [CLEAR] wr. na deg$_x$(RI); ša di; ša di-di; ša di-di$_5$; ša di$_5$ Akk. ašāru; elēlu; hasāsu <u>šuš</u> [COVER] wr. šuš$_2$; šuš; šuš$_5$ Akk. ašāru; erēpu; katāmu; sahāpu; sehpu; šaqû ša lubši ePSD: ašar samāti <u>kisaĝĝala</u> [STRONGHOLD] wr. ki-saĝ-ĝal$_2$-la Akk. ašar dimāti; ašar samāti	wašaru "to sink down" ذرا (لسان العرب) وذر (لسان العرب) وثر (مقاييس اللغة) وَثْرَةُ (القاموس المحيط) وثر (لسان العرب) وشَرَ (القاموس المحيط) مذر (لسان العرب) مَذِرَتِ (القاموس المحيط) مذر (الصّحَاح في اللغة) مشر (لسان العرب) مسر (الصّحَاح في اللغة) مسر (لسان العرب)

			ePSD: wašaru ri [IMPOSE] wr. RI; ru Akk. bâ'u; emēdu; nadû; nasāku; ramû; rehû; tarû; wašaru ePSD: wašru dun [HUMBLE] wr. dun_5-na Akk. wašru ePSD: esēru pag [ENCLOSE] wr. pag Akk. esēru; šutanuhu ePSD: esēru; lawû niĝin [ENCIRCLE] wr. niĝin2; niĝin Akk. esēru; lawû; sahāru; târu; târu; sahāru; şâdu ePSD: ešēru si sa [STRAIGHTEN] wr. si sa2; si si-sa2 Akk. ešēru; šutēšuru AALD: mašāru (v.) يمشط (الملابس)، ينسحب (على الارض)، يدفع حول، يسحب حول، يؤجل؟ (يهجر) AALD: wašāru (See ašāru) AALD: ašāru (v.) يحرر AALD: *ašru (s. m. and f.) (ašaru, išru) الاشارة، المكان، الموقع، المنطقة، البلاد، المدينة، المكان المقدس ašar šumšu: هنا وهناك	مَسَرَهُ (القاموس المحيط) أشِرَ (القاموس المحيط) أشر (لسان العرب) أثر (لسان العرب) شور (لسان العرب) شارَ (القاموس المحيط) سرو (الصّحّاح في اللغة) سرر (لسان العرب) الأَسْرُ (القاموس المحيط) هسر (لسان العرب) أسر (لسان العرب)
54	*áš-šá-te*	256[T1]	aššatu dam [SPOUSE] wr. dam "spouse" Akk. aššatu; mutu	أست (لسان العرب) أَسْتُ (القاموس المحيط)
55	*áš-ši-šu-ma* *áš-šá-áš-šu-ma* *áš-šá-áš-šu-ma* áš-ši-a-šú-ma *iš-šá-a* *iš-šá-am-ma* *iš-ši* *iš-ši* *iš-ši* *iš-šu-ú*	249[T1] 257[T1] 283[T1] 14[P] 312[T10] 312[T10] 165[T11] 276[T11] 306[T11] 104[T11]	See also *nu-us-su* See also *ši-tas-si* See also *ú-še-şu-ú* See also *it-ti-si* See also *i-šu-ú* See also *is-su-ú* AALD: ašāšu (v.) يسبب uššuššu uššuššu، يقبق، يضطرب، في يأس الاذي ، يؤذي شخصا AALD: ašāšu (v.) ešešu يمسك (بشبكة)، يغمر، يغرق AALD: ašâtu (s.) سائق العربة AALD: ašannu (s.) الجندي AALD: asumātanu (s.) الطير	شَشا (لسان العرب) شيص (مقاييس اللغة) الشِّيصُ (القاموس المحيط) أشأ (لسان العرب) الوَشْيُ (القاموس المحيط) وشي (لسان العرب) أشش (لسان العرب) هسس (العباب الزاخر) هسس (لسان العرب) هَشَّ (القاموس المحيط) هشش (الصّحّاح في اللغة) هشش (لسان العرب) خبط (العباب الزاخر) نهش (مقاييس اللغة) نهس (العباب الزاخر) أسي (الصّحّاح في اللغة) أسا (لسان العرب) أسو (مقاييس اللغة) سوس (لسان العرب) وهس (لسان العرب) وعس (مقاييس اللغة) الوَعْسُ (القاموس المحيط) وعس (لسان العرب) عَسَّ (القاموس المحيط)

				عسس (العباب الزاخر) عس (مقاييس اللغة) عسو/ي (مقاييس اللغة) عَسا (القاموس المحيط) عسا (لسان العرب) عسس (لسان العرب)
56	*áš-šú*	264[T10] 265[T10] 276[T10] 120[T11]	See *šá* See *šá-a-šú* AALD: aššum (conj.) (aššu) بسبب، بالرغم من، لذلك، ذلك AALD: aššum (prep.) (aššu, ašši, aššumi, aššumma) بخصوص، بالاضافة الى، بسبب كذا، فيما يتعلق <u>Note:</u> áš-šú = á-šú = há-šú = that, those = [هذو] أذو = ذلك، هذا، ذلك لأن، هذا لأن	
57	*a-ṭe-eḫ-ḫa-a* *a-ṭe-eḫ-ḫa-a* *i-ṭe-eḫ-ḫa-a* *i-ṭe-ḫ-ḫa-a* *i-ṭe-eḫ-ḫa-a* *i-ṭe-eḫ-ḫa-a* *uṭ-ṭè-eḫ-ḫa-a*	129[T1] 156[T1] 144[T1] 144[T1] 165[T1] 183[T1] 277[T11]	ṭehû <u>teĝ</u> [APPROACH] wr. teĝ$_3$; teĝ$_4$ "(to be) near to; to approach" Akk. ṭehû <u>tehi</u> [APPROACH] wr. tehi$_2$; tehi "to approach" Akk. ṭehû	طخخ (لسان العرب) طَحا (القاموس المحيط) طحح (لسان العرب) طوح (لسان العرب) الطَّخُّ (القاموس المحيط) حطأ (لسان العرب) طحا (لسان العرب)
58	*at-ta-bak* *at-ta-bak* *at-ta-bak*	66[T11] 160[T11] 316[T11]	ePSD: tabāku <u>bala</u> [TURN] wr. bal; bil$_2$ Akk. elû; nabalkutu; nakāru; naqû; palû; tabāku	بقق (لسان العرب) بكك (الصّحاح في اللغة) بكّ (مقاييس اللغة) بكك (الصّحاح في اللغة) بَكَّهُ (القاموس المحيط) باكَ (القاموس المحيط) بكك (لسان العرب)
59	*at-ti* *at-ti* *at-ti* *at-ta*	95[T1] 258[T1] 285[T1] 20[P]	See also *ka-ti* AALD: atta (pron.) (attu) أنت، مفرد مذكر AALD: atti (pron.) (see atta) أنت، مفرد مؤنث	
60	*ba-aš-lat*	229[T11]	ePSD bašālu <u>šeĝ</u> [COOK] wr. šeĝ$_6$ Akk. bašālu	البَسْلُ (القاموس المحيط) بسل (لسان العرب) خمم (لسان العرب)
61	BÀD BÀD-*šú* BAD BÀD	11[T1] 13[T1] 318[T10] 137[T11]	ePSD: BAD <u>bad</u> [OPEN] wr. bad; ba; be$_2$ "(to be) remote; to open, undo; to thresh grain with a threshing sledge" Akk. be'ēšû; nesû; petû <u>barag</u> [SPREAD] wr. BAD; ba-ra-ge; ba-ra-ga; ^{ba}barag$_2$; KISAL^{ra} "to spread out" Akk. uşşû; šuparruru <u>mud</u> [BLOOD] wr. mud; mud$_2$ "blood" Akk. dāmu <u>ulal</u> [OVEN] wr. ulal "oven" Akk. tinūru <u>ziz</u> [INSECT] wr. ziz; ziz$_3$; ziz$_4$; za-az "an insect" Akk. sāsu; ākilu	بعد (مقاييس اللغة) بعد (لسان العرب) بيض (مقاييس اللغة) بيض (الصّحاح في اللغة) بيض (لسان العرب) بيد (مقاييس اللغة) بود(لسان العرب) بادَ (القاموس المحيط)
62	*ba-lá-ṭu* *ba-lá-ṭi* *bul-liṭ* *ib-luṭ*	41[T1] 41[T1] 26[T11] 176[T11]	balāṭu <u>til</u> [LIVE] wr. til$_3$ "to live; to sit (down); to dwell" Akk. ašābu; balāṭu AALD: balāṭu (s.) الحياة، العيش، الصحة الجيدة 2) طول الحياة، مدى الحياة 3) السنوات القادمة 4) الاحتياط، التوفير	بلا (لسان العرب) بلل (لسان العرب) بلو/ي (مقاييس اللغة) بلط (لسان العرب) بلط (العباب الزاخر)

			AALD: balāṭu (v.) يتحسن، يتماثل للشفاء 2) ينشط، بصحة تامة، يستمر، يدوم 3) يحيا، يبقى حيا، يهرب، يعيش، يحصل على طعام See: balittu, balitti	دهر (لسان العرب) See *da-ar* بلط (مقاييس اللغة) البَلاطُ (القاموس المحيط)
63	*bal-ta* *bal-ti-šú*	236[T1] 258[T11]	ePSD: biltu baltu dih [WEED] wr. ^{ĝeš}dih$_3$; dih$_3$; ^{ĝeš}tehi "a weed with thorns" Akk. baltu bāštu teš [PRIDE] wr. teš$_2$ "pride" Akk. bāštu AALD: baltu (see baštu) AALD: baštu (s.) الوقار، الكبرياء، حسن المنظر، الجلال، الغرور	بلت (لسان العرب) بتل (لسان العرب) بأس (مقاييس اللغة)
64	*BI* baṣāṣu	296[T11]	ePSD: BI bad [OPEN] wr. bad; ba; be$_2$ Akk. be'ēšû; nesû; petû biz [TRICKLE] wr. bi-iz; biz Akk. baṣāṣu dug [POT] wr. dug; dug$_x$(BI) Akk. karpatu e [SPEAK] wr. e; na-be$_2$-a; be$_2$; ne; da-me; na-be$_2$; e$_7$ Akk. atwû; dabābu; qabû ešemen [ROPE] wr. ešemen; ešemen$_2$; e-šen; ešemen$_3$; ešemen$_5$ Akk. keppû; mēlultu kaš [BEER] wr. kaš; kaš$_2$ Akk. šikaru ePSD: baṣāṣu biz [TRICKLE] wr. bi-iz; biz Akk. baṣāṣu	بيز (لسان العرب) بوز (لسان العرب) بأز (لسان العرب) بازَ (القاموس المحيط) بصا (لسان العرب) وبص (لسان العرب) بصص (لسان العرب)
65	*bi-rit* *bi-rit* *bi-rit* *bi-ri-it* *bi-ri-in-ni*	53[T1] 57[T1] 210[T11] 5[P] 202[T11]	birītu dalbana [SPACE] wr. dal-ba-na "intermediate space; property held in common" Akk. birītu murub [MIDDLE] wr. murub$_6$; murub$_4$; murub$_2$; murub; murub$_3$ "middle; female genitals, vulva; buttocks, rump; knob; mouth; gate (of city or large building); space between, distance; link; hips" Akk. abullu; birītu; bişşūru; pinku; pû; qablu; qinnatu; ûru	بون (لسان العرب) بون (الصّحّاح في اللغة) بين (لسان العرب)
66	*bir-ki-a-šú* *bir-ka-a-šú*	200[T1] 200[T1]	burgû burgia [OFFERING] wr. bur-gi$_4$-a; bur-ra-gi$_4$-a "an offering" Akk. burgû AALD: birku (s.) (burku) الركبة AALD: burku (s.) العدّاء، الراكض	برك (لسان العرب) برخ (لسان العرب) البَرْخُ (القاموس المحيط) برخ (مقاييس اللغة)
67	*bi-tuš-šú*	117[T1]		طوس (لسان العرب) توس (لسان العرب)
68	*bu-lim* *bu-la* *be-lí-ia* *be-lí* *bil-šú-ma*	111[T1] 260[T10] 32[T11] 33[T11] 253[T11]	ePSD: bēltu ereš [LADY] wr. ereš Akk. bēltu; šarratum nin [LADY] wr. nin; ga-ša-an; ga-ša$_2$-an; ka-ša-an Akk. bēltu; bēlu ugunu [LADY] wr. ugunu$_2$ Akk. bēltu ePSD: bēlu en [LORD] wr. en; u$_3$-mu-un; umun Akk. bēlu	بأل (لسان العرب) بول (لسان العرب) البَعْلُ (القاموس المحيط) بعل (لسان العرب)

			<u>lugal</u> [KING] wr. lugal; lu_2-gal Akk. bēlu; šarru <u>nin</u> [LADY] wr. nin; ga-ša-an; ga-$ša_2$-an; ka-ša-an Akk. bēltu; bēlu būlu (s) (1) قطيع من الماشية، الاغنام او الخيول (2) حيوانات برية	
69	*BÚR-ár*	245^{T1}	See also *i-pa-áš-šar*	برر (لسان العرب) لبِرُّ (القاموس المحيط) برَّ (مقاييس اللغة) بأر (لسان العرب)
70	*bu-şa*	259^{T10}	būşu <u>kir</u> [HYENA] wr. kir_4 "hyena" Akk. būşu	البَوْصُ (القاموس المحيط)
71	*bu-še-e-šú*	96^{T11}	See *i-ba-áš-ši*	
72	*bu-uḫ-re-e-ti*	127^{T11}	See *nap-ḫar* AALD: *buhhuru (v.) يبخّر، يحمي AALD: *buhra (adv.) ببخار، بحرارة AALD: *buhrītu (adj.) مُبخِر، طبق حار	بهر (مقاييس اللغة) البُهْرُ (القاموس المحيط) بهر (لسان العرب) بخر (مقاييس اللغة) بخر (الصّحّاح في اللغة) البَخْرُ (القاموس المحيط) بخر (لسان العرب)
73	*bu-ú-ri* *bu-ú-ru* *bu-ú-ri* *bu-ra* *bu-ú-ru*	39^{T1} 39^{T1} 130^{T1} 303^{T11}	ePSD: būrtu <u>pu</u> [WELL] wr. pu_2 Akk. asurrû; būrtu; šuplu <u>tul</u> [FOUNTAIN] wr. tul_2; |LAGAB×TIL| Akk. būrtu; hirītu; kalakku	بأر (لسان العرب) بور (لسان العرب)
74	*^{d}30*	281^{T10} 282^{T10}	See ^{d}Sin	
75	*da-'-um-mat* *da-'-um-mati*	107^{T11} 107^{T11}	ePSD: da'āmu <u>kukku</u> [DARK] wr. ku_{10}-ku_{10}; $kukku_5$ "(to be) dark" Akk. da'āmu	دوم (لسان العرب) دهم (لسان العرب)
76	*da-ar* *da-riš*	248^{T10} 167^{T11}	See also *du-ur-šú* ePSD: dārû <u>dari</u> [ETERNAL] wr. da-ri_2; da-ri; du-ri Akk. dārû	دهر (مقاييس اللغة) دهر (مقاييس اللغة) دهر (الصّحّاح في اللغة) دهر (لسان العرب)
77	*da-du-šú* *da-du-ka*	186^{T1} 186^{T1}	See also *DU.DU-ku* AALD: dādu (s.) المغازلة	ددن (لسان العرب) الدَّدَنُ (القاموس المحيط) ددا (لسان العرب)
78	*DAGAL-ti* *DAGAL-tim*	40^{T1} 40^{T1}	ePSD: dağal <u>dağal</u> <u>[WIDE]</u> (745x: ED IIIb, Old Akkadian, Lagash II, Ur III, Early Old Babylonian, Old Babylonian, unknown) wr. dağal; dam-gal; di-am-ga-al; da-ma-al Akk. rupšu	دجل (لسان العرب) دقل (لسان العرب)
79	*da-la-pi* *da-la-pi* *dal-pu-ma* *ta-ad-da-li-ip* *da-la-pi*	255^{T10} 255^{T10} 283^{T10} 297^{T10} 298^{T10}	ePSD: dalāpu igi lib [AWAKE] wr. igi lib; igi lib4 Akk. dalāpu <u>Note:</u> igi lib = old face dalāpu = walks slowly = be awake (at night) = aging = elderly	IGI LIB See *IGI.DU.*^{MEŠ} دَلَفَ (القاموس المحيط) دلف (لسان العرب) حصص (لسان العرب) lib لحب (الصّحّاح في اللغة)

80	*DAM* *DAM* *da-mu*	271[T1] 267[T1] 312[T11]	See *DUMU* See also *áš-šá-te*	
81	*DANNA*	301[T11]	ePSD: DA.NA <u>dana</u> [UNIT] wr. da-na; danna; dana$_2$ Akk. bêru	طعن (لسان العرب) ظعن (مقاييس اللغة) ظعن (لسان العرب) شوط (لسان العرب) فرسخ (لسان العرب)
82	*dan-nu* *dan-nu* *dan-nu* *dan-nu* *dan-nu* *dan-nu-us-su* *da-an* *da-an* *dan-na* *dan-niš*	33[T1] 141[T1] 268[T1] 272[T1] 291[T1] 42[T1] 124[T1] 249[T1] 238[T1] 232[T10]	See also *ik-ta-bi-it* ePSD: dannu <u>kalag</u> [STRONG] wr. kal-ga; kalag; kal-la Akk. dannu; kubbû <u>lirum</u> [STRENGTH] wr. lirum; lirum$_3$; lirum$_2$; lirum$_6$; lirum$_7$; lirum$_8$ Akk. abaru; dannu; emûqu; gāmiru; kamiru; kirimmu; umašu; šapşu; šitnunu; šitpuşu <u>urun</u> [EXALTED] wr. urun$_x$(EN); u$_{18}$-ru; uru; uru$_{15}$ Akk. dannu; šapsu; şīru AALD: danniš (adv.) (see danānu) بعظمة، بقسوة، كثيرا جدا	دنن (لسان العرب) الدَّنُّ (القاموس المحيط) ذأن (لسان العرب) دين (مقاييس اللغة) ذعن (لسان العرب) دعن (لسان العرب) الضَّنَنُ (القاموس المحيط) ضنن (لسان العرب) دعث (لسان العرب)
83	*^{d}a-num* ^{d}AN	93[T1]	<u>See Part 2.2.2</u> See also *EN* *Ancient Mesopotamian Gods and Goddesses*: http://oracc.museum.upenn.edu/amgg/listofdeities/an/index.html ePSD: AN <u>an</u> [SKY] wr. an Akk. šamû <u>an</u> [SPADIX] wr. a$_2$-an; an Akk. sissinnu <u>diĝir</u> [DEITY] wr. diĝir; dim$_3$-me-er; dim$_3$-me$_8$-er; dim$_3$-mi-ir; di-me$_2$-er Akk. iltu; ilu <u>ilu</u> [GOD] wr. ilu Akk. ilu	انن (لسان العرب) عنن (لسان العرب) عَنَّ (القاموس المحيط) عني (مقاييس اللغة) عنا (لسان العرب)
84	*^{d}a-nun-na-ki*	319[T10] 103[T11]	<u>See Part 2.2.3</u> See also *^{d}í-gì-gì* *a-nun-na* see ^{d}a-num Ki see *KI-tim* *Ancient Mesopotamian Gods and Goddesses*: http://oracc.museum.upenn.edu/amgg/listofdeities/anunna/index.html	
85	*^{d}a-ru-ru*	94[T1]	<u>See Part 2.2.4</u> See also *DINGIR.MAḪ*	رير (مقاييس اللغة) الرَّيْرُ (القاموس المحيط) رير (الصّحاح في اللغة) رير (لسان العرب)
86	*^{d}é-a* *^{d}é-a*	242[T1] 19[T11]	<u>See Part 2.2.5</u> See *^{d}nu-dím-mud*	
87	*^{d}en-ki-dú*	103[T1]	<u>See Part 2.2.6</u>	كَأَدَ (القاموس المحيط) كأد (لسان العرب)

			Wikipedia: *https://en.wikipedia.org/wiki/Enkidu* *Mythology Dictionary*: http://www.mythologydictionary.com/enkidu-mythology.html *en-ki* see ^{d}*nu-dím-mud* ePSD: abnu na [STONE] wr. na_4; na; $^{na}{}_4$na Akk. abnu niĝkiluha [STONE] wr. ^{ĝeš}niĝ$_2$-ki-luh-ha Akk. abnu za [BEAD] wr. za; za$_2$ Akk. abnu ePSD: kûtu algameš [STONE] wr. algameš Akk. algamišu; kûtu emerah [JUG] wr. emerah$_x$(|UD.SAL.HUB$_2$|); emerah Akk. kûtu AALD: kâdu (v.) يُزعج، يُقلق AALD: kīdu (s.) ريفي، شخص من خارج المدينة	كَدَأ (القاموس المحيط) كود (مقاييس اللغة) وكد (لسان العرب) كدا (لسان العرب) كدد (لسان العرب) كيد (مقاييس اللغة) كيد (الصّحّاح في اللغة) كيد (لسان العرب) كمد (لسان العرب) كتت (لسان العرب) كوت (لسان العرب) الكَعْتُ (القاموس المحيط) كتع (لسان العرب) وكع (لسان العرب) الكَتْأَةُ (القاموس المحيط) جعد (لسان العرب) جد (مقاييس اللغة) العَبْنُ (القاموس المحيط) عبنك (لسان العرب) عبن (لسان العرب) حبن (لسان العرب) عنك (مقاييس اللغة) عنك (لسان العرب) الأَنْكُ (القاموس المحيط)
88	^{d}*en-líl*	242^{T1}	See Part 2.2.7 See *EN* See *lu-bu-ši* See *i-tap-la-as* See *nim-ru* *Ancient Mesopotamian Gods and Goddesses:* http://oracc.museum.upenn.edu/amgg/listofdeities/enlil/ *Wikipedia:* https://en.wikipedia.org/wiki/Enlil ePSD: lillu lil [FOOL] wr. lil; $^{lu}{}_2$lil$_2$; lil$_3$; lil$_5$; lil$_8$ Akk. lillu lilû lillilgi [DEMON] wr. |LIL$_2$.LIL$_2$|-gi$_4$ Akk. lilû ePSD: zīqīqu lil [GHOST] wr. lil$_2$ Akk. zīqīqu ePSD: zīqīqu? sisig [BREEZE] wr. sig-sig; ^{tumu}si-si-ig; si-si-ga; sig$_3$-sig$_3$ Akk. mehû; zīqīqu?; šāru	زوق (الصّحّاح في اللغة) زقا (الصّحّاح في اللغة) زقق (لسان العرب) زيق (لسان العرب) لعب (لسان العرب) لألأ (الصّحّاح في اللغة) اللُّؤْلُؤُ (القاموس المحيط) ألّ (مقاييس اللغة) ألل (الصّحّاح في اللغة) ألل (لسان العرب) يلل (لسان العرب) اللَّيْلُ (القاموس المحيط) ليل (لسان العرب) الغُلُّ (القاموس المحيط) جن (مقاييس اللغة) جَنَّهُ (القاموس المحيط) جنن (لسان العرب) بلس (لسان العرب) لبس (لسان العرب) نمر (مقاييس اللغة) نمر (الصّحّاح في اللغة) نمر (لسان العرب)
89	^{d}*en-nu-gi*	17^{T11} 18^{T11}	See Part 2.2.8 *Wikipedia:* https://en.wikipedia.org/wiki/Ennugi ePSD: engû engiz [COOK] wr. engiz Akk. engişu; engû; nuhatimmu	نوج (لسان العرب) عنج (مقاييس اللغة) عنج (لسان العرب)

			العنج = التابع، الأمعة، الخادم دنجر عَنُج = الاله التابع، الأمعة، الخادم	
90	*ᵈèr-ra-kal* *ᵈèr-ra*	102[T11] 194[T11]	See Part 2.2.9 *Ancient Mesopotamian Gods and Goddesses:* http://oracc.museum.upenn.edu/amgg/listofdeities/erra/index.html	حرا (الصّحَاح في اللغة) هرو (مقاييس اللغة) الهِراوَةُ (القاموس المحيط) هرأ (لسان العرب) هرا (لسان العرب) هرق (لسان العرب) روق (لسان العرب) حرق (لسان العرب) عركل (لسان العرب) عرك (لسان العرب) حركل (لسان العرب) رقل (لسان العرب) ركل (مقاييس اللغة)
91	*ᵈGIŠ* *ᵈGIŠ-gím-maš* *ᵈbìl.ga.mes* *ᵐᵈGIŠ*-TUK *ᵐᵈGIŠ*-TUK	1[P] 3[T1] 204[T10] 204[T10] 207[T10]	See Part 2.2.10 See also *e-mu-qí* *Wikipedia:* https://en.wikipedia.org/wiki/Gilgamesh ePSD: bēlu en [LORD] wr. en; u_3-mu-un; umun Akk. bēlu lugal [KING] wr. lugal; lu_2-gal Akk. bēlu; šarru nin [LADY] wr. nin; ga-ša-an; ga-$ša_2$-an; ka-ša-an Akk. bēltu; bēlu	GIŠ جحش (لسان العرب) جحش (مقاييس اللغة) الجَحْشُ (القاموس المحيط) جحش (الصّحَاح في اللغة) جحس (العباب الزاخر) جشش (لسان العرب) جيش (مقاييس اللغة) جاشَ (القاموس المحيط) gím-maš جحمش (لسان العرب) جمش (مقاييس اللغة) جمش (لسان العرب) جمش (الصّحَاح في اللغة) جمس (مقاييس اللغة) جمس (الصّحَاح في اللغة) الجامُوسُ (القاموس المحيط) bìl بعل (لسان العرب) TUK توك (لسان العرب) تايَكُ (القاموس المحيط) تيك (لسان العرب) تكك (الصّحَاح في اللغة) تكك (لسان العرب)
92	*ᵈḫániš*	100[T11]	See Part 2.2.11 Gerald J. Davis. *Gilgamesh, The New Translation:* ḫaniš (god of destruction)	حنش (لسان العرب) حنس (لسان العرب) حنث (لسان العرب)
93	*ᵈḫum-ba-ba*	230[T10]	See Part 2.2.12 See also *E*	ḫuwawa حوا (لسان العرب) ḫumbaba

			Wikipedia: https://en.wikipedia.org/wiki/Humbaba	حوم (مقاييس اللغة) الهَوْمُ (القاموس المحيط) همم (لسان العرب) اعْرَنْزَمَتْ (مقاييس اللغة)
94	*di-da-šú* *di-da-a-šú*	188^{T1}	See also *da-du-šú* CAD: dīdū (dādū) s. dual and pl.; (a piece of female apparel covering the hips);	دهده (لسان العرب)
95	*ᵈí-gì-gì*	174^{T11}	See Part 2.2.13 See also *ᵈa-nun-na-ki* *Wikipedia:* https://en.wikipedia.org/wiki/Humbaba *Ancient Mesopotamian Gods and Goddesses:* http://oracc.museum.upenn.edu/amgg/listofdeities/igigi/ *Christian Courier:* https://www.christiancourier.com/articles/986-gog-and-magog-what-is-the-meaning-of-revelation-20-8	أجَ (مقاييس اللغة) الأجيجُ (القاموس المحيط) أجج (لسان العرب) جأي (لسان العرب) نجل (مقاييس اللغة) نجل (الصّحاح في اللغة) مجل (لسان العرب) نجج (لسان العرب) مجج (لسان العرب)
96	*di-ma-a-a* *di-ma-a-šú*	139^{T11} 309^{T11}	ePSD: dimmatu isiš [SORROW] wr. i-si-iš; isiš$_3$ Akk. dimmatu; nissatu; ratāmu; tassistu; şiāhu; şīhu ePSD: er er [TEARS] wr. er$_2$; i-ra Akk. bikītu; dimtu	دمع (مقاييس اللغة)
97	*DINGIR.MAḪ* bēlet-ilī	49^{T1}	See Part 2.2.4 See also ᵈa-ru-ru See also *bu-lim* ePSD: MAH mah [GREAT] wr. mah; mah$_2$ Akk. kabtu; mādu; rabû; şīru Note: bēlet-ilī = بعلة (سيدة) الآلهة *DINGIR.MAḪ* = رقيقة وجميلة (سيدة) الإله	مه (مقاييس اللغة) مهه (لسان العرب)
98	*DINGIR-ma* *DINGIR-um-ma*	48^{T1}	ePSD: diĝir diĝir [DEITY] wr. diĝir; dim$_3$-me-er; dim$_3$-me$_8$-er; dim$_3$-mi-ir; di-me$_2$-er Akk. iltu; ilu *Wikipedia:* https://en.wikipedia.org/wiki/Dingir	دنج (لسان العرب) دمهج (لسان العرب) دنهج (لسان العرب) دملج (لسان العرب)
99	*di-pa-ra-a-ti*	103^{T11} 104^{T11}	ePSD: dipāru gi'izila [TORCH] wr. gi-izi-la$_2$ Akk. dipāru; gizillû iziĝar [TORCH] wr. izi-ĝar Akk. dipāru	دفر (لسان العرب) دبر (لسان العرب) ذفر (لسان العرب)
100	*ᵈiškur*	99^{T11}	See Part 2.2.14 *Ancient Mesopotamian Gods and Goddesses:* http://oracc.museum.upenn.edu/amgg/listofdeities/ikur/index.html	هدد (لسان العرب) أسك (لسان العرب) عسك (لسان العرب) أسق (لسان العرب) عسق (لسان العرب)

				عسقر (لسان العرب) عسكر (لسان العرب)
101	^{d}*iš-tar* ^{d}*I5* ^{d}*I5*	210^{T1} 78^{T1} 274^{T1}	See Part 2.2.15 *Wikipedia:* https://en.wikipedia.org/wiki/Inanna https://en.wikipedia.org/wiki/Ishtar *Ancient Mesopotamian Gods and Goddesses:* http://oracc.museum.upenn.edu/amgg/listofdeities/inanaitar/index.html "4-Point Star." *ReligionFacts.com.* 10 Nov. 2015. Web. Accessed 13 Aug. 2016. <www.religionfacts.com/four-point-star>	ستر (لسان العرب) السِّتْرُ (القاموس المحيط) أفنس (لسان العرب)
102	^{d}*lugal-bàn-da*	35^{T1}	See Part 2.2.16 See *LUGAL* See also *ú-um-mi-id-ma* *Wikipedia:* https://en.wikipedia.org/wiki/Lugalbanda ePSD: banda banda [CHILD] wr. $^{lu}{}_2$banda$_3{}^{da}$ "child" banda [JUNIOR] wr. banda$_3{}^{da}$ Akk. ekdu; şehru banda [QUOTIENT] wr. banda$_3$ Akk. bandû banda [SAGACITY] wr. banda$_3$ Akk. tašimtu banda [STANCHION] wr. ban$_3$-da; banda$_5$; banda$_4$ Akk. takšīru	البَنْدُ (القاموس المحيط) بند (الصّحّاح في اللغة) بند (لسان العرب) بدد (الصّحّاح في اللغة) بدد (لسان العرب) لعا (لسان العرب) جل (لسان العرب)
103	^{d}*ma-am-me-tum* ^{d}*ma-mi*	320^{T10} 320^{T10}	See Part 2.2.17 See *ma-a-ti* *Wikipedia:* https://en.wikipedia.org/wiki/Mamitu	متت (لسان العرب) ماتَ (القاموس المحيط)
104	^{d}*nin-ši-kù*	19^{T11}	See Part 2.2.5 See ^{d}*nu-dím-mud*	
105	^{d}*nin-sún* ^{d}*nin-sún-an-na*		See Part 2.2.18 See ^{f}*ri-mat-*^{d}*nin-sún*	
106	^{d}*nin-urta*	104^{T1}	See Part 2.2.19 *Wikipedia:* https://en.wikipedia.org/wiki/Ninurta *Mythology Dictionary*: http://www.mythologydictionary.com/ninurta-mythology.html	نور (لسان العرب) نمر (لسان العرب)
107	^{d}*nissaba*	60^{T1}	See Part 2.2.20	نسب (لسان العرب) نسب ندب (لسان العرب)

			See also *qa-na* *Mythology Dictionary*: http://www.mythologydictionary.com/mesopotamian-mythology.html#nissaba *Ancient Mesopotamian Gods and Goddesses:* http://oracc.museum.upenn.edu/amgg/listofdeities/nidaba/index.html AALD: nissabu (s.) (see nissaba) تعبير عن الحبوب، الحنطة	
108	^{d}*nu-dím-mud*	50[T1]	See Part 2.2.5 See *EN* See *KI-tim* *See A.*^{MEŠ} See *E* See ú-um-mi-id-ma See ^{giš}*KUN*$_{4}$ *Ancient Mesopotamian Gods and Goddesses:* http://oracc.museum.upenn.edu/amgg/listofdeities/enlil/ *Wikipedia* https://en.wikipedia.org/wiki/Enki ePSD: GI gi [ESSENCE] wr. gi; ^{šim}gi gi [JUDGMENT] wr. gi; gi$_{16}$ Akk. šipţu gi [REED] wr. gi Akk. qanû gi [TURN] wr. gi$_{4}$; gi Akk. lamû; târu muru [MAT] wr. ^{gi}muru$_{x}$ Akk. burû ePSD: IDIM eše [AREA UNIT] wr. eše$_{3}$; Akk. eblu idim [HEAVY] wr. idim Akk. kabtu idim [SPRING] wr. idim Akk. nagbu idim [WILD] wr. idim Akk. ekdu iri [DISEASE] wr. iri$_{8}$ Akk. rapādu kur [MOUNTAIN] wr. kur; Akk. erşetu; mātu; šadû; šadû ePSD: NU nu [GENITALIA] wr. nu Akk. lipištu nu [MAN] wr. nu Akk. awīlu ePSD: NA na [MAN] wr. na Akk. amēlu dāmu See *DUMU* ePSD: nešakku nu'ešak [PRIEST] wr. nu-eš$_{3}$ Akk. nešakku nasāku ri [IMPOSE] wr. RI; ru Akk. bâ'u; emēdu; nadû; nasāku; ramû; rehû; tarû; wašaru	nu نوى (الصّحَاح في اللغة) نوي (مقاييس اللغة) نوي (لسان العرب) نوأ (لسان العرب) نوي (لسان العرب) dím-mud دامَ (القاموس المحيط) دوم (مقاييس اللغة) دأم (لسان العرب) دوم (لسان العرب) ديم (لسان العرب) ^{d}EN.KI See EN See KI-tim ^{d}EN.KI-GA.KAM ^{d}EN.KI.G جعا (لسان العرب) الجَعْوُ (القاموس المحيط) جيأ (العباب الزاخر) جيا (لسان العرب) جأجأ (لسان العرب) جيأ (لسان العرب) جَاءَ (القاموس المحيط) خام (مقاييس اللغة) أرضٌ (القاموس المحيط) خوم (لسان العرب) ^{d}nin-ši-kù ^{d}niššiku سك (مقاييس اللغة) نسك (الصّحَاح في اللغة) النُّسْكُ (القاموس المحيط) نسك (لسان العرب) gašam جسم (لسان العرب) ^{d}IDIM أدم (مقاييس اللغة) الأَدَمَةُ (القاموس المحيط)

			<u>sag</u> [SCATTER] wr. sag_2; sag_3; sag_7 Akk. dâku; nasāku; nêru; sapāhu ePSD: madādu <u>aĝ</u> [MEASURE] wr. $aĝ_2$ Akk. madādu AALD: nù (adj.) (التملك) يعود لنا، لنا AALD: nu (nuk, nuku) اداة تتقدم الكلام المباشر بعد الافعال التي يكون فيها ضمير المتكلم AALD: EA (also aya, ayya) اله الحكمة الاكدي، يرتبط بالماء والخليقة، حامي المضطهدين	أدم (لسان العرب) kina كين (الصّحاح في اللغة) كين (لسان العرب) é-a حيا (لسان العرب) هيا (لسان العرب)
109	^{d}*šákkan*	109^{T1}	<u>See Part 2.2.21</u> See also *qa-na* *Wikipedia:* https://en.wikipedia.org/wiki/Sumugan AALD: šakkan (šakan, šumuqan) اله سومري	قنا (لسان العرب)
110	^{d}ši-du-ri		<u>See Part 2.2.22</u> See ^{f}*sa-bit*	
111	^{d}Sin	281^{T10}	<u>See Part 2.2.23</u> *Wikipedia:* https://en.wikipedia.org/wiki/Sin_(mythology) *Ancient Mesopotamian Gods and Goddesses:* *http://oracc.museum.upenn.edu/amgg/listofdeities/nannasuen/index.html* zu see *SU-šú*	سنن (لسان العرب)
112	^{d}*šúllat*	100^{T11}	<u>See Part 2.2.24</u> See aslo *uš-te-li* Gerald J. Davis. *Gilgamesh, The New Translation:* Sullat (god of despoilment (looting))	سلل (لسان العرب)
113	*DU.DU-ku* *du* *DU.DU-ku* *DU.DU-ku* *DU.DU.*^{MEŠ}*-ku*	28^{T1} 287^{T10} 232^{T10} 233^{T10} 249^{T11}	See also *da-du-šú* See also *ṭīṭa* See also *DU-ka* See also ^{d}*UTU.È* ePSD: du_{12}-du_{12} <u>du</u> [PLAY] wr. du_{12}-du_{12}; du_{12} Akk. lapātu; zamāru ePSD: du <u>du</u> [ALL] wr. du_3 Akk. kalāma <u>du</u> [BUILD] wr. du_3 Akk. banû; epēšu <u>du</u> [FISH] wr. $du_6{}^{ku}{}_6$ <u>du</u> [GO] wr. du Akk. alāku <u>du</u> [HEAP] wr. du_8 Akk. kamāru <u>du</u> [HOLD] wr. du_3	طيط (لسان العرب) دوا (لسان العرب) دعو (مقاييس اللغة) الدُّعاءُ (القاموس المحيط) دعا (لسان العرب) دعدع (الصّحاح في اللغة) الدَّعُّ (القاموس المحيط) دعع (لسان العرب) ضوا (لسان العرب) ضأضأ (لسان العرب) ضوض (مقاييس اللغة) حَضَّهُ (القاموس المحيط) دود (مقاييس اللغة) الدُّودَةُ (القاموس المحيط)

			du [LAMENT] wr. du$_9$-du$_9$ du [PLANT] wr. du$_3$ Akk. retû; zaqāpu du [PLATFORM] wr. du$_6$ Akk. di'u du [PLAY] wr. du$_{12}$-du$_{12}$; du$_{12}$ Akk. lapātu; zamāru du [PUSH] wr. du$_7$ Akk. nakāpu du [SPREAD] wr. du$_8$ Akk. epû; labānu; pehû du [SQUARE] wr. du$_7$ du [SUITABLE] wr. du$_7$ Akk. asāmu; naţû du [WHIRL] wr. du$_7$-du$_7$ Akk. sarû	
114	*DU-du-ú-ma*	228^{T10}	See also *nin-nem-dú-ma* *See also DU.DU-ku*	دعو (مقاييس اللغة)
115	DUG$_4$.GA DUG$_4$.GA DUG$_4$.GA DUG$_4$.GA	36^{T11} 162^{T11} 181^{T11} 177^{T11}	See *i-qab-bu-ú* ePSD: dug dug [BIRD] wr. dug$_3$^{mušen}; du^{mušen} dug [GOOD] wr. dug$_3$; ze$_2$-eb; du-uq Akk. ţābu dug [POT] wr. dug; dug$_x$(BI) Akk. karpatu dug [SPEAK] wr. dug$_4$ Akk. atwû; dabābu; epēšu; qabû ePSD: duga duga [AFFLICTION] wr. dug$_4$-ga duga [COMMAND] wr. dug$_4$-ga Akk. qibītu	ذَاقَ (القاموس المحيط) ذوق (مقاييس اللغة) دوج (لسان العرب) دعج (لسان العرب) دجج (لسان العرب) أضَجَّ (القاموس المحيط) ضجج (الصّحَاح في اللغة)
116	*^{dug}A.DA.GUR$_5$* adagurra	159^{T11}	See also *GÌR-šú* *See DUG$_4$.GA* ePSD: adaguru adagir [CONTAINER] wr. ^{gi}a-da-gir$_5$ Akk. adaguru AALD: adagurru (s.) (adakurru) (DUG.A.DA.GUR$_4$ and (UG.A.DA.GUR$_5$)اناء مدبب الاسفل خاص بالطقوس لحفظ الجعة او الحليب	الدَّجْرُ (القاموس المحيط) دجر (الصّحَاح في اللغة) دجر (مقاييس اللغة) دجر (لسان العرب) دقر (لسان العرب)
117	*DU-ka* *DU-ka*	274^{T11} 309^{T11}	See also *ta-ad-de-kan-ni* *See also DU.DU-ku*	دوا (لسان العرب) دعو (لسان العرب) دوك (لسان العرب) دعك (مقاييس اللغة) دَعَكَ (القاموس المحيط) دعك (لسان العرب)
118	*DÙ-ma* *DÙ-ma*	177^{T11} 181^{T11}	See also *up-piš* *See also DU.DU-ku*	ضوا (لسان العرب)
119	*dum-muq* *dam-qa-ta* *du-muq* *dam-qa* *da-me-eq-tum* *dum-qa* *dum-qa* *dum-qí*	62^{T1} 207^{T1} 252^{T11} 302^{T10} 302^{T10} 313^{T11} 314^{T11} 314^{T11}	ePSD: dumqu niĝsaga [GOODNESS] wr. niĝ$_2$-sag$_9$-ga Akk. dumqu sag [GOOD] wr. sag$_8$; sag$_9$; sag$_{10}$; šeg$_{10}$; sag$_{12}$ Akk. banû; damāqu; dumqu; ţābu ePSD: damāqu sag [GOOD] wr. sag$_8$; sag$_9$; sag$_{10}$; šeg$_{10}$; Akk. banû; damāqu; dumqu; ţābu zil [GOOD] wr. zil$_2$ Akk. damāqu	دمق (مقاييس اللغة) دمج (مقاييس اللغة) دمج (لسان العرب) دجم (لسان العرب) دَمَقَ (القاموس المحيط) دمق (لسان العرب) دقم (الصّحَاح في اللغة)
120	*DUMU* *DUMU-šú* *DUMU.^{MEŠ}*	68^{T1} 259^{T1} 86^{T11}	See *ma-rat* See also *šum-šú* ePSD: dumu dumu [CHILD] wr. dumu; du$_5$-mu Akk. māru	دما (الصّحَاح في اللغة) دم (مقاييس اللغة) دمم (الصّحَاح في اللغة) دمم (لسان العرب) دمي (لسان العرب)

			ePSD: dāmu dara [RED] wr. $dara_4$ Akk. dāmu kurun [BEER] wr. kurun; $kurun_2$; $kurun_3$ Akk. dāmu; kurunnu; ţābu mud [BLOOD] wr. mud; mud_2 Akk. dāmu sa [SINEW] wr. sa Akk. dāmu; erru; matnu; pitnu umun [BLOOD] wr. u_3-mun; u_3-mu-un; umun Akk. dāmu uš [BLOOD] wr. $uš_2$ Akk. dāmu uš [DIE] wr. $uš_2$ Akk. dāmu; mâtu; mūtu; uššu	دما (الصّحَاح في اللغة) ذمم (لسان العرب)
121	^{d}*UTU.È* ^{d}*UTU.È.A* ^{d}*UTU-ši*	40^{T1} 40^{T1} 314^{T10}	See Part 2.2.25 See also *şe-te* See also *şu-ḫi-šú* *Ancient Mesopotamian Gods and Goddesses:* http://oracc.museum.upenn.edu/amgg/listofdeities/utu/index.html ePSD: utu'e utu'e [SUNRISE] wr. utu-e_3 Akk. şīt šamši	شمس (لسان العرب) ضحي (مقاييس اللغة) ضحا (لسان العرب) وضح (لسان العرب) ضوأ (لسان العرب)
122	*du-un-qi*	313^{T11}	See also *dum-qa* See also *DINGIR-ma*	دنج (لسان العرب) دنق (مقاييس اللغة) دنق (لسان العرب)
123	*du-ur-šú* *du-ri* *du-ur*	13^{T1} 20^{U} 248^{T10}	See also *BÀD-šú* ePSD: dūru bad [WALL] wr. bad_3 Akk. dūru duri [FOREVER] wr. du-ri_2 Akk. dūru	الدارُ (القاموس المحيط) دور (لسان العرب) دور (مقاييس اللغة) دير (مقاييس اللغة) دير (لسان العرب)
124	*E* *E* *É* *É* *É* *É*	182^{T1} 209^{T11} 22^{T1} 210^{T1} 217^{T1} 308^{T10}	See also *é.an.na* ePSD: e e [HOUSE] wr. e_2; $\hat{g}a_2$; e_4 Akk. Bītu ePSD: bītu e [HOUSE] wr. e_2; $\hat{g}a_2$; e_4 Akk. bītu eš [SHRINE] wr. $eš_3$ Akk. bītu; eššu ĝa [HOUSE] wr. $\hat{g}a_2$; ma Akk. bītu	بيت (مقاييس اللغة) أحيا (لسان العرب) حي (مقاييس اللغة) حي (مقاييس اللغة) حيا (لسان العرب) أيي (مقاييس اللغة) أيا (لسان العرب) See *A*
125	*é.an.na* *é.an.na*	12^{T1} 16^{T1}	See also *E*	الأَيْنُ (القاموس المحيط) أين (الصّحَاح في اللغة)
126	*É.GAL*	96^{T11}	See *É* See *LUGAL*	الوَجَلُ (القاموس المحيط)
127	*É.GAR$_8$.*^{MEŠ}*-šá*	58^{T11}	See *i-gar*	
128	*e-be-eḫ* *né-bé-ḫi*	275^{T10} 275^{T10}	ePSD: ebīhu ebih [ROPE] wr. $Ebih_2$ Akk. ebīhu ePSD: nēbehu ešla [BAND] wr. $Eš_2$-la_2 Akk. markasu; nēbehu AALD: ebēhu (v.) (see ebīḫu, nēbihu) يعترض، يطوّق	نبخ (مقاييس اللغة) النَّبْخُ (القاموس المحيط) نبخ (لسان العرب)

			AALD: ebīḫu (s.) الحبل الثخين AALD: nē-be-ḫu (s.) (nē-ba-ḫu) الحزام ام النطاق، الفريز: نسيج صوفي ثخين	
129	*e-bir* *e-te-te-bi-ra* *e-bu-ra-am-ma*	40[T1] 253[T10] 45[T11]	See also *ib-ri* ePSD: ebēru asilala [JOY] wr. asila; asil-la$_2$; asil$_3$-la$_2$; asila$_3$; si$_{11}$-le$_2$; sila; asila$_x$(|EZEN×KASKAL|); asil$_x$(EZEN)-la$_2$; asil$_x$(EZEN)-le$_2$ Akk. ašilalû; ebēru; riāšu; rīšātu AALD: ebēru (v.) (epēru, habaru) يعبر (ماء)، يمتد الى ما وراء شيء، يمر ذهابا وايابا AALD: ebēru (v.) يدهن، يطلي الوجه AALD: ebēr (v.) (epēru, habāru) يعبر (النهر) AALD: eber nāri (s.) عبرالنهر AALD: ebūru (s.) الحصاد، المحصول، وفت الحصاد، الصيف AALD: ebūrû (adj.) صيف AALD: ebūrû (s.) بذور الحنطة	حبر (لسان العرب) عبر (لسان العرب)
130	*ed-de-et-ti*	283[T11]	ePSD: eddidu ad [BUSH] wr. ad$_5$; ad$_2$ Akk. ašāgu; eddidu; eddittu ePSD: eddittu ad [BUSH] wr. ad$_5$; ad$_2$ Akk. ašāgu; eddidu; eddittu	حد (مقاييس اللغة) حدد (لسان العرب)
131	*e-de-šú* *ú-te-ed-diš*	261[T11] 266[T11]	ePSD: edēšu gibil [NEW] wr. gibil; gibil$_4$ Akk. edēšu	حدث (مقاييس اللغة) حَدَثَ (القاموس المحيط) حدث (لسان العرب)
132	EDIN EDIN-*ia*	102[T1] 248[T1]	See also *ṣi-ri-ia* ePSD: eden eden [BACK] wr. eden "back, upper side" Akk. şēru eden [BIRD] wr. eden^{mušen}; da^{mušen} "a bird" eden [PLAIN] wr. eden "plain, steppe, open country" Akk. edinu	عدن (لسان العرب)
133	EGIR	209[T10]	See also *ár-ku-ú* ePSD: eĝir eĝir [BACK] wr. eĝir; eĝir$_5$(LUM); egir$_4$; eĝir$_6$(MURGU$_2$) Akk. arkatu	عجر (لسان العرب)
134	*ek-ke-mu*	244[T11]	ePSD: ekkēmu gabkar [THIEF] wr. ga-ab-kar Akk. ekkēmu	عكم (مقاييس اللغة) عكم (الصّحاح في اللغة) عكم (لسان العرب)
135	*el-lim* *el-lima* *e-li-ki* *a-lu-ú* *a-la-a* *e-liš* *i-lam-ma* *i-te-lu-ú* *i-te-la-a* *ul-te-la-an-ni*	12[T1] 18[T1] 184[T1] 229[T1] 229[T10] 79[T11] 98[T11] 115[T11] 141[T11] 200[T11]	See also UGU See also UL.A ePSD: eli dirig [EXCEED] wr. diri; RI Akk. atru; eli; rabû; kapāšu; zaqāru; šarūru; šūturu; lē'û ugu [SKULL] wr. ugu$_2$; ugu; ugu$_3$; ugu$_x$(|U.SAG|); ugu$_x$(|A.U.KA|); ugu$_x$(SAG@n@g) Akk. eli; muhhu; qaqqadu ilim [RADIANCE] (8x: Old Babylonian) wr. i-lim	حلل (لسان العرب) حال (لسان العرب) ألم (لسان العرب) سقم (مقاييس اللغة) علو (مقاييس اللغة) علا (لسان العرب) عَلَعَ (القاموس المحيط)

	el-li *i-lam-ma*	254^{T11} 306^{T11}	Akk. šalummatu; šaqummatu ePSD: alû <u>ala</u> [DRUM] wr. ^{kuš}a$_2$-la$_2$; ^{kuš}a-la; ^{kuš}ala Akk. alû <u>alĝar</u> [INSTRUMENT] wr. ^{ĝeš}al-ĝar; al-gar Akk. alû AALD: alû (elû): جهاز، وسيلة لرفع الماء AALD: ilimdu (or ilimtu) in ilimdumma epēšu (v.) (meaning uncertain) <u>Note:</u> a-la-a = 'Ala' علاء	
136	*e-mi-a* *e-mu-ú* *i-te-mi*	27^{P} 204^{T11} 245^{T10}	See also *UL.A* ePSD: emītu <u>ušbar</u> [IN-LAW] wr. ušbar; ušbar$_3$; ušbar$_2$ Akk. emu; emītu ePSD: immu <u>ud</u> [SUN] wr. ud Akk. immu; ummedu; umšu; šamšu; ūmu ePSD: emēmu <u>kum</u> [HOT] wr. kum$_2$; kum$_4$ Akk. emēmu ePSD: emû <u>eme</u> [~PLOW] wr. ^{ĝeš}eme Akk. emû <u>iri</u> [MAKE MANIFEST] wr. i-ri Akk. emû; šūpû ePSD: hāmū <u>anba</u> [LITTER] wr. an-ba Akk. hāmū <u>e</u> [CHAFF] wr. e$_3$ Akk. hāmū	حمأ (لسان العرب) حم (مقاييس اللغة) حما (لسان العرب) حمم (لسان العرب) عمم (لسان العرب) العَمُّ (القاموس المحيط) عمي (لسان العرب) عَمِي (القاموس المحيط) عمى (الصحاح في اللغة) العَمُّ (القاموس المحيط)
137	*em-qet* *en-qet*	259^{T1} 259^{T1}	See also *e-niq* ePSD: emqu <u>igiĝaltuku</u> [WISE] wr. igi-ĝal$_2$-tuku Akk. emqu <u>usandu</u> [WISE] wr. usandu; usandu$_x$(|NUNUZ.AB$_2$×AŠGAB|) Akk. emqu <u>Note:</u> al-Jiburi rule: emqet = enqet	عمق (لسان العرب)
138	*e-mu-qí*	124^{T1}	ePSD: emûqu <u>lirum</u> [STRENGTH] wr. lirum; lirum$_3$; lirum$_2$; lirum$_6$; lirum$_7$; lirum$_8$ Akk. abaru; dannu; emûqu; gāmiru; kamiru; kirimmu; umašu; šapṣu; šitnunu; šitpuṣu <u>usu</u> [STRENGTH] wr. usu Akk. emûqu ePSD: emūqu <u>gu</u> [FORCE] wr. gu$_2$ Akk. emūqu <u>ne</u> [STRENGTH] wr. ne$_3$ Akk. emūqu	عمق (لسان العرب) حمق (لسان العرب)
139	*EN* *EN* *EN.^{MEŠ}* *EN-šá* *EN-šu-nu*	29^{T1} 79^{T1} 79^{T1} 259^{T1} 279^{T10}	See also *^{d}a-num* ePSD: EN <u>en</u> [LORD] wr. en; u$_3$-mu-un; umun Akk. bēlu <u>en</u> [PRIEST] wr. en Akk. entu; enu <u>enna</u> <u>[UNTIL]</u> wr. en-na; an-ma; en; en$_7$ Akk. adi <u>urun</u> <u>[CLEVER]</u> wr. urun$_x$(EN) Akk. naklu	عن (مقاييس اللغة) عَنَّ (القاموس المحيط) عن (مقاييس اللغة) عنن (لسان العرب) عني (مقاييس اللغة) عنا (لسان العرب)

			<u>urun</u> <u>[EXALTED]</u> wr. urun$_x$(EN); u$_{18}$-ru; uru; Akk. dannu; šapsu; ṣīru	
140	*e-nin-na* *e-nin-na* *e-nin-na-ma*	96[T1] 315[T11] 198[T11]	ePSD: inanna <u>adal</u> [EXCLAMATION] wr. a-da-al; a-da-lam; i-da-al; i-da-lam; i-da-al-la; i-da-la; i-da-la$_2$; i-dal; i-dal-am$_3$; i-dal-la Akk. ašarma; inanna ePSD: ennittu <u>šulalum</u> [PUNISHMENT] wr. šul-a-lum Akk. ennittu <u>ineš</u> [NOW] wr. i$_3$-ne-eš$_2$ Akk. inanna ePSD: enūma <u>ud</u> [WHEN] wr. ud Akk. enūma AALD: *enna (adv.) الان AALD: *eninni (adv.) see inanna الحين، الان AALD: *eninna (adv.) see inanna الحين، الان AALD: *enin (adv.) see inanna الحين، الان AALD: *enūma (adv.) see inūma حينما AALD: *enēnu (v.) يئن، يطلب الرحمة ، يصلي AALD: *enēnu (v.) (henēnu) يحن، يرحم AALD: *enēnu (v.) يعاقب AALD: *eninnu (s.) see enēnu الحنين، العطف AALD: *ennu (s.m.f.) see enēnu الحنين، الرحمة، الاستحسان	حنن (لسان العرب) حنا (لسان العرب) حين (لسان العرب)
141	*e-niq* *ni-iq-qu* *ni-qa-a* *ni-qu-ú* *ni-qit-ti*	36[T1] 69[T11] 157[T11] 157[T11] 295[T11]	See also *SÍSKUR* See also *ni-kit-ti* ePSD: naqû <u>bala</u> [TURN] wr. bal; bil$_2$ Akk. elû; nabalkutu; nakāru; naqû; palû; tabāku <u>siškur</u> [PRAYER] wr. siškur$_2$; siškur Akk. karābu; naqû; nīqu AALD: enēqu (v.): يرضع AALD: ēniqu (adj.): رضاعة الطفل AALD: niqittu معنى غير اكيد AALD: niqittu (see nigītu) AALD: niqītu (see nigītu) AALD: nigītu (s.) (or nikītu, niqītu, nigittu, nikittu, niqittu) الخشب العطري	نقق (لسان العرب) نيق (لسان العرب) نوق (لسان العرب) نقا (الصّحاح في اللغة) نقا (لسان العرب) نَقِيَ (القاموس المحيط) نقي (مقاييس اللغة) نجو (مقاييس اللغة) نقت (لسان العرب) نقت (الصّحاح في اللغة) النَّقْتُ (القاموس المحيط) النَّقْتُ: اسْتخْراجُ المُخّ. نقه (لسان العرب) أنق (لسان العرب) عنق (مقاييس اللغة)
142	*e-pi-i*	221[T11]	ePSD: epû <u>du</u> [SPREAD] wr. du$_8$ Akk. epû; labānu; pehû	عفو (مقاييس اللغة) عفا (الصّحاح في اللغة) عفا (لسان العرب) العَفْوُ (القاموس المحيط)
143	*e-ṣe-en-ši* *e-ṣe-en-ši* *e-ṣe-en-ši* *e-ṣe-en-ši* *i-ṣi-nu* *i-ṣi-nu* *i-te-ṣe-en* *i-te-ṣi-in*	81[T11] 82[T11] 83[T11] 84[T11] 161[T11] 162[T11] 305[T11] 305[T11]	ePSD: ṣanāhu <u>šag sur</u> [HAVE DIARRHEA] wr. šag$_4$ sur Akk. ṣanāhu; ṣubburu ePSD: ṣenu <u>azig</u> [VIOLENCE] wr. a$_2$-zig$_3$ Akk. ṣenu <u>niĝazig</u> [VIOLENCE] wr. niĝ$_2$-a$_2$-zig$_3$ Akk. ṣenu ePSD: eṣēnu <u>ur</u> [SMELL] wr. ur$_5$ Akk. eṣēnu	عسن (الصّحاح في اللغة) عسن (لسان العرب) عصن (لسان العرب) أسن (لسان العرب) صنا (لسان العرب) الصِنُّ (القاموس المحيط) صنن (الصّحاح في اللغة) صنن (لسان العرب)

			AALD: şênu (v.) يحمّل مركبا، يحمّل حمولة، يكوّم\يكدّس الطعام على المنظدة أو الوقود في المجمرة AALD: şēnu (adj.) محمل AALD: şēnu (adj.) شرير AALD: eşēnu (v.) يأسن، يشم (رائحة)، يشم رائحة كريهة، يجعل شيئا ما ذا رائحة كريهة AALD: eşēnnu (s.) العفن، التخمر	
144	*ESIR*	263^{T10}	Se also *kup-ra* ePSD: esir esir [BITUMEN] wr. esir$_2$; esir; esir$_2$(|LAGABxHAL|) Akk. iţţû; kupru esir [FISH] wr. esir$_x$(LAK173)$^{ku}{}_6$; esir$_3$$^{ku}{}_6$; LAK173 Akk. šēnu esir [SHOE] wr. ^{kuš}e-sir$_2$; e-sir$_2$; ^{kuš}esir$_3$; ^{kuš}esir$_4$; ^{kuš}esir$_5$; LAK173 Akk. šēnu esir [STREET] wr. e-sir$_2$; e-sir Akk. sūqu Note: ESIR = قار; Kupur = قير	حسر (لسان العرب) عضر (مقاييس اللغة) عسر (لسان العرب) قسر (لسان العرب) العُسْرُ (القاموس المحيط) عصر (مقاييس اللغة) عصر (الصّحّاح في اللغة) العَصْرُ (القاموس المحيط) عصر (لسان العرب)
145	*ESIR.ḪI.A*	263^{T10}	See *ESIR*	*ḪI.A* حيا (لسان العرب) خوى (الصّحّاح في اللغة) خَوَتِ (القاموس المحيط) خوا (لسان العرب)
146	*es-su-ú*	22^{T1}	See also *ḫa-as-su* AALD: esû (s.) (see issû, esû) حفرة ترابية، كلمة سومرية دخيلة	حسا (لسان العرب)
147	*eţli* *eţ-lu-tum* *it-lu-tum*	77^{T1} 21^{P} 21^{P}	ePSD: eţlu ĝuruš [MALE] wr. ĝuruš Akk. eţlu mes [HERO] wr. mes Akk. eţlu mu [MANLY] wr. mu$_6$ Akk. eţlu šuba [MULTICOLOURED] wr. šuba; Akk. bitrāmu; ellu; eţlu; ramku šul [YOUTH] wr. šul Akk. eţlu	عطل (لسان العرب) عتل (لسان العرب) حطل (لسان العرب)
148	*e-zu-ub* *e-te-zib*	69^{T11} 318^{T11}	ePSD: ezēbu pag [LEAVE] wr. pag Akk. ezēbu taka [ABANDON] wr. tak$_4$ Akk. ezēbu; uhhuru; šêtu	عزب (مقاييس اللغة) العَزَبُ (القاموس المحيط) عزب (لسان العرب)
149	*ez-zu* *it-ta-ziz-za* *iz-za-az* *i-zu-uz-zu* *ta-az-ziz-ma* *iz-za-az* *i-te-ziz*	34^{T1} 200^{T1} 251^{T1} 310^{T10} 7^{T11} 202^{T11} 173^{T11}	ePSD: ezzu huš [REDDISH] wr. huš; huš$_2$ Akk. ezzu sumur [ANGRY] wr. sumur; sumur$_x$(KA) Akk. ezzu; šamru sur [FURIOUS] wr. Akk. ezzu ePSD: izuzzu gub [STAND] wr. gub Akk. izuzzu	حزز (لسان العرب) الحَزُّ (القاموس المحيط) أزز (لسان العرب) عزا (لسان العرب) عزز (لسان العرب) عَزَّ (القاموس المحيط)
150	^{f}*ḪUL* ^{f}*ḪUL*	120^{T11} 121^{T11}	See also *ḪA.LA* See also *lu-mu-un* See also *na-áš* ePSD: HUL hulu [BAD] wr. hul; hul$_3$ Akk. abātu ša īni; bēšu; lapātu ša īni; şabru; lemnu; masku; qallu; sarru; zāmânû hulu [NARROW] wr. hul Akk. pašqu hulu [RUINATION] wr. hul Akk. šalputtu	الخَلُّ (القاموس المحيط) خلا (لسان العرب) خلل (لسان العرب) خيل (لسان العرب) حلل (لسان العرب) حول (مقاييس اللغة) حول (الصّحّاح في اللغة) حول (لسان العرب) حال (لسان العرب)

			ePSD: halû gug [MOLE] wr. gug Akk. halû; pendu AALD: *hâlu (v.) يحلل، يصبح سائلا ، يتحلل، ينضج AALD: hâlu (v.) يرتجف، يرتعش، يتضور، يتلوى AALD: hâlu (v.) معنى غير معروف AALD: hâlu (s.) see hayyātu, hīlū (عند الولادة) تكون في المخاض	هول (مقاييس اللغة) هول (الصّحَاح في اللغة) هول (لسان العرب)
151	^{f}ri-mat-^{d}nin-sún ^{f}ri-mat-^{d}nin-sún-an-na ^{f}ri-mat-^{d}nin- súmun ^{f}ri-mat-^{d}nin- súmun -na	36^{T1} 36^{T1} 36^{T1} 36^{T1}	See Part 2.2.18 ^{d}nin-sún ^{d}nin-súmun ^{d}NIN.GUL *Wikipedia*: https://en.wikipedia.org/wiki/Ninsun *Ancient Mesopotamian Gods and Goddesses:* http://oracc.museum.upenn.edu/amgg/listofdeities/ninsumun/index.html ePSD: nin nin [LADY] wr. nin; ga-ša-an; ga-ša$_{2}$-an; ka-ša-an Akk. bēltu; bēlu nin [SISTER] wr. nin$_{9}$ Akk. ahātu ePSD: GUL gul [DESTROY] wr. gul; gu-ul Akk. abātu; hepû; naqāru; sapānu isin [STALK] wr. išin; i$_{3}$-si-na; e-si-na; isin$_{x}$(|ŠE.IGI.TUR|); isim$_{2}$; isim$_{3}$ Akk. išīnu si [UNMNG] wr. si$_{23}$; si$_{5}$ sumun [COW] wr. sumun$_{2}$; u$_{3}$-sumun$_{2}$ Akk. rīmtu sumun [VESSEL] wr. sumun$_{2}$; u$_{3}$-sun$_{2}$ Akk. narţabu ePSD: sun$_{2}$ sumun [COW] wr. sumun$_{2}$; u$_{3}$-sumun$_{2}$ Akk. rīmtu sumun [VESSEL] wr. sumun$_{2}$; u$_{3}$-sun$_{2}$ Akk. narţabu ePSD: nigal nigal [RADIANCE] wr. ni$_{2}$-gal Akk. namrīru; namurratu	ريم (لسان العرب) نيس (العباب الزاخر) مسن (لسان العرب) سمن (لسان العرب) أسن (لسان العرب) سنن (لسان العرب) نسم (لسان العرب) NIN.GUL نجل (مقاييس اللغة) النَّجْلُ (القاموس المحيط) نجل (الصّحَاح في اللغة) نجل (لسان العرب) جول (لسان العرب)
152	^{f}sa-bit sa-bit ^{d}ši-du-ri	258^{T10} 258^{T10}	See Part 2.2.22 See *BÀD* (dūru) ePSD: sabû si [FILL] wr. si Akk. mullû; sabû; sâbu AALD: sibûtu (s.) (sību) (see sabû) الحانة ، النُّزلُ AALD: sību (s.) (in bīt sībi) (see sabû) الحانة ، النُّزلُ	سدر (لسان العرب) سَبَأَ (القاموس المحيط) سبأ (الصّحَاح في اللغة) سبأ (لسان العرب) سَبَى (القاموس المحيط) سبي (لسان العرب) سبي (مقاييس اللغة)
153	^{f}šam-ḫat ^{f}ša-am-ka-tim ^{f}ša-am-ka-at ^{f}ša-am-ka-tum	140^{T1} 135^{P} 140^{P} 172^{P}	ePSD: šamhu hili [LUXURIANT] wr. hi-li; hilib$_{2}$ Akk. kuzbu; šamhu	شمخ (مقاييس اللغة) شمخ (لسان العرب) سمح (لسان العرب)

			ePSD: šammāhu šagmah [INTESTINE] wr. ^{uzu}šag$_4$-mah Akk. šammāhu	
154	*ga-na*	209^{T11} 221^{T11}	ePSD: gana gana [COME ON!] wr. ga-na; gana Akk. gana	جني (مقاييس اللغة) جني (الصّحّاح في اللغة) جَنَى (القاموس المحيط) جنأ (مقاييس اللغة) جنأ (لسان العرب)
155	*gar-nu-šu-ma* *qí-re-en-ni*	11^{U} 216^{T1}	garānu gar [HEAP] wr. gar "to heap up" Akk. garānu gu gur [PILE UP] wr. gu$_2$ gur "to pile up" Akk. garānu AALD: garnu (see qarnu): (القرن (للحيوان	قرن (الصّحّاح في اللغة) بيغ (مقاييس اللغة) قرن (مقاييس اللغة) قرن (لسان العرب) جرن (لسان العرب)
156	*gat-ti* *ga-at-ti* *gat-ta-šú*	29^{T1} 16^{U} 50^{T1}	AALD: gattu (see kattu): التمثال، الشكل، الهيئة AALD: kattu (see gattu and kû) AALD: kû (adj.) (kûm, kuāu, kuwāu) f. (kattu, kuātu, kuwātu) pl. (kuttun) يعود اليك، لك AALD: gattu (see gādu): AALD: gādu (s.) (see gattu) اسم لنهر الفرات Note: tu = du	جثا (لسان العرب) جث (مقاييس اللغة) جذا (لسان العرب) لجُثْوَةُ (القاموس المحيط) القَتْوُ (القاموس المحيط)
157	^{ĝeš}ERIN ^{ĝeš}ERIN ÉRIN.^{MEŠ}	24^{T1} 230^{T10} 68^{T11}	ePSD: EREN eren [CEDAR] wr. ^{ĝeš}eren; eren; ^{šim}eren; ^{šimĝeš}eren; ^{ĝeš}hu-ri$_2$-in; ^{ĝeš}e-re-ne; hu-ri$_2$-in^{mušen} Akk. erēnu šeš [UNMNG] wr. šeš$_4$ "" šeš [WEEP] wr. šeš$_4$; še$_8$-še$_8$; še$_8$; šeš$_2$; šeš$_x$(|A.IGI|); šeš$_3$; še$_x$(|IGI×A|) Akk. bakû ePSD: ERIN$_2$ erin [PEOPLE] wr. erin$_2$; eri-na; erin$_9$ Akk. ṣābu erin [YOKE] wr. erin$_2$; ^{ĝeš}erin$_2$ Akk. ṣamādu; ṣimittu lah [DRY] wr. lah$_2$ "to dry" Akk. šābulu sur [HARNESS] wr. sur$_5$; sur$_x$(ERIN$_2$) Akk. šuqallulu zalag [SHINE] wr. zalag; zalag$_2$; su-lu-ug; sulug Akk. ebbu; namāru; nûru	عرن (مقاييس اللغة) عرن (لسان العرب) ظمخ (لسان العرب) سمق (لسان العرب) أرن (مقاييس اللغة) أرِنَ (القاموس المحيط) ارن (الصّحّاح في اللغة) أرن (لسان العرب)
158	^{ĝeš}GU.ZA	271^{T10}	ePSD: guza guza [CHAIR] wr. ^{ĝeš}gu-za; gu-za; gu$_2$-za; ^{ĝeš}guza; ^{ĝeš}aš-te Akk. kussû	الجَعْزُ (القاموس المحيط) جعز (لسان العرب) جوز (لسان العرب) جَزَعَ (القاموس المحيط) جزع (لسان العرب)
159	GEŠTIN karānu	73^{T11}	ePSD: karānu ĝeštin [VINE] wr. ĝeštin; ^{ĝeš}ĝeštin; mu-tin; mu-ti-in Akk. karānu AALD: *karānu (s.) (kiranu) الكرم، الكحول، كرمة العنب، العنب Note: al-Jibouri rule: karmu -> karnu	جعا (لسان العرب) كرم (لسان العرب)
160	^{ĝeš}TIR	230^{T10}	ePSD: TIR tir [BOW] wr. tir; ^{ĝeš}tir tir [FOREST] wr. tir; ^{ĝeš}tir Akk. luhummû; qištu tir [FORESTER] wr. $^{lu}{}_2$tir; tir tir [PLANT] wr. $^{u}{}_2$tir	طهر (لسان العرب) طير (مقاييس اللغة) طحر (لسان العرب) طَحْمَرَ (القاموس المحيط) طَحَرَتِ (القاموس المحيط) قوس (لسان العرب)

			ePSD: qištu tir [FOREST] wr. tir; ^{ĝeš}tir Akk. luhummû; qištu ePSD: qīštu niĝba [GIFT] wr. niĝ$_2$-ba Akk. qīštu u [GIFT] wr. u Akk. qīštu AALD: qâšu (v.) (qiāšu) يمنح، يقدم هبة qišti See *KASKAL*	كشش (لسان العرب) قشش (لسان العرب) قسس (الصّحّاح في اللغة) قسا (لسان العرب) الدَّوْسُ (القاموس المحيط) غيب (لسان العرب)
161	*GEŠTU.^{MIN}-šú*	205^{T1}	See also *ḫa-as-su* See also *ú-zu-un-šú* See also *ŠU.MIN-šá* ePSD: ĝeštug ĝeštug [EAR] wr. ĝeštug$_2$; ^{ĝeš}ĝeštug; ĝeštug; ĝeštug$_3$; muštug$_2$; mu-uš-tug$_2$; mu-uš-tug Akk. hassu; uznu; uznu; ţēmu ĝeštug [FISH] wr. ^{ĝeš}ĝeštug$^{ku}_6$; ^{ĝeš}ĝeštug$_2{}^{ku}{}_6$	جسس (العباب الزاخر) جوس (لسان العرب) حطأ (العباب الزاخر)
162	*GI*	301^{T10}	See also *qanê* See also *qa-na* EPSD: GI gi [ESSENCE] wr. Gi; ^{šim}gi gi [JUDGMENT] wr. Gi; gi$_{16}$ Akk. šipţu gi [KILL] wr. Gi$_4$ Akk. dâku gi [REED] wr. Gi Akk. qanû gi [THICKET] wr. ^{ĝeš}gi Akk. ? gi [TURN] wr. Gi$_4$; gi Akk. lamû; târu	جحح (لسان العرب) جحا (لسان العرب)
163	*GI$_6$* *GI$_6$* *GI$_6$.^{MEŠ}*	86^{T1} 239^{T1} 194^{T1}	See also *mu-ši* ePSD: ĝi ĝi [BIRD] wr. ĝi$_6{}^{\text{mušen}}$ ĝi [NIGHT] wr. ĝi$_6$ Akk. mūšu	غيا (لسان العرب)
164	*gíl-la-ti* *gíl-lat-šú*	186^{T11} 186^{T11}	ePSD: giltû ĝešdi [RUNG] wr. ^{ĝeš}di$_5$ Akk. giltû ePSD: galātu buluh [FEAR] wr. bu-luh; bu-lu-uh$_2$; bu-lu-uh$_3$; buluh Akk. galātu	غلو/ي (مقاييس اللغة) غَلاَ (القاموس المحيط) غلل (لسان العرب) غيل (لسان العرب) جول (لسان العرب) جأل (لسان العرب) جالَ (القاموس المحيط)
165	*GIM*	106^{T1}	See also *ki-ma* ePSD: agin agin [THUS] wr. a-gin$_7$ "thus" Akk. kī ePSD: gi gi [JUDGMENT] wr. gi; gi$_{16}$ "judgment" Akk. šipţu	جيا (لسان العرب) جوم (لسان العرب)
166	*GÌR-šú* *GÌR-^{MEŠ}-šú* *lu-ug-ri-šum-ma* *GÌR-^{MEŠ}-šú* *GIR$_4$* *ge-er*	56^{T1} 128^{T1} 220^{T1} 255^{T1} 66^{T11} 79^{T11}	See also *ši-pi-šú* See also *ki-i-ri* ePSD: GIR gir [ANGER] wr. gir$_{10}$ Akk. uzzu gir [FISH] wr. gir; gir$^{ku}_6$ Akk. šahû	جعر (مقاييس اللغة) الجَعْرُ (القاموس المحيط) جعر (لسان العرب) جأر (لسان العرب) جرجر (الصّحّاح في اللغة) جحر (لسان العرب)

	gi-ir	79^{T11}	gir [GIFT] wr. ^{gi}gir Akk. šerku gir [JAR] wr. ^{dug}gir$_{16}$; gir$_{9}$ "a large jar" Akk. kirru gir [OVEN] wr. gir$_{4}$ Akk. kīru gir [RUNNER] wr. gir$_{5}$; gir$_{7}$ Akk. šānû gir [SLIP] wr. gir$_{5}$ gir [STRANGER] wr. gir$_{5}$ Akk. ubāru[foreigner] gir [UNMNG] wr. gir$_{14}$ "?" gir [YOKE] wr. gir$_{11}$ Akk. şamādu ePSD: ĝiri ĝiri [DAGGER] wr. ĝiri$_{2}$; ^{urud}ĝiri$_{2}$; me$_{2}$-er; me-er; me-ri Akk. naglabu; patru ĝiri [FOOT] wr. ĝiri$_{3}$; me-ri; ĝiri$_{16}$ Akk. šēpu ePSD: gerû gabal du [HOSTILE] wr. ga-ba-al du$_{3}$ Akk. gerû AALD: šēpu (s.f) 1) القدم، الرِّجل 2) الذات، الشخص 3) الدخول ، التقدم، الهجوم 4) النقل، الطريق 5) المرتبة، المنزلة 6) اثر القدم، طبعة القدم	جير (مقاييس اللغة) جير (لسان العرب) جر (مقاييس اللغة) جمم (الصّحّاح في اللغة) الجَرُّ (القاموس المحيط) جرر (لسان العرب) وظف (لسان العرب) الرَّجُلُ (القاموس المحيط) الأَصْلُ (القاموس المحيط) الساقُ (القاموس المحيط) سوق (لسان العرب) رجل (لسان العرب) غور (لسان العرب) الغَوْرُ (القاموس المحيط) غور (مقاييس اللغة) غرر (لسان العرب)
167	^{giš}GAG.^{MEŠ} sikkāt	64^{T11}	ePSD: gag gag [NAIL] wr. ^{ĝeš}gag; gag; ^{urud}gag Akk. sikkatu; ūşu gag [POCK] wr. gag Akk. sikkatu ePSD: sikkatu gag [NAIL] wr. ^{ĝeš}gag; gag; Akk. sikkatu; ūşu gag [POCK] wr. gag Akk. sikkatu sahin [PEG] wr. sa-hi-in Akk. sikkatu sahindu [YEAST] wr. sa-hi-in-du$_{3}$; sa-hi-in; ^{šem}sah$_{7}$-hi-in Akk. sahindu; sikkatu ePSD: sakkuttu saĝkud [REED PIPE] wr. ^{gi}saĝ-kud Akk. sakkuttu	سكت (الصّحّاح في اللغة) السَّكْتُ (القاموس المحيط) سكت (لسان العرب) جوج (لسان العرب) See *gú-gal-la-šú-nu*
168	^{giš}KUN$_{4}$ *mu-kin* UKKIN UKKIN *kun-nu-nu*	15^{T1} 44^{T1} 271^{T10} 7^{T11} 116^{T11}	ePSD: kun$_{4}$ kuĝ [STAIR] wr. ^{ĝeš}kuĝ$_{5}$; kun$_{4}$; ^{ĝeš}kuĝ$_{4}$; kun$_{5}$; ^{ĝeš}kuĝ$_{x}$(LUM) Akk. askuppu; simmiltu ePSD: kun$_{5}$ kuĝ [STAIR] wr. ^{ĝeš}kuĝ$_{5}$; kun$_{4}$; ^{ĝeš}kuĝ$_{4}$; kun$_{5}$; ^{ĝeš}kuĝ$_{x}$(LUM) Akk. askuppu; simmiltu ePSD: kânu gin [ESTABLISH] wr. gin$_{6}$; gi-na; gi-in; ge-en; gin Akk. kânu; kīnu ePSD: kuninu buniĝ [TROUGH] wr. ^{ĝeš}buniĝ; ^{gi}buniĝ$_{x}$(|A.LAGAB×A|); buniĝ; ^{gi}buniĝ; ^{ĝeš}buniĝ$_{2}$; ^{ĝeš}buniĝ$_{3}$; kunin Akk. kuninu; pattû AALD: kânu (v.) (kuānu)	صمل (لسان العرب) كون (لسان العرب) وكن (لسان العرب) الكِنُّ (القاموس المحيط) كن (مقاييس اللغة) كنن (الصّحّاح في اللغة) كنن (لسان العرب) القَنُّ (القاموس المحيط) قنن (لسان العرب) مكن (لسان العرب)
169	^{giš}MÁ ^{giš}MÁ-*ma* ^{giš}MÁ-*ma*	24^{T11} 89^{T11} 94^{T11}	*See A.^{MEŠ}* *Wikipedia:* https://en.wikipedia.org/wiki/Noah%27s_Ark	طبق (لسان العرب) كفف (لسان العرب) قفف(لسان العرب) فلك (لسان العرب)

			worldwideflood.com: http://worldwideflood.com/ark/what_shape/ark_box.htm *Strong's Concordance:* http://biblehub.com/hebrew/8392.htm ePSD: ma ma [BURN] wr. ma_5-ma_5; ma_5 ma [SHIP] wr. ma_2; $^{ĝeš}ma_2$ Akk. eleppu ma [WEAPON?] wr. $^{ĝeš}ma_2$ Akk. mekû ePSD: MA ĝa [HOUSE] wr. ĝa2; ma Akk. bītu ĝen [GO] wr. ĝen; ma Akk. alāku mada [LAND] wr. ma-da; ma Akk. erşetu; mātu peš [FIG] wr. ĝešpeš3; peš; peš3; mupeš3 Akk. tittu ePSD: eleppu ma [SHIP] wr. ma_2; $^{ĝeš}ma_2$ Akk. eleppu ePSD: pilku in [SECTOR] wr. in Akk. pilku induba [BOUNDARY] wr. in-dub-ba; im-dub-ba Akk. pilku	شحن (لسان العرب) شخن (لسان العرب) شهن (لسان العرب) أبق (لسان العرب) علب (لسان العرب) موه (لسان العرب) موأ (العباب الزاخر) المَعْوُ (القاموس المحيط) ماعَ (القاموس المحيط) ميع (لسان العرب) مع (الصّحاح في اللغة) معع (لسان العرب)
170	*^{giš}má-gi-il-la*	272[T11]	ePSD: magillu magilum [BOAT] wr. $^{ĝeš}ma_2$-gi_4-lum; $^{ĝeš}ma_2$-gi-lum; $^{ĝeš}ma_2$-gi-la_2 Akk. magillu	أجل (لسان العرب) مجل (مقاييس اللغة) مجل (الصّحاح في اللغة) مَجَلَتْ (القاموس المحيط) مجل (لسان العرب) صحف (العباب الزاخر) صحف (لسان العرب)
171	*^{giš}su-us-su-ul*	68[T11]	ePSD: sassu KIKAL [BOTTOM] wr. KI.KAL Akk. sassu AALD: sussullu (s.) الصندوق أو وعاء من الخشب نادرا من المعادن الثمينة (سلة)	الشَّسْلَةُ (القاموس المحيط) شتِل (لسان العرب) شَتَّلَتْ (القاموس المحيط) التَّتَلُ (القاموس المحيط)
172	*gít-ma-lu* *gít-ma-lu* *gít-ma-lu* *gít-ma-lu* *gít-ma-lu*	35[T1] 37[T1] 61[T1] 211[T1] 218[T1]	ePSD: gitmālu rum [PERFECT] wr. rum Akk. gitmālu šar [PERFECT?] wr. $šar_2$ Akk. gitmālu ušum [SNAKE] wr. ušum Akk. ašaredu; bašmu; gitmālu Note: Possible derivation path: كَمل اكْتمل كتْتمل and جَمل اجْتمل جتْتمل	كمل (لسان العرب) جمل (لسان العرب)
173	GÚ GÚ GÚ-*ia*	39[T1] 12[T11] 166[T11]	ePSD: gu gu [BIRD] wr. $gu_2^{mušen}$ gu [CORD] wr. gu Akk. qû gu [EAT] wr. gu_7 Akk. akālu gu [ENTIRETY] wr. gu_2 Akk. nagbu; napharu gu [FORCE] wr. gu_2 Akk. emūqu gu [NECK] wr. gu_2 Akk. ahu; kišādu; tikku gu [PULSE] wr. gu_2 gu [SQUARE] wr. gu_7	الجَوُّ (القاموس المحيط) جوأ (لسان العرب) جوا (لسان العرب) جعا (لسان العرب)

			gu [VOICE] wr. gu$_3$ Akk. rigmu AALD: gû (s.) معنى غير معروف	
174	GU$_4$.^{MEŠ} GU$_4$	71^{T11} 108^{T11}	See also GÚ ePSD: gu$_4$ gud [OX] wr. gud; gu$_3$-ra Akk. alpu; lī'um	هلف (مقاييس اللغة) هلف (لسان العرب) علف (العباب الزاخر) علف (لسان العرب) جد (مقاييس اللغة) جدد (لسان العرب)
175	GUB-az	279^{T1}	See also ez-zu ePSD: gub gub [BATHE] wr. gub$_2$ Akk. ramāku gub [STAND] wr. gub Akk. izuzzu gub [~SHEEP] wr. gub	جوب (لسان العرب) جبز (مقاييس اللغة) جبس (العباب الزاخر)
176	gú-gal-la-šú-nu	17^{T11} 18^{T11}	ePSD: gugallu gugal [INSPECTOR] wr. ku$_3$-gal$_2$; gu$_2$-gal; ku$_6$-gal$_2$ Akk. gugallu	الجاجَةُ (القاموس المحيط) جَأَجَ (القاموس المحيط) جوج (لسان العرب) عيج (لسان العرب)
177	GÚR-sa	58^{T11}	ePSD: gur gur [CIRCLE] wr. Akk. kippatu; šumutu gur [LIFT] wr. gur$_3$-ru; guru$_3$; gur; gur$_{17}$; guru$_6$ Akk. našû; nāšû gur [REAP] wr. gur$_x$(|ŠE.KIN|); gur$_{10}$; gur$_x$(|ŠE.KIN.KIN|) "to reap" Akk. eṣēdu gur [RIM] wr. ^{ĝeš}gur$_2$ Akk. kippatu gur [SHIELD] wr. gur$_{21}$; ^{kuš}buru$_4$^{mušen}; ^{e}ur$_2$ gur [TOOL] wr. ^{ĝeš}gur$_8$ gur [TURN] wr. gur Akk. sahāru; târu gur [UNIT] wr. gur; gur$_9$ Akk. kurru; namandu	جرر (لسان العرب) جور (مقاييس اللغة) جور (لسان العرب)
178	GURUŠ.^{MEŠ} GURUŠ.TUR	67^{T1} 76^{T1}	See also eṯli ePSD: GURUŠ ĝuruš [MALE] wr. ĝuruš Akk. eṯlu ePSD: TUR ban [UNIT] wr. ba-an; ban$_2$; ban$_3$; ba-an-AŠ; ^{dug}ban$_3$ " Akk. sūtu banda [QUOTIENT] wr. banda$_3$ Akk. bandû banda [SAGACITY] wr. banda$_3$ Akk. tašimtu dumu [CHILD] wr. dumu; du$_5$-mu Akk. māru suhuš [OFFSHOOT] wr. suhuš$_x$(TUR); suhuš$_2$ tur [CHILD] wr. tur "(young) child" Akk. šerru tur [SMALL] wr. tur; tu Akk. ṣehērum ePSD: batultu kisikil [WOMAN] wr. ki-sikil; ^{lu}$_2$ki-sikil; mu-tin; mu-ti-in Akk. ardatu; batultu	غرس (لسان العرب) غَرَسَ (القاموس المحيط) batultu بتل (لسان العرب) بتل (مقاييس اللغة) TUR طور (لسان العرب) تور (لسان العرب) تأر (لسان العرب)
179	gu-za-lá-šú-nu GU.ZA.LÁ.^{MEŠ} gu-za-lu-ú	17^{T11} 101^{T11} 101^{T11}	See also ^{ĝeš}GU.ZA ePSD: guzallu ašbaltum [STATUS] wr. ^{lu}$_2$aš-bal-tum Akk. ašpaltu; guzallu guzal [SCOUNDREL] wr. gu$_2$-zal; gu$_3$-zal Akk. guzallu;	الجَزْلُ (القاموس المحيط) جزل (لسان العرب) ضرم (لسان العرب) جذل (لسان العرب)

			ishappu; ahurrû; nû'u hara [RUFFIAN] wr. $hara_3$ Akk. guzallu; ishappu ePSD: guzalû guzala [OFFICIAL] wr. gu-za-la_2 Akk. guzalû	
180	ḪA.LA	310[T10]	See also ^{f}ḪUL ePSD: hala hala [SHARE] wr. Ha-la; hal Akk. zittu ePSD: HAL hal [DIVIDE] wr. hal-ha; ha-la; hal Akk. barû; halālu; nazālu; petû; pirištu; zâzu; šahālu	الخَلُّ (القاموس المحيط) خلا (لسان العرب) خلل (الصّحاح في اللغة) خلل (لسان العرب) خول (لسان العرب) خيل (لسان العرب)
181	ḫa-a-a-al-ti	132[T11]	See also a-lit-ti	حول (لسان العرب) حال (لسان العرب)
182	ḫa-an-ši	57[T11]	ePSD: hanšat ya [FIVE] wr. ia_2 Akk. hanšat	خمس (مقاييس اللغة) حنث (لسان العرب)
183	ḫa-an-ṭiš	110[T11] 233[T11]	See also ú-ḫa-am-ma-ṭu AALD: ḫanṭiš (adv.) see ḫamaṭu بسرعة، حالا، فجأة	خَنَطَهُ (القاموس المحيط) حنط (العباب الزاخر) حنط (لسان العرب)
184	ḫa-as-su ḫas-su ḫi-is-sa-as it-te-eḫ-su it-taḫ-su lu-ú-uḫ-su-sa-am-ma aḫ-su-sa-am-ma ḫa-si-sa aḫ-ḫi-is	2[T1] 2[T1] 22[T11] 115[T11] 115[T11] 167[T11] 167[T11] 202[T1] 317[T11]	ePSD: hasāsu na deg [CLEAR] wr. na deg_x(RI); ša di; ša di-di; ša di-di_5; ša di_5 Akk. ašāru; elēlu; hasāsu si [REMEMBER] wr. si Akk. hasāsu ePSD: hasīsu ĝizzal [EAR] wr. ĝizzal; $gizzal_2$ Akk. hasīsu; uznu; uznu; nešmû ePSD: hassu; uznu ĝeštug [EAR] wr. $ĝeštug_2$; ^{ĝeš}ĝeštug; ĝeštug; $ĝeštug_3$; $muštug_2$; mu-uš-tug_2; mu-uš-tug Akk. hassu; uznu; uznu; ṭēmu	خسس (العباب الزاخر) خسس (لسان العرب) هسا (لسان العرب) وهس (العباب الزاخر) هسس (العباب الزاخر) هسس (لسان العرب) هَسَّهُ (القاموس المحيط) حسا (لسان العرب) حسو/ي (مقاييس اللغة) حسس (الصّحاح في اللغة) حسس (لسان العرب) حس (مقاييس اللغة) الحَسُّ (القاموس المحيط)
185	ḫa-bi-lu-LÙ	113[T1]	See aslo LÙ ePSD: habālu heše [OPPRESSED] wr. $heš_5{}^{še}{}_3$; haš Akk. habālu; kalû AALD: habbilu (adj) (see habālu) (2) شرير مخالف للقانون (1) شرير (شيطان، عفريت)	خبل (لسان العرب) حبل (لسان العرب)
186	ḫa-di-'-a ḫa-di-'-ú-a ḫad[ad]-di-'-i	234[T1] 234[T1] 265[T10]	See also e-du-ú ePSD: hadû lib [RICH] Akk. hadû; hidiātu; râšu; rāšû; rīšātu šag hul [HAPPY] wr. $šag_4$ hul_2 Akk. hadû AALD: *hadû (adj.) هاديء، لطيف، طيب AALD: *hadû (v.) (huddû, nahdû) ؛ يرحب، يكون سعيدا، يكون موافقا يَهتدي، يُوافق، يَسعَد	خدد (لسان العرب) حدأ (لسان العرب) هَدَأَ (القاموس المحيط) هدأ (العباب الزاخر) هدأ (لسان العرب) هدأ (لسان العرب) هدي (مقاييس اللغة) هدى (الصّحاح في اللغة) الهُدى (القاموس المحيط) هدي (لسان العرب)
187	ḫar-gal-li-šu	25	AALD: ḫargullu (ḫargallu): قفل، خطام يستخدم لسد فم الحيوان، كلمة سومرية دخيلة	حرجل (لسان العرب) خرق (لسان العرب)

			CAD: A set of metal rings used to hold the metal bar in palce	خرقل (لسان العرب)
188	*har-ra-na*	10^{U}	See also *ur-ḫa* ePSD: harrānu kaskal [WAY] wr. kaskal Akk. harrānu šušer [ROAD] wr. šu-še-er Akk. harrānu; nasīkātu	حرن (لسان العرب) حَرَنَتِ (القاموس المحيط)
189	*ḫa-ṣi-nu* *ḫa-ṣi-in-nu* *ḫa-aṣ-ṣi-nu* *ḫa-aṣ-ṣi-nu-um-ma*	278 278 29^{P} 31^{P}	ePSD: haṣṣinnu hazin [AX] wr. ^{urud}ha-zi-in; ^{urud}ha-zi; ^{urud}ha-zi_2-in Akk. haṣṣinnu	خصن (لسان العرب) خصن (مقاييس اللغة) حصن (لسان العرب)
190	*ḫa-ṣi-pi* *ḫa-ṣi-pi* *ḫa-ṣi-ip*	301^{T10} 307^{T10} 307^{T10}	ePSD haṣābu haš [BREAK] wr. Haš Akk. haṣābu; šebēru ePSD haṣāṣu ša [SNAP] wr. $Ša_5$ Akk. haṣāṣu ePSD haṣbu? hazbum [TERRACOTTA] wr. ^{dug}ha-az-bu-um Akk. haṣbu? ePSD haṣbu tugguza [TEXTILE] wr. Tug_2-guz-za; tug_2-gu-zaAkk. Haṣbu AALD: ḫasāpu (v.) ينتف (الشعر)؛ يزيل (طابوق)	هصص (لسان العرب) هصا (لسان العرب) هصم (لسان العرب) هصر (لسان العرب) حسف (لسان العرب) حصب (لسان العرب) خصف (لسان العرب) حصف (لسان العرب)
191	*ḫe-ru-ú* *ú-ḫar-ru-ú*	39^{T1} 130^{T1}	ePSD: harāru harra [DUG?] wr. har-ra "dug?" Akk. harāru šab [TRIM] wr. šab Akk. barû ša uzu; esēpu; harāru; harāṣu; harāṣu; eṣēru; harāṣu; šarāmu; nakāsu; šahāhu ePSD: herû bal [DIG] wr. ba-al; bal; bal_3; bal_4; pe-el Akk. herû dun [DIG] wr. dun Akk. herû AALD: *hurru (s.m.) الخرُّ، الحُفرة AALD: *hirru (s.m.) الخرُّ، الحز AALD: hirû (see herû) حفر، نبش، استخرج AALD: hirītû (s.) الخندق، القناة، الشق	حور (لسان العرب) حور (مقاييس اللغة) خُرْوَةُ (القاموس المحيط) خرت (لسان العرب) حري (لسان العرب) حرو/ي (مقاييس اللغة) خرر (لسان العرب) حرر (لسان العرب)
192	*ḪI.LI*	231^{T1}	ePSD: HI HI [CVNE] wr. HI dub [KNEE] wr. dub_3; ze_2-eb dug [GOOD] wr. dug_3; ze_2-eb; du- Akk. ṭābu hi [MIX] wr. hi Akk. balālu ePSD: HI.LI hili [LUXURIANT] wr. hi-li; $hilib_2$ Akk. kuzbu; šamhu hili [WIG] wr. hi-li	حيا (الصّحَاح في اللغة) الحِيُّ (القاموس المحيط) ليا (مقاييس اللغة) لِيأ (العباب الزاخر) ليا (لسان العرب) حلا (لسان العرب)
193	*ḫi-rat*	77^{T1}	ePSD: hīrtu ĝidlam [SPOUSE] wr. ĝidlam; $ĝidlam_2$; $ĝidlam_3$ Akk. hā'iru; hīrtu	خير (الصّحَاح في اللغة)
194	*ḫi-ṣib*	44^{T11}	AALD: ḫiṣbu (s.) الخصب، إنتاج وفير، إنتاج؛ الفرج (للمرأة)	خَضَبَهُ (القاموس المحيط) خضب (لسان العرب) خصب (الصّحَاح في

				(اللغة) الخِصْبُ (القاموس المحيط) خصب (لسان العرب)
195	*ḫi-šiḫ-tu* *ḫi-šiḫ-tum* *ḫu-šaḫ-ḫu*	56[T11] 65[T11] 193[T11]	ePSD: hišihtu a'aš [SUPPLIES] wr. a_2-$aš_2$ Akk. hišihtu ePSD: hušahhu sugu [NEED] wr. su-gu_7 Akk. hušahhu AALD: hisihtu (s.) See hasahu الحاجة، العوز؛ المتطلبات، التجهيزات الضرورية؛ وصف حاجة مفيدة ومحبوبة	هيث (الصّحَاح في اللغة) هثي (لسان العرب) هتت (الصّحَاح في اللغة) هتت (لسان العرب) حت (مقاييس اللغة) حتت (الصّحَاح في اللغة) حتت (لسان العرب) حَتَّه (القاموس المحيط) حثث (الصّحَاح في اللغة) حثث (لسان العرب) حضض (لسان العرب) بضض (لسان العرب)
196	*ḫi-ṭi* *ḫi-ṭa-a-šú*	185[T11]	ePSD: hiṭītu luĝa [DAMAGE] wr. luĝa; $luĝ_2$ Akk. hiṭītu; šillatu	الخَطَءُ (القاموس المحيط) خطأ (الصّحَاح في اللغة) خطأ (لسان العرب)
197	*ḫur-sa-a-ni* *ḫur-sa-an-nu*	38[T1] 38[T1]	ePSD: hursānu hursaĝ [MOUNTAIN] wr. hur-saĝ; $PA.DUN_3$ Akk. hursānu	حرس (لسان العرب)
198	*Ì.GIŠ* *Ì+GIŠ*	68[T11]	ePSD: GIŠ ĝeš [TREE] wr. ĝeš; mu; u_5 Akk. işu ePSD: I.GIŠ i'iz [NUMEROUS] wr. i-iz Akk. mādu i'iz [SEED] wr. i-iz Akk. zēru ePSD: iĝeš iĝeš [OIL] wr. i_3-ĝeš ePSD: ĝeš ĝeš [PENIS] wr. $ĝeš_3$; mu Akk. išaru; zikaru ĝeš [SIXTY] wr. $geš_2$; mu-uš "sixty" ĝeš [TREE] wr. ĝeš; mu; u_5 Akk. işu ePSD: šamnu i [OIL] wr. i_3; u_5; u_2 Akk. tallum; šamnu li [OIL] wr. li_2 Akk. šamnu u'u [STONE] wr. ${}^{na}{}_4u_2$-u_2 Akk. šamnu Note1: Ì+GIŠ = i-iz = i'iz = إجز = إيز = harvest = (حبوب) المحصود Note2: Ì+GIŠ = i-iz = i'iz = إإز = living source = (سبب العيش) أزاء Note3: Ì+GIŠ = i-iz = i'iz = [يغيس] إغيس = seeds Note3: Ì+GIŠ = E+GIŠ = جِش (حياة) حي = plant life = seeds Note4: i+ĝeš = E+ĝeš = [جِش] غيس (ماء) حي = seed [plant] water = vegetable oil	جزز (لسان العرب) أزا (لسان العرب) جش (مقاييس اللغة) جشش (لسان العرب) غيس (مقاييس اللغة) غسن (لسان العرب) الغَيْسانِيُّ (القاموس المحيط) عيا (لسان العرب) أيي (مقاييس اللغة) حيا (لسان العرب) See E سَمِنَ (القاموس المحيط) سمن (لسان العرب)
199	*Ì.NUN*	272[T10]	ePSD: inun	المومُ (القاموس المحيط)

	ẖimēti		inun [GHEE] wr. i_3-nun AALD: *ẖimētu (s.) الحم: الشحم بعد تحميصه؛ الدهن Note1: m <-> n; ن <-> م Note2: Ì.NUN = Ì.MUM = fat liquid = حمم = (ماء الشحم) حي موم = السمن	موم (لسان العرب) حمأ (لسان العرب) حم (مقاييس اللغة) حما (لسان العرب) حمم (لسان العرب) حنس (لسان العرب) حمس (لسان العرب)
200	*ia-a-ši* *ia-a-ši* *ia-a-ši* *ia-a-ši*	216[T1] 264[T10] 39[T11] 200[T11]	See also *ia-ti* AALD: yâši (pron.) (yâšim, yâšu, yâša, ayâši, also: yâšia, yâšinu) ضمير تملك متصل مفرد، لي AALD: yâšinu (pron.) ضمير تملك متصل جمع، لنا، الينا	
201	*ia-ti* *ia-a-ti-ma* *ia-a-ti-ma* *ia-a-tú*	13[P] 3[T11] 4[T11] 37[T11]	See also *ia-a-ši* AALD: yâti (pron.) (yâtia) ضمير تملك منفصل مفرد AALD: yâtinu (pron.) ضمير تملك منفصل جمع	
202	*i-ba-'-u* *i-ba-'-ú* *tu-ba-'-ú* *ú-ba-'-ú*	106[T11] 106[T11] 208[T11] 111[T11]	ePSD: bâ'u dib [PASS] wr. dib; dib_2; di-ib Akk. bâ'u; etēqu ri [IMPOSE] wr. RI; ru Akk. bâ'u; emēdu; nadû; nasāku; ramû; rehû; tarû; wašaru ur [DRAG] wr. ur_3 Akk. bâ'u; kapāru; šabāṭu	بغي (مقاييس اللغة) بغا (لسان العرب) بَوَأ (العباب الزاخر) بوأ (لسان العرب)
203	*i-ba-áš-ši* *i-ba-áš-šu-ú* *ib-šú-nim-ma* *ta-ba-áš-ši* *ib-šu-nik-ka* *ib-ba-šú-nim-ma* *i-ba-áš-ši* *i-ba-áš-ši* *i-ba-ši*	120[T1] 225[T1] 247[T1] 207[T1] 261[T1] 6[P] 311[T10] 315[T10] 215[T10]	ePSD: bašû ĝal [BE] wr. $ĝal_2$; ma-al; $^{ga}{}_2gal_2$ Akk. bašû; šakānu ePSD: būšu immal [PROPERTY] wr. $immal_3$ Akk. būšu; makkûru; maršītu; ṭuhhudu kibšur [PLENTIFUL] wr. kibšur Akk. bāšītu; būšu; makkûru; maršītu niĝšu [GOODS] wr. $niĝ_2$-šu Akk. būšu AALD: ibašši (see bašu) محتمل ان تعني نعم؛ أكيد، بالتأكيد AALD: bāšû (adj.) (see bašû) باق، جاهز	با (لسان العرب) بتأ (لسان العرب) بشش (لسان العرب) بعث (مقاييس اللغة) بثث (لسان العرب) بثّ (مقاييس اللغة)
204	*ib-ba-ti-iq* *ú-bat-ti-iq*	187[T11] 292[T11]	ePSD: batāqu šu dag [ABANDON] wr. šu dag Akk. batāqu	فتق (مقاييس اللغة) فتق (لسان العرب) بتك (مقاييس اللغة) بَتَكَهُ (القاموس المحيط)
205	*ib-ri*	268[T1]	See also *e-bir* ePSD: ibru guli [FRIEND] wr. gu_5-li; gu-li; gu_7-li Akk. ibru	أَبَرَ (القاموس المحيط) أبر (لسان العرب) أفر (مقاييس اللغة) أفر (لسان العرب)
206	*ÍD* *ÍD-ma* *ÍD.*[MEŠ]	312[T10] 74[T11] 205[T11]	See also *nāru* ePSD: id id [RIVER] wr. id_2; id_3; id_6; id_7; id_5 Akk. nāru	حيد (لسان العرب)
207	*i-dab-bu-bu-uš*	250[T10]	ePSD: dabābu di [SPEAK] wr. di Akk. atwû; dabābu; qabû dug [SPEAK] wr. dug_4 Akk. atwû; dabābu; epēšu; qabû e [SPEAK] wr. e; na-be_2-a; be_2; ne; da-me; na-be_2; e_7	طبب (لسان العرب) دبب (الصّحّاح في اللغة) دَبَّ (القاموس المحيط) دبب (لسان العرب)

			Akk. atwû; dabābu; qabû AALD: dabābu (v.) يتكلم، يتاول، يناقش، يتآمر، يقدم افادة، يرفع قضية، ينصب مكيدة، يطالب، يعترض، يتأمل، يفترض	
208	*^{id}pu-rat-ti*	12^{T11}	Euphrates River = River of fresh water	فرت (لسان العرب)
209	*i-du-ú* *id-du-ú* *it-ta-di* *it-ta-du* *i-de* *i-de* *i-de* *at-ta-di-šú* *ta-ad-di-šú* *at-ta-di-šú* *at-ta-di-iš* *id-du-ma* *ud-du-ú* *ul-te-du-ú* *at-ta-’-id* *at-ta-di* *ú-ta-ad-da-a* *i-de-e-ma* *i-di-ia* *ud-da-áš-šú* *e-dak-ka* *lid-di-ka* *lid-di* *ud-du-šú* *ud-du-úš* *id-di-ma* *id-du-ú* *il-du-du-šu-ma* *i-da-a-a* *e-du-ú* *it-ta-di* *it-ta-di*	2^{T1} 21^{T1} 102^{T1} 102^{T1} 108^{T1} 259^{T1} 6^{U} 257^{T1} 265^{T1} 283^{T1} 283^{T1} 271^{T10} 322^{T10} 322^{T10} 34^{T11} 57^{T11} 113^{T11} 180^{T11} 201^{T11} 224^{T11} 236^{T11} 248^{T11} 255^{T11} 257^{T11} 257^{T11} 261^{T11} 272^{T11} 290^{T11} 311^{T11} 315^{T11} 228^{T11} 307^{T11}	See also *AD-šú* See also *ḫa-di-’-a* See also *šá-nu-’-ú-du* idu see *a-ḫi-ia* ePSD: edû <u>zu</u> [KNOW] wr. zu Akk. edû; lamādu ePSD: lamādu <u>zu</u> [KNOW] wr. zu Akk. edû; lamādu ePSD: na'ādu <u>saĝEZEN</u> [HEED] wr. sag-EZEN Akk. na'ādu AALD: *idû (v.) edû AALD: tuddû (v.) AALD: ta'ittu (v.) (na'ādu) AALD: edû (s.) إندفاع الماء، ارتفاع الماء، كلمة سومرية دخيلة	الهَدُّ (القاموس المحيط) هدد (الصّحاح في اللغة) هدد (لسان العرب) عد (مقاييس اللغة) عدد (لسان العرب) عدو (مقاييس اللغة) عدا (الصّحاح في اللغة) عَدا (القاموس المحيط) عدا (لسان العرب) يد (مقاييس اللغة) يدى (الصّحاح في اللغة) يدي (لسان العرب) أدي (مقاييس اللغة) أدّاه (القاموس المحيط) أدا (الصّحاح في اللغة) أدا (لسان العرب) أدد (لسان العرب) أدو (مقاييس اللغة) أيد (لسان العرب)
210	*i-gam-mar* *gam-rat* *gu-um-mur-ka* *gu-um-mur-ku*	29^{U} 77^{T11} 5^{T11} 5^{T11}	See also *ik-tap-píl* See also *uk-tam-ma-ru* ePSD: gāmiru <u>lirum</u> [STRENGTH] wr. lirum; lirum$_3$; lirum$_2$; lirum$_6$; lirum$_7$; lirum$_8$ Akk. abaru; dannu; emûqu; gāmiru; kamiru; kirimmu; umašu; šapşu; šitnunu; šitpuşu ePSD: gamāru <u>til</u> [COMPLETE] wr. til; til$_3$ Akk. gamāru; labāru; qatû AALD: gamāru (v.) يُبيد، ينهي، يهلك، يستنفذ، يطوق، يسيطر، يقود للنهاية، يدفع او يسلّم بالكامل، يحمل سوية، يركز، يستعمل كل قوته	جمر (مقاييس اللغة) جمر (الصّحاح في اللغة) الجَمْرَةُ (القاموس المحيط) جمر (لسان العرب)
211	*i-gar* *i-gar* *i-ga-ri*	21^{T11} 22^{T11} 222^{T11}	ePSD igāru <u>egar</u> [WALL] wr. e$_2$-gar$_8$; ba-ar; ba$_9$-ar$_2$ Akk. igāru	حجر (مقاييس اللغة) حجر (الصّحاح في اللغة) الحَجَرُ (القاموس المحيط)

			izid [WALL] wr. iz-zi; i-zi Akk. agû; igāru ePSD: egēru gilim [CROSS] wr. gilim; $gilib_x$(|GI%GI|)[ib]; gi_{16}-il; gil-gil[il] Akk. egēru; parāku AALD: igāriš (adv.) مثل حجارة، مثل جدار AALD: igartu (s.) الحجارة، الجدار او السور AALD: igāru (s.) الحجارة، جدار للبناء، السور الدائري، جانب السفينة AALD: igāru (s.) العقار، المرج	حجر (لسان العرب)
212	*IGI* *IGI* *IGI.DU.*[MEŠ]	31[T1] 274[T1] 37[U]	See also *pa-ni* See also *a-šá-rit-ti* ePSD: igi igi [EYE] wr. igi; i-bi_2; i-gi Akk. īnu igi [FACE] wr. igi; i-bi_2; igi_3; i-gi Akk. mahrum; pānû igi [QUALITY] wr. i-gi_8 igi [~MATHEMATICS] wr. igi ePSD: IGI DU igi gub [SEE] wr. igi gub Akk.?	الوَجْهُ (القاموس المحيط) وجه (مقاييس اللغة) حجا (لسان العرب) جيأ (لسان العرب) *DU* دوا (لسان العرب)
213	*i-ḫab-bu-bu*	187[T1]	ePSD: habbu umun [PIT] wr. $umun_{10}$; $umun_{11}$; $umun_{12}$; $umun_5$; $umun_6$ Akk. habbu; hammu	حبب (لسان العرب) ودد (لسان العرب) رنا (لسان العرب) الحُبُّ (القاموس المحيط)
214	*i-ḫi-iṭ-ma* *ḫi-iṭ-ma* *ḫa-a-a-iṭ* *ḫi-i-ṭi-ma* *ḫi-i-iṭ-ṭi-ma*	5[U] 19[T1] 41[T1] 324[T11] 324[T11]	ePSD: hā'iṭu luĝiadudu [NIGHT-WATCHMAN] wr. lu_2-$ĝi_6$-a-du-du; lu_2-$ĝi_6$-du-du Akk. hā'iṭu AALD: ḫaṭu (hadu, hiāṭu) (v.) 1) يراقب 2) يطلع، يفحص 3) يبحث، يتبع 4) يزن، يدفع 5) يتتبع AALD: hitmu (s.) قطعة من الفضة او الذهب بشكل ووزن معينين	حوط (لسان العرب) حاطَه (القاموس المحيط) حوط (الصّحّاح في اللغة) حطم (لسان العرب)
215	*iḫ-pi-šá*	108[T11]	ePSD: happu hab [MALODOROUS] wr. hab_2; hab Akk. alappānu; bīšu; ekēlu; happu AALD: ḫapši (s.) الذراع، القوة	حفا (لسان العرب) حَفَّ (القاموس المحيط) حفف (الصّحّاح في اللغة) حفف (لسان العرب)
216	*i-hu-uz?*	6[T1]	ePSD: hāzû šulu [BIRD] wr. šu-lu_2[mušen]; šu-nu[mušen] Akk. huqu; hāzû	حزا (لسان العرب) حَزَى (القاموس المحيط) حزو/ي (مقاييس اللغة)
217	*i-kád-dir*	69[T1]	AALD: kadāru (v.) 1) يتجبر، يتغطرس، يتحمس، ينشط 2) يحدث ضررا	كدر (لسان العرب) كأد (لسان العرب)
218	*ik-su-pu* *ik-su-pu* *ku-sa-pu* *ku-sa-pu*	301[T11] 319[T11] 301[T11] 319[T11]	ePSD: kasāpu pad [BREAK] wr. pad Akk. kasāpu	كسف (مقاييس اللغة) كسف (الصّحّاح في اللغة) الكِسْفَةُ (القاموس المحيط) كسف (لسان العرب)
219	*ik-ta-bi-it* *kab-ta-at* *kab-tu-ta* *kab-tu-ta* *ki-ba-a-ti*	8[P] 240[T10] 289[T10] 292[T10] 47[T11]	See also *i-qab-bu-ú* See also *dan-nu* ePSD: kabātu kul [HEAVY] wr. kul Akk. kabātu	خبب (لسان العرب) خبت (لسان العرب) كبد (لسان العرب) كبع (لسان العرب) كبو (مقاييس اللغة)

			ePSD: kabattu peš [THICK] wr. peš; peš$_5$; peš$_4$; peš$_6$ Akk. alādu; kabattu; līp līpi; mār māri; mērû; napāšu; šabāšu ur [LIVER] wr. ur$_5$ Akk. kabattu; ummatu ePSD: kibtu kib [WHEAT] wr. gig; gib Akk. kibtu ePSD: kabtu alim [BISON] wr. alim; e-lum Akk. ditānu; kabtu; kusarikku aratta [IMPORTANT] wr. aratta Akk. kabtu; tanattu dilmun [IMPORTANT] wr. dilmun Akk. kabtu; musukku; têrtu; šûpû dugud [HEAVY] wr. dugud Akk. kabtu idim [HEAVY] wr. idim Akk. kabtu mah [GREAT] wr. mah; mah$_2$ Akk. kabtu; mādu; rabû; şīru tukur [IMPORTANT] wr. tukur$_2$; tukur Akk. kabtu AALD: *kabātu(v.) (kabādu) يكبدُ، يثقل، يضخم، يسمن	كبا (لسان العرب) كبب (لسان العرب) كبت (مقاييس اللغة) كبت (مقاييس اللغة) كَبَتَهُ (القاموس المحيط) كبت (لسان العرب)
220	*ik-tal-du-ni* *ik-tal-da*	169[T1] 90[T11]	ePSD: kadādu ur [ANOINT] wr. ur$_5$ Akk. kadādu AALD: Kaldû (s.): الكلديين: اقوام سكنت بابل في الالف الاول قبل الميلاد Note: al-Jibouri rule: إكْتَلَدَ <- إكْتَدَّ	خلد (مقاييس اللغة) خلد (الصّحَاح في اللغة) قَلَدَ (القاموس المحيط) كلد (لسان العرب) كدد (لسان العرب)
221	*ik-tap-píl*	29[U]	See also *i-gam-mar* AALD: kapālu (v.) (qapālu) 1) يكبل، يلف 2) يضفر، يُشبك، يُحيط 3 يلف، يغلف 4) يظفر، يجتمع ضد شخص AALD: kabālu (v.) (see kibilitu, kubultu): يكبّل، يجمّد، يعيق الحركة، يشلّ الحركة	كفل (مقاييس اللغة) كفل (لسان العرب) قَفَلَ (القاموس المحيط) قفل (لسان العرب) كبل (مقاييس اللغة) كبل (لسان العرب)
222	*ik-ta-ri-iş*	102[T1]	ePSD: karāşu kid [BREAK] wr. kid$_2$; gir$_8$; kid$_4$; kid$_7$ Akk. karāşu tuk [BREAK] wr. tuk$_x$(|IM.KAD$_3$|) Akk. karāşu; nakāsu; naqāru; narābu ePSD: karāsu ša esir HIHI [PINCH] wr. HI.HI Akk. karāsu ša esir AALD: *qarāşu (s.) (karşu) القرض، الافتراء، الاتهام (أكل التهمة) AALD: *qarāşu (v.) (garaşu) يقرض، يقرص، يفرق، يكسر، الافتراء، يتهم، يكذب	قرض (لسان العرب) قرص (لسان العرب) كرص (لسان العرب) كرس (لسان العرب)
223	*ik-ta-su-ú*	251[T11]	ePSD: kasû a la [BIND] wr. a$_2$ la$_2$ Akk. kamû; kasû gazi [CONDIMENT] wr. gazi; gazi$_2$ Akk. kasû šu la [PARALYZE] wr. šu la$_2$ Akk. eşēlu; kasû ePSD: kasû; şimittu la [HANG] wr. la$_2$; la; lal$_2$ Akk. alālu; hanāqu; hiāţu; kamû; kasû; şimittu; kullumu; šaqālu; šuqalulu; zarû	كسع (مقاييس اللغة) كسع (لسان العرب) كسأ (الصّحَاح في اللغة) كسأ (العباب الزاخر) كسأ (لسان العرب) كسا (لسان العرب)
224	*IKU*	58[T11]	See also *nindan*	أكر (لسان العرب)

<table>
<tr><td></td><td></td><td></td><td>ePSD: iku
iku [UNIT] wr. iku Akk. ikû

Wikipedia:
The 'perfect acre' is a rectangular area of 43,560 square feet, bounded by sides 660 feet by 66 feet long (660 ft long × 66 ft wide), or 220 yards by 22 yards long (220 yd/ long × 22 yd wide), or 40 rods by 4 rods long. Thus, an acre is 160 square rods.
A dunam was the Ottoman unit of area equivalent to the Greek stremma or English acre, representing the amount of land that could be ploughed by a team of oxen in a day. The legal definition was "forty standard paces in length and breadth", but its actual area varied considerably from place to place, from a little more than 900 m² in Palestine to around 2500 m² in Iraq.

Note1: Possible areas for an Acre:
Modern Acre = 160 rods^2 = 43,560 ft^2 ~ 4046 m^2
Small Cubit Acre = 0.36 Hectare = 38750.1 ft^2 = 3600 m^2
Large Cubit Acre = 0.81 Hectare = 87187.7 ft^2 = 8100 m^2

Note2: Iraqi Dunam (~ Acre) ~ 27000 ft^2 = 2500 m^2

Note3: Noah Ship's possible demesions using smaller Cubit standard:

Diameter = 10 nindan = 10 rod = 165 ft = 50 m
Ship area = 78.5 rod^2 = 21382.46 ft^2 = 2375 m^2</td><td></td></tr>
<tr><td>225</td><td>i-lit-ti
i-lit-tu$_4$
i-lit-ta-šú</td><td>104^{T1}
174^{T1}
174^{T1}</td><td>ePSD: illātu; illatşâbi
ildum [BAND] wr. ildum$_2$; ildum Akk. illātu; illatşâbi; piqittişâbi; illat kalbi

AALD: illatu (s. f.) (illitu) القافلة، الحزمة، العائلة، الجماعة، الحشد</td><td>عيل (لسان العرب)
عول (لسان العرب)</td></tr>
<tr><td>226</td><td>il-li-kam-ma
il-li-kám-ma
il-la-kam-ma
il-lak
il-la-kak-kúm-ma
il-la-ku
il-la-ku
il-la-ku
il-lak
il-la-ka
im-tal-ku-ma
tam-ta-lik-ma
i-tal-lak
i-tal-lak
i-tal-lak
it-ta-na-lak
it-ta-lak
it-ta-na-al-lak
at-ta-na-al-la-ak
lul-lik
tal-li-ka</td><td>9^{T1}
9^{T1}
9^{T1}
31^{T1}
268^{T1}
100^{T11}
101^{T11}
260^{T11}
103^{T11}
209^{T11}
170^{T11}
184^{T11}
147^{T1}
323^{T11}
20^{P}
63^{T1}
63^{T1}
126
4^{P}
243^{T11}
243^{T1}</td><td>See also mil-ki
See also IM-tal-lak
See also ni-lu-ú

ePSD: alāku
dirig [FLOAT] wr. dirig Akk. alāku; mahāhu; mahāru; neqelpû
du [GO] wr. du Akk. alāku
ere [GO] wr. re; er; e-ra; er_x(|DU.DU|); re_6; re_7; er-re; i-ri Akk. alāku
ĝen [GO] wr. ĝen; ma Akk. alāku
sub [GO] wr. sub$_2$ Akk. alāku</td><td>ولق (لسان العرب)
ألق (لسان العرب)
علك (الصّحّاح في اللغة)
علج (لسان العرب)
ألك (لسان العرب)
لأك (لسان العرب)
لوك (لسان العرب)
لكك (لسان العرب)
رسل (لسان العرب)
المَلْأَكُ (القاموس المحيط)
بلغ (لسان العرب)</td></tr>
</table>

	tal-li-ka	250^{T11}		
227	*ILLU*	312^{T10}	See also *el-lim* *See also mi-la* ePSD: illu illu [WATER] wr. illu Akk. mû; mīlu; namba'u; zâbu	علو (مقاييس اللغة)
228	*il-pu-ut* *tal-tap-tan-ni-ma* *lu-pu-us-su-ma* *il-pu-us-su-ma*	202^{T11} 233^{T11} 216^{T11} 230^{T11}	See also *lib-ba-ti* ePSD: lapātu du [PLAY] wr. du_{12}-du_{12}; du_{12} Akk. lapātu; zamāru halam [FORSAKE] wr. ha-lam; gel-le-$eĝ_3$ Akk. halāqu; lapātu; lemnu; mašû šu dug [TOUCH] wr. šu dug_4 Akk. lapātu šu tag [TOUCH] wr. šu tag Akk. lapātu tag [TOUCH] wr. tag Akk. lapātu; rakāsu ePSD: lupputu šu la [DEFILE] wr. šu la_2 Akk. lu'û; lupputu AALD: lapātu (v.) (labātu) يلمس، يضع اليد بسوء نية، ينتهك الحرمات، يدنس المقدسات، يشوه السمعة، يهاجم، يؤذي، يضرب، يضايق، يدحر، يلعب بآلة وتري، يوسخ، يظلم، يحك، يفرق، يهيج Note: from *Lisan al-Arab:* m <=> f <=> b; t <=> s lafata = labata = lafasa = labasa = lamasa م <=> ف <=> ب؛ ت <=> س؛ لفت = لبت = لفس = لبس = لمس	لمس (لسان العرب) لفس (العباب الزاخر) لفت (مقاييس اللغة) لفت (لسان العرب) لفأ (الصّحاح في اللغة) لفأ (الصّحاح في اللغة) لفا (لسان العرب) لَفَأَه (القاموس المحيط)
229	*im-ba-ri* *im-ba-ri*	211^{T11} 214^{T11}	ePSD: imbaru muru [RAINSTORM] wr. $muru_9$; $muru_3$ Akk. imbaru; murû	عنبر (الصّحاح في اللغة) العَنْبَرُ (القاموس المحيط) عمبر (لسان العرب)
230	*im-ḫul-lu*	133^{T11}	See also *im-Ú-lu* ePSD: imhullu imhul [WIND] wr. im-hul Akk. imhullu	محل (لسان العرب) مخل (لسان العرب)
231	*IM-tal-lak* *IM.^{meš}*	18^{T1} 157^{T11}	See also *im-tal-ku-ma* See also *i-tal-lak* ePSD: im im [CLAY] wr. im Akk. ţīdu; ţuppu im [RAIN] wr. im; me-er Akk. zunnu; šāru im [RUN] wr. im_2 Akk. šānû	أمَ (مقاييس اللغة) اوم (لسان العرب) الأوامُ (القاموس المحيط) ومأ (لسان العرب) يمم (الصّحاح في اللغة) اليَمُّ (القاموس المحيط)
232	*im-ta-naq-qu-tú* *im-taq-qu-ta* *im-ḳ-u-ut* *im-ta-qu-ut* *im-ta-qu-tu₄* *im-ta-qut* *lim-qut-am-ma* *li-in-qu-tam-ma*	248^{T1} 248^{T1} 7^{P} 262^{T1} 262^{T1} 137^{T11} 295^{T1} 295^{T1}	See also ŠUB.MEŠ See also *e-niq* ePSD: maqātu šub [FALL] wr. šub Akk. habātu; maqātu; nadû Note: Derivation: مقا: إمتقا، إمقا، امتنقا and مقع: إمتقع، إمقع، امتنقع	مقع (لسان العرب) مقع (مقاييس اللغة) مقا (لسان العرب)
233	*im-ta-si* *im-tas-si* *lim-si*	101^{T1} 101^{T1} 254^{T11}	ePSD: mesû luh [CLEAN] wr. luh Akk. mesû	مس (مقاييس اللغة) المَشُّ (القاموس المحيط) مسا (لسان العرب)

				مسح (لسان العرب) معس (لسان العرب)
234	*im-Ù-lu*	133[T11]	See also *im-ḫul-lu* See also *ma-a-a-al* See also *rig-ma-šú* aya [CRY] wr. a; u_3 Akk. ahulap; nâqu u [AND] wr. u_3 Akk. u ePSD: U_4 u [BELLOW] wr. u_4 Akk. nagāgu; rigmu u [PURSLANE] wr. u_4 Akk. puhpuhu ud [IF] wr. ud Akk. šumma ud [STORM] wr. ud Akk. ūmu ud [SUN] wr. ud Akk. immu; ummedu; umšu; šamšu; ūmu ud [WHEN] wr. ud Akk. enūma ePSD: U_5 a'u [WATER] wr. a-u_2; a-u_3; a-u_5; u_3; u_5 u [RIDE] wr. u_5 Akk. hinnu; kašāšu; rakābu; rikbu; šagammu	عوا (لسان العرب) معل (لسان العرب) مأل (لسان العرب)
235	*i-mu-ru* *i-tam-ra* *i-ta-mar* *im-mar* *im-mar* *ta-mu-ru*	1[T1] 299[T1] 299[T1] 304[T10] 305[T10] 288[T1]	See also *ma-rat* ePSD: amāru igi bar [LOOK AT] wr. igi bar Akk. amāru; barû; naplusu igi duh [SEE] wr. igi duh Akk. amāru; naplusu; naţālu igi sig [SEE] wr. igi sig_{10} Akk. amāru; naplusu u dug [ADMIRE] wr. u_6 dug_4 Akk. amāru; barû	أمر (مقاييس اللغة) أمر (لسان العرب) رأي (لسان العرب)
236	*i-na-aţ-ţa-la* *aţ-ţu-la* *i-na-aţ-ţa-la* *ú-ţul* *at-ta-ţal* *i-na-aţ-ţa-lu* *i-na-aţ-ţa-la*	204[T1] 246[T1] 246[T1] 235[T1] 92[T11] 314[T10] 314[T10]	ePSD: naţālu igi duh [SEE] wr. igi duh Akk. amāru; naplusu; naţālu igi la [WATCH] wr. igi la_2 Akk. naţālu CAD: naṭālu (v.) to see ahead; to see, to watch; to examine;	طل (مقاييس اللغة) طلل (لسان العرب) الطَّلُّ (القاموس المحيط) طلل (الصّحاح في اللغة) نطل (لسان العرب) نتل (لسان العرب)
237	*i-nak-kir-šú* *nu-uk-ki-ra* *ú-nak-kar*	145[T1] 240[T1] 222[T1]	ePSD: nakāru bala [TURN] wr. bal; bil_2 Akk. elû; nabalkutu; nakāru; naqû; palû; tabāku kur [DIFFERENT] wr. kur_2; gur Akk. nakāru; šanû niĝkur [HOSTILITY] wr. $ni\hat{g}_2$-kur_2 Akk. nakāru	نكر (لسان العرب)
238	*i-nam-bu-ṭa*	35[U]	See also *nu-bat-ta* ePSD: nabāţu di [SHINE] wr. di_5 Akk. nabāţu had [BRIGHT] wr. ha-ad; had_2 Akk. ebbu; nabāţu; ellu mul [SHINE] wr. mul; mul_2; mul_4 Akk. kakkabu; mulmullu; nabāţu saĝ mu [SHINE] wr. saĝ mu_2-mu_2 Akk. nabāţu šun [SHINE] wr. $šun_2$ Akk. nabāţu ul [BRIGHT] wr. ul_4; ul_6 Akk. namru; nabāţu ePSD: nabâtu kun [SHINE] wr. kun_2 Akk. nabâtu	نبط (لسان العرب)

239	*i-pa-áš-šar* *i-pa-áš-šar*	1^{P} 40^{P}	See also *BÚR-ár* ePSD: pašāru bur [SPREAD] wr. bur$_2$; bur Akk. pašāru; šuparruru u'en [RELEASE] wr. u$_3$-en; u$_3$-en$_3$ Akk. pašāru	فسر (لسان العرب) فسر (مقاييس اللغة) فسر (مقاييس اللغة)
240	*i-pa-DA-áš-šum-ma*	150^{T11}	See also *i-pa-áš-šum-ma* ePSD: DA da [CVVE] wr. da "(compound verb verbal element)" da [LINE] wr. da "line, edge, side" dag [SIDE] wr. da "side; vicinity" Akk. idu AALD: uppadētu (s.) (uppudetu, appadētu, appudētu) المشرف، المراقب، المفتش	أفد (مقاييس اللغة) وفد (مقاييس اللغة)
241	*i-pi-ra-am-ma*	149^{T11}	ePSD: parāru ur [ROAM] wr. ur$_4$; ur-ru-ur Akk. parāru AALD: pirru (s.) المراقب على العمال	البَرَمُ (القاموس المحيط) فرر (لسان العرب) الفَرُّ (القاموس المحيط) فر (مقاييس اللغة) أفر (مقاييس اللغة) أفر (لسان العرب)
242	*ip-pu-un-na*	276^{T1}	See *ap-pi-šu* ePSD: appūna anga [MOREOVER] wr. an-ga Akk. appūna ganam [MOREOVER] wr. ga-nam Akk. appūna	أفن (مقاييس اللغة) أَفَنَ (القاموس المحيط) أفن (لسان العرب)
243	*ip-te-şi*	227^{T11}	See BABBAR See also *pa-tu* ePSD: peşû babbar [WHITE] wr. babbar$_2$; babbar Akk. peşû	بضّ (مقاييس اللغة) بضض (لسان العرب) فضض (لسان العرب) فصص (الصّحّاح في اللغة) فصي (لسان العرب) فعص (لسان العرب) فصع (مقاييس اللغة) فَصَعَ (القاموس المحيط) فصأ (لسان العرب)
244	*ip-tu* *pe-tu-ú* *ip-te* *pi-te-ma* *lip-ta-a* *pi-te-ma* *lu-up-te-ka* *ap-te* *ap-ti* *pa-tu* *lu-ú-up-te* *ap-tu-ú*	7^{T1} 7^{T1} 26^{T1} 38^{T1} 143^{T1} 181^{T1} 9^{T11} 137^{T11} 137^{T11} 140^{T11} 281^{T11} 316^{T11}	See also *pu-ut* See also *ip-te-şi* ePSD: petû bad [OPEN] wr. bad; ba; be$_2$ Akk. be'ēšû; nesû; petû ĝal taka [OPEN] wr. ĝal$_2$ taka$_4$; ĝal$_2$ taka$_x$(BALAG) Akk. petû ĝal [OPEN] wr. ĝal$_2$ Akk. petû hal [DIVIDE] wr. hal-ha; ha-la; hal Akk. barû; halālu; nazālu; petû; pirištu; zâzu; šahālu ePSD: petû ša pī kag bad [TALK] wr. ka bad; ka ba; ka bar Akk. petû ša pī; pûm ša ana atwî pīt puridim dub bad [GO SWIFTLY] wr. dub$_3$ bad Akk. pīt puridim pātu giguru [EDGE] wr. giguru$_3$; giguru Akk. pātu	بتت (لسان العرب) الفَتُّ (القاموس المحيط) فَتَحَ (القاموس المحيط) فتح (الصّحّاح في اللغة) فقح (لسان العرب) الفَتُّ (القاموس المحيط) فتت (لسان العرب) فتأ (لسان العرب) فثأ (لسان العرب) فتا (لسان العرب) فتي (مقاييس اللغة) فأت (لسان العرب) فطا (لسان العرب) فظا (لسان العرب) فضا (لسان العرب)

			pāţu zag [SIDE] wr. zag Akk. ahu; idu; imittu; ishu; mişru; pāţu AALD: pītu (s.) (see pitû) الفتحة، الثقب، الكسر	
245	*i-qab-bu-ú* *i-qab-bi* *i-qab-bi* *i-qab-bu-ú* *i-qab-bu-u* *iq-bu-ka* *lu-uq-bi-ka* *taq-ba-a* *ta-qab-ba-áš-šu-nu-tu* *aq-bu-ú* *i-qab-bi* *lu-uq-bi-ka*	46^{T1} 122^{T1} 134^{T1} 205^{T1} 205^{T1} 271^{T10} 10^{T11} 33^{T11} 38^{T11} 120^{T11} 181^{T11} 282^{T11}	See also *DUG$_4$.GA* ePSD: qabû di [SPEAK] wr. di Akk. atwû; dabābu; qabû dug [SPEAK] wr. Akk. atwû; dabābu; epēšu; qabû e [SPEAK] wr. e; na-be$_2$-a; be$_2$; ne; da-me; na-be$_2$; e$_7$ Akk. atwû; dabābu; qabû ePSD: eqbu masila [HEEL] wr. ma-sila$_3$ Akk. eqbu sila [HEEL] wr. sila "heel" Akk. eqbu AALD: *eqbu (s.) عَقِب الكاحل، الظِّلف، الحافر	عقب (لسان العرب) قوب (لسان العرب) قبب (لسان العرب) قَبَّ (القاموس المحيط) قبأ (لسان العرب) قبأ (الصّحّاح في اللغة) قَبَأَ (القاموس المحيط) قبأ (العباب الزاخر) قبا (الصّحّاح في اللغة) قبا (لسان العرب)
246	*iq-qé-lep-pa-a* *iq-qé-lep-pe*	313^{T10} 313^{T10}	ePSD: qalāpu bar [OUTSIDE] wr. Bar; ba-ra; bala; bur Akk. būdum; kabattu; kawûm; ahû; warkatu; qalāpu; salātu; šalāqu zil [BOIL] wr. Zil Akk. qalāpu; salāqu	قلف (لسان العرب)
247	*i-ram-šu-ma* *a-ram-šú-ma* *a-ram-šú-ma* *ta-ram-šú-ma* *ur-ta-'-a-am-mu* *a-ram-šú-ma*	241 256 284 298 300 33^{P}	ePSD: râmu ki aĝ [LOVE] wr. ki aĝ$_2$; kiĝ$_2$; ki-ga-aĝ$_2$; ki-ig-aĝ$_2$; ki-ig-ga-aĝ$_2$ Akk. râmu	رأم (لسان العرب) رأم (مقاييس اللغة)
248	*i-ra-muk*	304^{T11}	ePSD: ramāku a tu [WASH] wr. a tu$_{15}$; a tu$_{17}$; a tu$_5$ Akk. ramāku gub [BATHE] wr. gub$_2$ Akk. ramāku	رمك (مقاييس اللغة) الرَّمَكَةُ (القاموس المحيط) رمك (الصّحّاح في اللغة)
249	*i-rap-pu-da* *ta-rap-pu-ud* *ta-rap-pu-ud*	197^{T1} 208^{T1} 218^{T10}	See also *ra-pa-áš* ePSD: rapādu iri [DISEASE] wr. iri$_8$ Akk. rapādu šu dag [ROAM AROUND] wr. šu dag Akk. nagāšu; rapādu	رفد (لسان العرب) ربد (لسان العرب) ربذ (مقاييس اللغة) ربذ (لسان العرب) رفض (لسان العرب)
250	*ir-bu-ú* *ir-bu-ú* *ir-bu-ú* *ra-bu-tum* *ra-bu-ti*	145^{T1} 166^{T1} 187^{T1}	ePSD: rabû buluĝ [GROW] wr. buluĝ$_3$; buluĝ$_5$; bu-lu-ug; buluĝ Akk. rabû; tarbûtu gal [BIG] wr. gal; gu-la; gu-ul; gal-gal; ku-ul Akk. rabû gur [THICK] wr. gur$_4$; gur$_{14}$; gur$_{13}$ Akk. ebû; rabû; kabru kingal [OFFICIAL] wr. kingal; kin-gal Akk. mu'erru; rabû mah [GREAT] wr. mah; mah$_2$ Akk. kabtu; mādu; rabû; şīru	ربا (لسان العرب) ربب (لسان العرب)
251	*ir-ḫi-iş*	108^{T11}	ePSD: rahāşu a ĝar [IRRIGATE] wr. a ĝar Akk. rahāşu ĝiri ĝar [TRAMPLE] wr. ĝiri$_3$ ĝarAkk. rahāşu rah [BEAT] wr. rah$_2$; ra-ah Akk. dâku; diāšu; hepû; rahāşu; rapāsu ePSD: rahīşu lugud [LOCUS] wr. lugud$_4$ Akk. maškanu; rahīşu	رخص (مقاييس اللغة) رخص (لسان العرب) رهص (مقاييس اللغة) رهص (لسان العرب)
252	*i-ri-šá* *i-ri-šá*	161^{T11} 162^{T11}	See *lu-ur-ši* See also *ÌR-šú*	أرس (العباب الزاخر) ارس (لسان العرب)

	e-ri-šá	162^{T11}	ePSD: erešu <u>ir</u> [SCENT] wr. ir; ir$_7$ Akk. erešu; zūtu <u>irsim</u> [FRAGRANCE] wr. ir-si-im; ir-sim Akk. erešu ePSD: erēšu <u>al dug</u> [DESIRE] wr. al dug$_4$ Akk. erēšu <u>uru</u> [SOW] wr. uru$_4$; uru$_{11}$^{ru}; i-ru Akk. erēšu ePSD: erištu <u>niĝaldi</u> [REQUEST] wr. niĝ$_2$-al-di Akk. erištu	عرس (مقاييس اللغة) عرس (العباب الزاخر) عرس (لسان العرب)
253	*ir-ka-bu* *ir-tak-bu*	271^{T11} 272^{T11}	ePSD: rakābu? <u>ĝeš du</u> [COPULATE] wr. ĝeš$_3$ du$_3$ Akk. rakābu? ePSD: rakābu <u>dub nir</u> [EJACULATE] wr. dub$_3$ nir Akk. rakābu <u>šid</u> [RIDE] wr. šid$_3$ Akk. rakābu <u>u</u> [RIDE] wr. u$_5$ Akk. hinnu; kašāšu; rakābu; rikbu; šagammu ePSD: rakību <u>saman</u> [VESSEL] wr. saman$_x$(|A.PA.BI.SI.A.GA|) Akk. rakību; šikkatu	ركب (مقاييس اللغة)
254	*i-ru-um-ma* *ú-ru-ma* *ru-um-mi-i* *ur-tam-mi* *ur-tam-mu* *ir-tam-ma-am-ma* *ru-um-me*	117^{T1} 140^{T1} 180^{T1} 188^{T1} 188^{T1} 99^{T11} 187^{T11}	See also *ir/š-tag-gu-um* ePSD: ramû <u>ri</u> [IMPOSE] wr. RI; ru Akk. bâ'u; emēdu; nadû; nasāku; ramû; rehû; tarû; wašaru <u>tulu</u> [SLACKEN] wr. tu-lu; tu-ul Akk. ramû ePSD: ramīmu <u>mumun</u> [NOISE] wr. mu$_7$-mu$_7$ Akk. ramīmu; rigmu AALD: rummû: a verb meaning	رم (مقاييس اللغة) رمم (لسان العرب) رمأ (العباب الزاخر) رمأ (مقاييس اللغة) رمي (لسان العرب) رمي (مقاييس اللغة) روم (مقاييس اللغة) روم (الصّحّاح في اللغة) أرم (مقاييس اللغة) أرم (لسان العرب)
255	*i-sa-an-ni-qu*	142^{T1}	ePSD: sanāqu <u>dim</u> [CHECK] wr. dim$_4$ Akk. sanāqu <u>sir</u> [CHECK] wr. sir$_2$ Akk. sanāqu <u>us</u> [LEAN] wr. us$_2$ Akk. emēdu; sanāqu AALD: sanāqu (v.) 1) يكون مجاورا، يتلو، يربط 2) يقتضي الدفع، يجمع، يحشد 3) يقيم دعوة 4) يدقق، يشرف، يُعول عليه 5) يُخضع، يربط 6) يبلغ الى موقع 7) يقيم دعوة AALD: sanāqu (v.) يكون في فاقة، عوز	شَنَق (القاموس المحيط) شنق (مقاييس اللغة) شنق (لسان العرب) سنق (لسان العرب)
256	*i-sap-pan*	129^{T11}	AALD: sapānu (v.) (labānu) معنى غير معروف	سفن (مقاييس اللغة) سفن (لسان العرب)
257	*i-šat-ti* *i-ša-ti*	172^{T1} 176^{T1}	See also *i-tep-pir* ePSD: išātu <u>izi</u> [FIRE] wr. izi; izi$_2$ Akk. išātu; pendû ePSD: šatû <u>dun</u> [WARP] wr. dun; DUB$_2$ Akk. dêpu; kamādu; šatû	ذأت (لسان العرب) ذعت (لسان العرب) ذعت (الصّحّاح في اللغة) ذعَته (القاموس المحيط) ذعط (مقاييس اللغة) ستا (الصّحّاح في اللغة) السَّتا (القاموس المحيط)

			naĝ [DRINK] wr. naĝ "to drink" Akk. šatû ePSD: maštû anaĝ [DRINK] wr. a-naĝ Akk. maštû AALD: šatû (v.) يحيك، يغزل، يجدل، يرتبط بالمعركة، يرتبط بالكفاح AALD: šatû (v.) يشرب، يطفئ العطش، يفرغ الكأس، يمتص، يتشرب، يشرب مرارا، يبتلع الدواء	ستع (لسان العرب) ستي (لسان العرب) شيط (مقاييس اللغة) شيط (الصّحاح في اللغة) شيط (لسان العرب) شطأ (لسان العرب)
258	*iš-bu-u* *iš-bu-ú* *iš-bu-u* *iš-bu-ú*	195[T1] 195[T1] 254[T10] 254[T10]	ePSD: šebû lum [FRUIT] wr. lum Akk. enēbu; unnubu; namāru; šebû; šihu	شبا (لسان العرب) شبع (لسان العرب)
259	*iš-di* *il-di* *i-šid*	1[T1] 1[U] 98[T11]	ePSD: išdu dubla [TOWER] wr. dub-la$_2$ Akk. išdu; tublu dubur [FOUNDATION] wr. dubur; dubur$_2$ "base" Akk. išdu išdum [ROOT] wr. išdum$_x$(|DU@g|) Akk. išdu suhuš [FOUNDATION] wr. suhuš Akk. išdu ur [ROOT] wr. ur$_2$; ur$_5$ Akk. išdu; mešrêtu; sūnu; utlu	عضد (لسان العرب) أسد (مقاييس اللغة) علد (لسان العرب) علد (الصّحاح في اللغة) علد (مقاييس اللغة) شدد (لسان العرب)
260	*i-ši-ma* *i-ši* *i-šu* *i-ši* *i-šu* *i-šu-ú* *i-šim-ma* *i-šim-me* *i-šu-ú*	27[T1] 65[T1] 65[T1] 82[T1] 82[T1] 276[T10] 320[T10] 320[T10] 81[T11]	See *it-ti-šú* See *muš-te-'-ú* AALD: išû (v.)(yišûm) يطالب شخصا؛ مبني للمجهول: يتوقف، يكف عن ، يجد، يملك	اذذ (لسان العرب) أذي (مقاييس اللغة) إذا (لسان العرب) حذذ (لسان العرب) حذا (لسان العرب) حذا (الصّحاح في اللغة) أتي (لسان العرب)
261	*i-si-nu* *i-sin-na*	228[T1] 75[T11]	ePSD: isinnu ezem [FESTIVAL] wr. Ezem; i-ze-eĝ$_3$ Akk. Isinnu Note: al-Jibouri rule (m -> n) إزيم -> إزين	زيم (مقاييس اللغة) زين (لسان العرب)
262	*is-sà-qar-am*	38[P]	*See also iz-za-kàr-am*	سقر (لسان العرب) قارَ (القاموس المحيط) قرر (لسان العرب)
263	*is-su-kaš-šú*	293[T11]	See also *šag-ga-šá-a* ePSD: sakku idim [BLOCKED] wr. idim Akk. sakku; saklu; ulālu ePSD: sakāku ĝeštug la [DEAF] wr. ĝeštug$_2$ la$_2$ Akk. sakāku AALD: šakāšu see šagāšu	سكك (لسان العرب)
264	*iš-tén* *iš-tu* *iš-ta-at*	123[T1] 98[T11] 225[T11]	See also ul-tu ištēn diš [ONE] wr. Diš; de-eš-šu$_2$; di-id; di-t- Akk. ištēn ešda [ONE] wr. Eš$_3$-da Akk. ištēn ur [HE] wr. Ur$_5$; ur Akk. amtu; ištēn; mithāru; šû AALD: ištēn (num) (ištin, ilten, issen, istena, iltana, ...)	أني (لسان العرب) سته (لسان العرب) أست (لسان العرب) أَسْتُ (القاموس المحيط)

			(f. ištat, ištet, iltet, iltat, iltatan, iltena, ...) الاول؛ الاولى	
265	*iš-te-nem-ma-a* *il-te-né-mi* *iš-te-nem-me*	78^{T1} 14^{U} 93^{T1}	See also *še-me-šá* ePSD: namû adam [HABITATION] wr. a_2-dam Akk. namû aria [STEPPE] wr. a-ri-a Akk. harbu; namû AALD: nammattu (s.) see mâdu الزيادة Note1: سَمَعَ -> إسْتَمَعَ -> إسْتَتَمَعَ Note2: نمي -> إسْتَنَمي -> إلْتَنَمي Note3: سَنَأ -> إسْتَنَأ -> إلْتَنَأ	نمي (لسان العرب) نَمَا (القاموس المحيط) نأم (مقاييس اللغة) سنأ (الصّحَاح في اللغة) سنا (لسان العرب) سنع (مقاييس اللغة) سنم (لسان العرب) السَّنَعُ (القاموس المحيط) سنع (لسان العرب)
266	*i-šu-ṭa* *ta-šu-ṭa*	274^{T11} 279^{T11}	ePSD: ešītu suh [CONFUSE] wr. suh_3 Akk. ešītu AALD: šâṭu (v.) يشحط، يسحب، يجُر، يجهد نفسه AALD: šâṭu (v.) يشُط، يهمل، يغدر، يخون	شطط (لسان العرب) ثعط (لسان العرب) ثطط (لسان العرب)
267	*i-ta-ma-áš-šum-ma* *i-ta-ma-a* *it-ma-ma* *ta-mì-ma*	213^{T1} 299^{T1} 15^{T11} 19^{T11}	See also *taq-qa-šum-ma* See also *ma-a-ti* ePSD: tamāhu tab [GRASP] wr. tab Akk. tamāhu ePSD: tamāhu; kamû dab [SEIZE] wr. dab_5; dab; dab_5-dab_5; dab_x(|LAGAB×GUD|) Akk. sahāpu; tamāhu; kamû; şabātu ePSD: māmītu namNERU [OATH] wr. nam-NE.RU Akk. māmītu saĝba [OATH] wr. saĝ-ba; saĝ-ba-a Akk. māmītu	أتم (لسان العرب) تمم (لسان العرب)
268	*i-tap-la-as* *i-tap-lu-si* *ap-pa-al-sa* *ap-pal-sa-am-ma* *ap-pa-li-is*	14^{T1} 93^{T11} 134^{T11} 134^{T11} 140^{T11}	AALD: palāsu (v.) يحدق، ينظر، يتفحص، يسبب الهم والقلق والاثارة، يواجه	بلس (لسان العرب) البَلَسُ (القاموس المحيط) فلس (العباب الزاخر)
269	*i-tep-pir* *i-tep-pi-ir* *i-te-ep-pir* *i-tep-pir*	111^{T1} 253^{T1} 176^{T1}	See also *i-šat-ti* ePSD: ipru bubu'l [RATION] wr. bu-bu-l Akk. ipru ePSD: ippīru gigam [CONFLICT] wr. gigam Akk. ippīru inbir [CONFLICT] wr. inbir Akk. ippīru	تفر (لسان العرب) عفر (لسان العرب) فرا (لسان العرب)
270	*i-ṭib* *i-ṭi-bu* *i-ṭib* *ṭa-ab-ta* *ṭa-ab-tú* *ṭa-bat* *ṭa-a-ba*	112^{T1} 173^{T1} 173^{T1} 254^{T10} 254^{T10} 118^{T11} 162^{T11}	See also *i-ṭi-pi* See also *DÙG.GA* ePSD: ţābu dug [GOOD] wr. dug_3; ze_2-eb; du-uq Akk. ţābu kud [SWEET] wr. ku_7 Akk. dašpu; matqu; ţābu kurun [BEER] wr. kurun; $kurun_2$; $kurun_3$ Akk. dāmu;	طابَ (القاموس المحيط) طبي (مقاييس اللغة) طبي (لسان العرب) وطب (لسان العرب) طبب (لسان العرب) طيب (الصّحَاح في اللغة) طيب (الصّحَاح في اللغة)

	ṭa-a-bu *ṭa-a-bu-um*	256[T11] 256[T11]	kurunnu; ţābu lal [SYRUP] wr. lal_3 Akk. dišpu; matqu; ţābu sag [GOOD] wr. sag_8; sag_9; sag_{10}; $šeg_{10}$; sag_{12} Akk. banû; damāqu; dumqu; ţābu ePSD: ţubtu u [PEACE] wr. u_2 Akk. ţubtu Note: Quran: الطيّبات = الطِيبُ = الذبائح = المواشي الحيّة = الحيّة = الطيّبة	طيب (لسان العرب)
271	*i-ṭi-pi*	177[T1]	See also *i-ṭib*	طفو (مقاييس اللغة) طفا (الصّحّاح في اللغة) طفا (لسان العرب) طفأ (لسان العرب)
272	*it-qí*	60[T1]	See also *ap-pat* ePSD: itqu aka [FLEECE] wr. aka_3 Akk. itqu inna [FLEECE] wr. inna Akk. itqu suluhu [FLEECE] wr. suluhu; $suluhu_3$ Akk. itqu; kitītu; lamahuššû; raqqatu; sulumhû ePSD: etēqu dib [PASS] wr. dib; dib_2; di-ib Akk. bâ'u; etēqu	عتق (مقاييس اللغة) عتق (لسان العرب)
273	*it-ta-raq* *te-riq*	131[T11] 131[T11]	ePSD: tarqītu kankal [OIL-PROCESSING] wr. kankal Akk. tarqītu ePSD: raqāqu sal [THIN] wr. sal Akk. raqāqu AALD: tarāqu (v.) معنى غير معروف	رقق (لسان العرب) طرق (مقاييس اللغة) طرق (الصّحّاح في اللغة)
274	*it-taš-bu-ni* *it-taš-bu-ni* *it-ta-šab* *áš-bu* *ti-šab* *áš-bi* *áš-bu-ma* *áš-ba-ku* *áš-bi* *a-šib-ma* *uš-šab* *uš-te-ši-bu-in-ni* *it-ta-šab* *at-ta-šab*	170[T1] 171[T1] 203[T1] 230[T10] 271[T10] 126[T11] 210[T11] 42[T11] 205[T11] 40[T11] 206[T11] 308[T11] 138[T11]	See also *uš-bi-šú-nu* ePSD: ašābu dur [SIT] wr. dur_2 Akk. ašābu durun [SIT] wr. $durun_x$(|KU.KU|); durun; dur_2-ru-un Akk. ašābu til [LIVE] wr. til_3 Akk. ašābu; balāţu tuš [SIT] wr. tuš Akk. ašābu AALD: ušābu (see w/ašābu) AALD: ušbu (s.) (see w/ašābu; see ušpu) مكان الجلوس، المكان؛ مقياس زيت AALD: ušubtu (s.) (see w/ašābu) الكمين AALD: ašbu (adj.) (wašbu) (see ašābu) معيشة (في بيت)، كمقيم، ساكن (في مدينة)، يقيم، يحضُر	الوَثْبُ (القاموس المحيط) وثب (مقاييس اللغة) ثبب (لسان العرب) وثب (لسان العرب)
275	*it-ti-si*	198[T1]	ePSD: isiš isiš [SORROW] (27x: Old Babylonian) wr. i-si-iš; $isiš_3$ Akk. dimmatu; nissatu; ratāmu; tassistu; şiāhu; şīhu	تسا (لسان العرب) توس (لسان العرب) أسو (مقاييس اللغة) أسي (الصّحّاح في اللغة) أسا (لسان العرب)
276	*it-ti-šú*	45[T1]	See also *KI-ia*	أتو (مقاييس اللغة)

	mu-ti-šá *it-ti* *it-ti* *it-ti-ka* *it-ti-ia* *tu-ut-ta-a* *ut-ta* *a-a-i-ta* *a-a-ta* *is-si-a* *at-tan-nak-kúm-ma* *ta-at-tan-na-áš-šum-ma*	76^{T1} 110^{T1} 254^{T1} 266^{T1} 232^{T10} 208^{T11} 317^{T11} 317^{T11} 317^{T11} 317^{T11} 275^{T11} 280^{T11}	See *i-ši-ma* ePSD: itti ki [WITH] wr. ki Akk. itti ePSD: atû idu [DOORKEEPER] wr. i_3-du_8 Akk. atû pad [FIND] wr. pad_3 Akk. atû; nabû ePSD: ittu ĝiškim [SIGN] wr. ĝiškim Akk. giskimmu; ittu; tukultu šušer [SIGN] wr. šu-še-er Akk. ittu uludin [FORM] wr. $uludin_2$; uludin Akk. ittu; nabnītu ePSD: mutu dam [SPOUSE] wr. dam Akk. aššatu; mutu	أتو (الصّحّاح في اللغة) الأَتْوُ (القاموس المحيط) الوَتْيُ (القاموس المحيط) وتي (لسان العرب) أتت (لسان العرب) أتّ (مقاييس اللغة) أتي (مقاييس اللغة) أتي (الصّحّاح في اللغة) أتَيْتُه (القاموس المحيط) أتي (لسان العرب)
277	*i-zab-bi-lu* *i-zab-bi-lu*	54^{T11} 66^{T11}	ePSD: zabbīlu gabil [BASKET] wr. gab2-il2 Akk. zabbīlu ePSD: zabbilu gabilil [PORTER] wr. gab2-il2-il2 Akk. zabbilu	زبل (مقاييس اللغة) زبل (الصّحّاح في اللغة) الزِّبْلُ (القاموس المحيط) زبل (لسان العرب)
278	*i-zi-qam-ma*	110^{T11}	See aslo *uš-te-ziq* ePSD: ziqqu zig [THRESHOLD] wr. zig Akk. ziqqu	زقق (لسان العرب) زقم (مقاييس اللغة) زقم (لسان العرب)
279	KÁ KA KA KÁ-*šá* KÁ-*šá* KÁ-*ka*	26^{T1} 295^{T1} 316^{T10} 262^{T10} 263^{T10} 89^{T11}	*See aslo* KI-*tim* *See pa-a-šú* See also *qé-e* ePSD: KA KA [CVVE] wr. KA kan [GATE] wr. kan_4; KA Akk. bābu kag [MOUTH] wr. ka Akk. pû dug [SPEAK] wr. dug_4 Akk. atwû; dabābu; epēšu; qabû inim [WORD] wr. inim; e-ne- Akk. amatu uzga [TREASURE] wr. uz-ga; uz-ga-$še_3$; $uzug_x$(KA); uz-ga-ta; uzug; uz_3-ga; us-ga-ne; us-ga; uz-ga-ne; $uzug_x$(|AN.ZAG|); $usag_x$(|U.ŠA|); $^{sa}usag_x$(|U.ŠA|); $^{sa}usag_x$(|U.ŠA|)^{ki} Akk. sagû; sukku zu [SHARE] wr. $^{ĝeš}zu_2$; zu_2 Akk. šinnu zu [TOOTH] wr. zu_2 Akk. šinnu zuh [STEAL] wr. zuh Akk. šarāqu AALD: ka (pron. m.s.): ضمير المخاطب المذكر المفرد AALD: *ak (see kî): كـ (حرف تشبيه)	ك (لسان العرب) كيأ (لسان العرب) كيأ (العباب الزاخر) الكاءُ (القاموس المحيط) أكَأَ (القاموس المحيط) أكك (لسان العرب) كأكأ (لسان العرب) الوَكْوَكَةُ (القاموس المحيط) كوك (لسان العرب)
280	*ka-a-a-nam-ma*	127^{T1}	See also *a-na-ku-ma* See also *mamma* See also *an-ni-ta* AALD: anāma (see annāma) AALD: annāma (adv.) هكذا، أشبه AALD: annû (adv.) هذا، ذلك	كان (مقاييس اللغة) كأن (لسان العرب)
281	*ka-a-*NI*-pa!*	319^{T11}	See also *ik-su-pu*	نأف (مقاييس اللغة)

			See also *ku-sa-pa* ePSD: NI NI [~NET] wr. NI dig [PARALYZED] wr. dig Akk. rimûtu dig [SOFT] wr. dig Akk. labāku; narbu gur [THICK] wr. gur$_4$; gur$_{14}$; gur$_{13}$ Akk. ebû; rabû; kabru i [OIL] wr. i$_3$; u$_5$; u$_2$ Akk. tallum; šamnu li [OIL] wr. li$_2$ Akk. šamnu li [PRESS] wr. li$_2$; li$_9$ Akk. ruqqû lidga [VESSEL] wr. lid$_2$-ga; lid$_2$-da-ga; li-id-ga; lid$_2$; lidda; lidda$_2$ Akk. litiktu; namaddu; parsiktu mu [GOOD] wr. mu$_5$ Akk. banû sal [POLE] wr. sal$_3$ Akk. mudulu sul [MEAT] wr. su-la$_2$; sul$_2$ Akk. muddulu suš [GREASE] wr. suš$_2$; suš Akk. šēmu zaĝa [PRESS] wr. zaĝa(NI) Akk. za'u; ṣahātu ša šamni zal [PASS] wr. zal Akk. naharmumu; naharmuṭu; qatû; râbu zal [SHINE] wr. zal ePSD: naptanu bur [BOWL] wr. bur; $^{na}{}_4$bur Akk. abru; naptanu; nīqu; pūru kul [MEAL] wr. kul Akk. naptanu unu [MEAL] wr. unu$_2$; Akk. mākālu; naptanu; paššūru	نأف (العباب الزاخر) نأف (الصّحاح في اللغة) نأف (لسان العرب) كنف (الصّحاح في اللغة) كنف (العباب الزاخر) كنف (لسان العرب) نأي (مقاييس اللغة) نأي (لسان العرب) نيأ (مقاييس اللغة) نَيَّأَ (القاموس المحيط) نيأ (لسان العرب) نوي (مقاييس اللغة) نوى (الصّحاح في اللغة) نوي (لسان العرب)
282	*ka-a-ru*	248^{T11}	ePSD: kāru addir [FORD] wr. addir; dir; addir$_x$(|PA.GISAL.SI.A|); addir$_x$(|PA.GISAL.SI.A.PAD|) Akk. kāru; nēberu kar [HARBOR] wr. kar Akk. kāru piš [BANK] wr. Akk. kibru; kāru; nahallu	كعر (مقاييس اللغة) كَعِرَ (القاموس المحيط) كعر (لسان العرب) كار (مقاييس اللغة) خور (لسان العرب)
283	*ka-a-ši* *ka-a-šú* *ka-a-šá* *ka-a-šá* *ka-a-šú-nu* *ka-a-šá* *ka-a-šá* *ka-a-šá*	183^{T1} 272^{T1} 272^{T1} 10^{T11} 43^{T11} 207^{T11} 236^{T11} 283^{T11}	See also *šá-a-šú* See also *ka-ti* AALD: kâti (pron.) (kâta, kâtu) أنت مفرد، مذكر منصوب ومؤنث مجرور AALD: kuāti (pron.) (kuāta, kuwāti) AALD: kuāši (pron.) (kuāša, kuāši) see kâši أنت مفرد، مجرور، منصوب AALD: kâši (pron.) أنت، اليك، لك Note: ka لاشارة ومخاطبة الحاضر ka-a-šú لكَ، الذي لكَ، ما لكَ، لكُمَ (أذوك) ka-a-ši لكِ، الذي لكِ، ما لكِ، لكُم (أذيك) ka-a-šá لذاك، الذي لذاك، ما لذاك، لذاكمَ (أذاك)	ك (لسان العرب) كَذَا (القاموس المحيط) كنت (لسان العرب)
284	*ka-la-mu* *ka-la-a-mu* *lu-kal-lim-ka* *ka-la-ma* *ka-la-a* *ki-lal-la-an* *ka-li-ši-na* *ku-li-li* *ka-la-ma* *ka-li-šú-nu* *kul-lat*	2^{T1} 2^{T1} 234^{T1} 259^{T1} 259^{T1} 300^{T1} 251^{T10} 313^{T10} 27^{T11} 86^{T11} 135^{T11}	ePSD: Kalāma du [ALL] wr. du$_3$ "all" Akk. Kalāma du [PLATFORM] wr. du$_6$ Akk. di'u ePSD: kallatu egia [BRIDE] wr. e$_2$-gi$_4$-a Akk. kallatu AALD: *kilallān (prop.) (kilallūn, f. kilattān) كلاهما، الاثنان، الزوجان AALD: kalūlu (s.) كل شيئ؛ معنى غير اكيد AALD: *kalu (s.) (kulu) كلّ، باجمعه	كلل (الصّحاح في اللغة) كلل (لسان العرب) كلا (لسان العرب) كلأ (لسان العرب) كلأ (مقاييس اللغة) كلأ (الصّحاح في اللغة) كلأ (العباب الزاخر) كلم (مقاييس اللغة) كلم (لسان العرب)

	kal-lat	12[U]	AALD: kilīlu (s.) الاندفاع، التهور، الصخب؛ شريط الرأس، شرفة القلعة، الخاتم AALD: kilili (s.) (kulili, kililu, kulilu) البومة (طير)، العفريتة، الشيطانة	
285	*ka-ma-a-ti*	116[T11]	ePSD: kamû a la [BIND] wr. a_2 la_2 Akk. kamû; kasû ešela [BOUND] wr. ešela Akk. hanāqu; kalû; kamû la [HANG] wr. la_2; la; lal_2 Akk. alālu; hanāqu; hiāṭu; kamû; kasû; şimittu; kullumu; šaqālu; šuqalulu; zarû šu dab [CAPTURE] wr. šu dab_5 Akk. kamû šu du [BIND] wr. šu du_3 Akk. kamû AALD: kimītu (s.) (kimûtu) see also kamû الأسر AALD: kamû (v.) يأسر، يوقع في شرك، يلحق، يحصّن	كمت (لسان العرب) كمم (لسان العرب)
286	*ka-man-šú* *ka-man-ka*	227[T11] 239[T11]	ePSD: kamānu gidešta [LOAF] wr. gidešta Akk. kamānu Note: Anise = Sweet Cumin الآنيسُونُ = الكَمُونُ الحُلْوُ	كوم (مقاييس اللغة) كَمَنَ (القاموس المحيط) كمن (الصّحاح في اللغة) كمن (لسان العرب)
287	*ka-ra-bi* *ik-ru-bu* *ik-ru-ba* *i-kar-ra-ban-na-ši*	318[T10] 318[T10] 318[T10] 202[T11]	See also *tu-qar-ra-ab* ePSD: karābu siškur [PRAYER] wr. $Siškur_2$; siškur Akk. karābu; naqû; nīqu šu e [BLESS] wr. Šu e_3 Akk. waşû; palāhu; karābu šu mu [PRAY] wr. Šu mu_2 Akk. karābu	كرب (لسان العرب)
288	*kar-šu* *ka-ra-ši* *ka-ra-ši* *kar-ši-ka* *kar-ši-ia* *kar-ši-šú*	120[T1] 113[T11] 171[T11] 215[T10] 222[T10] 293[T10]	ePSD: karāšu karaš [CAMP] wr. karaš Akk. karāšu pagra [DISASTER] wr. $pagra_3$ Akk. karāšu ePSD: kar-šú (s. f.) (1) المعدة، البطن، الجسم (2) العقل، القلب، الخطة، الرعبة (3) الداخل او الجزء السفلي	كرث (مقاييس اللغة) كرث (لسان العرب) كرس (مقاييس اللغة) الكِرْسُ (القاموس المحيط) كرس (لسان العرب) كرش (مقاييس اللغة) الكِرْشُ (القاموس المحيط) كرش (لسان العرب)
289	*ka-šid* *ka-ši-id* *ik-šu-da-niš-šu* *ik-šu-du-nim-ma* *ak-šu-dam-ma* *ka-šá-a-du* *ka-šá-a-di* *ka-šá-di* *ka-šá-a-di* *i-kaš-šá-du* *ka-šá-di-šú* *ik-ta-na-ša-da*	42[T1] 42[T1] 234[T10] 320[T10] 258[T10] 130[T11] 130[T11] 130[T11] 147[T11] 260[T11] 172[T11] 15[U]	ePSD: kašādu sa dug [ARRIVE] wr. sa_2 dug_4 Akk. kašādu sa [EQUAL] wr. sa_2; sa_x(ZAG); se_3 Akk. kašādu; mašālu; šanānu AALD: kašādu (v.) يقصد، يبلغ؛ يسيطر، ينتصر، يأسر، يطارد، يتقدم، يمسك، يباغت، ينفي، يعتقل؛ يساوي، يكن كافيا؛ AALD: kāšidu استيلاء، سيطرة AALD: kišdu (s.) الاكتساب AALD: kašdu (n.; v.; adj.) نجاح، انجاز؛ يحرز، يحقق؛ كاف، ملاءم	كسأ (الصّحاح في اللغة) كسأ (العباب الزاخر) كَسَدَ (القاموس المحيط) كَشَدَهُ (القاموس المحيط) كشد (لسان العرب) قسد (لسان العرب) قصد (مقاييس اللغة) قصد (الصّحاح في اللغة) قصد (لسان العرب)
290	KASKAL	168[T1]	*See also har-ra-na* See also *ur-ḫa* ePSD: kaskal kaskal [BASKET] wr. [gi]kaskal kaskal [WAY] wr. kaskal Akk. harrānu	شكل (لسان العرب) قسس (لسان العرب)

291	*ka-šú-šú*	111^{T11}	See also *ki-ik-ki-šú* ePSD: kašāšu u [RIDE] wr. u_5 Akk. ^{hinnu}; kašāšu; rakābu; rikbu; šagammu AALD: kašāšu (v.) يتسلط، يُخضع، يتطلب AALD: kašāšu (v.) معنى غير معروف	كتا (لسان العرب) كثأ (لسان العرب) كشش (العباب الزاخر) كشش (لسان العرب) كسس (العباب الزاخر) كسس (لسان العرب) كذذ (لسان العرب) كثث (لسان العرب)
292	*ka-ṣu-ú*	303^{T11}	ePSD: kaşû niĝsed [COLD] wr. $ni\hat{g}_2$-sed Akk. kaşû	قصو/ي (مقاييس اللغة) قصع (مقاييس اللغة) القَصْعَةُ (القاموس المحيط) قصع (لسان العرب)
293	*ka-ti*	17^{P}	See *at-ti* See also *ka-a-ši*	ك (لسان العرب) كَذَا (القاموس المحيط)
294	*ka-tim-tú* *kàt-ma*	7^{T1} 127^{T11}	See aslo *šab-ba* See also *KI-tim* ePSD: katāmu dul [COVER] wr. dul; dul_9; dul_5; dul_x(DUN_3) Akk. katāmu lu [MIX] wr. lu; lu_3 Akk. balālu; dalāhu; katāmu sul [COVER] wr. su-ul Akk. katāmu šag sag [AFFLICTED] wr. $šag_4$ sag_3 Akk. şurup libbi; katāmu šuš [COVER] wr. $šuš_2$; šuš; $šuš_5$ Akk. ašāru; erēpu; katāmu; sahāpu; sehpu; šaqû ša lubši	كتم (مقاييس اللغة) كَتَمَهُ (القاموس المحيط) كتم (الصَّحَاح في اللغة) كتم (لسان العرب) كظم (مقاييس اللغة) كظم (لسان العرب)
295	*KI.SIKIL-ta* ardata	302^{T10}	See also *KASKAL* ePSD: ardatu kisikil [WOMAN] wr. Ki-sikil; $^{lu}{}_2$ki-sikil; mu-tin; mu-ti-in Akk. ardatu; batultu unu [GIRL] wr. Unu_2 Akk. ardatu ePSD: ardu arad [SLAVE] wr. $Arad_2$; arad; ar_3-tu; e-re Akk. ardu subur [SLAVE] wr. Subur Akk. ardu	سقل (لسان العرب) صقل (لسان العرب) قصل (لسان العرب) قصمل (لسان العرب)
296	*kib-ru* *kib-ra-a-ti* *kib-ra-a-tum* *ki-bir* *kib-ra-a-ti* *kib-ri* *kib-ri-šú*	33^{T1} 41^{T1} 41^{T1} 59^{T11} 140^{T11} 277^{T11} 293^{T11}	See also *kup-ra* ePSD: kabru gur [THICK] wr. gur_4; gur_{14}; gur_{13} Akk. ebû; rabû; kabru ePSD: kibru piš [BANK] wr. $piš_{10}$ Akk. kibru; kāru; nahallu ePSD: kibrat arbatu anubda [QUARTER] wr. an-ub-da; ub-da Akk. kibrat arbatu AALD: kibrû (s.) (kubarû) رجل كبير AALD: kibru s.) (kipru) الضفة، شاطئ البحر ، حافة نهاية الشئ، منطقة، معنى غير معروف منطقة (kibrāt ebrēm)، يشير الى الجهات الاربعة للكون، حافة او نهاية AALD: kibrātu (s.) (f. Pl.)	كبر (لسان العرب)
297	*ki-ik-ki-šú* *ki-ik-ki-ši*	20^{T11} 20^{T11}	ePSD: kikkišu gidua [FENCE] wr. gi-du_3; gi-du_3-a Akk. kikkišu	كشش (لسان العرب) كسس (العباب الزاخر)

	ki-ik-ki-š	21[T11]	gisig [FENCE] wr. gi-sig; gi-sig_7 Akk. kikkišu ePSD: kiššu garadin [BUNDLE] wr. garadin; $garadin_4$ Akk. kiššu; kurullu sa [BUNDLE] wr. sa; ^{gi}sa Akk. kiššu AALD: kisû (s) دعامة جدارية على طول البناء، المسطبة او جدار المدينة، كلمة سومرية دخيلة	كسس (لسان العرب) كأكأ (لسان العرب)
298	*ki-i-ri*	66[T11]	ePSD: kūru dinig [KILN] wr. dinig; $dinig_3$; di-ni-ig Akk. kūru; nappašu; nappāhu kur [WOOD] wr. ^{ĝeš}kur; $^{ĝeš}kur_4$ Akk. kūru; kiskibirru ePSD: kirru gir [JAR] wr. $^{dug}gir_{16}$; gir_9 Akk. kirru	كير (لسان العرب) كور (لسان العرب)
299	*ki-ma* *ki-ma* *ki-i* *kī-ma* *ki-ki-i* *ki-a-am* *ki-mi*	13[T1] 17[P] 207[T1] 244[T10] 244[T10] 33[T11] 35[T11]	See also *GIM* See also *KÁ* See also *KI-tim* ePSD: kī agin [THUS] wr. a-gin_7 Akk. kī AALD: *ak (see kî): ك (حرف تشبيه) AALD: ka (pron. m.s.): ضمير المخاطب المذكر المفرد AALD: kî (conj.) (kê, akî, akê) متى، حالا، بعد، اذا، في حالة، فيما اذا، ذلك، بسبب، طبقا، كما، مجرد هكذا AALD: kî (prep.) (kê, akî, akê) مثل، كما، طبقا، بطريقة، بدلا من، متطابق، بطريقة مماثلة AALD: kî (inter.) (kê, akî, akkī, akê) كيف؟ AALD: akkīma (inter.) كيف؟ AALD: kīkî (inter.) (kēkê, kīkiya) كيف؟ AALD: kīma (conj.) كما، حالا، فورا، متى، طبقا لـ، ذلك، فيما اذا، بسبب، باعتبار، اذا، ولذلك AALD: kīma (inter.) كم AALD: kīma (prep.) مثل، بطريقة، طبقا لـ، متطابق، بدلا ما، في مكان ما AALD: kīam (adv.) (kīa, kīamma, kīa'm, kâm, kêm, kâ) هكذا، بهذا الاسلوب؛ كيف AALD: kīašu (adv.) (kīaša) مثل ذلك	ك (لسان العرب) كيأ (لسان العرب) كيأ (العباب الزاخر) كيا (لسان العرب) أيُّ (القاموس المحيط)
300	*KIMIN* *KIMIN* *KIMIN*	115 227[T10] 84[T11]	See also *e-şe-en-ši* ePSD: ki-mu kimu [STORAGE] wr. ki-mu	كوم (لسان العرب) كمن (مقاييس اللغة) كمن (لسان العرب) كمي (مقاييس اللغة)
301	*kim-ti-ia*	85[T11]	See also *ki-ma* ePSD: kimtu imria [CLAN] wr. im-ri-a; im-ru-a; im-ru Akk. kimtu	الكِيمُ (القاموس المحيط)
302	*KIRI*	22[T1]	See also *KUR* See also *ú-qur* ePSD: kirû kiri [ORCHARD] wr. $^{ĝeš}kiri_6$; $kiri_6$ Akk. kirû	كرا (لسان العرب) كير (لسان العرب)
303	*ki-rim-mi-ki* *ku-ru-um-ma-ti-šú*	180[T1] 221[T11]	ePSD: kirimmu lirum [STRENGTH] wr. lirum; $lirum_3$; $lirum_2$; $lirum_6$; $lirum_7$;	قرم (الصّحّاح في اللغة) قرم (مقاييس اللغة)

	ku-ru-um-ma-ti-šú *ku-ru-um-mat-su* *ku-ru-um-me-ti-ka*	223[T11] 225[T11] 235[T11]	lirum$_8$ Akk. abaru; dannu; emûqu; gāmiru; kamiru; kirimmu; umašu; šapṣu; šitnunu; šitpuṣu kurummatu kurum [RATION] wr. kurum$_6$ Akk. kurummatu šukur [RATION] wr. PAD; šukur$_2$ Akk. kurummatu AALD: kirimmu (s.) الحضن: وضع ذراعي الام عند حضن طفلها	كرم (لسان العرب) كرم (الصّحّاح في اللغة) الكَرْمُ (القاموس المحيط) كرم (مقاييس اللغة)
304	*ki-ṣir* *ki-iṣ-ri* *ki-iṣ-ru* *ki-iṣ-rù*	104[T1] 125[T1] 248[T1] 7[P]	See also *ESIR* See also *ik-su-pu* See also *ak-te-šìr* ePSD: kiṣru zukešed [RENT] wr. zu$_2$-keš$_2$ Akk. kiṣru zukešed [TROOP] wr. zu$_2$-keš$_2$; zu$_2$-keš$_2$-ra$_2$ Akk. kiṣru ePSD: kirṣu imkid [PIECE] wr. im-kid$_2$ Akk. kirṣu ePSD: kaṣāru aga kar [DEFEAT] wr. aga kar$_2$; aga$_3$ kar$_2$ Akk. kalû; kaṣāru kad [TIE] wr. kad$_5$; kad$_4$; kad$_6$; kad$_8$ Akk. harādu; harāsu; kaṣāru zu kešed [GATHER] wr. zu$_2$ keš$_2$ Akk. kaṣāru; rakāsu	كسر (مقاييس اللغة) كسر (الصّحّاح في اللغة) كسر (لسان العرب) كَسَرَهُ (القاموس المحيط) قسر (لسان العرب) قسر (مقاييس اللغة) قنسر (لسان العرب) قشر (لسان العرب) كصر (لسان العرب) خصر (لسان العرب) قصر (لسان العرب)
305	*KI-tim* *KI-ia* *KI-šú-nu*	62[T1] 317[T11] 320[T10]	See also *KÁ* See also *ki-ma* See also *it-ti-ia* ePSD: KI gagar [GROUND] wr. gagar Akk. qaqqaru ki [PLACE] wr. ki Akk. ašru; erṣetu; mātu; qaqqaru; šaplû ki [WITH] wr. ki Akk. itti ePSD: KITA kita [LOWER] wr. ki-ta Akk. šaplû ePSD: KITUM kitum [BURIAL] wr. ki-tum$_2$	ك (لسان العرب) كيا (لسان العرب) كعا (لسان العرب) كعع (لسان العرب) كعم (لسان العرب) كتم (لسان العرب) قعا (لسان العرب) قعع (لسان العرب) قوع (لسان العرب) erṣetu أرض (مقاييس اللغة) الأرضُ (القاموس المحيط) أرض (لسان العرب)
306	*KÙ.BABBAR*	82[T11]	ePSD: KU KU [STRENGTHEN] wr. KU Akk. asāqu ePSD: KU$_3$ kug [METAL] wr. kug kug [PURE] wr. kug Akk. ellu ePSD: BABBAR babbar [WHITE] wr. babbar$_2$; babbar Akk. peṣû peṣû See *ip-te-ṣi*	قها (الصّحّاح في اللغة) وكي (لسان العرب) كو (مقاييس اللغة) كوي (لسان العرب) بهر (لسان العرب) تبر (لسان العرب)
307	*KÙ.SIG$_{17}$*	83[T11]	ePSD: kugsig kugsig [GOLD] wr. kug-sig$_{17}$ Akk. hurāṣu *KÙ* See *KÙ.BABBAR*	عسجد (لسان العرب) ذهب (مقاييس اللغة) سوج (لسان العرب)

308	*KU$_6$.^{MEŠ}-ma* *KU$_6$.^{HÁ}*	44^{T11} 124^{T11}	See also *qù-du-du* ePSD: ku$_6$ kud [FISH] wr. ku$_6$ Akk. nūnu ePSD: HA gir [UNMNG] wr. gir$_{14}$ "?" haX [CONTAINER] wr. ha-X kud [FISH] wr. ku$_6$ Akk. nūnu ePSD: HA.IB HA.IB [FISH?] wr. HA.IB	كود (مقاييس اللغة) كود (لسان العرب) هيب (مقاييس اللغة) nūnu نون (مقاييس اللغة) نون (الصّحّاح في اللغة) سمك (لسان العرب)
309	*ku-da-ni*	226^{T10}	ePSD: kūdanu (kūdannu) anšeĝirnun [EQUID] wr. anše-ĝir$_2$-nun Akk. kūdanu AALD: kūdanu (s.) نوع من البغال	كَدِنَ (القاموس المحيط) كدن (لسان العرب)
310	*ku-kit-ti*	67^{T1}	ePSD: kittu niĝzid [RIGHTEOUSNESS] wr. niĝ$_2$-zid Akk. kittu kīttu niĝgina [TRUTH] wr. niĝ$_2$-gi-na; niĝ$_2$-gen$_6$-na Akk. kīttu	قوق (لسان العرب) كوك (لسان العرب) خوخ (لسان العرب)
311	*kup-ra* *ku-up-ri*	55^{T11} 66^{T11}	See also *ESIR* See also *kib-ru* ePSD: kupru esir [BITUMEN] wr. esir$_2$; esir; esir$_2$(|LAGABxHAL|) Akk. iţţû; kupru esirhia [BITUMEN] wr. esirhia Akk. kupru	القَفْرُ (القاموس المحيط) قفر (الصّحّاح في اللغة) قفر (لسان العرب) كفر (مقاييس اللغة) كفر (لسان العرب) قير (لسان العرب)
312	*ku-pu-ud-ma*	286^{T10}	AALD: kapādu (v.) (kapātu) (see kuppudu) يتآمر، يخطط، يتحايل، يعتني AALD: kappidu (adj.) (see kapādu) متلهف؟	كفت (لسان العرب)
313	*KUR-i* *KUR-da* *KUR-ú* *KUR-ú* *KUR-ú* *KUR.KUR.^{MEŠ}*	39^{T1} 172^{T1} 143^{T11} 144^{T11} 145^{T11} 251^{T10}	See also *KIRI* See also *ka-šid* ePSD: kur kur [BURN] wr. kur Akk. napāhu kur [DIFFERENT] wr. kur$_2$; gur Akk. nakāru; šanû kur [ENTER] wr. kur$_9$; kur$_x$(DU); kur$_x$(LIL) Akk. erēbu kur [MOUNTAIN] wr. kur; kir$_5$ Akk. erşetu; mātu; šadû; šadû kur [UNIT] wr. kur$_2$; gur$_2$ kur [WOOD] wr. ^{ĝeš}kur; ^{ĝeš}kur$_4$ Akk. kūru; kiskibirru	قور (الصّحّاح في اللغة) قور (لسان العرب) رسا (لسان العرب) قعر (لسان العرب) كور (لسان العرب) الكُورُ (القاموس المحيط) كور (مقاييس اللغة) صقع (لسان العرب) الكَرْدُ (القاموس المحيط) كرد (لسان العرب) قرد (لسان العرب)
314	*ku-ru-un-nu*	73^{T11}	ePSD: kurunnu kurun [BEER] wr. kurun; kurun$_2$; kurun$_3$ Akk. dāmu; kurunnu; ţābu	كرن (مقاييس اللغة) كرن (الصّحّاح في اللغة) كرن (لسان العرب)
315	*KÙŠ* *KUŠ.^{MEŠ}-šú-nu* *KUS.^{MEŠ}-šu-ma*	57^{T1} 261^{T10} 264^{T11}	See also *am-ma-ti* *See also muš-šu-kàt* See also *maš-ku-ú* ePSD: kuš kuš [CHANNEL] wr. kuš$_3$ Akk. rāţu kuš [DEVASTATION] wr. kuš$_7$ Akk. naspantu kuš [MALT-FLOUR] wr. kuš$_7$ Akk. kukkušu	قوس (لسان العرب) كوس (لسان العرب) قعس (لسان العرب) الكَعْسُ (القاموس المحيط) كعث (الصّحّاح في اللغة) خوس (مقاييس اللغة) خيس (مقاييس اللغة) خيس (العباب الزاخر)

			kuš [OFFICIAL] wr. kuš$_7$ Akk. kizû kuš [SKIN] wr. kuš Akk. mašku; zumru kuš [SUMMER] wr. kuš$_7$ Akk. qēṣu kuš [UNIT] wr. kuš$_3$ Akk. ammatu	كوش (لسان العرب)
316	*ku-uk-ki* *ku-uk-ku-šá*	46^{T11} 273^{T10}	See also *KÁ* ePSD: kukkušu kuš [MALT-FLOUR] wr. Kuš$_7$ Akk. Kukkušu mel [MALT-FLOUR] wr. Mel Akk. Kukkušu zidmilla [FLOUR] wr. Zid$_2$-milla Akk. Kukkušu ePSD: kukku gug [CAKE] wr. gug$_2$ Akk. kukku; niqû nindagug [CAKE] wr. ninda-gug$_2$ Akk. kukku	الكَيْكَةُ (القاموس المحيط) كيك (لسان العرب) كعك (لسان العرب)
317	*ku-zu-ub-šá* *ku-uz-ba*	143^{T1} 237^{T1}	ePSD: kuzbu hili [LUXURIANT] wr. hi-li; hilib$_2$ Akk. kuzbu; šamhu	الكُزْبُ (القاموس المحيط) قزب (لسان العرب) قضب (لسان العرب) قصب (لسان العرب) قصب (مقاييس اللغة) كذب (لسان العرب)
318	*la-am*	8^{T1} 243^{T1}	AALD: lām (see lāma) before, from قبل AALD: lāma (conj. & prep.) before, from قبل	لم (مقاييس اللغة) لمم (لسان العرب) لأم (مقاييس اللغة) لأم (لسان العرب)
319	*la-an* *la-an?* *la-an-šá* *la-an-ši*	34^{U} 52^{T1} 60^{T11}	AALD: lānu (S.) جسم، شكل، مظهر، تمثال (شخص)، هيئة، حجم	لهن (لسان العرب) لانَ (القاموس المحيط) اللَّوْنُ (القاموس المحيط) لون (مقاييس اللغة) لون (لسان العرب) لعن (لسان العرب) لعن (مقاييس اللغة) لعن (الصّحَاح في اللغة)
320	*la-be*	218^{T10}	See also *UR.MAḪ.*^{MES} ePSD: labbu ur [DOG] wr. ur; ^{ĝeš}ur Akk. kalbu; labbu ePSD: lābu piriĝ [LION] wr. piriĝ; piriĝ$_3$; bi$_2$-ri-iĝ$_3$; ^{ĝeš}piriĝ; piriĝ$_2$ Akk. lû; lābu; nēšu; rīmu	اللَّبُوُّ (القاموس المحيط) لبأ (الصّحَاح في اللغة)
321	*la-bir-ma*	13^{T11}	See also *lap-nu* ePSD: labāru libir [OLD] wr. libir Akk. labāru sumun [OLD] wr. sumun Akk. labāru; nutāpu; sumkīnu til [COMPLETE] wr. til; til$_3$ Akk. gamāru; labāru; qatû gamāru see *i-gam-mar* Note: labāru = labānu	لبن (لسان العرب)
322	*lap-nu* *lap-ni*	56^{T11} 56^{T11}	See *la-bir-ma*	لفأ (لسان العرب) لبن (لسان العرب)

			ePSD: lapnu sum [POOR] wr. sum_5 Akk. lapnu ukur [POOR] wr. $ukur_3$ Akk. lapnu AALD: lapnu see labnu (s.) AALD: lubānu see lupānu AALD: lupānu (s.) اللوز الحلو AALD: lupnu See lapānu الفقر AALD: lapānu (v.) see lapnu, lupnu يفقر	
323	*la-sa-an-šú*	201^{T1}	ePSD: lāsimu lukaš [RUNNER] wr. lu_2-$kaš_4$ Akk. lāsimu ePSD: lasāmu hub sar [RUN] wr. hub_2 sar Akk. lasāmu	لسم (مقاييس اللغة) لسم (لسان العرب) زم (مقاييس اللغة) لسن (مقاييس اللغة) لسن (لسان العرب)
324	*le-ta-šú* *le-ti-šu* *le-et*	59^{T1} 37^{U} 258^{T10}	See also *TE.*^{MES}*-a-a* ePSD: lētu te [CHEEK] wr. te Akk. lētu	لحا (لسان العرب) لحت (لسان العرب) لَيْتَ (القاموس المحيط) لَيْتَ (القاموس المحيط) ليت (لسان العرب)
325	*lìb-ba-šú* *lìb-ba-šá* *lib-bi-šú* *lìb-ba-šú* *lib-ba-šu* *lìb-ba-šú* *lìb-bi* *lìb-ba-šú*	97^{T1} 100^{T1} 112^{T1} 173^{T1} 173^{T1} 177^{T1} 209^{T1} 214^{T1}	See also *lib-ba-ti* ePSD: libbu lib [HEART] wr. lib Akk. libbu lipiš [INNARDS] wr. lipiš; $lipiš_x$(|AB_2.$ŠA_3$|) Akk. libbu; uzzu; ṣurru šag [HEART] wr. $šag_4$; ša; $ša_3$-ab Akk. libbu	لهب (لسان العرب) لحب (الصّحَاح في اللغة) لبب (لسان العرب)
326	*lib-ba-ti* *lìb-ba-a-te*	174^{T11} 174^{T11}	See also *lib-ba-šú* ePSD: libbātu murgu [RAGE] wr. $murgu_3$ Akk. libbātu	لَبَتَ (القاموس المحيط) لبت (لسان العرب)
327	*li-di-lu* *e-dil*	262^{T10} 318^{T10}	ePSD: edēlu ur [SHUT] wr. ur_3 Akk. edēlu; kidinnu CDA: edēlu (v.) يُغلِق	العَدْلُ (القاموس المحيط) عدل (مقاييس اللغة) عدل (لسان العرب)
328	*li-diš*	261^{T11}	ePSD: dêšu lu [ABUNDANT] wr. lu Akk. dêšu; kamāru ePSD: dišu uli'a [PLANT] wr. u_2-li-a^{sar} "a plant" Akk. dišu	الدَّأْصُ (القاموس المحيط) دأظ (لسان العرب) دأض (لسان العرب)
329	*li-ig-gél-ta-a* *i-te-gél-ta-a* *i-te-gél-ta-a-ma*	216^{T11} 230^{T11} 230^{T11}	ePSD: giltû ĝešdi [RUNG] wr. $^{ĝeš}di_5$ Akk. giltû ePSD: galātu buluh [FEAR] wr. bu-luh; bu-lu-uh_2; bu-lu-uh_3; buluh Akk. galātu	الوَجَلُ (القاموس المحيط) وجل (الصّحَاح في اللغة) جأل (لسان العرب)
330	*lil-li* *li-la-a-ti*	270^{T10} 47^{T11}	See also *^{d}en-líl* ePSD: lillu lil [FOOL] wr. lil; $^{lu}{}_2lil_2$; lil_3; lil_5; lil_8 Akk. lillu ePSD: lilû	يلل (لسان العرب) اللَّيْلُ (القاموس المحيط) ليل (لسان العرب)

			lillilgi [DEMON] wr. |LIL$_2$.LIL$_2$|-gi$_4$ Akk. lilû	
331	*lil-lid* *i'-al-du* *al-du* *ul-la-da*	30^{T1} 47^{T1} 47^{T1} 123^{T11}	ePSD: alādu peš [THICK] wr. peš; peš$_5$; peš$_4$; peš$_6$ Akk. alādu; kabattu; līp līpi; mār māri; mērû; napāšu; šabāšu ugu [BEAR] wr. ugu; ugu$_4$ Akk. alādu utud [BEAR] wr. tud; u$_3$-tu; tu-ud Akk. alādu	الوَلَدُ (القاموس المحيط) ولد (لسان العرب)
332	*lil-qé* *li-qé-e* *il-qé* *il-qu-ú* *ta-al-qu* *il-qu-in-ni-ma* *li-qé-šu-ma* *el-qe-šú-ma* *le-qa-a*	181^{T1} 182^{T1} 189^{T1} 296^{T10} 297^{T10} 206^{T11} 253^{T11} 35^{P} 127^{T11}	ePSD: leqû deg [COLLECT] wr. deg$_x$(RI) Akk. ahāzu; laqātu; leqû; nasāhu šu teĝ [ACCEPT] wr. šu teĝ$_4$; šu teĝ$_3$ Akk. leqû; mahāru	لَقِيَهُ (القاموس المحيط) لقى (الصّحَاح في اللغة) لقا (لسان العرب)
333	*liš-ẖu-uţ* *liš-ẖu-uţ*	143^{T1} 164^{T1}	ePSD: šahāţu gud [JUMP] wr. gu$_4$-ud; gud$_2$ Akk. qarrādu; šahāţu tug sig [STRIP] wr. tug$_2$ sig$_9$ Akk. šahāţu	سحط (لسان العرب) سطح (لسان العرب) شحط (لسان العرب)
334	*liš-ta-an-na-nu-ma* *ši-na-šú*	98^{T1} 35^{U}	ePSD: šanānu sa [EQUAL] wr. sa$_2$; sa$_x$(ZAG); se$_3$ Akk. kašādu; mašālu; šanānu ePSD: šinnu gug [TOOTH] wr. gug; gug$_6$ Akk. nišik kalbi; šinnu zu [SHARE] wr. ^{ĝeš}zu$_2$; zu$_2$ Akk. šinnu zu [TOOTH] wr. zu$_2$ Akk. šinnu	سنن (لسان العرب)
335	*LÚ* *LÚ* *LÚ* *la-le-e-šú* *lul-la-a* *lul-la-a* *la-la-šá* *la-la-a-šá* *ul-lu-la* *e-le-'-i-a* *la-'-i* *il-ti-'i* *LÚ-ut-tim* *LÚ.U$_{18}$.LU-ú* *LÚ.U$_{18}$.LU-a*	17^{T1} 95^{T1} 235^{T1} 61^{T1} 178^{T1} 185^{T1} 195^{T1} 195^{T1} 199^{T1} 250^{T1} 255^{T1} 9^{P} 307^{T10} 318^{T10} 318^{T10}	See aslo *a-me-lu-tu* See also *ma-a-a-al* ePSD: LU lu [ABUNDANT] wr. lu Akk. dêšu; kamāru lu [MIX] wr. lu; lu$_3$ Akk. balālu; dalāhu; katāmu lug [DWELL] wr. lug; lug$_x$(LUL) lug [TWIST] wr. lu-gu$_2$; lug; lum Akk. zâru udu [SHEEP] wr. udu; e-ze$_2$ Akk. immeru lu [FISH] wr. lu$_2{}^{ku}{}_6$ lu [FLARE] wr. lu$_9$ Akk. napāhu lu [PERSON] wr. lu$_2$; mu-lu; mu-lu$_2$; lu$_{10}$; lu$_6$ Akk. amēlu; ša ePSD: lē'û a ĝal [STRONG] wr. a$_2$ ĝal$_2$ Akk. lē'û atuku [POWERFUL] wr. a$_2$-tuku Akk. igigallu; lē'û da [WRITING BOARD] wr. ^{ĝeš}da Akk. lē'û ePSD: LULU lulu [BIRD] wr. lu$_7$-lu$_7{}^{lu}{}_2{}^{mušen}$; lu$_7$-lu$_2{}^{mušen}$ Akk. awīlānu lulu [MAN] wr. lu$_2$-lu$_7$; lu$_2$-lu$_7{}^{lu}$ Akk. amēlu; lullû ePSD: LU$_2$.LUL lulul [LIAR] wr. lu$_2$-lul Akk. sarru ePSD: LU$_2$.LUL.LUL lulullul [LIAR] wr. lu$_2$-lul-lul	لعا (لسان العرب) لعو (مقاييس اللغة) لعل (لسان العرب) لأي (لسان العرب) لَعَلَّ (القاموس المحيط) علل (لسان العرب) عل (مقاييس اللغة)

			ePSD: LU$_2$-ULU$_3$ lulu [MAN] wr. lu$_2$-lu$_7$; lu$_2$-lu$_7^{lu}$ Akk. amēlu; lullû ePSD: lullû lulu [MAN] wr. lu$_2$-lu$_7$; lu$_2$-lu$_7^{lu}$ Akk. amēlu; lullû ePSD: la'û henzer [CHILD] wr. henzer Akk. ašpaltu; la'û; lakû; šerru ePSD: lalû lala [PLENTY] wr. la-la; a-la; la Akk. lalû me [DESIRE] wr. me "desire" Akk. lalû ePSD: alālu a'allari [EXCLAMATION] wr. a-al-la-ri; a-li-ri Akk. alālu ellum [SONG] wr. e-el-lu; e-el-lum Akk. alālu la [HANG] wr. la$_2$; la; lal$_2$ Akk. alālu; hanāqu; hiāţu; kamû; kasû; şimittu; kullumu; šaqālu; šuqalulu; zarû AALD: lala'u, lali'u (see lalû) AALD: lalû (s.) الطفل الرضيع	
336	^{lú}*AD.KID* atkuppu	51^{T11}	ePSD: AD.KID adKID [WEAVER] wr. ad-KID; ad-kup$_5$ Akk. atkuppu	عتك (مقاييس اللغة) العَدْكُ (القاموس المحيط)
337	*lu-bu-ši* *lu-bu-uš-ti* *la-biš* *la-bis* *lu-bu-uš-ti* *lu-bu-uš-tú* *la-biš*	109^{T1} 109^{T1} 109^{T1} 274^{T10} 258^{T10} 258^{T10} 258^{T11}	ePSD: lubuštu i [CLOTHING] wr. i$_6$ Akk. lubuštu lubuštum [CLOTHING] wr. lu-bu-uš-tum Akk. lubuštu	لبث (الصّحّاح في اللغة) لبد (لسان العرب) لبس (مقاييس اللغة) لَبِسَ (القاموس المحيط) لبس (العباب الزاخر) لبس (لسان العرب)
338	*LUGAL* *GAL-tú* *GAL-i*	17^{T1} 94^{T1} 295^{T1}	See also *meš-ra-a* ePSD: lugal lugal [KING] wr. lugal; lu$_2$-gal Akk. bēlu; šarru ePSD: gal gal [BIG] wr. gal; gu-la; gu-ul; gal-gal; ku-ul Akk. rabû	جلل (لسان العرب)
339	*lul-tuk*	298^{T11}	See also *ul-taḫ-ḫi* ePSD: litiktu kab [TEST] wr. kab$_2$; kab$_x$(|SAG×A|) Akk. latāku; litiktu lidga [VESSEL] wr. lid$_2$-ga; lid$_2$-da-ga; li-id-ga; lid$_2$; lidda; lidda$_2$ Akk. litiktu; namaddu; parsiktu ePSD: latāku kab [TEST] wr. kab$_2$; kab$_x$(|SAG×A|) Akk. latāku; litiktu Note: hataka => lahtaka => lultahaka حَتَكَ => لَحْتَكَ => لأُلْتَحُكَ	هتك (لسان العرب) حَتَكَ (القاموس المحيط) حتك (لسان العرب) الحَكُّ (القاموس المحيط) الجَرَبُ (القاموس المحيط)
340	^{lú}*MÁ.LAḪ$_4$* ^{lú}*MÁ.LAḪ$_4$* *ma-la-ḫi*	70^{T11} 95^{T11} 247^{T11}	ePSD: MA$_2$.LAL mala [BOAT] wr. ma$_2$-la$_2$; ^{ĝeš}ma$_2$-la$_2$; ^{gi}ma$_2$-la$_2$	ملع (مقاييس اللغة) ملع (لسان العرب) ملح (مقاييس اللغة)

			ePSD: malahhu malah [SAILOR] wr. ma$_2$-lah$_5$; ma$_2$-lah$_4$; ma$_2$-lah$_6$; $^{lu}{}_2$ma$_2$-lah$_5$; $^{lu}{}_2$ma$_2$-lah$_4$; $^{lu}{}_2$ma$_2$-lah$_6$ Akk. malahhu	ملح (لسان العرب)
341	*lu-mu-un*	214^{T10}	See also ^{f}*ḪUL* ePSD: lemnu halam [FORSAKE] wr. ha-lam; gel-le-eĝ$_3$ Akk. halāqu; lapātu; lemnu; mašû hulu [BAD] wr. hul; hul$_3$ Akk. abātu ša īni; bēšu; lapātu ša īni; ṣabru; lemnu; masku; qallu; sarru; zāmânû luhulĝal [EVILDOER] wr. lu$_2$-hul-ĝal$_2$ Akk. lemnu ePSD: lemuttu niĝhulu [EVIL] wr. niĝ$_2$-hul Akk. lemuttu AALD: lumun libbi (s.) (see lemēnu) الاسى، الحزن، الكآبة، الغضب، الكسوف AALD: lemēnu (v.) (lemānu) يواجه حظا سيئا، يتحول الى شرير (مع قلب كمفعول به)، يجعل الاطراف يعادي بعضهم بعضا	لأم (الصّحّاح في اللغة) اللُّؤْمُ (القاموس المحيط) لأم (لسان العرب)
342	^{lú}*NAGAR*	50^{T11}	ePSD: NAGAR alla [OAK] wr. alla Akk. allānu nagar [CARPENTER] wr. nagar Akk. nagarum ePSD: naggāru šukara [CARPENTER] wr. $^{lu}{}_2{}^{ĝeš}$šu-kara$_2$; ^{ĝeš}šu-kara$_2$ Akk. naggāru	نجر (لسان العرب)
343	*lu-ú*	97^{T1} 29^{T11} 30^{T11}	ليكن له، ليكن لها	
344	*lu-ur-ši* *lu-ur-ši-ma* *ri-ši-šú*	296^{T1} 297^{T1} 278^{T10}	ePSD: rašû lidim [GET] wr. lidim Akk. rašû tuku [ACQUIRE] wr. tuku Akk. rašû	رسس (العباب الزاخر) رسي (مقاييس اللغة) رسا (لسان العرب) رسس (لسان العرب)
345	*lu-us-kut*	244^{T10}	AALD: sakātu (v.) (sukkutu) يسكت، يصمت	سكت (مقاييس اللغة) سكت (لسان العرب)
346	*MÁ.MUG.*^{MEŠ}	79^{T11}	See ^{giš}*MÁ* *See also tar-kul-li* ePSD: MUG mug [WOOL] wr. mug Akk. mukku	موج (مقاييس اللغة) المَوْجُ (القاموس المحيط) موج (لسان العرب) مَعَجَ (القاموس المحيط) معج (لسان العرب)
347	*ma-a-a-al* *mi-lu-la* *ú-ma-al-xx* *a-lit-ti* *ma-li-ti* *ma-a-a-li-ia*	232^{T1} 264^{T10} 265^{T10} 117^{T11} 117^{T11} 245^{T11}	See also *LÚ* *See also ni-lu-ú* ePSD: mayyaltu kinud [BEDROOM] wr. ki-nud Akk. mayyaltu; mayyālu maršum [BED] wr. ^{ĝeš}mar-šum Akk. maršu; mayyaltu silig [BED] wr. ^{ĝeš}silig Akk. mayyaltu ePSD: mēlultu enedi [GAME] wr. e-ne-di Akk. mēlultu ešemen [ROPE] wr. ešemen; ešemen$_2$; e-šen; ešemen$_3$; ešemen$_5$ Akk. keppû; mēlultu	مالَ (القاموس المحيط) آلَ (القاموس المحيط) ألت (لسان العرب) ميل (مقاييس اللغة) مأل (لسان العرب) مأل (مقاييس اللغة) عالَ (القاموس المحيط) مهل (لسان العرب) معل (مقاييس اللغة) مَعَلَ (القاموس المحيط) معل (لسان العرب)

			mēlû <u>ĝešil</u> [TREETOP] wr. ĝeš-il$_2$ Akk. mēlû <u>sukud</u> [HEIGHT] wr. sukud Akk. mēlû AALD: mēlelu (s.) (mēlulu) اللعبة AALD: melēlu (v.) يرقص، يقفز	
348	*ma-ak-ku-ru* *ma-ak-ku-ra*	26^{T11}	ePSD: makkuru <u>niĝGA</u> [PROPERTY] wr. niĝ$_2$-GA; mu-un-gur$_{11}$; mu-un-gar$_3$ Akk. makkuru	مقر (لسان العرب) مكر (لسان العرب)
349	*ma-a-ti* *ma-a-ti* *ma-a-tum* *ma-a-tum* *ma-a-tu* *mi-tum* *mi-i-tum* *mu-ta* *mu-tum* *mu-ti* *mu-ú-tu* *mu-tum* *mu-tum* *mu-ú-tum* *mu-tum*	1^{T1} 3^{T1} 251^{T1} 49^{T11} 252^{T1} 316^{T10} 316^{T10} 239^{T10} 104^{T1} 303^{T10} 304^{T10} 304^{T10} 307^{T10} 245^{T11} 245^{T11}	See also *i-ta-ma-áš-šum-ma* ePSD: mātu <u>kalam</u> [LAND] wr. kalam; ka-na-aĝ$_2$; ka-naĝ Akk. mātu <u>ki</u> [PLACE] wr. ki Akk. ašru; erşetu; mātu; qaqqaru; šaplû <u>kur</u> [MOUNTAIN] wr. kur; Akk. erşetu; mātu; šadû; šadû <u>mada</u> [LAND] wr. ma-da; ma Akk. erşetu; mātu <u>mim</u> [SPACE] wr. mim$_2$ Akk. mātu <u>muš</u> [SPACE] wr. muš$_3$ Akk. mātu ePSD: mâtu <u>ug</u> [DIE] wr. ug$_7$; ug$_5$; ug$_x$(|BAD.BAD|) Akk. mâtu <u>uš</u> [DIE] wr. uš$_2$ Akk. dāmu; mâtu; mūtu; uššu ePSD: mūtu <u>namuš</u> [DEATH] wr. nam-uš$_2$ Akk. mūtānu; mūtu <u>uš</u> [DIE] wr. uš$_2$ Akk. dāmu; mâtu; mūtu; uššu	موت (لسان العرب) متت (لسان العرب) ماتَ (القاموس المحيط) مثث (لسان العرب) أثّ (مقاييس اللغة) ميث (لسان العرب)
350	*ma-gir* *am-gur*	213^{T1} 33^{T11}	ePSD: magāru <u>šeg</u> [AGREE] wr. še Akk. magāru	مجر (لسان العرب) عقل (لسان العرب)
351	*ma-ḫa-zi* *ma-ḫa-zu*	43^{T1} 43^{T1}	ePSD: māhāzu <u>kišupeš</u> [LOCUS] wr. ki-šu-peš; ki-šu-peš$_5$ Akk. māhāzu <u>zig</u> [TOWN] wr. zig$_x$(|PA.GI|) Akk. māhāzu	حوز (لسان العرب) مخخ (لسان العرب)
352	*ma-ḫir* *ma-ḫar* *maḫ-ri* *mi-iḫ-ra* *mi-iḫ-ri* *ma-ḫar* *tul$_5$-ta-maḫ-ri-šu* *tul$_5$-ta-maḫ-ri-šu* *tul$_5$-ta-maḫ-ḫa-ri-šu* *ul-tam-ḫi-ri-šú* *uš-tam-ḫi-ir-šú* *ul-tam-ḫi-raš-šú* *ul-tam-ḫi-ra-šú* *ul-ta-maḫ-ḫar-šú* *uš-ta-ma-ḫa-ru* *im-ta-ḫir*	97^{T1} 45^{P} 100^{T11} 103^{T11} 103^{T11} 120^{T11} 254^{T1} 258^{T1} 285^{T1} 285^{T1} 114^{T1} 266^{T1} 290^{T1} 290^{T1} 41^{U} 59^{T11}	See also *mit-ḫa-riš* ePSD: mahāru <u>BU'I</u> [FACE] wr. BU-I Akk. mahāru <u>dirig</u> [FLOAT] wr. dirig Akk. alāku; mahāhu; mahāru; neqelpû <u>gaba ri</u> [CONFRONT] wr. gaba ri Akk. mahāru <u>gaba rugu</u> [OPPOSE] wr. gaba ru-gu$_2$ Akk. mahāru <u>rugu</u> [WITHSTAND] wr. ru-gu$_2$ Akk. mahāru <u>saĝ gi</u> [BLOCK] wr. saĝ gi$_4$ Akk. hašû?; mahāru <u>šu gid</u> [ACCEPT] wr. šu gid$_2$ Akk. mahāru <u>šu teĝ</u> [ACCEPT] wr. šu teĝ$_4$; šu teĝ$_3$ Akk. leqû; mahāru <u>šu tutu</u> [WITHSTAND] wr. šu tu-tu Akk. mahāru ePSD: mihru <u>kunzida</u> [WEIR] wr. kun-zid-da; kun-zi Akk. mihru	مهر (لسان العرب) مخر (لسان العرب) مخر (الصَحَاح في اللغة) مخر (مقاييس اللغة) مَخَرَتِ (القاموس المحيط) خرت (لسان العرب)
353	*mam-ma* *mam-ma* *mim-mu-ú* *ma-am-ma* *mim-ma*	14^{T1} 17^{T1} 28^{T1} 304^{T10} 315^{T10}	See also *man-nu* ePSD: mamma <u>name</u> [SOMEBODY] wr. na-me Akk. mamma	ما (لسان العرب)

	mim-mu-ú *mim-ma*	48[T11] 81[T11]	ePSD: mammān luname [SOMEONE] wr. lu$_2$-na-me Akk. mammān ePSD: mimma niĝ [THING] wr. niĝ$_2$; aĝ$_2$ Akk. bušu; mimma niĝnam [ANYTHING] wr. niĝ$_2$-nam Akk. mimma ul [ANYTHING] wr. ul$_4$ Akk. mimma AALD: mimmu الممتلكات، كل شيء، الحصة او الجزء، ضمير تملك متصل Note1: man-ma -> mamma Note2: mim-ma = min-ma	
354	*man-nu* *man-ni-ia* *man-ni-iá* *man-nu-um-ma* *am-me-ni* *am-mi-ni* *mi-na-a* *mi-na-a* *mi-na-tu-ka* *mi-na-tu-šá* *mi-na-tu-šú* *mu-na-a* *im-nu-ú*	45[T1] 311[T11] 311[T11] 179[T11] 208[T1] 213[T10] 257[T10] 296[T10] 3[T11] 29[T11] 29[T11] 235[T11] 171[T11]	See also *mamma* *See also um-ma* ePSD: mannu aba [WHO?] wr. a-ba Akk. mannu ePSD: minû enam [WHAT] wr. en-nam Akk. minû ePSD: mīnu anam [WHAT] wr. a-na-am$_3$ Akk. mīnu ePSD: mīnum ana [WHAT?] wr. a-na; ta; ta-a Akk. mīnum ePSD: minûtu šid [COUNT] wr. šid Akk. minûtu; mišlānū uttu [COUNT] wr. uttu$_2$ Akk. minûtu AALD: minītu (s.) (manītu) الحجم الاعتيادي للشيء، الرقم الاعتيادي، اللحظة، الطول، الحساب؛ في حالة الجمع: الجسم، الشكل، الحجم، النسبة، الصحة AALD: ammīni (interr) see mīnu AALD: minsu (interr) (see mīnu) ماذا؟ ما ذلك؟ AALD: ammēnim (interr) لماذا AALD: ammēni (interr) لماذا AALD: mīna (interr) see mīnu AALD: min (interr) see mīnu AALD: mīnamma (interr) see mīnu AALD: mīnammi (interr) see mīnu AALD: mīna (interr) see mīnu AALD: mīnu (interr) لاي شيء ،لاي سبب ، لماذا، ماذا، كلما AALD: mêš (interr) (see ayiš) أين AALD: manan (interr) لماذا Note1: manû -> مَن هو <- مَنّوَ Note2: minû -> مِن اي شيء <- مِنّوَ	من (الصّحّاح في اللغة) ممَنَّ (القاموس المحيط) منن (الصّحّاح في اللغة) منن (لسان العرب) منأ (لسان العرب) منا (الصّحّاح في اللغة) منع (لسان العرب) مني (لسان العرب) مأن (الصّحّاح في اللغة) المَأْنَةُ (القاموس المحيط) مأن (لسان العرب)
355	*man-za-zu*	150[T11]	ePSD: manzazu ĝišgal [STATION] wr. ĝišgal Akk. manzazu AALD: nazūzu (s.) (هور) اجمة القصب AALD: nazāzu (v.) (nasāsu) النَّزيز، يصرخ بصوت عالي ومستمر، يخشخش، يتمايل، يصدر صوت مثل الغثاء	النَّزُّ (القاموس المحيط) نزز (لسان العرب)

			AALD: nūzu (s.) معنى غير معروف AALD: nuzzû (v.) (nunzû) معنى غير معروف AALD: nuzzumu (adj.) معنى غير معروف	
356	*ma-rat* *ma-ri*	77[T1] 135[T1]	See also DUMU See also *i-mu-ru* ePSD: mārtu dumumunus [DAUGHTER] wr. dumu-munus Akk. mārtu ePSD: māru amar [YOUNG] wr. amar Akk. būru; māru dumu [CHILD] wr. dumu; du_5-mu Akk. māru dumunita [SON] wr. dumu-nita Akk. māru hibira [SON] wr. hibira Akk. māru AALD: mu'āru (s.): الرجلُ، البطلُ AALD: mu'irru (s.) (see âru): الآمر، المدير AALD: âru (v.) يذهب، يتقدم، يحكم، يسيطر AALD: *māru (s.) (mar'u, mer'u) المرء، الابن، السليل (2) الابن، يستخدم مخاطبة الادنى تعبيرا عن المدة والحب	مرر (لسان العرب) مور (الصّحاح في اللغة) مور (مقاييس اللغة) مور (لسان العرب) مار (لسان العرب) مرأ (لسان العرب) مرا (لسان العرب) قرآن (الكهف 15:21)
357	*mar-ḫi-ti-šú* *mar-ḫi-is-su*	212[T11] 215[T11]	See also *ma-rat* AALD: marhītu (s.) see rehû (الزوجة، السرية (المحظية AALD: rehû (v.) (rahû) يُخصِب، يحَمَل، يصب، يسكب على، يقهر، يلقّح، يُخَصّب	مره (مقاييس اللغة) مَرِهَتْ (القاموس المحيط) رها (لسان العرب)
358	*mar-ṣa-a-ti* *mar-ṣu* *mar-ṣa-a-ti* *mar-ṣu-ti*	28[T1] 15[U] 232[T10] 252[T10]	ePSD: marāṣu gig [SICK] wr. gig Akk. marāṣu; marṣu tur [ILL] wr. tur_5 Akk. marāṣu; murṣu	مرض (لسان العرب)
359	MAŠ.DÀ.[MEŠ]-*ma*	110[T1]	ePSD: mašda mašda [GAZELLE] wr. maš-da_3; $maš_2$-da_3 Akk. ṣabītu mašda [STONE] wr. $^{na}{}_4$maš-da	مثد (لسان العرب)
360	MÁŠ.GI_6	246[T1]	See also *šu-na-te-ka* See also *šu-ut-ta* MAŠ.MI mašĝik [VISION] wr. maš-$ĝi_6$; $maš_2$-$ĝi_6$ GI_6 see *mu-ši*	شجا (لسان العرب) شَجاهُ (القاموس المحيط) شجج (لسان العرب) سجج (لسان العرب) مشج (مقاييس اللغة) مأش (لسان العرب) المَشُّ (القاموس المحيط) ميش (لسان العرب) مشج (لسان العرب)
361	*maš-ḫa-an-da*	274[T10]	AALD: mašḫandu (s.): معنى غير اكيد AALD: mašḫu (s.): الرداء AALD: mašḫurannu (s.): الرداء	
362	*maš-qa-a* *áš-qí*	111[T1] 74[T11]	ePSD: mašqītu ugu [WATERING PLACE] wr. ugu_2 Akk. mašqītu; mikru ePSD: mašqû asig [VESSEL] wr. a-sig Akk. mašqû epig [VESSEL] wr. epig Akk. mašqû	مشق (مقاييس اللغة) المَشْقُ (القاموس المحيط) مشق (لسان العرب) سقي (لسان العرب)
363	*ma-ti-ma-a* *im-ma-ti-ma*	270[T10] 308[T10]	See also *am-ma-ti*	مَتَى (القاموس المحيط) متى (الصّحاح في اللغة)

	im-ma-ti-ma *im-ma-ti-ma*	309^{T10} 310^{T10}	ePSD: mati meta [WHENCE?] wr. me-ta Akk. ayyānu; mati ePSD: matīma udmeda [EVER] wr. ud-me-da Akk. matīma AALD: mati (conj.) (immati, immat, ammate, matima) متى، حالما، اين، كلما AALD: mati (inter. adv.) (mati, mat, immati, immat) mati (mat, matim) متى؟ (نفي) ابدا، اخيرا immati (immat) متى؟، كلما، دائما AALD: mattimê (conj.) (immatimê) متى، حالما، كلما AALD: matima (inter.; adv.) متى؟، دائما (نفي) ابدا، كلما (في الماضي) احيانا متى؟، في اي وقت (مستقبل) AALD: mattimeni (adv.) دائما AALD: immatima (see mati) (adv.) متى AALD: immati (see mati) (adv.) متى AALD: immat (see mati) (adv.) متى AALD: immatimê (see mati) (adv.) متى، كلما AALD: *ammati (interr) see mati متى Note1: Whence = where from; from where Whence = from what place التى منها لذلك؛ الذى منه؛ من اجل ذلك؛ من اين؛ من حيث = Note2: matimā = until when = الى متى = مِن متى = متى ما	متى (لسان العرب)
364	*me-e*	254^{T11}	See aslo *A.*^{MES} AALD: mû (s. pl. only) (mā'ū) AALD: mû (s.)	موه (لسان العرب) موأ (لسان العرب) موأ (العباب الزاخر) موا (لسان العرب)
365	*MEŠ* *MAŠ*	22^{T1} 56^{T1}	ePSD: MAŠ ba [HALF] wr. ba$_3$; ba$_7$ Akk. bāmtu; mišlu; šalāšā maš [BORDER] wr. maš Akk. miṣru maš [GOAT] wr. maš$_2$; maš Akk. bīru; urīṣu maš [INTEREST] wr. maš; maš$_2$ Akk. ṣibtu maš [PURE] wr. maš; maš$_3$ Akk. ellu maš [TWIN] wr. maš "twin" Akk. māšu sa [HALF] wr. sa$_9$ Akk. mišlu zipah [UNIT] wr. zipah$_2$; zipah; zipah$_x$(|ŠU$_2$.BAD|); šu-pah Akk. ūṭu maš [PLANT] wr. ^{ĝeš}maš maš [TILE] wr. ^{dug}maš "a drainage tile" Akk. mišlānū maš [TREE] wr. ^{ĝeš}maš "a tree" Akk. giṣṣu ePSD: MES kišib [HAND] wr. kišib-la$_2$; kišib Akk. rittu kišib [SEAL] wr. kišib$_3$; kišib; $^{na}{}_4$kišib Akk. kunukku mes [BLACKNESS] wr. mes; ^{ĝeš}mes Akk. ṣulmu mes [HERO] wr. mes Akk. eṭlu mes [TREE] wr. ^{ĝeš}mes Akk. mēsu	مَأسَ (القاموس المحيط) مأس (لسان العرب) ميش (مقاييس اللغة) ميش (لسان العرب) مشش (لسان العرب) مش (مقاييس اللغة) ميس (لسان العرب)
366	*meš-ra-a* *ša-ru-ú* *šá-ru-u*	45^{T11} 55^{T11} 55^{T11}	See also *NÍG.TUKU-ma* See *LUGAL*	سرا (لسان العرب) ثرا (لسان العرب) شرى (الصّحّاح في اللغة)

			ePSD: šarû gutuku [PERFECT] wr. gu$_2$-tuku Akk. gitmalu; šarû luniĝtuku [RICH] wr. lu$_2$-niĝ$_2$-tuku Akk. šarû niĝtuku [RICH] wr. niĝ$_2$-tuku Akk. šarû AALD: mašrû (s.) (mešrû) الثروة، الرفاهية، اسم وصفي للنخلة AALD: mašrītu (s) (see šaru) الثروة	شري (لسان العرب) شرع (الصّحَاح في اللغة) شرع (لسان العرب) يسر (لسان العرب)
367	*mi-in-di* *mìn-de-ma*	17^{P} 39^{T11}	See *i-du-ú* See also ú-um-mi-id-ma ePSD: mindê iginzu [AS IF] wr. i-gi$_4$-in-zu; i-gi$_4$-in-zu$_7$; i-gi-in-zu; i$_3$-gi$_4$-in-zu Akk. mindê AALD: minde (adv.) (midde) (see idû): perhaps; since; ربما، ممكن، من يدري، من يقول Note: al-Jibouri rule: middi -> mindi مدِّ -> مِنْدِ	منذ (لسان العرب) مُنْذُ (القاموس المحيط)
368	*mil-ki* *mil-ki* *mil-ki* *mil-ku* *ma-lik* *ma-lik* *ma-lik* *ma-li-ku* *ma-li-ku* *ma-li-ki* *ma-lik-šú-nu* *mi-lik-šú*	146^{T1} 277^{T10} 198^{T11} 198^{T11} 295^{T1} 296^{T1} 297^{T1} 296^{T1} 297^{T1} 276^{T10} 15^{T11} 198^{T11}	See il-li-kam-ma ePSD: mālaku ki'enDU [WATERCOURSE] wr. ki-en-DU Akk. mālaku malaku [~MEAT] wr. ma-la-ku Akk. mālaku ePSD: malāku ad gi [ADVISE] wr. ad gi$_4$ Akk. malāku šag kušu [SOOTHE] wr. šag$_4$ kuš$_2$-u$_3$ Akk. ?; malāku ePSD: milku ĝalga [FORETHOUGHT] wr. ĝalga; ma-al-ga Akk. milku; ţēmu sa [ADVICE] wr. sa$_2$ Akk. milku	ملك (مقاييس اللغة) ملك (لسان العرب) لكم (لسان العرب)
369	*mìn-di-na*	259^{T10}	See also *UR.MAH̲.*^{MES} ePSD: mindinu ug [LION] wr. ug; ug$_x$(|PIRIG×ZA|) Akk. mindinu; nešu; ūmu AALD: mindina (s.) (middinu, mandinu) الاسد؟ Note: al-Jibouri's rules: maddin -> mandin; مَدّين -> مَندين	مَدَنَ (القاموس المحيط) مدن (لسان العرب)
370	*mìn-du-da* *min-du-da*	29^{T11}	See ú-um-mi-id-ma Note: al-Jibouri rule: midduda -> minduda مِدُّدَ -> مِنْدُدَ	
371	*mit-ḫa-riš* *mit-ḫa-riš* *mit-ḫur* *mit-ḫu-rat*	5^{T1} 5^{U} 30^{T11} 136^{T11}	See also *ma-ḫir* ePSD: mithartum ibsi [SQUARE] wr. ib$_2$-si$_8$; ib$_2$-si; ib-si$_2$ Akk. mithartum	متخ (لسان العرب) متح (لسان العرب)

			ePSD: mithāru ur [HE] wr. ur_5; ur Akk. amtu; ištēn; mithāru; šû ePSD: mithurtu hamun [HARMONY] wr. ha-mun Akk. mithurtu AALD: mitẖāriš (adv.) 1) كل واحد، الى نفس المدى او الدرجة 2) في كل مكان، اجمالا، في كل مناسبة، كل مرة، في المجموعة (الكل سوية)	
372	*ᵐpu-zu-ur-ᵈKUR.GAL* puzur-amurri	95[T11]	See Part 2.2.27 See Part 2.2.29 See also *ᵐur-ᵈšánabi* See *pu-zu-ur* See *ᵈen-líl* See *KUR* See *LUGAL* *Wikipedia:* https://en.wikipedia.org/wiki/Kur	كرج (مقاييس اللغة) الكَرَجُ (القاموس المحيط) كرج (لسان العرب) عمر (مقاييس اللغة) العَمْرُ (القاموس المحيط) عمر (لسان العرب)
373	*mu-ab-bit*	34[T1]	ePSD: abātu gul [DESTROY] wr. gul; gu-ul Akk. abātu; hepû; naqāru; sapānu	عبط (لسان العرب) أفت (لسان العرب) أَبِتَ (القاموس المحيط) أَبت (لسان العرب)
374	*ᵐu-bar-tu-tu* *ᵐubara-ᵈtu-tu*	208[T10] 23[T11]	See Part 2.2.28 *Wikipedia:* https://en.wikipedia.org/wiki/Ubara-Tutu ePSD: ubāru ubar [FOREIGNER] wr. u-bar Akk. ubāru ePSD: [foreigner] gir [STRANGER] wr. gir_5 Akk. ubāru [foreigner]	عبر (لسان العرب) لمك (لسان العرب) tu-tu توت (لسان العرب) توث (لسان العرب)
375	*mu-du-ú* *mu-da-at* *mu-da-a-tú* *mu-da-at* *mu-da-at* *mu-di-a-at*	214[T1] 259[T1] 259[T1] 286[T1] 15[P] 37[P]	*See i-du-ú*	
376	*ᵐUD-ZI-tim* *ᵐUD-ZI* ᵐUta-napišti *ú-tu-ur-na-pu-uš-ti* *a-tar-ẖa-sis* *at-ra-ẖa-sis*	42[T1] 42[T1] 7[U] 49[T11] 197[T11]	See Part 2.2.30 See also *ni-ip-šu* See also *UD* See also *šá* See also *ẖa-as-su* See also *mu-tir* *Wikipedia:* https://en.wikipedia.org/wiki/Atra-Hasis *Mythology Dictionary:* http://www.mythologydictionary.com/atrahasis-	عطا (لسان العرب) أتي (لسان العرب) العَوْدُ (القاموس المحيط) عود (مقاييس اللغة) عطر (مقاييس اللغة) العِطْرُ (القاموس المحيط) عطر (الصّحاح في اللغة) عطر (لسان العرب) عتر (مقاييس اللغة) عتر (الصّحاح في اللغة) عتر (لسان العرب) ترر (لسان العرب) تور (لسان العرب)

			mythology.html ePSD: zi zi [LIFE] wr. zi; ši; ši-i Akk. napištu ePSD: atru dirig [EXCEED] wr. diri; RI Akk. atru; eli; rabû; kapāšu; zaqāru; šarūru; šūturu; lē'û	زيا (لسان العرب) زوي (لسان العرب) ذا (لسان العرب) ذيا (لسان العرب) نفس (العباب الزاخر)
377	*muḫ-ḫi-šú* *muḫ-ḫi-šá* *me-ḫu-ú* *me-ḫu-ú* *mi-ḫu-ú* *me-ḫu-ú*	252[T1] 59[T11] 109[T11] 129[T11] 129[T11] 131[T11]	ePSD: muhhu ugu [SKULL] wr. ugu_2; ugu; ugu_3; ugu_x(|U.SAG|); ugu_x(|A.U.KA|); ugu_x(SAG@n@g) Akk. eli; muhhu; qaqqadu ePSD: mehû mir [WIND] wr. mir; ^{tumu}mir Akk. ištānu; mehû sisig [BREEZE] wr. sig-sig; ^{tumu}si-si-ig; si-si-ga; sig_3-sig_3 Akk. mehû; zīqīqu?; šāru ulu [WIND] wr. ulu_3^{lu}; $^{tumu}ulu_3^{lu}$; $^{tumu}ulu_3$; u_{18}-lu; $^{tumu}ulu_2$ Akk. alû; mehê šūti; šūtu; mehû	مخخ (لسان العرب) محو (مقاييس اللغة) محا (لسان العرب) محح (لسان العرب) محت (لسان العرب) موخ (لسان العرب) ميح (لسان العرب)
378	*MUL.*[MEŠ] *MUL*	247[T1]	mul [SHINE] (129x: ED IIIb, Lagash II, Ur III, Old Babylonian) wr. mul; mul_2; mul_4 "star; to shine, radiate (light); arrow; to radiate (branches)" Akk. kakkabu; mulmullu; nabāṭu	ملل (لسان العرب)
379	*mun-tal-ku*	21[T1]	See *il-li-kam-ma* AALD: muntalku (adj.) 1) مدروس، حكيم 2) مستشار Note: al-Jibouri rule: ألك >> مُتَألَكَ >> مُنتالَكَ >> مُنتَلَكَ	ألك (لسان العرب)
380	*MUNUS-šú*	204[T11]	*See sin-niš-ti* Note2: munus = nu-nus = مؤنث Note2: munus = nu-nus = مؤنس	
381	*MU-ra* *MU-ár* *MU-ár*	206[T1] 245[T1] 259[T1]	See also *i-zak-ka-ra* ePSD: mu mu [SOUND] wr. mu_7	مار (لسان العرب) مور (لسان العرب) موأ (لسان العرب)
382	*^{m}ur-^{d}šánabi*	247[T11]	See Part 2.2.27 See Part 2.2.29 See *URU* See *^{m}pu-zu-ur-^{d}KUR.GAL* See also *zu-um-bé-e* See also *šit-tin-šú* *Role Playing in Sumer and Akkad:* http://galmartu.perso.sfr.fr/roleplay/sumerakkad/urshanabi.php *Andrew. R. George:* http://eprints.soas.ac.uk/20636/1/Urshanabi.pdf šinipu	ذنب (مقاييس اللغة) الذَّنَبُ (القاموس المحيط) ذنب (الصّحاح في اللغة) السَّنَبَةُ (القاموس المحيط) السُّنْبُكُ (القاموس المحيط) سنبه (لسان العرب) سنبت (لسان العرب) هنبك (لسان العرب) سنب (لسان العرب)

			<u>šanabi</u> [TWO-THIRDS] wr. šanabi "two-thirds" Akk. šinipu	
383	*MURUB$_4$-šá*	64^{T11}	See *qab-li* ePSD: murub <u>murub</u> [MIDDLE] wr. murub$_6$; murub$_4$; murub$_2$; murub; murub$_3$ Akk. abullu; birītu; biṣṣūru; pinku; pû; qablu; qinnatu; ûru <u>murub</u> [PRIEST] wr. murub; murub$_3$ Akk. ēnu	ورب (لسان العرب)
384	*MUŠ*	305^{T11}	See also *mu-ši* ePSD: MUŠ <u>muš</u> [SNAKE] wr. muš Akk. ṣēru <u>šahan</u> [UNMNG] wr. šahan; šahan$_2$ "" <u>šer</u> [ACQUISITION] wr. šer$_{10}$ <u>šuba</u> [STONE] wr. šuba$_3$; $^{na}{}_4$šuba; šuba$_4$; šuba$_x$(MUŠ); šuba$_x$(|MUŠ.ŠA|) Akk. šubû	موس (لسان العرب) ميس (العباب الزاخر)
385	*MUŠEN.^{MEŠ}* iṣṣūrāti	44^{T11}	See *uṣ-ṣir* ePSD: mušen <u>mušen</u> [BIRD] wr. mušen; mu-ti-in; mu-tin Akk. iṣṣūru ePSD: mušenburu <u>mušenburu</u> [FLOCK] wr. mušen-buru$_5$ ePSD: mušgu <u>mušgu</u> [BIRD] wr. muš-gu$_7{}^{mušen}$	iṣṣūru عصر (لسان العرب) *MUŠEN* شعن (لسان العرب) سعن (لسان العرب) وشع (لسان العرب) العَشّةُ (القاموس المحيط) عش (مقاييس اللغة) عشش (الصّحّاح في اللغة) عشش (لسان العرب)
386	*mu-še-zib* *ú-še-zeb* *uš-te-né-zeb-ka*	268^{T1} 272^{T1} 272^{T1}	ePSD: šūzubu <u>šu kar</u> [SPARE] wr. šu kar Akk. šūzubu	شذب (لسان العرب)
387	*mu-ši* *mu-ši* *mu-ši-ti-ia*	69^{T1} 232^{T1} 3^{P}	See also *GI$_6$* ePSD: mūšu <u>ĝi</u> [NIGHT] wr. ĝi$_6$ Akk. mūšu AALD: mūšu (adv.) (mūšam, mūšamma) مساءأ، في المساء AALD: mišu (s.) الليل AALD: mašu (v.) يمضي الليل AALD: miši (s.) الجنود	مَأسَ (القاموس المحيط) مأس (لسان العرب) مسي (مقاييس اللغة) مسا (لسان العرب) موس (لسان العرب) ميس (العباب الزاخر) مشي (لسان العرب)
388	*muš-šu-kàt* *maš-ku-ú* *maš-ki-šu-ma*	226^{T11} 252^{T11} 255^{T11}	See also *KUŠ.^{MEŠ}-šú-nu* also see *maš-qa-a* ePSD: mašku <u>kuš</u> [SKIN] wr. kuš Akk. mašku; zumru AALD: mašku (see masku) AALD: masku (adj.) (mašku) f. masiktu, mašiktu) سيء، رديء، فاسد اخلاقيا، قبيح	المَشْقُ (القاموس المحيط) مسك (الصّحّاح في اللغة) المَسْكُ (القاموس المحيط) مسك (لسان العرب)
389	*muš-te-'-ú* *i-še-'-a*	41^{T1} 214^{T1}	UM See *AMA*	سدع (لسان العرب) سدع (مقاييس اللغة)

	taš-ú *téš-'-UM* *še-'-i*	7^{T11} 7^{T11} 25^{T11}	ePSD: ašra še'û ki kiĝ [SEEK] wr. ki kiĝ$_2$ Akk. ašra še'û ePSD: se'û šu us [PUSH OPEN] wr. šu us$_2$ " Akk. se'û AALD: še'û يبحث، يفتش، يسبر، يتفحص، يدقق، يمعن النظر، يتوق، يطمح، يحن الى، يشفق	السَّدْعُ (القاموس المحيط) صدع (لسان العرب) المِسْتَعُ (القاموس المحيط) سأي (لسان العرب) سَعَى (القاموس المحيط) سعا (لسان العرب)
390	*mu-tir* *lu-tar-ru-ka* *i-ta-ár* *ta-ta-ár* *i-tar-ri* *i-tu-ram-mu* *i-tu-*[ra]*ram-mu* *ut-ter-ru* *i-tur-ma* *i-tu-ra* *i-tu-ram-ma* *i-tu-ram-ma* *li-tur* *li-tur* *lu-tur* *ta-ri-šú*	43^{T1} 209^{T1} 275^{T11} 280^{T11} 156^{T11} 203^{T1} 203^{T1} 107^{T11} 119^{T11} 135^{T11} 149^{T11} 152^{T11} 217^{T11} 218^{T11} 300^{T11} 307^{T11}	ePSD: târu gi [TURN] wr. gi$_4$; gi Akk. lamû; târu gur [TURN] wr. gur Akk. sahāru; târu ePSD: târu; târu; sahāru niĝin [ENCIRCLE] wr. niĝin$_2$; niĝin Akk. esēru; lawû; sahāru; târu; târu; sahāru; şâdu ePSD: tarû ri [IMPOSE] wr. RI; ru Akk. bâ'u; emēdu; nadû; nasāku; ramû; rehû; tarû; wašaru	وتر (لسان العرب) تر (مقاييس اللغة) أتر (لسان العرب) ترر (لسان العرب) تور (لسان العرب) التُّوْرُ (القاموس المحيط) أتر (لسان العرب) تأر (لسان العرب) تير (لسان العرب) متر (لسان العرب) بتر (لسان العرب)
391	*mut-tak-pu*	30^{T1}	See also *nag-ba* See also *na-aq-ba* AALD: *takāpu (v.) يثقب، يغرز AALD: muttakkipu (adj.) see nakāpu مَخروق (بقرن، بسكين) AALD: muttakpu (adj.) see nakāpu مَخروق (بقرن، بسكين)	ثقف (لسان العرب) ثقب (لسان العرب)
392	*mu-uş-şi-ma* *ú-şi* *ú-şa-a*	184^{T1} 175^{T11} 218^{T11}	ePSD: aşû e [LEAVE] wr. e$_3$; i; e Akk. aşû; erēbu; mahû; rubbû; zarû; šakāku ePSD: uşşu ku [PLACE] wr. ku Akk. nadû; uşşu ePSD: uşşû barag [SPREAD] wr. BAD; ba-ra-ge; ba-ra-ga; [ba]barag$_2$; KISAL[ra] Akk. uşşû; šuparruru	عص (مقاييس اللغة) عصو/ي (مقاييس اللغة) عصص (لسان العرب) العَصُّ (القاموس المحيط) عصا (لسان العرب) وأص (لسان العرب) هَصَا (القاموس المحيط) هصا (لسان العرب) وهص (لسان العرب) أصا (القاموس المحيط) أصا (لسان العرب) أصص (لسان العرب) أصَّهُ (القاموس المحيط) وصي (لسان العرب) مصص (لسان العرب) مضض (لسان العرب)
393	*NA$_4$* *NA$_4$* [MEŠ]	34^{T1} 289^{T11}	ePSD: na na [CVNE] wr. na na [MAN] wr. na Akk. amēlu na [PESTLE] wr. [na]$_4$na Akk. na'u na [STONE] wr. na$_4$; na; [na]$_4$na Akk. abnu	نَاءَ (القاموس المحيط)
394	[na4]*NA.RÚ.A*	10^{T1}	See *NA$_4$*	النَّرْوَةُ (القاموس المحيط)
395	[na4]*ZA.GÌN*	27^{T1}	See also *uq-na-ti*	زاغَ (القاموس المحيط)

			See also NA$_4$ ePSD: zagin zagin [LAPIS] wr. za-gin$_3$; $^{na}{}_4$za-gin$_3$ Akk. uqnû	زيغ (لسان العرب)
396	*na-aq-ba*	1^{U}	See also *nag-ba* See also *mut-tak-pu* ePSD: nakāpu du [PUSH] wr. Akk. nakāpu saĝ sag [TREMBLE] wr. saĝ sag$_3$ Akk. nakāpu	نقب (مقاييس اللغة) النَّقْبُ (القاموس المحيط) نقب (لسان العرب)
397	*na-bu* *ú-nam-bi* *ú-nam-ba*	47^{T1} 118^{T11} 118^{T11}	ePSD: nabû gu de [SAY] wr. gu$_3$ de$_2$ Akk. ?; nabû; šasû pad [FIND] wr. pad$_3$ Akk. atû; nabû še [CALL] wr. še$_{21}$ Akk. nabû Note: únambi = únanbi = únnabi	نَبَّ (القاموس المحيط) نبب (لسان العرب) نبو (مقاييس اللغة) نبأ (لسان العرب) نبا (الصّحّاح في اللغة) نَبَا (القاموس المحيط) النَّبَأ (القاموس المحيط) نبا (لسان العرب)
398	*na-di-ma* *na-da-at* *i-nam-din-an-ni* *i-nam-du-ú*	278^{T1} 6^{T11} 133^{T1} 293^{T10}	ePSD: nadû gurud [THROW] wr. gurud; gurud$_2$ Akk. nadû ku [PLACE] wr. ku Akk. nadû; uşşu ri [IMPOSE] wr. RI; ru Akk. bâ'u; emēdu; nadû; nasāku; ramû; rehû; tarû; wašaru šub [FALL] wr. šub Akk. habātu; maqātu; nadû ePSD: nadānu šum [GIVE] wr. šum$_2$; ze$_2$-eĝ$_3$ Akk. nadānu	ندأ (لسان العرب) نَدَأَهُ (القاموس المحيط) ندي (مقاييس اللغة) ندي (لسان العرب) نَدَّ (القاموس المحيط)
399	*nag-ba*	1^{T1}	See also *na-aq-ba* See also *mut-tak-pu* ePSD: nagbu gu [ENTIRETY] wr. gu$_2$ Akk. nagbu; napharu idim [SPRING] wr. idim Akk. nagbu AALD: naqābu (v.) (naqāpu) يَنْقُب، يفض البكارة، يغتصب AALD: naqāpu see nakāpu v. and naqābu AALD: nakāpu (v,) (naqāpu) ينطح، يناطح، يجرح بقرن، يتاخم	نجف (مقاييس اللغة) النَّجَفُ (القاموس المحيط) نجف (العباب الزاخر) نجف (لسان العرب) نجب (مقاييس اللغة) نجب (لسان العرب) نكف (مقاييس اللغة) نكف (العباب الزاخر) نقف (لسان العرب)
400	*na-gu-ú*	141^{T11}	ePSD: nagû niĝin [DISTRICT] wr. niĝin$_5$; niĝin$_x$(|LAL$_2$.SAR|); niĝin$_9$ Akk. nagû	نجو (مقاييس اللغة) نَجَا (القاموس المحيط) نجا (الصّحّاح في اللغة) نجا (لسان العرب)
401	*nam-maš-še-e* *nam-maš-šá-a* *nam-maš-se-e* *nam-se-e*	112^{T1} 260^{T10} 260^{T10} 253^{T11}	ePSD: nammaštû gilim [RODENT] wr. gilim$_2$; Akk. nammaštû niĝki [HERD] wr. niĝ$_2$-ki Akk. nammaštû ePSD: namsû niĝ'esir [WASH-BASIN] wr. ^{gi}niĝ$_2$-esir$_2$-ra Akk. namsû Note: علي بن ابي طالب: "كل وعاء يضيق بما جُعِل فيه، إلا وعاء العلم فإنه يتسع"	نمش (لسان العرب) نمس (لسان العرب) وعي (لسان العرب)
402	*nap-ḫar*	6^{T1}	AALD: nabharu (s.) 1) المجموع، الحاصل، اجمالي 2) الكل، الكون، المجموع الكلي	بحر (لسان العرب)

403	*nāru*	313[T10]	See also *ÍD* ePSD: nāru id [RIVER] wr. Id_2; id_3; id_6; id_7; id_5 Akk. nāru nab [MUSICIAN] wr. Nab Akk. nāru nar [MUSICIAN] wr. Nar Akk. nāru	نعر (لسان العرب) نهر (لسان العرب)
404	*né-bé-ru*	248[T11]	ePSD: nēberu addir [FORD] wr. addir; dir; $addir_x$(|PA.GISAL.SI.A|); $addir_x$(|PA.GISAL.SI.A.PAD|) Akk. kāru; nēberu ma'addir [FERRYBOAT] wr. ma_2-addir; ma_2-$addir_x$(|PAD.DUG.GIŠ.SI|) Akk. nēberu; elep igri	عبر (لسان العرب) العَذْرُ (القاموس المحيط) عدر (لسان العرب)
405	*né-me-qí*	6[T1]	né-me-qu (s.) (see emqu) الخبرة، المعرفة، المهارة، البراعة	نمق (مقاييس اللغة) نمق (لسان العرب) نَمَقَ (القاموس المحيط)
406	*né-re-bé-e-ti* *né-re-bé-e-tum* *i-te-ru-ub* *e-ru-ub*	38[T1] 38[T1] 274 89[T11]	See also *ir-bu-ú* *See also a-ri-bi* ePSD: erēbu e [LEAVE] wr. e_3; i; e Akk. aşû; erēbu; mahû; rubbû; zarû; šakāku kur [ENTER] wr. kur_9; kur_x(DU); kur_x(LIL) "to enter" Akk. erēbu ePSD: nērubu kar [FLEE] wr. kar Akk. ekēmu; eţēru; mašā'u; nērubu kas dug [RUN] wr. kas_4 dug_4 Akk. lasāmu; nērubu kas kar [RUN] wr. kas_4 kar Akk. lasāmu; nērubu AALD: nerēbu (nerēbtu) see erēbu (s.) طريق الدخول، المدخل، الممر الجبلي	هرب (لسان العرب) عرب (مقاييس اللغة) أرب (مقاييس اللغة) أرب (لسان العرب) نير (مقاييس اللغة) نحر (لسان العرب)
407	*né-šá*	259[T10]	See *UR.MAH̱.[MES]* ePSD: nešu; ūmu ug [LION] wr. ug; ug_x(|PIRIG×ZA|) Akk. mindinu; nešu; ūmu ePSD: nēšu piriĝ [LION] wr. piriĝ; $piri\hat{g}_3$; bi_2-ri-$i\hat{g}_3$; [ĝeš]piriĝ; $piri\hat{g}_2$ Akk. lû; lābu; nēšu; rīmu urmah [LION] wr. ur-mah Akk. nēšu; urmahhu Note: al-Jibouri's rules: missu -> nisu; ميسُ -> نيسُ	نعس (لسان العرب) المَيْسُ (القاموس المحيط)
408	*ni!-kás* *ni!-kás* *ni-kás* *ni-kás*	56[T1] 58[T1] 36[U] 37[U]	See also *NÌG.KA₉* ePSD: nikkassu niĝŠID [ACCOUNT] wr. $ni\hat{g}_2$-ŠID; $ni\hat{g}_2$-ŠID-ma Akk. nikkassu AALD: nakāsu (v.) 1) ينكس، يقطع اشجار 2) يقطع،يفصل 3) يقلل 4) يذبح، يقتل	نقص (لسان العرب) نقص (مقاييس اللغة) قصص (لسان العرب) نكس (لسان العرب)
409	*ni-du-ku* *a-du-ka*	231[T10] 259[T10]	ePSD: dâku gaz [KILL] wr. gaz; gaz_2; kaz_8 Akk. dâku; habātu; hašālu;	دكك (الصّحّاح في اللغة) دكك (لسان العرب)

			kaşāşu; pa'āşu; šagāšu gi [KILL] wr. gi_4 "kill" Akk. dâku rah [BEAT] wr. rah_2; ra-ah Akk. dâku; diāšu; hepû; rahāşu; rapāsu sag [SCATTER] wr. sag_2; sag_3; sag_7 Akk. dâku; nasāku; nêru; sapāhu	
410	*NÌG.KA₉*	56[T1]	See also *ni!-kás* ePSD: nig [PLOW] (2x: Old Babylonian) wr. ^{ĝeš}nig; ^{kuš}nig Akk. kalbatu; kurussu ša epinni	نجخ (لسان العرب)
411	*NÍG.TUKU-ma*	25[T11]	See also *meš-ra-a* ePSD: niĝ niĝ [THING] wr. $niĝ_2$; $aĝ_2$ Akk. bušu; mimma ePSD: TUK du [PLAY] wr. du_{12}-du_{12}; du_{12} Akk. lapātu; zamāru tuku [ACQUIRE] wr. tuku Akk. rašû	نعج (لسان العرب) نأج (لسان العرب) نوج (لسان العرب) تأق (لسان العرب) تأق (الصّحَاح في اللغة) تاقَ (القاموس المحيط) توق (مقاييس اللغة) توق (لسان العرب)
412	*ni-ip-šu* *ni-piš* *i-nap-pu-uš* *i-nap-pu-uš* *na-pis-su* *nu-up-pu-us* *na-piš-ti* *na-piš-tú* *nap-šá-a-ti* *nap-pa-šá-am-ma* *ni-piš* *nu-up-pu-us*	13[T1] 13[T1] 211[T11] 214[T11] 182[T1] 106[T1] 26[T11] 26[T11] 27[T11] 137[T11] 305[T11]	ePSD: nipšu peš [TUFT] wr. $peš_6$ Akk. nipšu ePSD: napīšu paĝ [BREATHE] wr. pa-$aĝ_2$; pa-an Akk. napīšu paĝta [BREATH] wr. pa-$aĝ_2$-ta Akk. napīšu AALD: nipšu (s.) النفس، الشخير AALD: nipšu (s.) خصلة الصوف، الزغب المنفوش، مشط الصوف AALD: nabāsu (s.) (nabassu, napāsu, nabāšu): Red died wool AALD: napīštu (s.) (naputšu, napulu, napšatu, nupšatu, napaštu, napaltu) النفس، الحياة، الحيوية، النشاط؛ الصحة؛ الكائن الحي؛ النفس (الهواء)؛ شخص، شخص ما؛ حيوانات القطيع؛ الجسم؛	نفش (لسان العرب) نفش (مقاييس اللغة) نفث (لسان العرب) نبث (لسان العرب) النَّبْشُ (القاموس المحيط) نبش (مقاييس اللغة) نبس (لسان العرب) نفس (العباب الزاخر) نفس (لسان العرب)
413	*ni-is-sa-tu* *ni-is-sa-tu* *ni-is-sa-ta* *ni-is-sa-ti*	215[T10] 222[T10] 267[T10] 126[T11]	See also *SAG.PA.LAGAB* See also *nu-us-su* ePSD: nissatu isiš [SORROW] wr. i-si-iš; $isiš_3$ Akk. dimmatu; nissatu; ratāmu; tassistu; şiāhu; şīhu ug [LAMENTATION] wr. ug_2 Akk. nissatu zarah [WAILING] wr. zarah Akk. nissatu AALD: nissatu (niššatu) (s.) الاسى، القلق، الكآبة؛ النحيب	نسأ (لسان العرب) نسس (لسان العرب) نسس (العباب الزاخر) النَّسُّ (القاموس المحيط)
414	*ni-kit-ti*	295[T11]	See also *ni-qit-ti* ePSD: nukkatu nug [PLANT] wr. nug; nug_2 Akk. nukkatu AALD: nikittu (see nigītu) AALD: nikītu (see nigītu) AALD: nikittu (s.) (see nakādu) الخوف، القلق، المأساة، الوضع الخطر	نكه (مقاييس اللغة) نَكِدَ (القاموس المحيط) نكد (لسان العرب) نجأ (لسان العرب)
415	*ni-lu-ú* *a-né-el-lam-ma*	228[T10] 247[T10]	See aslo *ma-a-a-al* ePSD: na'lu	نحل (لسان العرب) نحل (مقاييس اللغة) نأل (لسان العرب)

			<u>aĝizzal</u> [DISEASE] wr. a-ĝizzal$_x$(|GIŠ.TUG$_2$.PI.ŠIR$_2$t.SIL$_2$|) Akk. na'lu AALD: nâlu (v.) (niālu) يستلقي، يضطجع، يستلقي مرارا ، يتمدد، يسجى، يُمدد في القبر، يحفظ بالملح او الرمل، يدفن See also mayāltu, mayālu, nayālu, nīlu (adj.) AALD: na'lu (ne'lu) (s.) المرض	نول (لسان العرب) نيل (لسان العرب)
416	*NIM.*^{meš}	165^{T11}	See also *zu-um-bé-e* See also *uš-ti-nim-ma* ePSD: NIM <u>dih</u> [CHAOS] wr. dih$_3$; ^{ĝeš}dih$_3$ Akk. sahmaštu <u>dih</u> [WEED] wr. ^{ĝeš}dih$_3$; dih$_3$; ^{ĝeš}tehi Akk. baltu <u>nim</u> [BUZZ] wr. nim <u>nim</u> [FLY] wr. nim Akk. zumbu <u>nim</u> [HIGH] wr. nim Akk. šaqû <u>tum</u> [UNMNG] wr. tum$_2$; tum$_4$ ""	الوَنيمُ (القاموس المحيط) ونم (الصّحاح في اللغة) ونم (لسان العرب) نوم (لسان العرب) نيم (مقاييس اللغة) نمم (لسان العرب)
417	*nim-ru* *nim!-ri* *nim-ri* *na-ma-a-ri* *nam-ri-ir-ri-šú-nu* *nam-ru*	226^{T10} 226^{T10} 259^{T10} 48^{T11} 105^{T11} 107^{T11}	ePSD: nimru <u>nemur</u> [LEOPARD] wr. nemur$_x$(|PIRIG.TUR|); ^{ĝeš}nemur$_x$(|PIRIG.TUR|) Akk. nimru ePSD: namrīru <u>nigal</u> [RADIANCE] wr. ni$_2$-gal Akk. namrīru; namurratu ePSD: namru <u>dadag</u> [BRIGHT] wr. dadag; dag$_2$ Akk. ebbu; ellu; namru <u>pirig</u> [BRIGHT] wr. pirig$_2$; pirig$_3$ Akk. namru <u>ul</u> [BRIGHT] wr. ul$_4$; ul$_6$ Akk. namru; nabāṭu <u>zabar</u> [BRONZE] wr. zabar; zabar$_3$ Akk. ebbu; hutpu; kakku; mušālu; namru; qû; sappu; siparru	النَّمِرَةُ (القاموس المحيط) نمر (مقاييس اللغة) نمر (الصّحاح في اللغة) نمر (لسان العرب)
418	*ni-muš* ^{kur}*ni-muš* *ni-muš* *ni-muš* *ni-muš* ni-ṣir	142^{T11} 143^{T11} 144^{T11} 145^{T11} 146^{T11}	<u>See Part 2.2.31</u> See also *nam-maš-še-e* *See also ni-ṣir-ta* *Wikipedia:* https://en.wikipedia.org/wiki/Mount_Nisir *Wikipedia:* https://en.wikipedia.org/wiki/Noah%27s_Ark إسماعيل بن عمر بن كثير القرشي الدمشقي. البداية والنهاية. http://library.islamweb.net/newlibrary/display_book.php?idfrom=20&idto=24&bk_no=59&ID=25	نظر (لسان العرب) نمس (لسان العرب) الجَيِّدُ (القاموس المحيط) جود (لسان العرب) كسا (لسان العرب) أجأ (لسان العرب) أجأ (العباب الزاخر)
419	*ni-na-ru*	229^{T10}	ePSD: nêru <u>sag</u> [SCATTER] wr. sag$_2$; sag$_3$; sag$_7$ Akk. dâku; nasāku; nêru; sapāhu <u>saĝ ĝeš ra</u> [KILL] wr. saĝ ĝeš ra Akk. nêru	نحر (مقاييس اللغة) نَحْرُ (القاموس المحيط) نحر (لسان العرب) حرب (لسان العرب)
420	*nindan*	56^{T1}	See also *iku* ePSD: nindanu <u>nindan</u> [POLE] wr. nindan; nindan-DU Akk. nindanu	ندد (الصّحاح في اللغة) نطط (العباب الزاخر) نطط (لسان العرب)

			ePSD: NINDA$_2$ gur [UNIT] wr. gur; Akk. kurru; namandu AALD: nindakku see nindanu AALD: nindanu (S.) مقياس للطول=12 ذراع؛ كلمة سومرية دخيلة Note: Rod (also Pol) = 5.5 yards = 16.5 ft ~ 5 m Small Cubit (arm length, from elbow to tip of middle finger) ~ 1.4 ft ~ 16.8 in Nindan = 12 Cubits = 16.75 ft ~ 5 m	
421	*NINDAN.TA.ÀM* *NINDAN.TA.ÀM* *NINDAN.ÀM*	58^{T11} 59^{T11} 59^{T11}	See *nindan* See *TA.ÀM*	
422	*nin-nem-dú-ma*	31^{T10}	See also *DU-du-ú-ma* ePSD: nīnu menden [WE] wr. me-en-de$_3$-en Akk. nīnu	نحن (لسان العرب)
423	*ni-pi-iḫ*	35^{U}	AALD: niphu (s.) النفخ، الشروق 2) الوهج، الحريق الهائل، اللهيب 3) غير جدير بالثقة، زائف 4) زائد	نفح (مقاييس اللغة) نفح (لسان العرب) لفح (لسان العرب) نفخ (لسان العرب) نفخ (مقاييس اللغة)
424	*ni-ṣir-ta* *ni-šir-ti-šú* *ni-ṣir-ti*	7^{T1} 26^{T1} 9^{T11}	See also *ṣirti* ePSD: nişirtu paphal [SECRET] wr. pap-hal Akk. nişirtu; pušqu	صرر (لسان العرب) صري (لسان العرب) نصر (لسان العرب) نطر (لسان العرب) نظر (لسان العرب)
425	*ni-šu-ú-a-a-ma* *te-né-še-e-ti*	123^{T11} 135^{T11}	See *also ÚG.*^{MEŠ} See *also nu-us-su* ePSD: nišu uĝ [PEOPLE] wr. uĝ$_3$ Akk. nišu ePSD: nišū umia [PEOPLE] wr. u$_2$-mi-a Akk. nišū	أنس (لسان العرب)
426	*nit-tab-ba-lu*	79^{T11}	See also *ub-la* See also *bu-lim* ePSD: tabiltu dabiltum [POT] wr. ^{dug}da-bil$_2$-tum Akk. tabiltu AALD: tabālu (v.) يَنقُل، يُقصي، يَحرم، يَنقل بالقوة، يُجبِر، يُميت، يطرح (رياضيات)، يُكلّف (الثمن)، يأخذ للاستعمال، يمتص، يختفي، يُبعد AALD: tābalu (s.) الارض الجافة Note: Southern Iraq accent: *tibilla* تبلّة rope harness used to clime palm trees	تبل (لسان العرب)
427	*nu-bal-li-ia*	131^{T1}	ePSD: nahbalu esad [TRAP] wr. ^{ĝeš}es$_2$-ad Akk. nahbalu	نبل (لسان العرب)
428	*nu-bat-ta*	302^{T11}	See also *i-nam-bu-ṭa* See also *ú-rid* AALD: nubattu (adv.; n.) (nabattu?) المساء، وقت المساء، إقامة	نوب (الصّحّاح في اللغة) النَّوْبُ (القاموس المحيط) نوب (لسان العرب) ورد (لسان العرب)

			مؤقتة، البقاء طوال الليل، ليلة، عشية الوليمة، ليلة الاحتفال AALD: nubtu (s.) النحلة العسّالة	
429	NUMUN	27T11	See *ze-ru-tum* ePSD: numun numun [GRASS] wr. $^{u}{}_{2}$numun$_2$; $^{u}{}_{2}$|ZI&ZI|; šu-mu; $^{u}{}_{2}$|A.ZI&ZI|; $^{u}{}_{2}$|ZI&ZI.A|; $^{u}{}_{2}$|ZI&ZI.EŠ$_2$.ŠE|; šu-mu-un Akk. elpetu numun [INSECT] wr. numun$_3$ Akk. kalmatu; nāpû numun [SEED] wr. numun Akk. zēru	نوم (لسان العرب) نعم (لسان العرب) الانعام 141-143 (قرآن)
430	*nu-ru-ub*	126T11	See also *né-re-bé-e-ti* ePSD: narābu kid [SOFTEN] wr. kid$_7$ Akk. narābu tuk [BREAK] wr. tuk$_x$(|IM.KAD$_3$|) Akk. karāşu; nakāsu; naqāru; narābu AALD: nurbu (s.) (see narābu) النقطة الرّطبة، طري، الجزء الرطب؛ معنى غير معروف AALD: narābu (v.) يصبح رطبا، نديا، مريحا، ناعما؛ يُميع، يُسيل، يُلين	نرب (مقاييس اللغة) نرب (لسان العرب)
431	*nu-uḫ-šam-ma*	43T11	AALD: nuḫšu (adj.) (naḫāšu) وَفرة، كَثرة، انتعاش	النَّحْسُ (القاموس المحيط) نحس (الصّحّاح في اللغة) نحس (العباب الزاخر) نحس (لسان العرب) نهش (لسان العرب) نهس (لسان العرب) نخس (العباب الزاخر) نَخَسَ (القاموس المحيط) نخس (لسان العرب)
432	*nu-us-su* *ú-ni-iš-šú-ma* *ú-ni-is-su-ma* *nu-uš-šá-šú* *i-na-aš-šam-ma* *i-na-šá-a* *na-áš* *na-a-ši* *na-ši* *na-ši* *na-ši* *na-ši-ma*	250T1 9P 9P 9P 315T11 315T11 143T11 143T11 50T11 51T11 55T11 204T11	See also *ni-is-sa-tu* See also *áš-ši-šu-ma* ePSD: našû gaĝ [CARRY] wr. gaĝ$_x$(IL$_2$); ga-aĝ$_3$ Akk. našû gur [LIFT] wr. gur$_3$-ru; guru$_3$; gur; gur$_{17}$; guru$_6$ Akk. našû; nāšû il [RAISE] wr. il$_2$; il$_5$; il$_2^{li}_2$ Akk. našû ePSD: nasû asilal [DISTANT] wr. asilal Akk. duppuru; nasû ePSD: enšu hunu [WEAK] wr. hu-nu; hu-hu-nu Akk. enšu; hašāru AALD: nussusu (v.) (nuzzuzu, nuššušu) ينوس، ينثر الشعر، يهزّ الذيل، يصفّق الاجنحة، يهزّ الطفل AALD: nâšu (pron.) (niāšim, niāši, nâšu, nayāš) الينا، لنا AALD: nāšiānu (s.) see našû (المُرحَل) الشخص المنقول	حنص (لسان العرب) نصص (لسان العرب) نص (مقاييس اللغة) حَنَصَ (القاموس المحيط) النَّيْصُ (القاموس المحيط) نيص (لسان العرب) نوص (لسان العرب) نضض (لسان العرب) نوش (لسان العرب) نشش (لسان العرب) نسأ (لسان العرب) نسس (لسان العرب) نسس (العباب الزاخر) نس (مقاييس اللغة) نوس (لسان العرب) نوس (مقاييس اللغة) النَّسُّ (القاموس المحيط)
433	PA-*ad-di-'-i*	265T10	See also *pa-a-šú* *See also ḫad^{ad}-di-'-i* ePSD: PA sag [BEAT] wr. sag$_3$; sag$_2$ Akk. mahāşu	PA فأ (مقاييس اللغة) فا (لسان العرب) PA-*ad-di-'-i*

			sag [SCATTER] wr. sag$_2$; sag$_3$; sag$_7$ Akk. dâku; nasāku; nêru; sapāhu ePSD: PA PA [POUCH] wr. PA$_5$ ad-di-'-i see i-du-ú	فَدَاهُ (القاموس المحيط) فدي (مقاييس اللغة) فدى (الصّحَاح في اللغة) فدي (لسان العرب)
434	*pa-as-su*	50^{T11}	ePSD: pāšu giĝ [AX] wr. giĝ$_4$; ^{urud}giĝ$_4$ "ax, adze" Akk. pāšu tun [AX] wr. ^{urud}tun$_3$; tun$_3$ "ax, adze" Akk. pāšu	فأس (لسان العرب)
435	*pa-a-šú* *pi-i* *pi-i*	122^{T1} 295^{T1} 205^{T11}	See also *KÁ* ePSD: pû kag [MOUTH] wr. ka Akk. pû murub [MIDDLE] wr. murub$_6$; murub$_4$; murub$_2$; murub; murub$_3$ Akk. abullu; birītu; bişşūru; pinku; pû; qablu; qinnatu; ûru pu [MOUTH] wr. pu$_3$ Akk. pû AALD: pû (pā'u, pī'u) الفم، القرار، الامر، الاعتراف، وجهة التظر	الفاءُ (القاموس المحيط) فيأ (لسان العرب) فأ (مقاييس اللغة) فا (لسان العرب) فوه (لسان العرب) الفاهُ (القاموس المحيط) فوه (الصّحَاح في اللغة)
436	*pag-ri-šú* *pa-gar-šú* *pa-gar-šú*	49^{T1} 199^{T1} 251^{T11}	See also *şa-lam* ePSD: pagru adda [CORPSE] wr. adda; adda$_2$; ad$_x$(|LU$_2$@s×BAD|); ad$_x$(|BAD.LU$_2$|); ad$_x$(|LU$_2$×GAM|); ad$_x$(|LU$_2$@s|); $^{a-da}$adda$_x$(|LU$_2$@g.UŠ$_2$|) Akk. pagru; šalamtu	فقر (لسان العرب)
437	*pa-ni* *pa-nu-šú* *pa-ni-ka* *pa-an* *pa-an* *pa-an* *pa-ni* *pa-nu* *pa-nu-šá* *pa-nu-šú* *pa-nu-u-a* *pa-nu-ú-a* *pa-na-su* *pa-na-as-su*	31^{T1} 116^{T1} 138^{T1} 218^{T10} 285^{T10} 314^{T10} 314^{T10} 314^{T10} 314^{T10} 314^{T10} 254^{T10} 254^{T10} 250^{T11} 250^{T11}	See *IGI* ePSD: pānû igi [FACE] wr. igi; i-bi$_2$; igi$_3$; i-gi Akk. mahrum; pānû	فني (لسان العرب) فانٍ (القاموس المحيط) فنن (الصّحَاح في اللغة) فنن (لسان العرب) الفَنُّ (القاموس المحيط) فنس (العباب الزاخر) الفَنَسُ (القاموس المحيط) فنس (لسان العرب)
438	*pa-rak-ki*	5^{U}	ePSD: parakku barag [DAIS] wr. barag; bara$_{10}$; bara$_6$; bara$_7$; bara$_8$ Akk. parakku; šarru; šubtu	فَرَقَ (القاموس المحيط) فرق (مقاييس اللغة) فرق (لسان العرب) فرك (لسان العرب) فرك (مقاييس اللغة)
439	*par-şi*	44^{T1}	See also *pu-ri-su* ePSD: parşu biluda [RITUALS] wr. biluda; bi$_3$-lu$_5$-da; bi-lu-da$_{10}$; pi-lu$_8$-da Akk. parşu; pilludû ĝarza [RITES] wr. ĝarza; mar-za; ĝarza$_2$ Akk. parşu unugi [RITES] wr. unugi Akk. parşu	فرص (مقاييس اللغة) فَرْصَةُ (القاموس المحيط) المَقْلُ (القاموس المحيط) فرص (لسان العرب) فرض (لسان العرب)

440	*pár-si-gu*	257[T11]	AALD: parsīgu (see barasigû and paršīgu) AALD: parsikku (see paršīgu) AALD: paršīgu (s.) الحزام، الوشاح (يستعمل احيانا لتزيين الرأس)	الفِرْسِقُ (القاموس المحيط) البُرْزَجُ (القاموس المحيط) زأبِر (لسان العرب) الخَزُّ (القاموس المحيط) القُرْطَقُ (القاموس المحيط) قرطق (لسان العرب)
441	*pe-et-tim-ma*	230[T11]	See also *pi-te-ma* ePSD: pēmtum <u>udub</u> [COAL] wr. u$_3$-dub$_2$; udub Akk. pēmtum AALD: pēntu (s.) (pēmtu) الفحم النباتي، الجذور	فتي (لسان العرب)
442	*per-ti-šú*	60[T1]	AALD: pertu (pirtu) (s.f) الشعر	فرا (لسان العرب)
443	*pi-ḫe* *pe-ḫi-i* *lip-ḫu-ú*	89[T11] 95[T11] 263[T10]	ePSD: pehû <u>du</u> [SPREAD] wr. du$_8$ Akk. epû; labānu; pehû <u>henzer</u> [BLOCK] wr. henzir Akk. pehû AALD: pehû (v.; adj.) يعيقُ، يسدّ، يغلف، يحجز، يخزن سرا، يطيّن، يغلق، يكسو، يلحمُ؛ مسدود، مغلق	حنز (لسان العرب) فيح (لسان العرب) فهه (لسان العرب) البَخْوُ (القاموس المحيط) الفَحَا (القاموس المحيط) بزر (الصّحّاح في اللغة) فحا (الصّحّاح في اللغة) فحا (لسان العرب)
444	*piš-šá-ti*	76[T11]	See *up-piš* See *ABZU* ePSD: piššatu <u>iba</u> [RATION] wr. i$_3$-ba Akk. piššatu ePSD: pištu <u>in</u> [ABUSE] wr. in; e-mu Akk. pištu <u>u</u> [ABUSE] wr. u Akk. pištu	فثث (لسان العرب) فسس (لسان العرب) فصا (الصّحّاح في اللغة) فصأ (لسان العرب) فصص (لسان العرب)
445	*pi-til-ta*	54[T11]	ePSD: pitiltu <u>šusar</u> [STRING] wr. šu-sar; ^{urud}šu-sar Akk. pitiltu	فتل (لسان العرب)
446	*pi-tir* *pi-ti-ir*	22[T1] 23[T1]	ePSD: pitru <u>hirim</u> [DITCH] wr. hirim Akk. ittû; miţru; pitru AALD: pitru (s.) المنطقة الخالية	البَتْرُ (القاموس المحيط) بتر (لسان العرب) فتر (مقاييس اللغة) فتر (لسان العرب) نصف (مقاييس اللغة)
447	*pu-ri-di-šú*	57[T1] 210[T11]	See also *pu-ri-su* ePSD: purīdu <u>pah</u> [LEG] wr. pah Akk. purīdu AALD: purīdu (S) (piīdu, puriddu) الرجل ، قياس ثُلث الذراع	برد (لسان العرب) الفَرْدُ (القاموس المحيط) فرد (الصّحّاح في اللغة) فرد (مقاييس اللغة) فرد (لسان العرب)
448	*pu-ri-su* *pi-riš-ti* *ap-ta-ra-as-si* *ap-ta-ra-as-su* *ap-ta-ra-as* *pa-ri-su* *pi-riš-ti* *pi-riš-ti* *pa-ri-sa*	56[T1] 10[T11] 62[T11] 62[T11] 63[T11] 65[T11] 196[T11] 197[T11] 276[T11]	See also *par-şi* See also *pu-ri-di-šú* See also *AD.ḪAL* ePSD: pirištu <u>hal</u> [DIVIDE] wr. hal-ha; ha-la; hal Akk. barû; halālu; nazālu; petû; pirištu; zâzu; šahālu <u>kiši</u> [SECRET] wr. kiši$_{12}$ Akk. pirištu <u>uraš</u> [SECRET] wr. uraš Akk. pirištu	برس (لسان العرب) الفَرَسُ (القاموس المحيط) فرس (الصّحّاح في اللغة) فرس (العباب الزاخر) فرس (لسان العرب)

			ePSD: pirsānu <u>tuba</u> [UNMNG] wr. tuba$_3$ Akk. pirsānu ePSD: pursû <u>burzi</u> [BOWL] wr. bur-zi Akk. pursû AALD: pirsu (s.) (see parāsu) الفصل، القطع، القسمة AALD: parāsu (v.) يقطع، يسد، يصد، يخمد، يعيق، يوقف، يوزع، يحصص، يقسم اعداد، ينسحب، ينسحب، يبتعد، يفطم، يصدر حكما، يتخذ قرارا، يحقق، يعتني، يقرر، AALD: parīsu (s.) (parissu, parrisu; parāsu) (pl. parīsātu) الوتد، الخازوق، لوح خشبي ثخين AALD: parīsu (s.) (see parāsu)مقياس حجم = نصف كور، اناء	
449	*pu-uḫ-ḫu-rat* *paḫ-ru* *paḫ-ri* *i-pa-aḫ-ḫur* *pu-ḫur* *ip-taḫ-ru* *ú-paḫ-ḫa-rak-kúm-ma*	252^{T1} 278^{T1} 278^{T1} 49^{T11} 120^{T11} 163^{T11} 207^{T11}	ePSD: pahāru <u>NINDAMEKAR</u> [UNMNG] wr. |NINDA$_2$×ME+GAN$_2$@t| "?" Akk. pahāru; redû ša kiškattê <u>bahar</u> [POTTER] wr. bahar$_2$; bahar$_3$; bahar; bahar$_4$; LAK742; LAK747 Akk. pahāru <u>dul</u> [GATHER] wr. du$_6$-ul Akk. pahāru <u>gu kin</u> [GATHER] wr. gu$_3$ kin; gu$_3$ kin$_5$ Akk. pahāru <u>gu si</u> [ASSEMBLE] wr. gu$_2$ si Akk. pahāru <u>šugalanzu</u> [POTTER] wr. šu-gal-an-zu Akk. pahāru ePSD: puhru <u>dagan</u> [TOTALITY] wr. da-gan Akk. kullatu; puhru; riksu <u>kilib</u> [TOTAL] wr. kilib; kilib$_3$ Akk. napharu; puhru <u>puhrum</u> [ASSEMBLY] wr. pu-uh$_2$-ru-um; pu-uh$_3$-ru-um; pu-uh$_2$-rum; pu-uh-ru-um; pu-hu-ru-um Akk. puhru <u>unkin</u> [ASSEMBLY] wr. unkin; LAK649 Akk. puhru	فهر (لسان العرب) فهر (مقاييس اللغة) زيم (مقاييس اللغة) فخر (لسان العرب) فخر (مقاييس اللغة) فخز (لسان العرب)
450	*pu-uk-ku* *pu-uk-ki-šú* *pu-uk-ki* *i-pu-uk-ki*	66^{T1} 66^{T1} 83^{T1} 83^{T1}	See also *at-ta-bak* ePSD: pukku <u>ellag</u> [BALL] wr. ^{ĝeš}ellag Akk. pukku <u>hal</u> [STICK] wr. hal Akk. pukku <u>illar</u> [BALL] wr. ^{ĝeš}illar; illar Akk. pukku	بوك (لسان العرب) بكّ (مقاييس اللغة) بكك (لسان العرب) فك (مقاييس اللغة) فكك (لسان العرب) فوق (لسان العرب)
451	*pu-ut* *pu-ut* *pu-ut* *pu-ut* *pu-ut* *pūt* *pūt* *pu-ti* *pu-ut-ni-ma*	114^{T1} 115^{T1} 128^{T1} 155^{T1} 171^{T1} 123^{T1} 150^{T1} 12^{P} 202^{T11}	ePSD: pûtu <u>saĝki</u> [FOREHEAD] wr. saĝ-ki Akk. pûtu	فوت (لسان العرب) فوت (مقاييس اللغة)
452	*pu-uṭ-ṭe-er* *pu-uṭ-ṭe-er?*	23^{U} 25^{T1}	ePSD: paṭāru <u>duh</u> [LOOSEN] wr. duh; ze$_2$-eb Akk. paṭāru <u>tar</u> [CUT] wr. tar; tar^{ar} Akk. harāṣu; parāsu; paṭāru; sapāhu	فطر (مقاييس اللغة) الفَطْرُ (القاموس المحيط) فطر (لسان العرب) بطر (لسان العرب)
453	*pu-zu-ur* *ú-pa-az-zi-ru* *ip-zi-ru-nim*	44^{T11} 70^{T11} 6^{P}	ePSD: puzru <u>a'ur</u> [ARMPIT] wr. a$_2$-ur$_2$ Akk. puzru <u>gira</u> [CONCEALMENT] wr. gira Akk. puzru; šamû <u>puzur</u> [SECRET] wr. puzur$_4$; puzur$_5$; puzur; puzur$_2$	بزر (مقاييس اللغة) البَزْرُ (القاموس المحيط) بزر (لسان العرب) فزر (الصّحَاح في اللغة)

			Akk. puzru	فزر (مقاييس اللغة) فزر (لسان العرب) فرز (لسان العرب)
454	*qa-bal-tú* *qá-bal-ti* *qab-li* *qab-la*	179[T1] 179[T1] 111[T11] 131[T11]	See also *MURUB₄-šá* ePSD: qablu gu'ana [BATTLE] wr. guana Akk. qablu ib [HIPS] wr. ib_2 Akk. qablu murub [MIDDLE] wr. $murub_6$; $murub_4$; $murub_2$; murub; $murub_3$ Akk. abullu; birītu; biṣṣūru; pinku; pû; qablu; qinnatu; ûru sabad [BATTLE] wr. $sabad_2$; $sabad_3$; sad_2 Akk. qablu šab [HIPS] wr. šab Akk. qablu šen [BATTLE] wr. šen Akk. qablu; šašmu ula [BATTLE] wr. ula_2 Akk. qablu AALD: qablu (S.) الوسط؛ المركز	قبل (مقاييس اللغة) قبل (الصّحاح في اللغة) قَبْلُ (القاموس المحيط)
455	*qa-na* *qa-na* *qanê* *qin-nu* *ni-qan-na-nu*	56[T1] 36[U] 160[T10] 309[T10] 309[T10]	See also GI ePSD: qanû gi [REED] wr. gi Akk. qanû ePSD: qinnatu murub [MIDDLE] wr. $murub_6$; $murub_4$; $murub_2$; murub; $murub_3$ Akk. abullu; birītu; biṣṣūru; pinku; pû; qablu; qinnatu; ûru AALD: qanānu (v.) يعشعش؛ يؤسس بيتا، منزلا w/qinnu يبني عشا AALD: qanīnu (s.) العش، المأوى AALD: qanû (v.) يشتري، يتطلب، يحافظ AALD: qanû (s.) المهنة AALD: qanû (s.) القصب، الانبوب، السهم، قطعة الارض AALD: qannu (s.) حظيرة المواشي؛ المشرف على المواشي AALD: qinnu (s.) عش الطير، القرابة، العشيرة، العائلة AALD: qinītu (s.) (see qanû) الاكتساب، الممتلكات؛ الزوجة السرية، الزوجة ذات المرتبة الثانية AALD: qinnatu (s.) الشرج، المؤخرة AALD: qinniš (adv.) عكسي، خلفي	قنن (لسان العرب) القِنْوَةُ (القاموس المحيط) قنا (مقاييس اللغة) قنا (لسان العرب)
456	*qaq-qa-šú*	257[T11]	See also *SAG.DU* ePSD: qaqqadu saĝ [HEAD] wr. saĝ Akk. qaqqadu; rēšu saĝdu [HEAD] wr. saĝ-du; saĝdu Akk. qaqqadu ugu [SKULL] wr. ugu_2; ugu; ugu_3; ugu_x(|U.SAG|); ugu_x(|A.U.KA|); ugu_x(SAG@n@g) Akk. eli; muhhu; qaqqadu	القُوقُ (القاموس المحيط) قوق (لسان العرب)
457	*qar-du* *qu-ra-du* *qu-ra-di* *qu-ra-di* *qu-ra-du*	30[T1] 103[T1] 77[T1] 92[T1] 16[T11]	ePSD: qardu gardu [SOLDIER] wr. gar_3-du Akk. qardu	كرد (لسان العرب) قرد (لسان العرب) القَرَدُ (القاموس المحيط)
458	*qātī-ia*	132[T1]	ePSD: qātu	قتث (لسان العرب)

	iq-ti *qa-ti-ia-ma* *qa-tu-ú* *uq-ta-at-tu-ú*	258^{T10} 200^{T11} 214^{T10} 252^{T11}	silig [HAND] wr. silig$_2$; silig$_4$ Akk. lupnu; qātu; rittu šu [HAND] wr. šu; sum$_5$; šu-x Akk. qātu tibir [HAND] wr. tibir; tibir$_2$; tibir$_4$; tibir$_3$ "hand; fist" Akk. qātu; rittu; upnu ePSD: qatû til [COMPLETE] wr. til; til$_3$ Akk. gamāru; labāru; qatû zal [PASS] wr. zal Akk. naharmumu; naharmuţu; qatû; râbu	قتت (لسان العرب) قثا (لسان العرب) قوت (لسان العرب) القَتْوُ (القاموس المحيط) القَتُّ (القاموس المحيط) قتا (لسان العرب)
459	*qé-bé-ri*	236^{T10}	ePSD: qebēru ki tum [BURY] wr. ki tum$_2$ Akk. qebēru šu gur [ROLL UP] wr. šu gur Akk. qarāru; qebēru ePSD: qabru irigal [UNDERWORLD] wr. irigal; iri-gal; urugal$_2$ Akk. erşetu; qabru	قبر (لسان العرب)
460	*qé-e*	13^{T1}	See also *KÁ* See also *GÚ* ePSD: qû gu [CORD] wr. gu Akk. qû gunu [FLAX] wr. gu-nu Akk. qû sila [UNIT] wr. sila$_3$ Akk. mīšertu; qû zabar [BRONZE] wr. zabar; zabar$_3$ Akk. ebbu; hutpu; kakku; mušālu; namru; qû; sappu; siparru	قها (الصّحّاح في اللغة) قوا (لسان العرب) قيأ (لسان العرب)
461	*qí-iš-tim*	292^{T10}	ePSD: qiāšu ba [ALLOT] wr. ba Akk. qiāšu; zâzu šubarzi [PRESENT] wr. šu-bar-zi Akk. qiāšu	
462	*qud-du-ši*	12^{T1}	ePSD: qadištu lukur [PRIESTESS] wr. lukur Akk. nadītu; qadištu nugig [PRIESTESS] wr. nu-gig; nu-u$_8$-gig; mu-gi$_{17}$-ib; mu-gib$_3$ Akk. qadištu	قدس (لسان العرب)
463	*qù-du-du*	213^{T10}	ePSD: qadādu gurum [BEND] wr. gurum; gur$_8$; gur; gurum$_x$(GURUN) Akk. kanāšu; kanānu; kapāpu; qadādu	قدد (الصّحّاح في اللغة)
464	*qu-lip-ti* *qu-lip-tum*	307^{T11}	ePSD: qalāpu bar [OUTSIDE] wr. bar; ba-ra; bala; bur Akk. būdum; kabattu; kawûm; ahû; warkatu; qalāpu; salātu; šalāqu zil [BOIL] wr. zil Akk. qalāpu; salāqu	قلف (مقاييس اللغة) القِلْفُ (القاموس المحيط) قلف (الصّحّاح في اللغة) قلف (لسان العرب)
465	*qul-ti* *i-qul-ma* *i-qu-ul-ma* *lu-qul* *lu-qul*	104^{T1} 118^{T1} 118^{T1} 134^{T11} 244^{T10}	ePSD: qâlu me ĝar [MAKE SILENT] wr. me ĝar Akk. qâlu ePSD: qūlu me [SILENCE] wr. me Akk. qūlu niĝmeĝar [SILENCE] wr. niĝ$_2$-me-ĝar Akk. qūlu AALD: *qalālu (v.) يقلّ، يصبح قليلا، ضعيفا، خفيفا AALD: qallu (adj.) (qālu) (see qalālu) خفيف، من قيمة قليلة، صغير، قليل AALD: qallu (s.) see qalālu: العبد AALD: qâlu (v.) يصبح ساكنا، يبقى هادئا، يكون غافلا عن، غير منتبه، ينتبه، يلتفت الى، يصغي، يستمع الى AALD: qâlu (v.) (qiālu) (see qīlu adj.) 1) معنى غير معروف (2	قلل (لسان العرب) القُلُّ (القاموس المحيط) قهل (مقاييس اللغة) قول (لسان العرب) عقل (لسان العرب)

			qullu معنى غير معروف AALD: qīlu (adj.) منبطح؟، ميال الى؟، منكب؟	
466	*qu-um-mu-ú*	217[T10]	ePSD: qalû bil [BURN] wr. bil_2; bil_3; bil Akk. qalû niĝsasa [BURNING] wr. $ni\hat{g}_2$-sa-sa Akk. qalqallu; maqlû; qalû sa [ROAST] wr. sa Akk. qalû AALD: qummû see qu'û AALD: qammû (adj.) محمّص AALD: qammû (v.) يحرق، يشعل، يطحن، يحرش، يتلف (الاعداء) بالنار، يمحق، يُبطِل	قمي (لسان العرب) قمم (لسان العرب) قمأ (لسان العرب)
467	*ra*	38[U]	ePSD: RA ri [IMPOSE] wr. RI; ru Akk. bâ'u; emēdu; nadû; nasāku; ramû; rehû; tarû; wašaru	رعع (لسان العرب) رأي (لسان العرب) ريا (لسان العرب)
468	*ra-a-du*	129[T11]	See also *šá-a-ru* ePSD: rādu aĝar [RAINSHOWER] wr. $a\hat{g}ar_5$; $a\hat{g}ar_6$ Akk. rādu	رأد (مقاييس اللغة) رأد (الصَحّاح في اللغة) رأد (لسان العرب) رعد (مقاييس اللغة) رعد (لسان العرب)
469	*ra-a-ṭa* *ra-a-ṭa* *ra-a-ṭu*	288[T11] 316[T11]	ePSD: rāţu kuš [CHANNEL] wr. $ku\check{s}_3$ Akk. rāţu paršita [CHANNEL] wr. pa_5-$\check{s}ita_3$ Akk. rāţu šitan [WATER-CHANNEL] wr. $\check{s}ita_3$ Akk. rāţu	رَاطَ (القاموس المحيط) ورط (مقاييس اللغة) روط (العباب الزاخر) ريط (لسان العرب)
470	*ra-bé-e*	77[T11]	ePSD: ereb šamši utušuš [SUNSET] wr. utu-$\check{s}u_2$-uš; utu-$\check{s}u\check{s}_2$ Akk. ereb šamši	ربع (لسان العرب) ربي/أ (مقاييس اللغة)
471	*rab-ṣu*	116[T11]	See also *ra-pa-áš* ePSD: rabāşu šed [LIE] wr. $\check{s}e_{21}$; $\check{s}e_x(NA_2)$ Akk. itūlu; rabāşu	ربص (لسان العرب)
472	*ra-bu-tum* *ra-bu-ti*	232[T1] 232 [T1]	See also *ir-bu-ú* See also *né-re-bé-e-ti*	ربا (لسان العرب) ربب (لسان العرب)
473	*rag-ga-at* *i-rag-gi-ig-ki*	220[T11]	ePSD: raggu NERU [ENEMY] wr. NE.RU Akk. ayyābu; raggu luNERU [EVILDOER] wr. lu_2-NE.DU; lu_2-NE.RU Akk. raggu; ayyābu luniĝNERU [EVILDOER] wr. lu_2-$ni\hat{g}_2$-NE.RU Akk. raggu niĝNERU [EVIL] wr. $ni\hat{g}_2$-NE.RU; $ni\hat{g}_2$-NE.EREN Akk. raggu	راجَ (القاموس المحيط) روج (لسان العرب) نفق (لسان العرب)
474	*ra-ma-ni* *ram-ni-ia*	255[T10] 313[T11]	See also *i-ru-um-ma* ePSD: ramānu mete [ONE'S OWN] wr. me-te; ni_2-te Akk. ramānu ni [SELF] wr. ni_2 Akk. ramānu	رأم (لسان العرب) رأم (مقاييس اللغة)
475	*ra-pa-áš* *ú-rap-pi-šu* *ru-pu-us-sa*	202[T1] 242[T1] 30[T11]	See also *i-rap-pu-da* ePSD: rupšu daĝal [WIDE] wr. daĝal; dam-gal; di-am-ga-al; da-ma-al Akk. rupšu ePSD: rapāšu	رفص (لسان العرب) ربس (لسان العرب) رفس (لسان العرب) ربض (لسان العرب)

			<u>tal</u> [BROAD] wr. tal$_2$ Akk. rapāšu ePSD: rapāsu <u>ĝeš rah</u> [BEAT] wr. ĝeš rah$_2$ Akk. rapāsu <u>rah</u> [BEAT] wr. rah$_2$; ra-ah Akk. dâku; diāšu; hepû; rahāşu; rapāsu AALD: rupšu (s.) see rapāšu العرض، جزء من النمو الهرمي للكبد؛ اللعاب، الرُضاب AALD: ripšu (s.) see ribšu AALD: ribšu (s,) (see rabāšu) الدعوى، الشكوى (الطعن بأمر ما)	
476	*ra-šub-bu*	37^{T1}	ePSD: rašubbatu <u>nihuš</u> [APPEARANCE] wr. ni$_2$-huš Akk. rašubbatu <u>sulim</u> [RADIANCE] wr. su-lim; su-li$_2$-im Akk. šalummatu; rašubbatu	رسب (لسان العرب) رسب (مقاييس اللغة)
477	*raṭ-bat*	226^{T11}	ePSD: raţbu <u>duru</u> [WET] wr. duru$_5$; duru$_5$^{ru} Akk. labāku; raţbu	رطب (مقاييس اللغة) الرَّطْبُ (القاموس المحيط) رطب (لسان العرب)
478	*re-ba-a*	145^{T11}		
479	*re-e-šú* *re-ši-šú*	64^{T1} 221^{T11}	ePSD: rēšu <u>saĝ</u> [HEAD] wr. saĝ Akk. qaqqadu; rēšu	الشَّوْقُ (القاموس المحيط) شقق (لسان العرب) شهق (لسان العرب) رأس (لسان العرب) رأي (لسان العرب) ريا (لسان العرب)
480	*rig-ma-šú* *rig-mu* *ir/š-tag-gu-um*	306^{T10} 15^{U} 99^{T11}	See also *ir-tam-ma-am-ma* ePSD: rigmu <u>ad</u> [VOICE] wr. Ad Akk. rigmu <u>akkil</u> [NOISE] wr. Akkil; akkil$_2$ Akk. ikkillu; rigmu; tanūqātu; šīsu <u>ašša</u> [LAMENTATION] wr. Ašša$_2$ Akk. ikkillu; rigmu <u>gu</u> [VOICE] wr. Gu$_3$ Akk. rigmu <u>mumun</u> [NOISE] wr. Mu$_7$-mu$_7$ Akk. ramīmu; rigmu <u>šeg</u> [VOICE] wr. Še; šeg$_{10}$; šeg$_x$(|KA×KID$_2$|); šeg$_x$(|KA×LI|); šed$_{15}$; šeg$_{12}$ "voice, cry, noise" Akk. rigmu <u>teš</u> [VOICE] wr. Te-eš Akk. rigmu <u>u</u> [BELLOW] wr. U$_4$ Akk. nagāgu; rigmu <u>zipaĝ</u> [BREATH] wr. Za-pa-aĝ$_2$; zi-pa-aĝ$_2$ Akk. napištu; rigmu	رجم (مقاييس اللغة) رجم (لسان العرب)
481	*ri-i-mu*	30^{T1}	See also *AM* ePSD: rīmu <u>am</u> [BULL] wr. am Akk. rīmu <u>gudam</u> [BULL] wr. gud-am Akk. rīmu <u>piriĝ</u> [LION] wr. piriĝ; piriĝ$_3$; bi$_2$-ri-iĝ$_3$; ^{ĝeš}piriĝ; piriĝ$_2$ Akk. lû; lābu; nēšu; rīmu <u>Note:</u> stag, elk, antelope, deer, gazelle, ram:بقر الوحش، ظبي	ريم (لسان العرب)
482	*ri-ma-niš*	64^{T1}	See *ri-i-mu* See *nu-us-su*	

			Note: *ri-ma-niš* = *ri-ma+niš*	
483	*ri-šá-tum* *ri-šá-a-ti*	231^{T1}	ePSD: rīšātu asilala [JOY] wr. asila; asil-la$_2$; asil$_3$-la$_2$; asila$_3$; si$_{11}$-le$_2$; sila; asila$_x$(|EZEN×KASKAL|); asil$_x$(EZEN)-la$_2$; asil$_x$(EZEN)-le$_2$ Akk. ašilalû; ebēru; riāšu; rīšātu lib [RICH] Akk. hadû; hidiātu; râšu; rāšû; rīšātu ePSD: rišātu niĝmeĝar [JUBILATION] wr. niĝ$_2$-me-ĝar Akk. išdihu; rišātu	رشأ (الصّحّاح في اللغة) رشأ (لسان العرب) رشا (لسان العرب) ريس (مقاييس اللغة) ريس (لسان العرب)
484	*ru-ù'-ú-šú*	66^{T1}	ePSD: ru'u dusa [FRIEND] wr. du$_{10}$-us$_2$-sa; du$_{10}$-sa; du-us$_2$-sa; du$_2$-us$_2$-sa Akk. ru'u	رعي (لسان العرب) روع (لسان العرب)
485	*ru-uq-ta* *ru-ú-qí* *ru-ú-qa* *ru-qu-tu* *ru-uq-ti* *ru-ú-qí*	9^{T1} 42^{T1} 42^{T1} 300^{T10} 7^{P} 205^{T11}	See also *a-ni-ḫ* ePSD: rêqu sud [DISTANT] wr. sud; su$_3$-ud Akk. nesû; rêqu ePSD: nesû bad [OPEN] wr. bad; ba; be$_2$ Akk. be'ēšû; nesû; petû bul [BLOW] wr. bul$_4$; bul; bun; bul$_5$ Akk. edēpu; našāpu; nesû ri [DISTANT] wr. ri Akk. nesû sil [SPLIT] wr. si-il; zil; sil$_x$(|EZEN×LAL$_2$|); sil$_5$ Akk. nesû; šalātu sud [DISTANT] wr. sud; su$_3$-ud Akk. nesû; rêqu ePSD: nasû asilal [DISTANT] wr. asilal Akk. duppuru; nasû AALD: rūqu (adj) (f. rūqtu) 1) مسافة، بعد، بعيد جدا 2) مسافة (في الوقت) 3) لا يُختَرَق (متحجّر)، لا يُسبرُ غورُه، مُتعذر فهمُه AALD: nesû (v.) (našû, nasā'u) يتوقف (عن التقدم)، ينسحب، يغادر، يتراجع، ينكص، يَنفي، يهجر، يُبقي بعيدا، يُقصي AALD: nesû (adj.) (našû) بعيد، مسافة، عن بعد، متروع، منقول AALD: našû (v.) يرفع AALD: našû (adj.) مقام، مرفوع	نزو (مقاييس اللغة) نشأ (لسان العرب) نسأ (لسان العرب) نسا (لسان العرب) رقا (لسان العرب) الرَّوْكَةُ (القاموس المحيط) رقق (لسان العرب) روق (مقاييس اللغة) روق (الصّحّاح في اللغة) الرَّوْقُ (القاموس المحيط) روق (لسان العرب) ريق (لسان العرب)
486	*šá* *šú*		ePSD: ša lu [PERSON] wr. lu$_2$; mu-lu; mu-lu$_2$; lu$_{10}$; lu$_6$ Akk. amēlu; ša	ذ (لسان العرب) ذا (الصّحّاح في اللغة) ذا (لسان العرب) ذو (القاموس المحيط)
487	*ŠÀ* *SA.^{MEŠ}-ka*	148^{T1} 299^{T10}	See also *lib-bi-šú* See also *ši-ir-a-ni-ia* ePSD: ŠA šag [HEART] wr. šag$_4$; ša; ša$_3$-ab Akk. libbu ePSD: sa sa [SINEW] (68x: Old Babylonian) wr. sa Akk. dāmu; erru; matnu; pitnu	شأي (لسان العرب) سأي (لسان العرب)
488	*ṣa-a-a-du* *ṣa-a-a-du* *ṣa-a-a-du* *ṣa-a-a-di*	113^{T1} 116^{T1} 131^{T1} 162^{T1}	ePSD: ṣâdu niĝin [ENCIRCLE] wr. niĝin$_2$; niĝin Akk. esēru; lawû; sahāru; târu; târu; sahāru; ṣâdu	صعد (لسان العرب) ضدد (لسان العرب) صدد (لسان العرب) صيد (لسان العرب)
489	šá-am-ḫa-ku-ma	4^{P}	See also ^{f}*šam-ḫat*	سمخ (مقاييس اللغة)

				سمخ (لسان العرب) شمخ (مقاييس اللغة) شمخ (لسان العرب) سمح (لسان العرب)
490	*šá-a-šú* *šá-a-šú* *šá-a-šú* *šá-a-ši* *šá-a-ši* *šá-a-ši*	114[T1] 129[T1] 159[T1] 144[T1] 165[T1] 60[T11]	See also *ka-a-ši* See also *áš-šú* Note: Adding šá لاشارة ومخاطبة الغائب šá-a-šú (أذو ذا) لهُمَ، ماله، الذي له، له šá-a-ši (أذي ذا) لِهِم، مالها، الذي لها، لها šá-a-šá (أذا ذا) لذَام، ما لذا، الذي لذا، لذا	
491	*šá-at*	3[P]	ePSD: šāt mūši ĝi'unak [NIGHT] wr. ĝi$_6$-u$_3$-na Akk. šāt mūši	سوع (لسان العرب)
492	*ṣabatma* *ṣa-bat* *iṣ-bat-ma* *iṣ-bat* *uṣ-ṣab-bi-tu$_4$* *uṣ-ṣab-bi-ta* *ṣu-bat*	15[T1] 138[T1] 143[T11] 200[T11] 244[T11] 244[T11] 258[T11]	See also *ṣu-ub-bu* ePSD: ṣabātu dab [SEIZE] wr. dab$_5$; dab; dab$_5$-dab$_5$; dab$_x$(|LAGAB×GUD|) Akk. sahāpu; tamāhu; kamû; ṣabātu	ضبط (لسان العرب) الصَّبْطُ (القاموس المحيط) سبط (لسان العرب) ضبب (لسان العرب) ضَبَثْه (القاموس المحيط) صوب (لسان العرب)
493	*šá-bu-lat* *šab-ba*	225[T11] 127[T11]	See also *kàt-ma* ePSD: šābulu ah [DRY] wr. ah$_3$ Akk. abālu; šābulu lah [DRY] wr. lah$_2$ Akk. šābulu	ذَبَلَ (القاموس المحيط) ذبل (لسان العرب) ذب (مقاييس اللغة) ذبب (لسان العرب)
494	*šá-du-um-ma* *šá-di-im-ma* *šá-du-ú* *šá-di-i*	174[T1] 243[T1] 19[P] 37[T9]	ePSD: šadû gabiri [MOUNTAIN] wr. ga-bi-ri Akk. šadû gin [MOUNTAIN] wr. gin$_3$ Akk. šadû iš [MOUNTAIN] wr. iš Akk. šadû kur [MOUNTAIN] wr. kur; Akk. erṣetu; mātu; šadû; šadû	سدد (لسان العرب) سدد (الصّحّاح في اللغة) سدا (لسان العرب) سأد (لسان العرب) صدد (لسان العرب) سعد (لسان العرب) صعد (لسان العرب)
495	*SAG.DU*	257[T11]	See also *qaq-qa-šú* ePSD: saĝdu saĝdu [BEAM] wr. ^{ĝeš}saĝ-du; sag-du saĝdu [HEAD] wr. saĝ-du; saĝdu Akk. qaqqadu saĝdu [STONE] wr. $^{na}{}_4$saĝ-du	الصُّدْغُ (القاموس المحيط) سجد (لسان العرب)
496	*SAG.PA.LAGAB*	120[T1]	See also *ni-is-sa-tu* ePSD: SAG.PA saĝPA [POUCH] wr. saĝ-PA Akk. nēpeštu ePSD: SAG PA saĝ sag [TREMBLE] wr. saĝ sag$_3$ Akk. nakāpu ePSD: lagab lagab [BLOCK] wr. lagab; $^{na}{}_4$lagab Akk. upqu lagab [DEBT-NOTE] wr. lagab Akk. hišû lagab [EXCESS] wr. lagab Akk. atartu lagab [RAIL] wr. lagab Akk. kutlu	سغن (لسان العرب) سغل (لسان العرب) سغب (لسان العرب) لغب (لسان العرب) لجب (لسان العرب)
497	*šag-ga-šá-a* *šag-ga-a-šú*	179[T1] 179[T1]	ePSD: šagāšu gaz [KILL] wr. gaz; gaz$_2$; kaz$_8$ Akk. dâku; habātu; hašālu;	سجس (لسان العرب) شجذ (مقاييس اللغة)

	áš-gi-iš *liš-giš* *liš-giš*	72^{T11} 193^{T11} 195^{T11}	kaşāşu; pa'āşu; šagāšu ePSD: šaggāšu <u>sagaz</u> [ROBBER] wr. sa-gaz; sag-gaz " Akk. habbātu; šaggāšu ePSD: šagaštu <u>kilul</u> [MURDER] wr. ki-lul-la; ki-lul Akk. šagaštu	الشَّجْذَةُ (القاموس المحيط) شج (مقاييس اللغة) شجج (الصّحاح في اللغة) شجج (لسان العرب) سجا (الصّحاح في اللغة) سجا (لسان العرب) سجج (لسان العرب)
498	*šá-kin* *šá-kin* *ša-kin* *šá-kan* *taš-ku-nu* *taš-ku-nu* *taš-ku-nu* *taš-ku-nu* *liš-šá-kin-ma* *a-šak-ka-na* *a-šak-kan* *áš-kun* *áš-ku-un* *iš-ku-nu* *iš-šak-nu* *šak-nu* *iš-ta-kan* *iš-ta-kan* *lu-uš-kun* *ša-ak-na-ta-ma* *šak-na* *šak-nu* *ši-tak-ka-ni* *iš-tak-ka-ni* *šu-kun*	10^{T1} 228^{T1} 33^{U} 14^{T11} 188^{T11} 190^{T11} 192^{T11} 194^{T11} 193^{T11} 41^{T11} 41^{T11} 313^{T11} 313^{T11} 302^{T11} 317^{T11} 317^{T11} 148^{T1} 196^{T1} 245^{T11} 218^{T10} 128^{T1} 12^{T11} 221^{T11} 223^{T11} 138^{T1}	ePSD: šakānu <u>ĝal</u> [BE] wr. ĝal$_2$; ma-al; ${}^{ga}{}_2$gal$_2$ Akk. bašû; šakānu <u>ĝar</u> [PLACE] wr. ĝar; ĝa$_2$; ĝa$_2$-ar; ${}^{ĝa}{}_2$ĝar; ĝar^{ar}; mar; ${}^{ĝa}{}_2$ĝar^{ar} Akk. šakānu <u>sig</u> [PLACE] wr. sig$_9$; sig$_{10}$; si-ig Akk. šakānu	ثكن (مقاييس اللغة) ثكن (لسان العرب) دكن (لسان العرب) الدُّكْنَةُ (القاموس المحيط) دكن (مقاييس اللغة) سكن (الصّحاح في اللغة) سكن (لسان العرب)
499	*sa-ki-pu*	284^{T10}	ePSD: sakāpu <u>zag saga</u> [OVERTURN] wr. Zag saga$_{11}$ Akk. sakāpu; darāšu	سكف (لسان العرب)
500	*şa-lam* *şa-lam-šú* *şa-lim-tum*	49^{T1} 317^{T10} 98^{T11}	ePSD: şalmu <u>alan</u> [STATUE] wr. alan; ^{urud}alan Akk. şalmu <u>giggi</u> [BLACK] wr. giggi; gi$_6$-gi$_6$ Akk. şalmu ePSD: şulmu <u>mes</u> [BLACKNESS] wr. mes; ^{ĝeš}mes Akk. şulmu	ظلم (مقاييس اللغة) صلم (لسان العرب) صنم (لسان العرب)
501	*sa-me-ta-šu* *sa-me-ta-šá* *si-mat* *ši-ma-tú* *ši-im-ti-šú* *šim-ti* *ši-ma-tú* *šim-ti-šú-nu* *šá-mu-ut* *šá-mu-ut* *šá-mu-ut*	14^{T1} 14^{T1} 62^{T1} 222^{T1} 296^{T10} 320^{T10} 320^{T10} 320^{T10} 47^{T11} 88^{T11} 91^{T11}	See also *šum-šú* ePSD: simtu <u>mete</u> [APPROPRIATE THING] wr. me-te; te Akk. simtu <u>mete</u> [IMAGE] wr. me-te Akk. simtu ePSD: šimtu <u>zib</u> [MARK] wr. za$_3$; zib Akk. šimtu; şibbu ePSD:Akk. setu AALD: simtu (s.) السمة، الوجه، الشكل AALD: sīmtu (s.) (see šīmtu) الاجل	سمت (لسان العرب) سمت (مقاييس اللغة) السَّمْتُ (القاموس المحيط) دلل (لسان العرب) شيم (لسان العرب) شيم (مقاييس اللغة) وسم (لسان العرب)

			AALD: šīmtu (s.) عاقد العزم، القرار الالهي؛ المصير؛ الحظ، الحصة، المثير الشخصي؛ السلطة، الوصية، المثاق	
502	*šá-nu-'-ú-du* *ša-nu-'-ú-di*	29[T1] 16[U]	ePSD: nû'u guzal [SCOUNDREL] wr. gu_2-zal; gu_3-zal Akk. guzallu; ishappu; ahurrû; nû'u	نأد (لسان العرب) نأد (مقاييس اللغة)
503	*šá-pal* *šap-liš* *šap-li-šú-nu*	203[T1] 79[T11] 160[T11]	ePSD: šaplû ki [PLACE] wr. ki Akk. ašru; erşetu; mātu; qaqqaru; šaplû kita [LOWER] wr. ki-ta Akk. šaplû	سفل (الصّحّاح في اللغة) سفل (لسان العرب) ثفل (لسان العرب) ثفل (مقاييس اللغة)
504	*šap-ta-šú-nu*	127[T11]	ePSD: šaptu nundum [LIP] wr. nundum; šu-um-du-um Akk. šaptu tun [LIP] wr. tun_3 Akk. šaptu; suqtu	شف (مقاييس اللغة) الشَّفُّ (القاموس المحيط) شفف (لسان العرب) شفه (لسان العرب)
505	*šaq-qa-a*	58[T11]	AALD: sāqu (s.) جزء من الجسم AALD: šāqû (adj.) شاهق، عال، مرتفع، بارز، ناتئ، رفي، سام	شهق (لسان العرب)
506	*šá-qum-meš*	306[T11]	ePSD: šaqummatu ilim [RADIANCE] wr. i-lim Akk. šalummatu; šaqummatu išiu [SILENCE] wr. i-ši-u_5 Akk. šaqummatu lib [DAZED] wr. lib Akk. šaqummatu sig [SILENT] wr. si-ig; $šeg_5$ Akk. šaqummatu	سقم (لسان العرب)
507	*šár*	22[T1]	ePSD: *šár* šar [3600] (245x: ED IIIa, Ur III, Old Babylonian) wr. $šar_2$; šar; $šar_2$-$šar_2$ Akk. kiššatu; mâdu ePSD: šuššu šuš [SIXTH] wr. šuš Akk. šuššu AALD: šār (num.) (see šuššār) 1) 3600 2) المجموع الكلي.	سأر (لسان العرب) السُّؤْرُ (القاموس المحيط) السَّيْرُ (القاموس المحيط)
508	*šar-be*	217[T10]	šurīpu amagi [FROST] wr. amagi; $amagi_2$; $amagi_3$ "frost, ice" Akk. halpû; mammû; šurīpu halba [FROST] wr. $halba_2$; $halba_6$; halba; halpi "frost, ice, cold weather; (to be) cold" Akk. halpû; kuşşû; mammû; takşâtu; šurīpu šeg [FROST] wr. $šeg_9$; $šeg_4$ "snow; sleet; cold weather; frost, ice; burning, incineration; chills, shivers" Akk. šalgu; šurpu; šuruppû; šurīpu AALD: šarbum (s.) (sarbu, sarabu) الفصل الممطر، البارد (see šurīpu, šurīppu) AALD: šurīpu (s.) الجليد، الجماد	سرف (لسان العرب) السَّرْبُ (القاموس المحيط) سرب (لسان العرب) صرب (لسان العرب)
509	*šar-tu*	105[T1]	ePSD: šārtu munsub [HAIR] wr. munsub; $munsub_2$; $munsub_x$(|KA×SUHUR|); [su]munsub; [su]$munsub_2$; u_2-šu-p? Akk. šārtu; šārat zumri; gallābu	شعر (لسان العرب)
510	*šá-ru-uḫ* *šá-ru-ú /uḫ*	51[T1]	ePSD: šarhu sağtuku [SPLENDID] wr. sağ-tuku Akk. ašarēdu; šarhu	صرح (مقاييس اللغة) الصَّرْحُ (القاموس المحيط) سرح (لسان العرب) سرح (الصّحّاح في اللغة) السَّرْحُ (القاموس المحيط)
511	*se-bu-tum*	230[T11]	AALD: sebe (num) (seba) (f. sebet) سَبعة	سبع (لسان العرب)
512	*şe-eḫ-ret*	12[U]	See *şi-ri-ia*	صغر (مقاييس اللغة)

	li-ṣa-aḫ-ḫir *li-ṣa-aḫ-ḫir* *iṣ-ṣa-ḫir* *ṣu-uḫ-ri-ia-ma* *ṣe-eḫ-ri-ia-ma*	189[T11] 191[T11] 299[T11] 300[T11] 300[T11]	ePSD: ṣehērum tur [SMALL] wr. tur; tu Akk. ṣehērum ePSD: ṣehru banda [JUNIOR] wr. banda$_3$[da] Akk. ekdu; ṣehru genna [CHILD] wr. genna Akk. ṣehru; šerru ṣehrūtu zizna [WOMB] wr. zizna Akk. binītu; šassūru; ṣehrūtu	صغر (لسان العرب) الصّهْرُ (القاموس المحيط) صهر (الصّحّاح في اللغة) صهر (مقاييس اللغة) صهر (لسان العرب)
513	*še-er* *še-eri*	46[T11] 48[T11]	See also *uš-ta-aḫ-ri-ru* See also *UZU.*[MEŠ]*-šú-nu* See also *šèr-ri* See also *nim-ru*	
514	*še-me-šá* *še-me-šú* *i-šem-ma-a* *i-šem-me* *iš-me*	99[T1] 287[T11] 205[T1] 306[T10] 197[T11]	ePSD: šemû ĝeš tuku [LISTEN] wr. ĝeš tuku Akk. šemû	سمع (لسان العرب)
515	*še-ret-su* *še-ret-ka*	240[T1] 240[T1]	ePSD: šērtu šerda [CRIME] wr. šer$_7$-da; šer$_3$-da Akk. šērtu	شر (مقاييس اللغة) شرر (الصّحّاح في اللغة)
516	*še-riš* *še-riš* *še-ras* *šur-šum-me* *si-ri-šu*	69[T1] 86[T1] 86[T1] 272[T10] 73[T11]	See also *še-ret-su* ePSD: šuršu arina [ROOT] wr. e-ri$_2$-na; i$_3$-ri$_2$-na; erina$_8$; [ĝeš]arina; a-i$_3$-ri$_2$-na; [ĝeš]arina$_x$(|UR$_2$×A|)[na]; a-ri$_2$-na; a-ri$_8$-na; e-ri$_8$-na; i-ri$_8$-na; [ĝeš]arina$_x$(|I.LU$_2$@s.NA|); [ĝeš]arina$_x$(|LU$_2$@s.NA|) Akk. šuršu AALD: šuršummu (s.) (للجعة او الكحول) الحثالة، النفاية AALD: turšummum (s.) نوع من الكحول AALD: sarriš (adv.) (see sarāru) يغدُر، يخبُث	ضرس (مقاييس اللغة) ترس (لسان العرب) ترش (مقاييس اللغة) التَّرْشُ (القاموس المحيط) ترش (لسان العرب) سرس (لسان العرب) شرس (مقاييس اللغة) شرس (لسان العرب)
517	*šèr-ri*	255[T1]	See also *as-ḫur* ePSD: šerru bunga [CHILD] wr. bunga Akk. lagu; lakû; šerru genna [CHILD] wr. genna Akk. ṣehru; šerru henzer [CHILD] wr. henzer Akk. ašpaltu; la'û; lakû; šerru tur [CHILD] wr. tur Akk. šerru	سهر (مقاييس اللغة) سهر (لسان العرب)
518	*ŠEŠ.*[MEŠ]*-šú* *ŠEŠ.*[MEŠ]	32[T1] 310[T10]	See also *ši-tas-si* ePSD: šeš šeš [ANOINT] wr. šeš$_2$ Akk. pašāšu šeš [BIRD] wr. šeš[mušen] Akk. marratu šeš [BROTHER] wr. šeš Akk. ahu šeš [FISH] wr. šeš[ku]$_6$ "a fish" šeš [OBJECT] wr. [ĝeš]šeš Akk. šušû šeš [UNMNG] wr. šeš$_4$ "" šeš [WEEP] wr. šeš$_4$; še$_8$-še$_8$; še$_8$; šeš$_2$; šeš$_x$(|A.IGI|); šeš$_3$; še$_x$(|IGI×A|) Akk. bakû	سيس (لسان العرب)
519	*ṣe-te*	217[T10]	See also [d]*UTU.È* ePSD: ṣītu zig [RISE] wr. zig$_3$ Akk. dekû; gapāšu; tebû; ṣītu ziga [EXPENDITURE] wr. zi-ga Akk. ṣītu	ضوأ (لسان العرب)

			AALD: şetu (s.f.) الضوء، الظهور، الضياء (للشمس، والقمر، والنجوم)، المناخ شديد الحرارة والرطوبة، الشمس المشرقة	
520	*ši-bu-tum* *ši-bu-ti* *ši-ba* *ši-ba-am-ma* *ši-i-bu*	35^{T11} 54^{T11} 228^{T11} 298^{T11} 299^{T11}	See also *SIPA-ma* See also *ši-pa* ePSD: šību abba [FATHER] wr. ab; ab-ba; abba$_2$ Akk. abu; šību luki'inimak [WITNESS] wr. lu$_2$-ki-inim-ma Akk. šību šugi [SENIOR] wr. šu-gi$_4$; šu-gi Akk. šību ePSD: bīšu hab [MALODOROUS] wr. hab$_2$; hab Akk. alappānu; bīšu; ekēlu; happu AALD: šību (s.) الشيب، الكبر	ذيب (لسان العرب) ذوب (لسان العرب) شوب (لسان العرب) الشَّيْبُ (القاموس المحيط) شيب (مقاييس اللغة) شيب (الصّحَاح في اللغة) شيب (لسان العرب) بَيْشٌ (القاموس المحيط)
521	*SIG$_4$* *SIG$_4$-šú* *SIG$_4$-šu*	19^{T1} 20^{T1}	ePSD: šeg šeg [BRICK] (572x: ED IIIb, Old Akkadian, Lagash II, Ur III, Early Old Babylonian, Old Babylonian, unknown) wr. šeg$_{12}$; še-eb Akk. libittu	سجج (لسان العرب)
522	*si-ḫi-il-šú* *ú-saḫ-ḫal*	284^{T11} 284^{T11}	ePSD: sahālu te [PIERCE] wr. te Akk. sahālu ePSD: sahlû zahili [PLANT] wr. za$_3$-hi-li; za$_3$-hi-li^{sar}; ša$_3$-hi-li^{sar}; hi-li^{sar}?; za-hi-li; za-ha-e Akk. sahlû	سحل (مقاييس اللغة) سحل (الصّحَاح في اللغة) السَّحْلُ (القاموس المحيط)
523	*ši-i-ḫu* *ši-a-ḫi-šú*	37^{T1} 61^{T1}	ePSD: šihu lum [FRUIT] wr. lum Akk. enēbu; unnubu; namāru; šebû; šihu	ذيح (لسان العرب) ذيخ (لسان العرب) شيح (لسان العرب) شحح (لسان العرب) شيخ (لسان العرب) ضيح (لسان العرب)
524	*ši-ir-a-ni-ia*	256^{T10}	See also *SA.^{MEŠ}-ka* See aslo *UZU.^{MEŠ}-šú-nu*	سرع (لسان العرب)
525	*šikari*	272^{T10}	ePSD: šakāru si [DRUNK] wr. Si$_3$ Akk. šakāru AALD: šikāri (s.) (šikru) المسكّر، جعة مصنوعة من الحنطة AALD: šikari (s.) (šikru) in bit šikari "بيت الجعة" خانة مصنع الجعة AALD: šikari (s.) (šikru) in rab šikari الموظف المسؤول عن بيت الجعة	سكر (مقاييس اللغة) سَكِرَ (القاموس المحيط) سكرك (لسان العرب) سكر (لسان العرب)
526	*SILA*	277^{T1}	See also *su-ḳi-im* ePSD: sila sila [STREET] wr. sila; sila$_3$ Akk. sūqu	سيل (مقاييس اللغة)
527	*şīmāt*	234^{T10}	See also *sa-me-ta-šu* ePSD: şūmu immen [THIRST] wr. immen; immen$_2$ Akk. şamû; şūmu	صامَ (القاموس المحيط) صمت (لسان العرب)
528	*^{šim}GÍR*	160^{T11}	*GÍR* See *GÌR-šú* ePSD: šim	*šim* شمم (لسان العرب) الشَّمُّ (القاموس المحيط)

			šim [AROMATICS] wr. šim Akk. rīqu šim [BASIN] wr. šim	أوس (لسان العرب)
529	SIM^{mušen}	151[T11]	See See MUŠEN.^{MES} ePSD: sim sim [SWALLOW] wr. sim^{mušen}; še-en^{mušen}; še-na^{mušen} Akk. sinuntu	سوم (لسان العرب) سيم (لسان العرب)
530	ši-ni-pat-su	80[T11]	See also šit-tin-šú AALD: šinapš (v.) in šinapšumma epēšu معنى غير معروف AALD: šinnipātu See šinipu AALD: šinipu (num) (f. šinipiat, šinipât, šinipêt, šinnipât, šinnippât) (كلمة سومرية) ثلثان	سنف (العباب الزاخر) سنف (مقاييس اللغة) سنف (الصّحّاح في اللغة) السَّنْفُ (القاموس المحيط) سنف (لسان العرب) صدر (لسان العرب) الحَقَبُ (القاموس المحيط) حقو (مقاييس اللغة) الحَقْوُ (القاموس المحيط)
531	sin-niš-ti sin-niš-ti sin-niš-te sin-niš-ti	106[T1] 185[T1] 192[T1] 201[T11]	See also MUNUS-šú See also uq-na-ti ePSD: sinništu munus [WOMAN] wr. munus; nu-nus Akk. sinništu	نثا (لسان العرب) نَثِيثٌ (القاموس المحيط) نثث (لسان العرب) أنث (لسان العرب) نثث (لسان العرب) أنس (لسان العرب) نسأ (لسان العرب) نسا (لسان العرب)
532	ši-pa ši-pa	240[T11] 261[T11]	See also ši-ba	شأف (مقاييس اللغة) شأف (العباب الزاخر) شأف (لسان العرب)
533	SIPA-ma	71[T1]	ePSD: sipad sipad [BIRD] wr. sipad^{mušen} sipad [SHEPHERD] wr. sipad; su$_8$-ba; $^{lu}{}_2$sipad; šuba Akk. rē'û	سيب (لسان العرب)
534	ši-pi-šú šēpī-šú šēpī-šú še-pi-ia-a-ma še-pi-i-a	11[P] 289[T11] 292[T11] 41[T11] 41[T11]	See aslo GÌR-šú ePSD: šēpu ĝiri [FOOT] wr. ĝiri$_3$; me-ri; ĝiri$_{16}$ Akk. šēpu	ضيف (لسان العرب) ظفف (لسان العرب) وظف (لسان العرب)
535	ṣi-ri-ia ṣe-ri-ka	7[P] 6[T11]	See also EDIN See also ṣe-eḫ-ret ePSD: ṣeru LIL [PLAIN] wr. LIL$_2$ "plain" Akk. ṣeru ePSD: ṣēru aneden [STEPPE] wr. an-eden Akk. ṣēru eden [BACK] wr. eden Akk. ṣēru muš [SNAKE] wr. muš Akk. ṣēru sanimmara [BACK] wr. sa-nim-ma-ra Akk. ṣēru sug [BACK] wr. sug Akk. elītu; ṣēru	صحر (مقاييس اللغة) صحر (لسان العرب) صير (لسان العرب) ظهر (لسان العرب) ضهر (لسان العرب)
536	ṣirti ṣirtum	36[T1] 36[T1]	ePSD: ṣīru mah [GREAT] wr. mah; mah$_2$ Akk. kabtu; mādu; rabû; ṣīru umuš [EXALTED] wr. u$_2$-muš Akk. ṣīru urun [EXALTED] wr. urun$_x$(EN); u$_{18}$-ru; uru; uru$_{15}$	صرر (لسان العرب) صري (لسان العرب) صري (مقاييس اللغة) صر (مقاييس اللغة)

			Akk. dannu; šapsu; ṣīru	
537	*SÍSKUR*	163[T11]	ePSD: siškur siškur [PRAYER] wr. siškur$_2$; siškur Akk. karābu; naqû; nīqu ePSD: šakirû šakira [PLANT] wr. $^{u}_{2}$šakira$_3$; $^{u}_{2}$šakira; $^{u}_{2}$šakira$_x$(|URU×MIN+NI+GA|) Akk. šakirû	شكر (مقاييس اللغة) شكر (الصّحَاح في اللغة) الشُّكْرُ (القاموس المحيط) شكر (لسان العرب)
538	*ši-tas-si* *si-taš-ši* *is-su-ú* *i-šas-si*	27[T1] 27[T1] 98[T1] 117[T11]	See also *ŠEŠ.^{MEŠ}-šú* ePSD: šasû gu de [SAY] wr. gu$_3$ de$_2$ Akk. ?; nabû; šasû gu rah [SHOUT] wr. gu$_3$ ra-ah; gu$_3$ ra Akk. šasû AALD: šisītu (s) (tisītu, sisītu) (see šasû) 1) الصياح، البكاء 2) الاستدعاء الرسمي، التصريح، الاعلان AALD: šīsu (s) (tīsu) (see šasû) 1) الصياح 2) الاستدعاء الرسمي	سوس (العباب الزاخر) سوس (لسان العرب) سيس (لسان العرب) التَّيْسُ (القاموس المحيط) تيس (لسان العرب) وى (الصّحَاح في اللغة) طسس (لسان العرب)
539	*šit-tin-šú* *šit-ta-šú* *iš-šá-an-na-nu* *iš-tan-na-an* *šá-ni-nam-ma* *šá-ni-nam-ma* *šá-ni* *šá-niš* *šá-na-a* *šá-na-ta* *ú-šá-an-na-a*	48[T1] 48[T1] 45[T1] 45[T1] 65[T1] 278[T1] 31[P] 322[T10] 3[T11] 4[T11] 20[T11]	ePSD: šinnû sur [HALF] wr. sur; sur$_3$ Akk. šinnû; mišlu ePSD: šina min [TWO] wr. min; min$_3$; min$_6$ Akk. šina ePSD: šanû kur [DIFFERENT] wr. kur$_2$; gur Akk. nakāru; šanû šu gi [REPEAT] wr. šu gi$_4$ Akk. šanû AALD: šániš (adv.) للمرة الثانية، مرة اخرى، مشابه، ثانية؛ مختلف، بطريقة اخرى Note: al-Jibouri rule: šinta > šitta ثنتا ; šintin > šittin ثنتين	شنأ (لسان العرب) شنأ (العباب الزاخر) شَنَأَهُ (القاموس المحيط) شنع (لسان العرب) الذَّانُ (القاموس المحيط) ذين (لسان العرب) ثني (لسان العرب)
540	*ŠU.MIN-šá* *ŠU.MIN.^{MEŠ}-šá* *6-šu* *7-šú* *9-šú*	101[T1] 101[T1] 61[T11] 62[T11] 63[T11]	See also *qātī-ia* ePSD: šu šu [BASKET] wr. ^{ĝeš}šu$_4$ Akk. huppu šu [HAND] wr. šu; sum$_5$; šu-x Akk. qātu šu [HANDLE] wr. ^{ĝeš}šu "handle" šu [PESTLE] wr. $^{na}_{4}$šu-u Akk. šû šu [TOTALITY] wr. šu$_4$ Akk. kiššatu ePSD: MIN min [TWO] wr. min; min$_3$; min$_6$ Akk. šina	شوا (لسان العرب) منن (لسان العرب) يد (مقاييس اللغة) مهن (لسان العرب) شيع (مقاييس اللغة) شيع (لسان العرب)
541	*šu-'-ur* *šu-'-ru*	105[T1] 105[T1]	See *ú-ta-ad-da-ri* See *uš-te-še-ru*	
542	ŠUB.MEŠ	262[T1]	See also *im-ta-qu-ut* ePSD: ŠUB šub [FALL] wr. šub Akk. habātu; maqātu; nadû šub [LICK] wr. šub$_6$ šub [RUSH] wr. šub$_5$; šub$_x$(|ZI&ZI.EŠ$_2$|) Akk. šuppatu ePSD: ŠAB	سعب (لسان العرب) سأب (مقاييس اللغة) سأب (الصّحَاح في اللغة) سأب (لسان العرب) السُّوبَةُ (القاموس المحيط) شبا (لسان العرب) شَبا (القاموس المحيط) شبب (الصّحَاح في اللغة)

			šab [HIPS] wr. šab Akk. qablu šab [SEALING] wr. šab Akk. šipassu šab [TRIM] wr. šab Akk. barû ša uzu; esēpu; harāru; harāṣu; harāṣu; eşēru; harāṣu; šarāmu; nakāsu; šahāhu ePSD: ŠABA šaba [STONE] wr. $^{na}{}_4$ša-ba	شبب (لسان العرب) شوب (لسان العرب) نشب (الصّحّاح في اللغة)
543	*šubatu*	16[T1]	See also *it-taš-bu-ni* ePSD: šubtu ašte [CHAIR] wr. ašte$_2$; ^{ĝeš}aš-te; ^{ĝeš}iš-de$_3$ Akk. kussû; sukku; šubtu barag [DAIS] wr. barag; bara$_{10}$; bara$_6$; bara$_7$; bara$_8$ Akk. parakku; šarru; šubtu dag [DWELLING] wr. dag Akk. šubtu gunu [DWELLING] wr. gunu$_x$(|SI@g|) Akk. šubtu kituš [DWELLING] wr. ki-tuš Akk. mūšabu; šubtu unu [DWELLING] wr. unu$_6$; unu$_2$; unu Akk. mākalû; mūšabu; usukku; šubtu uru [SEAT] wr. uru$_5$ Akk. šubtu	وثب (لسان العرب) سبت (لسان العرب) ثبت (لسان العرب)
544	*šu-du-ud*	187[T11]	ePSD: šadādu gid [DRAG] wr. gid$_2$ Akk. diāšu; redû; šadādu	سدد (لسان العرب) شد (مقاييس اللغة) شدد (لسان العرب)
545	*şu-ḫi-šú*	165[T11]	See also *^{d}UTU.È* ePSD: şuhhu zu bir [LAUGH] wr. zu$_2$ bir$_9$ Akk. şuhhu	ضحي (مقاييس اللغة) ضحا (لسان العرب) ضحك (مقاييس اللغة)
546	*su-ḵi-im*	27[P]	Se also *SILA* ePSD: sūqu esir [STREET] wr. e-sir$_2$; e-sir Akk. sūqu sila [STREET] wr. sila; sila$_3$ Akk. sūqu tilla [STREET] wr. tilla$_2$; tilla$_3$; tilla; tilla$_4$; tilla$_5$; tilla$_x$(|AN&AN|) Akk. sūqu	سوق (لسان العرب) ساق (لسان العرب)
547	*šu-li-ma* *šul-me*	27[T11] 217[T11]	ePSD: šalāmu silim [HEALTHY] wr. silim Akk. šalāmu; šulmu ePSD: šullumu šu gi [REPAY] wr. šu gi$_4$ Akk. gimillu turru; šullumu	سلا (لسان العرب) سول (لسان العرب) سلف (لسان العرب) سلم (لسان العرب)
548	*šul-lul-ta-šú*	48[T1]	See also *šit-tin-šú* ePSD: šalašti peš [THREE] wr. peš Akk. šalašti AALD: šulšu (num.) (see šalāš) ثُلُث AALD: šulšu (adj.) (f. šulultu) ثالث AALD: šulšān see : šuššān (num.) الثلث AALD: šulšu (f. šulultu) ثالث	ثلث (لسان العرب) الثُّلُثُ (القاموس المحيط)
549	*şu-lul* *li-iş-lal* *iş-lal* *şa-li-lu*	33[T1] 184[T1] 191[T1] 239[T1]	ePSD: şalālu uku [SLEEP] wr. u$_3$ ku; u$_3$ ku$_4$ Akk. şalālu ePSD: şululu	صلل (لسان العرب) ضلل (لسان العرب) ظلل (لسان العرب)

	ṣu-ul-lil-ši	31[T11]	sumur [ROOF] wr. sumur; sumur$_2$; sumur$_3$ Akk. ṣululu ePSD:ṣulūlu andul [SHADE] wr. an-dul$_3$; an-dul$_7$ Akk. ṣulūlu saĝtab [PROTECTION] wr. saĝ-tab; sag-tab-ba Akk. rēṣu; ṣulūlu	
550	*šum-ma* *šum-ma* *šum-šu*	20[T1] 285[T11] 299[T11]	See also *um-ma* Se also *šum-šú* ePSD: šumma tukum [IF] wr. tukum Akk. surri; šumma tukumbi [IF] wr. tukumbi Akk. šumma ud [IF] wr. ud Akk. šumma ePSD: šammu u [PLANTS] wr. u$_2$ Akk. akalu; rîtu; šammu AALD: šumma (adv.) (preb.) عندما، في حين، الان؛ في الواقع، حقا، اذا، سواءً؛ فيما عدا، اذا اخدنا بنظر الاعتبار AALD: umma (enma, am-ma) اداة تسبق الكلام المباشر وغير المباشر "يقول" AALD: umā (adv.) الان Note: *šum-ma* = thumma: afterwards؛ at a later time ثمّ: بَعْدَ إِذْ؛ بَعْدَ أَنْ؛ بَعْدَ ما؛ بعدئذ؛ فى مابعد؛ فيما بعد؛ مِنْ بَعْدِ ما	وثَمَهُ (القاموس المحيط) ثوم (مقاييس اللغة) ثوم (لسان العرب) ثمم (الصّحّاح في اللغة) ثمم (لسان العرب)
551	*šum-šú* *šùm-šú* *šá-ma-mi* *šam-mi* *šam-mu* *šam-ma* *šam-ma-ma*	47[T1] 301[T10] 79[T1] 110[T1] 283[T11] 285[T11] 291[T11]	See also *šum-ma* See also *sa-me-ta-šá* ePSD: šumu mu [NAME] wr. mu Akk. šumu ePSD: šamû an [SKY] wr. an Akk. šamû gira [CONCEALMENT] wr. gira Akk. puzru; šamû un [HIGH] wr. un$_3$ Akk. elû; šamû; šaqû utah [HEAVEN] wr. utah Akk. šamû zigara [HEAVENS] wr. zigara Akk. šamû zikum [HEAVENS] wr. zikum Akk. šamû ePSD: šīmta šâmu nam tar [DECREE FATE] wr. nam tar Akk. šīmta šâmu ePSD: šīmtu nam [FATE] wr. nam; na-aĝ$_2$ Akk. šīmtu namtar [FATE] wr. nam-tar Akk. murṣu; namtaru; šīmtu AALD: šamû (s. f) (šamā'ū, šamāmū, šamū) السماء AALD: *š*āmutu (s.) (see *š*amû) التتابع، مواصلة البيع	سعم (لسان العرب) سوم (لسان العرب) سمم (لسان العرب) شمم (لسان العرب) شَمَا (القاموس المحيط) سما (لسان العرب)
552	*šu-na-te-ka* *šu-na-ta* *šu-na-ta*	244[T1] 245[T1] 197[T11]	*See also MÁŠ.GI$_6$* *See also šu-ut-ta*	شأن (لسان العرب) شأن (مقاييس اللغة) شون (لسان العرب) الشَّوْنَةُ (القاموس المحيط)
553	*šu-nu*	272[T11]	AALD: šunu (pron.) هم: جمع مذكر مرفوع، هولاء: جمع مذكر AALD: šunu (adj.) (see aššunu, iššunu, f. šunutu) \ يعود لهم	

			لهنّ	
554	*šup-šu-uḫ* *liš-tap-šiḫ*	9^{T1} 98^{T1}	See also *šup-šu-uq* ePSD: pašāhu <u>ni dub</u> [RELAX] wr. ni_2 dub_2 Akk. napāšu; pašāhu	فسح (لسان العرب)
555	*šup-šu-uq* *šup-šu-qu-ma*	10^{U} 78^{T11}	See also *šup-šu-uḫ* ePSD: pašqu <u>hulu</u> [NARROW] wr. hul Akk. pašqu AALD: ullu (adj.) المُعلّى، المُرقّى (الاله) AALD: pašāqu (v.): يصبح ضيقا، محدودا AALD: šupšuqu: يعاني من مصاعب، يكون في كرب	سفق (مقاييس اللغة) سفق (الصّحّاح في اللغة) سَفَقَ (القاموس المحيط) سفق (لسان العرب) بسق (الصّحّاح في اللغة) بسق (مقاييس اللغة) بشق (لسان العرب) فسق (مقاييس اللغة) الفِسْقُ (القاموس المحيط) فسق (لسان العرب) فشق (الصّحّاح في اللغة) الفَشْقُ (القاموس المحيط) فشق (مقاييس اللغة) فشق (لسان العرب)
556	*su-pu-ru* *su-pú-ri* *su-pu-ri* *su-pur* *ši-pir* *šip-ri* *ú-šab-ri-šum-ma*	11^{T1} 11^{T1} 321^{T11} 323^{T11} 185^{T1} 180^{T11} 197^{T11}	See also *ši-pir* ePSD: supūru <u>amaš</u> [SHEEPFOLD] wr. amaš; e_2-maš; a-maš; $^{e}{}_{2}$amaš Akk. supūru <u>rig</u> <u>[SHEEPFOLD]</u> (2x: Old Babylonian) wr. rig_{10} Akk. isru; tarbaşu ePSD: šipru <u>gašam</u> [WISE] wr. gašam Akk. mūdū; ummiānu; šipru	ظفر (مقاييس اللغة) الظُّفُر (القاموس المحيط) ظفر (لسان العرب) سفر (لسان العرب) سبر (مقاييس اللغة) سبر (لسان العرب) rig روج (لسان العرب)
557	*šu-pu-ú*	75^{T1}	ePSD: šupû <u>pa e</u> [APPEAR] wr. pa e_3 Akk. šupû ePSD: šapû <u>sir</u> [DENSE] wr. sir_2 Akk. šapû AALD: šupû (see ašibu, šubû, šumû) الافتراء، القذف، تشويه السمعة	سفا (لسان العرب) سبب (لسان العرب)
558	*šu-qu-rat*	273^{T1}	AALD: šūquru (adj.) f. šūqutru (see aqāru) ثمين، نفيس، رائع، مكّلف، قيّم AALD: šuqru (see šukru or šugru): Unknown meaning	زَكَرَهُ (القاموس المحيط) شقر (لسان العرب) ثقر (لسان العرب)
559	*šu-ri-ip-pak* ^{lú}*šu-ru-up-pa-ku-ú*	11^{T11} 23^{T11}	<u>See Part 2.2.32</u> See aslo šar-be *Wikipedia:* https://en.wikipedia.org/wiki/Shuruppak ePSD: pag <u>pag</u> [ENCLOSE] wr. pag Akk. esēru; šutanuhu <u>pag</u> [LEAVE] wr. pag Akk. ezēbu ePSD: pagû <u>SALI</u> [INSTRUMENT] wr. SA.LI Akk. pagû	شرب (الصّحّاح في اللغة) شَرِبَ (القاموس المحيط) شرب (لسان العرب) باكَ (القاموس المحيط) البَوْجُ (القاموس المحيط) بوج (لسان العرب) بعج (مقاييس اللغة) بعج (لسان العرب) بعك (لسان العرب) بعكك (الصّحّاح في اللغة)

560	*sur-qin-nu*	158[T11] 169[T11] 170[T11]	ePSD: sarāqu dub [HEAP] wr. dub Akk. sarāqu; šapāku AALD: surqinnu (s.) (surqīnu) see sarāqu القرابين	سرجن (لسان العرب) سرقن (لسان العرب) سرق (مقاييس اللغة) سَرَقَ (القاموس المحيط) سرق (لسان العرب)
561	*SU-šú* *ZU-šu*	198[T1] 198[T1]	See also *zu-um-ru-šú* See also *ZI.*[MEŠ] ePSD: su su [FLESH] wr. su "flesh; body; entrails (omen); body" Akk. zumru; šīru ePSD: zu zu [FLINT] wr. $^{na}{}_4$zu$_2$ "flint" zu [KNOW] wr. zu "to know; to learn" Akk. edû; lamādu zu [MATERIAL] wr. zu "type of building material" zu [SHARE] wr. ^{ĝeš}zu$_2$; zu$_2$ "plow share; blade of the hoe; point (of a battering ram)" Akk. šinnu zu [TOOTH] wr. zu$_2$ "tooth" Akk. šinnu	سنن (لسان العرب) سوا (لسان العرب) زوي (لسان العرب) زيا (لسان العرب)
562	*šu-su-ma*	230[T1]	AALD: šūsumu (adj.) (šussumu) see asāmu ملائم، مناسب، لائق	سما (لسان العرب) سسم (لسان العرب) بهم (لسان العرب) سأسم (لسان العرب) شيز (لسان العرب) دسم (لسان العرب) شوس (لسان العرب) رفع (لسان العرب)
563	*šu-tum₄-mi*	12[T1]	ePSD: šutummu šutum [STOREHOUSE] wr. $^{e}{}_2$šu-tum; šu-tum; šutum$_2$; šudum; šutum$_x$(|E$_2$.GI.NA.AB.HI|) Akk. šutummu	ذيت (لسان العرب)
564	*šu-tur* *šu-tu-ur*	29[T1] 29[T1]	ePSD: šūturu; lē'û dirig [EXCEED] wr. diri; RI Akk. atru; eli; rabû; kapāšu; zaqāru; šarūru; šūturu; lē'û AALD: šūturu (adj.) (šūturtu, atāru): اسمى، ارفع، فخم، رائع AALD: atāru (v.): يتجاوز بالعدد والحجم، يتفوق بالنوعية، يزيد، يتفوق	سطر (مقاييس اللغة) سطر (لسان العرب)
565	*ṣu-ub-bu* *ṣu-ub-bi* *ṣu-up-pi* *ṣu-up* *ṣú-pu* *iṣ-ṣa-pu*	19[T1] 324[T11] 21[U] 38[U] 256[T11] 265[T11]	See also *ṣabatma* AALD: ṣīpu (s.) (ṣību) (see ṣabû) التنقيع بالماء (الري)، القماش المصبوغ AALD: ṣuppû (v.) يحُك، يُدَلّك AALD: ṣuppû (see ṣubbû ṣubû) AALD: ṣupû (see ṣubû) AALD: ṣubbu (v.) (ṣuppu) 1) يبحث عن شيء من بعيد 2) يكون واعيا 3) يشكل فكرة، يعمل وفق خطة، ينجز AALD: subitu (s. f) منقع في الماء	صبأ (الصّحَاح في اللغة) صبأ (لسان العرب) صبغ (مقاييس اللغة) صب (مقاييس اللغة) صبا (لسان العرب) صبب (الصّحَاح في اللغة) صبب (لسان العرب) صوب (لسان العرب) صفو (مقاييس اللغة) صفا (لسان العرب) صفف (لسان العرب) صفف (العباب الزاخر) ضف (مقاييس اللغة) الضَّفْوُ (القاموس المحيط) ضفا (لسان العرب)
566	*šu-ut*	125[T11]	AALD: šūt (prep.) (see aššut) بخصوص، بسبب، فيما يتعلق AALD: šūt (pron.) هم: جمع مذكر	

			AALD: šūt (pron.) (see šūtu) هو: مذكر مفرد؛ ذلك: كما ورد آنفا: مذكر مفرد	
567	*šu-ut-bu-ú*	83[T1]	See also *te-bu-ú* Note: كان يسير العنق: هو سير فوق البطئ، وقيل هو ادنى المشي	السَّتْبُ (القاموس المحيط) عنق (الصّحّاح في اللغة) سبطر (لسان العرب)
568	*šu-ut-ta* *šu-ut-ta* *šit-ta* *šit-ti* *šit-tu* *šit-tum*	276[T1] 4[P] 254[T10] 254[T10] 211[T11] 232[T11]	See also *šu-na-te-ka* See also *MÁŠ.GI$_6$* ePSD: šuttu mamud [DREAM] wr. ma-mu$_2$; ma-mu Akk. šuttu ePSD: šittu ibtag [REMAINDER] wr. ib$_2$-tag$_4$ Akk. šittu u [SLEEP] wr. u$_3$ Akk. šittu udi [DAZED] wr. u$_3$-di Akk. kâru; šittu usag [SLEEP] wr. u$_3$-sa$_2$; u$_3$-di$_5$; u$_3$-sa-ga Akk. šittu AALD: šuttu[1] (s.) pl. šunātu MÁŠ.GI$_6$ الحُلم AALD: šuttu[2] (s.) الحُفرة	ثتت (لسان العرب) سطط (لسان العرب) شحط (الصّحّاح في اللغة) شَذَّ (القاموس المحيط) شَتَّ (القاموس المحيط) شتت (الصّحّاح في اللغة) شتت (لسان العرب) شطط (لسان العرب) شطط (الصّحّاح في اللغة) شع (مقاييس اللغة) شعع (لسان العرب)
569	*TA.ÀM*	141[T11]	ePSD: TA.A ana [WHAT?] wr. a-na; ta; ta-a Akk. mīnum ePSD: TA.|A.AN| ta'am [EACH] wr. ta-am$_3$	ظأم (لسان العرب) تأم (لسان العرب)
570	*ta-ad-de-kan-ni*	233[T11]	See also *DUG$_4$.GA* ePSD: dekû zig [RISE] wr. zig$_3$ Akk. dekû; gapāšu; tebû; ṣītu	دوك (مقاييس اللغة) دوك (لسان العرب) دكأ (لسان العرب) دَعَكَ (القاموس المحيط) دعك (لسان العرب) zig زأج (لسان العرب) زعج (لسان العرب) زعج (الصّحّاح في اللغة) زَعَجَهُ (القاموس المحيط)
571	*ta-at-til* *it-ti-lu* *ta-at-ti-lu*	209[T11] 222[T11] 236[T11]	ePSD: itūlu šed [LIE] wr. še$_{21}$; še$_x$(NA$_2$) Akk. itūlu; rabāṣu ePSD: utulu nud [LIE] wr. nud; nu$_x$(|HU.NA$_2$|) Akk. utulu	أتل (مقاييس اللغة) وتل (لسان العرب) تَلَّهُ (القاموس المحيط) تلل (لسان العرب)
572	*tab-ni-i* *bi-ni-i* *ib-ta-ni* *bi-nu-tú* *bu-nu-šú* *ba-na-at* *ta-ban-nu-ši* *ta-ban-nu-ši*	95[T1] 96[T1] 100[T1] 230[T1] 31[P] 320[T10] 28[T11] 29[T11]	ePSD: binītu binitum [BEAM] wr. ^{ĝeš}bi$_2$-ni-tum Akk. binītu zizna [ROE] wr. zizna$^{ku}{}_6$ Akk. binītu ePSD: banû dim [CREATE] wr. dim$_2$ Akk. banû du [BUILD] wr. du$_3$ Akk. banû; epēšu mu [GOOD] wr. mu$_5$ Akk. banû mud [CREATE] wr. mud Akk. banû sag [GOOD] wr. sag$_8$; sag$_9$; sag$_{10}$; šeg$_{10}$; sag$_{12}$ Akk. banû; damāqu; dumqu; ṭābu saĝ du [BEGET] wr. saĝ du; saĝ du$_{11}$; saĝ du$_3$ Akk. banû	بني (مقاييس اللغة) بني (لسان العرب) بنن (الصّحّاح في اللغة) بنن (لسان العرب) بُنْتُ (القاموس المحيط) بنت (لسان العرب)

573	*ta-ḫa-du* *aḫ-ta-du*	20^{P} 32^{P}	ePSD: hadû lib [RICH] Akk. hadû; hidiātu; râšu; rāšû; rīšātu šag hul [HAPPY] wr. šag$_4$ hul$_2$ Akk. hadû	خَتَدَ (القاموس المحيط) خَدِيَ (القاموس المحيط) أخد (لسان العرب) أخذ (لسان العرب)
574	*ta-ma-ti* *ta-ma-tim* *ta-ma-a-tum* *ta-ma-ta* *tam-ta-am-ma* *tam-tum* *tam-tum*	40^{T1} 40^{T1} 253^{T10} 134^{T11} 124^{T11} 255^{T11} 293^{T11}	ePSD: tâmtu ab [SEA] wr. ab; a-ab-ta Akk. tâmtu ePSD: ţamû zara [OVERLAP] wr. zara$_6$ Akk. nentû; ţamû	طمم (لسان العرب) طما (لسان العرب)
575	*tam-ši-ḫu*	23^{T1}	AALD: mašāḫu [1] (v.) 1) يقيس 2) يحسب 3) يقاس AALD: mašāḫu [2] (v.) (see misḫu) تندلع النار، يلمع بسطوع	مسح (لسان العرب)
576	*tap-pu-ú*	268^{T1}	ePSD: tappû man [COMPANION] wr. man Akk. tappû sadu [COMPANION] wr. sa-du$_3$ Akk. tappû tab [DOUBLE] wr. tab; tab$_4$ Akk. eşēpu; tappû taba [COMPANION] wr. $^{lu}{}_2$tab-ba Akk. tappû ePSD: tappûm anta [COMPANION] wr. $^{lu}{}_2$an-ta Akk. tappûm	وفي (لسان العرب) وفي (مقاييس اللغة)
577	*tap-pu-ut-ka*	287^{T10}	ePSD: patāqu budug [MOLD] wr. Bu-du-ug Akk. patāqu de [SHAPE] wr. De$_2$ Akk. patāqu AALD: pitakku (s.) بناية	فتق (لسان العرب) فتك (لسان العرب)
578	*taq-qa-šum-ma* *at-ta-qí* *e-te-et-qa* *e-te-et-ti-qa*	213^{T1} 157^{T11} 252^{T10} 252^{T10}	See also *it-qí* AALD: tanqītu (s.) (taqqītu) See naqû التنقية، التطهير AALD: aqû (v.) see waqû AALD: waqā'u (v.) see waqû AALD: waqû (v.) ينتبه uqqû ينتظر	تأق (لسان العرب) تأق (الصّحّاح في اللغة) تاقَ (القاموس المحيط) تقق (لسان العرب) تقي (لسان العرب) وقي (مقاييس اللغة) وقى (الصّحّاح في اللغة) وَقاهُ (القاموس المحيط) وقي (لسان العرب)
579	*ţa-ri-du*	226^{T10}	AALD: ţardu (adj.) (see ţarādu): منفي، مطارد، مبعد AALD: ţarīdu (s.) (see ţarādu): الطّرود، النَفيُّ، الابعاد، اللجوء AALD: ţarādu (vj.) (see ţurrudu): يَطرُد، يُرسُل، يُبعِد، يبعث، يُسمي، يدعو	الطَّرْدُ (القاموس المحيط) طرد (لسان العرب)
580	*tar-kul-li*	102^{T11}	See also *MÁ.MUG.*^{MES} ePSD: tarkullu targul [POLE] wr. targul; targul$_x$(|MA$_2$.KAK|) Akk. tarkullu	ترج (لسان العرب) عرف (لسان العرب) ركل (مقاييس اللغة) ركل (لسان العرب) رجل (لسان العرب)
581	*ţár-ra*	59^{T1}	ePSD: ziqnu sum [BEARD] wr. sum$_4$ Akk. ziqnu AALD: ţarru (adj) see darru AALD: darru (adj) (tarru) see darīru ملتحٍ، ذو لحية AALD: darīru (adj) ملتح، ذو لحية	ذقن (مقاييس اللغة) طر (مقاييس اللغة) الطَّرُّ (القاموس المحيط) طرر (لسان العرب)
582	*taš-ḫu-ti* *iš-ḫu-ut*	182^{T1} 190^{T1}	ePSD: šahātu ni teĝ [FEAR] wr. ni$_2$ teĝ$_3$ Akk. palāhu; šahātu	ثهت (لسان العرب) ثها (لسان العرب)

			su zig [FEAR] wr. su zig_3 Akk. šahātu	
583	ta-zi-im-ta-š	74^{T1} 78^{T1}	ePSD: tazzimtu i'utu [COMPLAINT] wr. i-utu; i-^{d}utu "complaint" Akk. tazzimtu	عظم (لسان العرب)
584	TE.^{MEŠ}-a-a TU^{mušen} TU^{mušen}	220^{T10} 148^{T11} 149^{T11}	See also le-ta-šú See also MUŠEN.^{MEŠ} ePSD: te te [CHEEK] wr. te Akk. Lētu ePSD: tum tum [BRING] wr. tum_3; tum_2 tum [CROSS-BEAM] wr. tum Akk. hurdatu tum [DOVE] wr. tum_{12}^{mušen} Akk. summatu tum [FISH] wr. $tum_{12}^{mušenku}_{6}$	طوي (مقاييس اللغة) طوي (لسان العرب) طوأ (العباب الزاخر) الطَّعامُ (القاموس المحيط) الطَّاءَةُ (القاموس المحيط) التَّوُ (القاموس المحيط)
585	te-bu-ú te-bu-ú te-bu-ú te-bi-ma te-bé-e-ma lit-ba-am-ma lit-ba-am-ma it-bé-ma it-bé-e-ma a-te-eb-ba-a	65^{T1} 66^{T1} 82^{T1} 194^{T1} 194^{T1} 189^{T11} 191^{T11} 245 274 248^{T10}	See also šu-ut-bu-ú ePSD: tebû šu zig [RAISE THE HAND] wr. šu Akk. nanduru; qātu našû; tebû zig [RISE] wr. zig_3 Akk. dekû; gapāšu; tebû; şītu AALD: ţebû (adj., v.) see tebû v. مغمور بالماء، غارق ؛ يُغرِق، يَغمُر	طبي (لسان العرب) بغا (لسان العرب) بغم (مقاييس اللغة) بغم (لسان العرب) وطب (لسان العرب) تعب (مقاييس اللغة) تعب (الصّحّاح في اللغة) تعب (لسان العرب) تَبَا (القاموس المحيط) تبا (لسان العرب) تبع (مقاييس اللغة) تبع (الصّحّاح في اللغة) تَبِعَهُ (القاموس المحيط) تبع (لسان العرب) تب (مقاييس اللغة) التَّبُّ (القاموس المحيط) تبب (الصّحّاح في اللغة) وتَبَّ (القاموس المحيط) تبب (لسان العرب) التَّلْبُ (القاموس المحيط)
586	te-di-qí te-di-qa	258^{T11}	ePSD: tēdīq bēlti pala [GARMENT] wr. ^{tug}$_{2}$$pala_3$; ^{tug}$_{2}$pala; ^{tug}$_{2}$$pala_2$ Akk. tēdīq bēli; tēdīq bēlti; tēdīq šarri AALD: tēdīqu (s.) see edēqu رداء الاحتفال (الطقوس الدينية)، ملابس فاخرة للاحتفال	حدق (مقاييس اللغة) حدق (لسان العرب)
587	ţè-e-ma	8^{T1}	ePSD: ţēmu dimma [THOUGHT] wr. dim_2-ma; dimma Akk. ţēmu ĝalga [FORETHOUGHT] wr. ĝalga; ma-al-ga Akk. milku; ţēmu ĝeštug [EAR] wr. $ĝeštug_2$; ^{ĝeš}ĝeštug; ĝeštug; $ĝeštug_3$; $muštug_2$; mu-uš-tug_2; mu-uš-tug Akk. hassu; uznu; uznu; ţēmu nam [THOUGHT] wr. nam_2 Akk. ţēmu umuš [PLANNING] wr. umuš Akk. ţēmu	طيع (لسان العرب) طوع (لسان العرب) طحم (لسان العرب) طحم (مقاييس اللغة) طَحْمَةُ (القاموس المحيط) طيم (لسان العرب) طيم (الصّحّاح في اللغة) طعم (لسان العرب) العَقْلُ (القاموس المحيط)
588	te-me-en-nu	19^{T1}	ePSD: temennu temen [FOUNDATION] wr. temen Akk. temennu	أمن (لسان العرب) ضمن (لسان العرب) طمن (لسان العرب)

			AALD: temmennu (temennu, temmennu): وثيقة اساس، الكتابة، الاسس، مصطبة الاسس، كلمة سومرية دخيلة	
589	*tí-iṭ-ṭi-ra-áš-šú*	22^{P}	See also *ú-ta-ad-da-ri* See also *ṭár-ra*	طرأ (لسان العرب)
590	*ṭīṭa* *ṭi-iṭ-ṭiš* *ṭi-iṭ-ṭi*	102^{T1} 245^{T10} 119^{T11}	See also *ṭè-e-ma* ePSD: ţīdu; ţuppu im [CLAY] wr. im Akk. ţīdu; ţuppu AALD: ţīţu (s.) a qualification of beer im See *e-mi-a*	الطِينُ (القاموس المحيط) سيع (لسان العرب) طوب (لسان العرب) طأ (مقاييس اللغة) طآ (لسان العرب) ط (لسان العرب) طيط (لسان العرب) الطُّوطُ (القاموس المحيط) الطُّوطُ (القاموس المحيط) طوط (لسان العرب) طوط (العباب الزاخر) طين (لسان العرب)
591	^{túg}*ÍB.LÁ.*^{MES}	227^{T1}	ePSD: TUG$_2$ dul [COVER] wr. dul; dul$_9$; dul$_5$; dul$_x$(DUN$_3$) Akk. katāmu i [CLOTHING] wr. i$_6$ Akk. lubuštu mur [DRESS] wr. mur$_{10}$ Akk. labāšu taškarin [BOXWOOD] wr. ^{ĝeš}taškarin; taškarin Akk. taskarinnu tugX [GARMENT] wr. tug$_2$-X tug [TEXTILE] wr. tug$_2$ Akk. şubātu umuš [PLANNING] wr. umuš Akk. ţēmu ePSD: ibla ibla [BELT] wr. ^{kuš}ib$_2$-la$_2$; $^{tug}{}_2$ib$_2$-la$_2$	طوق (لسان العرب) الطَّوْقُ (القاموس المحيط) توج (لسان العرب) حبل (الصّحّاح في اللغة)
592	*tuḫ-ḫu* *tuḫ-ḫi*	273^{T10} 273^{T10}	ePSD: tuhhu duh [BRAN] wr. Duh; dah-hu Akk. Tuhhu	طحا (لسان العرب) طحي (لسان العرب)
593	*tukul-ti* ^{giš}*TUKUL.*^{MEŠ}*-šú*	32^{T1} 65^{T1}	See also *tukul-ti* ePSD: tukul tukul [WEAPON] wr. ^{ĝeš}tukul; tukul Akk. kakku ePSD: tukultu e [TRUST] wr. e$_7$ "trust" Akk. tukultu ĝiškim [SIGN] wr. ĝiškim Akk. giskimmu; ittu; tukultu ĝiškimti [TRUST] wr. ĝiškim-ti Akk. tukultu nir [TRUST] wr. nir Akk. tukultu ePSD: kakku gug [STICK] wr. gug$_6$ Akk. kakku rig [STICK] wr. rig$_3$ Akk. kakku šita [WEAPON] wr. šita$_2$; ^{ĝeš}šita$_2$; ^{ĝeš}šita$_4$; ^{ĝeš}šita$_x$(|KAK.GIŠ|) Akk. kakku tukul [WEAPON] wr. ^{ĝeš}tukul; tukul Akk. kakku udug [WEAPON] wr. udug$_2$; u$_3$-dug$_4$; u$_2$-tu-ug Akk. kakku	ثقل (لسان العرب) كهكه (لسان العرب) تَكِلَ (القاموس المحيط)(كلت (لسان العرب) وكل (لسان العرب) ثكل (مقاييس اللغة) ثكل (لسان العرب)
594	*tu-le-šú*	34^{U}	ePSD: tulû ubur [BREAST] wr. ubur; ubur$_2$; u$_3$-bur; u$_2$-bi-ur Akk. tulû	طلع (مقاييس اللغة) تلع (الصّحّاح في اللغة) التَّلْعَةُ (القاموس المحيط) تلع (لسان العرب) تول (لسان العرب)

				ثلل (لسان العرب) تل (مقاييس اللغة) تلا (لسان العرب) طلا (الصّحّاح في اللغة) طلي (لسان العرب)
595	*tul-tab-ši-ma-a*	81[T1]	ePSD: bašāmu sur [FORM] wr. sur "to form" Akk. bašāmu	بضم (لسان العرب) بذم (لسان العرب)
596	*tul-tu*	237[T10]	See also *tu-le-šú* ePSD: tûltu KAmuš [WORM] wr. KA-muš Akk. tûltu AALD: tultu (s.) الحفرة، الوجرة AALD: tūltu (s.) (tu'iltu, tu'issu, tūldu) الدودة، اليرقة، برج، كوكب	تعل (لسان العرب) الثُّوَلُ (القاموس المحيط) ثول (لسان العرب)
597	*tup-šen-na* *tu-up-ni-in-na*	24[T1] 22[U]	ePSD: ţuppu dub [TABLET] wr. dub Akk. ţuppu ePSD: tupšinnu dubšen [CHEST] wr. dub-šen Akk. tupšinnu ePSD: šennu šendili [EWER] wr. ^{urud}šen-dili$_2$ Akk. šennu	دبس (لسان العرب) طبس (لسان العرب) طوب (لسان العرب)
598	*tu-qar-ra-ab* *qer-bi-is-sú* *qer-bi-is-šú* *qer-bu-šú* *qer-bu-uš*	300[T10] 13[T11] 13[T11] 63[T11] 63[T11]	See also *ka-ra-bi* ePSD: qerēbu kunu [APPROACH] wr. Ku-nu "to approach" Akk. qerēbu; sanāqu ša nakri	قرب (مقاييس اللغة) قرب (الصّحّاح في اللغة) قَرُبَ (القاموس المحيط) قرب (لسان العرب)
599	*tu-qu-un-ti* *tu-qu-un-tú*	5[T11] 5[T11]	See also *qa-na* ePSD: tuqumtu ĝešla [BATTLE] wr. ĝeš-la$_2$ Akk. anantu; tuqumtu u [DEFEAT] wr. u$_8$; u$_2$ Akk. tuqumtu AALD: tuqumtu (s.) (tuquntu, tuquttu, tuqmatu) المعركة، الحرب، القتال AALD: *tuqqunu (adj.) نوعية متقنة، ملائمة، مناسبة Note: al-Jibouri rule: tuquttu -> tuquntu; tuqumtu -> tuquntu	قمم (الصّحّاح في اللغة) قمم (لسان العرب) تقق (لسان العرب) تقن (مقاييس اللغة) تقن (لسان العرب)
600	*tu-ra-ẖa*	260[T10]	ePSD: turāhu durah [GOAT] wr. durah$_x$(DARA$_4$); durah Akk. turāhu	ترح (لسان العرب)
601	*tur-ti-né-ed-di*	267[T10]	ePSD: redû us [FOLLOW] wr. us$_2$ Akk. diāšu; redû; šadādu	ردأ (العباب الزاخر) ردأ (لسان العرب) رَدَى (القاموس المحيط) ردي (مقاييس اللغة) ردي (لسان العرب)
602	*u$_4$-um* *u$_4$-um* *u$_4$-ma* *u$_4$-me* *u$_4$-mi-šam* *u$_4$-mi-šam*	47[T1] 97[T1] 115[T1] 115[T1] 228[T1] 29[U]	ePSD: umšu ud [SUN] wr. ud Akk. immu; ummedu; umšu; šamšu; ūmu AALD: umiša (adv) يوميا، يوما بيوم	الأوامُ (القاموس المحيط) أوم (لسان العرب) يوم (لسان العرب) عوم (لسان العرب)

	u_4-mi-šam-ma *u_4-me-šu-ma*	71^{T11} 208^{T11}		
603	*ub-la* *ub-la* *ub-lu* *i-ba-li*	8^{T1} 312^{T10} 312^{T10} 312^{T11}	ePSD: ibilu amsiharran [CAMEL] wr. am-si-har-ra-an Akk. ibilu amsikurak [CAMEL] wr. am-si-kur-ra Akk. ibilu ePSD: babālu de [BRING] wr. de_6; ga; de_3; ir; de_2 Akk. babālu ePSD: abālu ah [DRY] wr. ah_3 Akk. abālu; šābulu ePSD: eblu eš [ROPE] wr. $eš_2$ Akk. eblu eše [AREA UNIT] wr. $eše_3$; $eše_2$ "a unit of area; a unit of volume" Akk. eblu AALD: abālu[1] (v.) (babālu, wabālu): يجلب، يحمل، يسيطر، يحمل جنينا، يُوجه، يُدير، يربك، يشوش، يتلاعب، يناقش، يجادل، يفهم، يخدع AALD: abālu[2] (v.) (babālu, wabālu): يجف، يذبل AALD: ūbilu (s.) (abālu): porter الساعي، حامل البريد AALD: ubilu (see ābilu) AALD: ābilu (s.) (abālu) bearer, carrier Note: abala ~ ʿabala ~ ẖabala ~ habala; أبل ~ عبل ~ حبل ~ هبل	العَبْلُ (القاموس المحيط) عبل (لسان العرب) عبل (مقاييس اللغة) عبل (الصّحّاح في اللغة) أبل (لسان العرب) أبل (مقاييس اللغة) حبل (مقاييس اللغة) حبل (الصّحّاح في اللغة) الحَبْلُ (القاموس المحيط) حبل (لسان العرب) هبل (مقاييس اللغة) هبل (الصّحّاح في اللغة) وبل (لسان العرب) وبل (مقاييس اللغة)
604	UD UD.^{MEŠ}-*ka* U_4.^{MEŠ}-*ka* UD.^{MEŠ}-*šú*	228^{T1} 300^{T10} 300^{T10} 322^{T10}	See also *u_4-um* ePSD: UD ud [STORM] wr. ud Akk. ūmu ud [IF] (2x: unknown) wr. ud Akk. šumma ud [WHEN] (29x: ED IIIb, Old Akkadian, Lagash II, Ur III, Old Babylonian) wr. ud Akk. enūma ud [SUN] (29106x: Lagash II, Ur III, Old Babylonian) wr. ud Akk. immu; ummedu; umšu; šamšu; ūmu	عود (لسان العرب)
605	UD.DA	137^{T11}	See also ^{d}UTU.È ePSD: udda udda [STAND] wr. ud-da Akk. manzaltu	ضوأ (لسان العرب) عضا (لسان العرب)
606	UDU.NÍTA.^{MEŠ}	72^{T11}	See *i-du-ú* ePSD: udu-$nita_2$ udunita [RAM] wr. udu-$nita_2$ ePSD: udu udu [SHEEP] wr. udu; e-ze_2 Akk. Immeru ePSD: nita nita [BIRD] wr. $nita_2^{mušen}$ "a bird" nita [MALE] wr. $nita_2$; nita; $nita_x$(|ARAD×KUR|) Akk. zikaru	نحت (لسان العرب) النَّيْتُ (القاموس المحيط) نوت (لسان العرب) عدا (لسان العرب)
607	ÚG.^{MEŠ}	44^{T1} 111^{T11} 113^{T11}	See also *ni-šu-ú-a-a-ma* ePSD: uĝ	عجا (لسان العرب) عجج (لسان العرب) عج (مقاييس اللغة)

			<u>uĝ</u> [PEOPLE] wr. $uĝ_3$ Akk. nišu	
608	*ug-da-áš-šá-ár* *gaš-ru* *ug-da-áš-šá-ru* *ug-da-áš-šá-ri*	64[T1] 75[T1] 212[T1] 212[T1]	ePSD: gašru <u>ir</u> [MIGHTY] wr. ir_9; ir_3 Akk. gašru	جسر (لسان العرب) الْجَسْرُ (القاموس المحيط) جدس (لسان العرب) درس (لسان العرب) الدَّسْرُ (القاموس المحيط)
609	*UGU* *UGU-ki*	18[T1] 184[T1]	ePSD: ugu <u>ugu</u> <u>[BEAR]</u> wr. ugu; ugu_4 Akk. alādu <u>ugu</u> <u>[CVNE]</u> wr. u_2- <u>ugu</u> <u>[FOOD]</u> wr. u_2-gu_7 Akk. mākālu <u>ugu</u> <u>[PASTURE]</u> wr. u_2-gu_7 Akk. merītu <u>ugu</u> <u>[SKULL]</u> wr. ugu_2; ugu; ugu_3; ugu_x(|U.SAG|); ugu_x(|A.U.KA|); ugu_x(SAG@n@g) Akk. eli; muhhu; qaqqadu <u>ugu</u> <u>[WATERING PLACE]</u> wr. ugu_2 Akk. mašqītu; mikru	أجّ (مقاييس اللغة) الأَجِيجُ (القاموس المحيط) أجج (لسان العرب) عجا (لسان العرب) عجج (لسان العرب) عج (مقاييس اللغة) عوق (لسان العرب) عوج (لسان العرب) الأَقْتُ (القاموس المحيط) عقو (مقاييس اللغة) عقق (الصّحَاح في اللغة) عقا (لسان العرب) عقق (لسان العرب) عق (مقاييس اللغة)
610	*ú-ḫa-am-ma-ṭu*	105[T11]	See also *ḫa-an-ṭiš* ePSD: hamāṭu <u>KA'izi</u> [BURNING] wr. KA-izi Akk. hamāṭu; šumû <u>ĝiri ul</u> [RUSH] wr. $ĝiri_3$ ul_4 Akk. hamāṭu <u>sar</u> [RUN] wr. sar Akk. hamāṭu; lasāmu <u>tab</u> [BURN] wr. tab; tab_2 Akk. hamāṭu; šamātu;	همط (لسان لعرب) خمط (مقاييس اللغة) خمط (الصّحَاح في اللغة) خَمَطَ (القاموس المحيط) خمط (لسان لعرب) حمط (لسان لعرب)
611	*ú-ḫal-li-qu* *ḫul-lu-uq*	43[T1] 122[T11]	ePSD: halāqu <u>halam</u> [FORSAKE] wr. ha-lam; gel-le-$eĝ_3$ Akk. halāqu; lapātu; lemnu; mašû <u>ugu de</u> [DISAPPEAR] wr. u_2-gu de_2; u_2-gu_3 de_2; ugu de_2 Akk. halāqu <u>uzahal</u> [DISAPPEARANCE] wr. u_4-za-hal; u_4-za-ha-al Akk. halāqu <u>zah</u> [DISAPPEAR] wr. zah_3; zah_2 Akk. duppuru; halāqu; nābutu; šerû	حلق (مقاييس اللغة) حلق (لسان العرب) خلق (مقاييس اللغة) خلق (لسان العرب) هَلَقَ (القاموس المحيط) هلق (لسان العرب) هلك (مقاييس اللغة) هلك (الصّحَاح في اللغة) هلك (لسان العرب)
612	*uḫ-tan-na-ba*	60[T1]	ePSD: hanābu <u>gu mer</u> [THRIVE] wr. gu_2 mar-mar; gu_2 me-er-me-er Akk. hanābu	حنأ (لسان العرب) حنب (لسان العرب) خنب (لسان العرب) هنب (لسان العرب)
613	*uk-tam-ma-ru*	254[T1]	See also *i-gam-mar* ePSD: kamāru <u>daparu</u> [DEFEAT] wr. daparu Akk. kamāru; karašû; šapşu <u>du</u> [HEAP] wr. du_8 Akk. kamāru <u>guru</u> [HEAP] wr. $guru_7$; gur_{11} "to heap up" Akk. kamāru; karû <u>kamar</u> [WOOD] wr. ^{geš}KA-mar; ka-mar Akk. kamāru <u>lu</u> [ABUNDANT] wr. lu Akk. dêšu; kamāru <u>tub</u> [SMITE] wr. tu_{11}; Akk. hatû; kamāru ePSD: kamiru <u>lirum</u> [STRENGTH] wr. lirum; $lirum_3$; $lirum_2$; $lirum_6$; $lirum_7$;	قمر (مقاييس اللغة) قمر (لسان العرب) غمر (لسان العرب) خمر (لسان العرب)

		lirum$_8$ Akk. abaru; dannu; emûqu; gāmiru; kamiru; kirimmu; umašu; šapṣu; šitnunu; šitpuṣu ePSD: kamaru ešla [TRAP] wr. ^{ĝeš}eš$_2$-la$_2$ Akk. kamaru gamar [FISH] wr. gamar^{ku}$_6$; ka-mar^{ku}$_6$; ga-mar^{ku}$_6$ Akk. kamaru AALD: kamāru الشّرك، الفخ، الاندحار، الابادة؛ يكدس، يكوم، يزيد	
614	*uk-tam-mi-is-ma* *uk-tam-me-es-ma* *uš-tak-mi-is*	138^{T11} 138^{T11} 201^{T11}	See also *ka-ma-a-ti* ePSD: kamāsu šukin dab [PROSTRATE] wr. šu-kin dab$_5$ Akk. kamāsu ePSD: kumāṣu dimuš [SHELTER] wr. dimuš Akk. kumāṣu; kušāru gud [NEST] wr. gud$_3$; ^{gi}gud$_3$ Akk. hīšu; kumāṣu; qinnu ePSD: kanāšu gu ĝal [SUBMIT] wr. gu$_2$ ĝal$_2$ Akk. kanāšu gu ĝar [SUBMIT] wr. gu$_2$ ĝar; gu$_2$ ĝa$_2$-ĝa$_2$ Akk. kanāšu gu ĝeš ĝal [SUBMIT] wr. gu$_2$ ĝeš ĝal$_2$ Akk. kanāšu gu ĝeš ĝar [SUBMIT] wr. gu$_2$ ĝeš ĝar; gu$_2$ giš ga$_2$-ga$_2$ Akk. kanāšu gurum [BEND] wr. gurum; gur$_8$; gur; gurum$_x$(GURUN) Akk. kanāšu; kanānu; kapāpu; qadādu AALD: *kamāsu (v.) يكمش، يجمع، يُحصّل؛ ينهي، يكمل، يجني شعيرا، يجمع، يحشد اشخاصا، يجهز AALD: *kamāsu (v.) (kamāṣu, kamāšu) يقرفص، يكمبص، يركع، ينوخ، يجعل شخصا يركع AALD: *kāmisu (s.) الذي يركع	كنبت (لسان العرب) كنبث (لسان العرب) كلبث (لسان العرب) كنس (لسان العرب) قنبص (لسان العرب) قبض (لسان العرب) قنص (لسان العرب) قمص (لسان العرب) قمس (لسان العرب) كمس (العباب الزاخر)
615	*uk-tin*	159^{T11}	See also ^{giš}*KUN$_4$*	كتن (مقاييس اللغة) الكَتَنُ (القاموس المحيط) كتن (لسان العرب)
616	*ul*		AALD: ul (u + lā) (see ula, lā) اداة النفي: لا (لم، ولن) AALD: ula (see u + lā) اداة للنفي: لا AALD: ūl فيما اذا .. أو šumma … ūl ؛ أو .. اما ūl … ūl ؛ اداة للعطف: أو AALD: ūla (ūlā) (ū + lā) (see ūlū) (see ul, uli, ulla, ullaman) اداة للعطف: او ؛ ūla … ūla اما .. أو	ليس (العباب الزاخر) إلاً (القاموس المحيط) ألاَ (القاموس المحيط) ألا (الصّحّاح في اللغة) إلا (لسان العرب) ألا (لسان العرب)
617	*UL.A*	27^{P}	See also *el-lim* See also e-mi-a See also *MÁŠ.GI$_6$* ePSD: ula ula [ANYTHING] wr. u$_3$-la ula [BATTLE] wr. ula$_2$ Akk. qablu ula [FEEBLE] wr. u$_2$-la$_2$ Akk. muqqu ePSD: ul mul [SHINE] wr. mul; mul$_2$; mul$_4$ Akk. kakkabu; mulmullu; nabāṭu ul [DISTANT] wr. ul; ul-li$_2$; ul-li Akk. ṣiātu	

618	*ul-tab-lak-ki-is-su-ma* *ú-ni-iš-šú-ma*	250[T1] 9[P]	ePSD: labāku dig [SOFT] wr. dig Akk. labāku; narbu duru [WET] wr. duru$_5$; duru$_5^{ru}$ Akk. labāku; raţbu Note: Derivation: إِلْتَبْلَكَ = إِسْتَبْلَكَ : بلك إِلْتَلْبَكَ = إِسْتَلْبَكَ : لبك	بَلَكَةُ (القاموس المحيط) بلك (لسان العرب) لبك (لسان العرب) اللَّبْكُ (القاموس المحيط)
619	*ul-taḫ-ḫi*	199[T1]	See also *lul-tuk* ePSD: lu'û šu la [DEFILE] wr. šu la$_2$ Akk. lu'û; lupputu šu pela [DEFILE] wr. šu pe-el-la$_2$; šu pel-la$_2$; šu pel$_2$-la$_2$ Akk. lu'û; qullulu ePSD: lu''û pel [DEFILE] wr. pe-el-la$_2$; pe-el Akk. lu''û; qalālu	لطه (لسان العرب) لطح (لسان العرب) لحت (لسان العرب) لتخ (لسان العرب) لطخ (لسان العرب)
620	*ul-te-eş-bi* *ni-iş-ba-tu-ma*	50[T1] 229[T10]	ePSD: aşābu tah [ADD] wr. tah Akk. aşābu ePSD: ešēbu; uššubu lam [FLOURISH] wr. lam; lam$_x$(LUM) Akk. ešēbu; uššubu ePSD: naşābu sub [RUB] wr. su-ub; sub; sub$_6$ Akk. naşābu AALD: ešēpu (see aşābu; aşāpu; waşābu, uşābu; uttaşşubu) Note: al-Jibury rules: uš-te-eş-bi > ul-te-eş-bi un-te-eş-bi > ul-te-eş-bi	وصب (لسان العرب) وصب (مقاييس اللغة) عصب (مقاييس اللغة) نصب (لسان العرب) لصب (لسان العرب)
621	*ul-tu* *ul-la-nu* *ul-tu* *ul-tu* *ul-tu* *ul-tu* *ul-lu-ú* *ul-la-nu-um-ma* *ul-la-nu-um-ma* *ul-la-nu-um-ma*	15[T1] 15[T1] 49[T1] 195[T1] 243[T1] 315[T10] 119[T11] 165[T1] 315[T10] 172[T11]	See also *iš-tén* See also *iš-di* *See also uš-šú-šú* See also *it-ti-šú* AALD: ultu: see ištu, išti, išdu (conj & prep) AALD: ištu see išdu and išti AALD: ištu (conj.) (uštu, ultu, ilti) منذ، بَعد، بقَدرِ، حالما AALD: ištu (prep.) (eštu, uštu, ultu, issu) من، نقطة في مكان او زمان خارج (مكان، حاجة، كمية)، منذ، بعد AALD: ištu (prep) مع AALD: ulanu: see hullu Note1: ultu = أول; ulan = أولون، أولين، أولان Note2: ultu ul-la-nu = أول الاولين Note3: ultu ulanu = أوّل الاولين Note4: ultu ulanuma = كأوّل اوّلِما؛ اول باول	أسس (لسان العرب) أول (مقاييس اللغة) أول (لسان العرب) وأل (لسان العرب)
622	*ú-ma-am*	86[T11]	ePSD: umāmu umamu [BEASTS] wr. u$_2$-ma-am; u$_2$-ma-mu Akk. umāmu	همم (لسان العرب) امم (لسان العرب)
623	*ú-maš-šá-lu* *maš-lu*	14[T1] 121[T1]	ePSD: mišlu ba [HALF] wr. ba$_3$; ba$_7$ Akk. bāmtu; mišlu; šalāšā niĝsura [~TABLET] wr. niĝ$_2$-sur-ra Akk. mišlu	مثل (لسان العرب) مذل (لسان العرب) مدل (لسان العرب)

			sa [HALF] wr. sa_9 Akk. mišlu sur [HALF] wr. sur; sur_3 Akk. šinnû; mišlu ePSD: mašālu sa [EQUAL] wr. sa_2; sa_x(ZAG); se_3 Akk. kašādu; mašālu; šanānu sig [EQUAL] wr. sig_{10} Akk. mašālu	مشل (لسان العرب)
624	*um-ma-ni-šú* *um-ma-nu* *um-ma-nu* *um-man-na-ti* *um-ma-nu* *um-ma-a-ni*	33^{T1} 253^{T1} 35^{T11} 71^{T11} 86^{T11} 86^{T11}	ePSD: ummānu ugnim [ARMY] wr. ugnim Akk. ummānu ummia [EXPERT] wr. um-mi-a; um-me-a Akk. ummānu	الأَمْنُ (القاموس المحيط) أمن (لسان العرب)
625	*um-ta-aţ-ţu*	201^{T1}	ePSD: maţû lal [SMALL] wr. lal; lal_2 Akk. maţû; tamţâtu	معط (العباب الزاخر) ميط (لسان العرب) مطا (لسان العرب) متا (لسان العرب)
626	*um-tal-li* *um-tal-li* *im-ta-li* *mi-la* *im-ta-li* *im-ta-la* *ma-la* *ma-la-a* *ma-lu-ú* *ma-le-šú* *ú-ma-al-la-a*	130^{T1} 256^{T10} 174^{T11} 312^{T10} 174^{T11} 174^{T11} 279^{T10} 231^{T1} 251^{T11} 254^{T11} 124^{T11}	See also *ILLU* ePSD: mullû si [FILL] wr. si Akk. mullû; sabû; sâbu ePSD: milu a'eštub [FLOODING] wr. a-eštub$^{ku}{}_6$ Akk. milu AALD: malû (s.) شعر اشعث، غير ممشط؛ المملوء، الملآن AALD: malû (v.) (malā'u) يملئ	ملا (لسان العرب) ملأ (العباب الزاخر) ملأ (لسان العرب) ملأ (العباب الزاخر)
627	*ú-na-as-saḫ* *i-na-as-saḫ*	102^{T11} 102^{T11}	ePSD: nasāhu bur [TEAR] wr. bur_{12}; bu_7 Akk. nasāhu deg [COLLECT] wr. deg_x(RI) Akk. ahāzu; laqātu; leqû; nasāhu dirig [TEAR] wr. dirig Akk. nasāhu suh [EXTRACT] wr. suh_5; suh Akk. nasāhu zi [CUT] wr. zi_2; zi; zi_x(|IGI@g|) Akk. baqāmu; barāšu; naţāpu; nasāhu	نسح (لسان العرب) نسخ (لسان العرب)
628	*ú-na-šá-qu* *ú-na-šá-ku*	255^{T1} 11^{P}	ePSD: našāqu ne sub [KISS] wr. ne su-ub; še su-ub Akk. našāqu ePSD: nasāqu igi saĝ [CHOOSE] wr. igi $saĝ_5$; igi saĝ; igi zag; igi sig_5? Akk. bêru; nasāqu igi suh [CHOOSE] wr. igi suh Akk. nasāqu	نشق (لسان العرب) نسق (لسان العرب)
629	UNUG^{ki} UNUG^{ki} UNUG^{ki} UNUG^{ki}	11^{T1} 18^{T1} 321^{T11} 323^{T11}	See Part 2.2.33 See also Uruk^{ki} *Wikipedia:* https://en.wikipedia.org/wiki/Uruk *Online Biblical Hebrew Dictionary:* http://www.abarim-publications.com/Meaning/Erech.html#.V7Xf8qJ0P30	عنج (مقاييس اللغة) عنج (لسان العرب) عنق (مقاييس اللغة) العُنْقُ (القاموس المحيط) عنق (لسان العرب) عرق (مقاييس اللغة)

630	*ú-nu-tú*	316^{T11}	See also *an-ni-ta* ePSD: unūtu akar [IMPLEMENT] wr. ^{ĝeš}a$_2$-kar$_2$ Akk. unūtu niĝguna [UTENSILS] wr. niĝ$_2$-gu$_2$-na Akk. unūtu šukara [TOOL] wr. ^{ĝeš}šu-kara$_2$ Akk. unūtu AALD: unūtu (s) (anūtu, enūtu) الادوات، ادوات الاكل، البضائع، الشحنة، العدّة، اثاث، اواني، امتعة Libbi unūt الاحشاء الداخلية	عنن (لسان العرب)
631	*up-piš* *ú-pi-šú* *up-p-uš* *i-pu-uš-ma* *e-peš* *i-pu-uš-ma* *ep-ši-šu-ma* *ep-ši-šú-ma* *i-pu-šu-nik-ka* *e-peš* *ep-pu-uš* *i-pu-šú* *lu-pu-uš* *i-te-pu-uš* *e-te-pu-uš* *ni-ip-pu-šá* *ip-pu-uš* *ip-pu-šú* *i-pa-áš-šum-ma*	11^{T1} 11^{T1} 106^{T1} 122^{T1} 133^{T1} 134^{T1} 185^{T1} 185^{T1} 269^{T10} 5^{T11} 34^{T11} 165^{T11} 243^{T11} 314^{T11} 314^{T11} 308^{T10} 308^{T10} 75^{T11} 150^{T11}	See also *i-ba-áš-ši* See also *pe-tu-ú* See also *i-pa-DA-áš-šum-ma* ePSD: epēšu ak [DO] wr. ak; a Akk. epēšu du [BUILD] wr. du$_3$ Akk. banû; epēšu dug [SPEAK] wr. dug$_4$ Akk. atwû; dabābu; epēšu; qabû AALD: epēšu (n.) العبث، العمل، النشاط، السحر الشرير AALD: epēšu (v.) 1) بدون مفعول به مباشر: ينتشر، ينجز، يعمل، ينشط، ينشأ 2) مع المفعول به المباشر: يعالج، يصنع، ينشأ، يبني AALD: ipšu (s.) (epšu) see epēšu AALD: pašamu (v.) يُحيي؟ ، يُرجِع؟ du$_3$ See *DU.DU-ku* dug See *DUG$_4$.GA*	عبس (لسان العرب) عفس (مقاييس اللغة) عفس (لسان العرب) عبش (لسان العرب) عفش (لسان العرب) العَبْشُ (القاموس المحيط) أبس (العباب الزاخر) أبس (لسان العرب) أبش (لسان العرب) الأَبْشُ (القاموس المحيط) جفل (مقاييس اللغة) فيش (لسان العرب) بشا (لسان العرب) فشا (لسان العرب) بسأ (لسان العرب) بسا (لسان العرب) عفث (الصّحّاح في اللغة) عبث (لسان العرب) عبد (الصّحّاح في اللغة) العَبْدُ (القاموس المحيط) عبد (لسان العرب) بسس (لسان العرب) أبث (الصّحّاح في اللغة) حبش (لسان العرب) هبش (لسان العرب) حبس (لسان العرب) حبس (العباب الزاخر) حفش (لسان العرب) حفش (مقاييس اللغة) AK أَكَأَ (القاموس المحيط) عكك (لسان العرب)
632	*uq-na-ti*	33^{U}	See also $^{na}{}_{4}$*ZA.GÌN* ePSD: uqnû zagin [LAPIS] wr. za-gin$_3$; $^{na}{}_{4}$za-gin$_3$ Akk. uqnû	عقن (لسان العرب) عقا (لسان العرب) عقو (مقاييس اللغة)
633	*ú-qur* *qaq-qar* *qaq-qa-ri* *qaq-qa-ru* *qa-ru-ra*	24^{T11} 41^{T11} 314^{T11} 314^{T11} 155^{T11}	ePSD: naqāru dag [DEMOLISH] wr. dag Akk. naqāru; sukuptu ed [ASCEND] wr. ed$_3$; |UD×U+U+U.DU| Akk. arādu; elû; naqāru; šegû gul [DESTROY] wr. gul; gu-ul Akk. abātu; hepû; naqāru; sapānu kid [DEMOLISH] wr. kid$_7$ Akk. naqāru	قور (لسان العرب) القُرُّ (القاموس المحيط) قرا (لسان العرب) قارَ (القاموس المحيط) نقر (لسان العرب) وقر (لسان العرب) عقر (مقاييس اللغة)

			suhur [SCRATCH] wr. suhur Akk. ekēku; naqāru tuk [BREAK] wr. tuk$_{x}$(|IM.KAD$_{3}$|) Akk. karāşu; nakāsu; naqāru; narābu ePSD: aqāru kal [RARE] wr. kal Akk. aqāru sag [RARE] wr. sag$_{10}$; sag$_{8}$ Akk. aqru; aqāru ePSD: qaqqaru gagar [GROUND] wr. gagar Akk. qaqqaru ki [PLACE] wr. ki Akk. ašru; erşetu; mātu; qaqqaru; šaplû u [EARTH] wr. u Akk. qaqqaru ePSD: qarāru hal [ROLL] wr. hal-hal; hal Akk. qarāru kir [GROVEL] wr. kir$_{3}$ Akk. qarāru šu gur [ROLL UP] wr. šu gur Akk. qarāru; qebēru	عقر (الصّحّاح في اللغة) عقر (لسان العرب) قرر (لسان العرب)
634	*UR.BAR.RA*	191^{T11}	ePSD: barbaru urbara [WOLF] wr. ur-bar-ra Akk. barbaru	هرر (لسان العرب) البِرُّ (القاموس المحيط) برر (لسان العرب) أرب (لسان العرب)
635	*UR.GI$_{7}$*	116^{T11}	See also *UR.MAḪ.^{MES}* ePSD: UR.EŠ$_{2}$ urgir [DOG] wr. ur-gir$_{15}$ Akk. kalbu	عرس (مقاييس اللغة) عرس (العباب الزاخر) عرس (لسان العرب) عرج (الصّحّاح في اللغة) عرج (لسان العرب)
636	*UR.MAḪ.^{MES}* *UR.MAḪ*	231^{T10} 314^{T11}	See also *né-šá* See also *la-be*	عرم (مقاييس اللغة) عرم (الصّحّاح في اللغة) عرم (لسان العرب) هرم (مقاييس اللغة) الهَرَمُ (القاموس المحيط)
637	*ú-rak-ki-is*	289^{T11}	ePSD: rakāsu kešed [BIND] wr. keš$_{2}$ Akk. rakāsu sir [BIND] wr. sir$_{3}$; sir$_{2}$ Akk. rakāsu tag [TOUCH] wr. Akk. lapātu; rakāsu zu kešed [GATHER] wr. zu$_{2}$ keš$_{2}$ Akk. kaşāru; rakāsu	ركس (مقاييس اللغة) ركس (العباب الزاخر) ركس (لسان العرب) ركز (مقاييس اللغة) رَكَزَ (القاموس المحيط)
638	*ur-ḫa* *ar-ḫi* *ar-ḫa-tum* *lul-tar-ri-iḫ* *ir-ḫi* *i-re-ḫi* *i-re-eḫ-ḫi* *ur-ri-iḫ* *ur-ru-ḫiš* *ir-ḫu-ú* *ur-ḫi-šú*	9^{T1} 36^{T1} 13^{U} 221^{T1} 194^{T1} 194^{T1} 194^{T1} 221^{T1} 303^{T10} 232^{T11} 260^{T11}	See also *KASKAL* See also *har-ra-na* ePSD: urhu harran [ROUTE] wr. har-ra-an Akk. mētequ; urhu ePSD: arāhu ul [HASTEN] wr. ul$_{4}$ Akk. arāhu; hamāţu; harāpu ePSD: arhu ab [COW] wr. ab$_{2}$ Akk. arhu; littu immal [COW] wr. immal$_{2}$; im-ma-al; immal; immal$_{x}$(|NUN.LAGAR|) Akk. arhu; littu itud [MOON] wr. itud; itud$_{x}$(|UD.AN.ŠEŠ.KI|); i$_{3}$-ti; iti$_{7}$; i-ti; itud$_{x}$(|UD@s|); itud$_{x}$(|UD×BAD|) Akk. arhu šilam [COW] wr. šilam; $^{ab}{}_{2}$šilam; $^{ab}{}_{2}$šilam$_{2}$; ša$_{3}$-lam; šallam$_{2}$; $^{ab}{}_{2}$NUN.LAGAR Akk. arhu; littû	رح (مقاييس اللغة) رحي (مقاييس اللغة) رهأ (لسان العرب) رها (لسان العرب) الرَّهْوُ (القاموس المحيط) رها (الصّحّاح في اللغة) رحا (لسان العرب) رحح (لسان العرب) أرخ (لسان العرب) رخخ (لسان العرب) رخو (مقاييس اللغة) كَرَحَيْتُها (القاموس المحيط) روح (لسان العرب) حرح (لسان العرب) الحَرُّ (القاموس المحيط)

			ePSD: rehû a ri [IMPREGNATE] wr. a ri Akk. rehû ĝeš dug [COPULATE] wr. ĝeš$_3$ dug$_4$ Akk. rehû ri [IMPOSE] wr. RI; ru Akk. bâ'u; emēdu; nadû; nasāku; ramû; rehû; tarû; wašaru AALD: rehû (v.) (rahû) يُخصِب، يحَمِّل، يصب، يسكب على، يقهر، يلقّح، يُخَصّب	
639	*ur-ra* *ur-ra* *ur-ki* *ur-ri* *ur-ri* *e-ra* *ÌR-šú* *ur-ra* *ur-ri* *ú-ri*	69^{T1} 86^{T1} 181^{T1} 194^{T1} 235^{T10} 284^{T10} 37^{T11} 128^{T11} 128^{T11} 136^{T11}	See also URU ePSD: UR lu [PERSON] wr. lu$_2$; mu-lu; mu-lu$_2$; lu$_{10}$; lu$_6$ Akk. amēlu; ša šuzi [UNMNG] wr. šuzi Akk. ? teš [PRIDE] wr. teš$_2$ Akk. bāštu teš [UNITY] wr. teš$_2$ ur [DOG] wr. ur; ^{ĝeš}ur Akk. kalbu; labbu ur [HE] wr. ur$_5$; ur Akk. amtu; ištēn; mithāru; šû ur [MAN] wr. ur Akk. amēlu ur [SERVANT] wr. ur ePSD: erû; urrû sug [EMPTY] wr. sug$_4$ Akk. erû; urrû; riāqu AALD: erâ (adv.) (aria, iria, irâ) جنب الى جنب	عور (الصّحّاح في اللغة) عور (لسان العرب) عرر (لسان العرب) عرا (لسان العرب)
640	*ur-rad-ma* *ú-rid*	42^{T11} 304^{T11}	ePSD: arādu ed [ASCEND] wr. ed$_3$; |UD×U+U+U.DU| Akk. arādu; elû; naqāru; šegû AALD: *arādu (v.) (warāda, eredu) يردّ، يزل (ارضا، تلا، نهرا)، يهبط، يخسر، يتخلى، يترك، يهجر، يستسلم، يذعن، يُعلّق، ينقل، يُزيل	أرض (لسان العرب) عرض (لسان العرب) عرد (لسان العرب) رد (مقاييس اللغة) ردد (لسان العرب) ورد (الصّحّاح في اللغة) ورد (مقاييس اللغة) الوَرْدُ (القاموس المحيط) ورد (لسان العرب)
641	*ur-ta-aş-şa-nu*	229^{T1}	ePSD: raşānu zulun [HAVE A POWERFUL VOICE] wr. zu-lu-un Akk. raşānu	رصن (لسان العرب) رصن (مقاييس اللغة) رَصَنَهُ (القاموس المحيط) حفي (مقاييس اللغة) حفا (لسان العرب)
642	*ur-tag-gi-ib-ši*	61^{T11}	AALD: rugbu (s.) (rugubu) العَليّة، الشُرفة، الغُرفة العُليا AALD: ruggubu (s.) (بيت) مسقوف AALD: ruggubu (v.) يَسقف AALD: rugbūtu see ruqbubu	رجب (مقاييس اللغة) رجب (الصّحّاح في اللغة) رَجِبَ (القاموس المحيط) رجب (لسان العرب)
643	URU URU URU-*ku-nu-ma* URU^{ki}	22^{T1} 35^{T11} 40^{T11} 327^{T11}	See also *ur-ra* ePSD: uru iri [CITY] wr. iri; iri^{ki}; uru$_2$; uru$_{11}$; iri$_{11}$ "city" Akk. ālu	وأر (لسان العرب) أري (مقاييس اللغة) أري (الصّحّاح في اللغة) أري (لسان العرب) أرر (لسان العرب) أور (لسان العرب)
644	Uruk^{ki}	10^{P} 28^{P}	See UNUG^{ki}	
645	*ú-šá-az-na-nak-ku-*	43^{T11}	ePSD: zanānu	مزن (الصّحّاح في اللغة)

	nu-ši *ú-šá-az-na-na-ku-nu-ši*	47[T11]	sur [PRESS] wr. sur; sur$_{8}$ Akk. natāku; zanānu; ṣahātu; ṣarāru šeĝ [RAIN] wr. šeĝ$_{3}$; šeĝ$_{x}$(|IM.A.A|); šeĝ$_{x}$(|IM.A.AN|) Akk. nalāšu; zanānu	مزن (لسان العرب) زنن (الصّحاح في اللغة) زنن (لسان العرب)
646	*ú-šab-ri-šum-ma*	197[T11]	See *ši-pir*	
647	*ú-šal-pi-tu* *nu-šal-pi-tu*	43[T1] 230[T10]	ePSD: šalputtu hulu [RUINATION] wr. hul Akk. šalputtu	سَلَفَ (القاموس المحيط) سلف (العباب الزاخر) سلف (مقاييس اللغة) لهن (لسان العرب) سلب (لسان العرب) سلب (مقاييس اللغة)
648	*ú-šar-di* *šá-a-ru*	103[T11] 129[T11]	ePSD: SAR sar [RUN] wr. sar Akk. hamāṭu; lasāmu sar [SMOKE] wr. sar ePSD: šāru im [RAIN] wr. im; me-er Akk. zunnu; šāru sisig [BREEZE] wr. sig-sig; ^{tumu}si-si-ig; si-si-ga; sig$_{3}$-sig$_{3}$ Akk. mehû; zīqīqu?; šāru šutur [UNMNG] wr. šu-tur Akk. šāru	سعر (لسان العرب)
649	*uš-bi-šú-nu*	170[T1]	See also *it-taš-bu-ni* AALD: ušultu (s.) العشبُ؛ الحشيشُ Note: al-Jibouri's rule: ušubtu -> ušultu; عُشُلتو <- عُشُبْتو	العِسْكِبَةُ (القاموس المحيط) الإِسْبُ (القاموس المحيط) أسب (لسان العرب) عسب (لسان العرب) أشب (مقاييس اللغة) أشب (الصّحاح في اللغة) أشب (لسان العرب) شبا (لسان العرب) وشب (لسان العرب) عشب (لسان العرب)
650	*ú-še-ṣu-ú* *ú-še-ṣi-ma* *ú-še-ṣi-ma* *ú-še-ṣi-ma*	232[T1] 148[T11] 151[T11] 154[T11]	See also *mu-uṣ-ṣi-ma* AALD: šūṣû (adj.) protruding?, turned out? (see aṣû)	شَصِيَ (القاموس المحيط) شصا (لسان العرب) الشَّظَى (القاموس المحيط) شوظ (لسان العرب) شوص (مقاييس اللغة) الشَّوْصُ (القاموس المحيط) شوص (لسان العرب) شوس (لسان العرب)
651	*uš-ni-lu*	131[T1]	See also *šit-tin-šú*	ثني (لسان العرب)
652	*uṣ-ṣir* *iṣ-ṣi-ru* *e-ṣir-ši* *eṣ-ri*	49[T1] 317[T10] 60[T11] 221[T11]	ePSD: eṣēru ĝeš hur [DRAW] wr. ĝeš hur Akk. eṣēru hur [SCRATCH] wr. hur Akk. eṣēru murgu [DRAW] wr. murgu Akk. eṣēru	صرر (الصّحاح في اللغة) صر (مقاييس اللغة) الصِّرَّةُ (القاموس المحيط) الأَصْرُ (القاموس المحيط) أصر (لسان العرب) صير (لسان العرب)
653	*uš-šú-šú*	21[T1]	See also *ul-tu* See also *iš-tén*	أسس (لسان العرب)
654	*uš-ta-aḫ-ri-ru* *uš-ḫa-ri-ir* *šu-ḫar-ra-as-su* *uš-ḫa-ri-ir*	116[T1] 118[T1] 106[T11] 133[T11]	See also *as-ḫur* ePSD: šīru su [FLESH] wr. su Akk. zumru; šīru	سحر (مقاييس اللغة) السَّحْرُ (القاموس المحيط) سحر (الصّحاح في اللغة) سحر (لسان العرب)

	uš-ḫa-ri-ir-ma	133[T11]	uzu [FLESH] wr. uzu; uzu(LAK350) Akk. šīru kiĝnim [MEAL] (7x: Old Babylonian) wr. kiĝ$_2$-nim Akk. naptan šērti ePSD: naptan līliāti kiĝsig [MEAL] wr. kiĝ$_2$-sig; kiĝ$_2$-sig$_7$; kiĝ$_2$-sig$_{17}$; kiĝ$_2$-sig$_x$(SAR) Akk. naptan līliāti AALD: šuharrura (v.) (šahurruru, šuhurruru, šuhruru) يدوخ، يصيب بالدوران، يصبح: ساكنا، خدران مع خوف؛ يخمد، يهمد AALD: šuharrura (adj.) سكوت؟ AALD: šuharriš (adv.) (or šuhurriš) في خدر، ساكن، هادئ Note: šuharrura = šú + ḫarrura (heat) = ذو حَرَرُ (حرارة)	شحر (لسان العرب) الشَّحْرُ (القاموس المحيط) حرر (لسان العرب)
655	*uš-te-li* *SAL* *i-šal-lal* *SAL-lu* *šal-lu* *uš-te-li* *sa-lat-ia* *ú-še-li* *ú-šal-lu* *uš-te-la-an-ni* *uš-te-li*	132[T1] 20[P] 303[T10] 316[T10] 316[T10] 85[T11] 85[T11] 86[T11] 136[T11] 200[T11] 201[T11]	ePSD: šalālu ir [PLUNDER] wr. ir Akk. šalālu sur [SPIN] wr. sur Akk. ţawû; šalālu ePSD: ašlu ninni [REEDS] wr. [u]$_2$ninni$_5$ Akk. ašlu ePSD: šalātu sil [SPLIT] wr. si-il; zil; sil$_x$(|EZEN×LAL$_2$|); sil$_5$ Akk. nesû; šalātu ePSD: ušallu usal [MEADOW] wr. u$_2$-sal; u$_8$-sal; SAL.|LAGAB×(GUD+GUD)|.DI?; |LAGAB×(GUD+GUD)|.DI.UD.SAL? Akk. aburriš; ušallu	سعل (مقاييس اللغة) وسل (مقاييس اللغة) وسل (لسان العرب) سلت (لسان العرب) السَّلُّ (القاموس المحيط) سلل (لسان العرب) أسل (مقاييس اللغة) الأَسَلُ (القاموس المحيط) سل (مقاييس اللغة) أسل (لسان العرب)
656	*uš-te-še-ru*	168[T1]	See also *ú-ta-ad-da-ri* ePSD: šurrû tab [BEGIN] wr. tab Akk. šurrû ePSD: šurru gu gid [LEAN] wr. gu$_2$ gid$_2$ Akk. šurru gu la [LEAN OVER] wr. gu$_2$ la$_2$ Akk. šurru	شر (مقاييس اللغة) الشَّرُّ (القاموس المحيط) سرر (لسان العرب) ذرا (لسان العرب) ذرأ (لسان العرب) ذرا (الصّحّاح في اللغة) ذرر (لسان العرب)
657	*uš-te-ziq* *ul-te-ziq*	255[T10] 255[T10]	ePSD: ešqu rib [SURPASSING] wr. rib; ri-ba Akk. ešqu; šūtuqu AALD: esēku (see esēqu) AALD: ezēqu (see esēqu) AALD: esēqu (v.) يرسم، يَسِمُ، ينحت نقشا جداريا	عزق (لسان العرب) عسك (لسان العرب) عَسِكَ (القاموس المحيط) أزق (لسان العرب) ازِقَ (القاموس المحيط) أزَق (مقاييس اللغة)
658	*uš-ti-nim-ma* *it-ti-lam-ma*	24[P] 24[P]	See also *NIM.*[meš] Note: al-Jibouri rule: ittinama -> ittilama	نأم (لسان العرب) نوم (لسان العرب)
659	*ú-ṭa-ab-ba-aḫ* *uṭ-ṭàb-bi-iḫ*	261[T10] 71[T11]	ePSD: ţābihu ĝirila [BUTCHER] wr. ĝiri$_2$-la$_2$ Akk. ţābihu flay	طبح (لسان العرب) طبخ (لسان العرب) طبخ (مقاييس اللغة)
660	*ú-ta-ad-da-ri* *uš-ta-dir* *in-na-dir* *ul-ta-dir*	67[T1] 84[T1] 118[T1] 30[U]	See also *ši-ir-a-ni-ia* See also *uš-te-še-ru* ePSD: adaru?	حدر (لسان العرب) حذر (مقاييس اللغة) أدر (مقاييس اللغة) در (مقاييس اللغة)

	a-dur *te-ed-dira-aš-x-šú*	238^{T10} 22^{P}	saĝ bala [SHAKE] wr. saĝ bala Akk. a-da-ru? ePSD: adāru ildag [POPLAR] wr. ^{ĝeš}ildag$_2$; ^{ĝeš}ildag$_4$; ildag$_2$; ^{ĝeš}ildag$_3$; ^{ĝeš}ildag; ^{ĝeš}ildag$_x$ Akk. adāru; ildakku kana [DARK] wr. kana$_6$; kana$_5$; kana$_3$ Akk. adāru ePSD: idirtu sumug [DARKNESS] wr. su-mu-ug; su$_2$-mu-ug Akk. idirtu AALD: šu'ru (šuhru, šūru): حاجب العين AALD: adāru (v.) (See: adirtu, adiru) يقلق، يسبب الازعاج او الخوف	ندر (لسان العرب) ذعر (لسان العرب) ذأر (لسان العرب) الذَّورُ (القاموس المحيط) أدر (لسان العرب) أطر (لسان العرب) الدارُ (القاموس المحيط) درى (الصّحَاح في اللغة) دَرَأَهُ (القاموس المحيط) دري (مقاييس اللغة) دري (لسان العرب) درأ (لسان العرب)
661	*ut-ta-as-si-iḫ* *i-šá-aḫ-ḫi* *is-su-uḫ-šú* *is-su-uḫ-a*	131^{T1} 156^{T11} 291^{T11} 291^{T11}	ePSD: šahāhu dirig [FALL] wr. dirig Akk. qâpu; šahāhu šab [TRIM] wr. šab Akk. barû ša uzu; esēpu; harāru; harāşu; harāşu; eşēru; harāşu; šarāmu; nakāsu; šahāhu ePSD: suhhu sah [MAT] wr. sah Akk. suhhu	سخا (لسان العرب) سها (لسان العرب) سح (مقاييس اللغة) سحا (الصّحَاح في اللغة) سحا (لسان العرب) سحح (لسان العرب)
662	*ú-um-mi-id-ma* *i-mi-du* *i-te-mid* *e-mid* *e-mid*	12^{P} 13^{P} 142^{T11} 185^{T11} 186^{T11}	ePSD: emēdu ri [IMPOSE] wr. RI; ru Akk. bâ'u; emēdu; nadû; nasāku; ramû; rehû; tarû; wašaru us [LEAN] wr. us2 Akk. emēdu; sanāqu ePSD: madādu aĝ [MEASURE] wr. aĝ$_2$ Akk. madādu ePSD: mādu i'iz [NUMEROUS] wr. i-iz Akk. mādu mah [GREAT] wr. mah; mah$_2$ Akk. kabtu; mādu; rabû; şīru ePSD: mādūtu didli [SEVERAL] wr. didli Akk. mādūtu AALD: nēmedu (nēmadu) (see emēdu): المساعدة، منصة الطقوس AALD: mandidūtu (see mādidūtu) AALD: manididu (see mādidu) AALD: middatu (s.) (mindatu, maddatu, mandatu) (pl. middātu, mindātu, miniātu see madādu) مقياس للحجم؛ مقياس للطول، المساحة، المنطقة، الوقت؛ القصبة: مقياس للطول وتساوي 550 ياردة	عمد (مقاييس اللغة) عمد (لسان العرب) أمد (لسان العرب) مدي (مقاييس اللغة) مدى (لسان العرب) مدد (الصّحَاح في اللغة) مدد (لسان العرب)
663	*UZU.^{MEŠ}-šú-nu* *UZU.^{MEŠ}-šú*	261^{T10} 252^{T11}	See also *ši-ir-a-ni-ia* See also *še-er* ePSD: UZU uzu [FLESH] wr. uzu; uzu(LAK350) Akk. šīru	عزا (لسان العرب) عزا (لسان العرب) عض (مقاييس اللغة) عضو (مقاييس اللغة) عضه (لسان العرب) عضا (لسان العرب)
664	*ú-zu-un-šú*	242^{T1}	See also *GEŠTU.MIN-šú* ePSD: uznu ĝeštug [EAR] wr. ĝeštug$_2$; ^{ĝeš}ĝeštug; ĝeštug; ĝeštug$_3$; muštug$_2$; mu-uš-tug$_2$; mu-uš-tug Akk. hassu; uznu; uznu; ţēmu ĝizzal [EAR] wr. ĝizzal; gizzal$_2$ Akk. hasīsu; uznu; uznu; nešmû	أذن (لسان العرب) وزن (لسان العرب)

665	*uz-zu-ḫu*	227[T1]	AALD: zahû (s.) الرداء، الكساء	زها (لسان العرب)
666	*ZABAR*	25[T1]	ePSD: zabar zabar [BRONZE] wr. zabar; zabar₃ Akk. ebbu; hutpu; kakku; mušālu; namru; qû; sappu; siparru	زبر (لسان العرب)
667	*ze-ru-tum* *ze-ru-tu* *ze-er-ma* *i-ze-er-an-ni-ma* *li-zer-ka*	311[T10] 311[T10] 26[T11] 39[T11] 248[T11]	See also *NUMUN* ePSD: zēru i'iz [SEED] wr. i-iz Akk. zēru numun [SEED] wr. numun Akk. zēru šenumun [SEED] wr. še-numun Akk. zēru ePSD: zêru gu bar [DISLIKE] wr. gu₂ bar Akk. zêru gu du [NEGLECT] wr. gu₂ du₃ Akk. zêru hulu gig [HATE] wr. hul gig Akk. zêru AALD: zērāti (s. pl. only) (zērūtu) (see zerû) العداوة، البغضاء AALD: zerû (v.) (ze'āru) يكره، يبغض، يتجنب، يكون مكروها	زحر (لسان العرب) زأر (لسان العرب) زير (لسان العرب) زور (لسان العرب) زغر (لسان العرب) زهر (لسان العرب) زعر (لسان العرب) زعبر (لسان العرب)
668	*ZI.*[MEŠ] *ZI.*[MEŠ]	25[T11] 84[T11]	See also *SU-šú* See also *šá* See *ni-ip-šu* Zi see [m]*UD-ZI-tim*	نفس (العباب الزاخر) ذيا (لسان العرب) ذا (لسان العرب)
669	*zik-ri* *zik-ri* *zi-kir-šú* *zik-ru* *zi-kir* *zi-ik-ri* *i-zak-ka-ra* *i-zak-ka-ra* *iz-za-kàr-am* *iz-za-kàr-am* *iz-za-kàr-am*	79[T1] 80[T1] 96[T1] 100[T1] 100[T1] 100[T1] 134[T1] 161[T1] 2[P] 16[P] 38[P]	See also *MU-ra* ePSD: zikru zikru [NAME] wr. zi-ik- Akk. zikru ePSD: zikaru duri [MALE] wr. duri Akk. zikaru ĝeš [PENIS] wr. ĝeš₃; mu Akk. išaru; zikaru nita [MALE] wr. nita₂; nita; nitaₓ(|ARAD×KUR|) Akk. zikaru pap [RELATION] wr. pap Akk. abu; ahu; ašarēdu; zikaru pil [MALE] wr. pil₆ Akk. zikaru urum [MALE] wr. urum₃ Akk. zikaru	ذِكر (لسان العرب) الذِّكْرُ (القاموس المحيط) ذكر (مقاييس اللغة)
670	*zi-mu-ú-ka*	214[T10]	See also *zu-um-ru-šú* ePSD: zīmu muš [FACE] wr. muš₃; muš₂ Akk. zīmu mušme [FACE] wr. muš₃-me Akk. zīmu; būnu rein AALD: zīmu (s.) الوهج (للنجوم)، المظهر، الهيئة، الرونق، البهاء	زم (مقاييس اللغة) زمم (لسان العرب)
671	*ziq-qur-rat*	158[T11]	ePSD: zaqāru dirig [EXCEED] wr. diri; RI Akk. atru; eli; rabû; kapāšu; zaqāru; šarūru; šūturu; lē'û Note: ziqqurrat = zayqūrah = زيقورة ziqqurrat = şayqūrah = sayqūrah = زيقورة، سيقورة، صيقورة	زيق (لسان العرب) صقر (مقاييس اللغة) الصَّقْرُ (القاموس المحيط) صقر (لسان العرب)
672	*zu-um-bé-e*	163[T11]	See also *NIM.*[meš]	ذبب (لسان العرب) ذب (مقاييس اللغة) زب (مقاييس اللغة)

			AALD: zumbu (s.) (zubbu, zunbu) الذبابة، حُلية من الاحجار الكريمة بشكل الذبابة	الزَّبَبُ (القاموس المحيط) زبب (لسان العرب) زنب (لسان العرب) زَنِبَ (القاموس المحيط)
673	*zu-um-me*	249^{T11}	ePSD: zamû zage [FOREMOST] wr. zag-e$_3$ Akk. ašarēdu; zamû; āşītu zamû Akk. ašarēdu; zamû; āşītu AALD: zummu (v.) يفتقر، يخطئ، يتجنّب، يكون مُشتقا، مستنتجا؛ يُسّبب تجَنُّب، ؛ يُسّبب الاشتقاق	زمع (مقاييس اللغة) الزَّمَعَةُ (القاموس المحيط) زمع (لسان العرب)
674	*zu-um-ru-šú* *zu-mur-šú*	105^{T1} 256^{T11}	See also *ZU-šu* See also *zi-mu-ú-ka* ePSD: zumru kuš [SKIN] wr. kuš Akk. mašku; zumru su [FLESH] wr. su Akk. zumru; šīru	ثمر (لسان العرب) زمر (لسان العرب) زمر (مقاييس اللغة) ضمر (الصّحّاح في اللغة)
675	*zu-'u-na* *zu-u'-na* *za-nin-u* *za-ni-n*	231^{T1} 237^{T1} 288^{T10} 294^{T10}	ePSD: za'ānu šu tag [DECORATE] wr. šu tag Akk. za'ānu grace ePSD: zanānu sur [PRESS] wr. sur; sur$_8$ Akk. natāku; zanānu; şahātu; şarāru šeĝ [RAIN] wr. šeĝ$_3$; šeĝ$_x$(|IM.A.A|); šeĝ$_x$(|IM.A.AN|) Akk. nalāšu; zanānu AALD: zāninu (adj., s.) (see zanānu) سقوط المطر؛ المجهز، المزود؛ التجهيز	الزِينةُ (القاموس المحيط) زين (لسان العرب) زون (مقاييس اللغة) زأن (لسان العرب) زنأ (لسان العرب) زنا (لسان العرب) زنن (لسان العرب) زون (لسان العرب) وزن (لسان العرب)

Part 3

Latin Transliterations

1

Tablet 1
The Standard Babylonian Edition

Latin Transliteration by

Andrew R. George
SOAS University of London

Department of the Languages and Cultures of the Near and Middle East
The Standard Babylonian Epic of Gilgamesh
Sources of the Standard Babylonian poem
http://www.soas.ac.uk/nme/research/gilgamesh/standard/

TABLET I

Siglum	*Museum number* *Distribution of lines by column*		*Plate in George Bab. Gilg. Epic*
	NINEVEH		
B_1	K 913+2756+2756E+2756F+6541+81-7-27, 93		36–40
B_2	K 2756A+2756B+13874		37–9
B_3	K 2756C		37
	i **1**–2 (B_1), 3–18 (B_3)	iv **149**–63 (B_2), 179–**200** (B_1)	
	ii **48**–51 (B_1), 100–**101** (B_2)	v 202–**251** (B_1(+)B_2)	
	iii 107–20 (B_1), 142–**148** (B_2)	vi 260–**300**, colophon (B_1)	
F_1	K 2756D+20778		41
F_2	K 7017		41
F_3	K 8584		41
F_4	K 12000Q		41
	i 3–14 (F_3)	iv **168**–76 (F_2), 180–205 (F_1)	
	ii 63–74 (F_3)	v 242–5, 252–66 (F_1)	
	iii 160–**167** (F_2)	vi 299–**300**, colophon (F_4)	
P	K 4465+9245+22153+Sm 2133		42–5
	ii 55–62, 75–**121**	iv **173**–**220**	
	iii **122**–46, 157–**172**	v **221**–48, 251–65	
	NIMRUD		
g	IM 67577 (ND 4405/4)		46
	i 19–54	[rev. not extant]	
	ii 111–15, 120–4		
	BABYLON		
d_1	Rm 785+956+1017+BM 34248+34357		47
d_2	K 15145 (Rm)		47
	i **1**–17 (d_1(+)d_2)	v unplaced traces (d_1)	
	ii **56**–73 (d_1)	–	
h	BM 34916+35419		48–9
	i 7–53	v **211**–17, 228–9, 235–43	
	ii 80–111	vi **259**–**300**	
n	BM 37163+F 234		50
	iii **97**–101	iv 194–**200**	
o	BM 38538		50
	i **1**–2	vi 286–**300**, colophon	
x	VAT 17234		51
	ii 72–89	iv 172–96	
	iii unplaced	v 229–42	

URUK

cc IM 76973 (W 22744/1 b) 52

ii 99–103	iv 158–63
–	v 208–17

Score transliteration

1	B_1	i 1	[ ]-⸢a⸣-ti
	B_1	col.	[šá nag-ba i-mu-ru i]š-di ma-a-ti
	d_1	i 1	[i]š-⸢di⸣ ma-a-[ti]
	o	i 1	[i]š-di ma-[a]-t[i]
2	B_1	i 2	[ḫ]as?-s[u]
	d_1	i 2	[-ti i-du]-⸢ú ka⸣-la-mu ḫa-as-[su]
	o	i 2	[ ] ⸢ka-la-a?-mu? ḫas⸣-[su]
3	B_3	i 1'	[^{d}GIŠ-gím-maš šá n]ag-⸢ba i-mu-ru⸣ [ ]
	F_3	i 1'	[-b]a ⸢i⸣-[ ]
	d_1	i 3	[ ] i-mu-ru iš-di ma-⸢a⸣-[ti]
4	B_3	i 2'	[-t]i i-du-ú ka-l[a-]
	F_3	i 2'	[ ] i-du-⸢ú⸣ [x (x) x]
	d_1	i 4	[i-d]u-ú ka-la-mu ḫa-a[s-su]
5	B_3	i 3'	[x x]x-ma mit-ḫa-riš p[a-]
	F_3	i 3'	[ ]-ḫa-riš [ ]
	d_1	i 5	[-ḫ]a-riš pa-x[x]
6	B_3	i 4'	[nap-ḫ]ar né-me-qí ša ka-la-a-mi [ ]
	F_3	i 4'	[ ] šá ka-la-ma ⸢i⸣-[x x]
	d_1	i 6	[ ] šá ka-la-mu [x (x)]
7	B_3	i 5'	[ni]-ṣir-ta i-mur-ma ka-ti-im-t[i]
	F_3	i 5'	[ ] ka-tim-tú i[p-te]
	d_1	i 1'	[-m]a ka-tim-ti ip-⸢tu⸣
	h	i 1'	[-m]a ⸢ka⸣-t[im-]
8	B_3	i 6'	[u]b-la ṭè-e-ma šá la-am [ ]
	F_3	i 6'	[l]a-am a-⸢bu⸣-b[i]
	d_1	i 2'	-a]m a-bu-bu
	h	i 2'	[-m]u [ ]
9	B_3	i 7'	[u]r-ḫa ru-uq-ta il-li-kam-ma a-ni-iḫ ⸢u/ù⸣ [ ]
	F_3	i 7'	[-ká]m-ma a-ni-iḫ ù šup-[ ]
	d_1	i 3'	[-m]a a-ni-iḫ u šup-šu-uḫ
	h	i 3'	[r]u-uq-tum il-la-kam-ma a-n[i-]

10	B_3	i 8'	[šá-k]in i-na ^{na_4}NA.RÚ.A ka-lu ma-na-a[ḫ-]
	F_3	i 8'	[ ]-e ka-lu ma-⸢na-aḫ⸣-t[i]
	d_1	i 4'	[m]a-⸢na⸣-aḫ-ti
	h	i 4'	[ ] i-na na-re-e ka-lu m[a-]
11	B_3	i 9'	[up-pi]š BÀD šá UNUG^{ki} su-p[u-ri]
	F_3	i 9'	[š]á ⸢UNUG⸣^{ki} su-pú-⸢ri⸣
	d_1	i 5'	[s]u-pu-ru
	h	i 5'	⸢ú⸣-pi-šú BÀD šá UNUG^{ki} s[u-]
12	B_3	i 10'	[šá é].⸢an⸣.na qud-du-ši šu-tum$_4$-mi e[l-lim]
	F_3	i 10'	[ ] el-⸢lim⸣
	d_1	i 6'	[ ] e[l$^?$]-⸢lim⸣
	d_2	i 1'	[qu]d-⸢du-ši⸣ š[u-]
	h	i 6'	šá é.an.na qud-du-šu šu-tùm-mu [ ]
13	B_3	i 11'	[a-mur B]ÀD-šu šá ki-ma qé-e n[i-x x]
	F_3	i 11'	[-i]p-š[u$^?$]
	d_2	i 2'	[-š]ú šá ki-ma qé-⸢e⸣ [ ]
	h	i 7'	a-mur du-ur-šú šá ki-ma qé-e ni-ip-š[u$^?$]
14	B_3	i 12'	[i-tap-la-a]s sa-me-ta-šu šá la ú-maš-šá-l[u]
	F_3	i 12'	[ ]-⸢lu⸣ [ ]
	d_2	i 3'	[-a]s sa-me-ta-šá š[á]
	h	i 8'	i-tap-la-as sa-me-ta-šá šá la ú-maš-šá-lu mam-ma
15	B_3	i 13'	[$^{gi]š}$KUN$_4$ šá ul-tu u[l$^{!?}$-]
	d_2	i 4'	[KU]N$_4$ š[á]
	h	i 9'	ṣa-bat-ma ^{giš}KUN$_4$ šá ul-tu ul-la-nu
16	B_3	i 14'	[é.a]n.na šu-b[at]
	d_2	i 5'	[.n]a šu-[ ]
	h	i 10'	qit-ru-ub ana é.an.na šu-bat ^{d}15
17	B_3	i 15'	[l]a ú-maš-š[á-]
	d_2	i 6'	[ ] ⸢la ú⸣-[ ]
	h	i 11'	šá LUGAL ár-ku-ú la ú-maš-šá-lu LÚ mam-ma
18	B_3	i 16'	[ ] ⸢šá⸣ U[NUG^{ki}]
	h	i 12'	e-li-ma ina$^?$ UGU BÀD šá UNUG^{ki} IM-tal-lak
19	**g**	i 1'	[ ]-⸢iṭ⸣-[ ]
	h	i 13'	te-me-en-nu ḫi-iṭ-ma SIG$_4$ ṣu-ub-bu
20	**g**	i 2'	[SI]G$_4$-šu la ⸢a⸣-[ ]
	h	i 14'	šum-ma SIG$_4$-šú la a-gur-⸢rat⸣
21	**g**	i 3'	[i]d-du-ú ⸢7⸣ [ ]
	h	i 15'	u uš-šú-šú la id-du-ú 7 ⸢mun⸣-tal-ku

22	**g**	i 4'	[^{giš}KIR]I.MEŠ šár es-su-⸢ú⸣ pi-t[ir]
	h	i 16'	[šár] ⸢URU⸣ [šár ^{giš}]⸢KIRI$^{?}$⸣.[MEŠ] ⸢šár es⸣-[s]u-ú GÉŠ.U.GÉŠ.U.GÉŠ.U É ^{d}15
23	**g**	i 5'	[3 šár] ù pi-ti-ir UN[U]G^{ki} ta[m-]
	h	i 17'	[^{k}]^{i} tam-ši-ḫu
24	**g**	i 6'	[ ] ^{giš}tup-šen-na šá ^{gi}[^{š}ERIN]
	h	i 18'	[ ] šá ^{giš}ERIN
25	**g**	i 7'	[ ]x ḫar-gal-li-šu šá ZAB[AR]
	h	i 19'	[-š]ú šá ZABAR
26	**g**	i 8'	[pi-te-m]a$^{?}$ KÁ šá ni-ṣir-ti-[ ]
	h	i 20'	[ ] šá ⸢ni-ṣir-ti⸣-šú
27	**g**	i 9'	[i-š]i$^{?}$-ma ṭup-pi ^{na4}ZA.GÌN ši-tas-si
	h	i 21'	[x (x)]x ⸢ṭup-pi⸣ ^{n}[^{a4}] si-taš-ši
28	**g**	i 10'	[ ]-ú ^{d}GIŠ-gím-maš DU.DU-ku ka-lu mar-ṣa-a-ti
	h	i 22'	[mim-m]u-ú ^{d}GIŠ-⸢gím⸣-[-ka]m ka-la mar-ṣa-a-tum
29	**g**	i 11'	[šu-t]u-ur UGU LUGAL.MEŠ šá-nu-'-ú-du EN gat-ti
	h	i 23'	[šu-t]ur UGU LUGAL.M[EŠ šá-nu]-⸢'⸣-ú-du EN gat-ti
30	**g**	i 12'	[qa]r-du lil-lid UNUG^{ki} ri-i-mu mut-tak-pu
	h	i 24'	[qa]r-du lil-li-du ⸢UNUG^{ki}⸣ AM ⸢mut⸣-tak-pu
31	**g**	i 13'	[i]l-lak ina pa-ni a-šá-red
	h	i 25'a	[i]l-lak ina IGI a-šá-red :
32	**g**	i 14'	[a]r-ka ⸢il⸣-lak-ma tukul-ti ŠEŠ.MEŠ-šú
	h	i 25'b	ár-ku il-⸢lak⸣ tukul-ti ŠEŠ.MEŠ-šú
33	**g**	i 15'	[k]ib-ru dan-nu ṣu-lul um-ma-ni-šú
	h	i 26'	kib-ri dan-nu ṣu-lul um$^{!}$-ma-ni-šú
34	**g**	i 16'	⸢a⸣-gu-ú ez-zu mu-ab-bit BÀD NA_4
	h	i 27'	a-gu-ú ez-zu mu-ab-bit ⸢BÀD⸣ NA_4
35	**g**	i 17'	[ri-m]u šá ^{d}lugal-bàn-da ^{d}GIŠ-gím-maš gít-⸢ma⸣-lu e-mu-qí
	h	i 28'	AM šá ^{d}lugal-bàn-da ^{d}GIŠ-gím-maš gít-ma-lu e-mu-qí
36	**g**	i 18'	[e-ni]q ar-ḫi ṣir-ti ^{f}ri-mat-^{d}nin-sún
	h	i 29'	e-niq ÁB ṣir-⸢tum⸣ šá ^{f}ri-mat-^{d}nin-sún-an-na
37	**g**	i 19'	[ši-ḫ]u ^{d}GIŠ-gím-maš gít-ma-lu ra-šub-bu
	h	i 30'	ši-i-ḫu ^{d}⟨GIŠ⟩-gím-maš gít-ma-lu ra-šub-bu
38	**g**	i 20'	[pe-t]u-ú né-re-bé-e-ti šá ḫur-sa-a-ni
	h	i 31'	pe-tu-ú né-re-bé-e-tum šá ḫur-sa-an-nu

39	**g**	i 21'	[ḫe-ru]-ú bu-ú-ri šá GÚ KUR-i
	h	i 32'	ḫe-ru-ú bu-ú-ru šá GÚ KUR-i
40	**g**	i 22'	[e-b]ir a-ab-⌜ba ta⌝-ma-ti DAGAL-ti EN ^{d}UTU.È
	h	i 33'	⌜e⌝-bir a-ab-ba ta-ma-tim DAGAL-tim EN ^{d}UTU.È.A
41	**g**	i 23'	[ḫa-a]-a-iṭ kib-⌜ra⌝-a-ti muš-⌜te⌝-ʾ-ú ba-lá-ṭi
	h	i 34'	ḫa-a-a-iṭ kib-ra-a-tum muš-te-ʾ-ú ba-lá-⌜ṭu⌝
42	**g**	i 24'	[ka]-ši-id dan-nu-⌜us!⌝-su! a-na ^{m}UD-ZI ru-ú-qí
	h	i 35'	ka-šid dan-nu-us-su ana UD-ZI-tim ru-⌜ú⌝-qa
43	**g**	i 25'	[mu-t]ir ⌜ma-ḫa⌝-zi ana aš-ri-šú-nu šá ú-ḫal-li-qu a-bu-bu
	h	i 36'	mu-tir ma-ḫa-⌜zu⌝ ana áš-ri-⌜šu⌝-nu šá ú-šal-⌜pi!-tu a-bu-bu⌝
44	**g**	i 26'	[mu-ki]n p[ar-ṣ]i ana ÙG.MEŠ a-pa-a-ti
	h	i 37'	⌜mu-kin⌝ par-ṣi ana ⌜ÙG⌝.[M]EŠ ⌜a⌝-[ ]
45	**g**	i 27'	[ ] ⌜it-ti⌝-šu iš-šá-an-na-nu a-na LUGAL-ti
	h	i 38'	man-nu it-ti-šú ⌜iš⌝-tan-na-an [ ]
46	**g**	i 28'	[ ] ⌜d⌝GIŠ-gím-maš i-qab-bu-ú a-na-ku-ma LUGAL
	h	i 39'	ù ki-i ⌜d⌝GIŠ-gím-maš i-qab-bu-⌜ú⌝ [ ]
47	**g**	i 29'	[^{d}GIŠ-gím-m]aš ⌜ul!⌝-tu u_4-um iʾ-al-du na-bu šum-šú
	h	i 40'	^{d}GIŠ-gím-maš ul-tu u_4-mu al-du [ ]
48	B_1	ii 1	šit-tin-šú DINGIR-ma [ ]
	g	i 30'	[-š]ú DINGIR-ma šul-lul-ta-šú a-me-lu-tu
	h	i 41'	[ši]t-⌜ta⌝-šú DINGIR-um-ma ⌜šul-lul⌝-t[a-]
49	B_1	ii 2	ṣa-lam pag-ri-šú [ ]
	g	i 31'	[ ]-ri-šu DINGIR.MAḪ ⌜uṣ⌝-ṣi[r]
	h	i 42'	[pa]g-ri-šú DINGIR.M[AḪ]
50	B_1	ii 3	⌜ul-te⌝-eṣ-bi g[at-]
	g	i 32'	[ ] gat-ta-šú ⌜^{d}nu⌝-dím-[mud]
	h	i 43'	[-e]ṣ-bi gat-t[a-]
51	B_1	ii 4	[x x] ⌜da?⌝-x-[ ]
	g	i 33'	[x x x]x-na šá-ru-uḫ [ ]
	h	i 44'	[x x x] ⌜e?⌝-ni šá-ru-ú/uḫ! [ ]
52	**g**	i 34'	[x x x x l]a-na x x ú [ ]
	h	i 45'	[x x x]x la-a-nu [ ]
53	**g**	i 35'	[x x] bi-rit [ ]
	h	i 46a'	[x x bi-ri]t? x x x x [ ]
54	**g**	i 36'	[ ]x x[ ]

A newly discovered fragment confirms the overlap of two lines in line-numeration reported as possible in the edition (pp. 540–1): see S. M. Maul, *Das Gilgamesch-Epos* (Munich, 2005) 156 on i 52. Ll. 55–6 in the edition and this transliteration are thus the same as 53–4.

55	P	ii 2	[ ]x[ ]
56	P	ii 3a	[ ] ⸢nindan⸣ pu-ri-su :
	d_1	ii 1	NÍG.KA$_9$ GÌR-šú 1/2 nindan p[u-ri-is-su]
57	P	ii 3b	⸢6⸣ [ ]
	d_1	ii 2	⸢6⸣ KÙŠ bi-rit {ras.} p[u-ri-di-šú]
58	P	ii 4a	[ ]-te-šú :
	d_1	ii 3	[x K]ÙŠ a-šá-rit-ti š[á]
59	P	ii 4b	ṭàr-r[a]
	d_1	ii 4	[ṭà]r-ra le-ta-šú GIM šá [ ]
60	P	ii 5	[-š]u uḫ-tan-n[a-]
	d_1	ii 5	[it-q]í per-ti-šú uḫ-tan-n[a-ba kīma ^{d}nissaba]
61	P	ii 6	[g]ít-ma-l[u]
	d_1	ii 6	[ina] ⸢ši-a⸣-ḫi-šú gít-ma-⸢lu la⸣-l[e-e-šú]
62	P	ii 7a	[ ]-⸢muq⸣!?
	d_1	ii 7	i-na si-mat KI-tim du[m-muq]
63	F_3	ii 8	⸢i⸣-[ ]
	d_1	ii 8	i-na su-pu-r[u] šá UNUG^{ki} šu-ú it-t[a-lak]
64	F_3	ii 9	u[g-]
	d_1	ii 9	ug-da-áš-šá-ár ri-ma-niš šá-qu-ú re-⸢e?⸣-[šú]
65	F_3	ii 10	⸢ul i⸣-šu [ ]
	d_1	ii 10	ul i-ši šá-ni-nam-ma te-bu-ú ^{giš}TUKUL.[MEŠ-šú]
66	F_3	ii 11	ina ⸢pu⸣-uk-ku [ ]
	d_1	ii 11	i-na pu-uk-ki-šú te-bu-ú ru-ù'-⸢ú⸣-[šú]
67	F_3	ii 12	⸢ú-ta⸣-ad-d[a-]
	d_1	ii 12	[ú]-⸢ta-ad-da⸣-ri GURUŠ.MEŠ šá UNUG^{ki} ina ku-k[it-ti]
68	F_3	ii 13	ul ú-maš-[šar]
	d_1	ii 13	[ ] ⸢d⸣GIŠ-gím-maš DUMU ana A[D-šú]
69	F_3	ii 14	[ur-r]a ù [mu-ši]
	d_1	ii 14	[-š]i i-kád-dir še-r[iš]
70	F_3	ii 15	[^{d}GIŠ-gí]m-maš x[ ]
	d_1		om.

71	F_3	ii 16	⸢šu-ú⸣ SIP[A-]
	d_1	ii 15	[-m]a$^{!?}$ šá UNUG^{ki} su-p[u-ri]
72	F_3	ii 17	⸢ul ú⸣-ma[š-šar ^{d}GIŠ-gím-maš]
	d_1		om.
	x	ii 1'	[ana] ⸢AMA⸣-[šá]
73	F_3		[(in one line with 72?)]
	d_1	ii 16	[ ] x x x-⸢ši-na ar⸣-[ ]
	x	ii 2'	[ ]-ši-na ár-[x (x)]
74	F_3	ii 18	⸢ta⸣-z[i-]
	x	ii 3'	[ ] UR$^{?}$ ḫi ina pa-n[i? x]
75	P	ii 17	[gaš-r]u [šu-pu-ú mu-du-ú]
	x	ii 4'	[-d]u-ú x [x]
76	P	ii 18	[ul] ú-maš-⸢šar⸣ [^{d}GIŠ-gím-maš]
	x	ii 5'	[^{f}]⸢GURUŠ.TUR a⸣-n[a mu-ti-šá?]
77	P	ii 19	⸢ma⸣-rat qu-r[a-di ḫi-rat eṭ-li]
	x	ii 6'	[-ra]t L[Ú.GURUŠ]
78	P	ii 20	[t]a-zi-im-ta-ši-na i[š-te-nem-]
	x	ii 7'	[ ]-ma-a ^{d}1[5]
79	P	ii 21a	[D]INGIR.MEŠ šá-ma-mi EN zi[k-ri :]
	x	ii 8'	[EN.M]EŠ zik-r[i]
80	P	ii 21b	[(in one line with 79)]
	h	ii 19	[x x]x x[ ]
	x	ii 9'	[ ]x ŠEŠ x x
81	P	ii 22	[t]ul$^{?}$-tab-ši-ma-a ri-ma kàd-ra [ina]
	h	ii 20	⸢tul⸣-tab-ši-ma ri-m[a]
	x	ii 10'	[i-n]a UNUG$^{⸢ki⸣}$ su-pú-rù
82	P	ii 23	[u]l i-šu šá-ni-nam-ma t[e-]
	h	ii 21	ul i-ši šá-ni-na[m-]
	x	ii 11'	[te-b]u-ú $^{giš⸢}$TUKUL.MEŠ-šú⸣
83	P	ii 24	[i]na pu-uk-ki šu-ut-bu-ú [ ]
	h	ii 22	i-pu-uk-[ ]
	x	ii 12'	[ ]-⸢ú$^{?}$⸣ ru-ù'-ú-šú
84	P		om.
	h	ii 23	uš-ta-d[ir eṭlūti šá UNUG^{ki}]
	x	ii 13'	[in]a ku-kit-ti

85	P	ii 25a	[u]l ú-maš-šar ^{d}GIŠ-gím-maš DUMU ana AD-šú :
	h	ii 24	ul ú-m[aš-]
	x	ii 14'	[ ] ana AD-šú
86	P	ii 25b	ur-ra u G[I$_{6}$ i-kád-dir]
	h	ii 25	ur-ru u m[u-šu]
	x	ii 15'	[ ] še-{ras.}-riš
87	P	ii 26	[š]u-ú SIPA-ma šá UNUG^{ki} s[u-]
	h	ii 26	šu-ú SI[PA]
	x	ii 16'	[s]u-pú-ru
88	P	om.	
	h	ii 27	^{d}GIŠ-gím-[maš]
	x	ii 17'	[ ]x-⸢a⸣-ti
89	P	ii 27	[š]u-ú re-'-ú-ši-na-ma u x[ ]
	h	ii 28	šu-ú SI[PA]
	x	ii 18'	[-ši-n]a?
90	P	ii 28	[g]aš-ru šu-pu-ú mu-du-ú [x x]
	h	ii 29	[g]a-áš-r[u]
91	P	ii 29	[u]l ú-maš-šar ^{d}GIŠ-gím-maš ^{f}GURUŠ.TUR a-na m[u-ti-šá?]
	h	ii 30	ul ú-[ ]
92	P	ii 30	[m]a-rat qu-ra-di ḫi-rat e[ṭ-li]
	h	ii 31	DAM [ ]
93	P	ii 31	[t]a-zi-im-ta-ši-na iš-te-nem-me ^{d}[a-num]
	h	ii 32	ta-z[i-]
94	P	ii 32a	⸢^{d}⸣a-ru-ru is-su-ú GAL-tú :
	h	ii 33	^{d}a-[ ]
95	P	ii 32b	at-ti ^{d}a-ru-ru tab-ni-[i LÚ]
	h	ii 34	at-[ ]
96	P	ii 33a	⸢e⸣-nin-na bi-ni-i zi-kir-šú :
	h	ii 35	⸢e⸣-ni[n-]
97	P	ii 33b	ana u$_{4}$-um lìb-bi-šú lu-u ma-ḫ[ir$^{?}$]
	h	ii 36	a-na x[ ]
	n	iii 1	[lì]b$^{?}$-ba-šú lu-ú m[a-]
98	P	ii 34	[l]iš-ta-an-na-nu-ma UNUG^{ki} liš-tap-š[iḫ]
	h	ii 37	liš-tan-n[a-]
	n	iii 2	[-ta]n-na-nu-ma UNUG$^{⸢ki}$ liš⸣-[ ]

99	P	ii 35a	⸢^{d}a⸣-ru-ru an-ni-ta ina še-me-šá :
	h	ii 38	^{d}a-r[u-]
	n	iii 3	[ ]⸢a⸣-ru-ru an-ni-t[i?]
	cc	ii 1'	[ ]-⸢e⸣-[ ]
100	B$_2$	ii 1'	[ ]-⸢bi-šá⸣
	P	ii 35b	zik-ru šá ^{d}a-nim ib-ta-ni ina ⸢lìb⸣-[ ]
	h	ii 39	zi-kir [ ]
	n	iii 4	[-i]k-ri šá ^{d}50 i[b-]
	cc	ii 2'	[-t]a-ni ana ⸢lìb⸣-b[i-]
101	B$_2$	ii 2'	[ ].MEŠ-šá
	P	ii 36a	[^{d}a-r]u-ru im-ta-si ŠU.MIN-šá :
	h	ii 40	⸢^{d}a-ru⸣-r[u]
	n	iii 5	[-r]u ⸢im-tas⸣-si [ ]
	cc	ii 3'	[-s]i ŠU.MIN.MEŠ-[ ]
102	P	ii 36b	ṭi-ṭa ik-ta-ri-iṣ it-ta-di ina EDI[N]
	h	ii 41	[ṭi]-⸢iṭ⸣-ṭi i[k-]
	n	iii 6	[ ] x [ ]
	cc	ii 4'	[i]t-ta-du ina ṣe-[ ]
103	P	ii 37a	[ina EDI]N ^{d}en-ki-dù ib-ta-ni qu-ra-du :
	h	ii 42	ina EDIN ^{d}en-k[i-]
	cc	ii 5'	[ ] ⸢qu-ra⸣-[ ]
104	P	ii 37b	i-lit-ti qul-ti ki-ṣir ^{d}nin-urta
	h	ii 43	i-lit$^{!}$-tu$_4$ mu-t[um$^{?}$]
105	P	ii 38a	[šu]-⸢ʾ⸣-ur šar-ta ka-lu zu-um-ri-šú :
	h	ii 44	[š]u-ʾ-ru šar-[ ]
106	P	ii 38b	up-pu-uš pe-re-tu GIM sin-niš-ti
	h	ii 45	[n]u-up-[pu]-uS p[e$^{?}$-]
107	B$_1$	iii 6	⸢i-ti-iq pér-ti⸣-[ ]
	P	ii 39	[i]-ti-iq pe-er-ti-šu uḫ-tan-na-ba ki-ma ^{d}nissaba
	h	ii 46	it-tí[q] per-t[i-]
108	B$_1$	iii 7	la i-de ÙG.ME[Š]
	P	ii 40a	[la] i-de ÙG.MEŠ u ma-tam-ma :
	h	ii 47	la ⸢i-de⸣ DINGIR.[(MEŠ)]
109	B$_1$	iii 8	lu-bu-ši la-biš [GIM]
	P	ii 40b	lu-bu-uš-ti la-biš GIM ^{d}šákkan
	h	ii 48	ù lu-b[u-]
110	B$_1$	iii 9	it-ti MAŠ.DÀ.MEŠ-ma ik-ka-⸢la⸣ [ ]
	P	ii 41	[i]t-ti MAŠ.DÀ.MEŠ-ma ik-ka-la šam-mi
	h	ii 49	it-ti x[ ]

Line	MS	Col.	Text
111	B_1	iii 10	it-ti bu-lim maš-qa-a ⸢i⸣-[ ]
	P	ii 42	[i]t-ti bu-lim maš-qa-a i-tep-pir
	g	ii 33	i[t-]
	h	ii 50	⸢it-ti⸣ [ ]
112	B_1	iii 11	it-ti ⸢nam-maš⸣-še-e A.MEŠ i-ṭib lìb-[ ]
	P	ii 43	[i]t-ti nam-maš-ši-e A.MEŠ i-ṭib lìb-ba-šú
	g	ii 34	it-t[i]
113	B_1	iii 12	ṣa-a-a-du ḫa-bi-l[u]
	P	ii 44	[ṣa]-⸢a⸣-a-du ḫa-bi-lu-LÚ
	g	ii 35	ṣa-⸢a⸣-[ ]
114	B_1	iii 13	i-na pu-ut maš-qí-i [šá]-⸢a⸣-šu uš-tam-ḫi-ir-š[ú]
	P	ii 45	[ina p]u-ut maš-qí-i šá-a-šú uš-tam-ḫi-ir-šú
	g	ii 36	ina p[u-]
115	B_1	iii 14	[1-e]n u$_4$-ma 2-a ù šal-[šá] ⸢i⸣-na pu-ut maš-qí-i KIMIN
	P	ii 46	[u]$_4$-me 2-a u šal-šá ina pu-ut maš-qí-i KIMIN
	g	ii 37	1-e[n]
116	B_1	iii15	[i-m]ur-šu-ma ṣa-a-a-du [-a]ḫ-ri-ru pa-nu-šú
	P	ii 47	[-š]u-ma ṣa-a-a-du uš-ta-aḫ-ri-ru pa-nu-šú
117	B_1	iii 16	[šu]-⸢ú⸣ u bu-li-šu [bi]-tuš-šu i-ru-um-ma
	P	ii 48	[ ] u bu-li-šú bi-tuš-šú i-ru-um-ma
118	B_1	iii 17	[in-na-d]ir uš-ḫ[a-ri-i]r i-qul-ma
	P	ii 49	[ ] uš-ḫa-ri-ir i-qu-ul-ma
119	B_1	iii 18	[ ]-⸢ba⸣-[šu pa-n]u-⸢šu⸣ ar-p[u]
	P	ii 50	[x x x] lìb-ba-šú pa-nu-šú ar-pu
120	B_1	iii 19	[ ]-⸢ši⸣-[šu]
	P	ii 51	[i-ba-áš-ši S]AG.PA.LAGAB ina kar-ši-šu
	g	ii 42	⸢i⸣-[ ]
121	P	ii 52	[r]u-qu-ti pa-nu-šú maš-lu
	g	ii 43	a-na [a-lik ur-ḫi]
			——————————————— P**g**
122	P	iii 1	ṣa-a-a-d[u pa-a-šú] i-pu-uš-ma i-qab-bi MU-r[a a-na a-bi-šú]
	g	ii 44	ṣa-⸢a⸣-a-[ ]
123	P	iii 2	a-b[i iš-té]n eṭ-lu šá il-l[i-ka ana pu-ut maš-qí-i?]
	g	ii 45	a-bi 1-[en]
124	P	iii 3	⸢i⸣-[na KUR d]a-an e-mu-q[í i-šu]
	g	ii 46	ina m[a-ti]
125	P	iii 4	[ki-ma ki-iṣ-ri] šá ^{d}a-nim dun-nu-n[a e-mu-qa-šu]
126	P	iii 5	[it-ta-na-al-la]k ina UGU KUR-i k[a-x x x]

127	P	iii 6	[ka-a-a-nam-m]a it-ti bu-lim [ik-ka-la Ú?]
128	P	iii 7	[ka-a-a-nam-ma G]ÌR.MEŠ-šú ina pu-ut maš-qí-⸢i⸣ [šak-na?]
129	P	iii 8	[pal-ḫa-ku-ma u]l a-ṭe-eḫ-ḫa-a a-na š[á-a-šu]
130	P	iii 9	[um-tal-li bu]-⸢ú⸣-ri šá ú-ḫar-ru-ú [ana-ku]
131	P	iii 10	[ut-ta-as-si-iḫ n]u-bal-li-ia šá uš-n[i-lu]
132	P	iii 11	[uš-te-li ina qātī-ia] bu-lam nam-maš-šá-a šá ED[IN]
133	P	iii 12	[ul i-nam-din-a]n-ni a-na e-peš ED[IN]
			———————————————— P
134	P	iii 13	[a-bu-šú pa-a-šú i-pu-uš-ma i-qab-b]i i-zak-ka-ra a-na ṣa-a-a-⸢du⸣
135	P	iii 14	[ma-ri KU]R UNUG^{ki} ^{d}GIŠ-gím-maš
136	P	iii 15	[ ]x e-lu EDIN-šu
137	P	iii 16	[ki-ma ki-iṣ-ri šá ^{d}a-nim dun-n]u-na e-mu-qa-a-šu
138	P	iii 17	[ṣa-bat ur-ḫa ina libbi UNUG^{ki} šu-ku]n pa-ni-ka
139	P	iii 18	[ ]x e-muq LÚ
140	P	iii 19	[a-lik ma-ri it-ti-ka ḫa-rim-tú ^{f}šam-ḫat] ú-ru-ma
141	P	iii 20	[ ] GIM dan-nu
142	B_2	iii 41	[e-nu-ma bu-lu i-sa-a]n-n[i-qu]
	P	iii 21	[a-na] maš-qí-i
143	B_2	iii 42	[ši-i liš-ḫu-uṭ lu-bu-š]i-ša-ma [lip-ta-a]
	P	iii 22	[ku-z]u-ub-šá
144	B_2	iii 43	[im-ma]r-⸢ši-ma⸣ i-ṭe-eḫ-ḫ[a-a a-na]
	P	iii 23	[š]á-a-ši
145	B_2	iii 44	i-nak-kir-šu bu-ul-šu [šá ir-bu-ú]
	P	iii 24	[UGU E]DIN-šu
146	B_2	iii 45	a-na mil-ki ša a-bi-šú [ ]
	P	iii 25	[ ]x x[(x)]
147	B_2	iii 46	ṣa-a-a-du i-tal-lak [ ]
148	B_2	iii 47	iṣ-bat ur-ḫa ina ŠÀ UNUG^{ki} iš-ta-[kan pa-ni-šu]
149	B_2	iv 1	[a]-⸢na?⸣ LUG[AL? ^{d}G]IŠ-gím-[maš]
150	B_2	iv 2	iš-tén e[ṭ-l]u šá [il-li-ka ana pu-ut maš-qí-i?]
151	B_2	iv 3	i-na KUR da-an ⸢e⸣-[mu-qí i-šu]
152	B_2	iv 4	ki-ma ki-iṣ-ri šá ^{d}a-nim ⸢dun-nu⸣-n[a e-mu-qa-šu]
153	B_2	iv 5	it-ta-⸢na⸣-al-lak ina UGU KUR-i k[a-x x x]
154	B_2	iv 6	ka-a-⸢a⸣-nam-ma it-ti bu-lim [ik-ka-la Ú?]
155	B_2	iv 7	ka-a-⸢a⸣-nam-ma GÌR.MIN-šú ina pu-ut maš-q[í-i šak-na?]
156	B_2	iv 8	pal-ḫa-ku-ma ul a-ṭe-eḫ-ḫa-a [a-na šá-a-šú]
157	B_2	iv 9	um-tal-li bu-ú-ri šá ú-ḫar-[ru-ú ana-ku]
	P	iii 36	u[m-]
158	B_2	iv 10	ut-[t]a-as-si-iḫ nu-bal-li-ia [šá uš-ni-lu]
	P	iii 37	u[t-]
	cc	iv 1'	u[t-]

159	B_2	iv 11	⸢uš⸣-te-li ina ŠU.MIN-ia bu-li nam-maš-š[á-a]
	P	iii 38	uš-[šá EDI]N
	cc	iv 2'	uš-t[e-]
160	B_2	iv 12	[u]l i-nam-din-an-ni a-na e-pe-[eš]
	F_2	iii 1'	[-š]i [EDIN]
	P	iii 39	ul [i-na]m-⸢din-na-an⸣-[ ] EDIN
	cc	iv 3'	ul i-[ ]
161	B_2	iv 13	[^{d}GI]Š-gím-maš a-na šá-šu-ma i-zak-ka-ra [ ]
	F_2	iii 2'	[ ] ṣa-a-a-⸢di⸣
	P	iii 40	^{d}GIŠ-⸢gím-maš⸣ a-na šá-šú-ma M[U-ra a-na ṣa-a]-a-di
	cc	iv 4'	^{d}GIŠ-g[ím-]
162	B_2	iv 14	[ ]-⸢du it-ti-ka⸣ ḫa-rim-tú ^{f}[ ]
	F_2	iii 3'	[š]am-ḫat ú-ru-ma
	P	iii 41	a-lik ṣa-a-a-di it-ti-ka ^{f}ḫ[a-] ú-ru-ma
	cc	iv 5'	a-lik ṣa-[ ]
163	B_2	iv 15	[-s]a-⸢ni⸣-q[u]
	F_2	iii 4'	[-q]u a-na maš-qé-e
	P	iii 42	e-nu-ma bu-lam i-⸢sa⸣-[ ] ana maš-qí-i
	cc	iv 6'	⸢e⸣-[ ]
164	F_2	iii 5'	[-t]a-a ku-zu-ub-šá
	P	iii 43	ši-i liš-ḫu-uṭ lu-bu-ši-š[á-ma lip]-⸢ta-a⸣ ku-zu-ub-šá
165	F_2	iii 6'	[-ḫ]e a-na šá-a-šá
	P	iii 44	im-mar-ši-ma i-ṭ[e-e]ḫ-ha-a a-na šá-a-ši
166	F_2	iii 7'	[-b]u-ú UGU EDIN-šu
	P	iii 45	i-nak-kir-šú bu-ul-šú š[á i]r-bu-ú UGU EDIN-šu
167	F_2	iii 8'	[ ]-tum šam-ḫat ú-ru-ma
	P	iii 46	il-lik ṣa-a-⟨a⟩-di it-ti-šú ⸢^{f}ḫa⸣-rim-ti ^{f}šam-ḫat ú-ru-ma
168	F_2	iv 1	[ ] ḫar-ra-nu
	P	iii 47	iṣ-⸢ṣab⸣-tu ur-ḫa uš-te-še-ru KASKAL
169	F_2	iv 2	[ ] ⸢ik⸣-tal-du-ni
	P	iii 48	ina šal-ši u_4-me ina A.ŠÀ a-dan-ni ik-tal-du-ni
170	F_2	iv 3	[-n]u it-taš-bu-ni
	P	iii 49	ṣa-a-a-du u ^{f}ḫa-rim-tu ana uš-bi-šú-nu it-taš-bu-ni
171	F_2	iv 4	[ ] it-taš-bu-ni
	P	iii 50	1-en u_4-ma 2-a u_4-ma ina pu-ut maš-qí-i it-taš-bu

172	F_2	iv 5a	[(in one line with 173) :]
	P	iii 51	KUR-da bu-lu maš-qa-a i-šat-ti
	x	iv 1'	[ ]-⸢lum⸣ [maš]-⸢qa⸣-[ ]
173	F_2	iv 5b	[ ] ⸢i⸣-ṭi-bu lib-ba-šú
	P	iv 1	KUR-da nam-maš-⟨še⟩-e A.MEŠ i-ṭib lìb-ba-šu
	x	iv 2'	[ ]-⸢e⸣ A.MEŠ i-ṭ[i-]
174	F_2	iv 6	[š]á-⸢du⸣-um-ma
	P	iv 2	ù šu-ú $^{⸢d⸣}$en-ki-dù i-lit-ta-šú šá-du-um-ma
	x	iv 3'	[-k]i-dù i-lit-t[a-]
175	F_2	iv 7a	[(in one line with 176) :]
	P	iv 3	it-ti MA[Š.D]À.MEŠ-ma ik-ka-la Ú
	x	iv 4'	[ ] ik-ka-lu [ ]
176	F_2	iv 7b	[i-te]p-pir
	P	iv 4	it-ti bu-lim maš-qa-a i-šat-ti
	x	iv 5'	[ ] ⸢maš⸣-qa-a i-te-e[p-pir]
177	P	iv 5	it-ti nam-maš-⸢še⸣-e A.MEŠ i-ṭib lìb-ba-šú
	x	iv 6'	[ ].MEŠ i-ṭi-pi l[ìb-]
178	P	iv 6	i-mur-šu-m[a] ^{f}šam-ḫat lul-la-a LÚ
	x	iv 7'	[ ]-ḫat lul-la-a ⸢a⸣-[me-la/lu]
179	B_1	iv 31	[ ] E[DIN]
	P	iv 7	GURUŠ šag-ga-⸢šá⸣-a šá qá-bal-ti EDIN
	x	iv 8'	[ ]-a-šú šá qa-bal-t[ú]
180	B_1	iv 32	[ ]-⸢um-mi-i⸣ ki-rim-mi-k[i]
	F_1	iv 11	[an-nu]-ú [ ]
	P	iv 8	an-nu-ú šu-ú ^{f}šam-ḫat ru-um-mi-i ki-rim-mi-ki
	x	iv 9'	[-ḫ]at ru-um-mi-i ki-rim-[ ]
181	B_1	iv 33	[-u]b-ki lil-qé
	F_1	iv 12	u[r-k]a pi-[ ]
	P	iv 9	ur-ki pi-te-ma ku-zu-ub-ki lil-qé
	x	iv 10'	u[r-ki] p[i-] ku-zu-ub-ki [ ]
182	B_1	iv 34	[ ]-⸢e⸣ na-pis-su
	F_1	iv 13	e taš-ḫu-t[i]
	P	iv 10	e taš-ḫu-ti li-qé-e na-pis-su
	x	iv 11'	⸢e taš⸣-ḫu-[ti] ⸢li⸣-qé-e na-p[i-]
183	B_1	iv 35	⸢im-mar-ki-ma i-ṭe-eḫ-ḫa-a⸣ a-na ka-a-ši
	F_1	iv 14	im-mar-k[i-]
	P	iv 11	im-mar-ki-ma i-ṭe-eḫ-ḫa-a ana ka-a-ši
	x	iv 12'	im-mar-ki-m[a] ⸢i-ṭe-eḫ⸣-ḫa-a a-n[a]

184	B_1	iv 36	lu-bu-ši-ki mu-uṣ-ṣi-ma UGU-ki li-iṣ-lal
	F_1	iv 15	lu-bu-⸢ši⸣-k[i]
	P	iv 12	lu-bu-ši-ki mu-uṣ-⸢ṣi⸣-ma UGU-ki li-iṣ-lal
	x	iv 13'	lu-bu-ši-ki ⸢mu-uṣ⸣-ṣi-ma e-l[i-]
185	B_1	iv 37	ep-ši-šu-ma lul-la-a ši-pir sin-niš-ti
	F_1	iv 16	ep-ši-šu-[ ]
	P	iv 13	ep-ši-šú-ma lul-[l]a-a ši-pir sin-niš-ti
	x	iv 14'	ep-ši-šú-ma lul-⸢la⸣-a ši-pir ⸢sin⸣-[niš]-⸢ti⸣
186	B_1	iv 38	i-nak-kir-šú bul-šú šá ir-bu-ú ina EDIN-šú
	F_1	iv 17	i-nak-kir-š[u]
	P	iv 14	i-nak-kir-šú bu-ul-šú š[á i]r-bu-ú ina EDIN-šú
	x	iv 15'	da-du-ka ⸢liḫ⸣-bu-bu ⸢e⸣-[l]i EDIN-šú
187	B_1	iv 39a	da-du-šú i-ḫab-bu-bu UGU EDIN-ki :
	F_1	iv 18	⸢da⸣-d[u-]
	P	iv 15	da-du-šú i-ḫab-b[u-b]u UGU EDIN-ki
	x	iv 16'	i-nak-kir-šú bu-[ú-l]u šá ⸢ir⸣-[bu]-ú ina EDIN-šú
188	B_1	iv 39b	ur-tam-mi ^{f}šam-ḫat di-da-šá
	F_1	iv 19a	[ur]-⸢tam$^{?}$-mi$^{?}$⸣-[:]
	P	iv 16a	ur-tam-mi šam-ḫat di-da-š[á :]
	x	iv 17'	ur-tam-⸢mu⸣ [^{f}]šam-ḫat [d]i-da-a-⸢šú⸣
189	B_1	iv 40	úr-šá ip-te-e-ma ku-zu-ub-šá il-qé
	F_1	iv 19b	[(in one line with 188)]
	P	iv 16b	[-z]u-ub-šá il-qé
	x	iv 18'	ur-⸢šú⸣ i[p-te-e-m]a ku-zu-ub-šú il-qé
190	B_1	iv 41	ul iš-ḫu-ut il-ti-qé na-pis-su
	F_1	iv 20	ul ⸢iš⸣-ḫu-ut [ ]
	P	iv 17	ul iš-ḫu-u[t -pi]s-su
	x	iv 19'	ul i[š-] ⸢il⸣-te-qé na-pi-is-su
191	B_1	iv 42	lu-bu-ši-šá ú-ma-ṣi-ma UGU-šá iṣ-lal
	F_1	iv 21	⸢lu-bu⸣-ši x[ ]
	P	iv 18	lu-bu-ši-š[á -m]a UGU-š[ú i]ṣ-lal
	x	iv 20'	[l]u-bu-š[i-šú] ⸢ú⸣-ma-aṣ-ṣi-ma UGU-šú ⸢iṣ⸣-lal
192	B_1	iv 43	i-pu-us-su-ma lul-la-a ši-pir sin-niš-te
	F_1	iv 22	⸢i-pu-us-su-ma⸣ [ ]
	P	iv 19	i-pu-u[s- -l]a-a ši-pir si[n-niš-t]i
	x	iv 21'	⸢i⸣-pu-u[s-su-m]a lul-la-a ši-pir sin-niš-t[i]
193	B_1	iv 44	da-du-šú iḫ-bu-bu UGU EDIN-šá
	F_1	iv 23	⸢da⸣-du-šu [ ]
	P	iv 20	da-d[u- -b]u UGU EDIN-[ ]
	x	iv 22'	da-⸢du⸣-[šú] iḫ-bu-bu ⸢UGU⸣ E[DIN-šú]

194	B_1	iv 45	6 ur-ri 7 GI$_6$.MEŠ ^{d}en-ki-dù te-bi-ma ^{f}šam-ḫat ir-ḫi
	F_1	iv 24	⸢6⸣ ur-ri ù ⸢7 GI$_6$⸣.MEŠ ^{d}e[n-]
	P	iv 21	⸢6⸣ u[r- -d]ù te-bi-ma šam-ḫat-ta i-re-[ḫi]
	n	iv 0'-1'	[ ] / [-b]i-⸢ma šam-ḫat i⸣-[re]-⸢eḫ⸣-[ḫi]
	x	iv 23-4'	6 ur-[ri] u 7 mu-šá-[a-ti] / [ ] te-bé-e-ma ^{f}š[am-]
195	B_1	iv 46a	ul-tu iš-bu-u la-la-šá
	F_1	iv 25	ul-tu iš-bu-[ ]
	P	iv 22	[ ]-⸢ú⸣ la-la-⸢šá⸣
	n	iv 2'	[-b]u-ú la-la-a-[šá]
	x	iv 25'	[-b]u-ú [ ]
196	B_1	iv 46b	pa-ni-šú iš-ta-kan ina EDIN bu-li-šú
	F_1	iv 26	pa-ni-šu iš-ta-ka[n]
	P	iv 23	[ ] a-na EDIN bu-li-š[u]
	n	iv 3'	[i]š-ta-kan a-na EDIN bu-lì-[šú]
	x	iv 26'	[-t]a-kan a-n[a]
197	B_1	iv 47	i-mu-ra-šu-ma ^{d}en-ki-dù i-rap-pu-da MAŠ.DÀ.MEŠ
	F_1	iv 27	i-mu-ra-šu-ma ^{d}en-ki-dù [ ]
	P	iv 24	[ ] ⸢i⸣-rap-pu-da MAŠ.DÀ.ME[Š]
	n	iv 4'	[-š]u-ma ^{d}en-ki-dù i-rap-pu-du MAŠ.DÀ.[MEŠ]
198	B_1	iv 48	bu-ul EDIN it-te-si ina ZU-šu
	F_1	iv 28	bu-ul ⸢EDIN⸣ it-ti-si [ ]
	P	iv 25	[-s]i ina SU-šú
	n	iv 5'	[EDI]N it-te-si ina zu-mur-i-[šú]
199	B_1	iv 49	⸢ul-taḫ-ḫi⸣-iD ^{d}en-ki-dù ul-lu-la pa-gar-šu
	F_1	iv 29	ul-taḫ-ḫi ^{d}en-ki-dù [ ]
	P	iv 26	[-d]ù ul-lu-la pa-gar-šú
	n	iv 6'	[-ḫ]a ^{d}en-ki-dù ul-lu-lu pa-gar-[šú]
200	B_1	iv 50	[ ]-⸢za⸣ bir-ka-a-⸢šú⸣ šá il-li-ka bu-⟨ul⟩-[šú]
	F_1	iv 30	it-ta-ziz-za bir-⸢ka-a⸣-š[u]
	P	iv 27	[-š]ú šá il-la-ka bu-ul-šú
	n	iv 7'	[-z]iz-za bir-ki-a-šú šá il-l[ak?-]
			———————————————— B
201	F_1	iv 31	um-ta-aṭ-ṭu ^{d}en-k[i-dù]
	P	iv 28	[u]l ki-i šá pa-ni la-sa-an-šú
202	B_2	v 2	[ ]-⸢sa⸣
	F_1	iv 32	ù šu-ú i-ši x[ ]
	P	iv 29	[r]a-pa-áš ḫa-si-sa
203	B_2	v 3	[ ]-šab ⸢ina šá-pal ḫa-rim⸣-ti
	F_1	iv 33	i-tu-^{ra}ram-mu i[t-]
	P	iv 30	[ ]-⸢ta⸣-šab ina šá-pal ^{f}ḫa-rim-ti

204	B_2	v 4	[-ṭ]a-la pa-ni-šú
	F_1	iv 34	^{f}ḫa-rim-tum [ ]
	P	iv 31	[ ] i-na-aṭ-ṭa-⸢la⸣ pa-ni-šá
205	B_2	v 5	[-qa]b-bu-u i-šem-ma-a GEŠTU.MIN-šú
	F_1	iv 35	ù ⸢šá!? ^{f}⸣ḫ[a-]
	P	iv 32	[-rim]-ti i-qab-bu-ú ⸢i⸣-šem-ma-a GEŠTU.MIN-šú
206	B_2	v 6	[-m]a MU-ra a-na ^{d}en-ki-dù
	P	iv 33	[^{f}ḫa-rim-tu a-n]a šá-šú-ma MU-ra a-na ^{d}en-ki-dù
207	B_2	v 7	[-d]ù ki-i DINGIR ta-ba-áš-ši
	P	iv 34	[dam]-⸢qa-ta ^{d}en⸣-ki-dù k[i-m]a DINGIR x x ⸢ba!⸣ ši
208	B_2	v 8	[-š]e-e ta-rap-pu-da EDIN
	P	iv 35	[a]m-me-ni it-ti nam-maš-š[e]-e ta-rap-pu-ud EDIN
	cc	v 1'	[ ]x x[ ]-pu-ud [EDIN]
209	B_2	v 9	[ ] ⸢lìb⸣-bi UNUG^{ki} su-pú-ri
	P	iv 36	al-ka lu-[t]ar-ru-k[a ana l]ìb-bi UNUG^{ki} su-pú-ri
	cc	v 2'	[-r]i-ka ana ⸢ŠÀ UNUG⸣^{ki} su-pur
210	B_2	v 10	[ ] ⸢^{d}a⸣-nim u ^{d}iš-tar
	P	iv 37	a-na É ⸢el⸣-lim mu-⸢šab⸣ ^{d}a-nim u ^{d}iš-tar
	cc	v 3'	[m]u-šá-bu šá ^{d}a-nu-um
210a	cc	v 4'	[ ]-ma ana ŠÀ UNUG^{ki} su-pur
210b	cc	v 5'	[ana é.an.n]a qud-du-šú mu-šá-bu šá ^{d}15
211	B_1	v 11	[^{d}GIŠ-gí]m-m[aš]
	B_2	v 11	[-l]u e-mu-qí
	P	iv 38	a-šar ⸢^{d}⸣[GI]Š-gím-maš gít-ma-lu e-mu-qí
	h	v 1	a-š[ar]
	cc	v 6'	[-g]ím-maš gít-ma-lu e-mu-qam
212	B_1	v 12	[A]M ug-da-⸢áš-šá⸣-[ru]
	B_2	v 12	[U]GU GURUŠ.MEŠ
	P	iv 39	ù ki-⸢i⸣ AM ug-⸢da⸣-áš-šá-ru UGU GURUŠ.MEŠ
	h	v 2	GIM [ ]
	cc	v 7'	[ ]-da-áš-šá-ri UGU GURUŠ.MEŠ
213	B_1	v 13	[-á]š-šum-ma ma-gi[r]
	B_2	v 13	[qa]-⸢ba⸣-a-a
	P	iv 40	i-ta-m[a]-áš-šum-ma ma-gir qa-ba-šá
	h	v 3	taq?-q[a?-]
	cc	v 8'	[-š]um-ma ma-gir qa-ba-a-[ ]

214	B_1	v 14	[ ] lìb-ba-šú i-še-⸢ʾ⸣-[ ]
	B_2	v 14	[-r]a
	P	iv 41	mu-du-⸢ú⸣ lìb-b[a-š]ú i-še-ʾ-a ib-ra
	h	v 4	mu-[ ]
	cc	v 9'	[l]ìb-ba-šú-ma i-še-ʾ-a ib-[ ]
215	B_1	v 15	[ ] ⸢a⸣-na šá-ši-ma MU-ra [ ]
	P	iv 42	^{d}en-ki-dù a-na šá-š[i-m]a MU-ra ⟨ana⟩ ^{f}ḫa-rim-[t]i
	h	v 5	^{d}e[n-]
	cc	v 10'	[-n]a šá-ši-ma MU-⸢ár ana ^{f}⸣[ ]
216	B_1	v 16	[ ] ^{f}šam-ḫat qí-ri-i[n-]
	P	iv 43	al-ki š[a]m-ḫat-ta ⸢qí⸣-re-en-[n]i ia-a-ši
	h	v 6	a[l-]
	cc	v 11'	[ša]m-ḫat ⸢qí⸣-r[i-]
217	B_1	v 17	[ ] el-lim qud-du-ši mu-šab ⸢^{d}⸣[ ]
	P	iv 44	a-na É ⸢el⸣-lim qud-⸢du⸣-ši mu-⸢šab⸣ ^{d}a-nim ^{d}⸢iš-tar⸣
	h	v 7	⸢a⸣-[ ]
	cc	v 12'	[ ] ⸢qud⸣-[ ]
218	B_1	v 18	[ ] ^{d}GIŠ-gím-maš gít-ma-lu [ ]
	P	iv 45	a-šar ⸢^{d}⸣GIŠ-gím-maš [gít-m]a-lu e-mu-qí
219	B_1	v 19	[k]i-i AM ug-da-áš-šá-ru UG[U]
	P	iv 46	ù ki-i A[M ug]-⸢da-áš⸣-[šá-ru] UGU GURUŠ.M[EŠ]
220	B_1	v 20	[-k]u lu-ug-ri-šum-ma da-an x[ ]
	P	iv 47	a-na-ku lu-ug-ri-šum-ma d[a-]x x x x
221	B_1	v 21	[x x]-ri-iḫ ina ŠÀ UNUG^{ki} a-na-ku-m[i]
	P	v 1	[UNU]G^{ki} a-na-ku-mi dan-nu
222	B_1	v 22	[x x]-um-ma ši-ma$^{!?}$-tú [ ]
	P	v 2	[ ]-tú ú-nak-kar
223	B_1	v 23	[šá i-n]a ⸢EDIN⸣ i'-al-du [ ]
	P	v 3	[da-a]n i-mu-qí i-šu
224	B_1	v 24	[x x] ⸢li-mu⸣-r[a pa]-⸢ni⸣-[ka]
	P	v 4	[-r]a pa-ni-ka
225	B_1	v 25	x[x] x[ ]-u i-[ ]
	P	v 5	[ ] i-ba-áš-šu-ú ana-ku lu i-de
226	B_1	v 26	a-[lik] ⸢^{d}⸣en-⸢ki-dù a⸣-[na UNUG^{ki}] su-p[ú-ri]
	P	v 6	[UNU]G^{ki} su-pú-ri
227	B_1	v 27	a-š[ar GU]RUŠ.MEŠ uz-[Í]B.LÁ.[ ]
	P	v 7	[-z]u-ḫu ^{túg}ÍB.LÁ.MEŠ

228	B_1	v 28	u_4-m[i-šam-m]a UD x[ ] i-sin-n[u]
	P	v 8	[š]á-kin i-sin-nu
	h	v 18	u[$_4$-]
229	B_1	v 29	a-ša[r ur-t]a-aṣ-ṣ[a-] a-lu-⸢ú⸣
	P	v 9	[-n]u a-lu-ú
	h	v 19	⸢a⸣-[ ]
	x	v 1'	[ ]-⸢ú⸣
230	B_1	v 30	ù ⸢f⸣[ḫar-ma]-a-ti [-m]a? bi-nu-t[ú]
	P	v 10	[š]u-su-ma bi-n[u-t]ú
	x	v 2'	[-n]u-tú
231	B_1	v 31	ḪI.LI [zu]-ʾu-n[a]-⸢a⸣ ri-šá-tu[m]
	P	v 11	[ma-l]a-a ri-š[á-a-t]i
	x	v 3'	[-š]a-ti
232	B_1	v 32	i-na ma-⸢a⸣-[a-a]l m[u-ši ú-š]e-ṣu-ú ra-bu-tu[m]
	P	v 12	[-ṣ]u-ú ra-[bu-tu]m
	x	v 4'	[ ]-bu-ti
233	B_1	v 33	^{d}en-ki-d[ù šá la] ⸢i⸣-[d]u-⸢ú⸣ ba-la-ṭ[a]
	P	v 13	[ ]-ú ba-l[á-ṭ]a
	x	v 5'	[ ]-lá-ṭi
234	B_1	v 34	lu-kal-lim-k[a ^{d}]GIŠ-gím-maš ḫa-di-ʾ-a L[Ú]
	P	v 14	[-d]i-ʾ-ú-a LÚ
	x	v 6'	[ ] a-me-lu
235	B_1	v 35a	a-mur šá-a-šú ⸢ú⸣-[ṭul pa-n]i-šú :
	P	v 15	[ ]-ṭul pa-ni-šú
	h	v 25	⸢a⸣-[ ]
	x	v 7'	[-n]i-šú
236	B_1	v 35b	eṭ-lu-ta ba-ni bal-ta i-[ši]
	P	v 16	[ba]l-ta i-ši
	h	v 26	GURU[Š-]
	x	v 8'	[ ] ⸢i⸣-ši
237	B_1	v 36	zu-ʾu-na k[u-u]z-ba ka-lu zu-um-r[i-šú]
	P	v 17	[k]a-lu SU-šú
	h	v 27	SU-[ ]
	x	v 9'	[-u]m-ri-šú
238	B_1	v 37	dan-na e-mu-qa e-li-ka i-[š]u
	P	v 18	[U]GU-ka i-ši
	h	v 28	da[n-]
	x	v 10'	[ ] i-ši

239	B$_1$	v 38	la ṣa-li-lu šá ur-ra ù GI$_6$
	P	v 19	[u]r-ra u GI$_6$
	h	v 29	la [ ]
	x	v 11'	[mūša u u]r-ra
240	B$_1$	v 39	^{d}en-ki-dù nu-uk-ki-ra še-ret-su
	P	v 20	[ ] še-ret-ka
	h	v 30	^{d}e[n-]
	x	v 12'	[-r]et-⸢ka⸣
241	B$_1$	v 40	^{d}GIŠ-gím-maš ^{d}UTU i-ram-šu-ma
	P	v 21	[ ] i-ram-šú-ma
	h	v 31	^{d}GI[Š-]
	x	v 13'	[ ]-⸢šú-ma⸣
242	B$_1$	v 41	^{d}a-nu-um ^{d}en-líl u ^{d}é-a ú-rap-pi-šu ú-zu-un-šú
	F$_1$	v 20	[ ]-šú
	P	v 22	[ ] ⸢^{d}é⸣-a ⸢ú⸣-[rap-p]i-šú ú-zu-un-šú
	h	v 32	^{d}⸢a⸣-[ ]
	x	v 14'	[ ]-šú
243	B$_1$	v 42	la-am tal-li-ka ul-tu šá-di-im-ma
	F$_1$	v 21	[-m]a
	P	v 23	[-l]i-ka u[l-t]u šá-di-ma
	h	v 33	la-[ ]
244	B$_1$	v 43	^{d}GIŠ-gím-maš ina ŠÀ UNUG^{ki} i-na-aṭ-ṭa-la šu-na-te-ka
	F$_1$	v 22	[-k]a
	P	v 24	[UN]UG^{ki} i-na-⸢ṭa⸣-lu šu-na-tu-ka
245	B$_1$	v 44	it-bé-ma ^{d}GIŠ-gím-maš šu-na-ta BÚR-ár MU-ra a-na AMA-šú
	F$_1$	v 23	[ ]-⸢šú⸣
	P	v 25	[ ] šu-na-tú BÚR-⸢ár⸣ MU-ár a-na AM[A-šú]
246	B$_1$	v 45	um-mi MÁŠ.GI$_6$ aṭ-ṭu-la mu-ši-ti-ia
	P	v 26	[ ].GI$_6$ aṭ-ṭu-⸢lu⸣ mu-ši-t[i-ia]
247	B$_1$	v 46	ib-šu-nim-ma MUL.MEŠ AN-e
	P	v 27	[-m]a MUL A[N-e]
248	B$_1$	v 47	GIM ki-iṣ-ru ša ^{d}a-⸢nim⸣ im-ta-naq-qu-tú e-lu EDIN-ia
	P	v 28	[ ]-⸢ma$^?$ im$^?$-taq$^?$-qu⸣-t[a UG]U [ ]
249	B$_1$	v 48	áš-ši-šu-ma ⸢da⸣-an e-li-ia
250	B$_1$	v 49	ul-tab-lak-ki-is-su-⸢ma⸣ ul e-le-ʾ-i-a nu-us-⸢su⸣
251	B$_1$	v 50	UNUG^{ki} ma-a-tum iz-za-az UGU-[šu]
	P	v 31	[i]z-⸢za⸣-[ ]

252	F_1	v 27b	[ ]-⸢ḫi⸣-šu
	P	v 32	[ma-a-tu pu-uḫ-ḫu-rat] in[a muḫ-ḫi-šú]
253	F_1	v 28a	[(in one line with 254)]
	P	v 33	[i-tep-pi-ir um-m]a-nu U[GU E]DIN-[šú]
254	F_1	v 28b	[ ] UGU-šu
	P	v 34	[GURUŠ.MEŠ uk]-tam-ma-ru UGU-[šú]
255	F_1	v 29	[ ].MEŠ-šu
	P	v 35	[ki-i šèr-ri la]-⸢ʾ⸣-i ú-na-šá-qu GÌR.[MEŠ-šú]
256	F_1	v 30	[a]ḫ-bu-ub
	P	v 36	[a-ram-šú-ma GI]M áš-šá-te UGU-šú aḫ-bu-[ub]
257	F_1	v 31a	[(in one line with 258)]
	P	v 37	[áš-šá-áš-šu-ma a]t-ta-di-šú ina šap-li-[ki]
258	F_1	v 31b	[ ]-ia
	P	v 38	[u at-ti tul$_5$-t]a-maḫ-ri-šu it-ti-[i]a
259	F_1	om.	
	P	v 39	[um-mi ^{d}GIŠ-gím-maš em-qet mu-d]a-at ka-la-ma i-de MU-ár ana EN-[š]á
	h	vi 1	[-ma]š en$^{!}$-qet mu-da-a-tú k[a-la-a i-de MU-ár ana DUM]U-šú
260	B_1	vi 9	[k]a-la i-de M[U-]
	F_1	v 32-3	[ ]-ma i-de / [ ] ^{d}GIŠ-gím-maš
	P	v 40	[m]u-da-at ka-la-ma i-de MU-ár ana ^{d}GIŠ-gí[m-m]aš
	h	vi 2	[⸢ri-mat-^{d}n]in-sún en-qet mu-da-a-[tú ka-la-a i-d]e / [MU-ár ana ^{d}GIŠ-gím-ma]š
261	B_1	vi 10	[ ] MUL.MEŠ [ ]
	F_1	v 34	[ ] AN-e
	P	v 41	[-k]a MUL AN-⸢e⸣
	h	vi 3a	[ib-š]u-nik-ka MUL AN-e :
262	B_1	vi 11	[i]m-ta-qu-ut e-lu [ ]
	F_1	v 35	[U]GU EDIN-ka
	P	v 42	[-n]im {šá} ŠUB.MEŠ UGU EDIN-ka
	h	vi 4	[ki]-⟨ma ki⟩-ṣir šá ^{d}a-nim im-ta-⸢qu⸣-t[u$_4$ -k]a
263	B_1	vi 12	[ ]-an e-l[i-ka]
	F_1	v 36	[ ] UGU-ka
	P	v 43	[ ]-⸢an⸣ UGU-ka
	h	vi 5	taš-ši-šu-ma ⸢da⸣-nu ⸢e⸣-[li-k]a
264	B_1	vi 13	[u]l te-le-ʾ-i-a n[u-]
	F_1	v 37	[ ]-ʾ-a nu-us-su
	P	v 44	[-s]u
	h	vi 6	tul-tab-lak-kit-su-ma ul ta-le-e-AN [ ]

265	B_1	vi 14	[-d]i-šu ina šap-[ ]
	F_1	v 38	[ša]p-li-ia
	P	v 45	[-i]a$^{!?}$
	h	vi 7	taš-šá-áš-šum-ma ⸢ta⸣-ad-di-šú ina ša[p-]
266	B_1	vi 15	[-ma]ḫ-ḫar-šu it-t[i-ka]
	F_1	v 39	[-t]i-⸢ka⸣
	h	vi 8	u a-na-ku ul-[ta]m-ḫi-raš-šú KI$^{!}$(DI)-[ ]
267	B_1	vi 16	[ ] ⸢e⸣-li-šú taḫ-[bu-ub]
	h	vi 9	ta-ram-šu-ma ⸢GIM⸣ DAM ⸢ta⸣-ḫab-bu-bu UGU-šú
268	B_1	vi 17	[ ]-pu-u mu-še-zib [ ]
	h	vi 10	il-la-⸢kak⸣-kúm-⸢ma dan⸣-nu tap-pu-ú mu-še-zib ib-ri
269	B_1	vi 18	[ ] ⸢e⸣-mu-qí i-[šu/i]
	h	vi 11	ina KUR da-an e-mu-qí-šú
270	B_1	vi 19	[d]un-nu-na e-mu-q[a-šu]
	h	vi 12	⸢ki-ma ki⸣-ṣir šá ^{d}a-nim du-un-nu-nu e-mu-qa-a-šú
271	B_1	vi 20	[ ] e-li-šú taḫ-b[u-ub]
	h	vi 13	⸢ta-ram-šu⸣-ma GIM DAM ta-ḫab-bu-bu UGU-šú
272	B_1	vi 21	[uš-te-n]é-zeb-ka ka-[a]-⸢šá⸣
	h	vi 14a	⸢šu$^{?}$-ú$^{?}$ dan⸣-nu ú-še-zeb ka-a-šú :
273	B_1	vi 22	[-m]ar/šu-qu-r]at šu-na-at-ka
	h	vi 14b	šá-ni-tum i-ta-mar šu-na-at-tú
274	B_1	om.	
	h	vi 15	[i]t-bé-e-ma i-te-ru-ub ana IGI ^{d}15 AMA-šú
275	B_1	vi 23	[ ] a-na AMA-šú
	h	vi 16	⸢^{d}⸣GIŠ-gím-maš ana šá-ši-ma MU-⸢ár⸣ ana AMA-šú
276	B_1	vi 24	[-t]a-mar šá-ni-ta šu-ut-ta
	h	vi 17	[i]p-pu-un-na-a AMA-a ⸢a⸣-ta-mar šá-⸢ni-tum⸣ MÁŠ.G[I_6]
277	B_1	vi 25a	[-t]i ⟨:⟩
	h	vi 18a	[ina SILA] šá UNUG^{ki} re-bi-tum :
278	B_1	vi 25b	⸢ḫa⸣-ṣi-nu na-di-ma UGU-šú paḫ-ru
	h	vi 18b	ḫa-ṣi-in-nu na-⸢di⸣-ma ⸢UGU⸣-šú / paḫ-ri
279	B_1	vi 26	[-t]um GUB-az UGU-šú
	h	vi 19	[UNUG^{k}]^{i} ma-a-tú iz-za-zu UGU-šú
280	B_1	vi 27	[-r]at ina muḫ-ḫi-šú
	h	vi 20a	[ma-a-tú puḫ]-ḫu-rat ina ⸢UGU⸣-šú :

281	B$_1$	vi 28	[um-ma]-nu UGU EDIN-šú
	h	vi 20b	i-te-ep-⸢pir⸣ [⟨ummānu⟩ UG]U EDIN-šú
282	B$_1$	om.	
	h	vi 21a	[GURUŠ.MEŠ u]k-⸢tam⸣-mar UGU-šú :
283	B$_1$	vi 29	[-m]a at-ta-di-šu ina šap-li-ki
	h	vi 21b	áš-šá-áš-šum$^{!}$-m[a at-ta-d]i-iš / [ina šap-l]i-ku
284	B$_1$	vi 30	[-m]a ki-i áš-šá-te UGU-šú aḫ-bu-ub
	h	vi 22	[a-ram-š]u-ma ki DAM ⸢UGU-šú aḫ⸣-[ ]
285	B$_1$	vi 31	[u at-ti t]ul$_5$-ta-maḫ-ḫa-ri-šu it-ti-ia
	h	vi 23	[ ]x tul-tam-ḫi-ri-šú [ ]-iá
286	B$_1$	vi 32	[-ma]š em-qet mu-da-at ka-lá-ma i-de MU-ra ana DUMU-šá
	h	vi 24	[e]n-qet mu-da-at ⸢ka-la-a⸣ i-de / MU-ár ana DUMU-šú
	o	vi 1'	⸢AMA ^{d}giš-gím-maš⸣ e[n-]
287	B$_1$	vi 33	[ ]-qet mu-da-at ka-lá-ma i-de MU-ra ana ^{d}GIŠ-gím-maš
	h	vi 25	[-^{d}ni]n-sún en-qet mu-da-a-tú ka-la-a i-de / MU-ár ana ^{d}GIŠ-gím-maš
	o	vi 2'	⸢^{f}ri-mat-^{d}nin-sún en-qet mu-d[a-at k]a-⸢la-ma i-de⸣ M[U-]
288	B$_1$	vi 34	[-n]u šá ta-mu-ru LÚ
	h	vi 26	[-i]n-nu ⸢šá ta⸣-mu-ru ib-ri
	o	vi 3'	[DUM]U$^{!}$ ḫa-ṣi-in-nu šá ta-mu-ru i[b-ru]
289	B$_1$	vi 35	[k]i-i áš-šá-te ta-ḫab-bu-ub UGU-šu
	h	vi 27	[-ra]m-šu-ma GIM D[AM] taḫ-bu-bu UGU-šú
	o	vi 4'	ta-ram-šu-ma GIM DAM ta-ḫab-bu-bu [ ]
290	B$_1$	vi 36	[u]l-ta-maḫ-ḫar-šú KI-ka
	h	vi 28	[ ] ul-tam-ḫi-ra-šú it-ti-ka
	o	vi 5'	u a-na-ku ul-ta-maḫ-ḫar-šú K[I-]
291	B$_1$	vi 37	[-m]a dan-nu tap-pu-u mu-še-zib ib-ri
	h	vi 29	[ ]-kak-kúm-ma dan-nu tap-pu-ú mu-še-zib ib-ri
	o	vi 6'	il-la-ka-ak-kúm-ma dan-nu tap-pu-ú mu-[ ]
292	B$_1$	vi 38	[-a]n e-mu-qí i-šu
	h	vi 30a	[ ] e-mu-qí-⸢šú$^{!}$⸣ :
	o	vi 7'	ina KUR da-an e-mu-qa ⸢i⸣-[ ]
293	B$_1$	vi 39	[-n]im dun-nu-na e-mu-qa-šu
	h	vi 30b	ki-ma ki-ṣir šá ^{d}a-nim dun-nu-nu / e-mu-qa-a-šú
	o	vi 8'	[k]i-ma ki-ṣir šá ^{d}a-nim dun-nu-na e-mu-q[a-]
294	B$_1$	vi 40	[-m]a MU-ár a-na AMA-šu
	h	vi 31	[-gí]m-maš ana šá-⸢šu⸣-ma MU-ár ana AMA-šú
	o	vi 9'	⸢^{d}⸣GIŠ-gím-maš ⟨ana⟩ šá-ši-ma MU-ár a-na A[MA-]

295	B$_1$	vi 41	[-l]i-ki GAL-i li-in-qu-tam-ma
	h	vi 32a	[p]i-i ^{d}en-líl ma-lik lim-qut-am-ma ⟨:⟩
	o	vi 10'	[u]m-ma ina KA ^{d}en-líl ma-lik lim-qut-a[m-ma]
296	B$_1$	vi 42	[a]-na-ku lu-ur-ši
	h	vi 32b	⸢ib⸣-ri ma-lik / ⸢ana⸣-[ku l]u-ur-ši
	o	vi 11'	[ib-r]i ma-li-ku a-na-ku lu-ur-[ ]
297	B$_1$	vi 43	[-l]i-ka a-na-ku
	h	vi 33	[lu-ur]-ši ib-ri ma-lik ⸢ana-ku :⸣
	o	vi 12'	[lu-u]r-ši-ma ib-ri ma-li-ku ⸢a⸣-[ ]
298	B$_1$	vi 44	[M]ÁŠ.GI$_6$.MEŠ-šu
	h	vi 34a	[i-t]a-mar šu-na-t[i-šu :]
	o	vi 13'	[i-tam-r]a šu-na-a-ti-[ ]
299	B$_1$	vi 45	[ ]-⸢maš⸣ i-ta-ma-a ana ^{d}en-ki-dù
	F$_4$	vi 1'	[ ]x [ ]
	h	vi 34b	[ša]m-ḫat ⸢šu⸣-na-at / [ ] ⸢^{d}en-ki⸣-[dù]
	o	vi 14'	[x (x) x ^{f}š]am-ḫat šu-na-ti ^{d}giš-gím-maš i-ta-ma-⸢a⸣ [ ]
300	B$_1$	vi 46	[k]i-lal-la-an
	F$_4$	vi 2'	[-m]u [ ]
	h	vi 35	[ur-ta-ʾ]-a-a[m-(mu) ki-lal-la-an :]
	o	vi 15'	[ur$^{?}$-ta$^{?}$-ʾ$^{?}$]-a-mu ki-lal-la-[an]

———————————————————— BF40

II 1	B$_1$	vi 47	[ ] ma-ḫar-šá
	F$_4$	vi 3'	[ ] a-š[ib$^{?}$]

A. R. George

2

Ugarit Fragments of Tablet 1
The Standard Babylonian Edition

Latin Transliteration by

Andrew R. George
SOAS University of London

The Gilgameš epic at Ugarit. Aula Orientalis 25 (2007) 237-254
http://eprints.soas.ac.uk/5654/

1	[*š*]*a na-aq-ba i-mu-ru il-di ma-t*[*i*]	// SB I 1
2	[*a*]*l-ka-ka-ti i-du-u ka-la-ma ḫa-[as-su]*	// SB I 2
3	⸢^{d}⸣*bìl.ga.mes ša na-aq-ba i-mu-ru* ⸢*il-di māti*(kur)⸣	// SB I 3
4	*[a]l-ka-ka-ti i-du-u ka-la-ma ḫa-as-s[u!]*	// SB I 4
5	⸢*i*⸣*-ḫi-iṭ-ma mit-ḫa-riš pa-rak-ki*! {x}	// SB I 5
6	*nap-ḫar né-mé-qí ša ka-la-ma i-de*	// SB I 6
7	*a-lik ḫarrān*(kaskal) *ú-tu-ur-na-pu-uš-ti* ⸢*ru-uq-ti*⸣	cf. SB I 42
8	*e-bi-ir a-ab-ba ta-ma-ta rapaš*(dagal)*-ta a-di ṣi-ti* ^{d}*šamši*(utu)^{ši}	// SB I 40
9	*ub-la ṭe-ma ša la-am a-bu-*[*b*]*i*	// SB I 8
10	*ḫar-ra-na ru-uq-ta illik*(gin)*-ma a-ni-iḫ ù šup-šu-uq*	// SB I 9
11	gar*-nu-šu-ma na-ru-*⟨*ú*⟩□*ka-lu ma-*⟨*na*⟩*-aḫ-*{ras.}*-ti*	// SB I 10
12	*ul ú-maš-šar* ^{d}bìl.ga.mes *kal-lat ṣe-eḫ-*⸢*ret*⸣ / *a-na mu-ti-*⸢*ša*⸣	// SB I 76
13	*šu-ú ri-im-ši*!*-na ši-na ar-ḫa-*⸢*tum*⸣	// SB I 73
14	*ta-zi-im-ta-ši-na il-te-né-mi* ^{d}*iš*$_{8}$-⸢*tár*!⸣	// SB I 78
15	*rig-mu mar-ṣu ik-ta-na-ša-da ana šamê*(an)^{e} *anim*(an)^{nim}	
16	*šu-tur a-na šarri*(lugal) *ša-nu-'-ú-di bēl*(en) *ga*!-⸢*at*! *-ti*⸣	// SB I 29
17	*qar-ra-du lil-lid ú-ru-uk ri-mu* x (x) x	// SB I 30
18	^{d}bìl.ga.mes *ša-nu-ú-di bēl*(en) *ga-*⸢*at*!⸣*-ti*	
19	*qar-ra-du lil-lid ú-ru-uk ri-mu mut-tak*!*-pu*	
20	*e-li* ^{d}*bìl.ga.mes muḫḫi*(ugu) *du-ri ša* ⸢*uruk*(unug)⸣^{ki} 21 *i-tal-lak*	// SB I 18
21	*te-me-na ḫi-iṭ libitta*(sig$_{4}$) *ṣu-up-pi*	// SB I 19
22	*pi-te-ma tu-up-ni-in-na ša* ^{giš}*erēni*(eren)	// SB I 24
23	*pu-uṭ-ṭe-er ḫar-gal-li-šú ša siparri*(zabar)	// SB I 25
24	*i-šam-ma ṭup-pi* $^{\text{na4!}}$*uqnî*(za.gìn.na) *ti-ša-*⸢*as*⸣*-si*	// SB I 27
25	*um-ma libitta*(sig$_{4}$)*-ša la a-gur-rat*	// SB I 20
26	*uš-ši-šú la id-du-ú* 7 *mu-un-tal-ku*	// SB I 21
27	*šár*^{ár} *ālu*(uru) *šár*^{ár} ^{giš}*kirâtu*(kiri$_{6}$)^{meš} *šár*^{ár} *es-sú-u pi-tir* ⸢*bīt*(é) *iš*$_{8}$*-tár*⸣	// SB I 22
edge		
28	*ša-la-áš*! *ša-ri ù pi-tir ú-ru-uk* x x x	// SB I 23
29	*ik-tap-píl* ^{d}bìl.ga.mes 50 *ru-'i*! / {*ru-'i*!}	
	u$_{4}$*-mi-šam i-gam-mar eṭlūti*!(guruš!)	
rev.		
30	*ul-ta-dir eṭlūti*(guruš!)^{meš} *ša uruk*(unug!)^{ki} *ina ku-*x x	// SB I 67 // 84
31	*ap-pat pe-er-ti-šu i*⟩*-ḫa-an-nu-ba kīma*(gim) ^{d}*niss*[*aba*]	// SB I 60 // 107
32	*i-nam*!*-bu-ṭa ši-na-šú ki-ma ni-pí-iḫ*! $^{\text{d!}}$*šá*!*-am*!*-š*[*i*]	
33	*ša*!*-kin pe-re-ta ki-i*! *uq-na-ti*	cf. SB I 106
34	11 *i-na am-ma-ti la-an-šú*	// SB I 52
	4 *i-na am-ma-tim* 35 *bi-rít tu-le-šú*	// SB I 53=55
36	*ni*!*-kás šēpā*(gìr)^{min}*-šu ù qa-na pu-ri-du-šu*	// SB I 56
37	*ni*!*-kás ašarēdū*(igi.du)^{meš} *ša le-ti-šu*	// SB I 58
38	*a-na ša ra a ṣu-up pa-ni-šu*	

3

Tablet 2 (lines 1-46)
The Old Babylonian Edition (Penn Tablet)

Latin Transliteration by

Andrew R. George
SOAS University of London

The Babylonian Gilgamesh Epic: Introduction, Critical Edition and Cuneiform Texts
Oxford University Press. 2003
http://eprints.soas.ac.uk/1603/

Morris Jastrow and Albert T. Clay
Yale University

An Old Babylonian Version of the Gilgamesh Epic.
Yale Oriental Series Vol. IV, 3. Yale University Press. 1920
http://www.gutenberg.org/ebooks/11000

1 it-bi-e-ma ^{d}Giš šú-na-tam i-pa-áš-šar
2 iz-za-kàr-am a-na um-mi-šú
3 um-mi i-na šá-at mu-ši-ti-ia
4 šá-am-ḫa-ku-ma at-ta-na-al-la-ak
5 i-na bi-ri-it it-lu-tim
6 ib-ba-šú-nim-ma *{ip-zi-ru-nim-ma}* ka-ka-bu šá-ma-i
7 [ki]-iṣ-rù *{x x-rum}* šá A-nim im-ḳu-ut a-na ṣi-ri-ia
8 áš-ši-šú-ma ik-ta-bi-it e-li-ia
9 ú-ni-iš-šú-ma *{ú-ni-is-su-ma}* nu-uš-šá-šú ú-ul il-ti-'i *{el-ti-'i}*
10 Uruk^{ki} ma-tum pa-ḫi-ir e-li-šú
11 it-lu-tum ú-na-šá-ku *{ú-na-šá-qu}* ši-pi-šú
12 ú-um-mi-id-ma pu-ti
13 i-mi-du ia-ti
14 áš-ši-a-šú-ma ab-ba-la-áš-šú a-na ṣi-ri-ki *{ṣe-ri-ki}*
15 um-mi ^{d}Giš mu-di-a-at *{mu-de-a-at}* ka-la-ma
16 iz-za-kàr-am a-na ^{d}Giš
17 mi-in-di ^{d}Giš šá ki-ma ka-ti
18 i-na ṣi-ri i-wa-li-id-ma
19 ú-ra-ab-bi-šú šá-du-ú
20 ta-mar-šú-ma [kima Sal(?)] ta-ḫa-du at-ta *{ta-mar-šu-ma ta-ḫa-du at-ta}*
21 it-lu-tum *{et-lu-tum}* ú-na-šá-ku ši-pi-šú
22 tí-iṭ-ṭi-ra-áš-[šú tu-ut]-tu-ú-ma *{te-ed-di-ra-aš!?-{x}-šu-ú-ma}*
23 ta-tar-ra-[as-su] a-na ṣi-[ri]-ia *{ta-tar-ra-⸢aš-šu a-na⸣ ṣi-⸢ri-ia⸣}*
24 [uš]-ti-nim-ma *{it-ti-lam-ma}* i-ta-mar šá-ni-tam
25 [šú-na]-ta *{it-be}* i-ta-wa-a-am a-na um-mi-šú
26 [um-mi] a-ta-mar šá-ni-tam
27 [šú-na-tu a-ta]-mar e-mi-a i-na su-ḳi-im *{x x x me-e UL.A i-na su-qi-im}*
28 [šá Uruk]^{ki} ri-bi-tim
29 ḫa-aṣ-ṣi-nu na-di-i-ma
30 e-li-šú pa-aḫ-ru
31 ḫa-aṣ-ṣi-nu-um-ma šá-ni bu-nu-šú
32 a-mur-šú-ma aḫ-ta-du a-na-ku
33 a-ra-am-šú-ma ki-ma áš-šá-tim
34 a-ḫa-ab-bu-ub el-šú
35 el-ki-šú-ma *{el-qe-šú-ma}* áš-ta-ka-an-šú
36 a-na a-ḫi-ia
37 um-mi ^{d}Giš mu-da-at [ka]-la-ma
38 [iz-za-kàr-am *{is-sà-qar-am}* a-na ^{d}Giš]
39 [^{d}Giš šá ta-mu-ru amêlu]
40 [ta-ḫa-ab-bu-ub ki-ma áš-šá-tim el-šú]
41 *{...}*
42 *{...}*
43 áš-šum uš-[ta]-ma-ḫa-ru it-ti-ka
44 ^{d}Giš šú-na-tam i-pa-šar
45 ^{d}En-ki-[dũ wa]-ši-ib ma-ḫar ḫa-ri-im-tim
46 ur-[šá ir]-ḫa-mu di-da-šá(?) ip-tí-[e] *{úr-ta-'a_4-mu ki-la-al-lu-un}*

4

Tablet 10 (lines 190-322)
The Standard Babylonian Edition

Latin Transliteration by

Andrew R. George
SOAS University of London

Department of the Languages and Cultures of the Near and Middle East
The Standard Babylonian Epic of Gilgamesh
Sources of the Standard Babylonian poem
http://www.soas.ac.uk/nme/research/gilgamesh/standard/

TABLET X

Siglum	*Museum number*		*Plate in George*
	Distribution of lines by column		*Bab. Gilg. Epic*
	NINEVEH		
K_1	K 3382+Rm 621		108–13
K_2	K 8579		109, 111
K_3	K 8589+Sm 1681		108–9, 112–13
	i **1**–30 (K_3, K_1)	iv **173**–95 (K_1)	
	ii 61–**111** (K_1)	v **221–277** (K_1, K_3)	
	iii **112**–25 (K_2), 131–**172** (K_1)	vi 296–**322**, colophon (K_3)	
	NIMRUD		
z	IM 67564 (ND 4381)		32–3
	i // 63–112	v variant text, see Chapter 7	
	ii // 196–230	vi // XI 304–328?	
	BABYLON		
b	BM 34160+34193+35174+35348+35413+35628		114–15
	i 19–46	v 260–94	
	ii 68–109	vi 311–**322**, colophon	
f	BM 34853+35546+Rm 751		116–17
	i **1**–17	v 239–61	
	ii traces of 2 unidentified lines	vi 292'–**322**, colophon	

Score transliteration

N.B. || signifies place of division into sub-column on MS K

1	D	catch-line	^{f}ší-d[u-ri sa-bi-t]um šá ina ⸢sa⸣-pan tam-ti áš-bat
	K_3	i 1	^{d}ší-du-ri sa-bi-tu[m || šá ina sa-pan tam-ti áš-bat]
	f	i 1	[t]am-tim áš-b[a-tu$_4$]
2	K_3	i 2	áš-bat-ma || [ ]
	f	i 2	[ ]x [x]
3	K_3	i 3	ib-šu-ši kan-nu ib-šu-ši x[ ]
4	K_3	i 4	ku-tu-um-mi kut-tu-mat-ma || x[ ]
5	K_3	i 5	^{d}GIŠ-gím-maš ut-tag-gi-ša[m]-ma || x[ ]
6	K_3	i 6	maš-ka la-biš || pu-l[uḫ$^{?}$-]
	f	i 6	[-lu]ḫ$^{?}$-tu[m x (x) x]

190	K_1	iv 17b	ù im-na ⸢nam/zi⸣-[ ]
191	K_1	iv 18	a-na-aṭ-ṭa-lam-ma || ul ia-[ú LÚ]
192	K_1	iv 19	a-na-aṭ-ṭa-lam-ma || u[l ia-ú LÚ?]
193	K_1	iv 20	a-⸢na-aṭ⸣-ṭa-lam-ma || [ul ia-ú LÚ?]
194	K_1	iv 21	[x x x i]a-ši x[ ]
195	K_1	iv 22	[x x x x] x x[ ]

The remainder of MS K col. iv, about 25 lines of tablet, is missing, leaving a gap of at least that in the text. Much of it is filled by MS **z** *col. ii:*

196	**z**	ii 1'	ul a-ia-⸢ú⸣ [ ]
197	**z**	ii 2'	ú-šar?-pa?-du [ ]
198	**z**	ii 3'	⸢^{lú}MÁ⸣.LAḪ$_5$ [ ]
199	**z**	ii 4'	a-mi-lu ⸢ša⸣ a-ta-[ ]
200	**z**	ii 5'	ša a-na-ṭal-la ul x[ ]
201	**z**	ii 6'	pi-qa-ma-a EDIN x[ ]
202	**z**	ii 7'	x x x ma x na-a ⸢ú⸣-[ ]
203	**z**	ii 8'	u[r]-na [x x]-ma it-ta-x[ ]
204	**z**	ii 9'	^{md}GIŠ-TUK a-na ⸢ka⸣-ri i[ṭ-ḫe]
205	**z**	ii 10'	⸢ú⸣-še-rid-ma ú?-la-[ ]
206	**z**	ii 11'	⸢ù⸣ [š]u-ú e-la-[m]a? it-ta-[ ]

———————————————— **z**

207	**z**	ii 12'	^{md}GIŠ-TUK a-na ša-š[u-m]a MU-á[r a-na ^{m}UD-ZI-(tim)]
208	**z**	ii 13'	[lib?]-⸢lu⸣-uṭ ^{m}UD-ZI DUMU ^{m}[u]-bar-t[u-tu ( )]
209	**z**	ii 14'	[(x)] x lu EGIR a-bu-⸢be šá ana⸣ da-[ ]
210	**z**	ii 15'	⸢a-bu⸣-be mi-na-a ana da-[ ]
211	**z**	ii 16'	[x x] x su me x ša x[ ]

———————————————— **z**

212	**z**	ii 17'	[^{m}UD-ZI a]-n[a š]a-šu-m[a M]U-ra a-n[a ^{md}GIŠ-TUK]
213	**z**	ii 18'	[am-mi-ni ak-la] ⸢le⸣-[ta]-ka qù-d[u-du pa-nu-ka]
214	**z**	ii 19'	[l]u-[m]u-u[n Š]À-[ka q]a-tu-ú [zi-mu-ú-ka]
215	**z**	ii 20'	⸢i⸣-ba-[š]i ni-is-[sa]-tu ina k[ar-ši-ka]
216	**z**	ii 21'	[a]-na a-⸢lik⸣ ar-[ḫ]i ru-qa-[ti pa-nu-ka maš-lu]
217	**z**	ii 22'	⸢i⸣-na A [šar-b]e u ⸢ṣe⸣-te [qu-(um)-mu-ú pa-nu-ka]
218	**z**	ii 23'	u pa-an la-be ša-ak-na-t[a-ma ta-ra(p)-pu-ud EDIN]

———————————————— **z**

219	**z**	ii 24'	^{md}GIŠ-TUK a-na ša-šu-m[a MU-ra a-na ^{m}UD-ZI-(tim)]
220	**z**	ii 25'	am-mi-ni la ak-la TE.MEŠ-[a-a la qù-du-du pa-nu-ú-a]
221	K_1	v 1	[zi]-mu-ú-a
	z	ii 26'	⸢la lu-mun lìb-bi⸣ la qa-t[u-ú]
222	K_1	v 2	[ina ka]r-ši-ia
	z	ii 27'	⸢la⸣ ib-⸢ba⸣-ši ni-is-sa-t[u]

223 K_1 v 3 [pa-nu-ú]-a la maš-lu
z ii 28' a-na a-lik ar-ḫi ru-qa-t[i]

224 K_1 v 4 [qu-um-mu]-⸢ú⸣ pa-nu-ú-a
z ii 29' ⸢i⸣-na A {AŠ?} šar-be u ṣe-te l[a]

225 K_1 v 5 [la a-r]ap-pu-ud EDIN
z ii 30' u [p]a-an la-be la šá-ak-na-[ku-ma]

———————————————————————— z

226 K_1 v 6 [ak-kan-nu šá KU]R nim-ru šá EDIN
z ii 31-32a' ib-ri ⸢ku⸣-da-ni ṭa-ri-[du] / nim!-ri ša EDIN

227 K_1 v 7 [ ] KIMIN
z ii 32b'-33' [^{md}en-ki-dù ib-ri] / ⸢ku⸣-da-ni ṭa-r[i-du]

228 K_1 v 8 [ni-l]u-ú šá-da-a
z ii 34' ⸢ša⸣ ni-nem!(DU)-du-⸢ú⸣-[ma]

229 K_1 v 9 [a]-⸢la⸣-a ni-na-ru
z ii 35' a-⸢la⸣-a ni-[iṣ-ba-tu-ma]

230 K_1 v 10 [nu-šal-pi-tu ^{d}ḫum-ba-ba šá ina ^{giš}T]IR ^{giš}EREN áš-bu
z ii 36' [nu-š]al-p[i-]

231 K_1 v 11 [ina né-re-bé-e-ti? šá KUR-i ni-d]u-ku UR.MAḪ.MEŠ
232 K_1 v 12 [ib-ri šá a-ram-mu-šú dan-niš it-ti-ia DU.DU-k]u ka-lu mar-ṣa-a-ti
233 K_1 v 13 [^{d}en-ki-dù ib-ri šá a-ram-mu-šú dan-niš it-ti-ia D]U.DU-ku KIMIN
234 K_1 v 14a [ik-šu-da-niš-šu šīmāt? amēlūti? :]
235 K_1 v 14b [6 ur-ri u 7 mu-šá-a-ti] UGU-šú ab-ki
236 K_1 v 15 [ul ad-din-šu a-n]a qé-bé-ri
237 K_1 v 16 [a-di tul-tu im-qu-tam ina ap-p]i-šu
238 K_1 v 17a [a-dur] ⸢:⸣

239 K_1 v 17b mu-ta ap-l[aḫ-ma a-rap-pu-ud E]DIN
f v 1' ⸢mu-tú⸣ [ ]

240 K_1 v 18a [a-mat ib-ri-ia kab?-t]a?-at UGU-ia :
f v 2' a-mat [ ]

241 K_1 v 18b ur-ḫa ru-qa-t[u a-rap-pu-ud EDI]N
f v 3' ⸢ur-ḫu⸣ [ ]

242 K_1 v 19a [a-mat ^{d}en-ki-dù] ib-ri-ia KIMIN :
f v 4' ⸢a-mat⸣ ^{d}e[n-]

243	K_1	v 19b	ḫar-ra-nu ⸢ru-qa⸣-t[u KIMIN]
	f	v 5'	⸢har⸣-ra-n[u]
244	K_1	v 20	[ki-ki-i l]u-us-kut ki-ki-i lu-qul [ana-ku?]
	f	v 6'	⸢ki⸣-ki-i [ ]
245	K_1	v 21a	[ib-ri š]á a-ram-mu i-te-mi ṭi-iṭ-ṭiš :
	f	v 7'	ib-ri [ ]
246	K_1	v 21b	^{d}en-ki-dù ib-r[i KIMIN]
	f	v 8'	[^{d}en-k]i-⸢dù⸣ i[b-]
247	K_1	v 22a	[ana-k]u ul ki-i šá-šu-ma-a a-né-el-lam-ma :
	f	v 9a'	[ana-ku] ul ki-i šá-a-šu-ma a-⸢né⸣-e[l-]
248	K_1	v 22b	ul a-te-eb-ba-a du-ur d[a-ar]
	f	v 9b'	[(in one line with 247)]
			———————————————— Kf
249	K_1	v 23	[^{d}]GIŠ-gím-maš ana šá-šu-ma || MU-ra ana ^{m}UD-Z[I]
	f	v 10'	⸢^{d}⸣GIŠ-gím-maš a-na šá-a-šu-ma ⸢MU⸣-r[a]
250*	K_1	v 24	[ana-ku] um-ma lul-lik-ma ^{m}UD-ZI ru-qa šá i-dab-bu-bu-uš lu-mu[r]
	f	v 11'	[ana]-ku um-ma lul-lik ^{m}UD-ZI ru-qí šá i-dab-b[u-]
251	K_1	v 25	[a]s-ḫur al-li-ka || ka-li-ši-na KUR.MEŠ
	f	v 12a'	[a]s-ḫur al-lak ka-li-ši-na KUR.KUR.MEŠ :
252	K_1	v 26	⸢e⸣-te-et-ti-qa || KUR.MEŠ mar-ṣu-ti
	f	v 12b'	e-te-et-qa [ ]
253	K_1	v 27	[u] e-te-te-bi-ra ka-li-ši-na ta-ma-a-tum
	f	v 13'	⸢ù⸣ e-te-eb-bi-ru ka-li-ši-na ta-m[a]-⸢a⸣-[ ]
254	K_1	v 28	[š]it-ta ṭa-ab-ta || ul iš-bu-u pa-nu-u-a
	f	v 14'	x-ku? um-ma : šit-ti ṭa-ab-⟨tú⟩ ul iš-bu-ú pa-⸢nu-ú⸣-[a]
255	K_1	v 29a	[u]š-te-ziq ra-ma-ni ina da-la-pu :
	f	v 15a'	ul-te-ziq ra-ma-ni ina da-la-pi :
256	K_1	v 29b	ši-ir-a-ni-ia SAG.PA.LAGAB um-tal-li
	f	v 15b'	ši-ir-a-ni-ia ⸢SAG.PA.LAGAB um⸣-[ ]

257 K_1 om.
f v 16' mi-na-a ak-te-šìr ina ma-⸢na-aḫ⸣-t[i-ia]

258 K_1 v 30 [ana le]-et sa-bit ul ak-šu-dam-ma lu-bu-uš-ti iq-ti
f v 17' ⸢ana⸣ le-et ^{f}sa-bit ul ak-šu-dam-ma lu$^{!}$-bu-uš-tú [ ]

259 K_1 v 31a [a-du-k]a a-sa bu-ṣa né-šá nim-ri mìn-di-na ⟨:⟩
f v 18' [a-du]k ⸢a⸣-[sa bu-ṣ]a né-e-šú nim-ri mìn-d[i-na]

260 K_1 v 31b a-a-la tu-ra-ḫa bu-la u ⸢nam-maš-šá-a šá EDIN⸣
b v 1' a-[ ]
f v 19' [-ḫ]u bu-lum nam-maš-⸢še⸣-e š[á]

261 K_1 v 32 [UZU.MEŠ]-šú-nu ak-kal KUŠ.MEŠ-šú-nu ú-ṭa-ab-[ba-aḫ?]
b v 2' UZU.ME[Š-]
f v 20' [M]EŠ-⸢šú-nu ú-ṭa$^{?}$-ab$^{?}$-ba$^{?}$⸣-[ ]

262 K_1 v 33a [.LA]GAB li-di-lu KÁ-šá :
b v 3' šá SAG.PA.L[AGAB]

263 K_1 v 33b ina ESIR.ḪI.A u ESIR ⸢lip$^{?}$⸣-[ḫu-ú? KÁ-šá?]
b v 4' ina ESIR.ḪI.⸢A⸣ [ ]

264 K_1 v 34 [ ]-a-ši mi-lu-la || la ⸢ú⸣-x[ ]
b v 5' áš-šú ia-a-š[i]

265 K_1 v 35 [áš-šú ia]-a-ši PA-ad-di-'-i ú-ma-a[l-]
b v 6' ia-a-ši PA-d[i-]

——————————————— Kb

266 K_1 v 36 [a-n]a šá-šu-ma MU-ra a-na [^{d}GIŠ-gím-maš]
b v 7' ^{m}ut-ZI-tim a-[ ]

267 K_1 v 37 [ ] ⸢^{d}⸣GIŠ-gím-maš ni-is-sa-ta tur-t[i-né-ed-di at-ta?]
b v 8' am-me-ni ^{d}GIŠ-g[ím-]

268 K_1 v 38 [DIN]GIR.MEŠ u a-me-lu-ti [ba-na-a-ta?]
K_3 v 1' šá ina U[ZU]
b v 9' šá ina UZU DINGIR.ME[Š]

269 K_1 v 39 [-k]a u AMA-ka i-pu-[ ]
K_3 v 2' šá GIM A[D-]
b v 10' šá ki-ma AD-ka [ ]

270	K_1	v 40	[-m]a ^{d}GIŠ-gím-maš ana li[l-li]
	K_3	v 3'	ma-t[i-]
	b	v 11'	ma-ti-ma-a ⸢^{d}⸣[ ]
271	K_1	v 41	[i]d-du-ma ti-x[ ]
	K_3	v 4'	^{giš}G[U.]
	b	v 12'	^{giš}GU.ZA ina UKKIN i[d-]
272	K_1	v 42	[ ]-šú ana lil-li šur-šum-me [ ]
	K_3	v 5'	na-a[d-]
	b	v 13'	na-ad-na-áš-šú ana [ ] / GIM Ì.NUN [ ]
273	K_1	v 43	[ ] ⸢ù⸣ ku-uk-ku-šá {šá} GIM [ ]
	K_3	v 6'	tuḫ-ḫ[i]
	b	v 14'	tuḫ-ḫu ⸢ù⸣ ku-uk-k[u-]
274	K_1	v 44	[-ḫ]a-an-da GIM [ ]
	K_3	v 7'	la-bi[š]
	b	v 15'	la-biš [m]aš-ḫa-an-d[a]
275	K_1	v 45	[né-b]é-ḫi e-b[e-eḫ]
	K_3	v 8'	ki-i [ ]
	b	v 16'	ù šá-a-šú GIM né-bé-[ ]
276	K_1	v 46	[ ]-⸢ú⸣ ⸢ma$^{?}$⸣-[li-ki?]
	K_3	v 8'	áš-šú [ ]
	b	v 17'	áš-šú la i-šu-ú [ ]
277	K_3	v 47	a-m[at]
	b	v 18'	a-mat mil-ki la i-š[u-ú]
278	b	v 19'	i-ši re-ši-šú ^{d}GI[Š-gím-maš]
279	b	v 20'	[x]-nu EN-šu-nu ma-la š[á$^{?}$]
280	b	v 21'	[x x] x x x ⸢AN⸣ x [ ]
281	b	v 22'	[x x] ^{d}30 u DINGIR.ME[Š]
282	b	v 23'	[ina] ⸢GI_6⸣ ^{d}30 il-lak [ ]
283	b	v 24'	[da]l-pu-ma DINGIR.MEŠ [ ]
284	b	v 25'	⸢e⸣-ra la sa-ki-pu x[ ]
285	b	v 26'	ul-tu pa-an šá-kin x[ ]
286	b	v 27'	at-ta ⸢ku⸣-pu-ud-ma x[ ]
287	b	v 28'	tap-pu-ut-ka a pi du$^{?}$ x[ ]
288	b	v 29'	šum-ma ^{d}GIŠ-gím-maš É DINGIR.MEŠ za-n[in-]
289	b	v 30'	É ^{d}15$^{!}$.MEŠ iḫ-x[ ]
290	b	v 31'	ši-na a-x (x) x-⸢uš⸣ DINGIR.MEŠ [ ]

291	b	v 32'	⸢a-na⸣ x x [x x] x x i-⸢pu-uš⸣ x[ ]
292	b	v 33'	[ ] ⸢a-na⸣ qí-⸢iš⸣-tim i-x[x (x) x]
293	b	v 34'	[ ] ⸢i⸣-nam-du-⸢ú⸣ [ ]
294	b	v 35'	[ ] ⸢AN?⸣ [ ]

The text of MS b breaks off here. About 17 lines of tablet are missing between the end of MS K col. v at l. 227. Since MS K is now less constrained for space it is unlikely to have doubled up many lines of poetry, and it is probable that we must assume there to be an overlap between the fragmentary end of MS b col. v and the equally poorly preserved first extant lines of MS f col. vi.

292*	f	vi 1'	[ ] x x
293*	f	vi 2'	[k]ar-ši-⸢šú⸣
294*	f	vi 3'	[ ]x za-⸢ni⸣-x
295	f	vi 4'	[ ]x a-me-lu-ti
296	K$_3$	vi 1'	[x (x) x i]l-qu-⸢ú || a-na⸣ [ ]
	f	vi 5'	[ ] ⸢a⸣-na ši-im-ti-šú
297	K$_3$	vi 2'	[x x t]a-ad-da-li-ip || mi-na-a [ ]
	f	vi 6'	[m]i-na-a ta-⸢al-qu⸣
298	K$_3$	vi 3'	[ina d]a-la-pi || tu-un-na-ḫ[a]
	f	vi 7a'	[t]u-un-na-[:]
299	K$_3$	vi 4'	⸢SA⸣.MEŠ-ka || ni-is-sa-t[a]
	f	vi 7b'	[S]A.MEŠ-ka SAG.PA.LAGAB tu-mál-⸢la⸣
300	K$_3$	vi 5'	ru-qu-tu || tu-qar-r[a-ab]
	f	vi 8'	[-t]u tu-qa[r-] UD.MEŠ-ka
301	K$_3$	vi 6'	a-me-lu-tum šá GIM GI a-pi [ ]
	f	vi 9'	[-tu]m šá k[i-ma GI a-p]i ḫa-ṣi-pi {x} šùm-šú
302	K$_3$	vi 7a'	eṭ-la dam-qa KI.SIKIL-ta da-me-eq-tum :
	f	vi 10a'	[ ] ⸢KI⸣.SIKIL da-m[i-]
303	K$_3$	vi 7b'	ur-[ru-ḫiš?]
	f	vi 10b'	[ ]-šú-nu-ma i šal-lal mu-ti
304	K$_3$	vi 8a'	⸢ul ma⸣-am-ma mu-ú-tu im-mar :
	f	vi 11a'	[ ] mu-tum im-m[ar :]
305	K$_3$	vi 8b'	ul ma-am-m[a ša mu-ti]
	f	vi 11b'	[i]m-⸢mar⸣ pa-ni-šú

Line	MS	Col.	Text
306	K_3	vi 9'	⌜ul ma-am-ma⌝ ša mu-ti || ri[g-ma-šú i-šem-me]
	f	vi 12a'	[ ] šá mu-tum rig-⌜ma-šú⌝ [ ]
307	K_3	vi 10'	ag-gu ⌜mu-tum⌝ || ḫa-[ṣi-ip] ⌜a⌝-m[e-lu-ti]
	f	vi 12b'	[ ] ḫa-ṣi-pi LÚ-ut-tim
308	K_3	vi 11a'	⌜im-ma⌝-ti-ma ni-ip-pu-šá É :
	f	vi 13a'	[-m]a ip-p[u]-uš É ⌜:⌝
309	K_3	vi 11b'	im-ma-ti-ma ni-qan-n[a-]
	f	vi 13b'	⌜im⌝-[-n]a-⌜nu⌝ qin-nu
310	K_3	vi 12'	⌜im⌝-ma-ti-ma ŠEŠ.MEŠ || i-zu-uz-[zu]
	f	vi 14'	[-t]i-ma ŠEŠ.MEŠ i-z[u-] ḪA.LA
311	K_3	vi 13'	⌜im⌝-ma-ti-ma ze-ru-tum || i-ba-áš-ši ina [KUR?]
	b	vi 1'	[m]a-x[(x)]
	f	vi 15'	[-t]i-ma ze-ru-tu i[b-] ⌜KUR?⌝
312	K_3	vi 14'	im-ma-ti-ma ÍD iš-šá-a || ILLU u[b-la]
	b	vi 2'	[ ] mi-lu ub-lu
	f	vi 16a'	[im-m]a-ti-ma ÍD iš-šá-am-ma mi-⌜la ub-lu$_4$⌝ [:]
313	K_3	vi 15'	ku-li-li || ⟨iq⟩-qé-lep-pa-a [ ]
	b	vi 3'	[-q]é-lep-pe ina ÍD
	f	vi 16b'	[k]u-li-⌜li⌝ [ ]
314	K_3	vi 16'	pa-nu-šá i-na-aṭ-ṭa-lu || pa-an ^{d}UTU-[ši]
	b	vi 4'	[ ]-aṭ-ṭa-lu pa-ni ^{d}UTU-ši
	f	vi 17'	[-š]ú i-na-aṭ-ṭa-la [p]a-an ⌜^{d}⌝[ ]
315	K_3	vi 17'	ul-tu ul-la-nu-um-ma || ul i-ba-áš-ši m[im-ma]
	b	vi 5'	[ ] ul-la-nu-um-ma ul i-ba-áš-ši mim-ma
	f	vi 18'	[ul-t]u ⌜ul-la⌝-nu-um-ma ul i-ba-áš-ši [ ]
316	K_3	vi 18'	SAL-lu ù mi-tum || ki-i a-ḫa-meš-[ma]
	b	vi 6'	[ ] u mi-i-tum ki-i KA a-ḫa-meš-ma
	f	vi 19'	[ ]-tum ki-i KA a-ḫa-m[eš-ma]
317	K_3	vi 19'	šá mu-ti || ul iṣ-ṣi-ru ṣa-la[m-šú]
	b	vi 7'	[-tu]m? ul iṣ-ṣi-ru ṣa-lam-šú
	f	vi 20a'	[-ṣ]i-⌜ru⌝ ṣa-lam-šú :

318	K$_3$	vi 20'	LÚ.U$_{18}$.LU-ú LÚ e-dil : ul-tu ik-ru-bu [x x]
	b	vi 8'	[L]Ú BAD ul ik-ru-ba ka-ra-bi ina KUR
	f	vi 20b'	LÚ.U$_{18}$.LU-a LÚ BAD ul ik-r[u-]
319	K$_3$	vi 21'	^{d}a-nun-na-ki DINGIR.MEŠ ‖ GAL.MEŠ pa[ḫ-ru]
	b	vi 9'	[ ] ⸢DINGIR.MEŠ GAL⸣.MEŠ paḫ-ru
	f	vi 21a'	[GA]L.⸢MEŠ paḫ⸣-ru :
320	K$_3$	vi 22'	^{d}ma-am-me-tum ba-na-at šim-ti KI-šú-nu ši-ma-tú i-ši[m-ma]
	b	vi 10'	⸢^{d}ma⸣-[ši]m-⸢ti-šú i-šim⸣-me
	f	vi 21b'	^{d}ma-mi ba-na-at šim-⸢ti⸣-šú-nu [ ]
321	K$_3$	vi 23'	iš-tak-nu mu-ta ‖ u ba-la-ṭ[a]
	b	vi 11'	il$^{!}$-ta-kan mu-t[i]-ṭu
	f	vi 22a'	[-l]a-⸢ṭu⸣ :
322	K$_3$	vi 24'	šá mu-ti ‖ ul ud-du-ú UD.MEŠ-šú
	b	vi 12'	šá mu-ú-tú ul ud-du-ú UD.MEŠ-šú ⸢šá-niš ul⸣-te-du-ú
	f	vi 22b'	šá mu-ú-tú ul ud-du-ú UD.MEŠ-šú š[á]-niš u[l-]
			———————————————— Kbf
(XI 1)		K$_3$	^{d}GIŠ-gím-maš ana šá-šu-ma MU-ra ana UD-ZI ru-qí
		b	^{d}GIŠ-gím-maš a-na šá-šu-ma MU-ár ana UD-ZI-tim ru-qí
		f	[-á]r ana ^{m}UD-ZI SUD

A. R. George

5

Tablet 11
The Standard Babylonian Edition

Latin transliteration by

Andrew R. George
SOAS University of London

Department of the Languages and Cultures of the Near and Middle East

The Standard Babylonian Epic of Gilgamesh
Sources of the Standard Babylonian poem
http://www.soas.ac.uk/nme/research/gilgamesh/standard/

TABLET XI

Siglum	*Museum number* / *Distribution of lines by column*		*Plate in George Bab. Gilg. Epic*
	NINEVEH		
C	K 2252+2602+3321+4486+Sm 1881		118–23
	i **1**–19, 54–**57**	iv **165**–219	
	ii **58**–63, 70–3, 80–5, 92–**108**	v **221**–35, 240–**278**	
	iii 113–27, 129–**164**	vi **279**–**328**, colophon	
J_1	K 3375		124–7
J_2	Rm 616		124
	i **1**–23 (J_2)	iv **167**–**229** (J_1)	
	ii 56–**107** (J_1)	v **230**–84 (J_1)	
	iii 110–**166** (J_1)	vi not extant	
T_1	K 7752+81-2-4, 245+296+460		128–30
T_2	Sm 2131+2196+Rm II 383+390+82-5-22, 316		128–9, 131
	i 29–**64** (T_2)	iv 224–**245** (T_1)	
	ii **65**–105 (T_{1-2}), 108–**123** (T_2)	v **246**–70 (T_2)	
	iii **124**–50 (T_1)	vi **298**–308, 315–19 (T_2)	
W_1	K 8517+8518+8569+8593+8595		132–6
W_2	K 8594+21502		136
W_3	K 17343		136
W_4	(Delitzsch B)		136
	i **1**–41 (W_1)	iv not extant	
	ii **57**–101 (W_1)	v 236–48, 254–**278** (W_1)	
	iii 143–62 (W_2, W_4), 165–**171** (W_3)	vi 299–**328**, colophon (W_1)	
	AŠŠUR		
b	VAT 10586		137
	181–202	242–74	
$\mathbf{c}_1$	VAT 11000		138–9
$\mathbf{c}_2$	VAT 11087		138–9
$\mathbf{c}_3$	VAT 11294		138–9
	i 45–**55** ($\mathbf{c}_1$)	ii unplaced traces ($\mathbf{c}_3$)	
	iii 133–53 ($\mathbf{c}_3$), 163–**171** ($\mathbf{c}_2$)	iv **172**–85 ($\mathbf{c}_2$)	
	NIMRUD		
z	IM 67564 (ND 4381)		33
	i // X 63–112	v variant text, see Chapter 7	
	ii // X 196–230	vi // 304–328?	
	BABYLON		
j	BM 35380		140–1
	i 5–29	v 219–36	
	ii 56–76	vi 289–319	

Score transliteration

1	C	i 1	^{d}GIŠ-gím-maš a-na šá-⸢šu⸣-ma MU-ra a-na ^{m}UD-ZI ru-ú-qí
	J$_2$	i 1	[ ] (traces) M[U-r]a [ ]
	W$_1$	i 1	[-⸢qí⸣
	K$_3$	catch-line	^{d}GIŠ-gím-maš ana šá-šu-ma MU-ra ana UD-ZI ru-qí
	b	catch-line	^{d}GIŠ-gím-maš a-na šá-šu-ma MU-ár ana UD-ZI-tim ru-qí
	f	catch-line	[-á]r ana ^{m}UD-ZI SUD
2	C	i 2	a-na-aṭ-ṭa-la-kúm-ma ^{m}UD-ZI
	J$_2$	i 2	[-a]ṭ-ṭa-la-kúm-ma [ ]
	W$_1$	i 2	[-ZI-t]im
3	C	i 3	mi-na-tu-ka ul ⸢šá⸣-na-a ki-i ia-ti-ma at-ta
	J$_2$	i 3	[ ]-⸢tu⸣-ka ul šá-na-a ki-⸢i⸣ [ ]
	W$_1$	i 3	[ ] ⸢ul šá-na⸣-a ⸢ki-i⸣ ia-a-ti-m[a at]-ta
4	C	i 4	ù at-ta ul š[á-n]a-ta ki-i ia-ti-ma at-ta
	J$_2$	i 4	⸢ù at-ta⸣ ul šá-na-ta ki-i [ ]
	W$_1$	i 4	[ ] ⸢ul⸣ šá-na-ta ki-i ia-ši-ma [at]-ta
5	C	i 5	⸢gu-um-mur-ka⸣ [lìb]-bi ana e-peš tu-qu-un-ti
	J$_2$	i 5	[gu-um-m]ur-⸢ka lìb⸣-bi ana e-[ ]
	W$_1$	i 5	[gúm-m]u[r]-⸢ku⸣ lìb-bi a-na e-peš t[u-q]u-un-tú
	j	i 5	[t]u-qu-un-ti
6	C	i 6	[-a]t e-lu ṣe-ri-ka
	J$_2$	i 6	[x]x a-ḫi ⸢na-da⸣-at e-l[u]
	W$_1$	i 6	[n]a-⸢da⸣-at-ta e-li ṣe-[ri]-ka
	j	i 6	[-l]u ṣe-ri-ka
7	C	i 7	[-m]a ina UKKIN DINGIR.MEŠ ba-la-ṭa taš-⸢ú⸣
	J$_2$	i 7	[at-t]a ⸢ki-ki-i⸣ ta-az-ziz-ma ina UKKIN DIN[GIR.MEŠ]
	W$_1$	i 7	[k]i-⸢ki-i ta-az-ziz-ma ina UKKIN DINGIR.MEŠ ba-la⸣-[ṭa té]š-ʾ-u$_{16}$(UM)
	j	i 7	[-zi]z-ma ina UKKIN DINGIR.MEŠ ba-⸢la⸣-ṭa taš-ú :
			———————— CJWj
8	C	i 8	[M]U-ra a-na ^{d}GIŠ-[ ]
	J$_2$	i 8a	[a-n]a šá-šu [MU-r]a ana ^{d}GIŠ-gím-maš :
	W$_1$	i 8	[^{m}U]D-ZI-tim ana šá-šu-ma MU-r[a a-na ^{d}GI]Š-gím-maš
	j	i 8	[M]U-⸢ra⸣ a-na ^{d}GIŠ-gím-maš

9	C	i 9	[ ] a-mat ni-ṣ[ir-ti]
	J_2	i 8b	lu-up-t[e-]
	W_1	i 9	lu-up-te-ka ^{d}GIŠ-gím-maš [-ṣ]ir-ti
	j	i 9	[-k]a ⌜^{d}⌝GIŠ-gí[m-m]aš a-mat ni-ṣir-ti
10	C	i 10	[a-n]a ka-a-šá lu-uq-b[i-ka]
	J_2	i 9	[-r]iš-ta šá DINGI[R.MEŠ k]a-a-š[á]
	W_1	i 10	ù pi-riš-ti šá DINGIR.MEŠ ka-a-šá l[u-uq-bi]-ka
	j	i 10	[-ri]š-ti šá DINGIR.MEŠ ka-a-šá lu-uq-bi-ka
11	C	i 11	[-d]u-šú at-[ta]
	J_2	i 10	[ ]-⌜ú⌝-ri-pak U[RU -d]u-[ ]
	W_1	i 11a	[U]RU šu-ri-ip-pak URU šá ti-du-šu at-ta :
	j	i 11	[x x (x) x-r]i-pak URU šá ti-du-šú at-ta
12	C	i 12	[ ]-ti šak-[nu]
	J_2	i 11a	[p]u-rat-t[i :]
	W_1	i 11b	x[-ra]t-ti šak-nu
	j	i 12	[x (x) x G]Ú ^{íd}pu-rat-ti šak-nu
13	C	i 13	[ ] DINGIR.MEŠ qer-bu-⌜šú⌝
	J_2	i 11b	[(in one line with 12)]
	W_1	i 12	[UR]U šu-ú la-bir-ma [ ]-šu
	j	i 13	[x š]u-ú la-bir-ma DINGIR.MEŠ qer-bu-uš
14	C	i 14	[ ]-⌜ba-šú-nu⌝ DINGIR.MEŠ GAL.MEŠ
	J_2	i 12	[ ] a-bu-b[i]
	W_1	i 13	[a-n]a ⌜šá-kan a-bu-bu ub-la lìb⌝-[ ].MEŠ
	j	i 14	[a-n]a šá-kan a-bu-bi ub-⌜la⌝ lìb-ba-šú-nu DINGIR.MEŠ GAL.MEŠ
15	C	i 15	[ ] ^{d}a-nu-um
	J_2	i 13a	[A]D-šú-nu [:]
	W_1	i 14a	[(in one line with 16) :]
	j	i 15a	[it]-ma-ma AD-šú-nu ^{d}a-num ⟨:⟩
16	C	i 16	[ ] ^{d}en-líl
	J_2	i 13b	[(in one line with 15)]
	W_1	i 14b	[-l]íl
	j	i 15b	ma-lik-šú-nu qu-ra-du ^{d}en-líl
17	C	i 17	[ ] ⌜^{d}⌝nin-urta
	J_2	i 14a	[(in one line with 18) :]
	W_1	i 15a	[(in one line with 18) :]
	j	i 16a	[g]u-za-lá-šú-nu ^{d}nin-urta ⟨:⟩

Line	MS	Col. line	Text
18	C	i 18	[^{d}e]n-nu-gi
	J_2	i 14b	[(in one line with 17)]
	W_1	i 15b	[-g]i
	j	i 16b	gú-⸢gal-la⸣-šú-nu ^{d}en-nu-gi
19	C	i 19	[ ]-⸢mì-ma⸣
	J_2	i 15	⸢d⸣nin-ši-k[ù]
	W_1	i 16	[^{d}]⸢nin-ši-kù ^{d}é⸣-[ ]
	j	i 17	^{d}nin-ši-kù ^{d}é-a it-ti-šú-nu ta-mì-ma
20	J_2	i 16	[a]-mat-su-nu [ ]
	W_1	i 17a	⸢a⸣-mat-su-nu ú-šá-an-na-⸢a ana ki⸣-i[k-ki-ši :]
	j	i 18	a-mat-su-nu ú-šá-an-na-a a-na ki-ik-ki-šú
21	J_2	i 17a	[k]i-ik-ki-š[u :]
	W_1	i 17b	[(in one line with 20)]
	j	i 19	ki-ik-kiš ki-ik-kiš i-gar i-gar
22	J_2	i 17b	[(in one line with 21)]
	W_1	i 18	[k]i-i[k-k]i-šu ši-me-ma i-ga-r[u]
	j	i 20	ki-ik-ki-šu ši-me-ma i-ga-ru ḫi-is-sa-as
23	J_2	i 18	[š]u-⸢ú⸣-[ ]
	W_1	i 19	[^{lú}šu-r]i-ip-pa-ku-ú DUMU ^{m}uba[ra-]
	j	i 21	^{lú}šu-ru-up-pa-ku-ú DUMU ^{m}ubara-^{d}tu-tu
24	W_1	i 20a	[ ] ⸢É⸣ bi-ni ^{giš}MÁ :
	j	i 22a	ú-qur É bi-nu ^{giš}MÁ 〈:〉
25	W_1	i 20b	muš-šìr ⸢NÍG⸣.[ ]
	j	i 22b	muš-šìr NÍG.TUKU-ma še-ʾ-i ZI.MEŠ :
26	W_1	i 21	[ma]-⸢ak-ku⸣-ra ze-er-ma na-⸢piš⸣-t[ú?]
	j	i 23	[m]a-ak-ku-ru ze-er-ma na-piš-ti bul-liṭ
27	W_1	i 22	[š]u-li-ma NUMUN nap-šá-a-ti ka-la-ma a-na lìb-bi $^{g[iš}$MÁ]
	j	i 24	[šu-l]i-ma NUMUN nap-šá-a-ti ka-la-ma ana ŠÀ ^{giš}MÁ
28	T_2	i 1a'	[(in one line with 29) :]
	W_1	i 23	[$^{gi]š}$MÁ šá ta-ban-nu-ši at-[ta]
	j	i 25a	[ ] ⸢šá ta-ban⸣-nu-šú ⸢at-ta⸣ 〈:〉

29	T_2	i 1b'	⌜lu⌝-[ ]
	W_1	i 24	[l]u-ú mìn-du-da mi-na-tu-⌜šá⌝
	j	i 25b	lu-ú ⌜mun-du-da mi-na-tu⌝-šú
30	T_2	i 2'	[ ]-⌜ḫur ru-pu-us⌝-sa [ ]
	W_1	i 25	[l]u-ú mit-ḫur ru-pu-us-sa ù mu-rak-šá
31	T_2	i 3'	[a]p-si-i šá-a-ši ṣ[u-]
	W_1	i 26	[k]i-ma ABZU šá-a-ši ṣu-ul-lil-ši
32	T_2	i 4'	[a-na-k]u i-de-ma a-zak-ka-r[a]
	W_1	i 27	[a]-na-ku i-de-ma MU-ra a-na ^{d}é-a be-lí-ia
33	T_2	i 5'	[am-g]ur be-lí šá taq-ba-a a[t-]
	W_1	i 28	[ ] be-lí šá taq-ba-a at-ta ki-a-am
34	T_2	i 6'	[at]-ta-'-id a-na-k[u]
	W_1	i 29	[ ] a-na-ku ep-pu-uš
35	T_2	i 7'	[ki-m]i lu-pu-ul URU um-ma-nu ⌜ù⌝ [ ]
	W_1	i 30	[u]m-ma-nu ù ši-bu-tum
36	T_2	i 8a'	[^{d}]⌜é⌝-a pa-a-šú i-pu-uš-ma DUG$_4$.GA :
	W_1	i 31a	[i]-⌜qab⌝-bi :
37	T_2	i 8b'	MU-[ra]
	W_1	i 31b	i-zak-ka-ra ana ÌR-šú ia-a-tú
38	T_2	i 9'	⌜ù⌝ at-ta ki-a-am ta-qab-b[a-áš]-⌜šú-nu-ti⌝
	W_1	i 32	[ ] ta-qab-ba-áš-šu-nu-tu
39	T_2	i 10'	[mì]n-de-ma ia-a-ši ^{d}en-líl i-[ze-er]-an-ni-ma
	W_1	i 33	[-l]íl i-ze-er-an-ni-ma
40	T_2	i 11'	[u]l uš-šab ina ⌜URU⌝-[ku]-nu-ma
	W_1	i 34a	[(in one line with 41) :]
41	T_2	i 12'	[ina] qaq-qar ^{d}en-líl ul a-šak-ka-n[a še-p]i-ia-a-ma
	W_1	i 34b	[-qa]r ⌜^{d}en-líl ul a-šak-kan še-pi-i-a⌝
42	T_2	i 13'	[ur-r]ad-ma ana ABZU it-ti ^{d}⌜é⌝-a [b]e-lí-ia áš-ba-ku
43	T_2	i 14'	[ana k]a-a-šú-nu ú-šá-az-na-[n]ak-ku-nu-ši nu-uḫ-šam-ma
44	T_2	i 15'	[ḫi-ṣib] MUŠEN.MEŠ pu-zu-ur KU$_6$.MEŠ-ma

45	T_2	i 16'	[ ] x x x x meš-ra-a e-bu-ra-am-ma
	$\mathbf{c}_1$	i 1'	i[l${}^{?}$-]
46	T_2	i 17'	[ ] ku-uk-ki
	$\mathbf{c}_1$	i 2'	ina ⸢še⸣-e[r]
47	T_2	i 18'	[ ]-šá-az-na-na-ku-nu-ši šá-mu-ut ki-ba-a-ti
	$\mathbf{c}_1$	i 3'	ina li-la-⸢a-ti ú⸣-[ ]
			———————————————— $T_2\mathbf{c}_1$
48	T_2	i 19'	[ ]-⸢e⸣-ri ina na-ma-⸢a-ri⸣
	$\mathbf{c}_1$	i 4'	mim-mu-ú ⸢še⸣-[ ]
49	T_2	i 20'	[ ] i-pa-aḫ-ḫur ma-a-[tum]
	$\mathbf{c}_1$	i 5'	ina KÁ a-tar-ḫa-s[is]
50	T_2	i 21'	[n]a-ši pa-a[s-su]
	$\mathbf{c}_1$	i 6'	${}^{\text{lú}}$NAGAR na-ši [ ]
51	T_2	i 22'	[n]a-ši a-b[a-an-šu]
	$\mathbf{c}_1$	i 7'	${}^{\text{lú}}$AD.KID na-ši [ ]
52	T_2	i 23a'	[(in one line with 53)] ⸢:⸣
	$\mathbf{c}_1$	i 8'	a-ga-si-li-ga-[ ]
53	C	i 1a'	⸢GURUŠ.MEŠ⸣ [:]
	T_2	i 23b'	${}^{\text{lú}}$GURUŠ.MEŠ ⸢i⸣-x[ ]
	$\mathbf{c}_1$	i 9'	ši-bu-ti i-[zab-]
54	C	i 1b'	[(in one line with 53)]
	T_2	i 24'	[ši-bu-ti i-zab-b]i-⸢lu⸣ pi-⸢til${}^{!?}$-ta⸣
	$\mathbf{c}_1$	i 10'	${}^{\text{lú}}$GURUŠ.MEŠ i-x[ ]
55	C	i 2'	šar-ru-⸢ú⸣ [ ]
	T_2	i 25'	[ ]-⸢ši⸣ kup-ra
	$\mathbf{c}_1$	i 11'	[š]á-ru-u na-[ ]
56	C	i 3'	lap-nu x[ ]
	J_1	ii 1'	[u]b-⸢la⸣
	T_2	i 26'	[ḫi-š]iḫ-tu ub-la
	j	ii 6a	lap-ni x[:]

Line	MS	Col./line	Text
57	C	i 4'	[i]na ḫa-an-ši u$_4$-mi [ ]
	J$_1$	ii 2'	[ ]-na-šá
	T$_2$	i 27'	[a]t-ta-di bu-na-šá
	W$_1$	ii 1	ina ḫa-an-ši ⸢u$_4$-me⸣ [ ]
	j	ii 6b	[(in one line with 56)]
58	C	ii 1	1.⸢IKU⸣ [GÚR]-sa [10] NINDAN.TA.À[M]
	J$_1$	ii 3'	[.G]AR$_8$.MEŠ-šá
	T$_2$	i 28'	[.À]M šaq-qa-a É.GAR$_8$.MEŠ-šá
	W$_1$	ii 2	1.IKU GÚR-sa 10 NINDAN.TA.À[M]
	j	ii 7	1.IKU GÚ[R-]
59	C	ii 2	10 NINDAN.ÀM ⸢im⸣-ta-[ ]
	J$_1$	ii 4'	[m]uḫ-ḫi-šá
	T$_2$	i 29'	[-ḫ]ir ki-bir muḫ-ḫi-šá
	W$_1$	ii 3	10 NINDAN.TA.ÀM im-ta-ḫir [ ]
	j	ii 8	10 NINDAN.TA.À[M]
60	C	ii 3	ad-di la-an-[šá]
	J$_1$	ii 5'	[ ] ⸢e⸣-ṣir-ši
	T$_2$	i 30'	[š]á-a-ši e-ṣir-ši
	W$_1$	ii 4	ad-di la-an-ši šá-a-ši [ ]
	j	ii 9	ad-di l[a-]
61	C	ii 4	ur-tag-gi-ib-š[i]
	J$_1$	ii 6a'	[(in one line with 62) (:)]
	T$_2$	i 31'	[-š]i a-na 6-šú
	W$_1$	ii 5a	ur-tag-gi-ib-ši a-na 6-šu ⟨:⟩
	j	ii 10	ur-tag-g[i-]
62	C	ii 5	[a]p-ta-ra-a[s-si]
	J$_1$	ii 6b'	[-s]u a-na 7-[š]ú
	T$_2$	i 32'	[ ] a-na 7-šú
	W$_1$	ii 5b	a[p-]
	j	ii 11	ap-t[a-]
63	C	ii 6	[qe]r-⸢bi-is⸣-s[u/s[ú]
	J$_1$	ii 7'	[ ] a-na [9-š]ú
	T$_2$	i 33'	[-r]a-as a-na 9-šú
	W$_1$	ii 6	qer-bi-is-sú ap-ta-ra-as [ ]
	j	ii 12	qer-bi-i[s-]

64	J_1	ii 8'	[l]u am-⸢ḫaṣ⸣
	T_2	i 34'	[ ] ⸢lu⸣ am-ḫas-si
	W_1	ii 7	^{giš}GAG.MEŠ A.MEŠ ina MURUB$_4$-šá lu-ú [ ]
	j	ii 13	^{giš}GAG.ME[Š]
65	J_1	ii 9'	[-t]i ad-[d]i
	T_1	ii 1	[ ]-d[i]
	W_1	ii 8	a-mur pa-ri-su ù ḫi-šiḫ-tum [ ]
	j	ii 14	a-mur pa-[ ]
66	J_1	ii 10'	[-ba]k a-n[a] GIR$_4$
	T_1	ii 2	[k]i-i-⸢ri⸣
	W_1	ii 9a	3 šár ku-up-ri at-ta-bak ana ki-i-ri :
	j	ii 15	6 šár ku-u[p-]
67	J_1	ii 11'	[ ] a-na lìb-bi
	T_1	ii 3	[ ] lìb-bi
	W_1	ii 9b	3 šár ESIR x[ ]
	j	ii 16	3 šár E[SIR]
68	J_1	ii 12'	[^{gi}]^{š}s[u-] ⸢šá i⸣-zab-bi-lu Ì.GIŠ
	T_1	ii 4	[-l]i šá ⸢i-zab⸣-bi-lu Ì+GIŠ
	W_1	ii 10	3 šár ÉRIN.MEŠ na-áš ^{giš}su-us-su-ul šá i-zab-b[i-]
	j	ii 17	3 šár ÉRIN.[ ]
69	J_1	ii 13'	[ ] Ì.GIŠ ⸢šá i⸣-ku-lu ni-iq-qu
	T_1	ii 5	[ ]-ku-lu ni-iq-qu
	W_1	ii 11	e-zu-ub šár Ì.GIŠ ⸢šá i-ku-lu⸣ n[i-]
	j	ii 18	e-zi-i[b]
70	C	ii 13	2 [ ]
	J_1	ii 14'	[ ] ⸢ú⸣-pa-az-zi-ru ^{lú}MÁ.LAḪ$_4$
	T_1	ii 6	[-a]z-zi-ru ^{lú}MÁ.LAḪ$_4$
	W_1	ii 12	2 šár Ì.⸢GIŠ⸣ [ ]
	j	ii 19	2 šár ú-[ ]
71	C	ii 14	a-n[a]
	J_1	ii 15'	[.ME]Š$^{?}$ uṭ-ṭàb-bi-iḫ GU$_4$.MEŠ
	T_1	ii 7a	[G]U$_4$.MEŠ :
	W_1	ii 13	a-n[a]
	j	ii 20	a-na um-m[an-]

72	C	ii 15	áš-g[i-]
	J_1	ii 16'	[ ].MEŠ u$_4$-mi-šam-ma
	T_1	ii 7b	áš-gi-iš UDU.NÍTA.MEŠ u$_4$-mi-šam-ma
	j	ii 21	áš-gi-i[š]
73	C	ii 16	s[i-]
	J_1	ii 17'	[ku-ru]-un-nu Ì.GIŠ ù GEŠTIN
	T_1	ii 8	[ ] Ì+GIŠ u GEŠTIN
	W_1	ii 15	[ ] ⸢ù?⸣ [ ]
	j	ii 22	si-ri-š[u]
74	J_1	ii 18'	[ ] ki-ma A.MEŠ ÍD-ma
	T_1	ii 9	[ ] ⸢A.MEŠ⸣ ÍD-ma
	W_1	ii 16a	[(in one line with 75) :]
	j	ii 23	um-ma-n[i? áš-qí]
74a	T_1	ii 10a	[ ]-ri :
75	J_1	ii 19'	[-š]ú ki-ma u$_4$-mi a-ki-tim-ma
	T_1	ii 10b	i-sin-na ip-pu-šú ki-i u$_4$-mi a-ki-tim-ma
	W_1	ii 16b	[-š]u? ki-i u[$_4$-]
	j	ii 24	i-sin-[ ]
76	J_1	ii 20'	[ ] piš-šá-ti qa-ti ad-di
	T_1	ii 11	[-š]á-ti qa-ti ad-di
	W_1	ii 17a	[(in one line with 77) :]
	j	ii 25	^{d}UT[U]
77	J_1	ii 21'	[r]a-bé-e ^{giš}MÁ gam-rat
	T_1	ii 12	[ ]-⸢e⸣ ^{giš}MÁ gam-rat
	W_1	ii 17b	[la-a]m ^{d}UTU ra-[ ]
78	J_1	ii 22'	[ ]x šup-šu-qu-ma
	T_1	ii 13	[ ] šup-šu-qu-ma
	W_1	ii 18a	[ ]-⸢qu-ma⸣ :
79	J_1	ii 23'	[ni]t-tab-ba-lu e-liš u šap-liš
	T_1	ii 14	[-b]a-lu e-liš u šap-liš
	W_1	ii 18b	⸢ge-er⸣ MÁ.MUG!.⸢MEŠ nit⸣-tab-ba-lu [ ]
80	C	ii 23	[-s]u
	J_1	ii 24'	[-l]i-ku ši-ni-pat-su
	T_1	ii 15	[ ] ⸢ši⸣-ni-pat-su
	W_1	ii 19	[-l]i-ku [š]i-ni-[ ]

CTW

81	C	ii 24	[-e]n-ši
	J_1	ii 25a'	[ ]-ši :
	T_1	ii 16a	[(in one line with 82) :]
	W_1	ii 20a	[mim-ma i-šu-ú] ⌜e-ṣe⌝-en-ši :
82	C	ii 25	[ ] KÙ.BABBAR
	J_1	ii 25b'	mim-ma i-šu-ú e-ṣe-en-ši KÙ.BABBAR
	T_1	ii 16b	[ ]-⌜ú⌝ i-ṣe-en-ši KÙ.BABBAR
	W_1	ii 20b	mim-ma i-šu-[-ṣ]e-⌜en⌝-[ ]
83	C	ii 26	[ ] KÙ.SIG_{17}
	J_1	ii 26'	[ ]-ṣe-en-ši KÙ.SIG_{17}
	T_1	ii 17a	[(in one line with 84) :]
	W_1	ii 21a	⌜mim-ma i⌝-š[u-ú] ⌜e-ṣe-en⌝-ši KÙ.SIG_{17} :
84	C	ii 27	[ ]-⌜ma⌝
	J_1	ii 27'	[-e]n-ši NUMUN ZI.MEŠ ka-la-ma
	T_1	ii 17b	[NUM]UN ZI.MEŠ ka-la-ma
	W_1	ii 21b	mim-ma i-š[u-ú KIMIN NUMU]N Z[I.MEŠ]
85	C	ii 28	[-i]a
	J_1	ii 28'	[ᵍⁱˢM]Á ka-la kim-ti-ia u sa-lat-ia
	T_1	ii 18	[ ]-ti-ia
	W_1	ii 22	uš-te-li a-[na] ŠÀ! ᵍⁱˢMÁ k[a- -t]i-⌜ia ù⌝ [ ]
86	J_1	ii 29'	[ME]Š um-ma-a-ni ka-li-šú-nu ú-še-li
	T_1	ii 19	[ ] ⌜ú⌝-še-li
	W_1	ii 23	bu-ul EDI[N] ⌜ú⌝-ma-am EDIN ⌜DUMU.MEŠ um⌝-ma-nu ⌜ka-li-šu⌝-n[u]
87	J_1	ii 30'	[ ] iš-ku-nam-ma
	T_1	ii 20	[-n]am-ma
	W_1	ii 24	a-dan-⌜na⌝ ᵈUTU iš-ku-[ ]
88	J_1	ii 31'	[-t]i ú-šá-az-na-an-nu šá-mu-ut ki-ba-a-ti
	T_1	ii 21	[-b]a-a-ti
	W_1	ii 25	ina še-er ku-u[k-k]i ina li-la-a-ti ú!-šá-az-na-nu šá-mu-t[u]
89	J_1	ii 32'	[ᵍⁱ]ˢMÁ-ma pi-ḫe KÁ-ka
	T_1	ii 22	[ ] KÁ-ka
	W_1	ii 26a	e-ru-ub ana [lì]b-bi ᵍⁱˢMÁ-ma pi-ḫe ᵍⁱˢMÁ :

90	J_1	ii 33'	[ ] ik-tal-da
	T_1	ii 23	[ ]-tal-da
	W_1	ii 26b	a-dan-nu šu-ú [ ]
91	J_1	ii 34'	[-t]i ú-šá-az-na-na šá-mu-ut ki-ba-a-ti
	T_1	ii 24	[-u]t ki-ba-a-ti
	W_1	ii 27	ina še-er ku-u[k-k]i ina li-la-a-ti i-za-an-na-nu šá-mu-tu k[i-]
92	C	ii 1'	[-m]i ⌜at-ta⌝-ṭal [ ]
	J_1	ii 35'	[ ] bu-na-šu
	T_1	ii 25	[b]u-na-šu
	W_1	ii 28a	šá u$_4$-mi at-t[a-ṭa]l bu-na-šu :
93	C	ii 2'	[ ] ⌜a⌝-na i-tap-lu-si pu-l[uḫ-]
	J_1	ii 36'	[p]u-luḫ-ta i-ši
	T_1	ii 26	[ ] i-šu
	T_2	ii 26	⌜u$_4$⌝-m[u]
	W_1	ii 28b	u$_4$-mu a-na i-tap-lu-si pu-lu[ḫ-]
94	C	ii 3'	[e-ru-u]b ana lìb-bi ^{giš}MÁ-ma [ ]
	J_1	ii 37'	[^{giš}M]Á-ma ap-te-ḫi ba-a-bi
	T_1	ii 27	[a]p-⌜te⌝-ḫi ba-a-b[i]
	T_2	ii 27	e-r[u-]
	W_1	ii 29	e-ru-u[b] ⌜a⌝-na ^{giš}MÁ-ma ap-⌜ti-ḫi⌝ ba-[a-bi]
95	C	ii 4'	[ana pe-ḫ]i-i šá ^{giš}MÁ ^{m}pu-zu-ur-^{d}[ ]
	J_1	ii 38'	[p]u-zu-ur-^{d}KUR.GAL ^{lú}MÁ.LAḪ$_4$
	T_1	ii 28	[-u]r-^{d}KUR.GAL ^{lú}MÁ.[LAḪ$_4$]
	T_2	ii 28	a-na p[e-]
	W_1	ii 30	a-na pe-ḫe-⌜e⌝ [šá ^{gi}]^{š}MÁ a-na pu-zu-⟨ur⟩-⌜^{d}KUR⌝.GAL ^{lú}[ ]
96	C	ii 5'	[É.GA]L at-ta-din [ ]
	J_1	ii 39'	[-di-i]n a-di bu-še-e-šú
	T_1	ii 29	[ ] a-di bu-⌜še-e⌝-[šú]
	T_2	ii 29	É.GA[L]
	W_1	ii 31	É.GAL at-[ta]-⌜din⌝ a-di bu-še-⌜e⌝-[šú]

———————————————————— CTW

97	C	ii 6'	[mim]-mu-ú še-e-ri [ ]
	J_1	ii 40'	[ ] ina na-ma-ri
	T_1	ii 30	[ ] ina n[a-]
	T_2	ii 30	mim-m[u-]
	W_1	ii 32	mim-mu-ú še-e-ri ina n[a-]

Line	MS		Text
98	C	ii 7'	⸢i⸣-lam-ma iš-tu i-šid AN-[ ]
	J_1	ii 41'	[A]N-e ur-pa-tum ṣa-lim-tum
	T_1	ii 31	[ ]-⸢pa⸣-[ ]
	T_2	ii 31	i-la[m-]
	W_1	ii 33	⸢i-lam-ma⸣ u[l-tu i-ši]d AN-e ur-pa-tum! ṣa-[ ]
99	C	ii 8'	^{d}IŠKUR ina lìb-bi-šá [ ]
	J_1	ii 42'	[ ] ir-tam-ma-am-ma
	T_2	ii 32a	^{d}IŠK[UR :]
	W_1	ii 34a	[ir/š-tag]-⸢gu-um⸣ [:]
100	C	ii 9'	^{d}šúllat u ^{d}ḫániš il-⸢la⸣-[ ]
	J_1	ii 43'	[i]l-la-ku ina maḫ-ri
	T_2	ii 32b	[(in one line with 99)]
	W_1	ii 34b	⸢^{d}šúllat⸣ u ^{d}ḫániš il-⸢la⸣-[ ]
101	C	ii 10'	il-la-ku GU.ZA.LÁ.MEŠ KUR-ú [ ]
	J_1	ii 44'	[.ME]Š KUR-ú u ma-a-tum
	T_2	ii 33a	il-l[a- :]
	W_1	ii 35	[gu-za-lu]-⸢ú⸣ KUR-⸢ú⸣ [ ]
102	C	ii 11'	⸢tar⸣-kul-li ^{d}èr-ra-kal ú-n[a-as-saḫ]
	J_1	ii 45'	[-g]al i-na-as-saḫ
	T_2	ii 33b	[(in one line with 101)]
103	C	ii 12'	il-lak ^{d}nin-⸢urta⸣ mi-iḫ-ra [ ]
	J_1	ii 46'	[-i]ḫ-ri ú-šar-di
	T_2	ii 34a	il-l[ak :]
104	C	ii 13'	^{d}a-nun-na-ki iš-šu-ú di-pa-[ ]
	J_1	ii 47'	[ ]-⸢ú⸣ di-pa-ra-a-ti
	T_2	ii 34b	[(in one line with 103)]
105	C	ii 14'	ina nam-ri-ir-ri-šú-nu ú-ḫa-am-ma-ṭu m[a-]
	J_1	ii 48'	[-a]m-ma-ṭu ma-a-tum
	T_2	ii 35	ina n[am-]
106	C	ii 15'	šá ^{d}IŠKUR šu-ḫar-ra-as-⸢su⸣ i-ba-'-⸢u⸣ [ ]
	J_1	ii 49'	[-b]a-'-ú AN-e
107	C	ii 16'	[mi]m-ma nam-ru ana ⸢da⸣-['-u]m-[mat] ut-te[r-ru]
	J_1	ii 50'	[-ma-t]i ut-ter-ru

108	C	ii 17'	[ir-ḫ]i-iṣ KUR GIM G[U_4]x iḫ-p[i-šá]
	T_2	ii 38	[-i]ṣ KUR GIM x[ ]
109	T_2	ii 39	⸢1⸣-en u_4-ma me-ḫ[u-ú]
110	J_1	iii 3	[ ] ⸢i-zi⸣-[-š]i KUR-a ⸢a⸣-[bu-bu?]
	T_2	ii 40	ḫa-an-ṭiš i-zi-qam-ma x[ ]
111	J_1	iii 4	[ki-m]a qab-li ⸢UGU⸣ ÙG.MEŠ ú-ba-'-ú [ka-šú-šú]
	T_2	ii 41	ki-ma qab-li UGU Ù[G.MEŠ]
112	J_1	iii 5a	⸢ul⸣ im-mar a-ḫu a-ḫa-šú :
	T_2	ii 42a	ul im-mar a-ḫu a-ḫa-šu :
113	C	iii 3b	[ ]-⸢da-a⸣ [ ] ina ⸢ka⸣-r[a-ši]
	J_1	iii 5b	⸢ul ú-ta-ad-da-a ÙG.MEŠ⸣ ina A[N-x]
	T_2	ii 42b	u[l]
114	C	iii 4	[ ] ⸢a⸣-bu-ba-am-ma
	J_1	iii 6	DINGIR.DINGIR ip-tal-ḫu a-bu-⸢ba⸣-am-[ma]
	T_2	ii 43	DINGIR.MEŠ ip-la-ḫu [ ]
115	C	iii 5	[ ] AN-e šá ^{d}a-nim
	J_1	iii 7	it-te-eḫ-su i-te-lu-ú ana AN-e šá ^{d}a-nim
	T_2	ii 44	it-taḫ-su i-te-lu-⸢ú⸣ [ ]
116	C	iii 6	[ ] ka-ma-a-ti rab-ṣu
	J_1	iii 8	DINGIR.MEŠ ki-ma UR.GI_7 kun-nu-nu ina ka-ma-a-ti rab-ṣu
	T_2	ii 45	DINGIR.MEŠ GIM UR.GI_7 kun-nu-n[u]
117	C	iii 7	[k]i-ma a-lit-ti
	J_1	iii 9	i-šas-si ^{d}iš-tar ma-li-ti
	T_2	ii 46	i-šas-si ^{d}iš-tar [ ]
118	C	iii 8	[ṭ]a-bat rig-ma
	J_1	iii 10	ú-nam-bi DINGIR.MAḪ ṭa-bat rig-ma
	T_2	ii 47	ú-nam-ba ^{d}be-let-DI[NGIR.MEŠ]
119	C	iii 9	[ ] lu-ú i-tur-ma
	J_1	iii 11	u_4-mu ul-lu-ú a-na ṭi-iṭ-ṭi lu-ú i-tur-ma
	T_2	ii 48	u_4-mu ul-lu-ú a-na ṭi-[ ]

Line	MS	Col./line	Text
120	C	iii 10	[-b]u-⌈ú⌉ ^{f}ḪUL
	J_1	iii 12	⌈šá a-na⌉-ku ina ma-ḫar DINGIR.DINGIR aq-bu-ú ^{f}ḪUL
	T_2	ii 49	áš-šú a-na-ku ina pu-ḫur DING[IR]
121	C	iii 11	[^{f}]ḪUL
	J_1	iii 13	⌈ki⌉-i ⌈aq⌉-bi ina ma-ḫar DINGIR.DINGIR ^{f}ḪUL
	T_2	ii 50	ki-i aq-bi ina pu-ḫur DI[NGIR]
122	C	iii 12	[ ]-ma
	J_1	iii 14	ana ḫul-l[u]-uq ÙG.MEŠ-ia qab-la aq-bi-ma
	T_2	ii 51	ana ḫul-lu-uq ÙG.MEŠ-i[a]
123	C	iii 13	[-m]a
	J_1	iii 15	a-na-ku-[u]m-ma ul-la-da ni-šu-ú-a-a-ma
	T_2	ii 52	ana-ku-um-ma ul-la-d[a]
124	C	iii 14	[-m]a
	J_1	iii 16	ki-i DUMU.MEŠ KU$_6$.ḪÁ ú-ma-al-la-a tam-ta-am-ma
	T_1	iii 1	ki-i DUMU.MEŠ K[U$_6$.]
125	C	iii 15	[ ]-šá
	J_1	iii 17	DINGIR.DINGIR šu-ut ^{d}a-nun-na-ki ba-ku-ú it-ti-šá
	T_1	iii 2	DINGIR.MEŠ šu-ut ⌈^{d}⌉[ ]
126	C	iii 16	[ ]-ti
	J_1	iii 18	DINGIR.MEŠ aš-ru áš-bi i-na bi-ki-ti
	T_1	iii 3	ina nu-ru-ub ni-is-⌈sa-ti ba⌉-k[u-ú it-ti-šá?]
127	C	iii 17	[-t]i$^{!?}$
	J_1	iii 19	kàt-ma šap-ta-šú-nu ⌈le-qa⌉-a bu-uḫ-re-e-ti
	T_1	iii 4	šab-ba šap-ta-šú-nu l[e-]
128	J_1	iii 20	6 ur-ra ⌈ù⌉ mu-šá-a-ti
	T_1	iii 5	⌈6⌉ ur-ri ù ⌈7⌉ [ ]
129	C	iii 19	⌈il⌉-l[ak]
	J_1	iii 21	il-lak šá-a-ru a-bu-⌈bu me⌉-ḫu-ú i-sap-pan KUR
	T_1	iii 6	⌈il⌉-lak šá-⌈a⌉-ru ra-a-du mi-ḫu-ú a-b[u-bu]
130	C	iii 20a	7-ú u$_4$-⌈mu ina ka-šá⌉-[a]-⌈du⌉ [:]
	J_1	iii 22a	se-bu-ú u$_4$-mu i-na ka-šá-a-⌈di⌉ [:]
	T_1	iii 7a	7-⌈ú u$_4$⌉-m[u ina k]a-šá-di :

131	C	iii 20b	⌜it⌝-ta-raq me-ḫu-ú [ ]
	J_1	iii 22b	⌜te$^?$-riq$^?$⌝ šu-ú a-bu-bu qab-la
	T_1	iii 7b	it-ta-raq m[i-]
132	C	iii 21	ša im-taḫ-ṣu GIM ha-[ ]-⌜ti⌝
	J_1	iii 23	šá im-taḫ-ṣu ki-ma ḫa-a-a-al-ti
	T_1	iii 8	šá i[m-taḫ]-ṣu GIM [ ]
133	C	iii 22	i-nu-uḫ A.AB.BA uš-ḫa-ri-ir im-ḫul-lu a-bu-bu ⌜ik⌝-lu
	J_1	iii 24	i-nu-uḫ A.AB.BA uš-ḫa-ri-ir-ma im-Ù-lu a-bu-bu ik-la
	T_1	iii 9	i-nu-⌜uḫ⌝ A.AB.BA uš-ḫa-ri-ir i[m-]
	c_3	iii 1'	[i]-nu-u[ḫ]
134	C	iii 23	ap-pal-sa-am-⌜ma⌝ u$_4$-ma šá-kin qu-lu
	J_1	iii 25	ap-pa-al-sa ta-ma-ta šá-kin qu-lu
	T_1	iii 10	ap-pal-sa-am-ma u$_4$-ma [ ]
	c_3	iii 2'	⌜ap⌝-[p]al-[ ]
135	C	iii 24	u kul-lat ⌜te⌝-né-še-e-ti i-tu-ra a-na ṭi-iṭ-ṭi
	J_1	iii 26	ù kul-lat te-né-še-e-ti i-tu-ra a-na ṭi-iṭ-ṭi
	T_1	iii 11	u kul-lat te-né-še-e-ti i-tu-[ ]
	c_3	iii 3'	u kul-⌜lat⌝ t[e]-n[é-]
136	C	iii 25	ki-ma ú-ri mit-ḫu-rat ú-šal-lu
	J_1	iii 27	ki-ma ú-ri mit-ḫu-rat ú-šal-lu
	T_1	iii 12	ki-ma ⌜ú⌝-ri mit-ḫu-ra[t]
	c_3	iii 4'	⌜ki-ma ú⌝-r[i]
137	C	iii 26	[a]p-ti nap-pa-šá-am-ma UD.DA im-ta-qut UGU BÀD ap-pi-ia
	J_1	iii 28	ap-te nap-pa-šá-am-ma UD.DA im-ta-qut UGU BÀD ap-pi-ia
	T_1	iii 13	ap-ti nap-pa-šá-am-ma UD.DA i[m-]
	c_3	iii 5'	ap-ti ⌜nap⌝-p[a-]
138	C	iii 27	[ ]-⌜me⌝-es-ma at-ta-šab a-bak-ki
	J_1	iii 29	uk-tam-mi-is-ma at-ta-šab a-bak-ki
	T_1	iii 14	uk-tam-mi-is-ma at-ta-[ ]
	c_3	iii 6'	uk-tam-me-es-m[a]
139	C	iii 28	[a]p-pi-ia ⌜il⌝-la-ka di-ma-a-a
	J_1	iii 30	UGU BÀD ap-pi-ia il-la-ka di-ma-a-a
	T_1	iii 15	UGU BÀD ap-[p]i-ia il-l[a-]
	c_3	iii 7'	UGU BÀD ap-pi-[ ]

Line	MS	Col.	Text
140	C	iii 29	[-r]a-⸢a-ti pa⸣-tu A.AB.BA
	J_1	iii 31	ap-pa-li-is kib-ra-a-ti pa-tu A.AB.BA
	T_1	iii 16	ap-pa-lis kib-ra-[a]-ti a-n[a]
	c_3	iii 8a'	ap-pa-lis kib-ra-a-tu pa-⸢a⸣-[:]
141	C	iii 30	[ ] ⸢i⸣-te-la-a na-gu-ú
	J_1	iii 32	a-na 12.TA.ÀM i-te-la-a na-gu-⸢ú⸣
	T_1	iii 17	a-na 14.TA.ÀM ⸢i⸣-te-l[a-]
	c_3	iii 8b'	[(in one line with 140)]
142	C	iii 31	[ ] ⸢i⸣-te-mid ^{giš}MÁ
	J_1	iii 33	a-na KUR ni-muš i-te-mid ^{giš}M[Á]
	T_1	iii 18	ana KUR ni-muš ⸢i⸣-te-[ ]
	c_3	iii 9a'	a-na ni-muš ⸢i⸣-te-mid ^{giš}⸢MÁ :⸣
143	C	iii 32	[ ] iṣ-bat-ma a-na na-a-ši ul id-din
	J_1	iii 34	KUR-ú ^{kur}ni-muš ^{giš}MÁ iṣ-bat-ma a-na na-a-ši ul i[d-din]
	T_1	iii 19	KUR-ú ni-muš ^{giš}M[Á iṣ-b]at-ma ⸢a⸣-[ ]
	W_2	iii 1'	[ ] ⸢a-na na-a⸣-[ ]
	c_3	iii 9b'	[(in one line with 142)]
144	C	iii 33a	[n]i-muš KIMIN :
	J_1	iii 35	1-en u$_4$-mu 2-a u$_4$-mu KUR-ú ni-muš K[IMIN]
	T_1	iii 20a	1-en u$_4$-ma 2 u$_4$-ma K[UR ni-m]uš KI[MIN :]
	W_2	iii 2a'	[K]IMIN :
	c_3	iii 10'	1-⸢en u$_4$⸣-ma 2-a u$_4$-[m]a [ ]
145	C	iii 33b	šal-šá u$_4$-ma 4-a u$_4$-ma KUR-ú KIMI[N]
	J_1	iii 36	šal-šá u$_4$-mu re-ba-a u$_4$-mu KUR-ú ni-muš KI[MIN]
	T_1	iii 20b	[(in one line with 144)]
	W_2	iii 2b'	3-šá u$_4$-ma 4-a u$_4$-ma KU[R]
	c_3	iii 11'	3-šá u$_4$-ma 4-a ⸢u$_4$-ma⸣ [ ]
146	C	iii 34a	[K]IMIN :
	J_1	iii 37	5-šú 6-šá KUR-ú ni-muš KI[MIN]
	T_1	iii 21a	5-šá 6-šá ⸢KUR-ú⸣ [ni-muš K]IMIN [:]
	W_2	iii 3a'	[-m]uš KIMIN :
	c_3	iii 12'	5-šá u$_4$-ma 6-šá u$_4$-ma [ ]
147	C	iii 34b	7-a u$_4$-ma ina ka-šá-a-di
	J_1	iii 38	7-a u$_4$-ma i-na ka-šá-d[i]
	T_1	iii 21b	[(in one line with 146)]
	W_2	iii 3b'	7-ú u$_4$-mu [ ]
	c_3	iii 13'	7-ú u$_4$-mu [i]na [ ]

CW**c**

148	C	iii 35a	⸢ú⸣-[-š]ar :
	J_1	iii 39a	ú-še-ṣi-ma TU^{mušen} ú-maš-šar :
	T_1	iii 22a	ú-še-ṣi-[:]
	W_2	iii 4a'	[-ša]r :
	c$_3$	iii 14'	[u-š]e-ṣi-ma TU^{mušen} ú-[ ]
149	C	iii 35b	il-lik TU^{mušen} i-pi-ra-am-m[a]
	J_1	iii 39b	il-lik TU^{mušen} i-tu-ram-m[a]
	T_1	iii 22b	[(in one line with 148)]
	W_2	iii 4b'	il-lik TU^{mušen} i-pi-[ ]
	c$_3$	iii 15'	[i]l-lik TU^{mušen} i-t[u-]
150	C	iii 36	man-z[a-]-šim-ma is-saḫ-r[a]
	J_1	iii 40	man-za-zu ul i-pa-áš-šum-ma is-saḫ-r[a]
	T_1	iii 23	[man-za]-⸢zu⸣ [ ]
	W_2	iii 5'	[ ]-pa-{DA}-áš-⸢šum⸣-ma is-s[aḫ-ra]
	c$_3$	iii 16'	[-z]u ul i-⸢pa-áš-šum?-ma⸣ [ ]
151	C	iii 37a	ú-[-ša]r :
	J_1	iii 41a	ú-še-ṣi-ma SIM^{mušen} ú-maš-šìr :
	W_2	iii 6a'	[S]IM^{mušen} ú-maš-š[ar :]
	c$_3$	iii 17'	[u-še]-ṣi-ma ⸢SIM^{mušen} ú⸣-[ ]
152	C	iii 37b	il-lik SIM^{mušen} i-pi-ra-a[m-ma]
	J_1	iii 41b	il-lik SIM^{mušen} i-tu-ram-m[a]
	W_2	iii 6b'	[il-li]k ⸢SIM^{mušen} i-pi⸣-r[a-]
	c$_3$	iii 18'	[il-li]k ⸢SIM^{mušen} i⸣-[ ]
153	C	iii 38	man-za-z[u -ši]m-ma is-s[aḫ-ra]
	J_1	iii 42	man-za-zu ul i-pa-áš-šum-ma is-saḫ-ra
	W_2	iii 7'	[ ]-SU u[l]
	c$_3$	iii 19'	[ ]-⸢pa-áš⸣-x[ ]
154	C	iii 39	ú-še-ṣ[i- -b]a [ ]
	J_1	iii 43	ú-še-ṣi-ma a-ri-bi ú-maš-šìr
	W_2	iii 8a'	[ ]-ri-ba ú-ma[š- :]
155	C	iii 40	il-lik ⸢a⸣-[-r]u-⸢ra⸣ š[á]
	J_1	iii 44	il-lik a-ri-bi-ma qa-ru-ra šá A.MEŠ i-mur-ma
	W_2	iii 8b'	[(in one line with 154)]

156	C	iii 41	ik-ka[l]
	J_1	iii 45	ik-kal i-šá-aḫ-ḫi i-tar-ri ul is-saḫ-ra
	W_2	iii 9a'	[ ]x-⸢ri?⸣ ul [:]
157	C	iii 42	⸢ú-še-ṣi⸣-[ ]
	J_1	iii 46	ú-še-ṣi-ma a-na 4 IM.MEŠ at-ta-qí ni-qa-a
	W_4	iii 1'	[n]i-q[u-ú]
158	C	iii 43	[á]š-ku[n]
	J_1	iii 47	áš-kun sur-qin-nu ina UGU ziq-qur-rat KUR-i
	W_4	iii 2'	[-r]at K[UR-i]
159	C	iii 44	⸢7⸣ u 7 [ ]
	J_1	iii 48	7 u 7 ^{dug}A.DA.GUR$_5$ uk-tin
	W_4	iii 3a'	[(in one line with 160) :]
160	C	iii 45	[ina š]ap-li-šú-nu [ ]
	J_1	iii 49	i-na šap-li-šú-nu at-ta-bak GI ^{giš}EREN u ^{šim}GÍ[R]
	W_4	iii 3b'	[ ] ^{giš}EREN! [u] ^{ši}[^{m}GÍR]
161	C	iii 46a	[DINGIR.M]EŠ i-⸢ṣi-nù i⸣-[:]
	J_1	iii 50a	DINGIR.MEŠ i-ṣi-nu i-ri-šá :
	W_4	iii 4a'	[(in one line with 162) :]
162	C	iii 46b	[(in one line with 161)]
	J_1	iii 50b	DINGIR.MEŠ i-ṣi-nu i-ri-šá DÙG.G[A]
	W_4	iii 4b'	[ ] ⸢e⸣-ri-šá ṭa-[a-ba]
163	C	iii 47	[DINGIR.ME]Š ⸢ki-i zu⸣-[ ]
	J_1	iii 51	DINGIR.MEŠ ki-ma zu-um-bé-e UGU EN SÍSKUR ip-taḫ-ru
	c_2	iii 1'	[DINGIR] ⸢ki-ma⸣ z[u-]
164	C	iii 48	[u]l-t[u]
	J_1	iii 52	ul-tu ul-la-nu-um-ma DINGIR.MAḪ ina ka-šá-di-šú
	c_2	iii 2'	[u]l-tu ul-⸢la⸣-n[u-]
165	C	iv 1	iš-ši NIM.MEŠ GAL.MEŠ šá ^{d}a-nu-um i-[ ]
	J_1	iii 53	iš-ši NIM.MEŠ GAL.MEŠ šá ^{d}a-num i-pu-šú ki-i ṣu-ḫi-šú
	W_3	iii 1'	[ ]-ḫi-šu
	c_2	iii 3'	[i]š-ši NIM.⸢MEŠ⸣ G[AL.]

166	C	iv 2	DINGIR.MEŠ an-nu-tum lu-ú ^{n}[$^{a}{}_{4}$]
	J$_1$	iii 54	DINGIR.MEŠ an-nu-ti lu-ú ^{na_4}ZA.GÌN GÚ-ia a-a am-ši
	W$_3$	iii 2'	[GÚ]-ia
	c$_2$	iii 4'	[DINGIR.M]EŠ an-nu-⸢tum⸣ l[u-]
167	C	iv 3	UD.MEŠ an-nu-tum lu-ú-uḫ-su-sa-a[m-]
	J$_1$	iv 1	UD.MEŠ an-nu-ti aḫ-su-sa-am-ma ana da-riš a-a am-ši
	W$_3$	iii 3'	[ ] am-SI
	c$_2$	iii 5'	[u$_4$-m]e an-nu-tum ⸢aḫ⸣-[ ]
168	C	iv 4	[DI]NGIR.MEŠ lil-li-ku-ni [ ]
	J$_1$	iv 2	DINGIR.MEŠ lil-li-ku-ni a-na sur-qin-ni
	W$_3$	iii 4a'	[(in one line with 169) :]
	c$_2$	iii 6'	[DINGI]R? lil-li-k[u-]
169	C	iv 5	⸢^{d}en⸣-líl a-a il-li-ka [ ]
	J$_1$	iv 3	^{d}en-líl a-a il-li-ka a-na sur-qin-ni
	W$_3$	iii 4b'	[ ]-ka ⟨ana⟩ sur-qí-ni
	c$_2$	iii 7'	[^{d}en-lí]l a-a il-⸢li⸣-ka [ ]
170	C	iv 6	áš-⸢šú⸣ la im-tal-ku-ma iš-k[u-]
	J$_1$	iv 4	áš-šú la im-tal-ku-ma iš-ku-nu a-bu-bu
	W$_3$	iii 5'	[ ]-ku-nu a-bu-bu
	c$_2$	iii 8'	[l]a im-tal-li-ku-[ ]
171	C	iv 7	u ÙG.⸢MEŠ-ia⸣ im-nu-ú [ ]
	J$_1$	iv 5	ù ÙG.MEŠ-ia im-nu-ú ana ka-ra-ši
	W$_3$	iii 6'	[ ] ⸢a⸣-na ka-⸢ra⸣-ši
	c$_2$	iii 9'	[ù Ù]G.MEŠ-ia im-nu-[ ]
172	C	iv 8	ul-tu ul-la-⸢nu-um-ma⸣ [ ]
	J$_1$	iv 6	ul-tu ul-la-nu-um-ma ^{d}en-líl ina ka-šá-di-šú
	c$_2$	iv 1	[-n]u-um-ma ^{d}e[n-]
173	C	iv 9	i-mur ^{giš}MÁ-m[a]
	J$_1$	iv 7a	i-mur ^{giš}MÁ-ma i-te-ziz ^{d}en-líl :
	c$_2$	iv 2	[i-m]u[r ^{giš}M]Á-ma ⸢i-te⸣-[ ]
174	C	iv 10	lib-ba-ti i[m-]
	J$_1$	iv 7b	lib-ba-ti im-ta-li šá DINGIR.DINGIR ^{d}í-gì-gì
	c$_2$	iv 3	[lìb-b]a-a-te im-ta-la šá ⸢DINGIR⸣.MEŠ [ ]

175	C	iv 11a	a-a-⸢um-ma⸣ ú-ṣ[i :]
	J_1	iv 8a	a-a-um-ma ú-ṣi na-piš-ti :
	c_2	iv 4	[a-a-n]u-um-ma ú-ṣu n[a-]
176	C	iv 11b	[(in one line with 175)]
	J_1	iv 8b	a-a ib-luṭ LÚ ina ka-ra-š[i]
	c_2	iv 5	[a]-⸢a⸣ ib-luṭ LÚ ina ka-⸢ra⸣-š[i]
			———————————— c
177	C	iv 12a	⸢^{d}nin⸣-urta ⸢pa-a⸣-[:]
	J_1	iv 9a	^{d}nin-urta pa-a-šú DÙ-ma DUG_4.GA :
	c_2	iv 6a	[^{d}nin-u]rta pa-a-šú DÙ-ma DUG_4.GA
178	C	iv 12b	[ ] ⸢qu-ra⸣-[ ]
	J_1	iv 9b	MU-ár ana qu-ra-di ^{d}en-l[íl]
	c_2	iv 6b	MU-ra ana qu-ra-di ^{d}en-[líl]
179	C	iv 13	[-u]m-ma š[á -m]a-ti i-⸢ba⸣-a[n-ni]
	J_1	iv 10	man-nu-um-ma šá la ^{d}é-a a-ma-tu i-ban-n[i]
	c_2	iv 7a	[-u]m-ma šá la ^{d}é-a a-mat i-ban-ni
180	C	iv 14	[ ]-⸢a⸣ i-[ ] ka-lu šip-r[i]
	J_1	iv 11	ù ^{d}é-a i-de-e-ma ka-la šip-r[i]
	c_2	iv 7b	u ^{d}é-a i-de-⸢e-ma⸣ k[al$^{?}$]
			———————————— c
181	C	iv 15a	[ ]-⸢šú DÙ⸣-ma [:]
	J_1	iv 12a	^{d}é-a pa-a-šú DÙ-ma DUG_4.GA :
	c_2	iv 8a	[p]a-⸢a⸣-šú [DÙ-m]a DUG_4.GA
	b	obv. 1a'	[-š]u DÙ-[.G]A ⸢:⸣
182	C	iv 15b	[MU-r]a ana qu-⸢ra⸣-[ ]
	J_1	iv 12b	MU-ár ana qu-ra-du ^{d}en-[líl]
	c_2	iv 8b	MU-ra ⸢ana qu⸣-ra-di ^{d}[en-líl]
	b	obv. 1b'	[M]U-[ ]
183	C	iv 16	[ ] ABG[AL] qu-r[a-du]
	J_1	iv 13	at-ta ABGAL DINGIR.MEŠ qu-ra-[du]
	c_2	iv 9	[ABGA]L DINGIR.MEŠ ⸢qu⸣-[ ]
	b	obv. 2a'	[ ] DINGIR.MEŠ ⸢qu-ra⸣-du :
184	C	iv 17	ki-⸢i⸣ [-t]a-li[k- -b]u-ba [ta]š-k[un]
	J_1	iv 14	ki-i ki-i la tam-ta-lik-ma a-bu-bu taš-k[un]
	c_2	iv 10	[ ]-⸢tal-lik⸣-ma a-b[u-]
	b	obv. 2b'	ki-ki-[i]

185	C	iv 18a	be-el ár-ni ⸢e⸣-[ ]-ṭa-šú :
	J_1	iv 15a	be-el ḫi-ṭi e-mid ḫi-ṭa-a-šú :
	$\mathbf{c_2}$	iv 11	[á]r-n[i] e-m[id]
	b	obv. 3a'	[ ]-mid ḫi-ṭa-⸢šu :⸣
186	C	iv 18b	[-t]i ⸢e-mid⸣ gíl[l-]
	J_1	iv 15b	be-el gíl-la-ti e-mid gíl-lat-[su]
	b	obv. 3b'	be-el gíl-l[a-]
187	C	iv 19	ru-um-me a-a i[b-b]a-ti-i[q] ⸢a⸣-a [ ]
	J_1	iv 16	ru-um-me a-a ib-ba-ti-iq šu-du-ud a-a i[r-mu]
	b	obv. 4'	[i]b-ba-⟨ti⟩-iq šu-⸢du⸣-ud [ ]
188	C	iv 20	am-ma-ki [ ] a-bu-b[u]
	J_1	iv 17a	am-ma-ku taš-ku-nu a-bu-ba :
	b	obv. 5a'	[-n]a a-bu-ba :
189	C	iv 21	UR.MAḪ lit-b[a- Ù]G.⸢MEŠ li-ṣa⸣-aḫ-ḫi-i[r]
	J_1	iv 17b	UR.MAḪ lit-ba-am-ma ÙG.MEŠ li-ṣa-a[ḫ-ḫir]
	b	obv. 5b'	UR.M[AḪ]
190	C	iv 22a	am-ma-ki taš-k[un a-bu-b]a :
	J_1	iv 18a	am-ma-ku taš-ku-nu a-bu-ba :
	b	obv. 6a'	[(in one line with 191) :]
191	C	iv 22b	UR.BAR.RA lit-ba-am-ma ⸢ÙG.MEŠ⸣ l[i-ṣa-aḫ-ḫir]
	J_1	iv 18b	UR.BAR.RA lit-ba-am-ma ÙG.MEŠ li-ṣa-[ḫi-ir]
	b	obv. 6b'	UR.BAR.[ ]
192	C	iv 23a	am-ma-ki taš-ku[n a-bu-b]a :
	J_1	iv 19a	am-ma-ku taš-ku-nu a-bu-ba :
	b	obv. 7a'	[(in one line with 193) :]
193	C	iv 23b	ḫu-šaḫ-ḫu liš-šá-kin-ma KUR liš-[giš]
	J_1	iv 19b	ḫu-šaḫ-ḫu liš-šá-kin-ma KUR liš-[giš]
	b	obv. 7b'	ḫu-ša[ḫ-]
194	C	iv 24a	am-ma-ki taš-ku[n :]
	J_1	iv 20a	am-ma-ku taš-ku-nu a-bu-ba :
	b	obv. 8a'	[(in one line with 195) :]
195	C	iv 24b	ᵈèr-ra lit-ba-am-ma KUR liš?-g[iš]
	J_1	iv 20b	ᵈèr-ra lit-ba-am-ma ÙG.MEŠ li[š]-⸢giš⸣
	b	obv. 8b'	ᵈèr-⸢ra⸣ [ ]

196	C	iv 25	ana-ku ul e[p-] pi-riš-ti DINGIR.⸢MEŠ GAL⸣.[MEŠ]
	J1	iv 21	a-na-ku ul ap-ta-a pi-riš-ti DINGIR.MEŠ GAL.MEŠ
	b	obv. 9'	[a]p-ta-a pi-riš-ti DINGIR.[ ]
197	C	iv 26	⸢at-ra-ḫa-sis⸣ [-ša]b-ri-šum-ma pi-riš-t[i DI]NGIR.M[EŠ]
	J1	iv 22	at-ra-ḫa-sis šu-na-ta ú-šab-ri-šum-ma pi-riš-ti DINGIR.MEŠ iš-me
	b	obv. 10'	[-s]is šu-na-ta ú-šab-[ ]
198	C	iv 27	[-š]u ⸢mil⸣-k[u]
	J1	iv 23a	e-nin-na-ma mi-lik-šú mil-ku :
	b	obv. 11'	[-m]a mi-[ ]
199	C	iv 28	[ ] ⸢a-na⸣ lìb-bi ^{giš}M[Á]
	J1	iv 23b	i-lam-ma ^{d}IDIM ana lìb-bi ^{giš}MÁ
	b	obv. 12'	[ ] ⸢^{d}⸣é-a LUGAL [ ]
200	C	iv 29	[ ]-⸢ni ia-a⸣-ši
	J1	iv 24	iṣ-bat qa-ti-ia-ma ul-te-la-an-ni ia-a-ši
	b	obv. 13'	[ ]-ma uš-te-la-a[n-]
201	C	iv 30	[si]n-niš-t[i]
	J1	iv 25	uš-te-li uš-tak-mi-is sin-niš-ti ina i-di-ia
	b	obv. 14'	[-n]iš-ti i[na]
202	C	iv 31	[ ]-ri-in-ni ⸢i⸣-[kar-r]a-[ ]
	J1	iv 26	il-pu-ut pu-ut-ni-ma iz-za-az ina bi-ri-in-ni i-kar-ra-ban-na-ši
	b	obv. 15'	[ ]-⸢az⸣ [ ]
203	C	iv 32	[ ] a-me-lu-tù[m-ma]
	J1	iv 27	i-na pa-na ^{m}UD-ZI a-me-lu-tùm-ma
204	C	iv 33	[ ] e-mu-ú ki-i DINGIR.ME[Š] na-[ ]
	J1	iv 28	e-nin-na-ma ^{m}UD-ZI u MUNUS-šú lu-u e-mu-ú ki-ma DINGIR.MEŠ na-ši-ma
205	C	iv 34	l[u-]-qí ina pi-i Í[D].ME[Š]
	J1	iv 29	lu-ú a-šib-ma ^{m}UD-ZI ina ru-ú-qí ina pi-i ÍD.MEŠ
206	C	iv 35	i[l-] ina pi-i ÍD.MEŠ uš-te-ši-bu-i[n-ni]
	J1	iv 30	il-qu-in-ni-ma ina ru-qí ina KA ÍD.MEŠ uš-te-ši-bu-in-ni

207	C	iv 36	[-n]a DINGIR.MEŠ ú-paḫ-ḫa-rak-⸢kúm⸣-[ma]
	J_1	iv 31	e-nin-na-ma ana ka-a-šá man-nu DINGIR.MEŠ ú-paḫ-ḫa-rak-kúm-ma
208	C	iv 37	[-b]a-ú tu-ut-ta-a ⸢at⸣-[ta]
	J_1	iv 32	ba-la-ṭa šá tu-ba-ʾ-ú tu-ut-ta-a at-ta
209	C	iv 38	[u]r-ri u 7 mu-šá-a-[ti]
	J_1	iv 33	ga-na e ta-at-til 6 ur-ri ù 7 mu-šá-a-ti
210	C	iv 39	[-r]it pu-ri-d[i-šú]
	J_1	iv 34	ki-ma áš-bu-ma ina bi-rit pu-ri-di-šú
211	C	iv 40	[ ]-uš UGU-[šú]
	J_1	iv 35	šit-tu ki-ma im-ba-ri i-nap-pu-uš UGU-šú
212	C	iv 41	[m]ar-ḫi-ti-⸢šú⸣
	J_1	iv 36	^{m}UD-ZI ana šá-ši-ma MU-ár ana mar-ḫi-ti-šú
213	C	iv 42	[ ] ba-la-ṭ[a]
	J_1	iv 37	am-ri ^{lú}GURUŠ šá i-ri-šú ba-la-ṭu
214	C	iv 43	[ ] UGU-[šú]
	J_1	iv 38	šit-tu ki-ma im-ba-ri i-nap-pu-uš UGU-šú
215	C	iv 44	[-Z]I ru-⸢ú⸣-[qí]
	J_1	iv 39	mar-ḫi-is-su ana šá-šu-ma MU-ár a-na ^{m}UD-ZI ru-qí
216	C	iv 45	[ ] ⸢LÚ⸣
	J_1	iv 40	lu-pu-us-su-ma li-ig-gél-ta-a LÚ
217	C	iv 46	[š]u[l-]
	J_1	iv 41	ḫar-ra-ni il-li-ka li-tur ina šul-me
218	C	iv 47	[-t]i-[ ]
	J_1	iv 42	KÁ.GAL ú-ṣa-a li-tur a-na ma-ti-šú
219	C	iv 48	[ ]-⸢šú⸣
	J_1	iv 43	^{m}UD-ZI ana šá-ši-ma MU-ár ana mar-ḫi-ti-šú
	j	v 1'	^{m}[ ]
220	J_1	iv 44	rag-ga-at a-me-lut-tu i-rag-gi-ig-ki

Line	MS	Col./line	Text
221	C	v 1	[g]a-na e-pi-i ku-ru-um-ma-ti-šú ši-tak-ka-ni ina re-ši-š[u]
	J_1	iv 45	ga-na e-pi-i ku-ru-um-⸢ma-ti-šú⸣ ši-tak-ka-ni ina re-ši-šú
	j	v 3'	g[a-]
222	C	v 2	[u] u_4-mi šá it-ti-lu ina i-ga-ri eṣ-ri
	J_1	iv 46	ù u_4-mi šá it-t[i-l]u ina i-ga-ri eṣ-r[i]
223	C	v 3	ši-i i-pi ku-ru-um-ma-ti-šú iš-tak-ka-ni ina re-ši-š[u]
	J_1	iv 47	ši-i e-pi ku-⸢ru⸣-um-⸢ma-ti-šú iš⸣-tak-ka-an ina r[e-ši-šú]
224	C	v 4	u u_4-mi šá it-ti-lu ina i-ga-ri ud-da-áš-š[ú]
	J_1	iv 48	⸢ù⸣ u_4-mi š[á i]t-ti-l[u ina i-g]a-ri ⸢ud⸣-[ ]
	T_1	iv 1'	[-š]ú
	j	v 6'	u/⸢ù⸣ [ ]
225	C	v 5	iš-ta-at šá-bu-lat ku-ru-um-mat-s[u]
	J_1	iv 49	[iš-t]a-⸢at⸣ [šá-b]u-lat ⸢ku-ru⸣-[ ]
	T_1	iv 2'	[-s]u
	j	v 7'	1-[et]
226	C	v 6a	2-tum muš-šu-kàt 3-tum raṭ-bat :
	J_1	iv 50a	[ ] ⸢3-tum raṭ⸣-bat [:]
	T_1	iv 3a'	[(in one line with 227) :]
227	C	v 6b	4-tum ip-te-ṣi ka-man-[šú]
	J_1	iv 50b	[(in one line with 226)]
	T_1	iv 3b'	[-ma]n-šú
	j	v 9'	⸢4⸣-[ ]
228	C	v 7a	5-tum ši-ba it-ta-di :
	J_1	iv 51a	[-d]i [:]
	T_1	iv 4a'	[(in one line with 229) :]
229	C	v 7b	6-tum ba-aš-[lat]
	J_1	iv 51b	[(in one line with 228)]
	T_1	iv 4b'	[-a]š-lat
230	C	v 8	se-⸢bu⸣-tum ina pe-et-tim-ma il-pu-us-su-ma i-⸢te⸣-gél-ta-⸢a⸣-[(ma) L]Ú
	J_1	v 1	[i]l-pu-us-su-ma ig-gél-ta-a LÚ
	T_1	iv 5'	[-t]a-a LÚ
	j	v 11'	⸢7⸣-[tum]
			———————— CT(k)

231	C	v 9	^{d}GIŠ-gím-maš a-na šá-šu-ma MU-ra a-na ^{m}UD-ZI [ru-ú]-qí
	J_1	v 2	[-m]a MU-ár a-na ^{m}UD-ZI ru-qí
	T_1	iv 6'	[r]u-ú-qí
	j	v 12'	⸢^{d}⸣[ ]
232	C	v 10	an-ni-miš šit-tum ir-⸢ḫu-ú⸣ e-l[i]-ia
	J_1	v 3	[i]r-ḫu-ú e-li-ia
	T_1	iv 7'	[ ] ⸢e⸣-li-ia
	j	v 13'	a[n-]
233	C	v 11	ḫa-an-ṭiš tal-tap-tan-ni-ma t[a- -n]i [at]-ta
	J_1	v 4	[-m]a ta-ad-de-kan-ni at-ta
	T_1	iv 8'	[a]t-ta
234	C	v 12	^{m}UD-⸢ZI a⸣-[na šá-šu-m]a [MU-ra] ⸢a⸣-na ^{d}G[IŠ-gí]m-maš
	J_1	v 5	[MU-r]a a-na ^{md}GIŠ-gím-maš
	T_1	iv 9'	[a-n]a ^{d}GIŠ-gím-maš
235	C	v 13	[-t]e-⸢ka⸣
	J_1	v 6	[al-kam-ma? ^{d}GIŠ-gím-m]aš mu-na-a ku-ru-um-me-ti-ka
	T_1	iv 10'-11'	[-ma]š mu-na-a / [ku-ru-u]m-ma-ti-ka
	j	v 16'	a[l$^{?}$-]
236	J_1	v 7	[u? u$_4$-mi? šá ta-at-ti-l]u lu-ú e-dak-ka ka-a-šá
	T_1	iv 12'	[-da]k-ka ka-a-šá
	W_1	v 1'	[ ] ⸢lu-ú?⸣ [ ]
	j	v 17'	u/⸢ù⸣$^{?}$ [ ]
237	J_1	v 8	[iš-ta-at šá-bu-lat] ku-ru-um-mat-ka
	T_1	iv 13'	[ ] ku-ru-um-mat-ka
	W_1	v 2a'	[-m]at-ka [:]
238	J_1	v 9	[šá-l]ul-tum raṭ-bat
	T_1	iv 14a'	[muš-šu]-⸢kàt 3-tum raṭ⸣-[ba]t ⟨:⟩
	W_1	v 2b'	2-tu[m]
239	J_1	v 10	[-t]e-ṣi ka-man-ka
	T_1	iv 14b'	4-tum ip-te-ṣi ka-man-ka
	W_1	v 3a'	[-k]a :
240	C	v 16	[b]a-a[š-lat]
	J_1	v 11	[-d]i 6-tum ba-aš-lat
	T_1	iv 15'	[-p]a it-ta-di ⸢6⸣-[t]um ba-aš-lat
	W_1	v 3b'	5-⸢tum⸣ ši-pa i[t-]

241	C	v 17	[ ] at-⸢ta⸣
	J_1	v 12	[-t]im-ma al-pu-ut-ka a-na-ku
	T_1	iv 16'	[7-tum in]a ⸢pe⸣-et-tim-ma te-et-[te-g]él-ta-a at-ta
	W_1	v 4'	[-e]t-te-gél-ta-[ ]
242	C	v 18	[ ]-ú-qí
	J_1	v 13	[ ] MU-ár a-na ^{m}UD-ZI ru-qí
	T_1	iv 17'	[^{d}GIŠ-g]ím-maš ana šá-šu-ma MU-ra ⸢a⸣-na ^{m}UD-ZI ru-ú-qí
	W_1	v 5'	[ ] ⸢a⸣-na ^{m}UD-Z[I]
	b	rev. 1'	[ ] MU-[ ]
243	C	v 19	[l]ul-lik
	J_1	v 14	[^{m}u]t-ZI a-a-ka-ni lul-lik
	T_1	iv 18'	[ki-k]i-i lu-pu-uš ^{m}ut-Z[I (a)]-⸢a⸣-i-ka-a lul-lik
	W_1	v 6'	[^{m}u]t-ZI-tim a-a-[ ]
	b	rev. 2'	[-p]u-uš ^{m}ut-Z[I]
244	C	v 20	[-k]e-mu
	J_1	v 15	[-t]a ek-ke-mu
	T_1	iv 19'	[x (x)].MEŠ-ia uṣ-ṣab-bi-tu_4 ek-ke-mu
	W_1	v 7a'	[-k]e-mu :
	b	rev. 3a'	[ ] ek-ke-mu :
245	C	v 21	[ ]-tum
	J_1	v 16	[-i]a a-šib mu-ú-tum
	T_1	iv 20'	[ina] É ma-a-a-li-ia ⸢a⸣-šib mu-tum
	W_1	v 7b'	ina É ma-a-a-[ ]
	b	rev. 3b'	i[na]
246	C	v 22	[-tù]m-ma
	J_1	v 17	[lu-u]š-kun šu-ú mu-tùm-ma
	T_1	v 1	ù a-šar [ ]
	W_1	v 8'	[-u]š-kun šu-⸢ú⸣ [ ]
	b	rev. 4'	[ ] lu-uš-kun [ ]
			———————————————— CTW**b**
247	C	v 23	^{m}⸢UD⸣-Z[I -l]a-ḫi
	J_1	v 18	[-r]a a-na ^{m}ur-šánabi ma-la-ḫi
	T_1	v 2	^{m}UD-ZI a-na [šá-šu-ma]
	W_1	v 9'	[-r]a a-na ^{m}ur$^{!}$-^{d}šánabi m[a-]
	b	rev. 5'	[ ]-ma i-zak-[k]a-ra [ ]

248	C	v 24	^{m}ur-šánabi k[a- -ze]r-ka
	J_1	v 19	[ ]-di-ka né-bé-ru li-zer-ka
	T_1	v 3	^{m}ur-šánabi ka-⸢a⸣-[ru]
	W_1	v 10'	[-b]é-[ ]
	b	rev. 6'	[l]id-di-ka ⸢né⸣-[b]é-ru [ ]
249	C	v 25	šá ina a-ḫi-šá D[U.]-me
	J_1	v 20	[DU.DU.M]EŠ-ku aḫ-šá zu-um-me
	T_1	v 4	šá ina a-ḫi-šá DU.[ ]
	b	rev. 7'	[.D]U.MEŠ-ku aḫ-⸢ša⸣ [ ]
250	C	v 26a	LÚ šá tal-li-ka p[a- :]
	J_1	v 21a	[-n]a-as-su :
	T_1	v 5a	LÚ šá ⸢tal-li⸣-k[a :]
	b	rev. 8a'	[ ]-⸢ka pa⸣-na-su [:]
251	C	v 26b	[ ]-šú
	J_1	v 21b	ik-ta-su-ú ma-lu-ú pa-gar-šú
	T_1	v 5b	[(in one line with 250)]
	b	rev. 8b'	[ik-t]a-su-ú m[a-]
252	C	v 27	maš-ku-ú uq-[-š]ú
	J_1	v 22	[-t]a-at-tu-ú du-muq UZU.MEŠ-šú
	T_1	v 6	⸢maš-ku-ú⸣ [ ]
	b	rev. 9'	[ ]-at-tu-ú [d]u-muq U[ZU]
253	C	v 28	li-qé-šu-ma [-m]a
	J_1	v 23	[^{m}u]r-šánabi ana nam-se-e bil-šú-ma
	T_1	v 7	[l]i-⸢qé-šu⸣-[ ]
	b	rev. 10'	[-šá]nabi ana nam-se-e [ ]
254	C	v 29	ma-le-šú ina me-⸢e⸣ [ ]
	J_1	v 24	[A.M]EŠ GIM el-li lim-si
	T_1	v 8	[m]a-le-šú ina A.⸢MEŠ⸣ [ ]
	W_1	v 15'	[GI]M e[l-]
	b	rev. 11'	[m]e-e ⸢ki-ma el⸣-li [ ]
255	C	v 30a	lid-di maš-ki-šu-ma [:]
	J_1	v 25a	[ ] li-bil tam-tum :
	T_1	v 9a	⸢lid⸣-di maš-ki-šu-ma li-[:]
	W_1	v 16a'	[lid-d]i maš-ki-šu-ma ⸢li-bil⸣ [ ] ⸢:⸣?
	b	rev. 12'	[-m]a li-bil [ ]

Line	MS	Ref.	Text
256	C	v 30b	⌜ṭa-a-bu ṣú-pu⌝ [ ]
	J_1	v 25b	ṭa-a-bu lu ṣa-pu zu-mur-šú
	T_1	v 9b	[(in one line with 255)]
	W_1	v 16b'	[ṭ]a$^{?}$-[bu]-⌜um$^{?}$ ṣú⌝-p[u]
	b	rev. 13a'	[z]u-m[ur]-šu :
257	C	v 31	lu-ú ud-du-u[š -g]u šá S[AG.D]U-šú
	J_1	v 26	[-d]u-uš pár-si-gu šá qaq-qa-di-šú
	T_1	v 10	lu-ú ud-du-u[š]
	W_1	v 17a'	[lu]-⌜ú⌝ ud-du-šú par-si-gi š[á SAG.D]U-šú :
	b	rev. 13b'	lu-ú [ud-d]u-u[š]-si-gu [ ]
258	C	v 32a	te-di-qí lu-ú l[a- -t]i-šú :
	J_1	v 27	[ ]-⌜ú⌝ la-biš ṣu-bat bal-ti-šú
	T_1	v 11	te-di-qí lu la-[ ]
	W_1	v 17b'	te-di-qa lu [ ]
	b	rev. 14a'	[ ] ṣu-bat ⌜bal-ti⌝-[:]
259	C	v 32b	a-di il-la-ku ana URU-šú
	J_1	v 28a	[an]a ⌜KUR⌝-šú (⟨:⟩)
	T_1	v 12a	a-di il-la-ku an[a (:)]
	W_1	v 18a'	[i]l-⌜la⌝-ku ana URU-šú :
	b	rev. 14b'	[(in one line with 258, or om.?)]
260	C	v 33a	a-di i-kaš-šá-d[u :]
	J_1	v 28b	a-di i-kaš-šá-du ana ur-ḫi-šú
	T_1	v 12b	[(in one line with 259)]
	W_1	v 18b'	a-di ⌜i⌝-[kaš-š]á-du a-na u[r-]
	b	rev. 14b'	[(om., or in one line with 258?)]
261	C	v 33b	[t]e-di-qu ši-pa a-a id-di-ma e-de-šú li-diš
	J_1	v 29	[ ]-⌜a⌝ id-di e-de-šú li-diš
	T_1	v 13	te-di-qu ši-pa ⌜a⌝-[ ]
	W_1	v 19'	[-p]a a-a id-⌜di⌝-[-š]u l[i-diš]
	b	rev. 15'	[i]d-di-ma [ ]
262	C	v 34	il-qé-šu-m[a an]a nam-se-e ú-bil-šu-ma
	J_1	v 30	[^{m}]ur-šánabi ana nam-se-e ú-bil-šu-ma
	T_1	v 14	il-qé-šu-ma [ ]
	W_1	v 20'	[-š]u-m[a ^{m}u]r-⌜šánabi a⌝-[ ] ú-[ ]
	b	rev. 16a'	[-s]e-e ú-bil-[:]

263	C	v 35	ma-le-šú ina [i]l-li ⸢im⸣-si
	J_1	v 31	[A.M]EŠ GIM el-li im-si
	T_1	v 15	ma-le-šu ina ⸢A⸣.[ ]
	W_1	v 21'	[m]a-le-šú ina ⸢A⸣.[ ]
	b	rev. 16b'	[(in one line with 262)]
264	C	v 36a	id-di KUŠ.[t]am-tum :
	J_1	v 32a	[ ] ⸢ú⸣-bil tam-tum :
	T_1	v 16	id-di KUŠ.[ ]
	W_1	v 22'	id-di KUŠ.MEŠ-š[u-ma]
	b	rev. 17a'	[ ] ⸢tam⸣-tum :
265	C	v 36b	ṭa-a-ba iṣ-ṣa-⸢pi⸣ SU-šú
	J_1	v 32b	ṭa-a-bu iṣ-ṣa-pi zu-mur-šú
	T_1	v 17	ṭa-a-bu [ ]
	W_1	v 23a'	ṭa-a-bu iṣ-ṣa-pu zu-mu[r-šú :]
	b	rev. 17b'	ṭa-[ ]
266	C	v 37a	ú-te-ed-di[š pár-si-gu šá SAG.DU-š]ú :
	J_1	v 33a	[S]AG.DU-šú :
	T_1	v 18	ú-te-ed-[ ]
	W_1	v 23b'	[(in one line with 265)]
	b	rev. 18a'	[ ]-šu : (or 267?)
267	C	v 37b	te-di-qa la-biš ṣu-bat bal-ti-šú
	J_1	v 33b	te-di-qa la-biš ṣu-bat bal-ti-šú
	T_1	v 19	te-di-qa [ ]
	W_1	v 24a'	te-di-qa la-biš ṣu-bat ba[l- :]
	b	rev. 18a'	see 266
268	C	v 38a	[a-di i]l-[la-ku ana URU-šú] ⸢:⸣
	J_1	om.	
	T_1	v 20a	⸢a⸣-di ⸢il⸣-[(:)]
	W_1	v 24b'	[(in one line with 267)]
	b	rev. 18b'	a-⸢di il-la-ku⸣ [ ]
269	C	v 38b	⸢i-kaš-šá-du⸣ ana ur-ḫi-šú
	J_1	om.	
	T_1	v 20b	[(in one line with 268)]
	W_1	v 25a'	⸢a⸣-di i-kaš-šá-⸢du⸣ ana ⸢ur-ḫi-šú :⸣
	b	om?	

270	C	v 39	[ ] li-diš
	J_1	om.	
	T_1	v 21	⸢te⸣-[ ]
	W_1	v 25b'	[(in one line with 269)]
	b	rev. 19'	[te-di-qu ši-pa a-a id-d]i-⸢ma e-de⸣-šu [ ]
271	C	v 40	[ ] ⸢^{giš}MÁ⸣
	J_1	v 34	[^{m}u]r-šánabi ir-ka-bu ^{giš}MÁ
	W_1	v 26a'	^{d}GIŠ-gím-maš u ^{m}u[r- :]
	b	rev. 20a'	[(in one line with 272) :]
272	C	v 41	^{giš}m[á-gi-il-la]
	J_1	v 35	[id]-du-ú šu-nu ir-tak-bu
	W_1	v 26b'	[(in one line with 271)]
	b	rev. 20b'	[^{gi}]^{š}m[á-gíl?]-⸢la⸣ id-du-[u?] šu-n[u]
			———————————— CW**b**
273	C	v 42	mar-ḫi-is-s[u]
	J_1	v 36	[M]U-⸢ár⸣ a-na ^{m}UD-ZI ru-qí
	W_1	v 27'	mar-ḫi-is-su ana šá-šu-⸢ma MU⸣-[ ]
	b	rev. 21'	[-za]k-ka-r[a]
274	C	v 43	^{d}GIŠ-gím-maš D[U$^{?}$]
	J_1	v 37	[ ] ⸢i⸣-na-ḫa i-šu-ṭa
	W_1	v 28'	^{d}GIŠ-gím-maš DU-ka i-n[a-]
	b	rev. 22'	[ ]-ḫa [ ]
275	C	v 44	mi-na-a ta-at-tan-⸢na-áš⸣-š[um-]
	J_1	v 38	[-m]a i-ta-ár ana KUR-šú
	W_1	v 29'	mi-na ta-at-tan-na-á[š-]
276	C	v 45	u šu-ú iš-ši pa-r[i-]
	J_1	v 39	[-r]i-sa ^{d}GIŠ-gím-maš
	W_1	v 30a'	⸢ù⸣ šu-ú iš-ši pa-ri-[:]
277	C	v 46	^{giš}MÁ uṭ-ṭè-eḫ-ḫa-⸢a⸣ [ ]
	J_1	v 40	[ ] ⸢a⸣-na kib-ri
	W_1	v 30b'	[(in one line with 276)]
278	C	v 47	^{m}UD-ZI a-na šá-šu-ma [MU-ár]
	J_1	v 41	[a-n]a ^{d}GIŠ-gím-maš
	W_1	v 31'	[^{m}UD-Z]I-⸢tim ana šá-šu⸣-m[a]
279	C	vi 1	⸢^{d}⸣GIŠ-gím-maš tal-⸢li⸣-ka ta-na-ḫa t[a-]
	J_1	v 42	[-ḫ]a ta-šu-⸢ṭa⸣

280	C	vi 2	mi-na-a at-tan-nak-kúm-ma ta-ta-ár ana [ ]
	J$_1$	v 43	[-á]r ana KUR-ka
281	C	vi 3a	lu-ú-up-te ^{d}GIŠ-gím-maš a-mat ni-ṣir-ti :
	J$_1$	v 44	[-ṣ]ir-ti
282	C	vi 3b	u AD.ḪAL š[á DINGIR.MEŠ]
	J$_1$	v 45	[ka-a-šá lu-u]q-bi-ka
283	C	vi 4	šam-mu šu-ú ki-ma ed-de-et-t[i]
	J$_1$	v 46	[š]á-k[i]n
284	C	vi 5	si-ḫi-il-šú GIM a-mur-din-nim-ma ú-sa[ḫ-ḫal]
	J$_1$	v 47	[ ]x
285	C	vi 6a	šum-ma šam-ma šá-a-šú i-kaš-šá-da qa-ta-a-k[a :]
286	C	vi 6b	[(in one line with 285)]
287	C	vi 7a	^{d}GIŠ-gím-maš an-ni-tú ina še-me-šú :
288	C	vi 7b	ip-ti r[a-a-ṭa]
289	C	vi 8	ú-rak-ki-is NA$_4$.MEŠ kab-tu-t[a a/ina šēpī-šú]
	j	vi 1'	⸢ú$^{?}$-rak$^{?}$⸣-[ ]
290	C	vi 9	il-du-du-šu-[m]a ana ABZ[U]
	j	vi 2'	⸢il⸣-du-⟨du⟩-⸢šu-ma⸣ [ ]
291	C	vi 10	šu-ú il-⸢qé⸣ šam-ma-ma is-s[u-uḫ-šú]
	j	vi 3'	⸢šu-ú⸣ i[l-q]é$^{?}$ šam-ma-m[a]
292	C	vi 11	ú-bat-ti-iq ⸢NA$_4$⸣.MEŠ kab-tu-t[a ina šēpī-šú]
	j	vi 4'	⸢ú⸣-[bat]-ti-iq NA$_4$.MEŠ kab-t[u-]
293	C	vi 12	⸢tam$^{?}$⸣-tum is-⸢su⸣-kaš-šú [ ]
	j	vi 5'	t[am-t]um is-su-kaš-šú a-⸢na kib-ri⸣-šú
			———————————————— Cj
294	C	vi 13	^{d}GIŠ-gím-maš a-na šá-šu-ma MU-r[a -ḫ]u
	j	vi 6'	⸢^{d}⸣[GIŠ]-gí[m]-maš a-na šá-šu-ma MU-ra a-na ^{m}ur-šánabi ma$^{!}$-la-ḫu
295	C	vi 14	^{m}ur-šánabi šam-mu an-nu-ú ša[m-]
	j	vi 7'	^{m}[ ] šam-mu an-nu-ú šam-mu ni-qit-ti
296	C	vi 15	šá LÚ ina lìb-bi-šú i-kaš-⸢šá⸣-d[u]
	j	vi 8'	[lì]b-bi-šú i-kaš-šá-du nap-šat$^{!}$(BI)-su

297	C	vi 16a	⸢lu-bil-šu⸣ ana lìb-bi UNUG^{ki} su-pu-r[i :]
	j	vi 9a'	[-š]u ana ŠÀ UNUG^{ki} su-pu-ri ⟨:⟩
298	C	vi 16b	[(in one line with 297)]
	T_1	vi 1	[-d]i$^?$ šam-ma lul-tuk
	j	vi 9b'	lu-šá-kil ši-ba-am-ma šam-ma lul-tuk
299	C	vi 17	⸢šum-šu?⸣ ši-i-bu iṣ-⸢ṣa⸣-[ ]
	T_1	vi 2	[-b]u iṣ-ṣa-ḫir LÚ
	W_1	vi 1'	[x]-šá [ ] (or 298–[299]?)
	j	vi 10'	[ ]-i-bi iṣ-ṣa-ḫir LÚ
300	C	vi 18	a-na-ku lu-kul-ma lu-tur a-[na]
	T_1	vi 3	[ ]-tur ana šá ṣu-uḫ-ri-ia-ma
	W_1	vi 2'	ana-⸢ku lu⸣-k[ul-ma lu-tur] ana ṣe-eḫ-ri-i[a-a-ma]
	j	vi 11'	[-ku]l-ma lu-tur a-na šá ṣu-uḫ-ri-ia-a-ma
301	C	vi 19a	a-na 20 DANNA ik-su-pu ku-sa-pu [:]
	T_1	vi 4a	[-p]u ku-sa-pa :
	W_1	vi 3a'	⸢ana 20⸣ DANNA ik-⸢su⸣-pu ku-sa-⸢pa :⸣
	j	vi 12'	[DAN]NA ik-su-pu ku-sa-pu
302	C	vi 19b	[(in one line with 301)]
	T_1	vi 4b	a-na 30 DANNA iš-ku-nu nu-bat-ta
	W_1	vi 3b'	ana 30 DANNA iš-[ ]
	j	vi 13'	[DAN]NA iš-ku-nu nu-bat-ta
303	C	vi 20	i-mur-ma bu-ra ^{d}⸢GIŠ⸣-g[ím-]
	T_1	vi 5	[^{d}G]IŠ-gím-maš šá ka-ṣu-ú A.MEŠ-šá
	W_1	vi 4'	[i-m]ur-ma bu-ú-ru ^{d}⸢GIŠ-gím-maš šá ka⸣-[ ]
	j	vi 14'	[b]u-ra ^{d}GIŠ-gím-maš šá ka-ṣu-ú A.MEŠ-⸢šá⸣
304	C	vi 21	ú-⸢rid⸣ a-na lìb-b[i-]
	T_1	vi 6	[-b]i-im-ma A.MEŠ i-ra-muk
	W_1	vi 5'	[ú-r]id ana lìb-bi-[ ]
	z	vi 1'	[-mu]k?
	j	vi 15'	[ ]-na lìb-bi-im-ma A.MEŠ i-ra-muk
305	C	vi 22a	MUŠ ⸢i-te-ṣi-in⸣ ni-piš [:]
	T_1	vi 7	[-i]n ni-piš šam-mu
	W_1	vi 6a'	[MU]Š i-te-ṣe-en n[i- :]
	z	vi 2'-3a'	[-i]n pi? / [ ]
	j	vi 16'	[-t]e-ṣi-in ni-piš šam-mu

306	C	vi 22b	[(in one line with 305)]
	T_1	vi 8	[-l]am-ma šam-ma i[š]-ši
	W_1	vi 6b'	[(in one line with 305)]
	z	vi 3b'-4a'	[ ]-la-ma / [ ]
	j	vi 17'	[šá-qum-m]eš i-lam-ma šam-mu iš-ši
307	C	vi 23a	⸢ina ta⸣-ri-šú [it-t]a-⸢di⸣ q[u- :]
	T_1	vi 9	[i]t-ta-di ⸢qu⸣-[lip-t]i
	W_1	vi 7'	[ina t]a-ri-⸢šu⸣ i[t-]
	z	vi 4b'-5'	[ ]-šu / [ ]-ta
	j	vi 18'	[ ] it-ta-di qu-lip-tum
308	C	vi 23b	[(in one line with 307)]
	T_1	vi 10	[-ma]š ⸢it⸣-t[a-]
	W_1	vi 8'	[ina] ⸢u$_4$⸣-me-⸢šu!-ma⸣ ^{d}GI[Š-gí]m-[ ]
	z	vi 6'	[-š]ab i-bak-ki
	j	vi 19'	[-m]a ^{d}GIŠ-gím-maš it-ta-šab i-bak-[k]i
309	C	vi 24a	[i]l-la-k[a :]
	W_1	vi 9a'	[UG]U BÀD ap-pi-šú DU-ka di-ma-⸢a-šú :⸣
	z	vi 7a'	[(om.?)]
	j	vi 20'	[a]p-pi-šú il-la-ka di-ma-a-šú
310	C	vi 24b	[(in one line with 309)]
	W_1	vi 9b'	x x[ ]
	z	vi 7b'	[ ] MÁ.LAḪ$_5$
	j	vi 21'	[x (x) x x-a]r ⸢ana⸣ ur-šánabi ma-la-ḫu
311	C	vi 25	[a-na ma]n-ni-ia ^{m}⸢ur⸣-šá[nabi]-⸢a⸣-a
	W_1	vi 10a'	[ana ma]n-⸢ni⸣-iá ^{m}ur-^{d}šánabi i-na-ḫa i-da-a-a ⸢:⸣
	z	vi 8'	[^{m}ur-šu-na-b]e e-na-ḫa Á-⸢a⸣
	j	vi 22'	[ ] ^{m}ur-šánabi i-na-ḫu i-⸢da⸣-a-a
312	C	vi 26	a-na man-ni-ia i-b[a- l]ìb-bi-ia
	W_1	vi 10b'	an[a]
	z	vi 9a'	[(in one line with 313)]
	j	vi 23a'	[-b]a-li da-mu lìb-bi-ia :
313	C	vi 27a	ul áš-kun dum-qa ana ram-ni-i[a :]
	W_1	vi 11'	[u]l áš-kun dum-qa a-[ ]
	z	vi 9b'-10a'	[ ] du-un-qi i!-⸢na?⸣ / [ ]
	j	vi 23b'	ul áš-ku-un dum-qa a-na x x x

Line	MS	Ref.	Text
314	C	vi 27b	[du]m-qí i-te-pu-uš
	W_1	vi 12'	[ana] UR.MAḪ šá qaq-qa-ri du-un-[qV] ⌜e⌝-te-[ ]
	z	vi 10b'	[as]-⌜sa-kan⌝ du-x x
	j	vi 24'	[qa]q-qa-ru dum-qa e-te-pu-⌜uš⌝
315	C	vi 28	e-nin-na a-na 20 DANNA [ ] ⌜i⌝-na-aš-šam-ma
	T_1	vi 15	[-m]a
	W_1	vi 13'	⌜e⌝-nin-na ana 20 DANNA e-du-⌜ú⌝ (i-na-a)š-šam-[ma]
	z	vi 11'	[i]-na-šá-a e-du-ú
	j	vi 25'	[DAN]NA e-du-ú i-na-aš-[ ]
316	C	vi 29	ra-a-ṭa ki-i ap-tu-⌜ú⌝ [at-t]a-bak ú-nu-tú
	T_1	vi 16	[-t]ú
	W_1	vi 14'	[r]a-a-ṭu ⌜ki-i⌝ ap-tu-⌜ú at-ta-bak⌝ ú-n[u-tú]
	z		[(om. or in one line with 317?)]
	j	vi 26'	[a]t-ta-bak ú-[ ]
317	C	vi 30	ut-ta a-a-i-ta šá ana KI-ia i[š-šak-nu] ana-ku lu aḫ-ḫi-is
	T_1	vi 17	[-i]s
	W_1	vi 15'	[ut-t]a a-a-⌜ta šá⌝ ana it-t[i- an]a-ku l[u]
	z	vi 12'	[ ]x-du is-si-a ša[k-n]u
	j	vi 27'	[-ša]k-nu ana-ku lu [ ]
318	C	vi 31a	u ^{giš}MÁ e-te-zib ina kib-ri :
	T_1	vi 18a	[(in one line with 319) :]
	W_1	vi 16a'	[ ]⌜MÁ e-te-zib⌝ ina ⌜kib-ri⌝ [:]
	z	vi 13a'	[(in one line with 319)]
	j	vi 28a'	[(in one line with 319) :]
319	C	vi 31b	ana 20 D[ANNA] ik-su-pu ku-sa-pa
	T_1	vi 18b	[-p]a
	W_1	vi 16b'	a[na]-p[u]
	z	vi 13b'	[ ] ka-a-NI-pa!
	j	vi 28b'	[DAN]NA ⌜ik-su⌝-p[u]
			——— **z**
320	C	vi 32a	ana 30 DANNA iš-ku-nu nu-bat-ta :
	W_1	vi 17a'	[ ] DANNA iš-ku-nu nu-bat-t[a :]
	z	vi 14a'	[-t]a
321	C	vi 32b	ik-šu-d[u-ni]m-ma ana lìb-bi UNUG^{ki} su-pu-ri
	W_1	vi 17b'	[(in one line with 320)]
	z	vi 14b'-15a'	ik-šu-⌜du⌝-ni-⌜ma⌝ / [-p]u-ri
			——— CW

Line	MS	Ref.	Text
322	C	vi 33	^{d}GIŠ-gím-maš a-na šá-šu-ma MU-ra a-⸢na⸣ ^{m}ur-šánabi ma-la-ḫi
	W$_1$	vi 18'	[^{d}GI]Š-gím-maš ana šá-šu-ma M[U-]
	z	vi 15b'-16'	^{md}GIŠ-TUK [a]-⸢na⸣ / [ ] ^{m}ur-šu-na-be
323	C	vi 34	e-li-ma ^{m}ur-šánabi ina UGU BÀD šá UNUG$^{⸢ki⸣}$ i-tal-lak
	W$_1$	vi 19'	[e-l]i-ma ^{m}ur-^{d}šánabi ina U[GU]
	z	vi 17'	[B]ÀD ša ⸢UNUG^{ki} su-pur i⸣-tal-lak
			———— z
324	C	vi 35a	te-me-en-na ḫi-i-ṭi-ma SIG$_4$ ṣu-ub-bi ⟨:⟩
	W$_1$	vi 20a'	[ ]-⸢na ḫi⸣-[i]-⸢iṭ⸣-[:]
	z	vi 18'	[ ] x x x
325	C	vi 35b	šum-ma ⸢SIG$_4$⸣-šú la a-gur-rat
	W$_1$	vi 20b'	[(in one line with 324)]
	z	vi 19'	[ ] x x x ub
326	C	vi 36	u uš-ši-šú la id-du-ú 7 ⸢mun⸣-tal-ki
	W$_1$	vi 21'	[ù] ⸢uš-ši-šu la⸣ i[d-]
	z	vi 20'	[ ] x [x] x x [x x] x
327	C	vi 37	1 šár URU^{ki} 1 šár ^{giš}KIRI$_6$.MEŠ 1 šár es-su-⸢ú⸣ pi-t[i-i]r É ^{d}iš-tar
	W$_1$	vi 22'	[šár U]RU^{ki} šár $^{gi[š}$KI]RI$_6$.M[EŠ š]ár [ ]
	z	vi 21'	[ ] x x x
328	C	vi 38	3 šár ù pit-ru UNUG^{ki} tam-[ši]-⸢ḫu⸣
	W$_1$	vi 23'	[3] šár u pi-t[i-i]r UNUG^{ki} [ ]
	z	vi 22'	[ ] x x x x
			———— CW
XII 1	C	vi 39	u$_4$-ma pu-uk-ku ina ⸢É⸣ ^{lú}NAGAR lu e-z[ib]
	W$_1$	vi 24'	[p]u-uk-ku ina É ^{lú}NAGAR lu-ú ⸢e⸣-[ ]

A. R. George

www.ingramcontent.com/pod-product-compliance
Lightning Source LLC
Chambersburg PA
CBHW081132300726
48982CB00005B/936
* 9 7 8 0 9 9 8 1 7 2 7 2 9 *